A HISTORY OF RUSSIAN

The history of ideas has played a central role in Russia's political and social history. Understanding its intellectual tradition and the way the intelligentsia have shaped the nation is crucial to understanding the Russia of today. This new history examines important intellectual and cultural currents (the Enlightenment, nationalism, nihilism and religious revival) and key themes (conceptions of the West and East, the common people and attitudes to capitalism and natural science) in Russian intellectual history. Concentrating on the Golden Age of Russian thought in the mid-nineteenth century, the contributors also look back to its eighteenth-century origins in the flowering of culture following the reign of Peter the Great and forward to the continuing vitality of Russia's classical intellectual tradition in the Soviet and post-Soviet eras. With brief biographical details of over fifty key thinkers and an extensive bibliography, this book provides a fresh, comprehensive overview of Russian intellectual history.

WILLIAM LEATHERBARROW is Emeritus Professor of Russian at the University of Sheffield.

DEREK OFFORD is Professor of Russian Intellectual History at the University of Bristol.

A HISTORY OF RUSSIAN THOUGHT

EDITED BY

WILLIAM LEATHERBARROW
AND
DEREK OFFORD

CAMBRIDGE
UNIVERSITY PRESS

CAMBRIDGE UNIVERSITY PRESS
Cambridge, New York, Melbourne, Madrid, Cape Town,
Singapore, São Paulo, Delhi, Mexico City

Cambridge University Press
The Edinburgh Building, Cambridge CB2 8RU, UK

Published in the United States of America by Cambridge University Press, New York

www.cambridge.org
Information on this title: www.cambridge.org/9781107412521

© Cambridge University Press 2010

First published 2010
First paperback edition 2012

A catalogue record for this publication is available from the British Library

Library of Congress Cataloguing in Publication Data
A history of Russian thought / edited by William Leatherbarrow and Derek Offord.
p.   cm.
Includes bibliographical references and index.
ISBN 978-0-521-87521-9 (hbk.)
1. Russia – Intellectual life – 1801–1917.   2. Russia – Intellectual life.   3. Soviet Union – Intellectual
life.   I. Leatherbarrow, William J.   II. Offord, Derek.   III. Title.
DK189.2.H57   2010
947–dc22
2009050369

ISBN 978-0-521-87521-9 Hardback
ISBN 978-1-107-41252-1 Paperback

Contents

Preface

Savrasov's famous painting *The Rooks have Returned*, which appears on the cover of this volume, was felt by the painter's contemporaries to convey an authentic, quintessential Russianness. Kramskoy, leader of the so-called *peredvizhniki*, a group of painters who chose subject-matter that they perceived to be of national significance, singled the painting out for special praise when it was displayed in 1871 at the group's first exhibition, on account of its possession of 'soul' (*dusha*). The birches in the foreground, to which the rooks have returned to build their nests as snow melts and nature's annual renewal begins; the as yet bleak landscape stretching into a boundless distance under the weak sun of early spring; the meandering river; the ramshackle signs of human habitation in the rural vastness, including the wooden hut from which a wisp of smoke is rising; and – at the painting's centre – the symbols of the Russian people's religiosity, the church's belfry and the onion-shaped domes: these images depict Russia's heartland with a simple lyricism that seemed peculiarly appropriate to a section of the cultural elite at that juncture in her history. They poignantly evoked one aspect of a nation that was reappraising its position in the contemporary world and striving to define its distinctive character.

And yet it was a far cry, as every educated viewer of the painting would have been aware, from a village near Kostroma in the Golden Ring of ancient towns around Moscow, where Savrasov's landscape was located, to the Baroque and Classical splendour of the modern capital city, St Petersburg. Founded at the beginning of the eighteenth century by the iron-willed ruler, Peter the Great (Peter I), who turned Russia's gaze towards Europe, subjugated church to state and embarked on the creation of an empire, St Petersburg was a counterweight to introspective, Orthodox Moscow. It looked towards the West and modernity. The clash of the civilisations represented by these two aspects of nineteenth-century Russia – rural and urban, traditional and modern, religious and secular, inward-looking and outward-looking – proved magnificently productive, especially in music and literature, as well as in painting, and in the corpus of thought on which it is the purpose of this volume to offer a new perspective.

The corpus of modern Russian thought has its origins no earlier than the eighteenth century, for it was only with Peter's rapid westernisation of the administration and nobility in the first quarter of that century that firm foundations were laid for the creation of a secular intellectual culture. The classical period of Russian thought, its Golden Age, which coincided with the most luxuriant flowering of Russian imaginative literature, was in the middle quarters of the nineteenth century. That is therefore where the centre of gravity of this volume lies. After a period of relative decline towards the end of the nineteenth century, when the utopian dreams of the Golden Age collapsed, it underwent a renaissance in the so-called Silver Age, in the first quarter of the twentieth century. By then, though, a more rigorous philosophical tradition had become established alongside the tradition of impassioned aesthetic, moral, social and political speculation which we characterise as 'thought' and on which this volume chiefly focuses. After the October Revolution – the philosophical and cultural ground for which had been thoroughly prepared by the radical thinkers of the nineteenth century – the more oppressive political conditions served first to restrict the area within which independent thinking could take place and then, in the Stalinist period, effectively to suppress such thinking. And yet ideas with which thinkers had grappled in the classical age continued to have reso- nance in the 1920s and early 1930s and then again from the early 1960s, and they developed in new directions.

We have not attempted in this volume to produce a history of Russian thought that is strictly chronological and more or less comprehensive, after the manner of the magisterial volume published some thirty years ago by Andrzej Walicki on the period from the Enlightenment to Marxism. Nor have we sought to privilege any of the individual thinkers who are usually deemed to be of exceptional importance or who have achieved particular prominence in historiography as a result of admiring treatment by Soviet or western scholars. In any case much has already been written on most of these thinkers (for example, Bakunin, Belinsky, Chaadaev, Chernyshevsky, Herzen, Karamzin, Khomiakov, Ivan Kireevsky and Radishchev). Instead we have aimed to provide, in Parts II and III of the volume, a fresh, sweeping characterisation of Russian thought by reference to some of its main intellectual currents and key themes and constructs. We then seek, in Part IV, to draw out the continuing vitality and significance of this intel- lectual tradition, in new circumstances, in the post-revolutionary era. We hope in the process to show that Russian thought has presciently addressed questions of contemporary and universal interest, such as the dilemmas of modernisation in backward nations, the importance to peoples of a sense of community and distinctive identity, the effects of crises of faith and the attractions and dangers inherent in systems of thought that offer comprehensive explanations of human experience.

In order to fill in the potential lacunae left by an approach that eschews strict chronology, the sustained intellectual biography of individuals and exhaustive enumeration of the representatives of each intellectual current, we have provided separately at the end of the volume concise information on some fifty major Russian thinkers. We also provide information there on a few of the leading classical writers, since their work was of cardinal importance to many thinkers (indeed, they themselves often ventured into the territory of 'thought') and since they may be unfamiliar to non-specialist readers, to whom the volume is intended to be accessible. Ten of the biographical entries have been written by Ruth Coates.

We have attempted to root the thought examined in the volume in a broad political, social and cultural context. For we believe that the subject cannot be properly understood without awareness of such factors as the late survival of absolutism, the retention by government of repressive powers that were falling away elsewhere in Europe, the survival of serfdom until 1861, Russia's associated political, social and economic backwardness and the growing tension between the state and an emergent public opinion. To this end, two contributors have furnished surveys, of the political and social order and of the history and nature of the intelligentsia respectively. These surveys follow our introductory overview of the subject in Part I. Further appropriate contextual material has been included within several of the individual chapters in Parts II, III and IV. The extensive bibliography refers readers to secondary sources that will furnish them with further information on political, social, economic, scientific, literary and other cultural contexts as well as to sources on Russian thought itself.

We do not mean, by taking this essentially historicist approach, to imply that we see no merit in the argument that texts yield various – some would say infinitely numerous – meanings to individual readers living at different times and in different places. Indeed, Part IV of the volume, in so far as it deals with the reception of classical Russian thought in post-revolutionary times, addresses the question of the evolving meaning of that body of thought. Nor do we suggest that the non-fictional texts that serve as vehicles for Russian thought should invariably be read as examples of pure intellectual enquiry. (Here the distinction that we have made between 'thought' and 'philosophy' might again be borne in mind.) On the contrary, many texts should be understood as highly subjective and polemical. They constituted the engagé journalism (*publitsistika*) with which the so-called 'thick' journals that played such an important part in nineteenth-century Russian intellectual life were packed. Such texts, no less than fictional texts, could be shaped by generic expectations, and they exhibited not a little literary craft. It is worth mentioning in this connection that many Russian thinkers and writers – Chernyshevsky, Dostoevsky, Gogol, Herzen, Karamzin, Khomiakov, Ivan Kireevsky, Pogodin, Pushkin, Radishchev, Shcherbatov, Tolstoy and Tiutchev are examples – moved easily back and forth across the boundaries between art, on the one hand, and non-fictional forms of writing, including *publitsistika*, on the other.

We take this opportunity, finally, to offer our warmest thanks to Linda Bree for her support of this project from its inception to completion and to Maartje Scheltens for her advice and assistance in the later stages of its production, to Christopher Feeney for his meticulous copy-editing of our manuscript and to Gareth Griffith for his assistance with compilation of the index.

WILLIAM LEATHERBARROW
DEREK OFFORD

Contributors

RUTH COATES is Senior Lecturer in Russian Studies and Head of Subject at the University of Bristol. Her research interests lie mainly in the fields of nineteenth- and early twentieth-century Russian literature and intellectual history and in particular in the impact of Russian Orthodox culture on secular Russian thought. She co-edited (with Natalya Pecherskaya) *The Emancipation of Russian Christianity* (1995) and is the author of the prize-winning monograph *Christianity in Bakhtin: God and the Exiled Author* (Cambridge University Press, 1998) and of articles on Bakhtin and Herzen, Bakhtin and hesychasm, Florensky, and Vladimir Solovev.

WAYNE DOWLER is Professor of History at the University of Toronto. He is a former editor of *Canadian Slavonic Papers*. His publications in Russian history include *Dostoevsky and Native Soil Conservatism* (1982), *An Unnecessary Man. The Life of Apollon Grigor'ev* (1995) and *Classroom and Empire. The Politics of Schooling Russia's Eastern Nationalities, 1860–1917* (2001). He is currently writing a history of Russia in 1913.

CHARLES ELLIS is a part-time lecturer at the Department of Russian Studies, University of Bristol, with a particular interest in the science and thought of eighteenth- and nineteenth-century Russia. He graduated in economics at Trinity College, Cambridge, and in Russian studies at the University of Bristol, where he went on to write his doctoral thesis, 'The Scientific Revolutions of Copernicus and Darwin and Their Repercussions on Russian Political and Sociological Writing' (2000). He has contributed essays on the full range of Lomonosov's work in the *Study Group on Eighteenth Century Russia Newsletter* (1997 and 1999) and an essay, 'Tolstoi, Great Men and the Mathematical Mechanics of History', in *Turgenev and Russian Culture: Essays to Honour Richard Peace* (2008).

G. M. HAMBURG is Otho M. Behr Professor of History at Claremont McKenna College, Claremont, California. He wrote the chapter 'Russian Political Thought 1700 to 1917' in the *Cambridge History of Modern Russia*, vol. II, edited by Dominic Lieven. He is also the author of *Boris Chicherin and Early Russian Liberalism, 1828–1866* (1992), editor of *Liberty, Equality and the Market. Selected Essays of Boris Chicherin* (1998) and co-author, with Thomas Sanders and Ernest Tucker, of *Russian–Muslim Confrontation in the Caucasus, 1829–1859* (2004). He is currently writing a history of Russian political thought, 1700–1917.

W. GARETH JONES is Professor Emeritus of Russian at Bangor University. He has written extensively on aspects of Russian eighteenth-century literature and thought and is the author of *Nikolay Novikov: Enlightener of Russia* (Cambridge University Press, 1984).

NIKOLAI KREMENTSOV is Associate Professor at the Institute for the History and Philosophy of Science and Technology at the University of Toronto. He is the author of *Stalinist Science* (1997), *The Cure: A Story of Cancer and Politics from the Annals of the Cold War* (2002) and *International Science between the World Wars: The Case of Genetics* (2005). His current research interests focus on the history of biomedical sciences in 1920s Russia.

WILLIAM LEATHERBARROW is Emeritus Professor of Russian at the University of Sheffield. He is the author of many books and articles on Dostoevsky and co-editor with Derek Offord of *A Documentary History of Russian Thought: From the Enlightenment to Marxism* (1987). His most recent book is *A Devil's Vaudeville: The Demonic in Dostoevsky's Major Fiction* (2005).

GARY SAUL MORSON is Frances Hooper Professor of Arts and Humanities at Northwestern University, Illinois. A member of the American Academy of Arts and Sciences since 1995 and a winner of best book of the year awards from the American Association of Teachers of Slavic and East European Languages (AATSEEL) and the American Comparative Literature Association, he has published over a hundred articles on topics in Russian and comparative literature. His books include *The Boundaries of Genre* (1981), *Hidden in Plain View: Narrative and Creative Potentials in 'War and Peace'* (1988), *Narrative and Freedom: The Shadows of Time* (1994) and *Seeing More Wisely: 'Anna Karenina' in Our Time* (2006). In 2008 he won AATSEEL's award for the profession's outstanding scholar.

DEREK OFFORD is Professor of Russian Intellectual History at the University of Bristol. His publications on Russian history, literature and thought include *Portraits of Early Russian Liberals: A Study of the Thought of T. N. Granovsky, V. P. Botkin, P. V. Annenkov, A. V. Druzhinin, and K. D. Kavelin* (Cambridge University Press, 1985), *The Russian Revolutionary Movement in the 1880s* (Cambridge University Press, 1986), *Journeys to a Graveyard: Perceptions of Europe in Classical Russian Travel Writing* (2005) and, with W. J. Leatherbarrow, *A Documentary History of Russian Thought: From the Enlightenment to Marxism* (1987).

RICHARD PEACE is Emeritus Professor of Russian at the University of Bristol. He has published widely on nineteenth-century Russian literature. Chief among his publications are *Dostoyevsky: An Examination of the Major Novels* (Cambridge University Press, 1971), *The Enigma of Gogol* (Cambridge University Press, 1981), *Chekhov: A Study of the Four Major Plays* (1983), a contribution to the *Cambridge History of Russian Literature* (Cambridge University Press, 1989), *Oblomov: A Critical Examination of Goncharov's Novel* (1991) and *The Novels of Turgenev: Symbols and Emblems* (2002).

DAVID SAUNDERS is Professor of the History of the Russian Empire at Newcastle University. A specialist on inter-ethnic relations, he also works on Russian social history, Russian-language historiography and connections between England and Russia. His principal publications are *The Ukrainian Impact on Russian Culture* (1985) and *Russia in the Age of Reaction and Reform 1801–1881* (1992).

JAMES SCANLAN is Emeritus Professor of Philosophy at The Ohio State University in Columbus, Ohio. He is best known as co-editor of the three-volume anthology *Russian Philosophy* (1965), translator of Peter Lavrov's *Historical Letters* (1967) and Michael Gershenzon's *A History of Young Russia* (1986), editor of *Russian Thought after Communism* (1994) and author of *Marxism in the USSR* (1985) and *Dostoevsky the Thinker* (2002).

DAVID SCHIMMELPENNINCK VAN DER OYE is Chair of the History Department and Professor of Russian History at Brock University in St. Catharines, Ontario, Canada. His research interests focus on eighteenth- and nineteenth-century Russian cultural, intellectual, diplomatic and military history. He is the author of *Toward the Rising Sun: Russian Ideologies of Empire and the Path to War with Japan* (2001), co-editor with Bruce Menning of *Reforming the Tsar's Army: Military*

Innovation in Imperial Russia (Cambridge University Press, 2004) and with John Steinberg *et al.* of *The Russo-Japanese War in Global Perspective: World War Zero* (2 vols., 2005–7). He is currently completing a book about Russian orientalism.

GALIN TIHANOV is Professor of Comparative Literature and Intellectual History and Co-Director of the Research Institute for Cosmopolitan Cultures at the University of Manchester. His publications include two books on Bulgarian literature (1994 and 1998), a book on Bakhtin, Lukács and the ideas of their time (2000), co-edited volumes on Bakhtin and the Bakhtin Circle (2000 and 2004) and on Robert Musil (2007), a guest-edited special issue of *History of Photography* on Russian avant-garde photography and visual culture (2000), as well as numerous articles on German, Russian and East European intellectual and cultural history and on cultural and literary theory.

DANIEL TODES is Professor at the Institute of the History of Medicine at The Johns Hopkins University. The author of *Darwin without Malthus: The Struggle for Existence in Russian Evolutionary Thought* (1989) and *Pavlov's Physiology Factory: Experiment, Interpretation, Laboratory Enterprise* (2002), he is currently completing a biography of Ivan Pavlov.

VERA TOLZ is Sir William Mather Professor of Russian Studies at the University of Manchester. She has published widely on various aspects of Russian nationalism and the relationship between intellectuals and the state under the communist regime. Her books include *Gender and Nation in Contemporary Europe* (co-editor, 2005), *Russia: Inventing the Nation* (2001), *European Democratization since 1800* (co-editor, 2000) and *Russian Academicians and the Revolution* (1997). She is currently completing a book on academic Orientology and identity politics in late imperial and early Soviet Russia.

Note on dates, transliteration and other conventions

In 1700 Peter the Great adopted the Julian calendar, which was eleven days behind the Gregorian calendar in the eighteenth century, twelve days behind in the nineteenth and thirteen days behind in the twentieth. The Gregorian calendar, which western states had begun to adopt in preference to the Julian calendar in 1582, was not adopted in Russia until 1918. In this book dates are given in the Old Style (OS; i.e. according to the Julian calendar) when the event to which reference is made takes place in pre-revolutionary Russia and in the New Style (NS; i.e. according to the Gregorian calendar) when it takes place outside Russia.

Dates in parentheses after the titles of works mentioned in the text are, unless otherwise stated, the dates of first publication, not dates of composition.

We have in most respects followed the system of transliteration used in *The Slavonic and East European Review*. The Russian letter ё has everywhere been transliterated as e. Russian surnames ending in -ский have been rendered by the commonly accepted English form -sky (e.g. Dostoevsky), except in citations and transliterated titles in the notes and bibliography. We have also used the common English form Yeltsin. The letter -й and the combination -ий at the end of Russian forenames have been rendered by -y, e.g. 'Aleksey', 'Vasily', rather than 'Aleksei', 'Vasilii' respectively, except in transliterated titles in the notes and bibliography. The Russian soft sign has not been transliterated at all except in common nouns that are left in their Russian form in the text and, again, in titles of Russian works in the notes and bibliography, in which cases it is rendered by an apostrophe, e.g. *artel'*, Gogol'. Russian words printed in pre-revolutionary orthography (e.g. the titles of eighteenth- and nineteenth-century journals) have been transliterated from their modernised form.

We have preferred transliterated forenames (e.g. Aleksandr, Pavel, Petr) to translated ones (Alexander, Paul, Peter), except in the case of monarchs and other members of the Russian royal family, who are familiar to the English-speaking reader from the translated form.

Places are referred to by the name that was in use in Russia at the time of the work or event in question (thus Tiflis, in pre-revolutionary times, instead of Tbilisi). The modern place-name, where it differs from the name used in the text, is given in brackets.

The Russian title of each journal, newspaper or almanac mentioned in the text is given in the list of journal titles on pp. xviii–xix.

Dates (OS) of reigns in eighteenth-, nineteenth- and early twentieth-century Russia

Peter I	(i.e. Peter the Great) 1672–1725, son of Tsar Alexis (ruled 1645–76); co-ruled with his half-brother Ivan V 1689–96 and sole ruler 1696–1725
Catherine I	1684–1727, Lithuanian peasant taken captive by the Russians in 1702; consort of Peter I from 1703 and his wife from 1712; reigned 1725–7
Peter II	1715–30, infant son of Prince Alexis (1690–1718), who was the son of Peter I; reigned 1727–30
Anna	1693–1740, daughter of Ivan V; reigned 1730–40
Elizabeth	1709–61, daughter of Peter I and Catherine I; reigned 1741–61
Peter III	1728–62, son of a daughter of Peter I and of Charles Frederick, Duke of Holstein-Gottorp; reigned 1761–2
Catherine II	(i.e. Catherine the Great) 1729–96, German princess who came to Russia as fiancée of the future Peter III; reigned 1762–96
Paul	1754–1801, son of Peter III and Catherine II; reigned 1796–1801
Alexander I	1777–1825, son of Paul; reigned 1801–25
Nicholas I	1796–1855, son of Paul and younger brother of Alexander I; reigned 1825–55
Alexander II	1818–81, son of Nicholas I; reigned 1855–81
Alexander III	1845–94, son of Alexander II; reigned 1881–94
Nicholas II	1868–1918, son of Alexander III; reigned 1894–1917

Russian titles of journals, newspapers and miscellanies

All Sorts	*Vsiakaia vsiachina*
Annals of the Fatherland: see *Notes of the Fatherland*	
Bag	*Koshelek*
Beacon	*Maiak*
Bell	*Kolokol*
Children's Reading for Heart and Mind	*Detskoe chtenie dlia serdtsa i razuma*
Citizen in Conversation	*Beseduiushchii grazhdanin*
Colloquy	*Beseda*
Contemporary	*Sovremennik*
Dawn	*Rassvet*
Day	*Den'*
Drone	*Truten'*
Elements. The Eurasian Review	*Elementy. Evraziiskoe obozrenie*
Epoch	*Epokha*
Forward!	*Vpered!*
Landmarks	*Vekhi*
Maritime Miscellany	*Morskoi sbornik*
Messenger of Europe	*Vestnik Evropy*
Morning Light	*Utrennii svet*
Moscow Collection	*Moskovskii sbornik*
Moscow Messenger	*Moskovskii vestnik*
Moscow Monthly Publication	*Moskovskoe ezhemesiachnoe izdanie*
Moscow News	*Moskovskie vedomosti*
Muscovite	*Moskvit'ianin*
New Way	*Novyi put'*
New World	*Novyi mir*

Northern Bee	*Severnaia pchela*
Notes of the Fatherland	*Otechestvennye zapiski*
Our Contemporary	*Nash sovremennik*
Out of the Depths	*Iz glubiny*
Painter	*Zhivopisets*
Problems of Idealism	*Problemy idealizma*
Problems of Literature	*Voprosy literatury*
Problems of Philosophy	*Voprosy filosofii*
Reading Library	*Biblioteka dlia chteniia*
Rumour	*Molva*
Rus (i.e. *Old Russia*)	*Rus'*
Russian Colloquy	*Russkaia beseda*
Russian Gazette	*Russkie vedomosti*
Russian Herald or *Russian Messenger*	*Russkii vestnik*
Russian Thought	*Russkaia mysl'*
Russian Wealth	*Russkoe bogatstvo*
Russian Word	*Russkoe slovo*
St Petersburg Learned Gazette	*Sankt-Peterburgskie uchenye vedomosti*
St Petersburg News	*Sankt-Peterburgskie vedomosti*
Signposts: see *Landmarks*	
Son of the Fatherland	*Syn otechestva*
Spark	*Iskra*
Telescope	*Teleskop*
Time	*Vremia*
Tocsin	*Nabat*
Tomorrow	*Zavtra*
Torches	*Fakely*
Under the Banner of Marxism	*Pod znamenem Marksizma*
Whistler	*Svistok*
World of Art	*Mir iskusstva*

PART I

Context

CHAPTER I

Introduction

William Leatherbarrow and Derek Offord

In chapter 2 of this volume David Saunders comments on how in the 1950s and 1960s 'Russian thought used to be fashionable', occupying centre stage in English-language historical writing. This association of 'Russian thought' with historical scholarship implicitly raises the question of what precisely is the subject we are attempting to address in this volume. Not all scholars would necessarily embrace the view that it is primarily a mode of Russian historical study, although all surely would acknowledge the close association between 'history' and 'thought'. The approaches (and even the titles) of some of the major English-language works on the subject betray this uncertainty. While the works of Nicholas Riasanovsky, Martin Malia, Marc Raeff and Richard Pipes, for example, consistently seek to locate Russian thought primarily within the context of social and political history, the three-volume anthology edited in the 1960s by James M. Edie, James P. Scanlan, Mary-Barbara Zeldin and George L. Kline suggests a much broader understanding in its title *Russian Philosophy*. It sets out to be the first historical anthology of 'Russian philosophical thought', and alongside examples of socio-political thought it includes metaphysical philosophy by thinkers such as Berdiaev, Shestov, Frank and Lossky, as well as the work of ecclesiastical and religious thinkers like the 'Russian Socrates' Skovoroda and the pre-revolutionary 'theologians' Fedorov and Solovev – figures who do not always find their way into other treatments of Russian thought. Nevertheless, the editors of *Russian Philosophy* do concede the important point that Russian speculation, even when apparently at its most abstract, has always been 'man-centred' and, unlike its western counterpart, non-professional and non-academic.[1] Its practitioners have emerged to a strikingly large degree from the literary world, rather than from the academic disciplines of philosophy or history, and their involvement with 'philosophy' has rarely been pure (in the sense of objective or non-committed). Although, as Galin Tihanov shows in chapter 14, a more mature philosophical tradition did emerge in the twentieth century, by and large Russian thinkers have wielded ideas not as keys to remote and abstruse truths, but as weapons in the struggle for moral, social, historical or political justice, a struggle that has motivated their entire quest for the meaning of life, nature and history and imbued it with personal commitment along with what Edie, Scanlan, Zeldin and Kline call 'a special intensity and an impatience with moderation'.[2]

A similar recognition of the 'close association' between philosophy and social thought informs Andrzej Walicki's seminal work *A History of Russian Thought from the Enlightenment to Marxism* (first English edition 1979). Walicki argues that philosophy failed to establish itself as an autonomous discipline partly because of its comparatively late appearance in a Russia where independent thought was strictly controlled, but also because growing awareness of pressing social problems 'distracted attention from issues not immediately related to social practice'.[3] Indeed, he goes further, asserting that any study of Russian thought that confined itself to pure philosophy (i.e. 'professional', 'formalistic' or 'academic' speculation) would 'give an impoverished picture of the history of Russian ideas' because of the lack of originality of such thought and its dependence on western European models: '[Russian thought's] striking originality can only be perceived when we examine it in the context of Russian intellectual history, i.e. from the point of view of the issues that were closest to the hearts of educated Russians, and felt by them to be the most relevant to the future of their country.'[4]

This notion of Russian thought as 'intellectual history' is taken up in the very title of Raeff's anthology (1966), which sets out to illustrate 'the writings and ideas that have helped to shape the social and political consciousness of modern Russia'.[5] Raeff's volume contains an illuminating introduction in which Isaiah Berlin (who did so much to promote awareness of and respect for Russian thought in the English-speaking world in the 1950s and 1960s) explores more fully the concept of intellectual history in its Russian context. Berlin argues that 'intellectual history' is not a clear or self-explanatory concept and that it lacks the precision of histories of ideas in more specific or technical disciplines such as political, economic, social, scientific, philosophical or mathematical thought. Instead, intellectual history deals with 'general ideas' that are in the air at a given moment and form the 'intellectual background' or 'climate of opinion' – 'beliefs, attitudes, and mental and emotional habits, some of which are vague and undefined, others of which have become crystallized into religious, legal, or political systems, moral doctrines, social outlooks, psychological dispositions, and so forth'.[6] In Russia such general ideas became the province of an emerging and increasingly isolated educated class (although 'class', with its implications of a distinct socio-economic layer, is the wrong word here) that seized upon the realm of thought as a means to articulate deep concerns that were denied expression in any other way. Such Russian practitioners of what has become known as 'social thought' (*obshchestvennaia mysl*) were for the most part truly amateurs in whatever intellectual fields – politics, economics, religion, law, philosophy, etc. – they inhabited, but they brought to those fields an intensity, immediacy, practicality and commitment unknown to the specialist, along with a willingness to apply their ideas to the solution of the most pressing problems of the age. As a result, according to Berlin, ideas 'played a greater and more peculiar role in Russian history than anywhere else', and the study of Russian thought can thus explain much more than we might expect about Russian behaviour.[7]

It may be argued, therefore, that the present volume is concerned less with ideas than with how those ideas were wielded by an intellectual minority that by the 1860s had become known as the Russian *intelligentsia*, but which had its origins much earlier in the Russian Enlightenment and the serving nobility of the eighteenth century. As Berlin has observed, the most striking characteristic of that minority was not the intellectual inventiveness of its members, but the seriousness with which it took the ideas of others and transformed them through the intensity of its own sense of mission: 'it surrendered itself to what it believed to be true with a lifelong singleness of purpose seldom known outside of religious life in the West'.[8] Elsewhere Berlin evocatively develops this analogy, writing that the concept of intelligentsia 'must not be confused with the notion of intellectuals. Its members thought of themselves as united by something more than mere interest in ideas; they conceived themselves as being a dedicated order, almost a secular priesthood, devoted to the spreading of a specific attitude to life, something like a gospel.'[9] A similar view is offered by Annenkov, who moved easily among the leading westernised intellectuals of the 1830s and 1840s and left in his memoirs an account of a gathering at the village of Sokolovo in the summer of 1845, a gathering that included Herzen and Granovsky and which Annenkov compared to 'a militant order of knights, which had no written charter', but which 'stood athwart the whole current of contemporary life'.[10] Likewise, the later observer of Russian intellectual life Mikhail Gershenzon also identified this dedicated, self-effacing, quixotic characteristic in the Russian intelligentsia:

When you picture in your mind the nature of the average Russian *intelligent* one typical feature immediately strikes you: that here is a person who above all else has from his earliest years been living *outside himself*, in a quite literal sense; that is to say, acknowledging as the only object worthy of his interest and concern something lying beyond his personality – the people, society or the state. Nowhere in the world does social opinion reign as despotically as among us, and for two-thirds of a century our social opinion has been founded upon acknowledgement of the supreme principle that to think about one's personality is egoism and somehow indecent. The only true man is he who ponders upon social matters, takes an interest in social questions, and works for the common good.[11]

G. M. Hamburg deals in detail with the complex and multifaceted nature of the Russian intellectual minority and the multiple meanings of the term 'intelligentsia' in chapter 3, where he brings lucidity to a confusing topic by carefully plotting the interaction of the different social venues in which various Russian intelligentsias operated from the eighteenth century onwards. This approach sheds new and welcome light on the shape of pre-revolutionary Russian cultural life, and it helps us to avoid traditional oversimplifications both in how we define the intelligentsia and in the qualities we ascribe to it. It is tempting here, though, to speculate further on what might have created the chivalric, cabalistic and dedicated qualities identified in the Russian intelligentsia (in the broadest sense of the term) by Annenkov, Gershenzon, Berlin and many others. Certainly, youth and a love of intrigue, along with a sense of the inadequacy of contemporary social and political life, must have drawn many into the clandestine discussion groups of the 1830s and 1840s, just as those same qualities had drawn a previous generation into the masonic lodges, where exclusivity and ritual stimulated the heady sense of being an elect with a mission. A clear, albeit fictional instance of the latter is to be found in Pierre Bezukhov in Tolstoy's *War and Peace*. The masonic lodges and political circles of the first four decades of the nineteenth century thus fulfilled, as Philip Pomper observes, a variety of complex social and psychological needs.[12] Moreover, many members of the eighteenth-century educated nobility and the nineteenth-century Russian intelligentsia must have been at least aware of their isolation as a social group, notwithstanding Hamburg's argument that sociability was a key factor in the spread of ideas and that alienation should not be seen as the sole motor of the intelligentsia's evolution. The spread of enlightenment among members of the nobility in the wake of western-isation had created a small educated elite and thus added a further layer to the estrangement of that class from those below. Such alienation from 'the masses' is, of course, an inevitable consequence of socially selective educa-tion, and it has been experienced by the intellectual minorities of other nations. What made the eighteenth-century educated Russian nobleman so different, along with his descendants among the nineteenth-century intelligentsia, was the completeness of their isolation. As well as being cut off from below (which almost certainly did not bother them), they were also to a certain extent estranged from above – denied a fully meaningful participation in Russian political life by the autocracy's insistence upon the indivisibility of monarchical power. What is more, government and educated public were eventually to part company in Russia, each becoming suspicious of and hostile to the aspirations of the other.[13] Saunders's account of the relationship between the Russian educated public and the key formal institutions of the state – authoritarianism and autocracy, the agencies of state repression, censorship, legal institutions and penalties, social and economic policy, education and official ideology and so forth – provides an illuminating perspective on that process.

The result of all this was the emergence of a peculiarly self-enclosed and self-conscious intellectual minority, acutely aware of the social and moral obligations imposed upon it by the privilege of enlightenment. Yet in any attempt to explain the deep sense of obligation shared by members of that minority, due account must be taken of a view argued by many (though not all) commentators – that the nineteenth-century Russian *intelligent* was, in Gershenzon's words, 'the direct descendant and heir of the Voltairean serf-owner'.[14] Raeff goes yet further, arguing that 'a straight line of spiritual and psychological filiation connects the servicemen of Peter the Great to the revolutionaries of the nineteenth century'.[15] In other words, the origins of the Russian intelligentsia and its cast of mind must be sought in the enlightened nobility of the eighteenth century, a class of people whose original *raison d'être* had been state service (the term 'servicemen' – *sluzhilye liudi* – was used to describe them), but who had gradually been emancipated from their service obligations to the state during the eighteenth century – a process significantly coterminous with the spread of enlightenment within that class.

The social composition of the Russian educated minority indeed changed significantly as it developed from the service nobility of the eighteenth century to the middle-class revolutionaries (*raznochintsy*) of the nineteenth.[16] Yet it would appear that the eighteenth-century nobleman's sense of an obligation to serve survived within that minority, evolving from a sense of duty to the state, through an engagement with more abstract concepts such as self-improvement, the common good (*obshchee blago*), patriotism, truth and justice, before finally settling into an awareness of, and commitment to, the Russian people. This process of discovery of the *narod* by a peculiarly obligated intellectual minority probably began with the return of noblemen to their estates following their emancipation from state service, and it was certainly accelerated by the spread of Enlightenment ideas on the rights of man and by the subsequent impact of Sentimentalism and Romanticism, with their preoccupation with the common man. But, as Derek Offord shows in chapter 11, it developed apace in the nineteenth century as Russian intellectuals constructed their own images of the Russian *narod* in their attempts to clarify their vision of the Russian nation and of their own role within it. From the Slavophiles' utopian vision of the people as the heart of an apolitical moral organism and the essence of Russia's national distinctiveness, via the Westernisers' assessment of the people as the potential beneficiaries of humanitarian improvement and emancipation on the basis of western ideas (and, ultimately, as the bearers of 'Russian socialism'), through to the near-worship of the common folk during the Populist movement of the 1870s – the Russian *narod* consistently lay at the heart of the Russian intelligentsia's efforts to refine its understanding of itself and its mission.

A variety of key ideas and concepts litters the path of the Russian intelligentsia's intellectual evolution, but to a large extent these all have their origins in the processes of westernisation and enlightenment that accompanied the emergence of a Russian educated elite. The cultural westernisation that marked the reign of Catherine the Great not only fostered the development of an educated, Europeanised elite who came to question the principles on which their native Russia had historically rested, but also provided an intellectual framework for that questioning. The key philosophical principles of the Age of Reason rested on a belief that the laws of nature underpinning the physical world were ultimately knowable and that man's increasing enlightenment would enable him first to understand and then to control the world he inhabited. Such faith in the power of reason and the perfectibility of man in turn coloured Enlightenment views on man's relationship to society, and it fostered the belief that societies were perfectible if based upon rational social relations and an enlightened code of law. The 'irrationality' and inhumanity of such traditional Russian institutions as autocracy and serfdom became all too apparent to those Catherine had sent to study abroad, and this contributed more than anything to political disaffection and the emergence of critical social thought. In chapter 4 of this volume Gareth Jones traces the processes of westernisation and enlightenment in Russia from the reforms of Peter the Great, relating them to the 'norms' of the European Age of Reason and showing how they penetrated all areas of Russian cultural life. Initially, educated society sought to propagate Enlightenment values in cooperation with the state, in the form of the 'enlightened despot' Catherine had initially appeared to be. But her response to the French Revolution and subsequent treatment of Radishchev for his criticisms of autocracy and serfdom in *A Journey from St Petersburg to Moscow* (1790) demonstrated clearly the limitations of autocracy's ability to reform itself and marked the beginning of 'the parting of ways' of government and educated public.

Jones recognises that although its central core 'was the urge to modify the way that men and women had traditionally thought and behaved', Enlightenment thought was kaleidoscopic in nature, even assuming conservative and religious forms. This reminds us that there has traditionally been a tendency in both English-language and Russian scholarship on Russian social thought to emphasise its liberal and radical manifestations. Although the increasing identification of the Russian nineteenth-century intelligentsia with reformist and revolutionary aims means that this emphasis is understandable (and, indeed, it is reinforced in this volume), there has been a tendency (in spite of the work of a number of scholars, most of them North American) to play down the extent and strength of Russian conservative thought in the classical period. Moreover, there is little justification for dismissing Russian conservative thought as mere obscurantism. In chapter 5 William Leatherbarrow attempts to restore some balance by addressing the nature of conservative thought between the Enlightenment and the Great Reforms of the 1860s. In arguing that Russian conservatism was much more than mere resistance to change, he seeks to identify its nature through consideration of the philosophy of history implicitly or explicitly expressed by key conservative thinkers of the period, as well as in their attempts to construct a unique cultural identity for Russia that would stand in opposition to the philosophical absolutes and universal concepts of social progress characteristic of the Enlightenment.

Conservative emphasis on a specifically Russian way that would confront and resist the processes of westernisation gained much support from Russia's triumph over Napoleon and the subsequent march on Paris. Russian national consciousness, already stimulated by the growth of Russian historical study (in particular, the work of Karamzin), was reinforced by the fact that Russia now found herself a major power at the heart of Europe and no longer merely a junior partner hungry for the crumbs from Europe's technological and cultural feast. Moreover, it was not only conservative thinkers who found themselves swept up in a tide of Romantic nationalism. The development of Russian Romanticism and the displacement of Enlightenment rationalism by metaphysical idealism in the course of the 1820s marked a major shift in the entire direction of Russian thought.

The nature of Russia and her relationship with the West, which had been an issue since the reign of Peter the Great, now came to dominate Russian social and historical thought. What was most striking was the way in which Russian thinkers of the period, Slavophiles as well as the so-called Westernisers, sought to refine their understanding of Russia against the templates they had constructed of the West. Indeed, as Vera Tolz argues in chapter 9, 'the West (*zapad*) had become the most important ingredient of modern Russian identity'. In her essay Tolz carefully traces the various spatial, cultural, political and economic images of the West constructed by Russian intellectuals as they developed their 'reactive nationalism' of national cultural and historical difference, a form of nationalism that was to become a model for national leaders in the colonial and post-colonial age.

The Russian intellectual's preoccupation with images of Europe should not be allowed to obscure the fact that at this time Russia was an imperial power with a history of expansion into both the south and the east. In a compelling image from his first 'Philosophical Letter', Chaadaev presented Russia as a sleeping giant suspended 'between the two great divisions of the world, between East and West, with one elbow resting on China and the other on Germany', a nation that should have united in its history 'the two principles of intellectual life, imagination and reason, and brought together in [its] civilisation the history of the entire globe'.[17] Chaadaev's image, along with his warning that Russia had so far failed to find any meaningful identity or role in the great drama of world history (a warning that was in many respects to set the agenda for Russian thought from that point on), remind us that Asia was also a lure for the Russian mind. David Schimmelpenninck van der Oye's essay clearly demonstrates how identification with the East became a further way of articulating distance from the West and of refining the sense of national character and place in the world. Ironically, the imperialist adventure also allowed Russia to qualify as part of Europe, in that having an empire strengthened her credentials as a European nation. Indeed, while many Russian thinkers sought to distance themselves from westerners, the very act of looking towards Asia made them feel very much European. Schimmelpenninck not only traces the impact of Eurasianism on Russian thinkers of the nineteenth and early twentieth centuries, but also shows how its resurgence in the post-communist period has contributed to a profound disillusionment with the West and to many Russians agreeing with the view of the film-director Mikhalkov that their nation is not Europe's backyard, but 'Asia's front door'.

From the point when the failure of the Decembrist Revolt in 1825 appeared to expose the limitations of Enlightenment thought and its faith in perfectibility on the basis of rational and legalistic principles, the Russian intellectual landscape was to be dominated for a generation by attempts to come to terms with the implications of German metaphysical idealism for Russian social reality. The ideas of Schelling, Fichte and, after 1837, Hegel underpinned the evolution of both westernising and Slavophile tendencies in the intelligentsia. Slavophiles, despite their increasing antipathy to western culture as a model for their own land, drew upon the organicism of such thought in order to articulate their vision of the Russian social order, a vision described in this volume in the essays by Leatherbarrow, Tolz and Offord. Less straightforward were the ways in which representatives of the westernising intelligentsia engaged with German idealism. Initially drawn to metaphysics as an escape from the depressing reality of post-Decembrist Russia, the Westernisers increasingly came to see the thought of Hegel in particular as a way of defining and justifying their relationship to that reality. The process is illustrated in the intellectual trajectory of Belinsky: detached from social and political realities by his discovery of Schelling, he initially saw those realities as the shortcomings of an imperfect and insubstantial physical world best forsaken for the world of the ideal as disclosed by aestheticism and art. Subsequently, on the basis of his understanding of Hegel, to whose ideas he was introduced by Bakunin, Belinsky endured a painful discovery of reality. At first, Belinsky found solace in the notion that history was the logical outcome of a supreme Idea evolving dialectically towards an absolute, for at a stroke it accounted for the negative aspects of reality and indicated the attitude that a rational man should adopt towards that reality – one of philosophical reconciliation. The result of this was an eccentric period in the life of one who was in due course to achieve lasting fame as a critic of reality: in the late 1830s Belinsky wrote several articles in which he called upon the individual to submit to the rationality of reality – even to such distasteful manifestations of it as Russian tsarist autocracy – or risk being crushed 'under the leaden weight of its gigantic palm'.[18] Such conservatism, however, went against the grain of Belinsky's proud and independent nature, and by 1840 he was beginning to manifest a growing distaste for reconciliation, repudiating his 'Hegelian' passivity and turning to the writings of European socialist thinkers in order to articulate an impassioned criticism of the reality he had tried so earnestly to vindicate.

In a letter to Botkin of 11 December 1840 Belinsky conceded that the flaw in his reading of Hegel had been his failure to develop 'the idea of negation as a no less sacred historical right, without which the history of mankind would become a stagnant, stinking swamp'.[19] Herzen, too, was soon to recognise the importance of negation, arguing that Hegel's thought was not a justification for passivity in the face of historical reality, but was in its dialectical nature the very 'algebra of revolution',[20] an idea that, as Daniel Todes and Nikolai Krementsov show in chapter 15, gained renewed significance with the advent of Marxism and 'dialectical materialism'. Such recognition of the importance of negation reflects a general evolution of the westernised intelligentsia of the 1840s and 1850s away from bootless metaphysical abstractions and towards an increasing radicalism based upon recognition of the need for action and the repudiation of tsarist reality. This process came to a head in the so-called 'nihilism' of the late 1850s and 1860s, when, as Richard Peace shows in chapter 6, a younger generation of thinkers led by Chernyshevsky, Dobroliubov and Pisarev disowned the inactivity of their 'fathers', the men of the 1840s, and espoused an unsentimental 'scientific' materialism as the basis for their rejection of the Russian status quo. The growth of nihilism was indissolubly linked to the processes of reform undertaken in post-Nicholaevan Russia, but intellectually it marked a firm rejection of the metaphysical idealism that had shaped so much Russian thought since the Decembrist Revolt and a return to the rationalism of the Enlightenment. Indeed, the 'men of the sixties' became known as 'enlighteners' (*prosvetiteli*), and their social thought is profoundly indebted to the materialist underpinnings of the Age of Reason and, in particular, to the utilitarianism of the British social philosophers Bentham and Mill.

As Peace argues, nihilism not only fed into the Russian revolutionary movement in obvious ways such as Bakunin's 'lust for destruction', but it also helped to shape the way in which Marxism was received in Russia (and not just by providing an earlier model of materialism as the basis for social change). Chernyshevsky's argument that Russia might be able to proceed directly to socialism from its current semi-feudal position, thus avoiding the European experience of industrialisation and capitalism, might well have reflected the broad conclusions of Herzen's 'Russian Socialism', but it also ran counter to the classical Marxist analysis of capitalism as a precondition of the transition to socialism. This in turn prompted a new phase in the by now familiar argument that Russia's historical social and cultural differences would ensure a future path of development different from that of the West. Wayne Dowler's essay carefully traces the 'controversy over capitalism'[21] that animated the Russian intelligentsia for much of the nineteenth century, showing how capitalism was seen not only as an economic system that had played a beneficial role in overcoming absolutist regimes in Europe and as the key to the West's material superiority, but also as a social formation that threatened to disrupt traditional Russian social arrangements and further pauperise the masses. From Herzen's *Letters from the Avenue Marigny* in 1847 through to the Russian Populism of the 1870s, capitalism afforded many Russian thinkers the means to argue that western conceptions of political economy afforded no basis for life in Russia, a view that was to bring them into conflict not only with Russian Marxists, but also with the reality of capitalist growth in their native land.

The resurgence of materialism that accompanied industrial development and the rise of capitalism in Europe was based upon a renewed respect for the achievements of science. The writings of Chernyshevsky reflect this by setting out to show that the rational scientific method was applicable not only to the world of nature, but also to that of man, and he identified 'rational egoism' as the basis of both individual behaviour and rational social development. To be sure, Chernyshevsky took the scientific method to absurd lengths in his attempts to explain the determinist nature of even the simplest human action, such as getting out of bed; but such absurdities should not blind us to the importance of 'science' in nineteenth-century Russian intellectual life. Charles Ellis traces the process of scientific enquiry in Russia from its relatively late beginnings in the reign of Peter the Great, when it served the drive for modernisation, through to its apotheosis in the 1860s, when, thanks largely to the impact of Darwinism, science came of age in Russian intellectual life and took its place alongside the anti-rationalist tradition in any proper understanding of the full development of Russian thought. Whereas in the eighteenth century scientific debate had been conducted in isolation from social and political debate, by the 1860s, as Ellis shows, it had become 'the leading factor in the re-examination of long-held religious, political and sociological assumptions' and, for many, the key to validating the fruits of all forms of speculation.

But not for all: just as the rational confidence of the Enlightenment had earlier given way to the anti-rationalist reaction of Romanticism, so many Russian intellectuals in the later decades of the nineteenth century came to feel disappointment at what they saw as the limitations of the scientific method. In part this fed into the 'subjective sociology' of Populists like Lavrov and Mikhailovsky, who sought to reconcile the objective truths disclosed by science with the subjective ideals for social improvement constructed by 'critically thinking' individuals possessed of a moral purpose. But after the failure of the Populists to win social and economic improvements for the masses or political concessions for themselves by any of the methods they employed, such disappointment also fed a revival of interest in metaphysical and religious speculation and a turn away from the 'heroic materialism' that had accompanied the technological confidence of

European culture in the nineteenth century. Ruth Coates's essay concentrates on the cultural conditions and intellectual backdrop that made possible the religious renaissance in Russia between the end of the nineteenth century and the advent of militant atheism following the Bolshevik Revolution. Drawing on Christopher Read's distinction between 'academic' and 'artistic' schools within this renaissance, Coates shows how Russian thinkers reacted to what she terms the 'ideological exhaustion' represented by a politically compromised Orthodox Church on the one hand and, on the other, a radical intelligentsia defeated by the failure of the Populist movement and the political reaction fostered by the regimes of Alexander III and Nicholas II. Those representatives of the religious renaissance who went on to survive the hostility of the Bolshevik regime formed part of the first wave of intellectual emigration. The émigré communities they established in the West served as a basis for the continuation of Russian religious thought in the twentieth century, a tradition that is now being rediscovered in post-Soviet Russia.

In his illuminating discussion of the relationship between the radical intelligentsia and a counter-tradition represented by some of the pillars of nineteenth-century Russian literature, Gary Saul Morson explores other ways in which Russian culture responded to what came to be seen as the limitations of radical Russian thought and practice. Whereas the radicals of the mid-nineteenth century onwards had come to espouse a sense of identity characterised by ideological orthodoxy, rationality, exclusivity, immoderate fervour and extremism in both behaviour and political aspirations, so the works of Turgenev, Tolstoy, Dostoevsky and Chekhov provided models designed to show that life was too complex to be embraced by the 'moral Newtonianism' of radical theory and practice. In the course of this antagonistic dialogue the literary counter-tradition developed a set of alternatives that emphasised anti-theoretism, open-endedness, sensitivity to particular cases and renewed respect for the wisdom of ordinary human practices. Russian literature's traditional preoccupation with 'the accursed questions' and its alertness to the polemics of the day has led some of its readers to the conclusion that it is a literature of ideas and, in many respects, a branch of Russian thought. While this is true to an extent – and our Preface suggests how many Russian writers moved easily between the world of fiction and that of social thought – it is also facile. Morson's chapter provides a much more complex and nuanced understanding of the dynamic relationship between Russian literature and thought in the 'Golden Age'.

The Golden Age of classical Russian thought has generally been held by scholars to be the period between the Enlightenment and the advent of

Marxism, a period in which Russia's burgeoning national consciousness along with the twin processes of westernisation and modernisation gave rise to vigorous debates about her social and political nature and her historical destiny. It might be expected that the translation of Marxism into the official ideology of the Soviet state would have brought about the end of such debates, along with the suppression of non-Marxist thought and the diminution of the intellectual heritage. To a certain extent this is indeed what happened, but the essay by Galin Tihanov demonstrates that the interaction of Marxist ideology with Russian intellectual life was by no means straightforward. His treatment of how Soviet Marxism responded to classical Russian thought and how the latter survived and was modified during the Soviet period, both in the Soviet Union and in émigré communities in the West, is one that is alert to nuances and transitions. In its conclusions it revisits the prevailing consensus that has assumed a total rupture with the Russian intellectual tradition during the post-revolutionary period. The treatment of dialectical materialism and Soviet science by Todes and Krementsov further demonstrates how, despite the changed nature of both state and intelligentsia in the Soviet period, ideas and ideologies continued to offer a cultural resource to be exploited in different ways by the parties concerned. In the post-Soviet period, as James Scanlan demonstrates in the Afterword to this volume, those same elements of continuity are further reinforced as contemporary Russia seeks to address the questions associated with national identity and purpose by reaching back to the very same debates that animated the intelligentsia during the classical period of Russian thought. Russian thought indeed 'used to be fashionable', but now it is fashionable again for those who seek to understand the Russia of today.

NOTES

1. James M. Edie, James P. Scanlan, Mary-Barbara Zeldin and George L. Kline, *Russian Philosophy*, 3 vols. (Chicago: Quadrangle, 1965), vol. I, p. ix.
2. Ibid., pp. x–xi.
3. Andrzej Walicki, *A History of Russian Thought from the Enlightenment to Marxism*, trans. Hilda Andrews-Rusiecka (Oxford: Clarendon Press, 1980), p. xiii.
4. Ibid., p. xiv.
5. Marc Raeff (ed.), *Russian Intellectual History: An Anthology* (New Jersey: Humanities Press, 1966), p. v.
6. Isaiah Berlin, 'Introduction' in ibid., p. 4.
7. Ibid., p. 5.
8. Ibid., p. 6.

9. Isaiah Berlin, *Russian Thinkers*, ed. Henry Hardy and Aileen Kelly (London: Hogarth Press, 1978), p. 117.

10. P. V. Annenkov, *Literaturnye vospominaniia* (Moscow: Gosudarstvennoe izdatel'stvo khudozhestvennoi literatury, 1960), p. 270.

11. M. O. Gershenzon, *Istoricheskie zapiski* (Moscow: Tipografiia I. N. Kushnereva, 1910), pp. 153–4.

12. Philip Pomper, *The Russian Revolutionary Intelligentsia* (New York: Crowell, 1970), p. 1.

13. See Nicholas V. Riasanovsky, *A Parting of Ways: Government and the Educated Public in Russia 1801–1855* (Oxford: Clarendon Press, 1976).

14. Gershenzon, *Istoricheskie zapiski*, p. 164.

15. Marc Raeff, *Origins of the Russian Intelligentsia: The Eighteenth-Century Nobility* (New York: Harcourt, Brace and World, 1966), p. 171.

16. The term 'middle class' as used here does not coincide with usage of the term in the West. The *raznochintsy* did not comprise a single distinct economic class, but were rather a variegated assortment of intellectuals below the level of the nobility.

17. P. Ia. Chaadaev, *Stat'i i pis'ma* (Moscow: Sovremennik, 1989), p. 47.

18. V. G. Belinskii, *Polnoe sobranie sochinenii*, 13 vols. (Moscow: Akademiia nauk SSSR, 1953–9), vol. III, p. 341.

19. Ibid., vol. XI, p. 576.

20. A. I. Herzen, *Sobranie sochinenii*, 8 vols. (Moscow: Pravda, 1975), vol. V, pp. 104–5.

21. The reference here is to the title of Andrzej Walicki's *The Controversy over Capitalism. Studies in the Philosophy of the Russian Populists* (Oxford University Press, 1969).

CHAPTER 2

The political and social order

David Saunders

The history of Russian thought used to be fashionable. Indeed, in the 1950s and early 1960s it occupied centre stage in English-language writing about Russian history. While Isaiah Berlin popularised it in Britain,[1] in the United States Nicholas Riasanovsky published on Slavophiles, Leopold Haimson on the ideological origins of Bolshevism, Marc Raeff on the ideas of the early nineteenth-century bureaucrat Speransky, Richard Pipes on the conservative Karamzin and Martin Malia on the liberal and proto-socialist Herzen.[2] Then, from the end of the 1950s, new academic exchange programmes permitted a few western scholars to study in the Soviet Union.[3] Those among them who gained admission to Soviet archives no longer had to confine their attention to the printed works of individual thinkers. When the studies of this new generation of scholars began to appear in print, the history of ideas began to take a back seat. Institutions and social groups, the prime concern of state archives, became a more frequent subject of anglophone monographs on Russian history than the intellectuals who had previously been in the ascendant. After the fall of the Soviet Union, when Russian archives came to be much more readily accessible to non-Russian scholars, concern for the history of ideas diminished still further. Thus anglophone work on Russian history since the Second World War may be said to consist of a phase of concentration on Russian thought followed by a phase of concentration on Russian politics and society. Although not every anglophone historian of Russia studied the history of ideas in the 1950s,[4] and although not all of them worked on majorities even when it became relatively easy to study in Russian archives,[5] intellectuals and the contexts in which they arose have, for the most part, been investigated serially rather than in parallel. Not a great deal of work has been done on the relationship between them.[6]

This chapter centres on that relationship. It suggests interactions between, on the one hand, Russia's political and social order in the eighteenth, nineteenth and early twentieth centuries (with some reference to earlier and later periods), and, on the other, 'thought' as defined by the editors in the Introduction to this book and as broken down chronologically and thematically in the chapters which follow. Unless one holds that texts can be read independently of the circumstances in which they are created (not a view taken here), it is reasonable to suppose that the perspectives of Russian thinkers constituted responses of one kind or another to the political and social order in which they arose. This chapter proposes three simple responses: conservatives tended to admire the world in which they found themselves, liberals sought to tinker with it and radicals were repelled by it. It tries to explain where these three sorts of thinker came from and how they found outlets for their views.

GOVERNMENT INSTITUTIONS

All Russian thinkers have grown up under political systems whose most striking feature was authoritarianism, or, to use the word most frequently employed in the Russian case, 'autocracy'. The Russian word for autocracy (*samoderzhavie*) did not originally imply overbearing power. In the sixteenth century, its principal connotation was independence from an external overlord. When Catherine the Great stated, in her instructions to the Legislative Commission of 1767–8, that '[t]he sovereign is autocratic [*samoderzhavnyi*]',[7] she probably meant only that she did not have to defer to any institutions below the throne. Not until the nineteenth century did autocracy come to be synonymous with oppression.[8] Nonetheless, after their final escape from Mongol tutelage towards the end of the fifteenth century Russia's rulers gave many indications that they would not willingly accept any further checks on their power. Changes in their official title encapsulated the growth in their confidence. Until the sixteenth century, they were Grand Princes. At his coronation in 1547, Ivan IV (the Terrible) formally became a 'tsar' (Caesar). At the end of the Great Northern War in 1721, Peter the Great declared Muscovy an empire and himself an emperor (*imperator*). The many succession crises of the years 1730–1825 demonstrated that people who aspired to influence policy in Russia knew they had to control the throne if they were to satisfy their ambitions. When Nicholas II took personal charge of Russia's armed forces at the height of the First World War in August 1915, he asserted a right to unmediated personal authority which no comparable monarch in Europe sought to exercise. Thus tsars continued to insist on their power until the end of the imperial period in February 1917. Surrogate tsars – General Secretaries of the Communist Party, Presidents of the Russian

Federation – often seemed to exert comparable degrees of power in the Soviet and post-Soviet periods.

It would not be true, of course, to say that Russian rulers have been deaf to advice. On the contrary, they have often permitted and sometimes encouraged advisory institutions. Discursive co-ordination of executive authority took place in the Boyar Duma in seventeenth-century Muscovy, in the Senate established by Peter the Great in 1711, in the State Council established by Alexander I in 1801 (to which he gave greater authority in 1810), in the Committee and Council of Ministers and various departments of the tsar's personal chancellery in nineteenth- and early twentieth-century Russia, in Unions of Towns and Zemstvos and a number of 'Special Councils' in the First World War and in the Politburo in the Soviet period.

Russian history has even witnessed instances of election. The country had intermittent 'Assemblies of the Land' in the sixteenth and seventeenth centuries, a representative Legislative Commission in 1767–8, 'Marshals of Nobility' elected by their peers at provincial and district level from 1775, urban corporations of a kind from 1785, forty-six provincial committees of noblemen elected in 1858 for the discussion of the abolition of serfdom, provincial and urban self-government from 1864 and 1870 respectively, an indirectly elected national Duma between 1906 and 1917, a genuinely and broadly representative 'Constituent Assembly' in January 1918 and a network of elected Soviet and Communist Party organisations below the level of the Politburo in which debate sometimes took place behind closed doors in the years 1917–91.

None of these subordinate agencies, however, significantly challenged the power of the key central authority. All of them were either manipulated by elements above them in the political hierarchy, or elected on narrow franchises, or short-lived or stillborn. 'Public opinion' (*obshchestvennost*) has had few dependable state-sanctioned political outlets in Russia. Until Gorbachev established the late Soviet 'Congress of People's Deputies' in 1989, Russia had no influential, potentially long-standing, central, all-class representative organs (and the promise of 1989 does not look so promising today).

Apart from permitting only infrequent exchanges of views at the highest executive level and usually denying the need for consensus in the preparation of legislative initiatives, Russian rulers have also been good at devising and maintaining powerful instruments for the implementation of their edicts. At the centre, they employed chanceries (*prikazy*) in the seventeenth century, colleges of government in the eighteenth century, ministries between 1802 and 1917 and, in the Soviet period, people's commissariats (which in due course became ministries again). In the provinces, they had military governors (*voevody*) in the seventeenth century, civilian governors (in the main) from the eighteenth century to 1917, regional and district secretaries of the Communist Party in the Soviet period and, since 1991, and after a brief period of election, centrally appointed regional governors.

Much of the enforcement of the autocrats' wishes, furthermore, has been the work not merely of bureaucrats but also of more or less openly repressive agencies and instruments: the armed forces, the secret police, censorship, prisons and a panoply of judicial and extra-judicial penalties.

Examples of the value of the armed forces to the regime in the maintenance of its conception of domestic order include the suppression of the revolt of the military colonists at Chuguev in eastern Ukraine in 1819, the Bezdna affair in the province of Kazan at the time of the abolition of serfdom in 1861, 'Bloody Sunday' in St Petersburg in January 1905, the massacre of workers on the Lena Goldfields in Siberia in April 1912 and the suppression of the strike in Novocherkassk in 1962.[9]

Russia's police agencies date back to Ivan the Terrible's sixteenth-century *oprichniki*, Fedor Romodanovsky's 'Preobrazhensky prikaz' in the early eighteenth century and Alexander I's ephemeral Ministry of Police (1811–19). Their continuous history, however, dates from 1826, when Nicholas I created the 'Third Department' of his personal chancellery, which in 1880 gave way to the Department of Police in the Ministry of Internal Affairs (the 'Okhranka', 1880–1917). Recent documentary publications make clear the range of Russian policemen's activities in the nineteenth and early twentieth centuries.[10] Highlights of their work included breaking up the Ukrainian 'Kirillo-Methodian Society' in 1847, suppressing the Petrashevsky Circle in 1849, rounding up the associates of Karakozov after his attempt to assassinate Alexander II in April 1866, infiltrating virtually every Russian revolutionary organisation from the 1880s to the end of the tsarist period and forging *The Protocols of the Elders of Zion*. The secret police of the Soviet and post-Soviet periods – Lenin's Cheka, Beria's NKVD, the late Soviet KGB and post-Soviet FSB – are notorious enough not to need special discussion, though it may be worth emphasising that the title of Orlando Figes's book *The Whisperers* captures very well a feature of Soviet society – whispering – for which they bear the principal responsibility.[11]

When publications were relatively few in number and issued mainly from government printing presses, the tsarist authorities did not require an elaborate system of censorship. To monitor literature, they needed only to keep their eye on private printing presses and prevent the importation of unwelcome material from abroad. Catherine the Great devoted more of her

time to promoting the development of Russian literary life than to imped-
ing it. After the outbreak of the French Revolution, however, she took
fright. In 1790 she sent Radishchev to Siberia for publishing *A Journey from
St Petersburg to Moscow*, an indictment of Russian social conditions. In 1792
she consigned the editor, publisher and writer Novikov to the Schlüsselburg
Fortress near St Petersburg. In September 1796 she closed down all private
printing presses and assigned the systematic monitoring of publications
from abroad to the Senate in St Petersburg and Moscow and various local
government agencies on the empire's Baltic, Polish and Black Sea frontiers.[12] Although Alexander I lifted Catherine's ban on private presses in
March 1801, he decreed in July 1804 that 'no book or composition may be
printed or put on sale in the Russian Empire without having been previously scrutinised by the censorship'.[13] This decree marked the start of the
continuous history of censorship in Russia.

Relatively mild at first, the state's scrutiny of potential publications became
much more severe in the reign of Nicholas I. Nicholas believed that the
Decembrist Revolt of 1825 with which his reign began had stemmed partly
from the failure of the regime to prevent the free circulation of opinion.
Accordingly, he promulgated the so-called 'Iron' censorship statute of June
1826, which, had it remained in force, would have closed down literary life
more or less for good. The decree of April 1828 which replaced it was only a
little less forbidding. It brought into being the long-lived 'Main Censorship
Administration' (*Glavnoe upravlenie tsenzury*), an agency of the Ministry
of Education which was responsible for local censorship committees in
St Petersburg, Moscow, Riga, Vilna (Vilnius), Kiev, Odessa and Tiflis
(Tbilisi) (as well as the Foreign Censorship Committee in St Petersburg,
which scrutinised imports). Many other government agencies – the
Ministries of Internal and Foreign Affairs, the Finance and War Ministries,
the Second and Third Departments of the tsar's personal chancellery – had
responsibility for censorship in their particular fields of competence. Thus,
under Nicholas, censorship was well-nigh ubiquitous. The tsar even created a
body whose sole purpose was to monitor images of the ruler and his family.
Censorship peaked, under Nicholas, in the last and most benighted part of
the reign, the period of the 'Buturlin Committee' (1848–55), an additional
body created by the tsar in the wake of the European revolutions of 1848 to
ensure that the other censorship agencies were being strict enough.[14]

Under Alexander II, conditions for writers became a little easier.
Although overall control of censorship was taken out of the hands of the
Ministry of Education and given to the Ministry of Internal Affairs in 1863
(a move which the Minister of Education thought would lead to greater

severity), new rules of April 1865 freed the editors of newspapers (in St Petersburg and Moscow) and the authors of certain sorts of book (the longer ones) from the need to submit their works to the censor prior to publication. What had once been the Main Censorship Administration now became the softer-sounding Main Press Administration (*Glavnoe upravlenie po delam pechati*). Editors, however, could still be notified by the authorities that their newspapers were running the risk of being shut down (three warnings led to closure), and books could still be prosecuted after publication. Substantial press freedom arrived in Russia only as a result of the revolution of 1905 (by virtue of edicts enacted in November 1905 and March and April 1906).[15] Even then the regime's relationship with writers remained uneasy, and military censorship supervened during the First World War.[16] The Provisional Government abolished censorship altogether in April 1917, but in October the Bolsheviks made clear where they stood on the subject when they closed down opposition newspapers within two days of taking power. Between then and 1991 the Soviet regime relaxed its hold on publications only intermittently and exceptionally.[17]

Thus for most of the nineteenth and twentieth centuries Russian thinkers had to bear in mind the probable difficulty of finding outlets for their views. Admittedly, Russian regimes have not necessarily been hostile to education (which requires printed matter), and attempts to suppress publications sometimes have the effect of stimulating them. When, however, it was illegal to criticise the dynasty (as it was in tsarist times), when a professor at Moscow University could lose his job for indirect involvement in the publication in 1848 of a critical late sixteenth-century English account of Muscovy,[18] when the Russian Empire's second most widely spoken language, Ukrainian, could be banned as a medium of publication (as it was between 1863 and 1905),[19] and when Akhmatova and Pasternak were unable to publish poetry under Stalin, it is reasonable to conclude that educated inhabitants of the Russian Empire and the Soviet Union had to think hard before contemplating lives in literature.

Penalties for thinking incorrectly could be severe. Although the Empress Elizabeth abolished capital punishment in Russia in 1754, her edict soon went by the board (in the cases, for example, of the people who murdered the Metropolitan of Moscow in 1771 and of the peasant rebel Pugachev in 1775). It did not survive Speransky's codification of Russian law in the early 1830s. Some ostensibly milder punishments – the lash, running the gauntlet – could lead to death anyway. Some penalties – lengthy periods of solitary confinement, Siberian exile with or without hard labour – could almost be said to have been worse than death. The first Siberian exile in Russian history is supposed to have been the bell at Uglich which Boris Godunov condemned in 1591 for trying to warn the inhabitants of the town that his minions were about to murder Crown Prince Dmitry. Novikov was so chastened by his experience of confinement in the Schlüsselburg Fortress in the 1790s that, after his release, he spent the last twenty years of his life more or less wholly on his estate. One of the reasons that Radishchev committed suicide in 1802 was probably that the Minister of Education had hinted to him, perhaps in jest, that the radicalism of a memorandum he had just submitted might get him sent to Siberia again. Although, by the standards of the time and in view of their demonstrable treason, it may not have been surprising that Nicholas I executed five of the Decembrists in 1826 and sent a hundred more to Siberia, the subjection of Dostoevsky (in 1849) and Chernyshevsky (in 1864) to mock public executions prior to lengthy periods of exile smacked of vindictiveness. The sentences which followed the 'Trial of the 193' in St Petersburg in 1877–8 and the many round-ups of Social Democrats in the mid-1890s were some of the highlights of later tsarist persecution. Pressure to conform was an even more strongly marked feature of the Soviet period. The show trials of 1936–8, the prosecution of the writers Siniavsky and Daniel in 1966, the expulsion of Solzhenitsyn from the Soviet Union in 1974 and the confinement of Academician Sakharov to Nizhnii Novgorod between January 1980 and December 1986 demonstrate that penalties for freedom of thought tended to be at least as far-reaching in twentieth-century Russia as they had been under the tsars.

SOCIAL POLICY

Apart from taking a firmly authoritarian view of politics, Russian rulers have also discouraged movement in society. Peasants were the overwhelming majority of their subjects until well into the twentieth century (between 69.8 per cent and 91.4 per cent of the total population in the tsarist census of January 1897, depending on who precisely is being counted).[20] They began losing their right of departure from the estates on which they worked in the middle of the fifteenth century, when edicts allowed them to leave only in a brief period either side of St George's Day (in November). They probably lost the right of departure altogether in 1592 or 1593, although the text of the relevant edict has never come to light.[21] Formalised in the Law Code of 1649, serfdom intensified in the following century and a half. Catherine the Great took over the estates of the monasteries in 1764 and extended serfdom to the Ukraine in 1783. Lords acquired the right to despatch recalcitrant peasants to Siberia in 1765. The various government pronouncements of the

first half of the nineteenth century which appeared to promise amelioration of
the peasants' lot were permissive rather than obligatory and bore little fruit.

Even the tsars' eventual abolitions of serfdom left a great deal to be
desired. The first, in the Baltic part of the empire between 1816 and 1819,
reduced peasants to indigence by failing to make land available to them.
The general abolition of February 1861 created almost as many problems as
it solved. Although this time the government did make land available to
peasants, the 'statutory charters' which defined the new boundaries tended
to favour the former owners. Nor did peasants receive their land allocations
free of charge. They had to make 'redemption payments', an arrangement
which saddled them with debt. Peasants did not receive their land allocations, moreover, as individuals or families. Ownership was vested in the
peasant commune (*mir* or *obshchina*), which meant that it continued to be
in strips in open fields rather than in the form of consolidated holdings. It
remained subject to communal decisions about times of sowing and har-
vesting, and also in some cases to periodic repartitioning in accordance with
changes in family size. Finally, peasants did not have recourse on peasant
matters to the new courts which the regime established shortly after the 1861
abolition. Dealt with in courts of their own (*volost'* courts), peasants
remained, in law as in economic matters, less than wholly independent
actors.

Peasant 'collective responsibility' (*krugovaia poruka*) was abolished in
1903 and the peasants' redemption payments in November 1905 (with full
effect from 1 January 1907). The 'Stolypin reforms' of November 1906 made
it possible for peasants to leave their communes and consolidate their
holdings in integrated farms. The government also promised additional
land to peasants who were willing to contemplate resettlement in Siberia or
the Far East. Peasant courts were abolished in 1912. These changes of the late
tsarist period were still taking effect when revolution broke out. Although,
in and just after 1917, peasants took over the estates of the gentry, they did
not convert them into multiple individual smallholdings. Perhaps because
the reforms of the previous decade had not had time to make their mark,
they applied traditional methods. As a result, 96 per cent of all rural families
were in communes in 1920.[22] At least twice in the 1920s (in 1923–4 and
1927–8), the young Soviet regime experienced crises of food supply because
the countryside would not part with its produce. Cities were not producing
industrial goods in sufficient quantities and at prices to suit the peasantry.
Centuries of mismanagement had fostered peasant recalcitrance.

Stalin, therefore, intervened decisively against the peasantry. In the
'collectivisation' process of the First Five-Year Plan (1928–32), he abolished

their communes (in 1930) and brought their landholdings under state control. In so doing, he put an end to whatever incipient liberation peasants had experienced since the abolition of serfdom in 1861. Russian peasants were probably little better off in the collective farms of Soviet times than they had been under serfdom. For most of the Soviet period they were not really full citizens. They were not granted internal passports, for example, at the point when the rest of the population was obliged to acquire them in November 1932. When they did finally receive them, in 1974, the reform was presented as a significant concession.[23]

Although Russia's other social groups have been less constrained than the peasantry, none of them has been wholly free from interference on the part of the state. Noblemen were probably as well placed as they were ever to be at the end of the sixteenth and beginning of the seventeenth centuries, when the extinction of the Moscow branch of the Riurikid dynasty created a power vacuum. Two boyars, Boris Godunov and Vasily Shuisky, held the throne for a few years at that time before a third, Michael Romanov, established the new dynasty. The rivalry of the Miloslavsky and Naryshkin clans after the death of Tsar Alexis Mikhailovich in 1676 gave the impression that prominent nobles were still the dominant force in the administration of the country, but the complex system of precedent (*mestnichestvo*) on which senior noblemen relied to keep out their inferiors was abolished in 1682, and Peter the Great's ascent to undivided authority in 1696 heralded an era in which service to the state came to be the principal feature of Russian nobility. Peter went far beyond his famous insistence on the shaving of beards and replacement of Muscovite by European clothing. In 1722 he made civil, military or court service obligatory and assigned all positions in these three branches of service a place on a new fourteen-point 'Table of Ranks'. Because the bottom six of the fourteen points conferred personal and the top eight hereditary nobility, the new system combined the stick and the carrot.

Whether the rewards that Peter's system offered were sufficiently attractive to offset the compulsion it entailed has been a matter of debate. When the tsar's grandson, Peter III, relieved nobles of the obligation to serve the state in 1762, many of them retired to their estates to enjoy what has been called 'the golden age of the Russian nobility' (the period between 1762 and the abolition of serfdom in 1861). When Catherine the Great incorporated nobles as an estate of the realm in her 'Charter to the Nobility' of 1785, it appeared that they had gained not only independence from the state, but also its respect. If, however, the retirements and the new legally defined rights of the later eighteenth century give the impression that Russian nobles were justified in feeling that they could do without the state, the impression needs to be modified. Who was ditching whom in 1762 is unclear.[24] Because many nobles needed the material rewards of government employment, the state could lift the obligation on them to serve (many of them would take jobs anyway). Because significant numbers of servitors were beginning to emerge from outside the ranks of the long-established nobility, landed noblemen who left government employ ran the risk of being supplanted by a new category of landless noble whose interests would be at odds with their own (a phenomenon which almost certainly played its part in the process which brought about the abolition of serfdom in 1861). Some noblemen who chose not to serve, furthermore, appear simply to have found the life of leisure frustrating, a phenomenon which may be embodied in the personality of the early nineteenth-century dissident Chaadaev and certainly finds expression in nineteenth-century fictional characters such as Turgenev's 'superfluous man' of 1851 and the hero of Goncharov's novel *Oblomov* of 1859. It should not be a surprise, therefore, that the nobles' 'golden age' ended badly, from their point of view, with the loss of their serfs in 1861. The state had been undermining them for decades. They did not adjust well to life without serfs. Having owned some 30.8 per cent of the land of European Russia just before the abolition of serfdom, they owned only 19.4 per cent in 1877, 13.7 per cent in 1905 and 10.2 per cent at the end of 1914.[25] Thus it can be argued that, slowly at first, then rather rapidly, they were in decline throughout the period on which this book concentrates. The Russian state brought them to heel.

Lest it seem, however, that in bringing pressure to bear on nobles the tsars were trying to reduce privilege, remove social barriers and encourage talent, it needs to be emphasised that these were not their concerns. Their interest lay in control. Just as peasants had to be kept in their place even after the abolition of serfdom, so nobles had to be kept in their place even when, as serf-owners, they were the crown's principal agents in the countryside. When Catherine the Great incorporated the gentry as an estate of the realm in 1785, she was not trying to liberate them, but rather to pin them down. Whereas until then they had enjoyed a certain licence, henceforward their rights and duties were to be defined. The empress issued a comparable charter to Russia's towns on the same day. She seems to have contemplated a further charter to the peasantry. Her goal in these edicts and potential edicts was to define the rights and duties of all her subjects by assigning all of them to specific categories. She had in mind an estate-based, as opposed to a class-based, society. Juridical definitions, not economic inter-connections, were to shape the world towards which she was moving.[26]

In western Europe, estate-based societies were undermined for good when the French Estates General agreed to vote by head rather than by estate in the summer of 1789. In the minds of Russian rulers, however, the vision of clearly delineated estates lived on into the nineteenth and twentieth centuries. Alexander I tried to legislate for the creation of an estate of 'free agriculturalists' in 1803. Nicholas I created the category of urban 'honoured citizen' in 1832 and legislated for the potential emergence of a category of 'obligated peasants' in 1842. Pre-revolutionary Russia hardly ever enacted social legislation which applied to everybody. One of the main reasons why the introduction of universal military conscription was controversial in 1874 was the very fact of its universality. The poll tax, paid only by peasants, survived until the mid-1880s. Income tax arrived in Russia only at the height of the First World War in 1916. At the end of the nineteenth and in the early twentieth centuries, Russia's last tsars were probably trying harder than ever to fit the population of the empire into the Procrustean bed of an estate-based rather than a class-based society.[27] The votes which brought the First Duma into being in 1906 were not equally weighted. When neither the First nor the Second Duma behaved in a manner acceptable to the regime, Prime Minister Stolypin rendered votes more unequal still by changing the electoral law. Estates of the realm were formally abolished only on 11 November 1917, two weeks after the Bolsheviks came to power. Even after that Stalin may have been trying, in the 1930s, to reintroduce something akin to them.[28] Russian governments have almost invariably sought to control not merely individuals, but society in the round.

OFFICIAL IDEOLOGIES

Apart from embodying their authoritarianism in government institutions and social policies, Russian rulers have also striven to impose ideologies on their subjects. Perhaps their most striking achievement in this regard was to turn to their advantage the hierarchy of the Russian Orthodox Church. The church–state tension which figures so prominently in the history of other European countries is barely discernible in Russia. The closest the country came to it was Alexis Mikhailovich's dispute with Patriarch Nikon in the 1660s, which ended with the consignment of the patriarch to an island in the White Sea and, in effect, the transfer of the church's ideological resources to the secular authority. Alexis made it possible for Russian rulers to turn their autocracy into a quasi-theocracy. In 1700 Peter the Great dispensed with patriarchs altogether, replacing them in 1721 with a state-controlled 'Holy

Synod' which ran the Orthodox Church until 1917. Although Orthodoxy remained a quintessential aspect of Russian identity, most of its priests and monks were mouthpieces of the monarchy (literally, in so far as priests read out tsarist edicts in church). *The Justice of the Monarch's Will*, the paper of 1722 in which Peter the Great's principal churchman, Feofan Prokopovich, justified the tsar's right to name his own heir, was essentially a Russian version of the argument for the divine right of kings. At her coronation in 1742, the Empress Elizabeth emphasised the crown's view of the relative priority of state and church by taking the crown from the hands of an archbishop and crowning herself (an action which all future tsars replicated).

In the nineteenth century, Nicholas I was perhaps the tsar who made most use of Orthodoxy as an ideological device. In 1833 his Minister of Education, Uvarov, circulated the key text of the doctrine which historians later dubbed 'Official Nationality'. 'Our general duty', it averred, 'consists of this: that the education of the people be conducted in conformity with the *supreme* intention of our *august monarch* in the united spirit of Orthodoxy, autocracy, and nationality.'[29] Analysts have made much of the words 'autocracy' and 'nationality' in this statement without always placing sufficient emphasis on the fact that 'Orthodoxy' preceded them. In March 1848, at a time of revolutionary upheaval in Europe, Nicholas I issued a violent tirade counterposing 'our Holy Rus' to the revolutionary countries of western and central Europe and affirming that 'our ancient cry, Faith, Tsar and Fatherland, will show us the way to victory even now'.[30] 'Faith, Tsar and Fatherland' in this pronouncement were synonyms for the three key words in the circular of 1833. A year later Nicholas spoke in comparable terms when sending his armies into Hungary.[31] When he declared war on the Ottoman Empire in 1853 and on Britain and France in 1854, he once more set himself against 'the revolutionists of all countries' and declared that Russia was fighting 'for the Christian faith, and for the defence of her co-religionists oppressed by implacable enemies'.[32]

Thus Nicholas relied heavily on religious motifs in his ideological declarations. Because Alexis Mikhailovich had won his battles with Patriarch Nikon nearly two centuries earlier, nineteenth-century tsars could be sure that they and the Russian Orthodox Church were of one mind. It is true that Nicholas's elder brother and predecessor, Alexander I, toyed with the idea of religious renewal, but the initiative proved to be short-lived.[33] The fact that the Orthodox Church was not an organisation which encouraged its adherents to think for themselves is perhaps best illustrated by its failure to publish a complete one-volume bible in modern Russian until 1876.[34] The publication of bibles in vernacular languages had been one of the most striking achievements of the sixteenth-century central and west European Reformations. That so much time had to elapse before an officially approved bible appeared in modern Russian was an indication of the extent to which the Orthodox Church had lost whatever capacity it once possessed for ideological leadership.

Tsars after Nicholas I usually made plain their commitment to authoritarianism less sanctimoniously than he. Indeed, when Karakozov fired on Alexander II in April 1866, the tsar's reaction was almost entirely practical: he abolished the governor-generalship of St Petersburg, dismissed his Minister of Education, appointed a much more dynamic police chief and promulgated an edict which greatly increased the power of his provincial governors.[35] When, nonetheless, The People's Will succeeded in assassinating him fifteen years later, his son Alexander III was a little more pompous. He made a public profession of 'faith in the strength and verity of autocratic power, which we have been called upon to maintain and defend, for the good of the people, against all encroachments upon it'.[36] Like his father, however, Alexander III soon turned to practicalities. In August 1881 he issued the 'Law on Reinforced Safeguard', a statute which marked the establishment of a police state whose key features survived until the end of the tsarist regime, and which, in the opinion of Richard Pipes, informed the authoritarianism of the Soviet Union.[37] In January 1895, three months after ascending the throne, Nicholas II told delegates from Russia's elected organs of local government that his response to their 'senseless dreams' about becoming involved in the domestic administration of the country was to '[L]et everyone know that whilst I shall dedicate all my powers to the well-being of the people, I shall maintain the principles of autocracy as firmly and unbendingly as my late never-to-be-forgotten father.'[38] The new, supposedly more liberal edition of the *Fundamental Laws of the Russian Empire* which Nicholas was nonetheless obliged to promulgate in April 1906 (as a result of the revolution of 1905) still opened with the resounding statement that 'the Russian State is one and indivisible' (which disappointed some of the majority non-Russian population of the empire), specified that legislative initiative belonged to the tsar (clause 8) and reserved to the tsar the right to circumvent the country's new parliament by legislating when it was not in session (clause 87).[39]

Thus tsars repeatedly made clear, sometimes in religious terms, sometimes not, that their ideology was strongly and avowedly directive. Few if any of them were non-interventionist, pragmatic, empirically inclined or detached. None gave the population much room for manoeuvre. In this, as in other respects, their Soviet successors imitated them; Martin Malia and

David Priestland are just two recent authors who have emphasised the importance to the Soviet regime of firm ideological commitment.[40]

RESPONSES

In the light of the foregoing, it ought to be easy to see why there were conservative thinkers in eighteenth-, nineteenth- and early twentieth-century Russia. They were the intellectuals who respected strong institutions, welcomed social control and deplored ideological dissidence. Two of them, Feofan Prokopovich and Uvarov, appeared in passing in the last section. Others will appear later in this book (notably in chapter 5). The present writer thinks first of the conservative 'statist school' in nineteenth- and early twentieth-century Russian-language historiography, a series of intellectuals from Karamzin to Kliuchevsky who, by contrast with 'populist' historians such as Shchapov, Kostomarov and Semevsky, put the state machine at the centre of the Russian historical process.[41] Various branches and representatives of Russian conservatism have been attracting scholarly interest in recent years.[42]

In theory, it is also not difficult to imagine why there were people in Russia who, on the one hand, wanted to tinker with the regime (liberals) or, on the other, sought to overthrow it (radicals). Not everyone, after all, values subordination and deference. A moment's reflection, however, brings to mind a conundrum in respect of liberals and radicals. In view of the fact that Russia's political and social structures both appear to have been strongly anti-libertarian, how did non-conservatives ever come into existence there? And how, having fallen prey to dissident ideas, did they manage to communicate them to others?

These questions need answering, for it can be argued that the thought of liberals and radicals has played a greater part in bringing about change in Russia than the revolutionary upheavals on which commentators usually concentrate. Mass disturbances have troubled Russia's rulers only occasionally. Although historians make much of Russia's four major peasant rebellions of the seventeenth and eighteenth centuries, of what Soviet scholars used to call the 'revolutionary situations' of 1859–61 and 1879–81 (times of great crisis which embodied many but not all of the prerequisites for revolution), of the revolutions of 1905 and 1917 and of the events which culminated in the collapse of the Soviet Union at the end of 1991, it is worth pointing out that there were no large-scale uprisings against the tsars between the execution of Pugachev in 1775 and the St Petersburg textile strikes of 1896–7, and none in the Soviet Union between the horrors of collectivisation in the early 1930s and the Gorbachev years of the late 1980s. For the most part, in other words, Russia has been upheaval-free. Ideological resistance on the part of liberals and radicals, however, has been more or less continuous there. It is hard to think of a time when rulers did not have their intellectual opponents. Even Stalin probably succeeded in closing down only the most overt signs of dissent.[43] Dissident Russian thought needs to be explained. How did it arise, and how did it find outlets?

EDUCATION

A major answer to the first of these questions lies in education. Russian rulers needed educated servants to exploit and run their domains, but education enables people to reflect critically on the world around them. Regimes could not guarantee that their servants would accept their values.

At first, Russia met her educational needs by importing trained foreigners. Tsar Alexis Mikhailovich formalised the pre-existing foreigners' quarter of Moscow, the *nemetskaia sloboda*, in 1652. General Patrick Gordon is only the best known of the early foreign advisers of the young Peter the Great. After Peter visited western Europe in 1697–8, the flow of foreigners into his homeland turned from a trickle into a stream. Many recent studies testify to the importance of foreigners in eighteenth-century Russia.[44] In its early days the Imperial Academy of Sciences, founded in 1724, was a sort of German fiefdom. The long-running 'Normanist controversy' in Russian historiography (a debate about the part played by Vikings in Russia's origins) was inaugurated in 1736 by Gottlieb Bayer, a German at the Russian Academy. The prolific Swiss mathematician Leonhard Euler spent a total of about thirty years in eighteenth-century St Petersburg. The Scotsman Samuel Greig was the most famous foreign sailor to serve Catherine the Great. The careers of Karl von Nesselrode, Minister of Foreign Affairs between 1816 and 1856, and of Egor Kankrin and Mikhail Reitern, Ministers of Finance under Nicholas I and Alexander II, testify to the fact that native German-speakers (from Germany proper as well as the Baltic provinces of the Russian Empire) continued to occupy significant positions in the Russian civil service in the nineteenth century. Vladimir Dal, the greatest of Russian lexicographers, was the son of a Dane. Even in the second half of the nineteenth century, when the tsarist regime was becoming more self-reliant, foreign engineers and industrialists figured prominently in Russian economic life. Charles Mitchell, an Aberdonian, built the first dedicated iron shipbuilding yard in St Petersburg in the early 1860s. John Hughes, a Welsh iron-founder, initiated coal-mining in the

Donbass in 1869. The Metro-Vickers trial of 1933 demonstrated among other things that foreigners were still significant in early Soviet industrial development. The tribulations of Shell and BP in the Russia of President Putin remind us that foreigners have played a significant part in the transformation of post-Soviet Russia.

Russia also sent natives abroad to receive the education they could not get at home. Boris Godunov, in 1602, may have been the first Russian ruler to send Russian students to foreign parts. In the eighteenth century, Russians of independent means enrolled at many of the universities of central and western Europe.[45] Catherine the Great systematised the practice of sending Russian sailors to learn their craft on British ships at the very beginning of her reign in 1762. Acting on a proposal of 1827 from Professor E. I. Parrot of Dorpat, Nicholas I initiated the nineteenth-century Russian government's practice of supporting Russian graduate students in lengthy periods of foreign study in order to prepare them for professorships at home. Although this practice peaked in the first half of the 1860s, it was still operational in 1915.[46] In the 1890s the chemist Mendeleev came to Britain on more than one occasion at Russian government expense to keep up with British scientific developments.[47] As we saw in the opening paragraph of the present essay, even the basically autarkic Soviet Union agreed to exchange a few students with western countries at the end of the 1950s.

Since virtually all the foreigners who entered Russian employ were more enlightened in their political opinions than their Russian masters, and since Russians who were educated in central and western Europe could pick up ideas there which were at odds with those which motivated their masters at home, there was an element of risk, from the point of view of challenges to Russian authoritarianism, in Russia's first two ways of procuring well-trained servants. On the other hand, neither the number of foreigners in Russia nor the number of Russians who have studied outside the country has ever been enormous. If Russia had been able to meet its need for educated people solely by importing the people it needed or sending Russians abroad, its regimes might have been able to keep in check whatever ideological challenges arose among the educated inhabitants of the country. Unfortunately, from the point of view of political and social stability, the country's need for educated people could not be satisfied so easily.

Gradually, therefore, Russia set up an educational network of her own. It is true that the tsars always fought shy of compulsory mass primary education, and that, according to the imperial census of 1897, literacy stood at a mere 21.1 per cent,[48] but even that small percentage meant that in a population of just over 125 million more than 25 million people were literate, and most of them were young, male and urban, the sort of people likeliest to pose problems for the regime. Higher education, furthermore, had developed more rapidly than primary schools. When Russia took over eastern Ukraine in the seventeenth century, it acquired the Kiev Academy, the largest educational establishment in tsarist hands prior to the early nineteenth century. The Empress Elizabeth founded Moscow University in 1755. After setting up new universities in Kharkov and Kazan in 1804 and revamping the originally non-Russian universities of Dorpat (Tartu) in Estonia and Vilna (Vilnius) in Lithuania, Alexander I set up St Petersburg University in 1819. Additional universities came into being elsewhere in the Russian Empire between the early nineteenth century and 1917.

Russian regimes would no doubt have been happy to educate their subjects to the highest possible standard if they could have been sure that, for example, Lobachevsky would confine his attention to mathematics, Pirogov to medicine, Mendeleev to chemistry, Pavlov to physiology and Vernadsky to geology (and, in the Soviet period, Sakharov to physics). It was never likely, however, that university-educated people would confine themselves to their specialisms. The 2,000 city-based Russian university students who spent the summer of 1874 'going to the people' in order to discover the condition of the Russian countryside a decade after the abolition of serfdom were only one of the most striking examples of the phenomenon of educated people turning from their fields of study to the wider problems of their society. University students were to be significant in all the revolutionary parties which came into being in the last years of tsarism.[49]

A CHANGING WORLD

If education gave potential liberals and radicals the means of expressing their thoughts, the changing world of the Russian Empire continually gave them pressing new problems to think about. The description of government institutions, social policies and ideologies with which this essay began was deceptive in so far as it gave the impression that Russian rulers had no interest other than maintaining the status quo. On the contrary, they also wanted to expand the frontiers of the state and make clear to neighbouring powers that they were a force to be reckoned with. These ambitions required barely controllable experimentation and modernisation. Russian thinkers were often responding not merely to their rulers' authoritarianism *tout court*, but to the effects of a combination of authoritarianism and expansionism.

Muscovy began conquering large numbers of non-Slavs in the sixteenth century, when Ivan the Terrible defeated the Tatars on the Volga. His successors acquired part of the Ukraine and the whole of Siberia in the seventeenth century; the southern shore of the eastern Baltic, the eastern half of the Polish–Lithuanian Commonwealth and the Crimea in the eighteenth century; Transcaucasia, Finland, Moldavia, the eastern coastline of the Black Sea and Central Asia in the nineteenth century; and in 1945 a surrogate empire in eastern Europe. Only after eastern Europe broke away from Moscow's tutelage in 1989 and the Soviet Union fell apart in 1991 did Russia revert to something like its seventeenth-century boundaries.

Some of the problems generated by empire were different in kind from the problems Russia was used to. Empire involved greater religious and ethnic variety. Until the mid-seventeenth century, Russia was a predominantly Slavonic and Orthodox country. By the end of the tsarist regime, Russians were in a minority in the population, the state contained as many Muslims as the Ottoman Empire and the Jews of the former Polish–Lithuanian Commonwealth had become a focus of Russian racism and were complicating relations between Russia and the USA.

In addition, the military requirements of empire had social and economic implications for the imperial heartland which would have strained any regime. Scholars have argued, for example, that both the sixteenth- and seventeenth-century origins and the nineteenth-century abolition of serfdom, the key distinguishing feature of the social structure of the tsarist empire, ought to be explained principally with reference to military matters.[50] These arguments run as follows. In the sixteenth and seventeenth centuries, peasants could not be allowed to forsake the estates of the regime's lesser servitors for those of grandees because the regime needed both sorts of landowner to staff its growing army. Therefore, peasants had to be tied down permanently. In the nineteenth century, on the other hand, removing more than a certain number of peasants from the land to serve in the army was impossible because of the highly labour-intensive nature of Russian peasant farming, and returning peasants to the land after short periods of service (then taking others and so in time giving the entire peasantry military training) was also impossible, because peasants with military training might be capable of overthrowing serfdom. Therefore, serfdom had to be abolished. The first of these arguments has been received more warmly than the second, but no one denies connections of one kind or another between serfdom and tsarist militarism.

In becoming an empire, finally, Russia put itself in competition with the rest of the world's Great Powers. The closer the contact, the more account Russian regimes had to take of foreign ideas and foreign realities, for only by understanding them could they compete with them. Foreign ideas and realities, however, could not be controlled to the extent that Russian regimes controlled domestic ideas and realities. They changed, sometimes dramatically – in the wake of the late eighteenth-century French Revolution, for example, and especially in the second half of the nineteenth century, when Britain's industrial revolution was replicated in a number of mainland European countries. Russia had to respond to these developments in order to keep up with her international competitors. This meant accepting some unwelcome phenomena: upwardly mobile peasants, downwardly mobile nobles, the emergence of an urban prole-tariat and, in Soviet times, a bureaucratic 'new class'. Many chapters of this book show Russian thinkers grappling with the changing world which Russian rulers were unable wholly to avoid.

OUTLETS

Although education and the stimulus of changes in the world around them may help to explain how liberals and radicals arose in Russia (for liberals and radicals were likeliest to put the two together and act on the mix), they do not explain how these nonconformists found ways of conveying their opinions to others. If Russian regimes were as authoritarian as the first part of this chapter made out, how did dissident intellectuals ever find outlets for their views?

An obvious answer to this question is that the rulers' methods of control left much to be desired. Although the number of bureaucrats per head of the population went up nearly sevenfold in Russia between 1796 and 1897,[51] it was never sufficiently high to enact the rulers' wishes in full. Nor were the tsars' servants always effective in their pursuit of their masters' goals. The censors, for example, blundered when they let through Chaadaev's first 'Philosophical Letter' in 1836, Chernyshevsky's subversive novel *What is to be Done?* in 1863 (at a time when its author was already in prison) and the Russian translation of volume one of Marx's *Capital* in 1872. The secret police probably did more to promote than to hinder the revolutionary movement at the beginning of the twentieth century when one of their agents, Zubatov, fostered trade unions (in the forlorn hope of controlling urban workers), and another, Azef, organised political assassinations (in order, he hoped, to win the con-fidence of assassins in the Socialist Revolutionary Party).

Mistakes, however, go only part of the way to explaining how liberals and radicals found ways of expressing themselves in Russia. Perhaps out

of self-confidence, some tsars betrayed a willingness to enter the ideological fray themselves. They permitted the expression of a wider range of
views than the ones they held themselves in order to win the ensuing
battles of ideas. But engaging with a range of ideas could have the effect of
opening Pandora's Box. When Catherine the Great corresponded with
Voltaire, Diderot and Grimm, it was not unreasonable of the thinkers
whom she was to prosecute, Novikov and Radishchev, to believe that
they, too, could discuss Enlightenment ideas. If Nicholas I 'felt it as part
of the mission of enlightened absolutism, which he had taken upon
himself, to encourage the flourishing of letters',[52] he may have done so
because, like Catherine, he hoped to turn literary ideas to his advantage.
I have argued elsewhere that this is precisely what he was trying to do
when, through Uvarov, he made the neologism *narodnost'* (nationality)
the third part of his policy platform of 1833 ('Orthodoxy, Autocracy,
Nationality').[53] If, however, he was indeed trying to draw the sting of a
word which had originated on the liberal end of the political spectrum, he
probably succeeded only in rendering the word more subversive than it
had been in the first place.[54]

Even rulers who had only a tenuous interest in ideology themselves
sometimes permitted liberals to voice their opinions because they realised
that they needed new ideas to revamp the management of their domains.
Thus Alexander I permitted Speransky, the 'Russian Montesquieu', to draw
up seminal papers on the reorganisation of Russian government in the years
of the Franco-Russian Alliance of 1807–12; and thus, after defeat in the
Crimean War, Alexander II allowed a senior official in the Finance Ministry
to ask how long the government intended to go on resisting the development of the industrial forces of the people,[55] and backed an entire cohort of
'enlightened bureaucrats' in legislating for the abolition of serfdom against
the wishes of virtually the entire Russian nobility.[56]

Outlets of the kind outlined so far, however, were available only to
moderates, the people whom, for convenience, I have collectively christened
'liberals'. No tsar, except perhaps in the brief period between the 1905
revolution and the First World War, and no Soviet leader from the point
when Stalin established his pre-eminence at the end of the 1920s, allowed
people with whom he or she disagreed strongly – the people whom, for
convenience, I dub 'radicals' – to express themselves freely. How, then, did
even these find outlets for their views? Broadly speaking, in one of two ways:
abroad (and therefore, up to a point, beyond the reach of Russia's repressive
agencies), and at home by risking everything (establishing oral networks,
publishing illegally, addressing the regime directly).

The history of Russian dissent outside Russia dates back at least to Prince Kurbsky in sixteenth-century Lithuania (who addressed vitriolic letters to Ivan the Terrible) and Kotoshikhin in seventeenth-century Sweden (who indicted the ceremonial of the court of Alexis Mikhailovich), but in the modern period it begins with Golovin's *Russia under the Autocrat Nicholas the First*, which came out in France and England in 1846, and Nikolay Turgenev's *Russia and the Russians*, a three-volume study of the Russia of Alexander I, which came out in France in 1847. Thereafter, to give only a few examples of the many that could be cited, Herzen ran *The Bell*, the most successful of all anti-tsarist periodicals, in London in the 1850s and 1860s; the Populist Stepniak-Kravchinsky published extensive indictments of the tsarist regime in London in the 1880s and 1890s; the Social Democrats published *The Spark* in Munich and other places in western Europe between 1900 and 1905; and, in the Soviet period, Boris Bazhanov, Walter Krivitsky and Viktor Kravchenko exposed the regime of Stalin in France, Britain and the United States before and after the Second World War. By the late Soviet period dissidents had coined a new word, *tamizdat* ('publication over there'), to describe the by then well-developed practice of smuggling manuscripts out of Russia for publication abroad.

Riskier even than *tamizdat* was its prototype *samizdat* ('self-publishing'), the phenomenon of uncensored publication inside Russia. In a pamphlet which his associates printed illegally and released in St Petersburg to coincide with his assassination of the tsar's chief of police in the summer of 1878, Stepniak-Kravchinsky declared that the socialist members of his party demanded 'the complete cessation of all prosecutions for the expression of any convictions whatever', 'the complete elimination of all arbitrary administrative behaviour' and 'a full amnesty for all political convicts': 'Do not infringe our human rights – that is all we want from you.'[57] Nothing so forthright could have appeared in print in late imperial Russia (or in Russia at many other points in its history) unless a few educated Russians had been prepared to throw caution to the winds. The revolutionaries of the late 1870s included a significant number of such people. In May 1878, for example, a few months before Stepniak-Kravchinsky's *démarche*, twenty-four of those who had just been found guilty in 'The Trial of the 193' declared in a letter to the authorities that, despite the lengthy sentences which awaited them, they remained 'enemies of Russia's prevailing system, which constitutes the misfortune and shame of our country, because in respect of economics it exploits the principle of labour in the interests of rapacious sponging and depravity and in respect of politics it sacrifices the labour, property, freedom, life and honour of every citizen to the whim of "personal discretion"'.[58] Boat-burning of this magnitude demonstrated that it was impossible to deny some thinking Russians a voice even when the regime might have thought that it had humiliated them completely.

CONCLUSION

The broad conclusion that arises from this survey is that Russian rulers have failed to solve the quandary of maintaining political and social control while continuing to develop their material resources. Whether the quandary has been of their own making is debatable. Perhaps, in an expanse of territory so vast, in difficult climatic conditions, when soil is poor and population density low, it is essential to create a strong central authority for developmental purposes. Whatever the reason, however, there can be no doubt that Russian rulers have invariably endeavoured to maintain their control while increasing the size of their domains, competing with other Great Powers and responding to the new social and economic challenges which the pursuit of the other goals has entailed. The upshot, so far as 'thought' is concerned, has been the cultivation, on the one hand, of state-orientated ideologists, but also the emergence of potentially non-state-orientated people with the intellectual tools to question both the outlook of their rulers and the structures they have tried to impart to government and society.

NOTES

1. Isaiah Berlin, *Russian Thinkers*, ed. Henry Hardy and Aileen Kelly (London: Hogarth Press, 1978), essays which, in the main, first appeared between 1948 and 1961.
2. Nicholas V. Riasanovsky, *Russia and the West in the Teaching of the Slavophiles: A Study of Romantic Ideology* (Cambridge, Mass.: Harvard University Press, 1952); Leopold H. Haimson, *The Russian Marxists and the Origins of Bolshevism* (Cambridge, Mass.: Harvard University Press, 1955); Marc Raeff, *Michael Speransky: Statesman of Imperial Russia 1772–1839* (The Hague: Martinus Nijhoff, 1957); Richard Pipes, *Karamzin's Memoir on Ancient and Modern Russia: A Translation and Analysis* (Cambridge, Mass.: Harvard University Press, 1959); Martin Malia, *Alexander Herzen and the Birth of Russian Socialism 1812–1855* (Cambridge, Mass.: Harvard University Press, 1961).
3. For some of the experiences of American historians in the USSR, see Samuel H. Baron and Cathy A. Frierson (eds.), *Adventures in Russian Historical Research: Reminiscences of American Scholars from the Cold War to the Present* (Armonk and London: M. E. Sharpe, 2003).

4. An outstanding exception was Donald W. Treadgold, *The Great Siberian Migration: Government and Peasant in Resettlement from Emancipation to the First World War* (Princeton University Press, 1957).

5. See G. M. Hamburg, *Boris Chicherin and Early Russian Liberalism 1828–1866* (Stanford University Press, 1992).

6. An important exception is Daniel R. Brower, *Training the Nihilists: Education and Radicalism in Tsarist Russia* (Ithaca and London: Cornell University Press, 1975). Because, in the Soviet Union, ideas always had to be related to the material context in which they arose, modern work in Russian pays more attention than work in English to the relationship between thinkers and society. See especially V. R. Leikina-Svirskaia, *Intelligentsiia v Rossii vo vtoroi polovine XIX veka* (Moscow: Mysl', 1971), her *Russkaia intelligentsiia v 1900–1917 godakh* (Moscow: Mysl', 1981), and V. Ia. Grosul, *Russkoe obshchestvo XVIII–XIX vekov: Traditsii i novatsii* (Moscow: Nauka, 2003). On the other hand, A. V. Sokolov, *Intelligenty i intellektualy v rossiiskoi istorii* (St Petersburg: SPbGUP, 2007), pays only a little attention to the socio-political hinterland of Russian thinkers.

7. S. Bertolissi and A. N. Sakharov (eds.), *Konstitutsionnye proekty v Rossii: XVIII–nachalo XX v.* (Moscow: Institut rossiiskoi istorii RAN, 2000), p. 249.

8. Isabel de Madariaga, 'Autocracy and sovereignty' in her *Politics and Culture in Eighteenth-Century Russia: Collected Essays* (London and New York: Longman, 1998), pp. 40–56.

9. V. A. Fedorov, *Soldatskoe dvizhenie v gody dekabristov 1816–1825gg.* (Moscow: MGU, 1963), pp. 43–71; Daniel Field, *Rebels in the Name of the Tsar*, 2nd edn (Boston, etc.: Unwin Hyman, 1989), pp. 30–111; Walter Sablinsky, *The Road to Bloody Sunday* (Princeton University Press, 1976); Michael Melancon, *The Lena Goldfields Massacre and the Crisis of the Late Tsarist State* (College Station: Texas A&M University Press, 2006); Samuel H. Baron, *Bloody Saturday in the Soviet Union: Novocherkassk, 1962* (Stanford University Press, 2001).

10. M. V. Sidorova and E. I. Shcherbakova (compilers), *Rossiia pod nadzorom: Otchety III otdeleniia 1827–1869* (Moscow: Rossiiskii fond kul'tury, 2006); E. I. Shcherbakova (compiler), *Agenturnaia rabota politicheskoi politsii Rossiiskoi imperii* (Moscow: AIRO-XXI and St Petersburg: Dmitrii Bulanin, 2006).

11. Orlando Figes, *The Whisperers: Private Life in Stalin's Russia* (London: Allen Lane, 2007).

12. A. M. Skabichevskii, *Ocherki istorii russkoi tsenzury (1700–1863gg.)* (St Petersburg: F. Pavlenkov, 1892), pp. 64–5.

13. T. S. Ilarionova *et al.* (compilers), *Vlast' i pressa v Rossii: K istorii pravovogo regulirovaniia otnoshenii 1700–1917: Khrestomatiia* (Moscow: Rossiiskaia akademiia gosudarstvennoi sluzhby pri Presidente Rossiiskoi Federatsii, 1999), p. 44.

14. Skabichevskii, *Ocherki*, pp. 216–389; Ilarionova, *Vlast' i pressa*, pp. 53–96; D. I. Raskin (principal ed.), *Vysshie i tsentral'nye gosudarstvennye uchrezhdeniia Rossii 1801–1917*, 4 vols. (St Petersburg: Nauka, 1998–2004), vol. II, pp. 50–2, vol. III, pp. 130–1; N. A. Grinchenko and N. G. Patrusheva (compilers),

Komitet tsenzury inostrannoi v Peterburge 1828–1917: Dokumenty i materialy (St Petersburg: Rossiiskaia natsional'naia biblioteka, 2006); S. I. Grigor'ev, *Pridvornaia tsenzura i obraz verkhovnoi vlasti 1831–1917* (St Petersburg: Aleteiia, 2007); V. P. Kozlov *et al.* (eds.), *Gosudarstvennost' Rossii: Slovar'-spravochnik*, 5 vols. (Moscow: Nauka, 1996–2005), vol. II, p. 328; vol. III, pp. 266–7; vol. IV, pp. 388–91.

15. Ilarionova, *Vlast' i pressa*, pp. 179–85, 187–93.

16. Dzh. Deili (Jonathan W. Daly), 'Pressa i gosudarstvo v Rossii (1906–1917gg.)', *Voprosy istorii*, 10 (2001), 25–45; Ilarionova, *Vlast' i pressa*, pp. 211–13.

17. For primary material on censorship in the Soviet period, see A. V. Blium (compiler), *Tsenzura v Sovetskom Soiuze 1917–1991: Dokumenty* (Moscow: ROSSPEN, 2004).

18. Richard Pipes, 'Introduction to Giles Fletcher's *Of the Russe Commonwealth* (1591)' in Pipes, *Russia Observed: Collected Essays on Russian and Soviet History* (Boulder, Col.: Westview Press, 1989), p. 32. The professor who lost his job was Osip Bodiansky.

19. A. I. Miller, *'Ukrainskii vopros' v politike vlastei i russkom obshchestvennom mnenii (vtoraia polovina XIX v.)* (St Petersburg: Aleteiia, 2000).

20. David Moon, 'Estimating the peasant population of late Imperial Russia from the 1897 census: a research note', *Europe-Asia Studies*, 48 (1996), 141–53.

21. V. I. Koretskii, *Zakreposhchenie krest'ian i klassovaia bor'ba v Rossii* (Moscow: Nauka, 1970), p. 123.

22. Dorothy Atkinson, *The End of the Russian Land Commune 1905–1930* (Stanford University Press, 1983), p. 209.

23. The principal synoptic accounts of the history of the Russian peasantry are Jerome Blum, *Lord and Peasant in Russia from the Ninth to the Nineteenth Century* (Princeton University Press, 1961), and David Moon, *The Russian Peasantry 1600–1930: The World the Peasants Made* (London and New York: Longman, 1999).

24. Except where otherwise stated, the remainder of this paragraph has in mind Marc Raeff, *Origins of the Russian Intelligentsia: The Eighteenth-Century Nobility* (New York: Harcourt, Brace and World, 1966); Paul Dukes, *Catherine the Great and the Russian Nobility* (Cambridge University Press, 1967); Robert E. Jones, *The Emancipation of the Russian Nobility 1762–1785* (Princeton University Press, 1973); I. V. Faizova, *'Manifest o vol'nosti' i sluzhba dvorianstva v XVIII stoletii* (Moscow: Nauka, 1999); and E. N. Marasinova, 'Vol'nost' rossiiskogo dvorianstva (Manifest Petra III i soslovnoe zakonoda-tel'stvo Ekateriny II)', *Otechestvennaia istoriia*, 4 (2007), 21–33. On the *douceur de vivre* which some nobles enjoyed between 1762 and 1861, see Priscilla R. Roosevelt, *Life on the Russian Country Estate: A Social and Cultural History* (New Haven: Yale University Press, 1995) and L. V. Ivanova (ed.), *Dvorianskaia i kupecheskaia sel'skaia usad'ba v Rossii XVI–XXvv.: Istoricheskie ocherki* (Moscow: URSS, 2000), pp. 178–394.

25. Geroid Tanquary Robinson, *Rural Russia under the Old Regime* (Berkeley and Los Angeles: University of California Press, 1932), pp. 63, 268, 270.

26. For the argument of this paragraph, see especially David M. Griffiths, 'Catherine II: the republican empress', *Jahrbücher für Geschichte Osteuropas*, 21 (1973), 323–44, and O. A. Omel'chenko, *'Zakonnaia monarkhiia' Ekateriny Vtoroi: prosveshchennyi absoliutizm v Rossii* (Moscow: Iurist, 1993).

27. Gregory L. Freeze, 'The soslovie (estate) paradigm and Russian social history', *American Historical Review*, 91 (1986), 11–36, and Madhavan K. Palat, 'Casting workers as an estate in late Imperial Russia', *Kritika: Explorations in Russian and Eurasian History*, 8 (2007), 307–48.

28. Sheila Fitzpatrick, 'Ascribing class: the construction of social identity in Soviet Russia', *Journal of Modern History*, 65 (1993), 745–70.

29. George Vernadsky (ed.), *A Source Book for Russian History from Early Times to 1917*, 3 vols. (New Haven: Yale University Press, 1972), vol. II, p. 564 (italics in the original).

30. 'Manifest: O sobytiiakh v zapadnoi Evrope', *Polnoe sobranie zakonov rossiiskoi imperii* (hereafter *PSZ*), 2nd series, 55 vols. (St Petersburg: Vtoroe Otdelenie Sobstvennoi Ego Imperatorskogo Velichestva Kantseliarii, 1830–84), vol. XXIII, part I, pp. 181–2, no. 22,087.

31. 'Manifest: O dvizhenii armii nashikh dlia sodeistviia Imperatoru Avstriiskomu na potushenie miatezha v Vengrii i Transil'vanii', *PSZ*, 2nd series, vol. XXIV, part I, p. 235, no. 23,200, 8 May 1849.

32. Vernadsky, *Source Book*, vol. II, pp. 538–9.

33. A. N. Pypin, 'Rossiiskoe bibleiskoe obshchestvo, 1812–1826' in his *Religioznye dvizheniia pri Aleksandre I* (St Petersburg: Gumanitarnyi proekt, 2000), pp. 20–303 (an essay first published in 1868); Raffaella Faggionato, 'From a society of the enlightened to the enlightenment of society: the Russian Bible Society and Rosicrucianism in the age of Alexander I', *Slavonic and East European Review*, 79 (2001), 459–87.

34. M. I. Rizhskii, *Istoriia perevodov Biblii v Rossii* (Novosibirsk: Nauka, 1978), p. 161.

35. P. A. Valuev, *Dnevnik*, 2 vols. (Moscow: Akademiia nauk SSSR, 1961), vol. II, pp. 114–16, 121, 131–2, 465, 467–9; A. V. Golovnin, *Zapiski dlia nemnogikh* (St Petersburg: Nestor-Istoriia, 2004), pp. 349–52; *PSZ*, 2nd series, vol. XLI, part I, pp. 953–4, no. 43,501, 22 July 1866.

36. Vernadsky, *Source Book*, vol. III, p. 680.

37. Ibid., vol. III, pp. 680–1; Richard Pipes, *Russia under the Old Regime* (Harmondsworth: Penguin, 1977), p. 305.

38. Aleksandr Bokhanov, *Nikolai II* (Moscow: Molodaia gvardiia, 1997), p. 105.

39. Marc Szeftel, *The Russian Constitution of April 23, 1906: Political Institutions of the Duma Monarchy* (Brussels: La Librairie encyclopédique, 1976), pp. 84, 85, 99.

40. Martin Malia, *The Soviet Tragedy: A History of Socialism in Russia, 1917–1991* (New York: Free Press, 1994); David Priestland, *Stalinism and the Politics of Mobilization: Ideas, Power, and Terror in Inter-war Russia* (Oxford University Press, 2007).

41. David Saunders, 'The political ideas of Russian historians', *Historical Journal*, 27 (1984), 757–71.

42. See, for example, A. I. Bokhanov *et al.* (eds.), *Rossiiskie konservatory* (Moscow: Russkii mir, 1997); K. B. Umbrashko, *M. P. Pogodin: chelovek, istorik, publitsist* (Moscow, IRI RAN, 1999); V. Ia. Grosul (ed.), *Russkii konservatizm XIX stoletiia: Ideologiia i praktika* (Moscow: Progress-Traditsiia, 2000); T. F. Prokopov (compiler), *Tainyi pravitel' Rossii: K. P. Pobedonostsev i ego korrespondenty; Pis'ma i zapiski 1866–1895* (Moscow: Russkaia kniga, 2001); M. N. Katkov, *Imperskoe slovo*, ed. M. B. Smolin (Moscow: Moskva, 2002); Andreas Renner, 'Defining a Russian nation: Mikhail Katkov and the "invention" of national politics', *Slavonic and East European Review*, 81 (2003), 659–82; O. A. Milevskii, *Lev Tikhomirov: Dve storony odnoi zhizni* (Barnaul: Altaiskii gosudarstvennyi universitet, 2004); and http://conservatism.narod.ru/bibl/1000.doc, the bibliographical section of a scholarly website hosted at Voronezh University (accessed 25 January 2008).

43. For the possibility that low-level dissent was ubiquitous under Stalin, see Sarah Davies, *Popular Opinion in Stalin's Russia: Terror, Propaganda and Dissent, 1934–1941* (Cambridge University Press, 1997).

44. Especially A. G. Cross, *'By the Banks of the Neva': Chapters from the Lives and Careers of the British in Eighteenth-Century Russia* (Cambridge University Press, 1997), and V. N. Zakharov, *Zapadnoevropeiskie kuptsy v rossiiskoi torgovle XVIII veka* (Moscow: Nauka, 2005).

45. S. A. Kozlov, *Russkii puteshestvennik epokhi Prosveshcheniia* (St Petersburg: Istoricheskaia illiustratsiia, 2003), pp. 78–137; A. Iu. Andreev, *Russkie studenty v nemetskikh universitetakh XVIII–pervoi poloviny XIX veka* (Moscow: Znak, 2005).

46. I. A. Kaloeva, *Izuchenie iuzhnykh slavian v Rossii v XVIII–pervoi polovine XIX v.* (Moscow: INION RAN, 2002), p. 55; R. G. Eimontova, *Russkie universitety na putiakh reformy: shestidesiatye gody XIX veka* (Moscow: Nauka, 1993), p. 199; A. E. Ivanov, *Uchenye stepeni v rossiiskoi imperii XVIIIv.–1917g.* (Moscow: IRI RAN, 1994), pp. 71–102.

47. For correspondence pertaining to his visits of 1894 and 1896, see London, The National Archives, Public Record Office, FO65/1481, folios 129, 130–2, 137, 139, 150, and FO65/1523, folios 172–3, 187.

48. P. Bechasnov, 'Kratkii obzor tsifrovykh dannykh' in N. A. Troinitskii (ed.), *Obshchii svod po imperii rezul'tatov razrabotki dannykh pervoi vseobshchei perepisi naseleniia, proizvedennoi 28 ianvaria 1897 goda*, 2 vols. (St Petersburg: Ministerstvo vnutrennikh del, 1905), vol. I, p. xvi.

49. See, for example, Susan K. Morrissey, *Heralds of Revolution: Russian Students and the Mythologies of Radicalism* (Oxford University Press, 1998).

50. Richard Hellie, *Enserfment and Military Change in Muscovy* (University of Chicago Press, 1971); Alfred J. Rieber, 'Alexander II: a revisionist view', *Journal of Modern History*, 43 (1971), 42–58.

51. P. A. Zaionchkovskii, *Pravitel'stvennyi apparat samoderzhavnoi Rossii v XIXv.* (Moscow: Mysl', 1978), p. 221.

52. Sidney Monas, *The Third Section: Police and Society in Russia under Nicholas I* (Cambridge, Mass.: Harvard University Press, 1961), p. 292.

53. David Saunders, 'Historians and concepts of nationality in early nineteenth-century Russia', *Slavonic and East European Review*, 60 (1982), 44–62.

54. See T. N. Zhukovskaia, 'S S Uvarov i Kirillo-Mefodievskoe obshchestvo ili krizis "ofitsial'noi narodnosti"' in R. Sh. Ganelin (ed.), *Otechestvennaia istoriia i istoricheskaia mysl' v Rossii XIX–XX vekov: Sbornik statei k 75-letiiu Alekseia Nikolaevicha Tsamutali* (St Petersburg: Nestor-Istoriia, 2006), pp. 196–207.

55. L. E. Shepelev (ed.), *Sud'by Rossii. Problemy ekonomicheskogo razvitiia strany v XIX–nachale XX vv.: Dokumenty i memuary gosudarstvennykh deiatelei* (St Petersburg: Spas-Liki Rossii, 2007), p. 63.

56. See W. Bruce Lincoln, *In the Vanguard of Reform: Russia's Enlightened Bureaucrats 1825–1861* (DeKalb: Northern Illinois University Press, 1982).

57. S. M. Stepniak-Kravchinskii, 'Smert' za smert'' in Stepniak-Kravchinskii, *Grozovaia tucha Rossii*, ed. B. Romanov (Moscow: Novyi kliuch, 2001), pp. 21–2.

58. B. S. Itenberg (ed.), *Revoliutsionnoe narodnichestvo 70-kh godov XIX veka: sbornik dokumentov*, 2 vols. (Moscow and Leningrad: Nauka, 1964–5), vol. I, p. 400.

CHAPTER 3

Russian intelligentsias

G. M. Hamburg

The word *intelligentsiia* appeared in the Russian language in the early eighteenth century, carrying the meaning 'alliance', 'compact' or 'agreement'.[1] By the 1730s, however, the poet Trediakovsky had associated the word root with the Latin word *intelligentia*, a word he translated into Russian as *razumnost'* (rationality). According to the linguist Viktor Vinogradov, Trediakovsky helped fix the basic semantic sense of the term *intelligentsiia* thereafter: that is, the word became associated with 'reason', 'rationality' and 'education'. In the mid-eighteenth century the freemason Johann Georg Schwartz often used *intelligentsiia* to connote the 'highest capacity of human beings as sentient creatures'. In the early nineteenth century the philosopher Galich incorporated it into his *History of Philosophical Systems* with the meaning 'rational spirit'.[2] In 1836 the term appeared in a diary entry by Zhukovsky, as a collective noun connoting members of Russia's educated Europeanised elite. According to the historian Sigurd Shmidt, Zhukovsky's concept of the intelligentsia connoted 'not only belonging to a certain socio-cultural milieu and having a European education, but also a certain moral outlook and behaviour – that is, *intelligentnost'* in the later meaning of the term'.[3] Still, so far as we know, uses of *intelligentsiia* as a collective noun remained infrequent until the 1860s: the first edition of Dal's comprehensive Russian dictionary (published 1863–8) contained no reference to the word.[4]

In the 1860s the word *intelligentsiia* established itself firmly in the literary and political lexicon. The liberal novelist Boborykin used it as a synonym of 'culture' or 'intelligence' in an 1866 essay in *The Russian Herald*.[5] Tolstoy employed it as a collective noun in *War and Peace* (1865–9) to denote the educated, Europeanised portion of Russian high society. The instructional fictional context of his use of the term was the famous opening scene in Anna Scherer's salon, wherein Pierre Bezukhov, recently returned from France, thrilled to the thought that 'here was gathered the entire intelligentsia of Petersburg'.[6] Tolstoy's cultural authority reinforced the term's currency, such that the second edition of Dal's dictionary (1880–2) defined it, 'used in the collective sense', as 'rational, educated, the intellectually developed portion of the populace'.[7] Thenceforth, the collective noun *intelligentsiia* retained that meaning through the turn of the century: in 1902 Mikhelson repeated Dal's 1881 definition verbatim.[8]

Meanwhile, the word *intelligentsiia* acquired a political colouration. As Nathaniel Knight has shown, in 1864 the censor Nikitenko compared Polish insurgents to Russian nihilists: 'Their intelligentsia is the same filth as ours – theirs is worse in fact, with its extra dose of Catholicism.'[9] In the 1870s the conservative journalist Katkov contrasted the simple, politically healthy Russian *narod* (people, nation) to the subversive, Europeanised *intelligentsiia*, a contrast that probably led him to assume in 1879, when the young Aleksandr Solovev tried to kill the tsar, that the assassin was 'an *intelligent* in a foreign top hat'.[10] In 1880, in his famous speech at the Pushkin monument in Moscow, Dostoevsky juxtaposed the common Russian *narod*, their intrinsic beauty and spirit, with the 'rootless' *intelligentsiia*, a purportedly alien and destructive element in national life. He accused the intelligentsia of 'not believing in the native soil, or in its innate strength, in Russia or in itself'.[11] As sometimes happens in politics when a certain group attaches a label to its opponents, Russian radicals did not initially use the word *intelligentsiia* as a self-description. Thus, the linguist Iury Sorokin has asserted that the words *intelligentsiia* and *intelligent* are not encountered in the works of Chernyshevsky, Dobroliubov and Pisarev.[12] Only in the 1870s did leading Populists such as Mikhailovsky and Tkachev proudly declare their membership in the *intelligentsiia*.[13]

In the twentieth century the term *intelligentsiia* continued to have the basic meaning of the educated or cultured part of the populace, but gradually the word was also associated with membership in the professions, with jobs that carried 'white collar' status. Ushakov's 1935 dictionary defined *intelligentsiia* as 'the social stratum of intellectual workers, of educated people'.[14] In the twentieth century *intelligentsiia* was also a contested political term. In the *Landmarks* anthology of 1909, disillusioned former radicals led by Struve and Berdiaev attacked the intelligentsia for its atheism, political maximalism, hostility to the state, lack of proportion and opposition to the rule of law.[15] In effect, *Landmarks* was a self-criticism of the *intelligentsiia* by several *intelligenty*. Between 1903 and 1940 the leadership of the Bolshevik party sought to define its relationship to the intelligentsia, with very uncertain results: on the one hand, party leaders happily embraced the intelligentsia to the degree that its members accepted Marxism and Soviet power; on the other hand, the party defined non-Bolshevik *intelligenty* as 'enemies of the people'. Thus, in 1922 Lenin ordered the exile from Russia of non-Bolshevik intellectuals.[16] Soviet newspapers of the late 1920s and early 1930s sometimes differentiated between the 'new' intelligentsia and the 'old' intelligentsia: the former consisted of loyal, Soviet-educated professionals, the latter of professionals educated in pre-Soviet schools who had held jobs under the old regime – that is, of 'former people'.[17] By 1935 Ushakov's dictionary carried a secondary definition of *intelligent* reflecting the Soviet regime's suspicion of independent thinkers: 'a person whose social behaviour is characterised by lack of will, by hesitations, by doubts'.[18]

INTELLIGENTSIAS

Confusion over the origin of the Russian word *intelligentsiia*, over its multiple meanings and its strategic place in the pre-1917 and post-1917 political lexicons has complicated the task of scholars trying to analyse the actual history of the intelligentsia. At times, scholars have opted to accept the basic definition of the term – 'the educated portion of the populace' – and therefore have asserted that the origins of the intelligentsia can be traced to the eighteenth century, when large numbers of the landed nobility received European educations.[19] Other scholars have chosen to define *intelligentsiia* more narrowly, in terms of its political orientation. They have posited that *intelligenty* were critical of the Russian social system, of the Orthodox Church and of the tsarist government. Although Russian scholars have usually claimed that the intelligentsia, in this narrower sense, came into being at some time in the eighteenth century,[20] many western historians have argued that the intelligentsia came into existence only in the 1840s or 1860s, when intellectuals articulated sharp attacks on the existing order.[21] Sometimes scholars have equated the intelligentsia with the revolutionary movement. According to this narrowest of definitions, *intelligenty* not only criticised the old order, they took up weapons against it or at least urged others to do so. As Boris Kolonitsky has pointedly observed, 'participants in the many discussions about the intelligentsia resemble a crowd engaged in a game where each player persists in playing according to his own rules'.[22]

In a short essay, one cannot hope to analyse the vast scholarship on the Russian intelligentsia, to sort out the numerous points of contention in the literature or to propose a new, 'definitive' approach to the intelligentsia's origins and turbulent history. The very attempt would force one to play in Kolonitsky's irrational game of multiple rules, and thus would properly invite ridicule: for if all players win the game as soon as they state their definition of *intelligentsia*, what is the point of playing? Instead, I propose here a different 'game' in which one takes with equal seriousness all previous definitions of the intelligentsia, the broadest as well as the narrowest. The object of the game is to identify the social venues in which Russian intellectuals operated, and thereby to understand how one intellectual group defined as intelligentsia related to others. Once this picture of Russian cultural realities is complete, we may also grasp more clearly how ideas circulated in the empire.

For heuristic purposes, let us agree to speak of an 'early intelligentsia' which came into existence in the eighteenth century as a by-product of state reformism and the spread of European education; a 'classical intelligentsia' which originated in the nineteenth century at some point between 1815 and 1860, and which adopted a systematically critical attitude towards some aspect(s) of the Russian social order; a 'revolutionary intelligentsia' which was a subset of the classical intelligentsia advocating the overthrow of the tsarist government; a 'zemstvo intelligentsia' (*zemskaia intelligentsiia*) generated between 1864 and 1900 by the hiring of experts whose task was to serve rural society and transform Russian life through gradual amelioration of social injustice; a 'professional intelligentsia' which encompassed the zemstvo intelligentsia, urban professionals hired by elected city councils and privately employed professionals; a pre-1861 'serf intelligentsia' (*krepostnaia intelligentsiia*) consisting of serfs trained as sophisticated artisans or as traders licensed to carry out commercial activity under the supervision of their lords; a post-1861 'village intelligentsia' (*sel'skaia intelligentsiia*) composed of literate peasants, such as village scribes, local school trustees and village priests; a post-1900 'intelligentsia from the people' (*narodnaia intelligentsiia*) connected to Russia's burgeoning book trade; and a 'new' or 'religious intelligentsia' which appeared in the late 1890s/first decade of the twentieth century and which repudiated the irreligion of some members of the 'classical intelligentsia'. Our enterprise, then, treats not so much the history of the Russian intelligentsia as the history of Russian intelligentsias.

THE EIGHTEENTH-CENTURY INTELLIGENTSIA

The origins of the early Russian intelligentsia had at least three preconditions. The first was the ongoing process of cultural interaction between Russia and the West, a process through which the Russian state sought to acquire knowledge of western science, to import into Russia useful military technology and to co-opt foreign 'experts' into Russian service. A parallel but also in some ways related component of the Russian–western interaction was Russian scrutiny and assimilation of western theology, a process accelerated by the importation into Russia of students from Ukrainian theological academies where the western scholastic tradition had been studied since the mid-seventeenth century.[23] The initial consequence of this complex cultural interaction was not the secularisation of Muscovite Rus, but rather the dynamic intermingling within Russian culture of western and eastern, secular and religious elements. Early Russian *intelligenty* internalised the tensions between different theological traditions and between lay and secular approaches to the world.

The second precondition for the origin of the early intelligentsia was the appearance and growth of print culture. The number of Russian books in print increased from a handful in the sixteenth century to 500 titles in 1689, to nearly 10,000 titles a century later. Gary Marker has argued that the struggle of the literary elites for access to print and of the political establishment to control that access 'established the institutional parameters for the evolution of Russian intellectual life as a whole in the eighteenth century'.[24] We might add that access to print was crucial for early *intelligenty* who sought to recruit allies through their publications, sometimes at risk to their own freedom.

The third precondition for the growth of the early intelligentsia was the existence of a *dirigiste* political culture that allowed intellectuals to believe that, once they had gained the ears of government leaders or had secured for themselves a high position in the official bureaucracy, they might influence state policy. Such a conviction did not have much purchase in seventeenth-century Muscovy, because the political system, dominated by the tsar and by boyar families, was less accessible to gentry intellectuals than was the Petrine system, which opened channels of influence to a broader portion of the country's educated elite.[25] The Petrine Table of Ranks system, as Iury Lotman has noted, tended to validate the prestige of high officials, just as the serf system encouraged among serf-owners 'a certain independence from the [central] political authorities'.[26] The result, by the time the eighteenth century came to a close, was that *intelligenty* began to pass their judgements with ever greater assertiveness, especially if they held high ranks in the bureaucracy but also if their positions as serf-owners had inculcated in them the habits of command. Of course, no one living in eighteenth-century Russia imagined himself or herself free from interference by the state, for there were no firm guarantees of individual rights. Still, among the educated elites the lack of juridical rights was moderated by a growing sense of personal prestige, social entitlement and relative autonomy.

The eighteenth century afforded educated Russians various venues of self-expression. Among the most precarious of these venues were circles of friends, of political functionaries, of like-minded *intelligenty* and, late in the century, of university students. Examples of such circles include the short-lived Learned Watch or 'scholarly retinue' (*uchenaia druzhina*) consisting of the historian Tatishchev, the satirist Kantemir and the churchman Prokopovich; the circle of Volynsky, which appeared in St Petersburg in the late 1730s; the circle of Novikov that appeared in 1767 on the staff of the imperial Legislative Commission; and the student group that crystallised in Leipzig in 1767 around Ushakov and Radishchev. None of these circles opposed the autocracy, but they all criticised some aspect of the existing political order. In 1730, the Learned Watch demanded an autocratic arrangement with greater power invested in the middling gentry, not in the more 'aristocratic' Supreme Privy Council.[27] Later that decade, Volynsky criticised political tyranny and defended religious toleration in the empire. In the 1760s the Novikov circle discussed how to improve peasants' living conditions, while the Ushakov–Radishchev circle rejected the petty despotism of the Russian educational inspector in Leipzig.[28] Each of these circles manifested one or more traits usually associated with the classical intelligentsia of the nineteenth century, but none stood far outside the penumbra of the government. Their members were usually political insiders who accepted the general direction of the Petrine reforms while disagreeing with some aspect of the reforms' implementation.

A second venue of intellectual self-expression in the eighteenth century was the noble country house. These domiciles, constructed in large numbers in central Russia following Peter's westernisation campaign, sometimes served as havens for historians and belletrists.[29] Thus, Tatishchev completed his history of Russia at the Boldino estate in Moscow province. At another estate Shcherbatov wrote his own Russian history and finished his attack on Russian modernisation, *On the Corruption of Morals in Russia*. Country houses were also the principal sites of Russian theatre in the provinces, and thus were places where *intelligenty* could produce and consume ideas. Eighteenth-century Russian plays, as Elise Wirtschafter has shown, emphasised the importance of civic and moral virtue, condemned injustice and sought to reconcile progressive ethical views with the existing social hierarchy.[30] Their message was perfectly calibrated by and for intellectuals embedded in the social hierarchy yet able to see its deficiencies.

Russian country houses were also the main work sites for the so-called 'serf intelligentsia' – the stratum of trained artisans who built furniture, fired porcelain, wove lace, loomed carpets, carved wood, fabricated jewellery and painted portraits for the pleasure of the serf-owning class. Although most Russian serfs laboured their entire lives on a single estate, some of them – like the portraitist Tropinin – developed a wide reputation for their art and were eventually freed from serf status. One serf artist, Soroka, dared in a painting of the Spasskoe estate in the 1840s to dramatise the social divide between the world of peasant fieldworkers and their landowner.[31] Given the social chasm between lord and peasant in Russia, the overlap between the early intelligentsia and serf intelligentsia was small, but both groups shared involvement in estate theatres: the elite *intelligenty* as writers and principal audience for the theatre, the serf *intelligenty* as actors, stage-hands, designers and the like.

A third venue of self-expression for eighteenth-century *intelligenty* was the masonic lodge. From the early eighteenth century to 1796 perhaps 3,000 people, mainly wealthy nobles, joined the freemasons in Russia. In the brotherhood they sought friendship, religious enlightenment and a life of virtue; lodge members often joined together in philanthropic activity such as supporting orphanages or engaging in famine relief.[32] Masonic societies weirdly combined strict hierarchy of organisation with an egalitarian ethos, arcane secrecy with public visibility. This exotic combination of traits made freemasonry an incubator of autonomous activity, independent-mindedness and secrecy, and thus a perceived threat to the state. Masonic lodges, with their commitment to social progress, were peculiarly receptive to utopian literature. Two of Kheraskov's utopian stories and Shcherbatov's *Journey to the Land of Ophir* were written under the influence of masonic doctrines of virtue.

Additional venues of self-expression for eighteenth-century intellectuals were learned societies and higher educational institutions, including the nascent Academy of Sciences and Moscow University. By mid-century the Academy had begun to promote ethnically Russian scholars such as Lomonosov to positions of prominence on its staff. The Academy sponsored the writing of Russian history, and it supported study trips abroad by Russian students in the sciences.[33] Moscow University, founded in 1755, attracted many of its students from elite noble families, but it also became a cultural space in which the values of early *intelligenty* were propagated. By the century's end it was known for its literary circles, translation groups, theatre and university press. The press, directed from 1779 to 1789 by Novikov, printed the newspaper *Moscow News* for nearly 4,000 subscribers. It also published roughly fifty academic titles a year and distributed them for sale in the city and provinces.[34] In spite of its elite student body, the university was a place 'where people of different Estates gathered under one roof.[35] The university's intellectual energy, enlightened outreach and 'democratic' ethos helped shape not only the early intelligentsia but also its nineteenth-century successors.

Together these venues of eighteenth-century self-expression – circles, country houses and theatres, masonic lodges, academic institutions and learned societies – constituted much of what some historians have christened 'Russian civil society'. On the broadest definition of *intelligentsiia* – 'the learned portion of society' – the early intelligentsia was substantially identical to civil society. Its membership must have numbered in the high hundreds or low thousands. If we were to count serf artisans as *intelligenty*, the intelligentsia's membership in the late eighteenth century must have run to several thousand individuals. Paradoxically, however, few serf artisans could be considered part of civil society, for they were generally not to be regarded as 'free subjects' and did not usually operate outside the tight boundaries of their masters' estates. Narrower definitions of the intelligentsia that demand of *intelligenty* principled criticism of existing social, political and religious arrangements reduce the intelligentsia to a handful of members and to an insignificant fraction of civil society. Only on the narrower definition of *intelligentsiia* does it make sense to think of *intelligenty* as somehow 'alienated' from the existing order. Even then, the postulate of their alienation can scarcely be taken seriously, since they were connected in so many ways to other members of society. Virtually all important early *intelligenty* were churchmen or state officials of some kind. Few of them renounced Christianity, whatever criticisms they may have made of the Orthodox Church; even freemasons like Novikov regarded masonry as consistent with Orthodoxy. Still fewer *intelligenty* wished to eliminate the autocracy. In general, the early intelligentsia was not an 'alien' body transplanted on to Russian soil, but an organic product of a culture in which native traditions and elements of western thinking were in dynamic interplay. If we take the broad definition of *intelligentsiia*, we can argue that its dramatic growth over the century was not a product of collective alienation from native ways, but of elite sociability.

THE NINETEENTH-CENTURY INTELLIGENTSIA

In the first half of the nineteenth century the intelligentsia, broadly defined as the educated public, gained many thousands of members. Meanwhile, between 1815 and the mid-1860s, there appeared several hundred members of the so-called 'classical intelligentsia' – that is, *intelligenty* who adopted a more-or-less systematically critical attitude towards some aspect of the existing order. Among these latter were a small number of radicals determined to overthrow the regime. These committed revolutionaries were the first members of the 'revolutionary intelligentsia', a group that grew quickly after 1815: from it came the Decembrist conspiracy, the radical Westernisers, the nihilists and Populists, and ultimately the left-wing political parties that in the early twentieth century challenged the autocracy. As we observed above, historians have sometimes reduced the history of the intelligentsia to the development of the revolutionary intelligentsia – a logical fallacy that substitutes *pars pro toto*. Here we shall focus both on the general evolution of educated society in the nineteenth century and on the social locations in which particular elements of that society expressed themselves. The overarching argument is that during the late imperial period the size of the educated public dramatically increased; the classical intelligentsia grew partly as a concomitant of the sheer vitality of the educated sector of society but also partly in response to the perceived deficiencies of the tsarist order. Late in the century, the classical intelligentsia, especially its revolutionary wing, divided itself into contending political parties. Thus, the very success of the classical intelligentsia was the precondition for its ultimate disintegration. Meanwhile, changing social conditions and the reforms of the 1860s created fertile ground for the appearance of new groups within the educated public: the so-called 'zemstvo' and 'technical' intelligentsias, the 'intelligentsia from the people' and also the 'new' or 'religious intelligentsia'.

In the nineteenth century intellectual self-expression continued to occur in the old venues. Many intellectual circles that appeared after 1815 played important roles in the history of the classical intelligentsia. To name only a handful, there were: in the 1810s and early 1820s the military circles and unofficial societies that served as foci for the future Decembrists; in the 1830s the circle of Nikolay Stankevich, which helped introduce Hegelian idealism to Bakunin, Granovsky, Belinsky and others; in the 1840s the circles of Westernisers and Slavophiles, which debated the proper foundations for a prospective new Russia; in the late 1840s the Petrashevsky circle, which developed a critique of serfdom and discussed plans for a democratic, socialist society; in the 1850s the circle of Aleksandr Stankevich, which helped generate Russian liberalism; in the 1870s the Chaikovsky and Fritsche circles, which inspired men and women to join the Populist movement; in the 1880s the Priiutino Brotherhood, which combined the 'cult of small deeds' and Tolstoy's ethical outlook to produce the incremental liberalism of Shakhovskoy and Vernadsky; and in the late 1890s the *Beseda* (*Colloquy*) circle, which acted as the organisational focus for gentry liberalism. The size of nineteenth-century circles varied from a handful of members (the two Stankevich circles, the Priiutino Brotherhood) to dozens of members (the Northern and Southern Societies, the Petrashevsky circle, the *Beseda* circle). One has the impression that the higher the social status of the participants, the easier it was for them to form larger circles, although size of membership was constrained by the need for secrecy in operations, by the desire of founding members to preserve social exclusivity or by the founders' high intellectual and/or ethical demands on members. On balance, nineteenth-century circles tended to be larger than eighteenth-century circles had been.

In the nineteenth century the noble country house continued to be an important seedbed of the intelligentsia. Herzen was radicalised by his domestic education, so that, at the age of thirteen, he swore an oath to uphold the Decembrists' legacy.[36] On the Priamukhino estate in Tver province, the future anarchist Bakunin developed a fierce sense of individual dignity, political autonomy and self-determination.[37] In Tambov province, Chicherin, the future Russian liberal, grew up in an intellectually engaged household, which emphasised the importance of personal virtue and social responsibility – two key components of his liberal outlook.[38] The Slavophiles Konstantin and Ivan Aksakov were raised on a country estate by a father who stressed the family's duties towards and dependence on the local peasantry.[39] In all these cases, estate life left a strong impression on the world-views of the *intelligenty* raised there. Several of these estates were significant sites of intellectual production: for example, several of Chicherin's philosophical tracts were written in the library of his Karaul estate.

Of course, not every estate was comfortable for the noble children educated there. Turgenev's mother, Varvara, persecuted her children, especially the future writer.[40] Dostoevsky's relationship with his father, after the family purchased the small Darovoe estate outside Moscow, was famously tense. In Turgenev's case, the family situation produced disgust at the serf order and for petty tyranny of any sort, though it did not make him antagonistic towards the Russian nobility or turn him into a social recluse. For Dostoevsky, who never fully identified himself as a Russian noble, brief exposure to estate life triggered alternating feelings of aversion towards the nobility and desire for social recognition by it. There were many estates, many family patterns and thus multiple links between estate life and the intelligentsia.

In the second half of the century, estates continued to be venues of self-expression for the nobility. Daniel Brower has shown that the majority of Russian nihilists were not *raznochintsy*, but nobles.[41] One of the key social constituents of Russian Populism was the 'repentant nobleman' (*kaiushchiisia dvorianin*) who, breaking with the social injustice of the serf era, 'went to the people' in 1873–4 to assuage feelings of moral culpability over serfdom.[42] At the height of Populism, the landed estate even became a laboratory for studying the peasantry and learning to live in harmony with peasants.[43] Throughout the emancipation era Tolstoy's experiments in popular education and his publishing projects in popular literature were centred at his Iasnaia Poliana estate; indeed, these enterprises would have been unthinkable outside its context. Later in the century, zemstvo liberalism, the Priiutino Brotherhood, the *Beseda* circle and the Kadet party all grew in part out of gentry perceptions of estate life.

In the nineteenth and early twentieth centuries, freemasonry played a role as venue for intellectual self-expression at two moments: before the Decembrist uprising and before the Russian Revolution of 1917. Militsa Nechkina has observed that nine members of the Union of Salvation were freemasons. She has also noted that in several respects (codes of secrecy, oaths of allegiance and hierarchical organisation) the Statutes of the Union of Salvation were patterned on the rules of a masonic lodge. In her opinion, the ethos of freemasonry therefore animated the Union of Salvation, even though a majority of the Union's members were not themselves masons.[44]

The problem of the intelligentsia, freemasonry and the Russian Revolution of 1917 has been little understood as well as heavily politicised. At least one respected scholar has argued that turn-of-the-century Russian freemasonry had nothing to do with left-wing politics, with plots to overthrow the monarchy or with the Revolution.[45] On the other hand, conservative Russian historians have estimated that, c. 1910, there were a hundred politically active masons in Russia; these historians have insisted that several masons participated in the 1916 conspiracy to arrest Nicholas II.[46] At the extreme are those who view the Russian Revolution as a consequence of western, Jewish, masonic plotting against crown and nation. Probably the soundest opinions in this debate belong to Boris Nikolaevsky and Vitaly Startsev, both of whom have suggested that, from 1912 to 1917, a Supreme Council of the Peoples of Russia, consisting of a dozen or so prominent liberal and left-wing politicians with masonic connections, periodically discussed national politics and the co-ordination of Duma tactics. In 1916 several members of the Council involved themselves in an effort to arrest Nicholas II, but, according to Nikolaevsky and Startsev, there is little evidence to suggest that in doing so they acted as masons or under the direction of the Supreme Council. Indeed, Russian freemasons generally opposed their lodges' involvement in revolutionary politics. Thus,

Nikolaevsky and Startsev have agreed that freemasonry played at least a minor political role in the decade before 1917, but neither of them has considered this role as decisive in the making of the Revolution.[47] A recent historiographical review has underlined the wisdom of scepticism about masonic involvement in the Revolution.[48]

The relevance of the debate about freemasonry and revolution to the history of Russian intelligentsias is straightforward: apparently, masonic lodges were clandestine sites where, between 1906 and 1916, left-wing *intelligenty* occasionally met to discuss political issues outside the normal scrutiny of their political factions. Freemasonry was not a central directory of revolutionary acts for the revolutionary intelligentsia, but rather a safe haven within the factionalised political sphere where opinions could be exchanged among *intelligenty* and co-ordination of political tactics might be explored.

Throughout the late imperial period, Russian universities were crucial sites for the intelligentsia. Nechkina has established that thirty-seven future Decembrists studied at Moscow University.[49] A generation later, as Herzen recalled in his memoirs, Moscow University was a place that 'raised students' civic-mindedness'.[50] In the 1850s and 1860s universities served Russian nihilists as staging points, where students gathered to discuss the injustices of the social order, the shortcomings of the government's reform programme and the possibilities of communal life; at the two universities in the capitals they elaborated the codes of behaviour and dress that came to constitute external signs of political radicalism.[51] In the 1870s hundreds of university students took part in the 'going to the people' (*khozhdenie v narod*).[52] In the 1880s and 1890s universities provided much of the leadership of the future Constitutional Democratic Party: Terence Emmons has shown that in 1905 twenty-one of forty members of the Kadet Central Committee were either professors or ex-professors.[53] In the protests precipitated by the February 1899 beating of St Petersburg University students, thousands of students across Russia took to the streets to express opposition to the government's heavy-handedness.[54] As the liberal professor of history Aleksandr Kizevetter noted, the university demonstrations surrounding the death of Tolstoy in 1910 and the disputed appointment of Kasso as Minister of Education in 1911 'did much to facilitate the shattering of the government's prestige'.[55] Thus, universities from early in the century onward were recruiting grounds for the revolutionary intelligentsia. That said, we must also remember that, in the first decade of the twentieth century, many students who joined anti-governmental protests at moments of political crisis looked anxiously forward to employment in the professions. Their

political militancy was perhaps more a *rite de passage* than a lifetime
commitment to the revolutionary movement: they regarded universities
pre-eminently as institutions of higher learning where professional skills and
accreditation might be acquired.[56] Thus, Russian universities and
post-secondary technical and pedagogical institutes were crucial sites both
for the revolutionary and the technical intelligentsias.

NEW VENUES OF SELF-EXPRESSION IN THE LATE NINETEENTH AND EARLY TWENTIETH CENTURIES

By the end of the nineteenth century, traditional venues of intellectual
self-expression had been augmented by new ones. Perhaps chief among
these were institutions of local self-government – the zemstvos and city
councils – established by the reforms of 1864 and 1870; new professional
organisations; a freer press and much expanded print culture; new religious
and philosophical societies; and, finally, political parties. Although it is
impossible to discuss these developments in detail here, one may nevertheless mention their connections to the history of the intelligentsia.

   Within zemstvos and city councils, Russian *intelligenty*, broadly defined,
participated in the kind of practical politics that had been off-limits to
preceding generations. The zemstvos raised taxes and planned for improvements to the local infrastructure (building roads and bridges), to community life (constructing and staffing schools and hospitals) and to agriculture
(through the employment of agronomists and statisticians). City councils
shouldered comparable duties with respect to urban infrastructures and
communities, but they also co-ordinated city activities with the central
government by quartering troops for the army, keeping public order in
difficult conditions and helping develop industry. Sometimes, when the
cooperative ethos broke down, there was conflict between local
self-governments and the central government. Natalia Pirumova has calcu-
lated that, between 1890 and 1902, over 240 zemstvo figures participated in
liberal protests against central government policies.[57] Meanwhile, in
Moscow between 1883 and 1913 two elected mayors were removed from
office by the central government – actions that led to protests by the city
council and by independent *intelligenty*.[58] In 1911, when a hundred professors left Moscow University in protest against the central government's
educational policies, they moved to the city-supported open university.[59] In
effect, by hiring the protesting professors, the city council indirectly supported a collective protest by *intelligenty* against the crown – an act almost
unthinkable even fifty years earlier.

Zemstvos and city councils were also among Russia's chief employers of teachers, doctors, nurses, paramedics, engineers, lawyers, statisticians and agronomists. In the zemstvo, such public servants were called the 'third element' but were also labelled the 'zemstvo intelligentsia'. Some of these employees occasionally collaborated with zemstvo boards on a common liberal platform, but, especially after 1905, they tended to pursue their own, more radical, political aims.[60] If politically active members of zemstvo boards were mostly centrists (that is, moderate conservatives or moderate liberals), the zemstvo intelligentsia included many left liberals, Populists and, more rarely, revolutionary radicals.[61]

In the late nineteenth and early twentieth centuries the number of professionals in Russia, including those employed by local self-governmental institutions and by other agencies, grew rapidly. The 1897 census counted roughly 17,000 doctors; by 1914 the Ministry of Internal Affairs had recorded licences for nearly 43,000 doctors. In addition, in 1914 there were 28,500 trained paramedics in the empire.[62] Between the early 1890s and 1914 the number of lawyers grew from 2,900 to 5,400; by 1916, if one counts lawyers and trained paralegals, the number of professionals licensed to practise before the bar reached 11,800.[63] Russian universities, polytechnic academies and professional schools trained thousands of engineers every year. In 1913–14, according to Vera Leikina-Svirskaia, state-supported post-secondary schools enrolled 27,000 engineers of various sorts.[64] By far the largest number of specialists worked in the field of education. According to Ben Eklof, the number of rural schoolteachers increased from about 24,000 in 1880 to 126,500 in 1911. If one adds primary schoolteachers from the cities, there were nearly 150,000 teachers in Russia in 1911.[65]

As one might expect, historians have disagreed about the appropriate classification for primary schoolteachers. Were they really professionals or not? Did they belong to the intelligentsia or not? According to Eklof, primary schoolteachers were generally competent to teach the rudiments of reading and writing, although, as the school system expanded in the countryside, so did the number of teachers with minimal qualifications. Eklof has labelled these teachers 'mere craftsmen'.[66] Scott Seregny has suggested that many teachers, not having an 'esoteric knowledge base', were nothing more than 'semi-professionals'.[67] However, Christine Ruane, an expert on urban primary schools, has insisted that urban teachers were part of Russia's professional intelligentsia.[68] Ruane's classification matches Russian scholarly parlance. In her 1986 book on the 'third element', Pirumova included teachers in the zemstvo intelligentsia. Leikina-Svirskaia, the most authoritative Russian scholar on the history of the professional intelligentsia, also included schoolteachers in that category.[69]

In the last decades of the old regime, Russian professionals struggled to organise themselves in professional societies and unions. In the second half of the nineteenth century, for example, doctors established and joined seventy societies, the largest of which were the Pirogov Society and the Russian Society for the Preservation of Popular Health. Russian paramedics (fel'dshery) organised their own societies, such as the All-Russian Union of Societies of Physicians' Assistants.[70] Lawyers established local bar associations and, in 1905, the Union of Lawyers. Engineers formed the Union of Engineers and Technicians in 1904. Although before 1905 the central government prohibited teachers from holding empire-wide congresses, this prohibition was ignored in 1896 and 1902, when teachers met illegally to discuss their common problems. In 1905, teachers established the Union of Public Schoolteachers, an organisation that by 1906 had over 13,000 members.[71] All these groups – doctors, paramedics, lawyers, engineers and teachers – had their own professional journals in which members expressed grievances as professionals and sometimes as imperial subjects. For example, paramedics demanded equal treatment with doctors, while teachers struggled for a living wage, but also for a rationalisation of the entire Russian school system. Yet all groups joined the Union of Unions in 1905, an organisation that demanded a genuinely representative system of government in the empire.[72]

The implications of this professional and political activity for the history of Russian *intelligenty* should be clear. Professional organisations, being committed to the spread of learning and to raising the popular standard of living, implemented in their own sphere of work one of the goals of the 'classical' intelligentsia: the social transformation of Russia. The political activity of these organisations in 1905 was aimed at dismantling traditional barriers to progress, including the autocracy. Again, the efforts of the professional intelligentsia seemed to grow organically out of the programme of the 'classical' intelligentsia. Yet this general picture of continuity masked sharp disagreements among professional groups and among the different intelligentsias of Russia. If we take the example of primary schoolteachers, we discover the unpleasant reality that, in many villages, teachers were objects of scorn by zemstvo doctors and by the 'village intelligentsia' (the local priest, scribes working for the village or *volost'* assembly, the local school trustee).[73] In 1902, many teachers had Populist sympathies – that is, they accepted Lavrov's ideal that the educated must serve the people; but teachers *en masse* still shied away from an open confrontation with the autocracy, either because they felt themselves vulnerable to governmental reprisal or because they feared the local peasants might attack them for their radicalism. Teachers' practical grievances – low salaries, for example – did not necessarily translate into larger political grievances.[74] The teachers' radicalism in 1905 was a momentary phenomenon brought about by the accumulation of their professional grievances, by pressures from the local peasants to change an unbearable social system and by encouragement from zemstvo radicals to confront the regime.[75]

The Russian press at the end of the old regime was freer than at any time in Russian history. This situation was the result of several factors, among them a decades-long struggle by the intelligentsia against censorship and the partial victory of revolutionary groups in securing civil liberties in 1905. However, two other factors stand out as well: the growth of literacy in the country and the sheer size of the publishing industry.

The spread of literacy was perhaps the most significant development in Russian cultural history. In 1847 roughly 10 per cent of peasants and 30 per cent of city dwellers were able to read. By 1917, 36 per cent of peasants and 64 per cent of city dwellers were literate.[76] The degree of literacy was higher among males and also higher among the young than the old. The 1920 census showed that 71 per cent of boys and 52 per cent of girls from twelve to sixteen years old were literate.[77] Increased literacy rates were correlated to the imperial investment in education – between 1879 and 1914 the number of rural primary schools increased from 22,700 to 108,280 – and owed much to the efforts of teachers described above.[78] But literacy rates were also driven up because Russian peasants came to believe that at least minimal competency in reading was an essential skill, especially for males.[79] Over time, as the mass of literate Russians increased, so did the demand for books to entertain, edify and enlighten them.

As Jeffrey Brooks has shown, much popular literature fell under the rubric of *lubochnaia literatura*, a Russian variant of European popular broadsides and chapbooks. Such books were short, simple to produce and relatively straightforward to distribute. They were written by authors mostly from the lower classes, including the peasantry, and were marketed by itinerant pedlars or petty merchants. The themes of this popular literature were various. Sometimes they unmasked superstitions or conveyed rudimentary scientific information: in such cases, they disseminated a world-view congenial to the 'classical' intelligentsia. More often, popular literature retold fairy tales, narrated fictional or real-life adventures or explained how to succeed in life. Not infrequently, *lubochnaia literatura* upheld the existing spiritual and political order and during wartime affirmed

Russian patriotism.[80] As Brooks has noted, there was an uneasy relationship between the 'classical' intelligentsia and the writers of popular literature. Certain popular writers recognised their debts to the 'classical' intelligentsia, yet sought to maintain their literary independence from it. On the other hand, classical *intelligenty* eyed popular authors nervously, seeing that *lubochnaia literatura* was often frivolous or delivered the 'wrong' (i.e. conservative) message.[81] Meanwhile, the audience that consumed such popular literature often thought of itself as an 'intelligentsia from the people' – still another category of intelligentsia to appear before 1917.[82]

By the last decades of the old regime the rate of growth of the publishing industry was remarkable. In 1900 there were 1,000 periodical publications in the Russian language; by 1915, that number had more than doubled. In 1897 there were 60 daily newspapers in the Russian language; by 1915, that number had increased to 569. Book production increased from 10,000 new titles in 1901 to 26,000 by 1913.[83] Since many members of the 'classical' intelligentsia contributed to these publications, one can justly claim that publishing venues of different types enabled them to reach a wider audience than ever before. However, as Louise McReynolds has shown in her study of Russia's mass circulation press, newspaper editors self-consciously vied with the intelligentsia for control over civil society. The commercial press – with its reports about crime, scandal, business affairs and entertainment – had purposes different from those of the 'classical' intelligentsia.[84] Occasionally, as in 1905, papers like *The Russian Word* took nationalist positions at odds with those of the 'classical' intelligentsia. Even if we agree that, after 1900, *intelligenty* enjoyed more freedom to publish than ever before, that freedom did not always translate to greater authority in the widened public sphere. Put another way, the intelligentsia (or intelligentsias) controlled part of civil society, but not all of it.

For a time in the middle of the nineteenth century, many leading *intelligenty* had identified themselves as irreligious. By the early twentieth century, however, this aspect of their identity was no longer secure. As Jutta Scherrer has shown, in the 1890s in St Petersburg a certain portion of the intelligentsia turned from the irreligion of the 1860s towards a new religious consciousness. The turn occurred under the influence of literary symbolists such as Merezhkovsky, Gippius, Blok and Bely, but also at the urging of those Russian philosophers (Struve, Berdiaev, Sergey Bulgakov, Frank) who abandoned Marxism for philosophical idealism. The result was the establishment in the capital of the St Petersburg Religious–Philosophical Meetings and the Religious–Philosophical Society.[85] A parallel process occurred in Moscow under the aegis of religious philosophers such as

Solovev, Grot, Troitsky and Chicherin. These thinkers established the Moscow Psychological Society; later, their descendants staffed the Vladimir Solovev Religious–Philosophical Society.[86] Since Scherrer defined *intelligenty* with respect to their function in society, she regarded the turn to a new religious consciousness as a process that occurred *within* the 'classical' intelligentsia: in her view, only values were transposed, not the social function of *intelligenty*.[87] Yet Scherrer has conceded that contemporaries saw the contradictions between the new religious consciousness and other groups in the intelligentsia as 'unbridgeable'.[88] For this reason, it may make sense to see intellectuals' turn to religion as the beginning of a 'new', religiously orientated intelligentsia distinct from the 'classical' intelligentsia of the nineteenth century.

The process of the development of political parties in Russia is now relatively well understood. However, the relationship between the intelligentsia(s) and the parties of the centre-left and left is a matter in serious dispute. As we have seen, university professors and university-trained cadres constituted a significant element of the Kadet leadership, but the Kadets also numbered in their leadership property owners of various sorts. Were they therefore a 'bourgeois' party, a party of progressive landowners and factory owners, or a party of intellectuals who ultimately betrayed propertied interests for socialism?[89] Meanwhile, some Russian historians have argued over whether the Menshevik party had been defined by the intelligentsia.[90] The role of the intelligentsia in shaping the Bolshevik party has also been bitterly contested, beginning with the Bolsheviks themselves.[91] In *What is to be Done?* Lenin made only passing references to the intelligentsia, but, according to Lars Lih, his general views of it were 'unflattering'. On the other hand, the French historian Alain Besançon has asserted that Bolshevik leadership emerged more or less in its entirety out of the intelligentsia ethos. According to Besançon, the 'core' of the Russian intelligentsia 'organised itself into a party'. Lenin's hatred of the intelligentsia was little more than a kind of self-loathing, analogous to the intelligentsia's purported loathing of civil society: 'they [intelligentsia and civil society] had become identical [in Lenin's mind], and liable in consequence to the same treachery'.[92] Besançon's position was simply a restatement of the general western historiographical approach linking the intelligentsia teleologically to Red October.

On the whole, the evidence suggests, radical parties offered *intelligenty* additional venues to convey their views to others and the possibility, under the right circumstances, to put those views into practice. In none of the major political factions were members from the intelligentsia and party membership entirely identical; within given party leadership groups *intelli-genty* played more or less prominent roles, but they were not necessarily the dominant players in the party. If we look across the spectrum of left-centre and left political parties, we can discern a few common convictions stemming from the creed of the 'classical' intelligentsia: opposition to social injustice and a desire to change society in a more humane direction; opposition to arbitrary rule and the hope of a more just system of government. Yet the existence of separate political parties entailed the danger that these remnants of the 'classical' intelligentsia would fight one another over their tactical and strategic differences in the pursuit of social justice. Thus, party organisations simultaneously represented for the 'classical' intelligentsia a way forward but also a dead end and disintegration.

CONCLUSION

By taking seriously both broader and narrower definitions of the Russian term *intelligentsiia*, historians may understand more clearly the contours of imperial Russia's cultural life. From Peter's time onwards, Russian intellectuals operated in the social venues open to them: informal circles, noble country houses, masonic lodges and academic societies. *Intelligenty* used these sites to express and refine their ideas; when possible, they published these ideas in the nascent press. The early intelligentsia played a large role in Russia's emergent civil society, although it should not be thought that intelligentsia and civil society were identical. A by-product of the early intelligentsia and of country-estate life more generally was the appearance of the serf intelligentsia, trained artisans who, by virtue of their humble social origins and of restrictions on their movement, stood almost wholly outside of civil society. In the nineteenth century, the broadly defined intelligentsia engendered the classical and revolutionary intelligentsias. These groups operated in the older venues for intellectual self-expression listed above, but also, by the late nineteenth century, in new venues – self-governing institutions, professional societies, the mass-circulation media and popular press, religious circles and political parties. Perhaps inevitably, the expansion of educated society and the search by groups of *intelligenty* for self-definition led to the appearance of other intelligentsias: the zemstvo intelligentsia, the technical intelligentsia, the village intelligentsia, the 'intelligentsia from the people' and the 'new' religious intelligentsia. By the end of the imperial period, the classical and revolutionary intelligentsias were in the process of disintegrating into rival political currents.

By grasping the chronological, social, political and cultural relationships among these various Russian intelligentsias, scholars may avoid oversimplifying the very complex process of Russia's cultural development. For example, we shall be less likely to treat the revolutionary intelligentsia as Russia's only intelligentsia; we shall be less likely to posit psychological alienation as the social motor of the intelligentsia's evolution and more likely to see the importance of sociability in the spread of intellectual currents across the empire; and we shall be less likely to interpret the history of the intelligentia(s) exclusively through a political lens. If we are alert, we shall be neither confused nor daunted by the conflicting connotations of the Russian word *intelligentsiia* or by early twentieth-century partisan disputes over the significance of the intelligentsia(s) in Russian life. Instead, we shall more easily accept the term's nuances and also the disputes over its application as semantic reflections of Russia's remarkably rich, variegated, if occasionally controversial and self-contradictory, cultural passage into modernity.

NOTES

1. Iu. S. Sorokin (ed.), *Slovar' russkogo iazyka XVIII veka. Vypusk 9* (Leningrad: Nauka, Leningradskoe otdelenie, 1997), p. 366.
2. V. V. Vinogradov, 'Intelligentsiia' in *Istoriia slov* (Moscow: Rossiiskaia Akademiia nauk, 1999), pp. 227–9; Galina N. Skliarevskaia, 'Russkie poniatiia "intelligentsiia", "intelligent": razmyshleniia o semanticheskikh transformatsiiakh' in Peter Thiergen (ed.), *Russische Begriffsgeschichte der Neuzeit. Beiträge zu einem Forschungsdesiderat* (Cologne, Weimar, Vienna: Böhlau Verlag, 2006), p. 436.
3. See V. A. Zhukovskii, 'Iz dnevnikov 1827–1840 godov', *Nashe nasledie* (Moscow: Iskusstvo, 1994), vol. X, p. 46; S. O. Shmidt, 'K istorii slova "intelligentsiia"' in Rossiiskaia Akademiia nauk. Institut russkoi literatury (Pushkinskii dom), *Rossiia, Zapad, Vostok. Vstrechnye techeniia* (St Petersburg: Nauka, 1996), pp. 409–17, here p. 413.
4. *Tolkovyi slovar' zhivogo velikorusskogo iazyka V. I. Dalia* (Moscow: Tipografiia A. Semena, 1863–8).
5. P. D. Boborykin, 'Mir uspekha. Ocherki parizhskoi dramaturgii (Pamiat' M. S. Shchepkina)', *Russkii vestnik* (August 1866), 637–89, (September 1866), 55–104. Boborykin's use of the term is discussed by Alan P. Pollard, 'The Russian intelligentsia: the mind of Russia', *California Slavic Studies*, 3 (1964), 1–6. Boborykin subsequently claimed to have coined the term *intelligentsiia*, a claim supported by the Granat *Entsiklopedicheskii slovar'* and *Bol'shaia sovetskaia entsiklopediia*. His purported status as originator of the term caused considerable confusion among western scholars who took the claim at face value since it was legitimated by major Russian reference sources.

6. Lev Tolstoi, *Polnoe sobranie sochinenii. Reprintnoe vosproizvedenie izdaniia 1928–1958 gg.*, 91 vols. (Moscow: Terra, 1992), vol. IX, p. 12.

7. *Tolkovyi slovar' zhivogo velikorusskogo iazyka Vladimira Dalia*, 4 vols. (St Petersburg: Tipografiia M. O. Vol'fa, 1881), vol. II, p. 46.

8. M. I. Mikhel'son, *Russkaia mysl' i rech': svoe i chuzhoe: opyt russkoi frazeologii. Sbornik obraznykh slov i inoskazanii*, 2 vols. (Moscow: Russkie slovari, 1994), vol. I, p. 377.

9. Aleksandr Nikitenko, *Dnevnik*, 3 vols. (Leningrad: Gosudarstvennoe izdatel'stvo khudozhestvennoi literatury, 1955), vol. II, p. 414, quoted in Nathaniel Knight, 'Was the intelligentsia part of the nation? Visions of society in post-emancipation Russia', *Kritika: Explorations in Russian and Eurasian History*, 7:4 (Fall 2006), 746.

10. V. A. Tvardovskaia, *Ideologiia poreformennogo samoderzhaviia (M. N. Katkov i ego izdaniia)* (Moscow: Nauka, 1978), pp. 176–7, 185.

11. F. M. Dostoevskii, 'Ob"iasnitel'noe slovo po povodu pechataemoi nizhe rechi o Pushkine', *Polnoe sobranie sochinenii*, 30 vols. (Leningrad: Nauka, 1972–90), vol. XXVI, p. 129; for a helpful analysis of Dostoevsky's view of the intelligentsia, see Derek Offord, 'Dostoevskii and the intelligentsia' in W. J. Leatherbarrow (ed.), *The Cambridge Companion to Dostoevskii* (Cambridge University Press, 2002), pp. 111–30.

12. Sorokin, *Razvitie slovarnogo sostava russkogo literaturnogo iazyka* (Moscow and Leningrad: Nauka, 1965), p. 145.

13. See Nikolai Konstantinovich Mikhailovskii, *Sochineniia*, 6 vols. (St Petersburg: Izdatel'stvo B. M. Vol'fa, 1897), vol. V, pp. 537–8; Knight, 'Was the intelligentsia part of the nation?', 753–4.

14. D. N. Ushakov, *Tolkovyi slovar' russkogo iazyka* (Moscow: Gosinstitut Sovetskaia Entsiklopediia, 1935), pp. 214–15.

15. *Vekhi. Sbornik statei o russkoi intelligentsii* (Moscow: Tipografiia V. M. Sablina, 1909).

16. Lesley Chamberlain, *Lenin's Private War: The Voyage of the Philosophy Steamer and the Exile of the Intelligentsia* (New York: St Martin's Press, 2007); Stuart Finkel, *On the Ideological Front: The Russian Intelligentsia and the Making of the Soviet Public Sphere* (New Haven: Yale University Press, 2007).

17. Sofiia Chuikina, *Dvorianskaia pamiat': 'byvshie' v sovetskom gorode (Leningrad, 1920–1930-e gody)* (St Petersburg: Izdatel'stvo Evropeiskogo universiteta v Sankt-Peterburge, 2006).

18. Ushakov, *Tolkovyi slovar' russkogo iazyka*, pp. 214–15.

19. An interesting recent example is the historian Simon Ilizarov, who has compiled a list of 850 eighteenth-century *intelligenty* involved in the creative arts and in the sciences in the city of Moscow. See S. S. Ilizarov, *Moskovskaia intelligentsiia XVIII veka* (Moscow: Ianus-K, 1999).

20. The great liberal historian Pavel Miliukov, for example, associated the birth of the intelligentsia with Tatishchev's efforts to justify a 'secular life' in the wake of the Petrine reforms. See P. N. Miliukov, *Ocherki po istorii russkoi kul'tury*, 3 vols. (Moscow: Izdatel'skaia gruppa 'Progress', 1993–5; reprint of 1930 edn),

vol. III, pp. 212–15. Ivanov-Razumnik spoke of isolated *intelligenty* in the fifteenth and sixteenth centuries, but dated the intelligentsia as a continuous phenomenon to the late eighteenth-century figures of Novikov, Fonvizin and Radishchev. See R. V. Ivanov-Razumnik, *Istoriia russkoi obshchestvennoi mysli. Individualizm i meshchanstvo v russkoi literature i zhizni XIX veka*, 2nd edn, 2 vols. (St Petersburg: Tipografiia M. M. Stasiulevicha, 1908), vol. I, introductory remarks, and *Chto takoe intelligentsiia?* (Berlin: Izdatel'stvo 'Skify', 1920), pp. 6–8. Berdiaev called Radishchev 'the first parent of the Russian intelligentsia' in *Russkaia ideia* (Paris: YMCA Press, 1971), p. 30.

21. Typical of this approach is Isaiah Berlin's four-essay cycle, originally published in *Encounter* under the title 'A marvellous decade' in 1955–6, and reprinted under the title 'A remarkable decade' in Berlin, *Russian Thinkers*, ed. Henry Hardy and Aileen Kelly (New York: Viking Press, 1978), pp. 114–209. In it, Berlin located the origins of the intelligentsia in the decade from 1838 to 1848. His basic periodisation was accepted by Martin Malia, 'What is the intelligentsia?' in Richard Pipes (ed.), *The Russian Intelligentsia* (New York: Columbia University Press, 1961), pp. 1–2, 11. James Billington dated the intelligentsia's origins to the period 1858–63 (see Billington, 'The intelligentsia and the religion of humanity', *The American Historical Review*, 675:4 (July 1960), 809, 812, 816). Marc Raeff's influential *Origins of the Russian Intelligentsia: The Eighteenth-Century Nobility* (New York: Harcourt, Brace and World, 1966) identified the first generation of the intelligentsia with the thinkers of Berlin's 'marvellous decade', even though he (Raeff) insisted that the intelligentsia was 'related genetically' to the eighteenth-century service nobility. Michael Confino argued that the first and only generation of *intelligenty* were the men of the 1860s (see Confino, 'On intellectuals and intellectual traditions in eighteenth- and nineteenth-century Russia', *Daedalus*, 101 (1972), 128–9).

22. Boris I. Kolonickij, 'Les identités de l'intelligentsia russe et l'anti-intellectualisme. Fin du XIXe–début du XXe siècle', *Cahiers du monde russe et soviétique*, 43:4 (October–December 2002), 601.

23. The most profound commentary on the Russian assimilation of western theology remains Father Georges Florovsky [Georgii Florovskii], *Puti russkogo bogosloviia* (Paris: YMCA Press, 1983).

24. See Gary Marker, *Publishing, Printing, and the Origins of Intellectual Life in Russia, 1700–1800* (Princeton University Press, 1985), pp. 14–15. On the number of Russian titles appearing annually in the early eighteenth century, see Sergei Pavlovich Luppov, *Kniga v Rossii v XVII veke* (Leningrad: Leningradskoe otdelenie 'Nauka', 1970), pp. 1–13.

25. I am well aware that the central government in Muscovy sometimes took into account the wishes of provincial gentry. On this phenomenon, see Valerie A. Kivelson, *Autocracy in the Provinces: The Muscovite Gentry and Political Culture in the Seventeenth Century* (Stanford University Press, 1996).

26. Iu. M. Lotman, *Besedy o russkoi kul'ture. Byt i traditsii russkogo dvorianstva (XVIII–nachalo XIX veka)* (St Petersburg: Iskusstvo, 1994), pp. 24–8.

27. For a discussion of Tatishchev's role, see Nil Popov, *V. N. Tatishchev i ego vremia* (Moscow: Tipografiia V. Gracheva, 1861), pp. 66–133.

28. On the 1767 Novikov circle, see Grigorii Panteleimonovich Makogonenko, *Nikolai Novikov i russkoe prosveshchenie XVIII veka* (Moscow: Gos. Izdatel'stvo khudozhestvennoi literatury, 1957), pp. 99–103; on Radishchev and Ushakov, see A. N. Radishchev, 'Zhitie Fedora Vasil'evicha Ushakova' in *Polnoe sobranie sochinenii*, 3 vols. (Moscow and Leningrad: AN SSSR, 1938), vol. I, pp. 161–72.

29. On this building programme, see Priscilla R. Roosevelt, *Life on the Russian Country Estate: A Social and Cultural History* (New Haven and London: Yale University Press, 1995), pp. xviii–xxi, 16–17.

30. Elise Kimerling Wirtschafter, *The Play of Ideas in Russian Enlightenment Theater* (DeKalb: University of Northern Illinois Press, 2003).

31. Roosevelt, *Life on the Russian Country Estate*, pp. 219, 246–60.

32. See Douglas Smith, *Working the Rough Stone: Freemasonry in Eighteenth-Century Russia* (DeKalb: University of Illinois Press, 1999).

33. For the mid-eighteenth-century Academy, see Valerii Ivanovich Osipov, *Peterburgskaia Akademiia Nauk i russko-nemetskie nauchnye sviazi v poslednei treti XVIII veka* (St Petersburg: PFA RAP, 1995).

34. Marker, *Publishing, Printing, and the Origins of Intellectual Life*, p. 126.

35. On Moscow University as 'cultural space', see I. P. Kulakova, *Universitetskoe prostranstvo i ego obitateli: Moskovskii universitet v istoriko-kul'turnoi srede XVIII veka* (Moscow: Novyi khronograf, 2006), pp. 207–8, 307–8.

36. A. I. Gertsen, *Byloe i dumy* (Moscow: Slovo, 2001), pp. 75–82.

37. On the Priamukhino estate and the Bakunins, see John Randolph, *The House in the Garden. The Bakunin Family and the Romance of Russian Idealism* (Ithaca and London: Cornell University Press, 2007), pp. 274–5.

38. On Chicherin's education, see *Vospominaniia Borisa Nikolaevicha Chicherina. Moskva sorokovykh godov* (Moscow: Izdanie M. i S. Sabashnikovykh, 1929).

39. The best book in English on Sergei Aksakov, father of the two Slavophiles, is Andrew Durkin, *Sergei Aksakov and Russian Pastoral* (New Brunswick: Rutgers University Press, 1983), p. 37.

40. See Edmund Wilson, 'Turgenev and the life-giving drop' in *A Window on Russia for the Use of Foreign Readers* (New York: Farrar, Strauss and Giroux, 1972), pp. 69–72.

41. Daniel Brower, *Training the Nihilists: Education and Radicalism in Tsarist Russia* (Ithaca: Cornell University Press, 1975).

42. Franco Venturi, *Roots of Revolution. A History of the Populist and Socialist Movements in Nineteenth-Century Russia*, trans. F. Haskell (London: Weidenfeld and Nicolson, 1960), especially pp. 469–506.

43. See Richard Wortman's portrait of Aleksandr Nikolaevich Engelgardt in his book *The Crisis of Russian Populism* (Cambridge University Press, 1967), pp. 35–60.

44. M. V. Nechkina, *Dvizhenie dekabristov*, 2 vols. (Moscow: AN SSSR, 1955), vol. I, pp. 105–6, 150–62.

45. See Aron Iakovlevich Avrekh, *Masony i revoliutsiia* (Moscow: Izdatel'stvo politicheskoi literatury, 1990), pp. 12–197, 339.

46. For a conservative take on the problem, see Viktor Stepanovich Brachev, *Russkoe masonstvo XX veka* (St Petersburg: Izdatel'stvo Stomma, 2000).
47. See B. I. Nikolaevskii, 'Russkie masony v nachale XX veka' in Iu. Fel'shtinskii (ed.), *Russkie masony i revoliutsiia* (Moscow: Terra, 1990), especially pp. 19–41; and V. I. Startsev, *Russkoe politicheskoe masonstvo nachala XX veka* (St Petersburg: Tret'ia Rossiia, 1996).
48. A. V. Sokolov, 'Istoriografiia, istochnikovedenie, metody istoricheskogo issledovaniia. Russkoe politicheskoe masonstvo 1910–1918 godov v otechestvennoi istoriografii', *Otechestvennaia istoriia*, 2004, no. 2, 139–53, here 149.
49. Nechkina, *Dvizhenie dekabristov*, vol. I, p. 96.
50. Gertsen, *Byloe i dumy*, p. 107.
51. See Abbott Gleason, *Young Russia: The Genesis of Russian Radicalism in the 1860s* (New York: Viking Press, 1980); Irina Paperno, *Chernyshevskii and the Age of Realism: A Study in the Semiotics of Behavior* (Stanford University Press, 1988); and Peter C. Pozefsky, *The Nihilist Imagination: Dmitrii Pisarev and the Cultural Origins of Russian Radicalism (1860–1868)* (New York: Peter Lang, 2003).
52. Boris Samuilovich Itenberg, *Dvizhenie revoliutsionnogo narodnichestva; narodnicheskie kruzhki i 'khozhdenie v narod' v 70-kh godov XIX v.* (Moscow: Nauka, 1965), pp. 148–58.
53. Terence Emmons, *The Formation of Political Parties and the First National Elections in Russia* (Cambridge, Mass: Harvard University Press, 1983), pp. 65–8.
54. Richard Pipes, *A Concise History of the Russian Revolution* (New York: Vintage Books, 1995), pp. 33–4.
55. A. A. Kizevetter, *Na rubezhe dvukh stoletii. (Vospominaniia 1881–1914)* (Prague: Izdatel'stvo Orbis, 1929), pp. 512–13.
56. The best treatment of the post-1900 student culture can be found in Samuel Kassow, *Students, Professors, and the State in Tsarist Russia* (Berkeley: University of California Press, 1989). Susan K. Morrissey, *Heralds of Revolution. Russian Students and the Mythologies of Radicalism* (New York: Oxford University Press, 1998) has argued that the overlap between the student body and the revolutionary intelligentsia was only temporary, since student status was itself transitory.
57. Natal'ia Mikhailovna Pirumova, *Zemskoe liberal'noe dvizhenie: sotsial'nye korni i evoliutsiia do nachala XX veka* (Moscow: Nauka, 1977); for a fuller catalogue of zemstvo disputes with the central government, see Boris Borisovich Veselovskii, *Istoriia zemstva za sorok let*, 4 vols. (St Petersburg: Izdatel'stvo O. N. Popovoi, 1909–13), especially vols. III and IV.
58. In 1883 the eminent historian Boris Chicherin was forced to resign as mayor after a speech at the coronation of Alexander III in which he called for collaboration between Russian cities and the central government. The central authorities interpreted him as calling for a constitution. See *Vospominaniia Borisa Nikolaevicha Chicherina. Zemstvo i Moskovskaia duma* (Moscow: Kooperativnoe obshchestvo 'Sever', 1934), pp. 233–52. In 1913 the central government failed to ratify the election of Prince Georgii L'vov as mayor. See

Robert W. Thurston, *Liberal City, Conservative State. Moscow and Russia's Urban Crisis, 1906–1914* (New York and Oxford: Oxford University Press, 1987), p. 80.

59. Thurston, *Liberal City, Conservative State*, pp. 163–73.
60. The shakiness of the alliance between zemstvo liberals and zemstvo *intelligenty* is explored by Nancy M. Frieden, 'The politics of zemstvo medicine' in Terence Emmons and Wayne S. Vucinich (eds.), *The Zemstvo in Russia. An Experiment in Local Self-Government* (Cambridge University Press, 1982), pp. 315–42.
61. The best book on the 'third element' is N. M. Pirumova, *Zemskaia intelligentsiia i ee rol' v obshchestvennoi bor'be do nachala XX v.* (Moscow: Nauka, 1986).
62. Vera Romanovna Leikina-Svirskaia, *Russkaia intelligentsiia v 1900–1917 godakh* (Moscow: Mysl', 1981), pp. 50–1.
63. Ibid., p. 78.
64. Ibid., p. 16.
65. Ben Eklof, *Russian Peasant Schools. Officialdom, Village Culture, and Popular Pedagogy, 1861–1914* (Berkeley: University of California Press, 1986), pp. 182–3.
66. Ibid., pp. 198–200.
67. Quoted ibid., p. 221.
68. Christine Ruane, *Gender, Class, and the Professionalization of Russian City Teachers, 1860–1914* (University of Pittsburgh Press, 1994).
69. Pirumova, *Zemskaia intelligentsiia*; Leikina-Svirskaia, *Russkaia intelligentsiia, passim.*
70. Leikina-Svirskaia, *Russkaia intelligentsiia*, pp. 52–3, 58.
71. Ibid., pp. 68–9.
72. Ibid., pp. 236–41.
73. Eklof, *Russian Peasant Schools*, pp. 220–1.
74. Ibid., pp. 243–6.
75. Scott Seregny, *Russian Teachers and Peasant Revolution: The Politics of Education in 1905* (Bloomington: Indiana University Press, 1989).
76. Boris Nikolaevich Mironov, *Sotsial'naia istoriia Rossii (XVIII–nachalo XX v.). Genezis lichnosti, demokraticheskoi sem'i, grazhdanskogo obshchestva i pravovogo gosudarstva*, 2 vols. (St Petersburg: Dmitrii Bulanin, 1999), vol. I, p. 527.
77. Jeffrey Brooks, *When Russia Learned to Read. Literacy and Popular Literature, 1861–1917* (Princeton University Press, 1985), p. 4.
78. Ibid., p. 38.
79. Eklof has noted that school attendance rates in the first two years of primary school were remarkably high, but that children rarely completed the third year of study. Only one in ninety students advanced beyond basic primary school; only one in five hundred enrolled in a secondary school. Eklof, *Russian Peasant Schools*, pp. 324–5, 330, 476–7.
80. Brooks, *When Russia Learned to Read*, pp. 59–294.
81. Ibid., pp. 85–7, 317–19.
82. Ibid., p. 318.
83. Leikina-Svirskaia, *Russkaia intelligentsiia*, pp. 122–3.

84. Louise McReynolds, *The News under Russia's Old Regime: The Development of a Mass-Circulation Press* (Princeton University Press, 1991).

85. Scherrer, *Die Petersburger Religiös-Philosophischen Vereinigungen. Die Entwicklung des religiösen Selbstverständnisses ihrer Intelligencija-Mitglieder (1901–1917)* (Berlin and Wiesbaden: Otho Harrassowitz, 1973), *passim*. See also her 'Intelligentsia, réligion, révolution: premières manifestations d'un socialisme chrétien en Russie, 1905–1907', *Cahiers du monde russe et soviétique*, 17:4 (1976), 427–66, 18:1/2 (1977), 5–32.

86. Randall Poole, *Neo-Idealist Philosophy in the Russian Liberation Movement: The Moscow Psychological Society and Its Symposium 'Problems of Idealism'* (Washington, DC: Kennan Institute for Advanced Russian Studies, 1996); Kristiane Burchardi, *Die Moskauer 'Religiös-philosophische Vladimir-Solov'ev Gesellschaft' (1905–1918), Forschungen zur osteuropäischen Geschichte*, 53 (Wiesbaden: Harrassowitz Verlag, 1998).

87. Scherrer, *Die Petersburger Religiös-Philosophischen Vereinigungen*, p. 38.

88. Ibid., p. 433.

89. Soviet historians commonly classified the Kadets as a 'bourgeois party' representing propertied interests of various sorts. However, an equally compelling case can be made that the Kadets closely resembled redistributionist European socialist parties and that their redistributionist economic platform emerged out of the intelligentsia milieu.

90. Ul'ia Urilov took the position that the Mensheviks had not been defined by the intelligentsia as a whole; rather, party leaders 'who were certainly representatives of the Russian intelligentsia defined its politics'. Ul'ia Khanukaevich Urilov, *Istoriia rossiiskoi sotsial-demokratii (men'shevizma)*, 3 vols. (Moscow: Vneshtorgizdat, 1996–2005).

91. Lih pointed out that, in *What is to be Done?* and subsequent writings, Lenin criticised the view that the Bolsheviks were an intelligentsia party. Lenin and Bogdanov either rejected the intelligentsia spirit altogether or claimed that the intelligentsia played only a marginal role in the party. See Lars T. Lih, *Lenin Rediscovered. 'What is to be Done?' in Context* (Leiden: Brill, 2006), pp. 532–6.

92. Alain Besançon, *The Intellectual Origins of Leninism*, trans. Sarah Matthews (Oxford: Basil Blackwell, 1981), pp. 111–12.

PART II

Intellectual currents

CHAPTER 4

Russia's eighteenth-century Enlightenment

W. Gareth Jones

The view once commonly held that the Enlightenment was a unified, bourgeois, anti-clerical and inherently revolutionary movement radiating out from its centre in Paris has given way to a kaleidoscopic picture of national varieties in which the continuous importance of religion and an array of political ideas and social attitudes are discerned. There could even be conservative and religious forms of Enlightenment. Its central core, however, was the urge to modify the way that men and women had traditionally thought and behaved, and to reform church and state institutions with the aim of bettering the human condition.

THE PETRINE AGE

For Russians the eighteenth century dawned with a calendar reform demonstrating that times had changed. Hitherto Muscovy had followed the traditional Byzantine way of counting years from the supposed creation of the world in 5509/8 BC. The year 7208 was for them the last to be officially recorded in this way. Henceforward, Peter the Great decreed, official records would adopt calendar years *Anno Domini* following the custom of the countries – Prussia, Holland and England – through which he travelled in 1697 on a journey that has been recognised as one of the key moments in a 'Chronology of the Enlightenment'.[1] However, it was not Peter I's journey that first allowed Russians, by absorbing western European influences, to participate in the process of the early Enlightenment. Throughout the seventeenth century, when rationalism, empiricism and experimental knowledge developed in an age of outstanding thinkers, including Bacon, Hobbes, Locke, Spinoza and Leibniz, western Europeans had made their way to Muscovy. Moreover, the young Peter had spent considerable time in Moscow's *nemetskaia sloboda*, a quarter set aside for foreign residents, where he gained firsthand experience of western technical expertise and a new outlook on social interactions. It is significant that these expatriates were in the main from the Protestant lands of northern Europe, and it was their homelands that prompted the course of Peter's journey in 1697. The fact that it was Protestant Europe that mediated the new ways of thought into Russia, it has been suggested by Marc Raeff, 'was to have a lasting effect'.[2]

Peter's mind had a practical rather than a philosophical bent, and he was unlikely to find prominent thinkers among Moscow's expatriate community, although the ideas that underpinned the latest western technology were present in the intellectual atmosphere permeating the foreigners' public consciousness. However, the Grand Embassy that left Moscow in 1697 was intended to garner advanced ideas as much as practical know-how. What Peter witnessed with his own eyes in the Dutch Republic and England was a flourishing merchant class, benefiting from a free exchange of ideas in the press and in public debate. In England, where he stayed from 10 January to 22 April 1698, he demonstrated his intellectual curiosity by visiting the Royal Observatory and the Royal Society, and by attending Anglican services and a Quaker meeting. He also went to the theatre and Parliament, institutions with which he was less impressed. He came to see more starkly what he had glimpsed in Moscow's foreign quarter: the degree to which Russians lagged behind the advanced economies and societies of western countries.

Inspired by his travel experiences, Peter decided to plunge his country into the process of general enlightenment that was spreading across Europe. On the periphery, including the Russian lands, that process had been one of slow seepage. It now became a flood at Peter's instigation. Peter did not merely decree a renumbering of the calendar on the western pattern. New Year's Day 1700 was to be marked in flamboyant style with a public firework display on Moscow's Red Square.[3] The spectacle was to be accompanied by rockets and salvoes from the muskets of the wealthier classes on Peter's orders. Lower orders were enjoined to cooperate in the festivities by providing flares and beacons. The contrast between this new, secular celebration and the traditional religious processions and pious homilies of previous Russian New Year's Days held on 1 September was manifest. This was an excellent example of the kind of visual show – statues, pictures and stage-sets were as effective as fireworks – that transmitted a new outlook on the world alongside the written word.[4] Peter certainly transformed the external appearance of Russian society by obliging the nobility to dress in western clothes and to become clean-shaven. Social graces were fostered among the youth by the inclusion of dancing, fencing and drawing in the curriculum of the Naval Academy. And the built environment was utterly changed as an elegant new capital with broad streets and squares, designed with the aid of western architects, arose in St Petersburg.

With his autocratic powers, Peter was the prime mover in this. And the expectation that any reform could be directed only from the top remained an enduring belief that would complicate the development of Russian social thought long into the future. The next step was to establish the mechanisms for the spreading of enlightenment. Peter's recruitment of foreign industrialists, military and naval experts and craftsmen might appear to have had a purely utilitarian purpose. But their advanced specialisms often depended on theoretical knowledge derived from the scientific revolution of the seventeenth century. As well as direct recruitment, Peter sought to train native Russians in the new way of thinking. This was achieved by despatching students abroad and, more importantly, by setting up training establishments at home staffed by foreign tutors. Among these expatriates were three British teachers of mathematical navigation: Henry Farquharson, Liddel mathematical tutor at Marischal College in Aberdeen, and Stephen Gwyn and Richard Grice, both students of the Royal Mathematical School attached to Christ's Hospital. An imperial ukase in January 1701 appointed Farquharson (1675–1739) head of the newly established Moscow Mathematics and Navigation School which was the forerunner of the Naval Academy (1716), where Farquharson was to become Professor of Mathematics at 'Russia's first serious scientific centre'[5] and where Iakov Brius (James Bruce) – claimed to be Russia's first Newtonian – established the country's first observatory. Both institutions initiated scientific publishing and inspired many technical and scientific enterprises in the early eighteenth century, as well as producing several generations of Russian explorers, cartographers, mathematicians, surveyors, engineers and naval experts, all essential for the spread of modernity.

Beyond the practical naval sphere, however, British influence was not widespread. The empiricism of English thinkers such as Bacon and Locke did not dominate the realm of ideas in Russia. For philosophical guidance Peter turned to Leibniz, with whom he corresponded, and it was he and Christian Wolff who were the tsar's most influential advisers on academic matters. They recommended for Russian service their personal pupils, who imported their own system of thought; the latter were the main conduit of Cartesian rationalism and natural law expounded by their teachers, Pufendorf and others. It has been argued that Russians were more receptive to Cartesianism, as presented to them, since it was not in conflict with traditional Christian teaching and its cosmology with its acceptance of the duality of mind and matter.[6] The Germans' ascendancy was marked in the foundation of the Academy of Sciences in 1725. Until the close of the century the Academy was dominated by Germans trained in German universities. Most Russian-based scientists and scholars with an international reputation, Müller, Euler, Schlözer, Pallas and Stählin, were connected with the Academy. Their work was not confined to the Academy's narrow scholarly interests; they received government commissions and crucially supported the work of other scientific and educational institutions, most notably the Cadet Corps (*Kadetskii korpus*), established in 1732 for the training of young noblemen.

THE LEARNED WATCH

The chief ideologist of the new outlook within the traditional sphere of Russian Orthodoxy was an outstanding Greek-Russian Orthodox cleric, the Ukrainian Feofan Prokopovich, a close collaborator of Peter I's. He has been seen as 'the first authentic voice in Russia of the Early Enlightenment'.[7] He was partially influenced by the western rationalism propagated by Leibniz and Christian Wolff,[8] and there is evidence that he was also acquainted with the works of Erasmus and Luther, of Buddeus and Bellarmine, of Descartes, of Galileo, Kepler, Bacon, Machiavelli, Grotius and Pufendorf, of Guicciardini, Hobbes and Locke.[9] The western influence was especially revealed in his *Justice of the Monarch's Will* (1722), which, while acknowledging divine right, sanctified by Scripture and Byzantine authorities, as the cornerstone of monarchical power, also reflected modern European natural law theory.[10] So Prokopovich stressed that the general will of the people (*vsenarodnaia volia*) endowed their ruler with power for the sake of the common good, thus forming a binding contract between the people and their ruler. The latter was beholden to God alone and did not require the church as intermediary. It has been suggested that Prokopovich may have been guided by Locke's view that the concerns of church and secular government should be separate. Prokopovich was in agreement with the view that the church's role should be limited to salvation by means of liturgy, ritual and dogma; education and social welfare should be the business of government. 'To maintain their subjects in felicity and to formulate for them every kind of good instruction for piety, and also for honest living': this for Prokopovich was the duty of tsars.[11]

Prokopovich's enlightened view of the separation of ecclesiastical and state powers was made manifest in the Ecclesiastical Regulation that established Peter the Great's church reform promulgated on 25 January 1721. It abolished the patriarchate, thus removing the figure of the patriarch as a possible rival to the tsar in gaining the affection of the Russian people, and replaced it with an 'Ecclesiastical College' soon renamed the Most Holy

All-Ruling Synod. As well as outlining a new form of governance for the church that subordinated it to the tsar, much emphasis was placed on the need for a new network of church schools in which secular learning, represented by the study of 'ancient and modern philosophers, astronomers, rhetoricians, historians, etc.', stood alongside that of the church fathers.[12] It was a document that embodied Peter's church reform, which in its recasting of a deeply rooted Russian institution may be considered the most radical in signalling a clean break with the past.[13] Most other reforms were imported additions to Russian society.

Prokopovich, who survived Peter the Great by a decade, resolutely defended the Petrine reforms and the tsar's reputation after his death, when Peter's legacy was in peril in the lackadaisical, often reactionary, short reigns of his successors Catherine I (1725–7) and Peter II (1727–30). Content to be a self-effacing interpreter of Peter's views during the tsar's lifetime, Prokopovich now used his position as a church dignitary to maintain the impetus of the Petrine enlightenment. He sought allies to assist him in this task and found them in the self-conscious grouping of the 'Learned Watch' (*uchenaia druzhina*), a grouping whose suggestive title was devised by him in 1730. Historically, *druzhina* designated a prince's armed force recruited as volunteers from the citizenry. The import of Prokopovich's phrase was unmistakable. He sought to enrol a like-minded group of men such as the poet-diplomat Kantemir (1708–44) and the historian-administrator Tatishchev (1686–1750), equipped not with arms but with pens, who would defend the memory of a prince to whom they owed allegiance and whose new vision for Russia was under attack from conservatives. It was Kantemir's first satire in 1729 that had prompted Prokopovich to use the phrase 'Learned Watch'. Directed against the 'disparagers of learning', it was a barbed denunciation of those who bridled at the enlightenment, the western sciences and church reforms that Peter had rooted in their society. Prokopovich responded with enthusiasm to the satire, circulating it widely with praise for its composer.[14] Four vivid characters served as the butt of Kantemir's satire. First is the cleric who sees enlightenment as the root cause of heresy and a threat to the church's wealth and authority. Second stands the representative of the gentry back-woodsmen who view the pursuit of new-fangled philosophy, physics, chemistry and medicine as a waste of time that could be better employed on exploiting one's estate; for him traditional lore was sufficient knowledge. The third sketch is of the sociable drunkard and the fourth of a giddy-headed fop, neither of whom sees any personal benefit in the new learning. The pen portraits were followed by a discourse on the perverted mores of the age when for so many in the church and the law there was a disdain for intellectual rigour and inner virtue, external trimmings being considered sufficient to exercise their calling. The satire is significant in that it indicates those spheres of Russian life that had been reformed by Russia's incipient Enlightenment, as well as revealing the nature and extent of the continuing opposition that had been emboldened by the removal of Peter's guiding hand.

It is worth noting that both Prokopovich and Kantemir had benefited from a western education. In 1698 Prokopovich, as an exceptionally gifted pupil in the Kiev Academy, was sent to pursue his studies at Jesuit colleges in Polish territory where he was obliged to become a Uniate and take Catholic orders. To complete his education he was sent to Rome, remaining there until his return to Kiev in 1702 where he reverted to Orthodoxy. During his three years in Rome he had been exposed to humanism with its rationalistic scepticism towards Roman Catholicism and to the works of the Reformation. He was a product of the 'Slavonic Renaissance', an amalgam of Polish–Latin and Russian elements that had flourished in Kiev in the seventeenth century and had seeped into Russian society after Kiev was incorporated into Muscovy in 1667. This has been seen as the fount of western Enlightenment on which Moscow first drew. Kantemir, born in Constantinople in 1708, was the son of Dmitry Kantemir, who as viceroy of Moldavia agreed to its annexation to Russia in 1711, following which the family moved to Russia, eventually taking up residence in the new capital of St Petersburg in 1719. Kantemir was nurtured in a family that spoke Greek and Italian and learnt Russian and Latin from tutors. In St Petersburg he received a broad education in mathematics, physics, philosophy and history from professors recruited from the West by Peter. Prokopovich and Kantemir, therefore, shared the distinction of being outsiders with a western education, attributes that they shared with the poet-academician Trediakovsky (1703–69), who had been born on the periphery, in Astrakhan, where his initial education was entrusted to Capuchin monks. After a period in Moscow's Slav-Greek-Latin Academy, he travelled westwards in 1723 to spend two years studying at The Hague and a further extensive period (1726–30) at the Sorbonne in Paris as a student of mathematics, philosophy and languages.

The 'Learned Watch' might be seen as a grouping of autonomous, like-minded individuals who had come together to exert their personal influence on society. However, it has been stressed that the outstanding personalities of the Enlightenment in Russia rarely accepted the spirit of western individualism and the political conclusions that flowed from it.[15]

The value and dignity of the educated citizen might be acknowledged by them, but in general (and this is seen in the case of Prokopovich's and Kantemir's 'Watch') there would be no advocacy of legal guarantees of individual rights, determined not by social privilege but by the simple possession of humanity, as the French *philosophes* argued. Again it was the German influence, Pietism and *Aufklärung* rather than the *Lumières*, that steered Russian thinking into a conception of individualism as 'enabling the person to enter into direct rapport with the sovereign autocrat without the mediation of juridically constituted, corporate bodies, as was the case in western and central Europe'.[16] Just as significant for the development of their enlightening ideas was the fact that they were all influential servants of the state. This close identification of such writers with state interests was a marked feature of Russian literary life until the close of the century.

The elevation of the virtues of civic duty, service and social responsibility over individual rights, inspired by German Pietists, was reinforced through the Academy of Sciences. It was dominated by products of the universities of Halle, Marburg and Leipzig, all centres of Pietism that continued to have a dramatic effect on society and government in Germany.[17] Originally Pietism was a religious revival that had swept through Lutheran Germany following the Thirty Years War. Its mission was to reform not only the Lutheran Church, but also the world. Frederick-William I of Prussia (1688–1740), Peter the Great's contemporary, had harnessed the movement's reformist enthusiasm for serving the poor and state welfare. It was Pietism that helped to convert the Prussian nobility into a bureaucracy at the service of the court. Its adherents, imbued with missionary zeal, saw Russia as a fertile field for proselytising, and the political stance that they had embraced in Prussia was in concord with the Petrine vision for the modernisation and development of his empire.

LOMONOSOV

A striking example of the product of the German connection was that of Lomonosov (1711–65), a native genius who towered over Russian intellectual life in the mid-century in both literary and scientific fields. Again he was an outsider of humble origins, born on the Russian periphery in a fishing community near the White Sea. In 1731 Lomonosov enrolled at Moscow's Slav-Greek-Latin Academy and was transferred for a brief period to the St Petersburg Academy of Sciences before being sent in 1736 to further his education in Marburg, where his intellectual horizons were established under Christian Wolff, the philosophic luminary of German Pietism. In moving from a humble provincial background to be trained as one of the new Russian meritocracy, Lomonosov was the most illustrious intellectual beneficiary of the westernisation policy. He was to remain in Marburg until 1741 with an interlude in Freiburg as a student of mining. Upon his return to St Petersburg he was appointed an assistant in the Academy of Sciences, where he established the Academy's first chemistry laboratory in 1748, following his appointment as Professor of Chemistry in 1745. From 1750 he enjoyed the patronage of Count Shuvalov, with whom he founded Moscow University in 1755. His most significant contribution to international science was his proof of the existence of an atmosphere on Venus, deduced from his observations of the transit of Venus in 1761.

His reputation in his lifetime, however, rested more on his contribution to Russian literature and the development of the Russian language. The spreading of enlightenment depended on the linguistic resources of its proponents; a rich vocabulary and a supple syntax were required for the expression of new ideas. Peter the Great had sensed the need for linguistic reform with his introduction of a new 'civic' typography in 1708–10, but no attempt was made to codify a register of Russian for secular use. Writers before Lomonosov had attempted to bring order into a Russian literary language in a state of flux, as elements from the traditional Church Slavonic, practical officialese and colloquial language coexisted uneasily. Kantemir had tried to free his language from the clunking fetters of Church Slavonic, but with only partial success. Trediakovsky, a timid innovator, also grappled with the problem of combining the colloquial with the traditional Slavonic. Lomonosov put forward a powerful argument in favour of a generally acceptable, coherent solution to the problem in his *Rhetoric* (1748), *Russian Grammar* (1755) and his essay 'Preface on the Value of Church Books in the Russian Language' (1757). His proposed doctrine recognised three 'styles', or registers: high, middle and low styles were defined by their relationship to church Slavonic, which predominated in the high style and was absent from the low style. The middle style allowed an amalgam of the vernacular with a discreet choice of Slavonicisms. The 'theory of the three styles', although rooted in the current conventional linguistic theory of France, was distinguished by its skilful adaptation to the Russian situation. Lomonosov's arguments were enthusiastically accepted, as numerous editions of the relevant works attest,[18] and would enable writers in the second half of the eighteenth century to employ a neutral, middle style sanctioned by a firm theoretical definition.

Earlier, while a student at Freiburg, Lomonosov had made a seminal contribution to the establishment of a reformed Russian system of syllabo-tonic versification that has lasted to this day. His 'Letter on the Rules of Russian Versification' was sent home to the Academy of Sciences together with his 'Ode on the Capture of Khotin', patterned on Boileau's 'Ode on the Taking of Namur', but also bearing the deep imprint, in its use of the accentual iambic tetrameter, of Johann Christian Günther's German ode on the peace of Passowitz between the Austrian and Ottoman Empires in 1718. Lomonosov used his new prosody not only for laudatory odes, but also for topics in natural philosophy and technology, such as his 'Evening Meditation on God's Greatness', expressing the scientist's sense of awe at observing the Northern Lights, and 'Epistle on the Value of Glass'.

Lomonosov's admiration for German scholarship, particularly for Wolff, whose influential textbook on physics appeared in his pupil's Russian version in 1746, was on the whole beneficial for the development of Russian thought. However, in one respect the deference to Wolff proved detrimental to the emergence of original Russian ideas. As early as 1739, a dissertation submitted to the St Petersburg Academy as proof of his progress in Marburg demonstrated Lomonosov's independence of mind. It outlined his 'corpuscular philosophy', or molecular theory, that sought to explain the nature of bodies by the properties of the 'corpuscles' that combined in their formation. He distanced himself from the belief in immaterial forces that informed Wolff's cosmology by claiming that the 'corpuscles' were solely physical and material entities defined by 'mass and shape'. Lomonosov's molecular materialism lay at the base of his philosophy. It inspired many of his intuitive scientific works, such as that on the conservation of matter and energy that anticipated Lavoisier. Yet Lomonosov, as a mark of his enormous respect for his mentor, refused even in the 1750s to promote his atomic theories by arguing against Wolff's monadism, although he was privately convinced that his proofs would refute the German's 'mystical teaching'. His forbearance and the continuing dominance of Wolffian influence meant that his insights had little immediate impact. Only late in the nineteenth century did Moscow University come to acknowledge the scope of its founder's intuitive scientific genius.

OTHER CULTURAL ACTIVITIES

It was not only the cerebral work of writers and scientists that contributed to the Enlightenment, but also collective cultural activities that fostered a sense of shared values among groups whose self-image was that of enlighteners of their society. It has been stressed that the personification of the state in Russia's rulers exerted immense influence on the development of Russian culture.[19] That influence was manifest and manifold in the case of Peter the Great. With his successors the scope and pace of the imperial drive may have waned. However, the increase in opportunities for social interaction on the European pattern introduced by Peter with his compulsory assemblies (*assamblei*) for nobles, training grounds to exercise proper etiquette, continued apace in the reigns of the three empresses, Anna (1730–40), Elizabeth (1741–61) and Catherine II (1762–96).

Under Anna national music institutions, such as the Winter Palace Opera House and music printing by the Academy of Sciences, were established. The placing of Italian opera at the centre of Russian court life was an indication of Anna's intention to westernise musical culture. For direction she turned away from the German musicians favoured by Peter to Italy, identified as one of the several 'Europes' adopted by Russia in its Enlightenment.[20] Francesco Araja was appointed as the first Italian *Kapellmeister* and a stream of Italian musicians were to follow in his footsteps throughout the century, with talented young Russians being sent to further their studies in Italy. What is remarkable is the degree of the Italians' acculturation as they took advantage of the richness of the Russian choral tradition in their contributions to the Orthodox liturgy.[21]

This happy melding of native and European traditions in musical life was not typical of the interaction between Russian and alien by the mid-century. Other cultural spheres lacked the foundation of a sturdy Russian heritage that music had been able to build upon. The dramatic theatre, for example, was in comparison late to make any impact on court life. Traditional theatre amounted to no more than crude fairground entertainments, often vilified by the church, and there was virtually no European-style theatre, apart from performances by foreign troupes, until Empress Elizabeth inaugurated the first public theatre in St Petersburg in 1756 under the direction of the poet and playwright Sumarokov (1718–77). The theatre flourished under Catherine II, who was herself a skilful playwright; she founded the Hermitage gallery with munificent purchases of complete western art collections and was an enthusiastic developer of parks and gardens in the English style.

Meanwhile, the unease of the nobility at the poverty of Russian high culture quickened the development of their national consciousness. Lomonosov gave vehement expression to this growing sense of the distinctiveness of being Russian, apparent in his determination to establish a Russian literary language and a distinct Russian prosody and in his role in the founding of a university in the old capital of Moscow, as well as in his fractious personal dealings with fellow German academicians. His fervent nationalism flared up in 1749 in a controversy on the origins of the Russian nation. Academician Müller traced the lineage of the first Russian rulers back to the Varangian princes, the Vikings who in the ninth century had been invited, according to the *Primary Chronicle*, to impose order on the strife-torn Russian lands. Lomonosov and others fiercely opposed this 'Normanist' theory of history; the discovery that the Scandinavians had created their first political organism 'came as a severe shock to their Russian self respect'.[22] Lomonosov sought historical compensation in eulogies of Peter the Great, such as his panegyric to him in 1755 to commemorate the coronation of Elizabeth. This has been seen as an important step in the process of mythologising Peter's reign. The myth became even more important than Peter's real achievement for subsequent Russian thought. The extolling of Peter's personal attributes by Lomonosov was crucial in reinforcing a political tradition of personal, goal-driven leadership. Even well into the nineteenth century Peter's innovations became a focal point in discussions on the nature of Russian society. 'Anyone who has wished to cast any philosophical glance on our past', wrote Kliuchevsky, 'has considered it an imperative of scholarly decency to express his judgement on Peter's activities.'[23]

ENLIGHTENMENT IN THE REIGN
OF CATHERINE THE GREAT

Catherine the Great, with whom for some authorities the Russian Enlightenment really began,[24] expressed her admiration for Peter in her 1766 plan for a bronze equestrian statue of the tsar. A sense of continuity and parity, if not a hint of pre-eminence, was conveyed in a poetic response to it that appeared in her 1769 moral weekly *All Sorts*: 'Peter gave us being, Catherine a soul.'[25] It was echoed in Kheraskov's line that 'Peter gave Russians bodies, Catherine – souls', used by Kliuchevsky to illustrate the difference between them as reformers.[26]

By the early years of Catherine's reign, as Wolffian influence began to wane, the ideas of the French *philosophes* had made their impact. It was seen in Kozelsky's *Philosophic Propositions*, published in 1768 at the Senate Press and described as 'the first systematic exposition of philosophical ideas by a Russian author'.[27] The 'propositions' were culled from Voltaire, Helvétius, Montesquieu, Rousseau and Diderot's reworking of Shaftesbury. No organised system emerged from the various propositions and no project for the reform of government. In concord with the general tenor of the French Enlighteners, Kozelsky appeared to be a rationalist supporter of natural law, a deist who did not see religion as the fount of morality, but maintained that social conduct and politics should be based on ethical principles. Meanwhile, Catherine engaged in spirited correspondence with the French *encyclopédistes* Diderot and Voltaire, and with Melchior Grimm. An important step in bringing the *Lumières* of France to Russia was the composition of her 'Instruction', or *Nakaz*, to the Legislative Commission that she convened in 1767. In the years between her arrival in Russia from Prussia in 1744, as bride for the Grand Duke Peter, and her accession in 1762 Catherine claimed to have read voraciously.[28] Political works that were a staple of her reading formed the basis of her 'Instruction'. Her most important source was Montesquieu's *Spirit of the Laws*, which supplied 294 articles out of the 526 in Part I of the 'Instruction'. A further 108 were drawn from Beccaria's *On Crimes and Punishments*. Other sources were the *encyclopédistes*, including d'Alembert, François Quesnay's *Natural Law* and even, albeit indirectly through Desnitsky, Adam Smith according to some, although this is disputed.[29] However, she did not retain their views uncritically, modifying them to suit her particular circumstances. One crucial point of variance was that while Montesquieu considered a noble class, defined by birth and a shared sense of honour, as a necessary intermediary between the ruler and the ruled in a balanced monarchical constitution, Catherine saw that intermediary role as the province of a service class, a bureaucracy serving the interests of the sovereign legislator. For support Catherine turned to the 'police science', or *Polizeiwissenschaft*, propounded by such writers as Bielfeld in his *Political Institutions*, and Justi, who wrote in the tradition of Christian Wolff's 'philosophic cameralism'.[30] 'Police' must not be understood in its modern, narrow sense; Catherine, in her heading to chapter 21 of the 'Instruction', equated it with 'Good Order', which embraced urban planning, public decency, health, consumer protection, employment legislation and general welfare.[31] There have been many conflicting views on the true nature of the 'Instruction' and of the Legislative Commission that it was designed to 'instruct', many prompted by the particular viewpoint of contemporaries and subsequent interpreters.[32] However, the deep impress of Enlightenment ideas must not be underestimated.

Neither must one undervalue the significance of the presentation of these ideas. The title 'Instruction' has misled commentators into perceiving the work as primarily a manual designed to provide an agenda for the Legislative Commission. But it was not merely a political manifesto. It was also the first substantial literary work by Catherine in a fruitful writing career. Literature for Europeans in the early eighteenth century was not limited to imaginative writing but embraced a broad field of discourses including divinity, history, philosophy and science.[33] It was not confined to the reader's private study but functioned as a social activity. A crucial audience for Montesquieu's works had been the Parisian salons presided over by influential hostesses, where works were read out, listened to and discussed in a social gathering. Significantly, the first critical response to the *Spirit of Laws* had been by Madame de Tencin, literary hostess to the luminaries of the Enlightenment, who recognised the belletristic character of the work.[34]

There was no equivalent in Russia to the Parisian literary salons, but Catherine seems to have been well aware that literature should be a social activity. Her early drafts of the 'Instruction' were read out to 'several persons of widely differing views ... Debates then ensued on every item.'[35] This initial introduction of the work to an elite group was a prelude to its presentation to the wide-ranging gathering of deputies from across the Russian Empire. The Commission consisted of over 500 representatives of the various estates. Once a month they listened to the 'Instruction' being read out in its entirety. Furthermore, fifty-four copies were distributed to various offices, and in 1768 the Senate decreed that in each office the 'Instruction' should be read out three times a year.[36]

The purpose of these public readings was to encourage debate among a broadened spectrum of society. Enlightenment was no longer the province of a tiny, beleaguered elite wedged close to the throne as Prokopovich's 'Learned Watch' had been. The awareness grew that progress not only depended on a stock of knowledge, but prospered through communication networks that dispensed, distributed and debated that knowledge. The publishing and reading of books, moral weeklies and journals, masonic lodges and travel all constituted enlightened sociability in Europe; Russia, encouraged by Catherine, was about to share fully in this enlightened sociability.

Western European literature provided most of the secular books published in Russian in Catherine's reign, as she sponsored an ambitious programme of translations that followed the publication of her 'Instruction', with the establishment in November 1768 of a Society for the Translation of Foreign Books headed by her literary secretary, Kozitsky. Generous subsidies were provided for the venture, which required professional, salaried translators. It remained in being until it was superseded by the Russian Academy of Letters in 1783. Within its first four years of existence the Society had published over forty titles including extracts from the *Encyclopédie* and works of Montesquieu and Voltaire.

Hard on the heels of the Society, Catherine, again with the aid of Kozitsky as editor, launched the first Russian moral weekly, *All Sorts,* modelled on Addison and Steele's *Spectator*, which had long been imitated across Europe. Isolated *Spectator* essays, mostly didactic in nature, had been translated into a variety of Russian publications from the 1720s onwards, but *All Sorts* was the first to reflect the *Spectator* model in which a fictional character presided as editor. In the case of *All Sorts* it was *Babushka*, or Granny. The nature of the material included in the weekly varied from the purely didactic to entertaining satirical sketches of coarse social manners and morals that required correction. The journal has been seen as another manifestation of Catherine's policy of 'official enlightenment'[37] or 'enlightened liberalism'[38] that sought to modify and mould public attitudes. It attempted to disabuse her subjects of the notion that the cause of social failings could be ascribed to the system or government; they were the consequence of perverted morals.[39] Her initiative was to be an invitation to other Russian writers to join with her in this new enterprise. 'I see an infinite posterity for *All Sorts*', wrote Granny in the first issue. 'I see it being followed by legitimate and illegitimate children.' Immediately it spawned a cluster of imitators.

By far the most successful was Novikov's *Drone*. Novikov (1744–1818), one of the early students at the Moscow University Gymnasium, had been drafted to serve in the Legislative Commission as a minute-taker for the committee formed to consider 'the middling sort of men'. The knowledge of the social issues gleaned there obviously served him well as social commentator in the new type of moral weekly. The appearance of a group of like-minded journals had signalled a widening of the constituency of arbitrators of social thought, and the closing numbers of *The Drone* in 1769, with a variety of vivid, thumbnail sketches under the heading 'Who Are My Readers?', hinted at an expanded reception for its message. However, the vagaries of an underdeveloped publishing system did not allow the moral weeklies to prosper, and they were short-lived. Novikov tried again in 1772 with a new moral weekly, *The Painter*. At the outset, he demonstrated his alignment with Catherine's own policies by identifying his efforts with the author of a new comedy, *Oh, Times!*, supposedly anonymous but generally ascribed to the empress herself. *Oh, Times!* ridiculed the obscurantist, vulgar provincial gentry resistant to the progressive measures of the new regime, and Novikov's *Painter* (significantly the editorial persona was now an honest craftsman rather than a nobleman) joined in the mocking. The introductory paper to the second part of *The Painter* reinforced the point that its editor was a committed supporter of the empress's policies. A tribute to Catherine from a naval chaplain recently returned from the Mediterranean expedition was followed by an extract from Frederick the Great's *Matinées royales* in which he explained how necessary writers were to a sovereign, confirming the power contemporary writers had newly acquired in becoming adjuncts to enlightened rulers.

The ideal projected by Novikov's moral journals was that of a caring monarchy intent on uniting all estates in a common endeavour to advance their society. Opposition came from provincial obscurantists, who had to be unmasked. The model citizen supported the monarch in exchange for the latter's care, and the 'truly noble nobleman' was he who had the total welfare of his serfs at heart. Conventional Russian thinking, as reflected by Novikov, had little truck with the bourgeois ideologies of western European Enlightenment advocating social relationships based on rational, impersonal legislation. Such views may have been advanced by the most original Russian thinkers of the time such as Desnitsky, but their arguments fell on deaf ears among their fellow citizens.[40] Although there was no hint of xenophobia in Novikov's writings, his moral weeklies counselled readers, as Russian patriots, to be discriminating in their acceptance of foreign influences, however beneficial. He derided the absurdities of unthinking Gallomania as much as did Fonvizin in his stage comedies *The Brigadier* (completed 1769) and *The Minor* (1782). A further indication of a growing confidence in Russia's sense of identity was Novikov's publication of two works, the *Essay at an Historical Dictionary of Russian Writers*, which included as many as fifty-four pre-Petrine writers, and the collection of historical archival documents in his *Ancient Russian Library*. He was recommended for the latter task by Prince Shcherbatov, who had been granted access to the State Archives in January 1770 in order to write a history of Russia. Shcherbatov, inspired by his researches into pre-Petrine Russia, was able to set Peter's achievements into a broad historical context, raising the question that was central to Russian thinkers in future years, namely whether indiscriminate, superficial aping of European manners, an unintended consequence of Peter's reforms, had led to a corruption of traditional virtues.[41]

How were the moral ills to be cured and a general sense of ethical responsibility to be restored? One way was to project the positive image of the 'true son of the fatherland' or the 'truly noble nobleman'. Forming such paragons was the aim of influential educational institutions such as the Cadet Corps and the Smolny Institute, where young ladies were groomed in the role of suitable partners for 'sons of the fatherland'. The portrayal of the latter in Novikov's introduction to his journal *The Bag* (1774) was based on the French *Encyclopédie* article 'Patriote', echoing its affirmation that 'to serve one's fatherland is not a fanciful duty, but an actual obligation' and suggesting that Russia's 'son of the fatherland' was a local variant of a pattern elaborated at the centre of the European Enlightenment.

However, the *Encyclopédie*'s secular 'patriot' was soon to be significantly modified. 'The Christian Patriot' was the title of the second half of a treatise, *Warheit der Religion*, by a Baltic German pastor, Gotthard Friedrich Stender (1714–96), directed against deists and 'Voltaireans' and published in a Russian translation in 1785 as *True Religion*.[42] An underlying trend in the purification of morals was the long-established and persisting influence of German Pietism, intent on reforming the individual on the basis of the seventeenth-century hermetic, mystical intellectual currents, termed the 'Rosicrucian Enlightenment' by Frances Yates, that found expression in the works of Johann Arndt and Jacob Böhme. The Pietism that made its way into Russia was not at odds with the Russian Orthodox Church. Indeed, its spirit of service and personal sentiment was most effectively spread by ecclesiastical schools. Furthermore, the Russian translators of German religious works were careful to select those that were free of dogmatic theology.

A crucial moment was Novikov's recruitment into freemasonry in St Petersburg in 1775. The lodge he was invited to join was presided over by Elagin, one of Catherine's most trusted advisers, and was aligned with the English variant of freemasonry imbued with a secular and rationalistic outlook that was in the mainstream of the approved *philosophe* Enlightenment. When obliged to explain his involvement with the craft during his interrogation after his arrest for subversion in 1792, Novikov stressed that in 1775 the masonic gatherings were tantamount to public, social occasions for prominent, principal noblemen and members of the educated service class committed to Catherine's reforms. No sooner had English masonry taken root in St Petersburg than its Russian adherents felt dissatisfied with its apparent superficiality. Elagin himself turned to a parallel system demanding a moral commitment and strict moral discipline from its members established by Baron Reichel, an expatriate German. Novikov embraced with enthusiasm this alternative to the convivial 'English' lodges. As he explained at his interrogation: 'We understood true masonry to be what led the way to moral correction by the shortest means in the path of Christian moral teaching.'[43] From now on he devoted his editorial and organisational energies to the masonic cause without ever thinking that his activities were in conflict with Catherine's reform policies. In 1777 Novikov published a masonic, philosophical journal, *Morning Light*, which enjoyed support from the church hierarchy and was intended to support charity schools.

A second important date was April 1779, when Novikov transferred his activities from St Petersburg to the old capital of Moscow. Here, with Catherine's approval, he was granted a ten-year lease of the ailing university press. Moscow, with a population twice that of St Petersburg and much less beholden to foreign influence, represented the old Russia and proved a fertile ground for Novikov's venture into publishing. In 1784 he took advantage of the decree on the setting-up of private presses to found the Typographical Company with the financial support of wealthy fellow masons. In the 1780s about a third of all Russian publications, and the most profitable, were those of an educational or historical nature. Collections by leading Russian writers appeared, as well as a variety of translations ranging from Bacon, Diderot, Locke, Rousseau and Voltaire to modern classics such as Corneille, Fielding, Klopstock, Lessing, Milton, Racine, Shakespeare and Sterne. Writers favoured by the masons such as Arndt and Böhme appeared but did not monopolise the output. In his choice of material Novikov showed that he had a broad rather than sectarian understanding of Russia's Enlightenment, and his *Moscow Monthly Publication*, established in 1781 and advertised as a continuation of *Morning Light*, also trod the middle ground, guarding against assaults from obscurantists on the one hand and extreme free-thinkers on the other.

Apart from literature, Novikov inspired joint social endeavours that have been seen as the beginnings of an autonomous civil society in Russia. The pietistic tradition of service persisting within Russian freemasonry was apparent in charitable educational groups alongside the reinvigorated university press. A Pedagogical Seminar was set up, funded by the Urals industrialist Demidov, which by 1782 supported thirty funded teachers under training. In 1781 a Society of University Alumni was formed whose aims were to practise personal responsibilities for society and pursue moral virtue. The following year a Translation Seminar was established with the aim of rendering moral works into Russian; six students were transferred from church seminaries. The same year saw them merged into the Friendly Learned Society, formally opened in November with the approval of the Moscow Governor-General and Archbishop Plato. Its benefactors were the same masons who had invested in the Typographical Company. One policy of the Friendly Learned Society was to have a vital bearing on the subsequent development of Russian literature and thought. Believing in the beneficial effect of travel, it sent gifted young graduates of the university to Europe at its expense. One of these was Karamzin, whose *Letters of a Russian Traveller* (1797–1801), based on a journey into Europe in 1789, proved to be a remarkable demonstration of the benefit of travel in broadening mental horizons. Karamzin was also given the opportunity to practise as a writer in the Society's *Children's Reading for Heart and Mind*, Russia's first educative magazine for children. There were also plans for a public apothecary and hospital, and provisions were made for large-scale famine relief following the drought of 1787. If these group initiatives indicated the stirrings of an autonomous civil society in Russia, it did not follow that participants were interested in establishing any independent political structures. They did not countenance freeing themselves from the patronage and tutelage of their sovereign.

It was Catherine who eventually distanced herself from their activities. She had little sympathy for freemasonry, treating it with amused disdain, as was evident in her three anti-masonic comedies, *The Deceiver* (1785), *The Siberian Shaman* (1786) and *The Deluded* (1786). Her displeasure with private initiatives became evident after 1784, when Novikov was charged with breaking copyright by reprinting for Moscow schools textbooks issued by the Imperial National Schools Commission. In December 1785 Catherine ordered an inventory of Novikov's publications to be made on the grounds that his presses were reputed to have printed 'many strange books'.[44] Archbishop Plato was ordered to examine Novikov's beliefs and the books for any signs that they concealed ideas 'not in concord with the plain and pure rules of our Orthodox faith and civil obligations'.[45] The campaign against freemasonry, now labelled the 'new dissent', continued until the lodges were closed in 1786. Catherine would have been alarmed at their close links with influential German Rosicrucians under Johann Christoph Wöllner, a high official in the reign of Frederick William II of Prussia, and their courting of her son and heir, Paul. It has also been argued that by demonstrating her antipathy to the 'new dissent', she also sought to reaffirm her support for the Orthodox Church, whose cooperation she had always assiduously cultivated.[46] Such cooperation was vital in the aftermath of the French Revolution, whose consequences forced Catherine to show a steel hand. In 1791 Novikov was arrested, interrogated and incarcerated in the Schlüsselburg Fortress. Catherine's waning trust in the Enlightenment was extinguished in 1792 with the arrest and condemnation to death of Radishchev, a sentence commuted to Siberian exile. The reason for the repression was her fury at his *A Journey from St Petersburg to Moscow*. Radishchev was in many ways a typical product of the Russian Enlightenment. From 1767–71, as one of an elite group of young Russians, he had studied law at Leipzig, where he came to know the works of Leibniz and Wolff and was enthused by French *philosophes* such as Helvétius, Rousseau and Mably. On his return to St Petersburg he translated Mably's *Observations on the History of Greece*, published for Catherine's Society for the Translation of Foreign Books in 1773 despite its evident republican sympathies. Prompted by the unveiling of Falconet's statue to Peter the Great in 1782, he wrote his 'Letter to a Friend in Tobolsk', the local Director of Economic Affairs, who had been a fellow student in Leipzig. Although fully supportive of Peter's reforms and without questioning his greatness, the 'Letter' did identify weaknesses in Peter's failure to safeguard individual liberty within a framework of civic law. Published in 1789, it caused Catherine to expostulate during Radishchev's interrogation that it was proof that he was a foremost supporter of the French Revolution. In fact Radishchev expressed bitter regret in his *Journey* that the Revolutionary National Assembly in France 'had violated the principles of freedom of speech'.[47] Freedom of the individual for Radishchev was derived from a social contract, defined by juridical relations based on rationality and self-interest. This belief in the abstract principles of Enlightenment thought permeated the *Journey* and the traveller's firsthand account of the social evils so evident in the Russian staging posts strung out between the two capital cities. Its faith in the spirit and efficiency of just laws recalled Catherine's own *Nakaz*. However, the *Journey* also reflected the other strand in Russian thinking: the belief in the efficacy of personal moral perfectibility. Radishchev had been an enthusiastic freemason and remained a bosom friend of Kutuzov, a fellow student in Leipzig and a leading light in Novikov's Moscow circle; the *Journey* was dedicated to Kutuzov. The effusive dedication was from a sentimental traveller, prey to the slightest tinge of emotional response to the iniquities of Russian reality encountered on his passage. The sentimental traveller was the true 'son of the fatherland' already depicted by Radishchev in his 'Discourse on What It Means To Be a Son of the Fatherland'. This had appeared in a short-lived 1789 monthly, *The Citizen in Conversation*, dedicated to 'The dearest, most beloved Fatherland of Russia' and with an epigraph taken from Catherine's *Nakaz* (chapter 6, 'On Laws in General', paragraph 57): 'We always act best when we do so willingly, freely and according to our Natural Inclination.' The image of the 'son of the fatherland', the 'truly noble nobleman', abjuring selfish and brutish behaviour, striving for moral perfection and dedicated to serving his society, had been impressed into Russian consciousness by the moral periodicals and dramas, but in the *Journey* it acquired a solipsistic intensity. The *Journey* was a disturbing, baffling mélange of rational, legalistic arguments and sentimental responses. It accounts for Pushkin's cool appraisal of Radishchev in 1836: 'Radishchev reflected the whole of French philosophy in his time: Voltaire's scepticism, Rousseau's philanthropy, the political cynicism of Diderot and Raynal, but all in a clumsy, misshapen form, as everything is twisted in the reflection of a distorting mirror. He is indeed the true representative of semi-enlightenment.'[48]

CONCLUSION

'Semi-enlightenment' may be too harsh a judgement. Russians had endeavoured to adapt new ways of thought to the reality of their society. The essential Enlightenment faith in reason and man's innate capability for perfecting social relationships and his individual moral behaviour was generally accepted. German science, philosophy, Pietism and masonic theory and practice had proved to be as compelling as the array of works by the French *philosophes*. There had been, from the days of Prokopovich's embattled 'Learned Watch', a steady expansion of the sector of society that saw itself as upholding and propagating the complex of Enlightenment values; its inclination was to do so in close cooperation with the state, present in the person of an enlightened sovereign. The French Revolution sundered this intimate relationship. The memory of Catherine's rejection of the supportive public sphere deepened its negative response to future tsars, particularly Paul I and Nicholas I, who were wary of an independent-minded citizenry. However, the concepts of the Enlightenment, if eclipsed, lay dormant within the educated service class, and the self-conscious elite of 'sons of the fatherland', if shunned, retained the potential of forming an active force in the shaping of Russian society.

NOTES

1. See Dorinda Outram, *The Enlightenment* (Cambridge University Press, 1995), p. xi.
2. Marc Raeff, 'The Enlightenment in Russia and Russian thought in the Enlightenment' in J. G. Garrard (ed.), *The Eighteenth Century in Russia* (Oxford: Clarendon Press, 1973), p. 26.
3. Lindsey Hughes, *Russia in the Age of Peter the Great* (New Haven and London: Yale University Press, 1998), p. 302.
4. See, for example, Thomas Crow, *Painters and Public Life in Eighteenth-Century Paris* (New Haven and London: Yale University Press, 1985).
5. W. F. Ryan, 'Navigation and the modernisation of Petrine Russia: teachers, textbooks, terminology' in Roger Bartlett and Janet M. Hartley (eds.), *Russia in the Age of the Enlightenment: Essays for Isabel de Madariaga* (London: Macmillan, 1990), p. 75.
6. Raeff, 'The Enlightenment in Russia', p. 30.
7. James Cracraft, *The Church Reform of Peter the Great* (London: Macmillan, 1971), p. 54.

8. Ibid., p. 30.
9. James Cracraft, 'Feofan Prokopovich' in Garrard (ed.), *The Eighteenth Century in Russia*, p. 76.
10. A. Lentin (ed.), *Peter the Great: His Law on the Imperial Succession in Russia, 1722. The Official Commentary* (Oxford: Headstart History, 1996), pp. 33–5, 41–5.
11. Quoted in Evgenii V. Anisimov, *The Reforms of Peter the Great: Progress through Coercion in Russia*, trans. John T. Alexander (Armonk and London: M. E. Sharpe, 1993), p. 23.
12. Cracraft, 'Feofan Prokopovich', p. 102.
13. Ibid., p. 75.
14. Antiokh Kantemir, *Sobranie stikhotvorenii* (Leningrad: Sovetskii pisatel', 1956), p. 62.
15. Marc Raeff, 'On the heterogeneity of the eighteenth century in Russia' in R. P. Bartlett, A. G. Cross and Karen Rasmussen (eds.), *Russia and the World of the Eighteenth Century* (Columbus, Ohio: Slavica, 1986), p. 670.
16. Ibid.
17. Christopher Clark, 'Piety, politics and society: Pietism in eighteenth-century Prussia' in Philip G. Dwyer (ed.), *The Rise of Prussia 1700–1830* (London: Longman, 2000), pp. 68–88.
18. *Svodnyi katalog russkoi knigi grazhdanskoi pechati XVIII veka 1725–1800*, 5 vols. (Moscow: Akademiia nauk SSSR, 1963–7), vol. II, pp. 168–9, 174–5.
19. Anisimov, *The Reforms of Peter the Great*, p. 224.
20. Raeff, 'The Enlightenment in Russia', p. 29.
21. Marina Ritzarev, *Eighteenth-Century Russian Music* (Aldershot: Ashgate, 2006), pp. 43–4.
22. Hans Rogger, *National Consciousness in Eighteenth-Century Russia* (Cambridge, Mass.: Harvard University Press, 1960), p. 210.
23. V. O. Kliuchevskii, *Sochineniia*, 8 vols. (Moscow: Gosudarstvennoe izdatel'stvo politicheskoi literatury, 1956–9), vol. IV, p. 201.
24. Andrzej Walicki, *A History of Russian Thought from the Enlightenment to Marxism*, trans. Hilda Andrews-Rusiecka (Oxford: Clarendon Press, 1980), p. 1.
25. Quoted by Viktor Zhivov, '"Vsiakaia vsiachina" i sozdanie Ekaterinskogo politicheskogo diskursa' in Roger Bartlett and Gabriela Lehmann-Carli (eds.), *Eighteenth-Century Russia: Society, Culture, Economy* (Münster: LIT Verlag, 2007), p. 254.
26. Kliuchevskii, *Sochineniia*, vol. IV, p. 202.
27. Walicki, *A History of Russian Thought*, p. 8.
28. Catherine the Great, *Memoirs*, trans. Katherine Anthony (New York: Tudor, 1935), p. 124.
29. Simon Dixon, *The Modernisation of Russia 1676–1825* (Cambridge University Press, 1999), p. 223.
30. Paul Dukes (ed. and trans.), *Russia under Catherine the Great*, vol. II, *Catherine the Great's Instruction (Nakaz) to the Legislative Commission, 1767* (Newtonville, Mass.: Oriental Research Partners, 1977), pp. 18–19.

31. Ibid., p. 109.
32. Isabel de Madariaga, *Russia in the Age of Catherine the Great* (London: Weidenfield and Nicolson, 1981), p. 162.
33. Terry Eagleton, *Literary Theory: An Introduction* (Oxford: Blackwell, 1983), p. 17.
34. Robert Shackleton, *Montesquieu: A Critical Biography* (Oxford University Press, 1961), p. 356.
35. Dukes, *Catherine the Great's Instruction*, p. 11.
36. *Nakaz imperatritsy Ekateriny II, dannyi kommissii o sochinenii proekta novogo ulozheniia*, ed. N. D. Chechulin (St Petersburg: Imperatorskaia Akademiia nauk, 1907), pp. cxiv–cxlvii.
37. Iu. D. Levin, *Epokha prosveshcheniia: iz mezhdunarodnykh sviazei russkoi literatury* (Leningrad: Nauka, 1967), p. 47.
38. Walicki, *A History of Russian Thought*, p. 15.
39. Zhivov, '"Vsiakaia vsiachina"', p. 263.
40. Walicki, *A History of Russian Thought*, p. 14.
41. See M. M. Shcherbatov, *On the Corruption of Morals in Russia*, ed. and trans. Anthony Lentin (Cambridge University Press, 1969).
42. Michael Schippan, 'Retseptsiia protestantskikh avtorov v Rossii v XVIII veke: (Spalding, Crugot, Stender)' in Bartlett and Lehmann-Carli (eds.), *Eighteenth-Century Russia*, pp. 244–6.
43. 'Dopros N. I. Novikova' in *N. I. Novikov i ego sovremenniki: Izbrannye sochineniia*, ed. I. V. Malyshev (Moscow: Akademiia nauk SSSR, 1961), p. 425.
44. N. I. Novikov, *Izbrannye sochineniia*, ed. G. P. Makogonenko (Moscow and Leningrad: Goslitizdat, 1951), p. 579.
45. *N. I. Novikov i ego sovremenniki*, pp. 577–8.
46. See Raffaella Faggionato, *A Rosicrucian Utopia in Eighteenth-Century Russia: The Masonic Circle of N. I. Novikov* (Dordrecht: Springer, 2004).
47. Alexander Radishchev, *A Journey from St Petersburg to Moscow*, trans. Leo Wiener, ed. Roderick Page Thaler (Cambridge, Mass.: Harvard University Press, 1958), p. 186.
48. A. S. Pushkin, *Polnoe sobranie sochinenii*, 9 vols. (Leningrad: Nauka, 1977–9), vol. VII, p. 245.

CHAPTER 5

Conservatism in the age of Alexander I and Nicholas I

William Leatherbarrow

In addressing the question of conservatism in Russia and in seeking to establish the nature of any Russian conservative 'tradition', the initial problem, as ever, is one of defining terms. Was 'conservatism' in nineteenth-century Russia simply, as its opponents might have argued, the expression of unwillingness on the part of those representing a historically privileged class to accommodate any changes that might diminish that class's advantages (especially those offered by land ownership and the institution of serfdom)? Was it hostility to any manifestation of political liberalism or radicalism that might unleash destructive social consequences, a sort of reversion to the safety of tradition in order to head off the spread of revolution in the wake of 1789 or the Decembrist Revolt of 1825? Was it inevitably associated with the tradition of autocracy, or was it – as Richard Pipes asserts – more broadly based?[1] Indeed, was it merely an inherited and unquestioning sense of the inviolability of what Shcherbatov, that eighteenth-century apologist of the old nobility, termed 'strict ancestral rules'?[2]

Or was Russian conservatism an altogether more positive phenomenon, securely grounded in a set of principles that were in turn rooted in the conviction that continuity was more important than change, that cultural and historical differences peculiar to individual nations were significant, and that only those circumstances and institutions validated by native tradition were truly justified and appropriate to Russia? In this regard, and as part of his argument that Russian conservatism should be seen not primarily as a reactive and reactionary political philosophy, but as an intellectual movement in its own right, Pipes establishes the following key principle:

Conservatism was by its very nature more diversified than liberalism. The liberals, who espoused the ideals of the Enlightenment, wished to change society in accord with certain principles which all of them held in common; liberty, equality, fraternity meant much the same thing in Greece and Spain, Russia and Germany, at least programmatically. Liberalism was international, cosmopolitan, and its adherents regarded the triumph of liberal ideals anywhere in the world as a personal triumph. Not so the conservatives. The conservatives did have in common certain basic attitudes, for their movements developed in reaction to the same set of circumstances; but their attention was focused on local, particular factors. The search for traditions, for roots, naturally took a different course in every country, depending on its conditions.[3]

Pipes's identification of a sense of historical difference as a key determinant of conservative thought suggests that one way of seeking to understand the conservative 'tradition' in Russia might be through the philosophy of history implicitly or explicitly expressed by representatives of that tradition. The enduring legacy of the Petrine reforms and the penetration of Enlightenment ideas into Russian intellectual life in the reign of Catherine the Great were the most significant factors in the emergence of history as a legitimate subject for theoretical debate among Russian thinkers of the late eighteenth century. They brought out into the open an implicit contradiction between views of Russia's development that broadly were either 'historicist' or 'ahistoricist' in their approach. The former privileged the importance of historical continuity and tradition in the evolution of a nation's specific and indigenous cultural and social features, while the latter emphasised universalism and rationalism and sought to reconceptualise and reconfigure Russia's historical path on the basis of alien institutions and philosophic principles which, although conceived on totally different historical and cultural soils, were deemed by virtue of their demonstrable rationality to be commonly applicable (and therefore of a higher order).[4] Peter the Great's willingness to sacrifice long-established Russian traditions and institutions in favour of western-inspired innovations that might better serve his modernising drive were matched by Catherine's initial belief that the ideas of the European Age of Reason might be transplantable to Russia with only beneficial consequences for Russian social and political life. Indeed, it is from the Age of Reason that the idea emerges that the concept of universality might be applicable not only to the objective laws of the material world, on the basis of which Peter sought to refine Russian technology, but also to the 'laws' governing mankind's social, political and cultural development.

Catherine's conviction that western European ideas might be applied to Russia from above by a strong and enlightened monarch was encouraged by the view, expressed by Diderot among others, that the Petrine reforms had cleared the ground by weakening any indigenous cultural and historical traditions that might interfere with such a revolution. Russia was thus in a privileged position to enact the spirit of the Enlightenment in a way that might prove difficult in lands where the power of tradition was undiminished. With Catherine's encouragement the progressive nobility of her time espoused ideas that were as diverse as the European thinkers whose works they read: Voltaire, Montesquieu, Beccaria, Rousseau, Mably, Priestley, Locke and the French *encyclopédistes* stand out among many others. Yet the various strands of Enlightenment thought shared a common belief that the laws of nature, upon which the physical world was erected, were ultimately knowable, and that man's increasing enlightenment would permit him first to understand and then to control the world around him. This faith in the power of reason and its role in the discoverability of underlying laws also coloured Enlightenment views of society and history and of man's relationship to them; and it fostered a universalist juridical world-view according to which societies were perfectible if based upon objectively rational social relations and an enlightened code of law. The potentially revolutionary implications of such ideas for societies based on local, traditional but 'irrational' social and political structures are all too clear, and by the end of her reign, fearful of the revolutionary consequences of the Age of Reason in Europe and the threat to her own position posed by the Pugachev revolt, Catherine had in some regards retreated into a conservative nationalism that emphasised not only the survival, but also the superiority, of the sort of Russian historical and cultural tradition characteristic of the pre-Petrine era. In this way she set both the terms and the opposing extremes of subsequent historical debate in Russia. Some, like Novikov, would reflect the ambiguity of Catherine's position by tempering their own advocacy of progressive European ideas with a keen sense of Russian patriotism and thus find themselves caught between universalism and national tradition. Others, such as Shcherbatov in his *On the Corruption of Morals in Russia* (not published until 1858), while steeped in Enlightenment ideals and supportive of the role of Peter the Great in Russian history, came to reject many innovations of the post-Petrine era and to affirm the superiority of traditional Russian institutions in terms that in many ways anticipated the ideas of Karamzin, ideas to be considered more fully later in this chapter.[5] On the other hand, the later part of Catherine's reign also saw in the work of Radishchev a full expression of the rationalistic universalism implicit in Enlightenment thought and neatly expressed in Hume's assertion that 'mankind are so much the same, in all times and places, that history informs us of nothing new or strange in this particular. Its chief use is only to discover the constant and universal principles of human nature.'[6] Although he occasionally appeared to pay lip-service to the role of national tradition in works such as 'A Discourse on What It Means To Be a Son of the Fatherland' (1789) and elsewhere,[7] Radishchev's world-view was rooted in the conviction that nature, virtue and society were founded upon abstract laws that had been revealed by reason and were immutable, universally valid and not subordinate to the specific historical quirks of any single nation. As Andrzej Walicki succinctly puts it: 'Although attempts have been made to discover elements of historicism in his world-view, these do not seem convincing. Radishchev boldly pitted an idealized Reason and Virtue against real history; his moral absolutism permitted no historical justification for stupidity or crime, no understanding of historical relativity.'[8] The indictment of Russian serfdom and autocracy in his *Journey from St Petersburg to Moscow* (1790) flows directly from the ahistoricism of Radishchev's thought, in which the western spirit of legalism, enshrined in the concepts of personal rights and natural and civil law, provided a yardstick for questioning the legality of such native institutions and their appropriateness in an age of reason.

KARAMZIN

Radishchev was not only a critic of the conditions of Catherine's reign, but also a product of those conditions. As a Russian nobleman he was acutely sensitive to the dangers inherent in the revolutionary overthrow from below of traditional institutions. He feared popular revolt and conceived the *Journey* not as a call to revolution, but as a warning to the Russian ruling classes that they must enact reforms and erect Russian society on rational foundations before they were swept away by the bursting dam of popular discontent. The work of Karamzin, on the other hand, served to emphasise the limits and dangers of reform from the point of view of a thinker keenly sensitive to Russian historical tradition and alert to national differences. His credentials in those respects were established by his writings on historical matters, culminating in a twelve-volume *History of the Russian State* that began to appear from 1818, and by his official role of government historian during the reign of Alexander I. His conservative nationalism was rooted, though, in the enduring horror provoked in him by the later stages of the French Revolution and the Jacobin terror, and it was formulated to reflect his alarm at the reforming processes initiated during the early years of Alexander's reign. Although to some extent a response to the anti-traditionalism of European Enlightenment philosophy, Karamzin's conservatism lacked a firm philosophical basis of its own. Instead, it sought to revalidate specific national social traditions and institutions at a time when they were under siege not only from Enlightenment insistence that they should demonstrate their appropriateness and rationality, but also from the reforms planned by Alexander's adviser Speransky. In this regard Pipes is right to argue that Karamzin represents Russian conservatism as a social, rather than intellectual or philosophical, phenomenon.[9] It is only from the advent of Romantic nationalism at the end of Alexander's reign that Russian conservatism can truly be said to have acquired a philosophical basis; and it took the Slavophiles' grounding in German idealism and Orthodox spirituality to raise Karamzin's reactive and pragmatic defence of the established order to the level of true historiosophy.

In his *Memoir on Ancient and Modern Russia* (1811) Karamzin took issue with the proposals emanating from Speransky's commission, arguing that they contained 'not a single idea derived from observation of the peculiar social complexion of Russia' and implying that the commission had failed to acknowledge 'that the laws of a nation must be an outgrowth of its own ideas, customs, habits, and special circumstances'.[10] In arguing that 'an old nation has no need of new laws'[11] and that Russia should seek instead to define its own social principles, Karamzin's *Memoir* sought to do the latter on the basis of the interdependence throughout Russian history of the institutions of autocracy, the nobility and serfdom. Much of the *Memoir* is given over to a vigorous defence of autocracy as the form of government most appropriate to Russia and of the nobility and serfdom as essential supports for that form. Karamzin's advocacy of autocracy as 'the Palladium of Russia' that has 'founded and resuscitated' the nation is based first on the initial premise of the *Memoir*, which asserts that '[t]he present is a consequence of the past. To judge the former one must recollect the latter.'[12] Historically, strong monarchical government has proved itself adept at holding together the diverse and extensive lands that comprise the Russian nation, whereas attempts to weaken such centralised control have led, as in the appanage period of Kievan Rus, to national disaster. Now, with Alexander I poised to sanction reforms designed to limit autocracy in Russia, Karamzin is quick to warn him of the lack of wisdom of such a move and its likely consequences:

If Alexander, inspired by generous hatred for the abuses of autocracy should lift a pen and prescribe himself laws other than those of God and of his conscience, then the true, virtuous citizen of Russia would presume to stop his hand, and to say: 'Sire! You exceed the limits of your authority. Russia, taught by long disasters, vested before the holy altar the power of autocracy in your ancestor, asking him that he rule her supremely, indivisibly. This covenant is the foundation of your authority, you have no other. You may do everything, but you may not limit your authority by law!'[13]

No matter how enlightened Alexander's support for the modernisation of Russia might be, the fact remains that 'it is dangerous to tamper with ancient political structures', and '[o]nly those laws are salutary which have for long been desired by the best minds of the country, and of which, so to say, the people have had a premonition'.[14] Traditional and patriarchal monarchical authority, unlimited by anything other than tradition, the monarch's own sense of virtue and responsibility and respect for public opinion, is what has always guaranteed social stability in Russia, and that authority asserts itself through the twin requirements of fear and reward. Rewards flow to those who provide loyal service to the tsar, but equally a 'salutary fear' of punishment is required in order to ensure public order. Indeed, an absence of fear is one of the most significant political evils of an age in which abstract legality and an emphasis upon citizens' rights has displaced fear of the sovereign.

Such views betray Karamzin's origins as a member of the gentry class that had historically benefited most from the rewards granted in return for loyalty. He is quick to assert that the gentry are an hereditary estate, whose role is to serve and provide support for the monarch and whose reward for such service is the right to own land and serfs: 'The people labour, the merchants trade, and the gentry serve, for which they are rewarded with distinctions and benefits, respect and comfort.' The gentry thus have traditionally played a major, but supportive role in Russian political life: 'The rights of the well-born are not something apart from monarchical authority – they are its principal and indispensable instrumentality by means of which the body politic is kept in motion.' Karamzin is scornful of the 'many-headed hydra of aristocracy', which would see the gentry's traditional relationship with the sovereign compromised by the aspiration to acquire political power for itself, but equally he is dismissive of the attempts of Peter the Great to break the traditional alliance between monarch and hereditary nobility through the creation of the Table of Ranks and the promotion of men of low birth to high office: 'Noble status should not depend on rank, but rank on noble status.'[15] Only the hereditary nobility have had time over the centuries to develop the appropriate sense of *noblesse oblige* that guarantees not only the inviolability of the sovereign's position, but also the well-being of the Russian serf.

Land and serf-ownership were seen by Karamzin as appropriate rewards for the gentry's loyal service, and in this regard his views are based on 'local' conditions that run counter to ahistoricist Enlightenment ideals concerning the rights of man. But Karamzin is not insensitive to the injustices of serfdom in practice, and he is quick to condemn those 'monstrous landowners' who have inhumanly trafficked in the serfs they own. However, he is insistent in his argument that the institution of serfdom, when humanely managed, has traditionally served the interests of all, providing economic benefits for the state and discipline and security for the agricultural worker. New plans for emancipation, while giving the peasants paper rights, would in reality plunge them into moral and economic chaos once freed from seigniorial discipline and work on the land 'which – and this is incontrovertible – belongs to the gentry'.[16] Once again, it is hard to overlook the class interests underpinning Karamzin's views, but it is only too easy to condemn his stance out of hand. We must always remember that he is not writing about autocracy, nobility and serfdom *in principle*. He might quote Montesquieu, whose works he studied, but his own views on those institutions are rooted in an admittedly idealised vision of how they have emerged and developed *in Russian conditions*. For Karamzin, as for other conservative Russian thinkers, those institutions have developed in response to the patriarchal principle that has historically supported Russian political and social structures.[17] For such thinkers, autocracy in Russia never arose from the seizure of political power by a tyrannical ruler, but was a responsibility handed to the autocrat by his people in moments of political crisis, such as the invitation to Riurik described in the primary chronicles and the election of Michael Romanov at the end of the Time of Troubles. The nobility evolved not as a jealous alternative to autocratic power, but as a class of loyal servitors whose role was to support the tsar in the discharge of his duties as father of the nation. And the common people, too, formed part of this organic family unity, as reflected in their adoption of the term of endearment *batiushka* (little father) to describe the tsar.

It is thus important to emphasise that Karamzin was no apologist for either the sort of despotism exercised by Alexander's predecessor, Paul, or the sort of reactionary obscurantism advocated by his successor, Nicholas I. Instead, he saw autocracy as undivided, rather than unlimited, power. It should not be weakened by being shared with unnecessary constitutional institutions, but neither should it be allowed to justify inhumane behaviour on the part of the autocrat, who must rule wisely and justly, remaining sensitive to public opinion and the need to maintain the personal freedom of the gentry. Nor would it be correct to conclude that, in spite of his advocacy of specifically Russian forms, Karamzin was anti-western in the way that many later conservative thinkers were (and here one might think of the Slavophiles' disparagement of the very principles of European culture). Indeed, as Pipes points out, until the later 1790s, when he turned to historical study and became aware of the importance of national differences, Karamzin had attributed such differences solely to the fact that nations were at different points on a single path of development towards universal goals.[18]

His study of history taught him the importance of Russia's adoption of the benefits offered by the West, but only in order the better to develop a uniquely national culture. As he wrote in an essay of 1802, 'On the Love of the Fatherland and on National Pride': 'A Patriot hastens to adapt to his fatherland all that is beneficial and useful, but he rejects slavish imitation in trivialities, offensive to national pride. One needs and one ought to learn: but woe to both the nation and the man who remain eternal pupils.'[19]

ROMANTIC NATIONALISM

Between the writing of Karamzin's *Memoir* and the accession of Nicholas I several factors emerged that were to impact significantly on the future complexion of Russian conservative thought. The first of these was the defeat of Napoleon and the subsequent growth of national self-consciousness, confidence and pride; the second was the flowering of Romanticism in Russia with its emphasis upon tradition, nationhood and the folk at the expense of the ahistoric universality of Enlightenment philosophy; and the third was the discovery of German idealist philosophy by Russian intellectuals. All these contributed to the emergence of what Walicki has termed 'anti-enlightenment trends' in early nineteenth-century Russia. The defeat of Napoleon led to a sense of Russian superiority and national messianism not only in Alexander himself (who retreated from his earlier enlightened reformism into a mystical nationalism that hardened into reaction, Christian fervour and the Holy Alliance with Prussia and Austria in 1815), but also among those thinkers who sought to emphasise Russia's distinctiveness from the rest of Europe and the sacredness of her mission as the defender of traditional and religious values.[20] The growth of Russian mysticism during this period (most notably in the form of mystical freemasonry and religious revival) reflects not only the above, but also a developing disenchantment with what increasingly came to be perceived as the limitations of western rationalism and its universal laws. To a certain extent this was a consequence of the general European Romantic revolt against the principles of eighteenth-century neo-classicism and the Age of Reason, but in Russia it also reflected the growing interest in German idealism that fostered a particular form of Romantic nationalism grounded in the *Naturphilosophie* of Schelling. It is best illustrated by the intellectual activities of a small group of thinkers known as the 'Wisdom-Lovers' (*liubomudry*), who emerged during the closing years of Alexander's reign and who helped set the agenda for Russian conservative thought for a generation to come.

The Society of Wisdom-Lovers was founded in 1823. Its key member was Odoevsky, best known for his work *Russian Nights* (1844), but it also contained the Romantic poet Venevitinov and the later Slavophile Ivan Kireevsky, among others. The poet Tiutchev, while not a member of the group, would certainly have been aware of its intellectual complexion through his mentor Raich, and many of his later poems give full and eloquent expression to the idealist world-view espoused by the Wisdom-Lovers. That world-view articulated a holistic vision of nature and the material world as merely an insubstantial veil concealing the world of the spirit, as well as implying a retreat from Enlightenment confidence in the universal applicability of rational analysis in favour of synthesis, the intuitive and the metaphysical.[21] This in turn fostered an entirely different approach to the understanding of history, which was no longer seen as a *mechanism* subject to discoverable rational laws and amenable to rational intervention. Instead, it was regarded as a living *organism* developing from potential to actuality and governed by a metaphysical principle (or 'spirit'). Man was thus no longer the enlightened architect of destiny, turning to his own ends the rational mechanics of nature and history; rather, he was an agent of historical development, a means for the realisation not of his own designs, but of those of the divine principle that animated all creation.

The view of the nation-state was similarly transformed in the Wisdom-Lovers' philosophy of nature and history. Whereas in Enlightenment aspirations the nation-state had been, in the words of the Decembrist Pestel, 'the totality or mass of the people',[22] merely a mechanical construct consisting of autonomous individuals held together by laws designed to protect the integrity of the individual while allowing the realisation of aims held in common, in the philosophy of the Wisdom-Lovers the nation was an organic whole, irreducible and much more than the sum of its parts. The individual was like a cell in that organism, at one with the common purpose and lacking meaning outside that purpose. Similarly, nations themselves formed part of a yet larger organism, that of history, in which each played its own distinctive role and made its own unique contribution. Such a view is clearly at odds with the rational universalism of Enlightenment thought, and it provides a 'cosmological' basis for the sort of historicism and celebration of national difference previously advocated on a more pragmatic basis by Karamzin and others. Moreover, while they are not intrinsically 'conservative' in any political sense, ideas such as those advocated by the Wisdom-Lovers are clearly capable of providing a rich philosophical medium for the cultivation of reactionary ideologies by others. Venevitinov's view that Russian culture had become imitative and that Russia should turn its back on Europe in order to develop a specifically national culture, along with Odoevsky's critique of western materialism and sense of Russia's mission to regenerate a spiritually bankrupt Europe, would find echoes not only among the later Slavophiles, but also among the architects of Official Nationality during the reign of Nicholas I.

OFFICIAL NATIONALITY

The 'Theory of Official Nationality', as it later became known, was in the words of Nicholas Riasanovsky 'a ramshackle affair'.[23] Designed to combat cosmopolitan Enlightenment ideas that had translated into revolution in Europe and the abortive Decembrist Revolt in Russia, the 'Theory' was a rearguard attempt to intellectualise reaction and restoration and proclaim the superiority of all things Russian. Apart from Nicholas himself, the main ideologists of Official Nationality were Nicholas's Minister of Education, Uvarov, and the nationalist thinkers Pogodin and Shevyrev, both professors at Moscow University. The theory was formally articulated as an official ideology by Uvarov in 1833, when he clearly signalled its central tenets as being 'Orthodoxy (*pravoslavie*), autocracy (*samoderzhavie*) and nationality (*narodnost*)'. These were to be the three pillars of all state education and propaganda, and they were subsequently taken up and disseminated by such conservative periodicals as *The Beacon*, *The Muscovite* and *The Northern Bee*, as well as by individual writers and journalists such as Senkovsky (who wrote under the pseudonym Baron Brambeus), Grech and Bulgarin. Indeed, as late as 1847 they were to form the basis of Gogol's infamous *Selected Passages from Correspondence with Friends*, seen by Belinsky as little more than a reactionary rant. They were identified by Uvarov as being the principles that not only defined and fortified Russian life, but also separated it from that of the West:

In the midst of the rapid collapse in Europe of religious and civil institutions, at the time of a general spread of destructive ideas, at the sight of grievous phenomena surrounding us on all sides, it was necessary to establish our fatherland on firm foundations upon which are based the well-being, strength, and life of a people; it was necessary to find the principles which form the distinctive character of Russia, and which belong only to Russia; it was necessary to gather into one whole the sacred remnants of Russian nationality and to fasten to them the anchor of our salvation.[24]

The appeal of Orthodoxy, autocracy and nationality for those anxious to construct an ideology of reaction and isolation is self-evident. The

Orthodox Church had provided a firm buttress to autocracy throughout much of Russian history, and Orthodoxy itself represented the spiritual separation of Russia from Catholic Europe. Moreover, the church's emphasis on ritual and worship, at the expense of cerebration and analysis, offered a welcome antidote to the Age of Reason and its destructive consequences. Similarly, Russian autocracy, in the idealised, patriarchal form already described by Karamzin (and reaffirmed in the hierarchical nature of creation implied in church teachings), was now advocated by Shevyrev and others as a unique and harmonious form of political life that allowed an unbroken unity of tsar and people, thus avoiding the dissension that had led in the West first to tyranny and then to revolt against that tyranny.[25] The tsar's authority derived from God, whereas that claimed by alternative forms of government derived from human, not divine, reason. The third principle, nationality (*narodnost*), is deeply ambiguous, not least because the Russian term *narod* may signify both the Russian *nation* (and thus imply conventional nationalism and chauvinism) and the Russian *people* (and thus reflect the preoccupation with the common folk characteristic of Romanticism). In practice, and despite the efforts of scholars such as Pogodin and Shevyrev to understand its true nature,[26] Official Nationality simply hijacked the latter aspect of the term in favour of the former, and *narodnost* eventually came to mean little more than an excuse for the glorification of all things Russian and a means for bolstering autocracy, defending serfdom and propagandising the status quo. It offered nothing in terms of new insights into the nature and role of the Russian people (whom it regarded merely as compliant material for the support of the Russian state), and it would be left to the major Slavophile thinkers to explore the philosophical richness of Romantic nationalism and tease out its full implications for Russia.

Of all the apologists of Official Nationality, Pogodin perhaps came closest to investing the term with some intellectual and moral depth, and in some respects he reflected the concerns of Slavophilism. His attachment to the ways of Russia did not blind him to the achievements of the West; nor did it prevent him from challenging gentry privilege and the institution of serfdom.[27] In an important essay on Peter the Great he managed the difficult task of recognising the achievements of Peter and of the processes of westernisation he had encouraged, while simultaneously seeking to identify the distinctive national principles that defined Russia, separated her from the West and justified the autocratic form of government she had adopted.[28] Pogodin's view of Russian history was informed by the organicism of German Romantic thought and he sought the distinctive features of the Russian nation not primarily to affirm their superiority, but in order to understand more fully Russia's role in the world historical order. In terms that anticipated ideas to be developed more challengingly by Slavophiles such as Khomiakov and Ivan Kireevsky, Pogodin saw the Russians as an essentially peace-loving and submissive people, whose history since the 'invitation to rule' extended to the Varangians had been characterised by a willingness to surrender political authority to others. This was in sharp contrast to the nations of Europe, which had been shaped by aggression, warfare, conquest, internecine struggle and now revolution. Although he was emphatic in his belief that the violent principles of western civilisation were inimical to those of Russia, Pogodin nevertheless viewed the reign of Peter the Great as a positive and natural stage in Russian history, rather than as a catastrophic shift that had forced Russian development along alien lines. Peter, he argued, had been right to seek to impose upon his subjects those western benefits that would secure Russia's future; otherwise the nation risked backwardness and marginalisation. Equally, the Russian people – obedient to their submissive nature – had been right to entrust their destiny once again to a powerful autocratic authority. This does not, though, imply slavish imitation or unqualified worship of the West, nor the ascendancy of foreign principles over those native to Russia. Indeed, in Pogodin's view, the questioning of European values following the defeat of Napoleon, the failure of the Decembrist Revolt and the adoption of Official Nationality marked the start of a new and higher stage for Russia. This stage would allow her to construct a richer national culture, grafting what had been newly learnt from Europe on to the rootstock of tradition, a tradition that had itself evolved through the assimilation of outside influences such as those of the Varangians and the Mongols.[29]

The most emphatic refutation of ideas such as these, as well as of the general sense of national superiority established by Official Nationality, came in the form of Chaadaev's first 'Philosophical Letter', written in 1829 and first published in the journal *Telescope* in 1836. Chaadaev's ideas on Russia's historical nature and relationship with the West can hardly be considered as representative of conservative Russian thought; but they did have a major effect on the subsequent development of conservative nationalism in Russia and must be considered briefly here. In his philosophy of history, elaborated on the same organicist basis of Romantic thought, the inherently 'submissive' nature of Russia identified by Pogodin and her capacity for the 'assimilation' of external cultural achievements were given a negative inflection; they were reconfigured as nothing more than the 'puerile frivolity' of an infant who reaches out for every new bauble offered by others. Moreover, far from being a uniquely harmonious nation whose cultural, social and political life should be glorified over that of the West, Russia represented 'a lacuna in the intellectual order' and was consigned in Chaadaev's analysis to the dustbin of history, as a nation that had failed to develop its own role and make its own contribution to the history of the world.

This is the natural consequence of a culture based wholly upon borrowing and imitation. With us there is no inner development, no natural progression: new ideas sweep away the old ones because they don't derive from them, but come to us from who knows where ... You would think, looking at us, that the general law of humanity has been revoked in our case. Alone in the world, we have given nothing to the world, taught the world nothing; we have not added a single idea to the fund of human ideas; we have contributed nothing to the progress of the human spirit, and we have disfigured everything we have taken of that progress. From the first instant of our social existence nothing has emanated from us for the common good of humanity; no useful idea has sprouted on the sterile soil of our fatherland; not a single great truth has sprung from our midst. We have never taken the trouble to invent anything ourselves, while from the inventions of others we have adopted only the deceptive appearances and useless luxuries.[30]

In a clear challenge to one of the central tenets of Official Nationality, Chaadaev blamed Russia's historical bankruptcy and isolation squarely on the fact that it had taken its religion from 'miserable, despised Byzantium'. This had condemned Russia's subsequent cultural evolution to one of isolation from the 'vivifying principle of unity' which, in the form of western Christianity, had animated the entire intellectual and moral development of European civilisation and made possible its great achievements: 'Thus, despite all that is incomplete, vicious and culpable in European society as it stands today, it is nonetheless true that the reign of God is realised in it in some way, because it contains the principle of indefinite progress and possesses the seeds and elements of all that is needed for this reign to be one day finally established on earth.'[31] In Chaadaev's philosophy of history Christianity is not merely a moral system 'conceived in the perishable forms of the human mind'; it also possesses a 'purely historical aspect', acting as a divine, eternal and universal power that leads humanity to convergence in the pursuit of a single purpose. Russia must seek to rectify its historical alienation from such universal reason not through further isolation and the misplaced national pride advocated by Official Nationality, but by the rejection of schism and recognition of its role in the European Christian order: 'We must repeat in our country the education of mankind from the very beginning.'[32]

This wholly negative view of Russian history was significantly modified in Chaadaev's 'Apologia of a Madman', written in 1837, a year after the

'Philosophical Letter' had brought down a hail of criticism, both official and unofficial, upon its author's head. It is tempting to see the 'Apologia' as a form of recantation in the face of that criticism, but it represented in reality a rethinking of Russia's history in the full light of the reign of Peter the Great. According to Chaadaev, Peter had seen Russia as a blank sheet of paper on which he wrote 'Europe and the West'. This had allowed Russia not only to join the historical process from which she had been isolated, but also to benefit from a past unencumbered by historical baggage. Russia's distinctive contribution lay not in her past, but in her future: 'History is no longer ours, it is true ... we could not begin the whole work of humanity again, but we can participate in its latest works. The past is no longer within our power, but the future belongs to us.'[33] The historiosophical basis of the first 'Philosophical Letter', with its emphasis on the divine underpinnings of history, together with the 'Apologia''s confident assertion that Russia's past isolation from Europe offered the key to her glorious future, were to form the starting-point for the thought of the major Slavophiles. True, they would reject Chaadaev's idea of universal reason unfolding through a process centred upon western civilisation, along with his admiration for Peter the Great and dismissal of Orthodoxy in favour of Catholicism. But in his view of the centrality of religion to the historical process the Slavophiles found the powerhouse of a Romantic nationalism far more sophisticated than any espoused by earlier conservative thinkers.

SLAVOPHILISM

Described by Riasanovsky as 'the fullest and most authentic expression of Romantic thought in Russia',[34] Slavophilism came to dominate the Russian conservative outlook for the rest of the Nicholaevan period. Its core vision, as well as its strengths and weaknesses, were revealed primarily in the writings of Khomiakov, Ivan Kireevsky and Konstantin Aksakov. Between them these three thinkers formulated a largely coherent body of doctrine embracing (albeit with varying degrees of success) personality, history, the relationship of Russia to the West, the processes of cognition and the nature of Russian society and culture. An essentially spiritual world-view structured on Orthodox Christianity lay at the heart of that doctrine, and it stood in opposition to the agnostic rationalism and materialism displayed by so many liberal pro-western thinkers. It was the Orthodox theologian Khomiakov who formulated the fundamental principles of the Slavophile theory of history, although Kireevsky and Aksakov contributed more to an explanation of how those principles impacted upon Russia's relationship with

Europe and upon the nature of her civil society. For Khomiakov, the differences between Russia and Europe were contemporary reflections of a historical dichotomy that had informed the entire evolution of the world. In his *Notes on Universal History*, a large but fragmentary work written over much of his career but published in three volumes only after his death, he wrote that 'freedom and necessity constitute the hidden principle around which all human thought is in various ways concentrated'.[35] Human history, and especially the history of its religions, thus illustrated the opposition of those principles, in that some nations and religions were founded on and embodied the principle of necessity, others the principle of freedom. Khomiakov termed the principle of necessity 'Kushite' (referring to Kush, the biblical name for present-day Ethiopia), while the principle of freedom was described as the 'Iranian' principle. Conceived by him initially as a way of categorising religious and cultural differences within the historical process, the contrast between Kushite and Iranian principles came to offer Khomiakov and his fellow Slavophiles a convenient basis on which to condemn western European culture and affirm that of Russia.[36] In Khomiakov's distinction Kushite nations, in thrall to the principle of necessity, expressed themselves through organisation, rationalism, materialism, analysis, the visual arts and the construction of imposing extraneous forms (e.g. sculpture and architecture); the Iranian principle of freedom, on the other hand, manifested itself in nations who prized free association, spontaneous creativity, spirituality, synthesis and the expression of inner meaning through poetry and song.

In Khomiakov's analysis the ancient Kushite principle of necessity, originating in the civilisations of Africa, Babylon and parts of Asia, had migrated into western European culture via the pagan Roman state and the Roman Church, with its preference for rationalism over spirituality. The Slav nations, on the other hand, headed by Russia and sustained by Orthodoxy, represented the most complete embodiment in the modern world of the Iranian principle of freedom. This allows us to reconfigure the Kushite/Iranian dichotomy in more revealing and more contemporary terms, and to understand it in relation to the contradiction between the rational universalism of the European Enlightenment and the Romantic nationalism that had manifested itself in Russian conservative thought since the end of Alexander's reign. For Khomiakov, as for other Slavophile thinkers who embraced his analysis, the Kushite nations of the West achieved social cohesion only through 'necessity' and submission to external force. This could be political force or the force of juridical law, but in either case it remained a force requiring the submission of the individual. Such societies were thus artificial constructs, mechanisms that attempted to balance the freedom of the individual with the requirement for social harmony. Russia, though, represented an Iranian nation whose social cohesion illustrated the principle of freedom. Order in Russia arose spontaneously and freely from within, and it reflected a shared vision of moral law rather than obedience to external necessity or contract. Russian society was thus an organic whole reflecting a natural harmony. Whereas in the West, especially in the wake of the Enlightenment, social theory had been dominated by the concept of the autonomous individual, with his rights and freedoms that had to be reconciled with those of other autonomous individuals and accommodated within an artificial construct called society, Khomiakov's 'social theory' was dominated by the concept of *sobornost'*. This is a word whose full meaning is difficult to replicate effectively in English. Khomiakov insisted that it was a rendition of the true meaning of the word 'catholic', which derived from the Greek *kata* (throughout) and *holos* (the whole) and thus meant 'according to all'. It also contains the Russian word *sobor*, meaning both 'gathering' and 'cathedral', and for Khomiakov Russian society, like the Russian church, 'is not a multitude of persons in their separate individuality, but a unity in the grace of God, living in a multitude of rational creatures, submitting themselves willingly to grace'.[37] In the Russian Orthodox Church 'man does not discover ... something alien to himself. He discovers himself in it, but a self which is not powerless in its spiritual solitude, but strong in its candid spiritual unity with its brethren and its Saviour', and the same was true of Russian society as a whole.[38] There was thus no contradiction in either the Russian church or Russian society between the aspirations of the individual and those of the whole; all were united in a single organism vivified by the spirit of God.

Just as such harmony was impossible in the mechanistic societies of the West, so it was absent from western churches. According to Khomiakov, Catholicism prioritised the will of the pope over individual freedom and thus offered unity without freedom, whereas the Protestant churches, those rebellious offspring of Catholicism, could offer only freedom without unity:

The grain of sand draws no new life from the heap into which it is cast by chance: such is the situation of man under Protestantism. The brick laid in the wall in no way changes or improves as a result of the place allotted it by the bricklayer's bevel: such is man's situation in the Roman Church. But each particle of matter assimilated in a living body becomes an inalienable part of the organism and acquires in the process new meaning and new life: such is man in the [Russian Orthodox] Church.[39]

The loss of organic unity and consequent atomisation of western European nations is more fully accounted for in the work of Ivan Kireevsky, who attributed it to the West's historical bases in the Roman Empire and Roman Christianity, in the primitive barbarian world that destroyed the Roman Empire and in ancient, pagan, classical civilisation. These had fostered, in his view, a culture based upon 'the triumph of rationalism over the tradition of immediate wisdom and inner, spiritual intelligence'.[40] This had prioritised individual reason, analysis and abstract intelligence over faith or any other form of shared synthesising wisdom, which in turn had led to the fragmentation of the societal 'unit' into autonomous and antagonistic individuals. Social atomisation was thus indissolubly linked to the fragmentation of personality and cognition. Conversely, the apprehension and achievement of a truly integrated reality was possible only on the basis of an integral personality and holistic cognition (*tsel'noe poznanie*). For Kireevsky such a capacity for integration and wholeness (*tsel'nost*) was what marked out ancient Russian society from that of the West, and at its heart stood the historical tendency of that society to organise itself on a communal basis sustained by the shared values of the Orthodox Church. Kireevsky's view of Russian society as a network of communes founded upon 'firm, unanimous and universal tradition', and within which the individual led an integrated and harmonious existence, is clearly an idealised one, and it owed much to Romanticism in its affirmation of wholeness and synthesis over individualisation and analysis. It is in some respects ironic that a vision emphasising Russia's difference from the West should be, in Walicki's words, 'only an interesting offshoot of European conservative romanticism'.[41] It is important, though, to establish the true nature of Slavophile conservatism and to differentiate it from the reactionary conservatism of Official Nationality. Apart from its somewhat more secure philosophical grounding, Slavophilism engendered a significantly different political programme. Whereas Official Nationality sought to justify and preserve the social and political status quo in Russia, Slavophilism sought change and was in many respects hostile to the post-Petrine Russia over which Nicholas presided. In Walicki's opinion, it was not so much a defence of the present as 'conservative utopianism' and 'romantic nostalgia for a lost ideal', and in that regard it could be argued that it posed no less significant a threat than Westernism to Nicholas's regime and its resistance to change.[42]

The utopian nature of Slavophile thought emerges in the work of Konstantin Aksakov, and especially in his memorandum on the internal state of Russia (written on the accession of Alexander II in 1855). The entire thrust of this document is regressive rather than conservative, in that Aksakov argues for the restoration of an idealised Russia that was lost as a consequence of Peter the Great's reforms. Insisting that the aspiration to political power on the part of the people is symptomatic of a nation's spiritual bankruptcy, he tries to show that events such as the Decembrist Revolt were the consequence of the infection of a Europeanised elite by principles alien to the true national spirit of pre-Petrine Russia. His account of that Russia is of a never-never land where freedom is freedom *from*, rather than *through*, politics, where monarchy is the only system that can guarantee the people such freedom (for all other political forms involve the people's participation to a greater or lesser extent), where the people leave state matters to the tsar and reserve unlimited spiritual freedom for themselves, where the monarch rules not despotically but as a benign, paternalistic custodian and where the relationship between ruler and people is based on the principle of mutual non-interference in each other's spheres. All this had been lost when Peter's westernising reforms began to encroach upon the people, and, once the principle of mutual non-interference had been ruptured, it was only a matter of time before the people sought to encroach upon the realm of the ruler and demand political participation. The only way to repair the ancient understanding between state and land, tsar and people, was to undo the effects of the Petrine period and return to the true principles of ancient Russia.[43]

CONCLUSION

Aksakov's memorandum does much to explain the subsequent disintegration of Slavophilism in the reign of Alexander II, since it showed how the movement's social basis in the gentry class and its Romantic theological, historiosophical and epistemological roots could translate only into the most naïve and backward-looking political solutions at a time when Russia cried out for modernisation and reform. The national backwardness revealed by Russia's defeat in the Crimean War and the processes of reform introduced by Alexander II posed questions in the 1860s that Slavophilism in particular and conservatism in general failed to confront adequately. The intellectual initiative passed to the Westernisers and in particular to a new generation of radicals that sought to strip out all untested traditions in the name of rational utilitarianism and wholesale social and political change. The Crimean campaign had also increased awareness among educated Russians of the plight of the southern Slav nations under Turkish occupation. This allowed classical Slavophilism to develop further emphasis on Slavic solidarity and facilitated its eventual evolution into Pan-Slavism and belief in Russia's mission to liberate and unite the Slavs in a process that would bring the 'light from the East' to illuminate and revive a moribund West. Another form of Romantic nationalism survived in the *pochvenni-chestvo* (native-soil conservatism) of Grigorev, Strakhov and Dostoevsky in the mid-1860s. Conceived partly in reaction against the 'nihilism' of Chernyshevsky and his fellow 'enlighteners', *pochvennichestvo* retained the Romantic emphasis on organicism, immediacy and intuition. It also retained, especially in the writings of Dostoevsky, the Slavophile critique of western European atomisation and over-reliance on pure reason. In his *Notes from Underground* (1864) Dostoevsky provided a compelling illustration of the corrosive effects of reason and individualism on both the personality and social harmony; in his account of his travels in Europe, *Winter Notes on Summer Impressions* (1863), he offered a telling analysis of the spiritual disintegration of the West; in his *Diary of a Writer*, written intermittently between 1873 and his death in 1881, he argued the case for Russian nationalism and Pan-Slavism; in his major novels he attempted to show that the moral and spiritual decline of Russia's westernised classes could be arrested only by a return to native tradition and Orthodoxy; while in the figure of Stavrogin (*The Devils*, 1872) he illustrated the tragedy of the *obshchechelovek*, the ahistoric 'universal man' stripped of national identity and thus of meaning. In the process Dostoevsky took the historical concerns of Russian conservatism to heights of intellectual and artistic sophistication unimagined by his predecessors; and as a result of the status he acquired in Russian intellectual life, as well as through his friendship with prominent establishment figures such as Pobedonostsev, he paved the way for a resurgence of conservative thought in the 1870s and beyond.

NOTES

1. Richard Pipes (ed.), *Karamzin's Memoir on Ancient and Modern Russia* (Cambridge, Mass.: Harvard University Press, 1959), p. x. Pipes argues that Russian conservatism's connection to Russian absolutism is a historical accident, and that 'it exists independently of governmental forms, and as such has lasting interest'.
2. Prince M. M. Shcherbatov, *On the Corruption of Morals in Russia*, ed. and trans. A. Lentin (Cambridge University Press, 1969), p. 113. Shcherbatov's arguments turn on his conviction that changing fashions and modish innovations in post-Petrine Russia had led to social debilitation, 'voluptuousness' (*slastostrastie*) and the erosion of a sense of *noblesse oblige* in the nobility (see p. 126).
3. Pipes, *Karamzin's Memoir*, p. 4.
4. The terms 'historicist' and 'ahistoricist' have been employed in a variety of contexts with different shades of meaning. It might be prudent to clarify at slightly greater length what the terms connote here. 'Ahistoricist' is used to

describe an intellectual system that embodies the assumption that its conclusions are absolute and universally applicable, and are not just confined to the particular historical and cultural circumstances in which they were first conceived. 'Historicist', on the other hand, refers to a framework that relativises such assumptions by its emphasis on local, rather than universal, conditions and by its insistence that intellectual and cultural forms that are the product of one set of historical or cultural conditions may not be readily imposed upon another, or indeed be compatible with it.

5. For a fuller treatment of Shcherbatov's ideas, see Marc Raeff, 'State and nobility in the ideology of M. M. Shcherbatov', *American Slavic and East European Review*, 19:3 (1960), 363–79.

6. *The Philosophical Works of David Hume*, ed. T. H. Green and T. H. Grose, 4 vols. (London: Longmans, Green, 1875), vol. II, p. 58.

7. See, for example, Allen McConnell, *A Russian Philosophe: Alexander Radishchev, 1749–1802* (The Hague: Martinus Nijhoff, 1964), p. 101 and *passim*.

8. Andrzej Walicki, *A History of Russian Thought from the Enlightenment to Marxism*, trans. Hilda Andrews-Rusiecka (Oxford: Clarendon Press, 1980), p. 44.

9. Pipes, *Karamzin's Memoir*, pp. 86–9.

10. Ibid., pp. 184–5.

11. Ibid., p. 187.

12. Ibid., pp. 200, 139, 103.

13. Ibid., p. 139.

14. Ibid., pp. 155, 153.

15. Ibid., pp. 200–1.

16. Ibid., p. 165.

17. See, in particular, the views of the apologists of Official Nationality and those of the Slavophile Konstantin Aksakov, to be discussed later.

18. Pipes, *Karamzin's Memoir*, p. 56.

19. Quoted ibid., p. 58.

20. As Walicki points out (*A History of Russian Thought*, p. 72), many Russians compared the defeat of Napoleon to the downfall of the Antichrist.

21. For a fuller treatment of the ideas of the Wisdom-Lovers, see Andrzej Walicki, *The Slavophile Controversy: History of a Conservative Utopia in Nineteenth-Century Russian Thought* (Oxford: Clarendon Press, 1975), pp. 64–82, and A. Koyré, *La Philosophie et le problème national en Russie au début du XIXe siècle* (Paris: Champion, 1929).

22. P. I. Pestel', 'Russian Law' in *A Documentary History of Russian Thought: From the Enlightenment to Marxism*, ed. W. J. Leatherbarrow and D. C. Offord (Ann Arbor: Ardis, 1987), p. 52.

23. N. V. Riasanovsky, *A Parting of Ways: Government and the Educated Public in Russia 1801–1855* (Oxford: Clarendon Press, 1976), p. 104. For a full account of Official Nationality, see also Riasanovsky's *Nicholas I and Official Nationality in Russia, 1825–1855* (Berkeley: University of California Press, 1959).

24. Cited in Riasanovsky, *A Parting of Ways*, p. 108.

25. S. P. Shevyrev, 'Vzgliad russkogo na sovremennoe obrazovanie Evropy', *Moskvitianin*, Part 1 (1841), 292–5. Cited in Riasanovsky, *A Parting of Ways*, p. 109.

26. For more on the role of Pogodin and Shevyrev, see N. Riasanovsky, 'Pogodin and Ševyrëv in Russian intellectual history', *Harvard Slavic Studies*, 4 (1957), 149–67.

27. Pogodin was himself the son of a serf.

28. The essay, entitled 'Petr Velikii', was first published in *Moskvitianin* in 1841 and republished in Pogodin's *Istoriko-kriticheskie otryvki*, 2 vols. (Moscow: Tipografiia Avgusta Semena, 1846–67), vol. I, pp. 333–63. For a fuller treatment of Pogodin, see two recent Russian studies: K. V. Umbrashko, *M. P. Pogodin: chelovek, istorik, publitsist* (Moscow: Institut rossiiskoi istorii RAN, 1999), and N. I. Pavlenko, *Mikhail Pogodin* (Moscow: Pamiatniki istoricheskoi mysli, 2003).

29. Pogodin, *Istoriko-kriticheskie otryvki*, vol. I, pp. 357–8.

30. Quoted in Leatherbarrow and Offord (eds.), *A Documentary History of Russian Thought*, pp. 70–3.

31. Ibid., p. 77.

32. Ibid., pp. 74–6.

33. *The Major Works of Peter Chaadaev*, ed. and trans. Raymond T. McNally (Notre Dame and London: University of Notre Dame Press, 1969), pp. 214–15.

34. Riasanovsky, *A Parting of Ways*, pp. 176–7. For a fuller treatment, see Riasanovsky's monograph, *Russia and the West in the Teaching of the Slavophiles* (Cambridge, Mass.: Harvard University Press, 1952).

35. A. S. Khomiakov, *Polnoe sobranie sochinenii*, 4th edn, 8 vols. (Moscow: Tipografiia I. N. Kushnereva, 1900–4), vol. V, p. 217.

36. For a full account of Khomiakov's historical views, see Walicki, *The Slavophile Controversy* (especially chapter 5) and P. K. Christoff, *An Introduction to Nineteenth-Century Russian Slavophilism: A. S. Xomjakov* (The Hague: Mouton, 1961).

37. Khomiakov, *The Church is One* (London: SPCK, 1948), p. 14.

38. Khomiakov, 'Po povodu poslaniia arkhiepiskopa parizhkogo', *Polnoe sobranie sochinenii*, 5th edn, 8 vols. (Moscow: Tipografiia I. N. Kushnereva, 1907), vol. II, p. 112. Translated in Leatherbarrow and Offord (eds.), *A Documentary History of Russian Thought*, p. 91.

39. Ibid.

40. I. V. Kireevskii, 'A Reply to A. S. Khomiakov' in Leatherbarrow and Offord (eds.), *A Documentary History of Russian Thought*, p. 81.

41. Walicki, *A History of Russian Thought*, p. 106.

42. Ibid., p. 107. For an alternative view, see Susanna Rabow-Edling, *Slavophile Thought and the Politics of Cultural Nationalism* (Albany: State University of New York Press, 2006).

43. The relevant section of Aksakov's memorandum may be found in N. L. Brodskii (ed.), *Rannie slavianofily* (Moscow: Izdatel'stvo I. D. Sytina, 1910), pp. 69–96.

CHAPTER 6

Nihilism

Richard Peace

Following the collapse of the repressive regime of Nicholas I and the debacle of the Crimean War it became clear that the time for mere reflection was over and that action was required to address the problems of Russia's backwardness in comparison with the countries of western Europe. At an official level there was much soul-searching as to the path Russia should now take. The new tsar, Alexander II, was intent on bringing the social structure of his country more into line with that of other European countries, and he embarked upon a programme of major modernisation and reform. However, his chief reform – the liberation of the serfs – was not without significant social costs. For a start it would lead to the decline of the hitherto powerful gentry class and weaken its cultural hegemony. Moreover, the harsh financial burden placed on the peasants, and their disillusionment with the land allocated to them, sparked disturbances in the countryside. Perhaps even more significantly, the unsatisfactory conditions of the emancipation had the effect of splitting the reform movement in the Russian intelligentsia. Liberals (who were mainly of gentry origin) were largely appeased, arguing that the emancipation was evidence of the government's good intentions and that any shortcomings could be addressed through a process of subsequent reform. A significant section of the intelligentsia was, however, radicalised by what they saw as the government's inability to make effective change, and it came to see the future as one of working against, rather than with, the regime in order to achieve progress. For these radicals – largely drawn from the middle-class *raznochintsy* and thus without a vested interest in the social status quo – the well-meaning idealism of the liberal gentry of the 1840s was an obstacle to progress that had to be swept aside in favour of a hard-headed and unsentimental realism that would affirm action rather than abstraction. Convictions needed to be verified in the crucible of scientific truth, and any that failed to measure up should be discarded. Much of this is reflected in Turgenev's novel *Fathers and Children*, and after the novel's publication in 1862 the terms 'nihilist' and 'nihilism' came into general use as pejorative descriptions of the 'new people' and their radical rejection of tradition and principles held merely on trust.

That a novel should be important for the development of Russian thought is not surprising, for, whereas philosophy ruled in nineteenth-century German universities, the regime of Nicholas I abolished university chairs of philosophy, replacing them with chairs in theology. Ideas went into unofficial debating circles or were diverted into literature and literary criticism, so that the critic Belinsky could claim a literary journal to be the equal of a university chair (*zhurnal stoit kafedry*).[1]

There was an even greater irony in Nicholas's attempt to substitute theology for philosophy; for it was precisely in this area, the theological schools and seminaries, that nihilism was born. Even later in the century these establishments were producing revolutionaries such as the future Stalin, and the 'new people' who came to the fore in the 1860s were nearly all seminary trained: Chernyshevsky, Dobroliubov, Pomialovsky and many more. This fact was so noticeable that the very word 'seminarist' became synonymous with 'nihilist'. Chernyshevsky and Dobroliubov ousted the so-called 'gentlemen's party' from the pages of the influential journal *The Contemporary* and made it their 'chair'. Its proprietor and chief editor jokingly referred to his editorial board as his 'consistory'.[2]

Why the ecclesiastical schools and seminaries turned out nihilists and revolutionaries may be seen in Pomialovsky's *Bursa Sketches* (1862–3). The *bursa* was the lower theological school and here the brutal beatings, filthy physical conditions and cynical teaching by rote of formulaic concepts, as described by Pomialovsky, led to a rebellious state of mind and a rejection of authoritarian, meaningless abstractions imposed as received wisdom.[3] At the same time the brighter pupils often had access to contraband literature – particularly Feuerbach's *Essence of Christianity* (the Russian version of which was actually dedicated to Russian seminarists).[4] This subversive work taught that man had surrendered his own godhead to some mythical creature beyond the skies, whereas man himself was god (*homo homini deus*) and should assume his true status. It was a doctrine in which practical reality ousted authoritarian abstractions. In the writings of Chernyshevsky the ideas of Feuerbach, in order to avoid censorship, would later be referred to as 'the anthropological principle'.[5]

After the Crimean War the question of education was very much to the fore. Back in the eighteenth century the development of schools had been an essential element in the establishment of Peter I's navy, and now, after a military defeat that had come from the sea, the navy's own official journal,

The Maritime Miscellany, led the educational debate; the 'nihilists' could follow in their wake. Dobroliubov used the pages of *The Contemporary* to put forward more liberal and practically orientated concepts of education, in particular fulminating against the use of corporal punishment. His colleague Chernyshevsky regarded literature itself as a form of education, arguing that it should be 'a textbook of life'.[6] Anxious that education should not remain in the abstract, Pomialovsky and others became involved in a Sunday school movement to teach lower-class children and adults the principles of literacy.[7] Dobroliubov regarded education and tyranny as polar opposites[8] and had the tyrannical teaching of the seminaries in his sights. In 'The Organic Development of Man in Connection with his Mental and Moral Activities' (1859) he attacked the dogma of the dualism of the body and the soul, asserting that the achievements of the natural sciences had shown the material unity of man. In this he was following German materialist thought – particularly the work of Moleschott and Vogt.

CHERNYSHEVSKY AND RATIONAL EGOISM

The materialist argument was further advanced by Chernyshevsky in his article 'The Anthropological Principle in Philosophy' (1860). Here again the argument is that science has replaced religion, and even 'gaps remaining in the scientific explanation of natural phenomena' do not justify 'the retention of remnants of a fantastic view of the world'.[9] Chernyshevsky argues against all idealistic concepts of reality. The world around us is exactly what everyone sees. Thus if you look into the eye of a person observing a tree, you will see reflected in that eye the very same image of the tree that you yourself see in reality. Moreover, psychological phenomena are merely another manifestation of matter. Just as water can exist in other physical states – ice and steam – but still remain H_2O, so what appear as different categories of state in man are, in effect, different functions of matter. It is this material nature of man which determines his actions, so that appearing to want to do something is merely a subjective impression accompanying an action dictated by material considerations. Chernyshevsky uses a banal analogy as illustration: in getting out of bed the leg to be put out first will be dictated not by will but by physical convenience. If, however, the subject puts out the other foot: 'here a simple substitution of one cause (physiological convenience) has replaced another (the thought of proving one's independence)'.[10]

Such arguments appear to deny free will, yet the material imperative of what is physically convenient may, as it were, pass from 'water' to 'steam':

material considerations of the 'will' may then be driven by what is in the subject's *actual* material interest. Reason itself is but a higher form of material processes, and it is at this point that the concept of rational egoism comes into play; for the short-term interest of the individual may not be to his or her ultimate advantage. Later, in Chernyshevsky's novel *What is to be Done?*, the two faces of egoism, rational versus non-rational, are skilfully juggled by Lopukhov, as he explains the realities of life to the receptive heroine Vera Pavlovna, while at the same time the ambiguity of his arguments can win the approval of her self-seeking, narrow-minded mother Maria Alekseevna.[11]

Perhaps 'rational egoism' has ambiguity at its very core. It derives from the 'enlightened self-interest' of the English utilitarian philosophers Bentham and Mill, but in its English interpretation it formed the ideological bulwark for free trade and a moral underpinning for capitalism. As a political doctrine it was first promoted by nineteenth-century liberals, but survives to the present day as a conservative mantra. However, in its Russian manifestation as 'rational egoism', it was interpreted in a radically different way: it became for Chernyshevsky and his followers the doctrine underpinning the ideal socialist society. In England the second element of the formula – 'self-interest' – was stressed. In the Russian version of 'rational egoism' it was the first, and so much so that rationality appeared to change the very nature of egoism itself and convert it into altruism. In Chernyshevsky's novel self-abnegation rules; for it is argued that man's true self-interest lies in taking into account the self-interest of others. It is on this basis that the truly communal self-interest of the perfect society is possible.

UTILITARIANISM AND AESTHETICS

Chernyshevsky took a keen interest in the writings of Mill. He translated, and commented on, his *Principles of Political Economy* and took the utilitarian yardstick of 'what is useful' as his own measure of what was 'good'.[12] Utilitarian values also influenced the attitude to art of Chernyshevsky and his colleague Dobroliubov. The problems of aesthetics play a dominant role in the writings of both. When Chernyshevsky was initially contemplating an academic career, aesthetics was the chosen field for his master's thesis 'The Aesthetic Relations of Art to Reality' (published in 1855). Typically, Chernyshevsky's approach stresses *reality*; it concentrates on the concrete at the expense of the abstract, and his famous dictum 'beauty is life' led him to assert that the creations of art are on a lower aesthetic level than the creations of the real world.[13] Aesthetically, life is always superior to art. Thus the pictorial representation of an apple cannot approach the beauty of a real apple. This dethroning of idealism (now in an aesthetic sense) again owes much to Feuerbach. An ideal, abstract depiction of beauty cannot be an adequate substitute for the beauty of reality itself – the world of things and matter. At the same time, if beauty is 'life', art must not merely reproduce it in its own inadequate way – it must interpret life. Art must not be content with its inadequate aesthetic face; it must go deeper and have ethical content. Here again we see the surfacing of rational values – an emphasis on understanding and analysis. Accordingly, Chernyshevsky tended to value literature above such art forms as painting, architecture and music. It is in this context that he could view a work of literature as 'a textbook of life' and here, in the propagandistic view of art, the emphasis on reality and the need to interpret it, we have the foundation of the doctrine of Socialist Realism, which in the following century would so dominate Soviet aesthetics.

From 1857 Dobroliubov was in charge of literary criticism at *The Contemporary*. His output was enormous, and he used his long reviews to advance his own ideas and those of Chernyshevsky. In 'What is Oblomovism?', his critique of Goncharov's novel *Oblomov*, Dobroliubov attacks the aesthetic of 'art for art's sake': 'We shall never agree that a poet wasting his talent on faultless depictions of charming little leaves and streams can have the same significance as one who, with equal talent, is capable of reproducing, for example, aspects of social life.'[14] Such statements seem merely to echo Chernyshevsky's view that a work of art should have content. Nevertheless, in a later essay, 'A Ray of Light in the Kingdom of Darkness' – his review of Ostrovsky's play *The Thunderstorm* – Dobroliubov clarifies his own philosophy as a critic. He distinguishes between two approaches to art: what he calls 'synthetic' criticism as opposed to 'analytic' criticism. The former sets out with a rigid set of norms, to be applied to every work under examination. It is, says Dobroliubov, the method of the recruiting sergeant, measuring peasant conscripts by a rule and pronouncing them fit or unfit.[15] In contemporary terms he sees belief in such artistic norms as typical of Slavophile critics, who demand the depiction of virtue in the Russian hero and values rooted in the old way of life. The Westernisers, on the other hand, are looking for an attack on superstition and on this same old way of life. Then there are critics of the 'art for art's sake' school, who measure a work by what they see as 'the eternal and universal demands of aesthetics'.[16] Similarly, there are also the widely divergent norms of Classicism and Romanticism. All such criticism, in Dobroliubov's terms, is 'synthetic' in that it attempts to build the bricks of a theory into a work of art, at the same time condemning anything that falls foul of the theory. There are very real dangers here:

It amazes us how revered people can consider accepting such a worthless, such a demeaning role for criticism. For restricting it by the application of 'eternal and general' laws of art to things which are particular and transient, by this very fact they condemn art to stagnation and impart to criticism a policing and bureaucratic sense.

In the Russian context this last statement has a very ominous ring, but Dobroliubov goes further:

Otherwise, how can one not see the difference between a critic and a judge? People are dragged into a court on suspicion of some misdeed or crime, and it is the judge's job to decide whether the accused is innocent or guilty; but surely a writer is not being accused of anything, when he is subjected to criticism? One thought that those times had already long gone, when being engaged with books was considered heresy and a crime.[17]

In pursuing this analogy with a court of law, Dobroliubov asserts that the critic should not be a judge passing sentence, but an advocate explaining the details of the case to the readers. In this role critics may use any means they see fit 'as long as they do not distort the essence of the matter'.[18] It is synthetic criticism, Dobroliubov claims, that is responsible for the continued existence of ignorance and credulity: 'Everywhere and in all things the synthesis reigns.' His own method, by contrast, is 'analytic':

We group together the data, consider the general sense of the work, indicate how it relates to the real world in which we live, come to our conclusion and attempt to present it in the best possible manner, but at the same time we always try to conduct ourselves in such a way that the reader may unconstrainedly judge between us and the author.[19]

Unfortunately, Dobroliubov himself did not always conform to these high standards in his own criticism.

Dobroliubov's views on practical criticism have been dwelt on at some length, not only because aesthetics is a central preoccupation of the so-called 'nihilists' and is entirely consonant with their mistrust of 'principles' in general, but also because his attack on aesthetic norms feeds into Pisarev's later, and more radical, 'demolition' of aesthetics as a science.[20] Yet there is also something positive in Dobroliubov's approach. Whereas Chernyshevsky's promotion of reality over art could be seen as laying the foundation for a later synthetic school of criticism, the doctrine of Socialist Realism, Dobroliubov's championship of analytic criticism could provide a countervailing approach. Thus in 1964, after Solzhenitsyn's story 'One Day in the Life of Ivan Denisovich' had been attacked in the Soviet press, the critic Vladimir Lakshin was able to follow in the shadow of Dobroliubov and launch a counter-attack on 'normative' (i.e. synthetic) criticism.[21]

LITERARY REFLECTIONS OF NIHILISM

Dobroliubov was not merely in charge of the literary criticism section of *The Contemporary*. From 1859 he was also responsible for a supplement which did much to foster the impression of the journal's negativity. *The Whistler* was a miscellany of prose and verse which mocked and pilloried rival journals and contemporary figures and events. Its many contributors wrote under pseudonyms, but Dobroliubov had overall charge. Very soon the epithet 'whistler' was to become synonymous with the later term 'nihilist'. Turgenev, who had been a regular contributor to *The Contemporary*, became increasingly disturbed at the new turn the journal was taking. Matters came to a head with the publication of Dobroliubov's review of his novel *On the Eve* under the title 'When Then Will the Real Day Come?' The review read as a thinly disguised call to revolution, which implicated Turgenev himself in the revolutionary message: 'For us, what the author *wished* to say is not as important as what was actually *said* by him, even unintentionally, simply as a consequence of reproducing the factuality of life truthfully.'[22] The critical approach of peering behind authorial intention may seem surprisingly modern for its time, but the intention it really hides is that of the critic himself. Turgenev used his influence with the journal's proprietor Nekrasov to try to have the review suppressed, or at least altered, but to no avail (although the official censor took his toll). Turgenev broke with the journal and, as others left, *The Contemporary* became more and more identified with the 'new people'.

To replace the lost literary talent Nekrasov turned to such plebeian writers as Pomialovsky, whose first novel *Bourgeois Happiness* (1860) was favourably compared to Turgenev's prose fiction and whose heroes were seen by some members of the younger generation as more acceptable than Bazarov in *Fathers and Children*.[23] The later novels of Pomialovsky, however, would portray the corrosive rationality of truly nihilistic heroes. Cherevanin, in *Molotov* (1861), is prey to a reductive ratiocination which leads him to find emptiness in every word. This is what he calls his 'grave-yard philosophy' (*kladbishchenstvo*) and it brings him to the awareness that there are 'terrible thoughts in the realm of ideas'. Ultimately, it is only conscience that prevents him from putting such 'terrible thoughts' into practice. However, Potesin in Pomialovsky's next novel, the unfinished *Brother and Sister* (1862; first published 1864), has no such scruples. He thinks he has found a rational weapon against conscience and can therefore act. In the development of nihilism the novels of Pomialovsky form an essential link between Turgenev's Bazarov and Dostoevsky's Raskolnikov in *Crime and Punishment*.[24]

Given Turgenev's hostility towards Dobroliubov, Bazarov was widely seen as a portrait of the young radical – particularly embarrassing for Turgenev as the much venerated critic had died in 1861, and, although Turgenev may not have invented the word 'nihilist', his novel had given the term a meaning and a life it had never had before. He was criticised on all sides: whereas those on the left, by and large, were incensed by the portrait of Bazarov, those on the right thought he had caricatured the older generation and presented Bazarov too sympathetically.[25] Nevertheless, Turgenev's portrayal of nihilism is seminal and in his own terms quite accurate. The key moment of definition comes in chapter 5 when, in response to his uncle's question as to who exactly Bazarov is, Arkady replies that his mentor is a nihilist. Arkady's father observes that the term must come from the Latin *nihil* and perhaps denotes someone who does not acknowledge anything. His uncle prefers the definition of someone who does not respect anything, but Arkady corrects them both: it is someone 'who regards everything from a critical viewpoint', and he then adds: 'A nihilist is a person who does not bow down before authorities of any kind, who does not accept a single principle on faith, however much respect surrounds such a principle.'[26]

Arkady's definition goes to the heart of the matter, and as we see Bazarov in action throughout the novel we understand the importance of science in underpinning this critical attitude to 'principles' in general. Bazarov, like Chernyshevsky and Dobroliubov, values science, certainly its experimental side, but unlike them he has actually taken a university course in the natural sciences and intends to become a doctor. On the Kirsanov estate he devotes much time to the dissection of frogs in order, as he tells a peasant boy, to understand the physical workings of the human body. The mumbo-jumbo theories of humours, herbs and minerals associated with traditional medicine and inherited from the ancients he dismisses with contempt, favouring facts which can be proved through experiment and scientific observation. Yet Bazarov goes further: his attitude to handed-down principles extends more generally beyond medicine. The world is seen as entirely one of matter, as it was for Chernyshevsky and Dobroliubov; all theories, all received wisdom must be subjected to rational analysis and put to the test of reality.

This is the philosophical basis for nihilism, but there is a practical step beyond this. In the argument between the generations in chapter 5 of the novel Bazarov talks of 'clearing the ground'.[27] Arkady's uncle asks a pointed question about action: 'Yes, acting, breaking things, but what sort of breaking is it when you don't even know why?' To this his nephew replies: 'We break, because we are a force.'[28] It is noticeable that in these discussions Bazarov himself is reticent about the need for destructive force, whereas his acolyte Arkady is not. This is suggestive of the development of nihilism itself: its ideologues, Chernyshevsky and Dobroliubov, were not directly implicated in violence, unlike those who succeeded them. Nevertheless, it was Turgenev's novel which gave the term its destructive image in the popular mind. In his article 'Apropos of *Fathers and Children*' Turgenev records that, when in May 1862 fires broke out in a poor market area of St Petersburg, he was accosted on the street with the words 'Look at what *your* nihilists are doing! They are burning St Petersburg!'[29] From this moment Turgenev's coining of the term became associated with the destructive violence of revolutionary terrorism. At the same time, it seems that Turgenev himself had such implications in mind. In a letter to a representative of the younger generation, Sluchevsky, he said of Bazarov: 'If he is called a nihilist, then one must read revolutionary.'[30]

It may be significant that Turgenev shared a common source of inspiration with Chernyshevsky and Dobroliubov. He, like them, owed a debt to the literary critic Belinsky. Indeed, *Fathers and Children* is dedicated to his memory, and there is perhaps more than a hint of Belinsky himself in the portrait of Bazarov, who like the famous critic is the son of a retired military doctor. In his attitude to life and literature Belinsky went through many ideological shifts, but it was his last phase, in which he stressed reality and realism in literature, that could appeal both to Turgenev and to the 'nihilists', though in different ways. Bazarov's famous rejection of working for future generations seems like an echo of a nihilistic moment in Belinsky: 'What is it to me that all will be well for my children or yours, if I find things so awful and through no fault of my own?' Even more significantly, during this last period of his life and thought Belinsky had pronounced negation to be his god.[31]

It was because of events of the previous year, namely the appearance of revolutionary pamphlets and student unrest, that the St Petersburg fires of May 1862 could be ascribed to 'nihilists'. The fires themselves split public opinion – were they the work of 'nihilists' or government *agents provocateurs*? At the same time, the government's quest for the origin of the pamphlets seemed to lead to *The Contemporary*. In July 1862 the journal was suspended for eight months, Chernyshevsky was arrested and the Sunday schools were closed down. Because of the lack of any real evidence against Chernyshevsky it was two years before he was brought to trial. During that period in the Peter and Paul Fortress in St Petersburg he wrote his extremely influential novel *What is to be Done?*, which because of bureaucratic incompetence was allowed out of the prison (as papers not relevant to the case) and immediately published in 1863 in the newly reopened *Contemporary*. The novel is Chernyshevsky's reply to *Fathers and Children*. The names of the two principal male characters, Kirsanov and Lopukhov, refer (one directly, the other indirectly) to the main characters of Turgenev's novel. Both are materialists and doctors who, like Bazarov, are more concerned with experimental science than with curing people. As Chernyshevsky comments: 'They are terribly keen to curse medicine ... they cut up frogs and every year perform autopsies on hundreds of corpses.'[32] Unlike Bazarov, whom many in the younger generation accused of egotistic pride, Chernyshevsky's heroes are followers of the doctrine of rational egoism. In the name Lopukhov there is an ironic reference to Bazarov's rejection of working for future generations – a time, he says, when *lopukh* (burdocks) will grow on his own grave.[33] Yet rational egoism encourages working for others, and the novel presents a picture of the perfect society of the future. Nevertheless, this society hardly suggests realistic comfort. It is housed in a glass palace, of which the Crystal Palace in London provides merely a hint, and is located, of all places, in the Arabian desert! It is the ultimate form of the commune, whose rational principles for the organisation of work and living are proclaimed throughout the novel.

The central figure of *What is to be Done?* is not a hero but a heroine, Vera Pavlovna. Through this figure Chernyshevsky projects a prime preoccupation of the nihilists – the emancipation of women, the so-called 'female question'. It is she who sets up a commune for exploited women on purely rational lines, yet on a non-rational level she also advances the ideological impact of the novel through a series of dreams – dreams of a personified revolution and of the society of the future. At a personal level, female emancipation allows Vera Pavlovna to abandon one husband (Lopukhov) for another (Kirsanov). When rejected by Odintsova, Bazarov had gone into a long sulk, but Lopukhov, guided by rational egoism, sees that his own long-term interest lies in purely rational behaviour: rational egoism dictates self-sacrifice to the interests of his friend and erstwhile wife.

The question of the 'honour' of the 'new people' is an issue. Bazarov, when challenged by a social superior, agrees to a duel – a concession to aristocratic codes condemned by most of the younger generation. The abstract concept of honour must be dealt with not through highfalutin principles, but practically. When Lopukhov has a confrontation on the street with a certain portly gentleman, he unceremoniously dumps him into a ditch.[34] Nevertheless, Lopukhov and Kirsanov are seen by Chernyshevsky as ordinary people; the real role model is the extraordinary figure of Rakhmetov – a man characterised by even greater self-abnegation (he sleeps on a bed of nails), a man dedicated to a cause, and that cause, it is suggested, is revolution. Rakhmetov is Chernyshevsky's answer to Bazarov, and that is perhaps why the names Kirsanov and Lopukhov (the one associated with 'camp-follower', the other with lack of future perspective) are given to the 'ordinary' heroes.

The impact of Chernyshevsky's novel on the younger generation was immense. Under its influence communes were set up. The most famous of these was the Znamenskaia Commune of the minor writer Sleptsov, a man influenced by both Chernyshevsky's ethics and his aesthetics (it is recorded that the penurious Sleptsov would buy an apple not to eat but to admire for its beauty).[35] The 'new women' often identified themselves by wearing blue-tinted glasses, having close-cropped hair and rejecting conventional marriage. In the minds of some, both men and women, the coded messages about revolution in Vera Pavlovna's dreams and the enigmatic figure of Rakhmetov struck home.

PISAREV: THINKING REALISTS AND THE DESTRUCTION OF AESTHETICS

An important contribution to nihilist thought was made by Pisarev, who in many respects differed from its other key advocates. Unlike Chernyshevsky and Dobroliubov, Pisarev came from an aristocratic background. Moreover, whereas Antonovich in *The Contemporary* had launched a bitter attack on Bazarov as the evil demon of our time (1862), Pisarev in the rival journal *The Russian Word* embraced Bazarov's values with enthusiasm (in such articles as 'Bazarov' (1862) and 'Realists' (1864)). He suffered the same fate as Chernyshevsky: in July 1862, he too was arrested and *The Russian Word* was suspended for eight months. On the face of it, the case against Pisarev was more serious: an illegal pamphlet, based on material provided by Pisarev hailing the downfall of the Romanov dynasty, had been published by Ballod, a well-to-do student of revolutionary leanings who had organised a clandestine printing press. Pisarev spent four and a half years in solitary confinement in the Peter and Paul Fortress but, through influence exerted by his mother, from his second year he was allowed to write and review articles for publication in order 'to support his family' (the official reason given). Thus such major contributions to nihilism as Chernyshevsky's novel and Pisarev's articles may be characterised as 'prison literature'. In the case of Pisarev the condition of solitary confinement may also have influenced the direction of his thought. There is a stronger emphasis on the isolated, individual ego than in many of his contemporaries, revealed particularly in his confessed self-identification with Bazarov, whom he saw as a tragic figure: 'The tragedy of Bazarov's situation lies in his complete isolation in the midst of all other living people.'[36]

The difference in class between Chernyshevsky and Pisarev ensured a radically different treatment at the hands of the authorities. Whereas Pisarev was allowed to write from prison and was finally released in 1866 (as a gesture to mark the marriage of the tsarevich), Chernyshevsky was forced to fall totally silent. Although the charges against him were trumped up, he went on to penal settlement and was not released until 1883 (and even then only to the provincial city of Astrakhan). Yet, the Ballod pamphlet notwithstanding, Chernyshevsky's novel, smuggled out of prison, may well have made him seem the more dangerous propagandist. Whatever the reason, the more radical nihilism of Pisarev had a voice, whereas that of Chernyshevsky was silenced, and Pisarev's views began to predominate in the thinking of the 'new people'.

Pisarev himself was greatly inspired by *What is to be Done?*, viewing it not so much as a polemical response to *Fathers and Children* but as a continuation and deepening of its ideas. The figure of Bazarov fascinated him throughout. In his review 'Bazarov' he had written: 'All our young generation with its ideas and its strivings can recognise itself in the characters of this novel.' If there were some minor distortions, they were those of a mirror, which might slightly alter the colour of objects but still reflect them in a recognisable way.[37] He returned to the theme in his article 'Realists', written from prison, confessing that 'Bazarov, from the very first moment of his appearance, attracted all my sympathy, and he continues to be a favourite of mine even now.'[38] If Antonovich had condemned the aristocratic behaviour of Bazarov,[39] Pisarev from his own more aristocratic viewpoint in solitary confinement could see things differently; for him real truth lay in individual human integrity, not in abstract philosophical systems imposed from without. He had already proclaimed the value of such egoism in 'The Scholasticism of the Nineteenth Century', an article written a year before his review of *Fathers and Children*:

If everybody were in the strict sense to be egoists by conviction – that is, were concerned only with themselves, and were to obey the dictates of feeling alone, without creating in themselves artificial concepts of an ideal and of duty, and did not interfere in the affairs of others – then truly one would live with more ease and freedom on this earth than now.[40]

Here the ego is said to be driven by feelings (rather than reason), and strangely it appears to anticipate Bazarov's most 'nihilistic' moment in the novel, when he confesses that it is feelings (*oshchushcheniia*) that have made him a nihilist.[41]

It was the integrity of the ego that Pisarev welcomed in Bazarov, an ego which refused to be swayed by the values of those around him and refused to acknowledge such abstractions as principles. For Pisarev the measure of morality lay within Bazarov himself – it was the regard that he had for his own personality, his feelings of self-worth: 'Bazarov would not steal a handkerchief for the very same reason that he would not eat a piece of rotting meat.'[42] At the same time, such egoism is rational: 'Very intelligent people ... understand that it is very advantageous to be honest, and that every crime from simple lying right up to murder is dangerous, and therefore inconvenient.'[43] Here morality is equated with 'calculation' (*raschet*), but whether intelligence or feeling is the guiding force of the ego, Pisarev's main concern is the ego itself. In Chernyshevsky's formulation, rational egoism, as displayed by the characters of *What is to be Done?*, actually becomes altruism, but for Pisarev the ego is the source of all values, whether it be guided by feeling or reason. This has important consequences, not only for Pisarev's interpretation of ethics, but also for his arguments on aesthetics.

In his 1862 review of Turgenev's novel, Pisarev defends Bazarov's ego-centred statement about not working for future generations,[44] but in 1865 in 'The Thinking Proletariat', having now read *What is to be Done?*, he revises this position: 'The ego which is true to itself will not shun work for the good of others.' 'The more profound the egoism [of the new people] becomes, the stronger grows their love for humanity.'[45] The world external to the ego could only be understood through science, and Bazarov was the right kind of scientist – a practical experimenter, not a theoretician. His dissection of frogs became emblematic for Pisarev: 'It is precisely here, in the dissected frog, that there lies the salvation and renovation of the Russian people.'[46] The 'new people' in Chernyshevsky's novel, Kirsanov and Lopukhov, appealed to Pisarev because, as doctors, they, too, were concerned more with practical experimentation than with received medical wisdom. No scientist himself, Pisarev was nevertheless impressed by the writings of materialists such as Moleschott, Vogt and Ludwig Büchner, who appeared to offer a purely physiological explanation of psychological processes. In his

'Physiological Sketches', following Moleschott and Vogt who identified thought with the simple movement of matter and subscribed to the view that *Der Mensch ist was er isst* – 'a man is what he eats', Pisarev argues that thought processes depend on the speed of the circulation of the blood and that mental characteristics can be related to diet (ideas that have again become fashionable).

Pisarev was fond of repeating that 'fame and illusions perish, facts remain'. Yet very often some of Pisarev's 'facts' were little more than speculation. Science for Pisarev would solve many problems. Not only was it a source of enlightenment much needed in backward Russia, but technical progress based on science would solve what he repeatedly stressed was the greatest moral problem: the shame of 'the starving and unclad'.[47] In its enlightenment role science would get rid of what Pisarev saw as the harmful effects of religion. Such ideas could not be expressed openly in print, but here the more neutral term 'prejudices' (*predrassudki*) could replace the word 'religion'. It is this euphemism that he employs in his original review of *Fathers and Children*: 'Bazarov has a thorough knowledge of natural science and medicine; and with their help he has knocked all prejudices out of his head.'[48] Reading Darwin also reinforced Pisarev's materialist view of man, and in 'Progress in the World of Animals and Plants' (1864) he became the chief populariser of Darwinian theory in Russia at the time.

Turgenev claimed to agree with Bazarov's ideas, except in one respect – his rejection of art,[49] and in his initial review of the novel Pisarev appears to concur with the author's own reservation, arguing that Bazarov in such matters speaks in ignorance and in haste. He has his own explanation: 'the flight from the abstractions of Hegelianism has made the younger generation start to persecute simple feelings and even purely physical sensations, such as the enjoyment of music'.[50] We are back again with the argument of feelings versus abstractions. But if at this stage he is attempting to give a psycho-materialist justification for aesthetic experience, he will later develop his arguments on 'feelings' into his well-known (infamous) doctrine of the destruction of aesthetics, ending up with views on art as extreme as those of Bazarov himself. Yet Pisarev claims merely to be interpreting Chernyshevsky's thesis on art and reality, accusing the 'disciple' Antonovich of distorting his master's doctrine. In Pisarev's view Chernyshevsky, in his thesis, had already pronounced the destruction of aesthetics as an abstract science, and back in 1861 Pisarev had already outlined his own position in 'The Scholasticism of the Nineteenth Century': 'personal impressions and only personal impressions can be the measure of beauty'.[51] Thus just as the ego through rationality is the judge of morality, so the ego through feeling is the judge of art. It is this latter argument which is developed in his highly polemical article of 1865, 'The Destruction of Aesthetics': 'One's own particular aesthetic is formed for each individual person, and it follows that a general aesthetic ordering personal tastes into obligatory unity becomes impossible.'[52] Pisarev compares aesthetic appreciation to love – each one loves in his or her own way, and just as there cannot be a general science of love so there cannot be a general science of aesthetics.[53]

So far so good, but Chernyshevsky, whose teaching Pisarev claims to be following, had clearly stated an aesthetic theory: beauty was to be equated with what was real, and the reality of what two people saw could not be in doubt – what any one person observed was exactly the same as it was reflected in the eye of another. Pisarev, however, appeared to believe in the old maxim 'beauty is in the eye of the beholder'; it did not inhere, as such, in the reality of the object itself – personal feeling intervened. Nonetheless, he could also claim the support of Chernyshevsky, inasmuch as the materialism of Chernyshevsky's doctrine, crudely interpreted, also destroyed aesthetics as an abstract science with general meaning: 'Given the definition of beauty that the author gives us, aesthetics, to our huge satisfaction, disappears into physiology and hygiene.'[54]

Although Pisarev's doubt about the possibility of establishing a science of aesthetics fits in well with Bazarov's rejection of principles and abstractions, he develops a view on the role of art which goes beyond that of Turgenev's nihilist hero. Art, he says, is the companion of luxury; it is a parasite that gets in the way of more vital considerations, and the most pressing of these is the great problem of 'the starving and unclad'. As things are, says Pisarev, hands which could be employed in the production of food for the starving are encouraged to make elegantly fine objects for the well fed. He argues, in words which sound like a premonition of Soviet aesthetic theory, that the temple of true art should be turned into the workshop of human thought, where research workers, writers, painters, each in their own way, can strive towards the great aim – the elimination of poverty and ignorance. The opposition of ethics to aesthetics – the substitution of ethical considerations for aesthetic criteria – is the most pronounced feature of Pisarev's anti-aestheticism. As his early writings show, he was far from being against the enjoyment of art, but he came to think that the price paid in order for art to be enjoyed by the few is too great when set beside human suffering.

Pisarev became the chief spokesman for the strong current of anti-aestheticism typical of the 'new people'. Bazarov himself had poured scorn on the 'fathers'' love of Pushkin, and Pisarev contended that both

Pushkin and Lermontov were rhymesters of consumptive girls and lieutenants, and that pastry was more to his taste. That he would rather be a Russian shoemaker than a Russian Raphael was a view also ascribed to him.[55] Such an approach to art links Pisarev with the English utilitarians, particularly Bentham and his view that 'quality of pleasure being equal, pushpin is as good as poetry'.[56] It also has overtones of puritanism, an identification Pisarev and his epigone Zaitsev were perfectly willing to accept.

However, it was the term 'nihilist', acknowledged by Bazarov, which Pisarev proudly accepted yet felt the need to gloss as 'thinking realist'. The nihilism of Bazarov concentrated on destruction – the old had to be cleared away before anything positive could be built. In 'The Scholasticism of the Nineteenth Century', published the year before Turgenev's novel, Pisarev had actually emphasised destruction even more strongly: 'This is the ultimatum of our camp: that which can be broken must be broken; that which withstands the blow is worthwhile, whatever flies into smithereens is rubbish. In any case, strike out left and right, no harm can come of this, or even be harm.'[57] Among those Russian institutions for which Bazarov had scant respect was the peasant commune. Chernyshevsky, along with Herzen, placed high hopes on that institution as an embryonic form of socialist society. Not so Pisarev, who in this respect is far closer to the condemnation voiced by Bazarov. His hopes for the future did not build on a backward-looking, primitive institution; they were firmly placed on science and western progress.

A trait of elitist arrogance seen in Bazarov was censured by many among the 'new people', yet the more aristocratic Pisarev demonstrated a similar undemocratic streak. Discussing the views of the poet Heine, he could write: 'the new Puritans of our time do not dream of any absolute equality'.[58] The 'thinking realists' formed a body of enlightened men and women, who saw all problems clearly and who would lead the masses to a better, more rational society. Their first goal, however, must be the elimination of the problem of 'the starving and unclad'. Thinking realists were to be drawn from all areas of society and would be an elite of minds, not a social elite. The image of such people could already be seen in Bazarov and the heroes of *What is to be Done?*

Chernyshevsky's novel began to impress Pisarev even more than *Fathers and Children*. In his first review of that novel he had complained that it contained no women who were Bazarov's equals. This was a significant omission in Pisarev's eyes, as he had always been a champion of women's rights (in his early years he had worked as a journalist on *The Dawn*, a journal mainly for women). Now in *What is to be Done?* he had found a true, positive portrait of the 'new woman', Vera Pavlovna, who fights the exploitation of women by organising a work cooperative, who exercises her right to freedom in love and who dreams prophetic dreams about revolution. Nevertheless, the true revolutionary in the novel is still a man – the puritanical Rakhmetov. 'The Thinking Proletariat', the article in which Pisarev discusses Chernyshevsky's heroes, had originally borne the title 'A New Type', and its concluding words make plain whom he has in mind: 'Wherever Rakhmetovs appear they shed bright ideas all round them and awaken living hope.'[59] At the same time, Pisarev has reservations. He does not endorse Rakhmetov's asceticism – he does not drink or have relations with women and even sleeps on a bed of nails. Pisarev feels there is a dangerous discrepancy between the ideals Rakhmetov stands for and the example he gives in his own life.[60]

Although in the Ballod pamphlet Pisarev had talked of giving the rotten house of Romanov and the St Petersburg bureaucracy one last push,[61] and had argued in his article on Heine that revolutions, terrible as they are, act like potentially harmful medicines such as mercury in curing a far more harmful disease (the reference is to syphilis),[62] nevertheless, like his hero Bazarov, he is not explicit on how the new order is to be brought about. Is it to be by the force of logic, by propaganda or is it to be full revolution? There are obvious constraints of censorship, but at the forefront of Pisarev's thinking is, perhaps, less the nature of a new state and the means of bringing it about, and more the elimination of an old but pressing problem: 'The ultimate aim of all our thinking and all activity of every honest person consists, nevertheless, in solving once and for all the inescapable problem of the starving and unclad; outside this problem there is definitely nothing worth one's concern, thought and efforts.'[63] It is in this emphasis on the elimination of a negative that Pisarev reveals himself as a true nihilist – it is Bazarov's 'clearing of the ground'.

DOSTOEVSKY AND NIHILISM

After an eight-month closure both *The Contemporary* and *The Russian Word* were allowed to resume publication early in 1863. *The Contemporary*, however, was without Chernyshevsky, whereas Pisarev was permitted to contribute from prison. The satirist Saltykov-Shchedrin was recruited to give direction to *The Contemporary*, and it soon became obvious that a gulf had opened up between the two main 'nihilist' journals. Dostoevsky, a keen observer of such matters, talked of a 'schism' in their ranks in an article principally aimed at Saltykov-Shchedrin.[64] We have already seen that literature itself was the main vehicle carrying on the debate over nihilism through a series of responses. *What is to be Done?* was a reply to *Fathers and Children*, and Pisarev's criticism reacted to both. Now Dostoevsky produced his own polemical response to *What is to be Done?* in his *Notes from Underground* (1864). Chernyshevsky's symbol of the future society, the Crystal Palace, is scathingly rejected by Dostoevsky's anti-hero, who 'nihilistically' destroys Chernyshevsky's principal doctrines one by one. Rational egoism is reduced to mere concern for a drop of one's own fat, the underground man's ego is projected as the least reliable guide to moral and sensible behaviour and mathematical reasoning itself is challenged. A more positive blow is struck for feminine worth when Dostoevsky shows that the prostitute Liza is the moral superior of his male protagonist. In *What is to be Done?*, by contrast, Kirsanov's attempt to save the prostitute Kriukova appears as patronising male condescension.[65] Lopukhov's example of asserting the honour of the 'new people' is mocked and parodied (with Gogolian overtones) in the underground man's strivings to improve his wardrobe before refusing to give way to an officer on the street. Nor does Pisarev escape. Darwinism is rejected, but at the same time the underground man adopts Pisarev's own arguments on art not promoting civilising values. Pisarev had used the examples of Nero and the Borgias as great lovers of art, but the underground man makes a similar argument against civilisation itself, pointing to the refined cruelty of Cleopatra and to more modern examples.[66] Although *Notes from Underground* engages in a polemic with nihilism, in a strange way it forms part of nihilism's legacy. Dostoevsky is employing its very own methods – destructive and reductive reasoning – to examine critically the received values, the 'principles' of nihilism itself: the underground man is a nihilistic anti-nihilist. This polemic is carried on throughout Dostoevsky's major novels, and nowhere more openly than in *Crime and Punishment* and *The Devils*. Indeed, Raskolnikov, the hero of the former novel, was identified by Dostoevsky's colleague Strakhov as 'a suffering nihilist'.[67]

Turgenev said that Dostoevsky was one of only two people who understood *Fathers and Children*; yet it is not known how he interpreted the novel – the letter giving his views has been lost. The 'fathers and children' theme is an obsessive strand in Dostoevsky's own writing, but worked in his own way. In *The Devils* he suggests not only a gulf between generations but also an ideological continuity: the intellectual of the 1840s, represented by Stepan Trofimovich, is the father of the nihilism of the following generation, as exemplified in his son Petr Stepanovich. In a less symbolic way

Turgenev, too, had suggested the theme of continuity. Bazarov's father likens his son's rejection of medical authorities to the attitude to outdated theories of his own generation, and Bazarov's chief antagonist, the 'father' Pavel Petrovich, speaks in similar terms about succeeding intellectual fashions ('Formerly there were Hegelianists, now nihilists.').[68] Even more telling is Turgenev's suggestion of a similarity of character between Bazarov and Pavel Petrovich. This 'father' appears to have almost a nihilistic streak himself: 'His soul, misanthropic in the French manner, foppishly dry and passionate, was incapable of dreaming.'[69]

CONCLUSION

Both Dostoevsky and Turgenev hint at placing the nihilism of the 1860s in a broader developmental context, as merely the plebeian expression of a long and more aristocratic tradition. The influences of the French scepticism and Byronism of an earlier age have been replaced by German materialism and English utilitarianism. The challenging of received opinions goes back at least to the eighteenth century. Chatsky, the hero of Griboedov's play *Woe from Wit*, with his devastating critique of Moscow society, may be seen as a more voluble aristocratic forerunner of Bazarov.[70] Even more far-reaching was Chaadaev's criticism of Russian history and culture in his first 'Philosophical Letter' of 1836. Nihilism on a more existential level may be found in the bleak poem which Pushkin wrote in 1828 on his birthday, proclaiming life to be a vain fortuitous gift, and Lermontov's view of life as an 'empty and stupid joke' in his poem of 1840.[71] These are sentiments close to the 'graveyard philosophy' of Pomialovsky's Cherevanin, and both Cherevanin and before him Goncharov's Oblomov come to similar nihil-istic conclusions about human progress when they contemplate history.[72] In his novel *Doctor Krupov* (1847) Herzen had projected a truly nihilistic and plebeian hero *avant la lettre*, and his own philosophy of the late 1840s and 1850s, as represented in *From the Other Shore* (1850), is imbued with a deep aristocratic nihilism.[73]

The more one looks at the matter, the more one realises that negation is a fundamental strand of Russian cultural life, and that the 'nihilism' of the 1860s is perhaps just its more radical efflorescence. Yet, Turgenev's novel marks a new moment of self-recognition, and the two events that many associated with the novel itself – the appearance of political pamphlets and the fires in St Petersburg – pointed to later developments: on the one hand, radical propaganda through literature and, on the other, violent direct action. Whereas the first was the only resort for early nihilists such as

Chernyshevsky, Dobroliubov and Pisarev, as well as for the Land and Liberty movement of the early 1860s, acts of destructive violence later became much more frequent, especially after the later (and quite separate) Land and Liberty organisation of the mid-1870s fragmented to produce the terrorist group The People's Will. Nihilism fed into the revolutionary movement, and its legacy can certainly be seen in the anarchism of Bakunin and his assertion that destruction was a positive force.[74] It shaped the way Marxism was received in Russia. The idea propagated by Chernyshevsky that Russia could leap directly from feudalism to socialism without experiencing an intervening bourgeois period found its way into the preface Marx and Engels wrote for the second Russian edition of the *Communist Manifesto*.[75] Lenin was an admirer of *What is to be Done?* and himself wrote an important work using Chernyshevsky's title.[76]

The literary tradition of critical evaluation and negation affected almost every writer in some way. Dostoevsky, as we have seen, used a nihilistic hero to debunk nihilism itself, but it is perhaps the case of Tolstoy that is the most notable. In much of his writing, particularly in later years, it is as though via the more aristocratic Pisarev the new plebeian version of the tradition has fused with that of aristocratic scepticism. Even in his earlier writing Tolstoy shows the same mistrust of medicine as Bazarov, and in *War and Peace* he debunks the idea that there is a 'science' of warfare, much as Pisarev had 'destroyed' the science of aesthetics.[77] Indeed, Tolstoy's puritanical, almost utilitarian attitude to aesthetics, as expressed in *What Is Art?* (1896), is very close to Pisarev's views on art. In his later years, when he devoted his energies to making boots, he almost seems to have adopted the famous dictum ascribed to Pisarev of preferring to be a Russian shoemaker rather than a Russian Raphael. This later period is Tolstoy's most polemical, and one of his pamphlets – 'What Then Must We Do?' – seems to echo the title of Chernyshevsky's novel. Most radical of all, and entirely consonant with the nihilists' attempts to dethrone 'prejudices', is Tolstoy's rational *reductio ad absurdum* of the celebration of the Eucharist in his novel *Resurrection*.[78]

The tradition extended into the Soviet period, with the underground literature of *samizdat* attacking and mocking the received wisdom and abstract concepts of official Russia. At the same time, the impact of Russian nihilism may be detected outside the borders of its own specific culture. The nihilists' attack on general principles and insistence on concrete expression seems to anticipate the dichotomy between 'essence' and 'existence' drawn by French Existentialists. Although it is highly unlikely that the author of *Nausea* was ever aware of Cherevanin's 'graveyard

philosophy', it is nevertheless true that Camus was an admirer of
Dostoevsky, and through this filter both Camus and Sartre were in touch
with this 'nihilistic' Russian tradition.[79] Indeed, at least one commentator,
Walter Kaufmann, in his book *Existentialism from Dostoevsky to Sartre*, has
hailed the first part of *Notes from Underground* as a precursor of
Existentialism itself.[80]

The nihilism of the 1860s was very much a literary phenomenon, whose
ideas were carried forward through novels and literary criticism. Although it
was not Turgenev who invented these ideas, his novel *Fathers and Children*
allotted a badge of identification to those who professed them – one which
Pisarev, among others, proudly wore. Moreover, Turgenev subtly suggested
the links of nihilism with the scepticism of previous generations, for as
Pisarev realised (when he argued that Bazarov and the earlier Byronic figure
of Pechorin 'were made of the same stuff' and saw the shade of Pechorin in
Pavel Petrovich): 'In the depths of his soul Pavel Petrovich is just the same
sceptic and empiricist as is Bazarov himself.'[81] At the same time, the
reception of the novel by those who linked it to the St Petersburg fires
was prophetic of the more practical and violent course nihilism would later
take. In further political developments the nihilists' championship of materialist philosophy prepared the ground for Marxism, and the literary doctrine of Socialist Realism would clearly have roots in the aesthetics
propounded by Chernyshevsky.

We have seen that, for all Bazarov's emphasis on reason, he is forced
ultimately to admit that his nihilism stems from feelings. A similar gulf is
apparent in Pisarev, even though he attempts to resolve the dichotomy by
arguing that 'the mind of the new people is in complete harmony with their
feeling, because neither mind nor feeling is distorted by chronic hatred of
the rest of humanity'.[82] Yet such harmony is illusory. It is feelings which in
the end bring about Bazarov's own downfall, and later acts of mindless
violence in Russian society suggest the chronic hatred which Pisarev was too
ready to dismiss.

On the positive side, the nihilism of the younger generation promoted a
critical attitude to outworn, received ideas and to life in general.
Dobroliubov's interest in education, and the whole Sunday school movement, found a reflection in Tolstoy's practical attempts at peasant education. Dobroliubov's own precepts for literary criticism were far-sighted and
basically sound. Pisarev's attitude to aesthetics was severe, but it promoted
thought and analysis of feeling and demanded a balance between aesthetics
and ethics. If, on the one hand, the corrosive rationality of Pomialovsky's
heroes appeared to dissolve conventional morality, Chernyshevsky's

concept of rational egoism (which was in fact self-abnegating altruism) led his heroes towards a strict personal morality. The whole movement's emphasis on ethics – on the rights of women, on 'the starving and unclad' and on the underprivileged in general – had a profound political impact, and its ideas, by whatever crooked paths, fed into the works of the two literary giants of the nineteenth century, Dostoevsky and Tolstoy. Through them they reached a wider world beyond.

NOTES

1. See F. Kuznetsov, *Nigilisty?: D. I. Pisarev i zhurnal 'Russkoe slovo'* (Moscow: Khudozhestvennaia literatura, 1983), p. 21.
2. *Shestidesiatye gody v vospominaniiakh M. Antonovicha i G. Eliseeva* (Leningrad: Academia, 1933), pp. 345–6.
3. N. G. Pomialovskii, *Polnoe sobranie sochinenii*, 2 vols. (Moscow and Leningrad: Academia, 1935). For a translation, see N. G. Pomyalovsky, *Seminary Sketches*, trans. Alfred Kuhn (Ithaca and London: Cornell University Press, 1973).
4. See Pomialovskii, *Polnoe sobranie sochinenii*, vol. II, p. 143.
5. See 'Antropologicheskii printsip v filosofii' in N. G. Chernyshevskii, *Sobranie sochinenii*, 5 vols. (Moscow: Izdatel'stvo 'Pravda', 1974), vol. IV, pp. 200–95. See also N. G. Chernyshevsky, *Selected Philosophical Essays* (Moscow: Foreign Languages Publishing House, 1953), pp. 49–135.
6. See Chernyshevskii, 'Esteticheskie otnosheniia iskusstva k deistvitel'nosti (Dissertatsiia)' in *Sobranie sochinenii*, vol. IV, p. 115.
7. Between 1859 and 1862 numerous schools were set up by private initiative on the 'free' day of Sunday, taking their name from the English phenomenon, but teaching literacy rather than religion. The government eyed them with suspicion and they were closed in 1862.
8. See 'Temnoe tsarstvo' in N. A. Dobroliubov, *Sobranie sochinenii*, 9 vols. (Moscow: Gosudarstvennoe izdatel'stvo khudozhestvennoi literatury, 1961–4), vol. V, p. 86. For a translation, see N. A. Dobrolyubov, *Selected Philosophical Essays*, trans. J. Fineberg (Moscow: Foreign Languages Publishing House, 1956), p. 309.
9. Chernyshevskii, *Sobranie sochinenii*, vol. IV, p. 235.
10. Ibid., pp. 249–50.
11. Chernyshevskii, *Chto delat'?: iz rasskazov o novykh liudiakh* (Leningrad: Nauka, 1975), pp. 67–71.
12. See the arguments of Lopukhov, ibid., part 8 of chapter 2, pp. 67–71.
13. Chernyshevskii, 'Esteticheskie otnosheniia' in *Sobranie sochinenii*, vol. IV, p. 117.
14. Dobroliubov, 'Chto takoe oblomovshchina' in *Sobranie sochinenii*, vol. IV, p. 313. See also *Selected Philosophical Essays*, p. 181.
15. Dobroliubov, 'Luch sveta v temnom tsarstve' in *Sobranie sochinenii*, vol. VI, p. 296. See also *Selected Philosophical Essays*, p. 556.

16. Ibid., p. 291. See also *Selected Philosophical Essays*, p. 550.
17. Ibid., pp. 292, 293. See also *Selected Philosophical Essays*, p. 552.
18. Ibid., p. 293. See also *Selected Philosophical Essays*, p. 553.
19. Ibid., p. 304. See also *Selected Philosophical Essays*, p. 564.
20. See D. I. Pisarev, 'Razrushenie estetiki' in *Sochineniia*, 4 vols. (Moscow: Gosudarstvennoe izdatel'stvo khudozhestvennoi literatury, 1956), vol. III, pp. 418–35.
21. V. Lakshin, 'Ivan Denisovich: Ego druz'ia i nedrugi', *Novyi mir*, 1 (1964), 223–45.
22. Dobroliubov, 'Kogda zhe pridet nastoiashchii den'?' in *Sobranie sochinenii*, vol. VI, p. 97. See also *Selected Philosophical Essays*, p. 390.
23. In a typical youthful reading circle of the 1860s, which strongly rejected the image of Bazarov, E. N. Vodovozova was advised to read the novels of Pomialovsky. See E. N. Vodovozova, *Na zare zhizni i drugie vospominaniia*, 2 vols. (Moscow and Leningrad: Khudozhestvennaia literatura, 1934), vol. II, pp. 134, 141.
24. Pomialovskii, *Polnoe sobranie sochinenii*, vol. I, pp. 184, 213–14.
25. Some of the diverse reactions to Bazarov may be seen in 'The contemporary reaction' in Ivan Turgenev, *Fathers and Sons*, ed. Ralph E. Matlaw, 2nd edn (New York: Norton & Company, 1989), pp. 195–236.
26. I. S. Turgenev, *Polnoe sobranie sochinenii i pisem*, 28 vols. (*Sochineniia*, 15 vols.; *Pis'ma*, 13 vols.) (Moscow and Leningrad: Akademiia nauk SSSR, 1961–8), *Sochineniia*, vol. VIII, pp. 215–16.
27. Ibid., vol. VIII, p. 243.
28. Ibid., p. 246.
29. Ibid., vol. XIV, p. 98.
30. Letter to K. K. Sluchevsky, 14/26 April 1862 in Turgenev, *Polnoe sobranie sochinenii*: *Pis'ma*, vol. IV, p. 380.
31. See Belinsky's letters of 1 March and 8 September 1841 to V. P. Botkin in *A Documentary History of Russian Thought: From the Enlightenment to Marxism*, ed. W. J. Leatherbarrow and D. C. Offord (Ann Arbor: Ardis, 1987), pp. 126, 128.
32. Chernyshevskii, *Chto delat'?*, p. 50.
33. Turgenev, *Polnoe sobranie sochinenii*: *Sochineniia*, vol. VIII, p. 325.
34. Chernyshevskii, *Chto delat'?*, p. 147.
35. Kornei Chukovskii, 'V. A. Sleptsov, ego zhizn' i tvorchestvo' in V. A. Sleptsov, *Sochineniia*, 2 vols. (Moscow: Gosudarstvennoe izdatel'stvo khudozhestvennoi literatury, 1957), vol. I, pp. 4–5.
36. Pisarev, 'Realisty' in *Sochineniia*, vol. III, p. 21.
37. Pisarev, 'Bazarov' in *Sochineniia*, vol. II, p. 7.
38. Pisarev, 'Realisty' in *Sochineniia*, vol. III, p. 21.
39. M. A. Antonovich, 'Asmodei nashego vremeni' in Turgenev, *Ottsy i deti* (St Petersburg: Gumanitarnoe agentstvo 'Akademicheskii proekt', 2000), pp. 243–87.
40. Pisarev, 'Skholastika XIX veka' in *Sochineniia*, vol. I, p. 119.
41. Turgenev, *Polnoe sobranie sochinenii*: *Sochineniia*, vol. VIII, p. 325.

42. Pisarev, 'Bazarov' in *Sochineniia*, vol. II, p. 10.
43. Ibid.
44. Ibid., pp. 11, 27.
45. Pisarev, *Sochineniia*, vol. IV, p. 20.
46. See E. Lampert, *Sons against Fathers: Studies in Russian Radicalism and Revolution* (Oxford: Clarendon Press, 1965), p. 301.
47. For example, Pisarev, 'Realisty' in *Sochineniia*, vol. III, p. 105.
48. Pisarev, *Sochineniia*, vol. II, p. 25.
49. Turgenev, 'Po povodu *Ottsov i detei*' in *Polnoe sobranie sochinenii: Sochineniia*, vol. XIV, pp. 100–2.
50. Pisarev, *Sochineniia*, vol. II, p. 25.
51. Ibid., vol. I. p. 116.
52. Ibid., vol. III, p. 420.
53. Ibid., p. 422.
54. Ibid., p. 423.
55. See Isaiah Berlin, *Russian Thinkers*, ed. Henry Hardy and Aileen Kelly (London: Hogarth Press, 1978), p. 208.
56. See J. S. Mill, *Utilitarianism: On Liberty, Essay on Bentham, together with Selected Writings of Jeremy Bentham and John Austin*, ed. Mary Warnock (London and Glasgow: Fontana, 1962), p. 123. Pushpin was a form of gambling popular in taverns.
57. Pisarev, *Sochineniia*, vol. I, p. 135.
58. Ibid., vol. IV, p. 234.
59. Ibid., p. 49.
60. Ibid., p. 45.
61. Pisarev, 'O broshiure Shedo-Ferroti' in *Sochineniia*, vol. II, p. 28.
62. Pisarev, *Sochineniia*, vol. IV, p. 229.
63. Pisarev, 'Realisty' in *Sochineniia*, vol. III, p. 105.
64. F. M. Dostoevskii, 'Gospodin Shchedrin, ili raskol v nigilistakh' in *Polnoe sobranie sochinenii*, 30 vols. (Leningrad: Nauka, 1972–90), vol. XX, pp. 102–4.
65. Cf. Dostoevskii, *Polnoe sobranie sochinenii*, vol. V, p. 175, and Chernyshevskii, *Chto delat'?*, p. 160.
66. Cf. Dostoevskii, *Polnoe sobranie sochinenii*, vol. V, pp. 105, 112, and Pisarev, *Sochineniia*, vol. III, p. 509.
67. See *F. M. Dostoevskii v vospominaniiakh sovremennikov*, ed. A. S. Dolinin, 2 vols. (Moscow: Izdatel'stvo 'Khudozhestvennaia literatura', 1964), vol. I, p. 430.
68. Turgenev, *Polnoe sobranie sochinenii: Sochineniia*, vol. VIII, p. 216.
69. Ibid., p. 252.
70. Despite the fact that Griboedov's play had long circulated in manuscript form, the full text was not printed until 1861 – the year before the publication of *Fathers and Children*.
71. The first line of the Pushkin poem is 'Dar naprasnyi, dar sluchainyi'; Lermontov's poem begins 'I skuchno i grustno, i nekomu ruku podat'. See A. S. Pushkin, *Polnoe sobranie sochinenii*, 4th edn, 10 vols. (Leningrad: Nauka,

1977–9), vol. III, p. 59; and M. Iu. Lermontov, *Sochineniia*, 6 vols. (Moscow and Leningrad: Izdatel'stvo Akademii nauk SSSR, 1954), vol. II, p. 138.

72. Cf. Pomialovskii, *Polnoe sobranie sochinenii*, vol. II. pp. 187–8 and I. A. Goncharov, *Sobranie sochinenii*, 6 vols. (Moscow: Izdatel'stvo 'Pravda', 1972), vol. IV, p. 63.

73. A. I Gertsen, *Izbrannoe* (Moscow: Izdatel'stvo 'Pravda', 1954), pp. 265–6.

74. M. A. Bakunin, 'The reaction in Germany, a fragment from a Frenchman' in *Michael Bakunin, Selected Writings*, ed. Arthur Lehning (London: Jonathan Cape, 1973), p. 58.

75. This is the theory of the *skachok* (leap), but, although Chernyshevsky was sometimes referred to as 'the Russian Marx', he was not a Marxist. Marx read his works, but it was left to the Russian Marxist Plekhanov to suggest to the authors of the *Communist Manifesto* that Russia might be a special case and could 'leap' from feudalism to socialism.

76. 'What is to be Done?' in *Essential Works of Lenin*, ed. Henry M. Christman (Toronto, New York, London: Bantam Books, 1971), pp. 53–175.

77. See the Epilogue, part 2, of *War and Peace*.

78. See *Resurrection*, chapter 39.

79. A possible conduit for this influence was the Russian émigré Shestov, who moved in these circles and was obsessed by Dostoevsky's *Notes from Underground*.

80. Walter Kaufmann (ed.), *Existentialism from Dostoevsky to Sartre* (Cleveland and New York: Meridian Books, 1956), p. 14.

81. Pisarev, *Sochineniia*, vol. II, p. 23.

82. Ibid., vol. IV, p. 25.

CHAPTER 7

Tradition and counter-tradition: the radical intelligentsia and classical Russian literature

Gary Saul Morson

No class in Russian history has had a more momentous impact on the destinies of that nation or indeed of the modern world.

Martin Malia on the classical Russian intelligentsia[1]

PART I: THE TRADITION

TRADITION AND COUNTER-TRADITION

In 1909, the critic Mikhail Gershenzon observed that 'in Russia, an almost infallible gauge of the strength of an artist's genius is the extent of his hatred for the intelligentsia'.[2] Largely true if somewhat exaggerated, Gershenzon's judgement provides the starting-point for this essay.

By and large, the most important ideas of Russian culture arose from an antagonistic dialogue between the radical intelligentsia and the great writers, with literary critics belonging to each group. On the one hand, we have the highly self-conscious tradition of *intelligenty* (members of the intelligentsia), whose patron saint was Chernyshevsky and which came to include Lavrov, Mikhailovsky, Nechaev, Lenin, Stalin and Trotsky. On the other, we have the counter-tradition of Tolstoy, Dostoevsky and Chekhov. Or again: Bakunin, Dobroliubov, Pisarev and Tkachev are answered by Solovev, Bakhtin and the contributors to the anthology in which Gershenzon's observation appears, *Landmarks* (1909).

Witnessing the danger of radical intelligentsia beliefs, the Russian counter-tradition developed a set of alternatives. Those alternatives probably represent the most durable contribution of Russian thought. Because both sides tended to extreme formulations, they framed issues sharply and made the stakes of intellectual debates especially clear. Russian intellectual history became a kind of uncontrolled experiment testing philosophical ideas.

WHAT IS THE INTELLIGENTSIA?

No recognised system of social analysis, either those known to the intelligentsia itself or those elaborated by modern sociology, makes provision for a 'class' held together only by the bond of 'consciousness', 'critical thought', or moral passion. (Malia)[3]

Virtually all commentators have stressed the difference between the meaning of the word 'intelligentsia' in English and its original meaning in Russian. A Russian *intelligent* was not what we think of as an 'intellectual' and the intelligentsia did not consist of people identified by their taste for independent thought. Quite the contrary, idiosyncratic views virtually disqualified one. We easily think of Tolstoy as an 'intellectual', but it would have seemed paradoxical to call him an *intelligent*. Neither would a well-educated mayor of Moscow qualify. But many barely literate people would.

To be sure, it is difficult to define the Russian term, in part because it was used in broader or narrower senses and in part because its meaning evolved. Especially in the last few decades of tsarist rule, it was possible, for instance, to use the word 'intelligentsia' to mean all educated and technically literate people, who might then be distinguished from the 'classical intelligentsia' that the contributors to *Landmarks* took as the object of their critique. Indeed, the main purpose of *Landmarks* was to transform the intelligentsia from its 'classical' meaning to a much broader one closer to that used in the West today. By the time of the Revolution the 'classical' intelligentsia was perceived as a distinct minority, almost an anachronism, which is another reason that its success in seizing power was not only not inevitable, as hindsight tends to deceive us into imagining, but quite surprising. Another reason that the term 'intelligentsia' had such varied usage was that the very question 'what is the intelligentsia?' often served as a surrogate for the question, how shall Russia be saved?

Despite these difficulties, it is possible to specify a group that virtually everyone would have considered members of the 'classical' intelligentsia. This group emerged more or less around 1860, with the generation of Chernyshevsky, although it was common to recruit retrospectively a few earlier figures – especially Belinsky and Bakunin – either as founders or immediate predecessors. For convenience, we may specify three defining characteristics.

THE FIRST CRITERION: IDENTITY

First, an *intelligent* identified above all *as* an *intelligent*. To be an *intelligent* was not like being a liberal, a professional or an Anglophile, each of which was compatible with a primary identity as (for instance) a nobleman. It was crucial for an *intelligent* to forsake all other allegiances in so far as they might conflict with one's identity as an *intelligent*. That, I take it, is the point of a witty question asked by Stepan Trofimovich in Dostoevsky's *The Devils*: is it wise to hire an engineer who, as a committed *intelligent*, believes in universal destruction? The very fact that Tolstoy used his title of Count was enough to exclude him.

The requirement to identify first of all as an *intelligent* meant that literature should be a form of propaganda. The writer served 'the cause', and all other goals – derisively referred to as 'aestheticism' or 'art for art's sake' – were seen as a form of aristocratic self-indulgence. Understandably, the best writers regarded such demands as incompatible with great art and as orders to lie. When critics insisted that Chekhov declare his 'tendency', he replied: 'do I not protest against lying ... from beginning to end? And is this not a tendency?'[4] As he well knew, for the intelligentsia it was not. The intelligentsia's dogmatic certainty offended Chekhov: 'It is easy to be pure when you are able to hate a devil you do not know and love a God whom it never occurs to you to doubt.'[5] If they ever gain the power they seek, Chekhov wrote, 'such toads and crocodiles will rule in ways not known even at the time of the Inquisition in Spain',[6] a comment that of course turned out to be an understatement.[7]

THE SECOND CRITERION: IDEOLOGY

An *intelligent* subscribed, without hesitation, doubt or scepticism, to a specific set of beliefs, 'each according to his own catechism', as Sergey Bulgakov observed.[8] Those catechisms varied from group to group and from age to age, but they always included a commitment to materialism, atheism, socialism and revolutionism. It was important not only to hold these beliefs but also to refuse to credit that anyone neither stupid nor venal could entertain any others. Indeed, one sign that an intelligentsia in the Russian sense has emerged from the educated, as has often happened, is precisely this refusal. From here to the Soviet treatment of dissidents as insane is but a step. Writers had to negotiate not just the tsar's censorship but also the intelligentsia's 'secondary censorship', as it was commonly called.

The intelligentsia thought of its beliefs as grounded in 'science', but its conception of science was in fact the opposite of science as we usually think of it. Intelligentsia 'science' was not, even in principle, an open-ended enquiry following the evidence wherever it might lead. Rather, the truth was given in advance. 'Science' meant not free enquiry but a commitment to a materialist metaphysics and the faith that an absolutely certain body of doctrine could redeem the world. It is precisely in the dissected frog that the salvation of the Russian people lies, proclaimed Pisarev, who was referring to Bazarov's conviction in Turgenev's *Fathers and Children* that there is no essential difference between people and frogs and that by dissecting one, a scientist can learn all about the other. In the Soviet period, such thinking led to the rejection of scientific theories on metaphysical grounds.[9]

Both for classical *intelligenty* and their Soviet heirs, advance criteria for truth were also political. Berdiaev referred to 'the almost insane tendency to judge philosophical doctrines and truths according to political and utilitarian criteria';[10] by 'utilitarian' he meant utility for making a revolution. Berdiaev continued:

love for egalitarian justice ... paralysed love for the truth and almost destroyed any interest in the truth ... The intelligentsia ... succumbed to the temptation of the Grand Inquisitor, who demanded the renunciation of truth in the name of man's happiness. The intelligentsia's basic moral premise is summed up by the formula: let truth perish, if its death will enable the people to live better and will make men happier; down with truth if it stands in the way of the sacred cry, 'down with autocracy'.[11]

Berdiaev and others stressed the danger of refuting theories by showing that they are insufficiently leftist. 'We developed police-search methods for judging philosophical endeavours and movements ... To refute philosophical theories on the ground that they do not favour Populism or Social Democracy is to scorn truth. No one will listen to a philosopher suspected of being "reactionary" (and what don't we call "reactionary"!), for no one is really interested in philosophy or truth *per se*.'[12] One sign that a culture has developed an intelligentsia in the Russian sense is precisely the prevalence of this kind of argument.[13]

Groups of Russian *intelligenty* might differ about how to realise socialism, but they never doubted the leading role of the intelligentsia itself. Like Raskolnikov in *Crime and Punishment*, they presumed their own superiority, their entitlement to rule and their 'right to transgress'. Dostoevsky foresaw that in intelligentsia ideology there would always be a passive 'people' that could be saved only by the efforts of *intelligenty* acting in its name. In *The Devils*, the *intelligent* Shigalev suggests as a final solution of the question the division of mankind into two unequal parts: 'One-tenth enjoys absolute liberty and unbounded power over the other nine-tenths. The others have to give up all individuality and … through boundless submission, will by a series of regenerations attain primeval innocence … "What I propose is not contemptible; it's paradise, an earthly paradise, and there can be no other on earth", Shigalev pronounced authoritatively.'[14]

THE THIRD CRITERION: INVERSE MANNERS

An *intelligent* was expected to live a certain kind of life: in large part, norms derived from Chernyshevsky's *What is to be Done?*, which was almost certainly the most widely read Russian literary work of the nineteenth century. Lenin declared that the book played a decisive role in turning him into a revolutionary.[15]

Serving as a 'how-to' book for daily conduct, *What is to be Done?* offered models for work, speech, dress, hair-style and sex. One commentator remembered: 'We made the novel into a kind of Koran.'[16] Noblemen took lessons in bad manners of the prescribed sort so as to be accepted into the intelligentsia. Or consider the story Joseph Frank tells of how Dostoevsky met his second wife. When his stenographer refused a cigarette, Dostoevsky realised that, since radicals were expected to smoke, she might not be a revolutionary. Why, he wondered, she might even believe in God – as, in fact, she did. Though educated, she was no *intelligentka*.[17]

This rigid code prescribed what might be thought of as *inverse manners*: it was *comme il faut* to be *comme il ne faut pas*. One simply had to have dirty fingernails, dress badly, flaunt one's inability to understand art and, in the case of women, call attention to one's promiscuity. The repulsive Kukshina in Turgenev's *Fathers and Children* self-consciously strains to perform all these radical duties, as if her prescribed hedonism felt like taking medicine.

The regulation of daily behaviour also signified that *everything is political*, and so no aspect of life should be left to its own devices. The *intelligent*, as Gershenzon observed, became a slave to politics and looked for political meaning in everything, a sort of 'tyranny of civic activism'.[18] Berdiaev called for 'not only political liberation but also liberation from the oppressive power of politics'.[19] If there is nothing outside the political, then there is no place for privacy, an individual self or a personal quest for meaning. On the contrary, as Gershenzon observed, 'the meaning of life was established beforehand, and it was the same for everyone, with no individual differences'.[20] No less than its theories, the intelligentsia's behavioural codes paved the way to totalitarianism. A group's belief that everything is political constitutes another sign that it has become an intelligentsia in the radical Russian sense.

HOW DID DOSTOEVSKY KNOW?

So far as I am aware, Dostoevsky was the only nineteenth-century thinker to foresee that the twentieth would be history's bloodiest and would engender the phenomenon we have come to call totalitarianism. In *The Devils*, Shigalev and Petr Stepanovich advocate a system of universal spying, the regulation of life to the smallest degree, the elimination of 'a hundred million heads' and (as in Mao's cultural revolution or Pol Pot's execution of the literate) the deliberate destruction of genius or talent, all in the name of equality. Petr Stepanovich explains: 'A high level of education and science is only possible for great intellects and these are not wanted ... Cicero will have his tongue cut out, Copernicus will have his eyes put out, Shakespeare will be stoned ... Complete equality! ... Only the necessary is necessary.'[21]

How did Dostoevsky know? The answer, I think, is that, having once been a conspirator himself, he grasped the mentality of the intelligentsia and projected what it would do should it ever gain power.

Dostoevsky was aware as well that the fervour sweeping the intelligentsia was essentially apocalyptic in character. Analysing Bolshevik rule, Berdiaev attributed its attempts to transform nature and human nature, as well as its desire to establish what we have come to call totalitarianism, to an essentially eschatological impulse, which he saw as a reflection (or distortion) of the Russian Orthodox tradition. He attached immense importance, therefore, to the fact that the conventional social origin for an *intelligent* was either seminarian or child of a priest – a description that applies to Chernyshevsky, Dobroliubov and Stalin. He therefore attributed great significance to the fascination early Bolsheviks and other *intelligenty* had for a thinker as strange as Fedorov, who saw humanity's easily achievable 'common task' as the resurrection of our 'fathers' by technological means that he referred to as 'the patrification of matter'. Because many molecules must have escaped the earth, Fedorov proposed space travel as a way to gather the necessary material for resurrection. Intellectual historians routinely point out that Tsiolkovsky, the founder of the Russian space programme, was a disciple of Fedorov.

For that matter, neither Dostoevsky nor Berdiaev was immune to eschatological fervour. For a brief period, Dostoevsky came to believe that the end of the world would literally arrive in months, and Berdiaev saw Bolsheviks as distorters of the Russian Orthodox apocalypticism that he valued.

REVOLUTIONISM

With its quasi-mystical belief in the transformative power of political ideology, the radical intelligentsia was inclined not just to revolution but to what Semen Frank called 'revolutionism'. One may accept revolution on purely tactical grounds, but 'revolutionism on principle'[22] involves the love of revolution as such. What really matters is the thrill of destruction, experienced as a kind of metaphysical jolt. Bakunin's aphorism – 'the will to destroy is also a creative will' – voices this sentiment and, as Frank explains: 'the qualifier "auch" [also] has long disappeared from this aphorism; destruction is no longer seen as *one* of the means of creation, but has been identified with it altogether ... Thus revolutionism merely reflects the metaphysical absolutisation of the value of destruction.'[23]

Russian terrorism also had a distinct metaphysical side: it implicitly affirmed the metaphysical freedom both of the victim (for why else would killing him matter?) and of the terrorist himself (for killing him). Indeed, Marxist historical determinists sometimes objected to terrorist ideology for just such implications.

For Petr Struve, the revolutionism of the intelligentsia was 'a moral error' because it sacrificed the lives of others without their consent, and a political error because 'it was based on the notion that society's "progress" need not be the fruit of human improvement, but could be instead a jackpot to be won at the gambling table of history'.[24] Struve's reference to gambling invokes a key simile of Dostoevsky's. In Dostoevsky's *The Gambler*, Aleksey plays roulette not for wealth but for the thrill of a moment in which one spin of the wheel could leave him either a pauper or a Rothschild. The normal laws of life are suspended, and winning represents a sort of instantaneous leap from necessity to freedom. Aleksey becomes addicted to such moments, and when he wins, he wastes the money so that he can eventually experience another one. In several of his novels, Dostoevsky discovers the same ecstasy in the instant just before an expected revolution, a murder or an epileptic seizure. As Bakhtin might say, each is a congealed 'suddenly'. For Prince Myshkin in *The Idiot*, such 'suddenlys' explain 'the extraordinary saying [in the Apocalypse] that *there shall be no more time*', but they are nevertheless 'a disease' leading inevitably to insanity.[25]

Both Aleksey and his opposite, the prosaic Englishman Mr Astley, explicitly identify gambling addiction with Russianness and Russianness with a taste for sudden change. Revolutionism and gambling both express a refusal to work, that is, to accomplish a long series of small tasks in order to accumulate wealth gradually, to improve one's character bit by bit or to reform society over time. Rather, everything must happen in a vertiginous 'suddenly'. As *The Gambler* concludes, Mr Astley observes: 'To my mind all Russians are like that, or disposed to be like that. If it is not roulette it is something similar. The exceptions are very rare. You are not the first who does not understand the meaning of work (I am not talking of your peasantry). Roulette is a game pre-eminently for Russians.'[26]

'I am not talking of your peasantry': Mr Astley characterises the mindset of the intelligentsia and all those educated people who dwell in its shadow.

PART II: THE COUNTER-TRADITION REPLIES

THEORETISM

The counter-tradition identified the intelligentsia's core error as its blind faith in theory or, to use Bakhtin's term, its 'theoretism'.[27] The theoretist regards historical, social and psychological facts as mere instantiations of timeless laws, the way the moon's position can be precisely determined using Newtonian mechanics. For the theoretist there is no 'surplus', nothing *left over* that the theory does not explain. If we do not have such a theory yet, we soon will: that is the faith (for Tolstoy, the superstition) of the intelligentsia.

Of course, such 'moral Newtonianism', as Elie Halévy famously called it, was not unique to Russia.[28] Thinkers as diverse as Marx, Bentham, Comte, Malinowski and Lévi-Strauss have all assumed that a social science in the strong sense is feasible, if not actually on the verge of realisation. What is special about the Russian intelligentsia was the depth and extremity of this faith, along with the belief that the theory was already sufficiently developed to be imposed immediately by force.

Critiques of moral Newtonianism of course existed outside Russia, but in response to the intelligentsia's extreme faith in theory Russian writers developed anti-theoretism with special profundity. We often speak of the Russian novel as ideological or philosophical, but it would be more accurate to speak of it as anti-ideological and anti-philosophical. Outside Russia, George Eliot, Joseph Conrad, George Orwell and others also wrote anti-philosophical novels of ideas, but such works *define* the Russian tradition as no other and arguably constitute its greatest achievement.

More recently, the anti-theoretist argument of the Russian novel has led to a renewed appreciation of the wisdom, typically overlooked by theorists, that is contained in ordinary practices. We see the Russian novel's direct influence on Wittgenstein, who in turn shaped Stephen Toulmin's argument that not just theoretical rationality (*episteme*) but also practical reason (*phronesis*) must play a role in solving human problems.[29]

THE MASTERPLOT

He was not a nihilist for nothing! (Turgenev, *Fathers and Children*)

The masterplot of the novel of ideas, perfected in Russia, tests the theory in which its hero believes not by constructing a logical critique but by tracing the theory's roots in biography and exploring its consequences in practice. An *irony of origins* shows how ideas purportedly based on 'science' actually derive from a psychic need, and an *irony of unwelcome outcomes* demonstrates that the world is much more complex than the theory has allowed.[30] In *Fathers and Children*, we see Arkady embracing nihilism because it makes him feel grown up and Bazarov, who believes love to be nothing but a physiological reaction, ensnared in the passion celebrated by the minnesingers and troubadours.

In *The Brothers Karamazov*, Ivan, who asserts that all is permitted and that even if there is such a thing as moral responsibility it pertains not to wishes but only to actions, comes to feel guilty for a crime he has merely desired. As the devil that haunts him points out, Ivan wants to justify amoralism itself with a moralistic theory: 'That's all very charming', the devil chides, 'but if you want to swindle why do you want a moral sanction for doing it? But that's our modern Russian [*intelligent*] all over. He can't bring himself to swindle without a moral sanction.'[31]

Such novels of ideas narrate *the overcoming of theoretism*. When Raskolnikov confesses, he still believes that his theory was correct even if he could not live up to it. He attains wisdom only when, in Siberia, he overcomes the theoretist mindset altogether: 'Life had stepped into the place of theory',[32] the author concludes. This change finally allows a new story to begin, 'the story of the gradual renewal of a man, the story of his gradual regeneration, of his gradual passing from one world into another, of his initiation into a new unknown life'.[33] The repetition of the word 'gradual' (*postepennyi*) contrasts with Raskolnikov's earlier taste for sudden or revolutionary transformation. The appreciation of a 'new unknown life' reflects his recognition that uncertainty and imperfect knowledge are constituent factors of human existence.

Ivan Karamazov regards it as a weakness that, notwithstanding his dark theory, he goes on living. 'In spite of logic', Ivan loves 'the sticky green leaves that open in the spring', a love that he attributes to a purely biological imperative – 'the force of the Karamazovs'. Alesha replies that what Ivan takes as weakness is in fact wisdom. Not theory but love of the sheer process of living justifies existence:

'I love the sticky leaves in spring ... It's not a matter of intellect or logic, it's loving with one's inside, with one's stomach ... Do you understand anything of my tirade, Alyosha?'
'I understand too well, Ivan ... I am awfully glad that you have such a longing for life ... I think everyone should love life above everything in the world.'
'Love life more than the meaning of it?'
'Certainly, love it, regardless of logic as you say, it must be regardless of logic; and it's only then one will understand the meaning of it.'[34]

Earlier in the novel, Father Zosima has told Madame Khokhlakova that although God, immortality and meaningfulness cannot be proven, one can become convinced of them if one lives a life of active love. One gets things the wrong way round if one demands reasons to live a good life. Rather, living a good life leads to faith stronger than any reasons. Proceed not from the top down, but from the bottom up: that is the constant lesson of Russian fiction.

If we live right, we can appreciate meaningfulness that we cannot express. Then existential problems are not solved but vanish. So Tolstoy's Levin discovers in *Anna Karenina* when he recognises 'not merely the pride of intellect, but the stupidity of intellect'.[35] The meaning he has sought has always been there, invisibly before his eyes, but unrecognised so long as he sought it in theory. 'And here is a miracle, the sole miracle possible, surrounding me on all sides, and I never noticed it! ... I have discovered nothing. I have found out only what I [already] knew.'[36] The novel teaches us to rediscover truths too familiar to remember.

The close of Wittgenstein's *Tractatus*, written under the influence of Dostoevsky and Tolstoy, echoes Levin's discoveries, at times almost word for word:

The solution of the problem of life is seen in the vanishing of the problem.

(Is this not the reason why those who have found after a long period of doubt that the sense of life became clear to them have been unable to say what constituted that sense?)

There are, indeed, things that cannot be put into words. They *make themselves manifest*.[37]

RETURN TO CASUISTRY

When he lives right, Levin also learns that he can arrive at ethical judgements better than any provided by theory. So does Pierre in *War and Peace*. In each novel, Tolstoy provides a long list of good ethical decisions that the hero learns to make without saying how he makes them. Levin now knows that he

must hire labourers as cheaply as possible; but to hire men in bond, paying them in advance less than the current rate of wages, was what he must not do, even though it was very profitable. Selling straw to the peasants in times of scarcity was what he might do ... but the tavern ... must be ignored ... To Petr, who was paying a moneylender ten per cent a month, he must lend a sum of money to set him free. But he could not let off peasants who did not pay their rent.[38]

And the list goes on, with no common principle identified. Tolstoy's point is that there is no such principle, for life is too complex for any ethical theory. We must rely instead on an *educated sensitivity to particular cases* – that is, to casuistry in the original sense of the word. Tolstoy's call for a revival of casuistry – reasoning by cases – has influenced contemporary ethical thought. As Albert Jonsen and Stephen Toulmin have argued, casuistry goes hand in hand with renewed respect for the unformalisable wisdom of practical reason (*phronesis*).[39] Though rejected as unphilosophical since the seventeenth century, practical reason and casuistry found a home in the realist novel, whose tacit moral assumptions Tolstoy made explicit and available.

When the discussion turns to the Eastern War, to which Levin objects even though most educated people across the political spectrum believed in it, Koznyshev asks Levin whether he would kill a Turk about to torture and murder a Bulgarian baby and, presuming he would, why he does not support Russian military efforts to prevent Turkish atrocities in Bulgaria. Why should it matter that the atrocities are happening at a distance?

Levin replies that he does not know what he would do in Koznyshev's hypothetical situation but would decide *on the instant*. Although this answer might seem intellectually unsatisfying – Levin gives no principle by which he would decide – for Tolstoy it is the right one. No principle *should* decide in advance because the particularities of the situation are too complex and variable to be foreseen and the consequences of a wrong decision either way are too great.

Tolstoy here makes several key anti-theoretist points. He stresses not only the superiority of educated moral sensitivity over principles, but also the sheer complexity and unpredictability of the world in which moral decisions must be made. If the world were like Newtonian astronomy, in which each moment is the automatic and predictable outcome of earlier moments, one could make decisions in advance and presentness would not be needed. But the world is not 'Newtonian' in this sense. Much more complicated than any ethical theory could accommodate, it more closely resembles battle as Kutuzov and later Prince Andrey understand it in *War and Peace* – too complex for any theory and often too surprising for advance judgements. Therefore, *presentness matters*. No matter what social scientific theory may assert, the radical contingency of things means there is always what Bakhtin thought of as 'surprisingness' and therefore always a need for what Tolstoy called 'moral alertness'.

Tolstoy's ideas about the relation of distance to ethical action are also crucial to this passage for two reasons. First, by a sort of moral inverse square law, the further we are from a situation the clearer it seems to be, while situations before our eyes – say, in our own family – tend to baffle us. The reason is that the greater the distance, the fewer contingencies we see and so the answers seem deceptively easy. Second, despite what most ethical theorists since the seventeenth century have argued, moral obligations must take into account persons. Kant notwithstanding, we do not owe the same moral debt and concern to people we have never met on the other side of the world as to our immediate family. Tolstoy here revives the Stoic idea that morality works by something resembling concentric circles. The further we get from our family, our neighbours and our community, the less moral obligation we actually have. Indeed, it is a moral error to assume that the same principles apply in near and distant cases.

THE TELESCOPE

At the end of *War and Peace*, Pierre abandons the quest for theory and focuses on the immense complexity of ordinary events taking place right before his eyes.

He felt like a man who, after straining his eyes to peer into the remote distance, finds what he was seeking at his very feet ... He had equipped himself with a mental telescope and gazed into the distance where the petty and commonplace that were hidden in the mists of distance had seemed to him great and infinite only because they are not clearly visible ... Now, however, he had learned to see the great, the eternal, the infinite in everything, and therefore, in order to look at it, to enjoy his contemplation of it, he naturally discarded the telescope through which he had till then been gazing over the heads of men, and joyfully surveyed the ever-changing, eternally great, and infinite life around him.[40]

The telescope is theory. Throughout the novel, Pierre has assumed that for meaning to exist, some theory must explain everything. When he believes he has such theory, life makes perfect sense, and when he does not, he despairs. As Raskolnikov lets life take the place of theory, so Pierre at last 'throws away the telescope'.

For the counter-tradition, with its respect for the wisdom of practice, the proper role of theory is never to dictate to experience; rather, it is a series of tentative generalisations from experience.

PROSAICS

These Russian heroes learn two closely related truths. First, the most important events in life are not grand and dramatic but small and ordinary. Second, time is always open and uncertainty pertains to the very nature of things. I like to call the combination of these two truths 'prosaics'. The exploration of prosaics constitutes the primary intellectual contribution of the Russian counter-tradition.

Let us consider several implications of prosaics.

First: the world is infinitely more complex than any theory

If time is open, the dream of a social science in the strong sense is entirely without foundation. For the author of *War and Peace*, all attempts to reduce events to a set of simple laws resemble either Pierre's numerology or General Pfuhl's 'science' of warfare. When Pfuhl wins, he claims the victory as validation of his supposed science, and when he loses, he claims the same!

The loss, it seems, always results from failure to execute his orders precisely, and, since orders can never be executed precisely, his theory is immune to disconfirmation. For Tolstoy, all purported social sciences, existing or to come, necessarily rely on one or another fallacy that – by something analogous to what Tolstoy calls 'stencil work' – excludes contrary evidence.

Second: the most important events and people are ordinary

As Kutuzov knows, battles are won not by commanders but by line officers, who can exploit the fleeting opportunities that no advance strategy could ever predict. In a key passage of *War and Peace*, we see Rostov take advantage of such an opportunity.

As with ordinary events, so with ordinary people: they are the ones who make the difference. In one of the novel's essays, Tolstoy identifies the apparently unremarkable Dokhturov as 'a noiselessly revolving transmission gear' that truly makes things happen. Historians barely mention Dokhturov, but 'it is this [very] silence about him that is the most cogent testimony to his merit'.[41]

In *Anna Karenina*, the noiselessly revolving transition gear is Dolly. If by the hero of a novel we mean the person who best represents the author's values, then the hero of *Anna Karenina* is Dolly. Anna, to be sure, is more dramatic, but Tolstoy's point is that we tend to identify true life with high drama whereas in fact it is a matter of prosaic moments and everyday efforts. In *War and Peace*, the outcome of the war is determined by ordinary people with no thought of acting 'historically' but whose efforts, taken together, matter far more than those of more dramatic figures who think of a grand historical narrative.

Third: perceptual fallacies lead us to mistake what really matters

To retrain our perception, Russian literature often places key characters and events at the margins, where we see but do not notice them precisely because they are so ordinary and do not stand out. But what if, in history and in individual lives, the sum total of ordinary events matters much more than the rare extraordinary ones? To identify noticeability with importance, Tolstoy writes, is like concluding from a view of a distant hill where only treetops are visible that the region contains nothing but trees.

Readers are often led to repeat the perceptual errors of characters, but because they can reread – go back and see how their perceptions and memory have misled them – they can learn to recognise perceptual fallacies and so to see what would otherwise remain hidden in plain view. I like to call this Russian device *open camouflage*, and its pedagogic point is to enable us to see more wisely. Both Tolstoy and Chekhov perfected versions of it.[42]

Fourth: the more finely we perceive a moment, the less it fits a pattern

One reason Russian novels are so long is that they try to see social and mental events with ever-increasing fineness. Tolstoy explains with an anecdote:

[The painter] Bryullov one day corrected a pupil's study. The pupil, having glanced at the altered drawing, exclaimed: 'Why you only touched it a tiny bit, but it is quite another thing.' Bryullov replied: 'Art begins where the tiny bit begins.'

That saying is strikingly true not only of art but of all life. One may say that true life begins where the tiny bit begins – where what seem to us minute and infinitely small alterations take place. True life is not lived where great external changes take place – where people move about, clash, fight and slay one another – it is lived only where these tiny, tiny, infinitesimally small changes occur.[43]

Turning to *Crime and Punishment*, Tolstoy contends that there never was a single moment when Raskolnikov decided to kill the old woman, which is why his search to understand the decision to murder is fruitless. The murder resulted not from a decision but from a *climate of mind* that was in turn shaped by countless tiny alterations of consciousness and small choices about quite other matters. Raskolnikov lived his true life

when he was lying on the sofa in his room, deliberating not at all about the old woman, nor even whether it is or is not permissible at the will of one man to wipe from the face of the earth another, unnecessary and harmful man, but whether he ought to live in Petersburg or not, whether he ought to accept money from his mother or not, and on other questions not at all relating to the old woman. And then ... the question whether he would or would not kill the old woman was decided. That question was decided – not when, having killed one old woman, he stood before another, axe in hand – but when he was doing nothing and was only thinking, when only his consciousness was active: and in that consciousness, tiny, tiny alterations were taking place ...

Tiny, tiny alterations – but on them depend the most immense and terrible consequences.[44]

Tolstoy was the supreme artist of 'tiny alterations'. The unsurpassed verisimilitude that has led critics to say that Tolstoy's works are not art but life derives largely from his ability to separate consciousness into finer and finer pieces. Where others see a simple, instantaneous action, Tolstoy describes a series of minute steps.

As Dostoevsky knew, Tolstoy alone has described Christian love of one's enemies in a psychologically plausible way, once in *War and Peace* (Prince Andrey) and once in *Anna Karenina* (Karenin). He did so, I believe, by dividing the transition to Christian love into a series of tiny steps, each of which plausibly follows from the preceding one; and having granted each step, we grant the result without ever having decided to do so.

Fifth: plot is an index of error

Where there is plot, life is lived badly. That, I take it, is what Tolstoy meant by his most famous sentence: 'All happy families resemble each other; each unhappy family is unhappy in its own way.' His notebooks for *Anna Karenina* and the text of *War and Peace* several times record a French proverb: 'Happy people have no history.' It is in that sense that happy people resemble each other. But unhappy people have a story, and each story is different.

That was also the idea that inspired Chekhov's great 'dramas of inaction'. Those who, like Uncle Vania, imagine that life must be eventful to be meaningful mistake what is really important, and the real heroine of the play – underappreciated, like Dolly – is the devoted but unromantic Sonia.

We tend to be most fascinated with high drama, and that fascination leads us to identify love with romance – the love of Romeo and Juliet, Tristan and Isolde or Anna and Vronsky – rather than the prosaic, family love of Levin and Kitty. For Tolstoy, it is the latter that really matters. As romance thrives on mystery, prosaic love cultivates daily intimacy. As *War and Peace* may be seen as an attack on the romanticisation of war, *Anna Karenina* discredits the romanticisation of love. Although we have long ceased to celebrate war, the ideology of romantic love is, if anything, even stronger than in Tolstoy's day.

THE RUSSIAN IDEA OF EVIL

Like good, most evil is ordinary and even (to use Hannah Arendt's word) 'banal'.[45] It derives primarily not from alien or mysterious sources, but from people like ourselves – indeed, from us. We witness, and are, its causes.

And so in *Crime and Punishment* Svidrigailov imagines hell not as Milton's Pandemonium but as a spider-infested bathhouse in the country. As the personification of evil, the devil in *The Brothers Karamazov* appears as the sort of companionable and witty person we all enjoy. He tells Ivan: 'I repeat, moderate your expectations, don't demand of me "everything great and noble" … You are really angry with me for not having appeared to you in a red glow, with thunder and lightning, with scorched wings, but have shown myself in such a modest form … How could such a vulgar devil visit such a great man as you!'[46]

For Dostoevsky, most evil derives not from the occasional monstrosity but from our daily wishes for harm to others. These wishes create the atmosphere in which crime is likely. They are more responsible for it than the actual criminal act, just as the person who douses a house with oil, not the one who happens to cause a spark, is primarily responsible for the ensuing fire. We all wish evil, which is why the Gospel tells us that wishes as well as actions have moral value and why Father Zosima insists that everyone is responsible. To reduce evil, we must improve not just social institutions but also ourselves by what Dostoevsky liked to call 'microscopic efforts'.

As Tolstoy wrote insightfully about *Crime and Punishment*, Dostoevsky wrote wisely about *Anna Karenina*. In it he discovered the idea of ordinary evil embodied in Stiva. Crucially, Stiva causes great harm without a shred of malice, but simply because he has trained himself not to notice whatever might interfere with his pleasure. For Tolstoy, evil not only is undramatic, it may be entirely negative. It does not even require evil wishes, just neglect. Most (if not the worst) evil derives from *in*action.

The fact that, like most of Stiva's acquaintances, readers usually find him congenial is precisely Tolstoy's point: if evil were not so attractive, we would not have so much of it. Dostoevsky understood Stiva in just this way, and it appears that the devil in *The Brothers Karamazov* is partly modelled after him.

THE PROSAIC VIEW OF TIME

Critics of the radical intelligentsia stressed that revolutionism leads to waste and the abandonment of ordinary decencies as somehow reactionary. The prosaic life we live every day is to be sacrificed to the epic deeds and utopian kingdom that ideology promises. In the prosaic view, by contrast, we owe our greatest obligation to people now alive.

For Bakhtin, the utopian mentality bleeds the present white because it 'always sees the segment of the future that separates the present from the end as lacking value; this separating segment of time loses its significance and interest, it is merely an unnecessary continuation of an indefinitely long present'.[47] But it is in just such a 'separating segment' that people actually live. For that matter, that is where they have always lived and will always live. The future is not a different kind of time, but just another present that has not yet arrived.

In contrast to the intelligentsia, Bakhtin contended that morality requires placing the greatest value on the present and the near future. To allow oneself either petty cruelty or revolutionary violence in the name of a glorious future means using politics to create an 'alibi' for responsibility. But 'there is no alibi', Bakhtin repeats; for what I can do at this moment, no one else can do, ever.

In perhaps his most famous lines, Herzen cautions against sacrificing living people for a utopian goal:

Do you truly wish to condemn all human beings alive to-day to the sad role of caryatids supporting a floor for others some day to dance on … or of wretched galley slaves, up to their knees in mud, dragging a barge filled with some mysterious treasure and with the humble words 'progress in the future' inscribed on its bows? … This alone should serve as a warning to people: an end that is infinitely remote is not an end, but, if you like, a trap; an end must be nearer – it ought to be, at the very least, the labourer's wage, or pleasure in the work done.[48]

THE BOURGEOIS VIRTUES

To respect everyday life, one must value the ordinary virtues and habits that sustain it. The intelligentsia typically rejected such virtues as 'bourgeois', an attitude its critics deemed another kind of aristocratic arrogance.

Gershenzon got into considerable trouble for his characterisation of intelligentsia attitudes towards daily life:

What has our intelligentsia's thought been doing for the last half-century? … A handful of revolutionaries has been going from house to house and knocking on every door: 'Everyone into the street! It's shameful to stay at home!' And every consciousness, the halt, the blind, and the armless, poured out into the square; not one stayed at home. For half a century they have been milling about, wailing and quarreling. At home, there is dirt, destitution, but the master doesn't care. He is out in public, saving the people – and that is easier and more entertaining than drudgery at home.[49]

Chekhov relentlessly criticised such contempt for ordinary decencies and bourgeois virtues. In his famous letter to his brother Nikolay, he wrote that 'people of culture must fulfil the following conditions':

1. They respect the human personality and are therefore forbearing, gentle, courteous, and compliant …

2. They are sympathetic not only to beggars and cats.
3. They respect the property of others and therefore pay their debts.
4. They ... do not lie even in small matters ... They don't pose ...
5. ... They do not say: 'I'm misunderstood!' ...
8. They develop an aesthetic taste. They cannot bring themselves to fall asleep in their clothes ... breathe foul air, walk across a floor that has been spat on ... ... Such are cultured people ... What you need is constant work.[50]

Respect property? Pay one's debts? Develop an aesthetic sense and respect not political activity but 'constant work'? As Chekhov well knew, such advice challenged intelligentsia precepts.

Chekhov's radical innovations in the drama derive from his prosaic values, above all his suspicion of grand gestures and his appreciation of inconspicuous goodness. Whereas most plays depict a dramatic world in which characters' dramatic actions are appropriate, the world of Chekhov's plays is as prosaic as our own, so dramatic actions appear as they really are, histrionic. Chekhov's major characters act as if they were characters in a play, which is ironic because they *are* characters in a play. The true heroes behave decently in the background. As in Tolstoy, if we value most the people who take up the most dramatic space, we have missed the author's central point. The key moral is given to Elena Andreevna, who gradually learns to overcome her taste for drama and high romance: 'Ivan Petrovich, you are an educated, intelligent man, and I should think you would understand that the world is being destroyed not by crime and fire, but by ... all these petty squabbles.'[51]

WORK

Chekhov and other counter-traditional thinkers faulted the ideologists for under-appreciating work. Semen Frank pointed out that the intelligentsia seemed to care only about the redistribution but not the creation of wealth, which requires productive work.

But it is a philosophical error and a moral sin to absolutise distribution and forget production or creation for its own sake ... It is time we finally understood that our life is not simply unjust, but is primarily poor and squalid, and that the poverty-stricken cannot become rich if they devote their attention solely to the equal distribution of their few pennies.[52]

Frank finds it significant that the intelligentsia pays the highest respect to 'journalists', who popularise and distribute knowledge, rather than to the scientists or writers who actually create it.

In the fiction of Tolstoy, Dostoevsky and (above all) Chekhov, the people who really matter are not those who move the plot, but those who work. In *Uncle Vania*, Sonia's labour produces the wealth to support the others' banal theorising and melodramatic posturing. The play's title tacitly points to her as the true but barely noticed hero: although she is not explicitly named, she alone could call Voinitsky 'Uncle Vania'.[53]

A passage in *Anna Karenina* that probably has no parallel in world literature describes the moment-to-moment psychology of labour as Levin learns to mow. The passage seems to be the first description of the psychological state that Mihaly Csikszsentmihalyi has called 'flow'.[54] Indeed, the novel measures how adequately characters understand life by their attitude to work. Even more than Levin, Dolly turns out to be, by this standard, the one who most surely grasps what life is all about. Though unpaid and unrewarded even by recognition, her work with her children can create in them the kind of depth that Vronsky, who has never had a family life, will always lack.

Most of Dolly's life consists of anxious labour to see that her children do not fall ill and die, are properly clothed and fed, are educated to prepare them for the future and, above all, become what she thinks of as 'decent' people. We are told that despite the cares that occupy her time, the children 'were even now repaying her in small joys for her sufferings. These joys were so small that they passed unnoticed, like gold in sand, and at moments she could see nothing but the pain, nothing but sand; but there were good moments too when she saw nothing but the joy, nothing but gold.'[55]

Like the causes of historical events in *War and Peace*, the most important moments in individual lives do not call attention to themselves but pass unnoticed like gold in sand. They remain openly camouflaged, hidden in plain view. Like everything truly important, they are too prosaic to form a plot and so even the reader can easily miss them.

OPEN TIME AND THE PROCESSUAL VIEW OF LIFE

Materialism and the dream of a social science have usually entailed a faith in closed time. By definition, time is closed if, at any given moment, one and only one thing can happen. Whatever does not happen could not happen. In this view, people may mistakenly perceive multiple paths and agonise over choice, but in fact the future is given, has in a sense already happened in the way that the ending of a novel is already there even if we are still only halfway through our reading.

The thinkers of the Russian counter-tradition tried to show that we live not in closed but in open time. For them, and for those whom they have influenced, possibilities really do outnumber actualities. As Stephen Jay Gould likes to say in describing his version of Darwinism, if we could play the tape over, identical situations might have different outcomes.[56] *Something else* might happen, and so each moment contains what Bakhtin calls 'eventness'.

The future does not exist at all until we make it, and we can choose to make one future rather than another. Herzen seems to initiate this line of argument in *From the Other Shore*: 'there is no libretto [to history]. If there were a libretto, history would lose all interest, become unnecessary, boring, ludicrous ... In history, all is improvisation, all is will, all is *ex tempore*; there are no frontiers, no itineraries.'[57]

Time is itself *ex tempore*. Tolstoy apparently had such passages in mind when, in *War and Peace*, he argued that history displays genuine contingency: events that (as Aristotle defined the term) could either be or not be. Sometimes things happen just 'for some reason', a favourite phrase of Tolstoy's. Nineteenth- and early twentieth-century thought tried to rescue social science by reducing contingent events to statistical laws. Random variations supposedly cancel each other out. But in recent decades chaos theory has returned to Tolstoy's point that sometimes contingencies do not cancel but concatenate in unpredictable ways.

Prince Andrey achieves wisdom when he recognises what Kutuzov has known all along: minute and unforeseeable incidents can interact in countless unpredictable ways that preclude 'scientific' deduction of outcomes. When Pierre tells Andrey that a good general can 'foresee all contingencies', Andrey replies: 'What are we facing tomorrow? A hundred million diverse chances which will be decided on the instant by whether we run or they run, whether this man or that man is killed.'[58] At his last council of war, Andrey asks himself:

'What science can there be in a matter in which, as in every practical matter, nothing can be determined and everything depends on innumerable conditions, the significance of which becomes manifest at a particular moment, and no one can tell when that moment will come?'[59]

'As in every practical matter': Tolstoy means this rejection of a science of war to apply to every conceivable social science. 'At a particular moment', 'on the instant': Tolstoy insists on presentness and the eventness of each moment, which is not simply an automatic result of earlier moments.

Dostoevsky's *Notes from Underground* polemicises against deterministic faith in laws, soon to be discovered, that could specify future events the way we can look up numbers in 'a table of logarithms to 108,000'.[60] Man would then be nothing but a 'piano key' or an 'organ stop' – until, that is, he decided to prove his freedom by disobeying the laws. After all, people, unlike inert objects, can know the laws that supposedly govern them, a complication that introduces an infinite regress of attempts to prove the laws false, new laws that predict those attempts and reactions to those new laws.

We need not to *live out* our lives, but to *live* them, so that our choices really matter. If the future is given, our actions are meaningless. 'If we concede that human life can be governed by reason', Tolstoy concluded, 'the possibility of life is destroyed.'[61] Dostoevsky repeatedly argued that for life to be meaningful, people must act under genuine uncertainty. The socialists do not see that if people received utopia in exchange for surprisingness, they would soon realise

that they had no life left, that they had no freedom of spirit, no will, no personality, that someone had stolen all this from them; they would see that their human image had disappeared ... People would realise that there is no happiness in inactivity, that the mind which does not labour will wither, that it is not possible to love one's neighbour without sacrificing something to him of one's own labour ... and that *happiness lies not in happiness but only in the attempt to achieve it.*[62]

For Bakhtin, the novel in general and Dostoevsky's polyphonic novel in particular convey the sense that there are more possibilities than actualities, that reality could have developed otherwise and that each personality could have developed differently. In a famous passage usually taken as directed against Marxist (or any other) determinism, Bakhtin writes:

An individual cannot be completely incarnated into the flesh of existing socio-historical categories. There is no mere form that would be able to incarnate once and forever all of his human possibilities and needs, no form in which he could exhaust himself down to the last word ... There always remains an unrealised surplus of humanness; there always remains a need for the future, and a place for his future must be found ... Reality as we have it in the novel is only one of many possible realities ... it bears within itself other possibilities.[63]

In his book on Dostoevsky, Bakhtin argues that Dostoevsky's novels show that:

A man never coincides with himself ... In Dostoevsky's artistic thinking, the genuine life of the personality takes place at the point of non-coincidence between a man and himself, at his point of departure beyond the limits of all that he is as a material being, a being that can be spied upon, defined apart from its own will, 'at second hand'.[64]

Beyond all that a person is as a 'material being' who can be defined at 'second hand', each person contains more than can be accounted for not only by any existing social science but also by any that could ever be developed. Moreover, the entire project of social 'Newtonianism' is not only doomed but also fundamentally immoral, inasmuch as the fundamental principle of morality, in Bakhtin's view, is to acknowledge each other person as non-coincident, as ultimately undefinable at second hand, and therefore as containing 'surprisingness' and a 'surplus of possibilities'. These are not only Bakhtin's own views but also the message he hears from the counter-tradition of Russian literature and thought.

PSYCHOLOGICAL COMPLEXITY

The radical intelligentsia's utopian politics typically presumed that human nature is both simple and infinitely malleable.[65] In Chernyshevsky's view, people inevitably pursue their greatest advantage; evil exists only because they mistake where their advantage lies. It follows that appropriate re-education could eliminate evil altogether.

Human nature is whatever social conditions make it. This view was already present in Locke and had been given political formulation by Helvétius. In the twentieth century, it was developed by Margaret Mead and Ruth Benedict and thrives today as 'social constructivism'. Quite remarkably, the century that began with the rediscovery of Mendelian genetics and ended with the human genome project saw the humanities and social sciences accept that our behaviour, unlike that of all other animals, owes nothing to our genetic heritage. We might call this view 'atheistic creationism'. It reflects the intelligentsia's aspiration to rule and remake society through its theoretical knowledge.

In its Marxist form, the assumption of infinite malleability led to totalitarian aspirations and the application of unprecedented force when human characteristics proved recalcitrant. Soviet rejection of genetics and Freudian psychology derive from the limits these theories apparently place on socialist remoulding, a conclusion that Freud himself drew in *Civilisation and Its Discontents*.

Thus, the very insistence that human psychology is irreducibly complex was, and in some circles still is, highly charged. Many western readers who admire the psychological depths of Russian novels often miss the point that such psychologising obviously challenged intelligentsia assumptions.

Russian writers' contributions to our understanding of thought and emotion have proved so numerous, profound and influential that it is impossible to describe them adequately here. They concern the dynamics of both conscious and unconscious; the ways in which the body does not just respond to but also shapes the stream of consciousness; the role of imperceptible contingencies in directing thoughts and feelings; and the manner in which memories shape perceptions in advance. They also include such counter-intuitive concepts as 'the egoism of suffering', 'disinterested obsequiousness' and self-destructive self-assertion; the many ways in which social conditions and choice can interact; and the nature of self-deception.[66]

Perhaps the most durable contributions concern the nature of intentionality. We usually assume, as Locke argued, that before we can act we must at some point have decided to do so. Russian literature repeatedly reveals the naïveté of this assumption. Sometimes intention evolves *along with* the action: a person may know at each moment what he is doing without knowing what he will do next. In such cases, a complete intention never exists at any single moment because intention is processual.

What is more, Dostoevsky observes after analysing one woman's processual intention, if the situation were repeated every moment could lead to many different outcomes, each of which 'could have happened and could have been done by this very same woman and sprung from the very same soul, in the very same mood and under the very same circumstances'.[67] If different actions could result from identical circumstances, then time is, by definition, open and determinism is false.[68] Here Dostoevsky's psychology and philosophy come together in an unexpected defence of freedom.

The infinite complexity of the human spirit demonstrates the absurdity of the radical intelligentsia's attempt to remake people and render them blissful in some preplanned ant-heap. In his review of *Anna Karenina*, Dostoevsky observes:

The Russian author's [Tolstoy's] view of guilt and transgression recognises that no ant-heap, no triumph of the 'fourth estate,' no abolition of poverty, no organisation, will save humanity from abnormality and, consequently, from guilt and transgression. This is expressed in a monumental psychological elaboration of the human soul, with awesome depth and force ... It is clear and intelligible to the point of obviousness that evil lies deeper in human beings than our socialist-physicians suppose; that no social structure will eliminate evil; that the human soul will remain as it has always been; that abnormality and sin arise from the soul itself; and finally that the laws of the human soul are still so little known, so obscure to science, so undefined, and so mysterious, that there cannot be either physicians or *final* judges.[69]

NOTES

1. Martin Malia, 'What is the intelligentsia?' in Richard Pipes (ed.), *The Russian Intelligentsia* (New York: Columbia University Press, 1961), p. 4.
2. Mikhail Gershenzon, 'Creative self-consciousness' in Marshall S. Shatz and Judith E. Zimmerman (eds. and trans.), *Signposts: A Collection of Articles on the Russian Intelligentsia* (Irvine: Schlacks, 1986), p. 60. This volume's title is more commonly translated *Landmarks*.
3. Malia, 'What is the intelligentsia?', p. 5.
4. As cited in Ernest J. Simmons, *Chekhov: A Biography* (Boston: Little, Brown, 1962), p. 168, letter of 7/8 October 1888.
5. Ibid., p. 168, letter of 11 September 1888.
6. Ibid., p. 165, letter of 27 August 1888.
7. Estimates of the number of lives claimed by the Inquisition in its history of three centuries in Spain, Portugal and the New World cover a range in the tens of thousands; for the period of Stalin's rule (or Mao's rule) in the tens of millions. See the classic study of Cecil Roth, *The Spanish Inquisition* (New York: Norton, 1964).
8. Sergey Bulgakov, 'Heroism and asceticism (reflections on the religious nature of the Russian intelligentsia)' in Shatz and Zimmerman (eds. and trans.), *Signposts*, p. 18.
9. For example, ideologists rejected the 'resonance' theory in chemistry (one cannot specify a single model for some molecules because they resonate between several) as a form of 'agnosticism' – that is, a denial of absolute certainty.
10. Nikolay Berdiaev, 'Philosophical verity and intelligentsia truth' in Shatz and Zimmerman (eds. and trans.), *Signposts*, p. 5.
11. Ibid., p. 6.
12. Ibid., pp. 6–7.
13. For an excellent study of a more recent group that pretty much became an intelligentsia in the classical Russian sense, see Tony Judt, *Past Imperfect: French Intellectuals, 1944–1956* (Berkeley: University of California Press, 1992). Judt cites Thomas Pavel's characterisation of this intelligentsia's 'refusal to listen' (cited on pp. 3–4).
14. Quoted from Fyodor Dostoevsky, *The Possessed* [*The Devils*], trans. Constance Garnett (New York: Modern Library, 1963), pp. 410–11.
15. N. Valentinov [N. V. Vol'skii], 'Chernyshevskii i Lenin', *Novyi zhurnal*, 26 (1951), 194.
16. Cited in Irina Paperno, *Chernyshevsky and the Age of Realism: A Study in the Semiotics of Behavior* (Stanford University Press, 1988), p. 27. Paperno's first chapter is a gold-mine of quotations of this sort.

17. See chapter 8 of Joseph Frank, *Dostoevsky: The Miraculous Years, 1865–1871* (Princeton University Press, 1995), pp. 151–69.

18. Gershenzon, 'Creative self-consciousness', p. 68.

19. Berdiaev, 'Philosophical verity and intelligentsia truth', p. 15.

20. Gershenzon, 'Creative self-consciousness', p. 67.

21. Dostoevsky, *The Possessed*, pp. 424–5.

22. Frank, *Dostoevsky: The Miraculous Years*, p. 145.

23. Ibid., p. 144.

24. Peter Struve, 'The intelligentsia and revolution' in Shatz and Zimmerman (eds. and trans.), *Signposts*, p. 125.

25. Quoted from Dostoevsky, *The Idiot*, trans. Constance Garnett (New York: Modern Library, 1962), p. 214.

26. Quoted from Dostoevsky, *The Gambler*, ed. Gary Saul Morson (New York: Modern Library, 2003), p. 178. I discuss this passage and the prosaic theme in my introduction to this edition, 'Writing like roulette'.

27. For a discussion of theoretism, the alibi, the surplus, eventness, surprisingness and related concepts in Bakhtin's thought, see Gary Saul Morson and Caryl Emerson, *Mikhail Bakhtin: Creation of a Prosaics* (Stanford University Press, 1990); the introduction to Morson and Emerson, *Rethinking Bakhtin: Extensions and Challenges* (Evanston: Northwestern University Press, 1989); and chapter 3 of Morson, *Narrative and Freedom: The Shadows of Time* (New Haven: Yale University Press, 1995).

28. Elie Halévy, *The Growth of Philosophic Radicalism*, trans. Mary Morris (Boston: Beacon, 1995), p. 6.

29. On the revival of practical reasoning, see Stephen Toulmin, *Cosmopolis: The Hidden Agenda of Modernity* (University of Chicago Press, 1992), and Toulmin, *Return to Reason* (Cambridge, Mass.: Harvard University Press, 2003). For the influence of Russian writers on Wittgenstein, see Alan Janik and Stephen Toulmin, *Wittgenstein's Vienna* (Chicago: Ivan R. Dee, 1996), and Ray Monk, *Ludwig Wittgenstein: The Duty of Genius* (New York: Penguin, 1990). I discuss the heritage of Tolstoy's ideas in diverse thinkers – Wittgenstein, Toulmin, Jane Jacobs, Stephen Jay Gould and others – in Morson, *'Anna Karenina' in Our Time: Seeing More Wisely* (New Haven: Yale University Press, 2007).

30. I first discussed 'the irony of origins' and 'the irony of outcomes' in Morson, *The Boundaries of Genre: Dostoevsky's 'Diary of a Writer' and the Traditions of Literary Utopia* (Austin: University of Texas Press, 1981).

31. Quoted from Dostoevsky, *The Brothers Karamazov*, trans. Constance Garnett (New York: Modern Library, 1950), pp. 789–90.

32. Quoted from Dostoevsky, *Crime and Punishment*, trans. Constance Garnett (New York: Modern Library, 1950), p. 531.

33. Ibid., p. 532; translation amended.

34. Dostoevsky, *The Brothers Karamazov*, p. 274.

35. Quoted from Leo Tolstoy, *Anna Karenina*, trans. Constance Garnett, revd Leonard J. Kent and Nina Berberova (New York: Modern Library, 1965), p. 831.

36. Ibid., p. 829.
37. Ludwig Wittgenstein, *Tractatus Logico-Philosophicus*, trans. D. F. Pears and B. F. McGuiness (London: Routledge, 1977), p. 73.
38. Tolstoy, *Anna Karenina*, p. 824.
39. See Albert R. Jonsen and Stephen Toulmin, *The Abuse of Casuistry: A History of Moral Reasoning* (Berkeley: University of California Press, 1988).
40. Quoted from Tolstoy, *War and Peace*, trans. Ann Dunnigan (New York: Signet, 1968), p. 1320.
41. Ibid., p. 1219.
42. I discuss 'open camouflage' (like 'prosaics', my own coinage) in *'Anna Karenina' in Our Time*.
43. Quoted from Tolstoy, 'Why do men stupefy themselves?' in *Recollections and Essays*, trans. Aylmer Maude (London: Oxford University Press, 1961), p. 81.
44. Ibid., pp. 81–2.
45. Hannah Arendt, *Eichmann in Jerusalem: A Report on the Banality of Evil* (New York: Viking, 1973).
46. Dostoevsky, *The Brothers Karamazov*, p. 786.
47. Mikhail Bakhtin, 'Forms of time and of the chronotope in the novel: notes toward a historical poetics' in *The Dialogic Imagination: Four Essays by M. M. Bakhtin*, ed. Michael Holquist, trans. Caryl Emerson and Michael Holquist (Austin: University of Texas Press, 1981), p. 148.
48. Alexander Herzen, *'From the Other Shore' and 'The Russian People and Socialism'*, trans. Moura Budberg and Richard Wollheim (Oxford University Press, 1979), pp. 36–7.
49. Gershenzon, 'Creative self-consciousness', p. 58.
50. Cited in Simmons, *Chekhov*, pp. 111–13, letter of March 1886.
51. Anton Chekhov, *Uncle Vanya* in *The Major Plays* (New York: Signet, 1964), p. 191.
52. Frank, *Dostoevsky: The Miraculous Years*, pp. 147–8.
53. These ideas are developed in Morson, 'Prosaic Chekhov: metadrama, the intelligentsia, and *Uncle Vanya*', *TriQuarterly* (Winter 1990–1), 118–59.
54. The classic study is Mihaly Csikszentmihalyi, *Flow: The Psychology of Optimal Experience* (New York: Harper, 1991). Csikszentmihalyi credits Tolstoy for the insight in Csikszentmihalyi, *Good Business: Leadership, Flow, and the Making of Meaning* (New York: Penguin, 2004), pp. 59–60.
55. Tolstoy, *Anna Karenina*, p. 277.
56. This is one of Gould's favourite points. See, for instance, Gould, *Wonderful Life: The Burgess Shale and the Nature of History* (New York: Norton, 1989) and *The Panda's Thumb: More Reflections in Natural History* (New York: Norton, 1982).
57. Herzen, *'From the Other Shore' and 'The Russian People and Socialism'*, p. 39.
58. Tolstoy, *War and Peace*, p. 930.
59. Ibid., p. 775.
60. Quoted from Dostoevsky, *'Notes from Underground' and 'The Grand Inquisitor'*, ed. and trans. Ralph Matlaw (New York: Dutton, 1960), p. 22.
61. Tolstoy, *War and Peace*, p. 1354.

62. Dostoevsky, *A Writer's Diary*, trans. Kenneth Lanz, 2 vols. (Evanston: Northwestern University Press, 1993–4), vol. I, p. 335.
63. Bakhtin, *Dialogic Imagination*, p. 37.
64. Bakhtin, *Problems of Dostoevsky's Poetics*, ed. and trans. Caryl Emerson (Minneapolis: University of Minnesota Press, 1984), p. 59.
65. This assumption still underlies rational choice theory and the economists' notion of 'economic man'.
66. The nature and dynamics of self-deception is Tolstoy's central concern in his portrayal of Anna Karenina, as I discuss in *'Anna Karenina' in Our Time*.
67. Dostoevsky, *A Writer's Diary*, vol. II, p. 1071.
68. In quantum physics, identical systems can produce different outcomes, a clear refutation of closed time. Although determinists have tried to dismiss such indeterminacies as too small to have a measurable effect, chaos theory suggests how even the smallest event can sometimes make a noticeable difference.
69. Dostoevsky, *A Writer's Diary*, vol. II, p. 477.

CHAPTER 8

Religious renaissance in the Silver Age

Ruth Coates

I am not sure who coined the phrase 'Russian religious renaissance'. Perhaps it was Nicolas Zernov, whose survey of the phenomenon is entitled *The Russian Religious Renaissance of the Twentieth Century*,[1] or perhaps he took over the term from one of its participants. For Zernov, the term 'religious renaissance' denotes the rebirth among the Russian intelligentsia of interest and participation in the Christian religion where these had been dead. If there is an allusion to the western European Renaissance at the beginning of the modern period, then this is an indication that the Russian religious renaissance took place on a high cultural level, that the return to faith incorporated a flowering of philosophy and the arts. However, this was more than a simple return to Russian Orthodoxy. Another intellectual historian of the Silver Age, Piama Gaidenko, also frequently likens the period to the European Renaissance, but in a negative sense (from her perspective), on account of its recourse to pagan culture and the aggressive humanism of many of its leading representatives.[2] And indeed, the Russian religious renaissance had, broadly speaking, two faces. When one looks at one set of texts it appears to represent a straightforward reversal of the ideological shift from theism to humanism that took place at the close of the Middle Ages, whereas another set indicates a more ambiguous (and ambivalent) religious awareness that sets itself in direct opposition to traditional Christianity and the church. In both cases, the new religious awareness began at the turn of the nineteenth and twentieth centuries and developed rapidly and intensely until the Bolshevik Revolution of 1917 destroyed the conditions under which it could flourish.

PARTICIPANTS IN THE RELIGIOUS RENAISSANCE

This chapter is about the cultural conditions and intellectual stimuli that made the Russian religious renaissance possible and helped determine the forms that it took. But I will start with a brief account of the main 'players' involved. Christopher Read's distinction between two 'schools', to be understood very loosely and with appropriate caveats about figures who do not properly fit into either, or who straddle both, still holds: the 'people whose means of expression was through scholarly articles' (I will call them for brevity's sake the 'academics'), and the 'creative writers' (whom I will refer to as the 'artists', although this camp included people who were primarily cultural critics or primarily 'thinkers').[3] A common focus for identifying the academics is the series of essay collections *Problems of Idealism* (1902), *Landmarks* (1909) and *Out of the Depths* (1918) to which various groupings of them contributed. They include: Sergey Trubetskoy, Professor of Hellenic Philosophy at Moscow University; his brother Evgeny, friend and biographer of Solovev; the Kantian jurist Novgorodtsev; Berdiaev, after the Revolution briefly Professor of Philosophy at Moscow University; Bulgakov, Professor of Political Economy at the universities of Kiev and Moscow; Frank, philosopher and lecturer at numerous universities; and Struve, publicist. Berdiaev, Bulgakov, Frank and Struve are commonly taken to be representative of the academics as a whole for their journey from Marxism via Kantian idealism to religious faith, but this is of course not a universal pattern. Beyond the essay collections one should also mention the Moscow quartet of Orthodox philosopher-theologians Elchaninov, Ern, the polymath Florensky and Sventitsky, plus the philosophers Karsavin, Lapshin, Losev and Nikolay Lossky. The list could continue. In the artistic camp, a similar focus might be the participants in the Religious–Philosophical Meetings of 1901–3 (the proceedings of most of them were published in the associated journal *The New Way*), or possibly contributors to the three-volume symposium *Torches* (1906–8). These are two overlapping Symbolist circles centred on Merezhkovsky, Gippius (Merezhkovsky's wife) and Filosofov, prime motivators behind the meetings, on the one hand, and, on the other, the 'mystical anarchists' Ivanov and Chulkov. Associated figures include Rozanov, the philosopher Shestov, the ubiquitous Berdiaev, Bely and to some extent Florensky. It is the academics who are associated with the return to traditional Christian values and to the church, while the artists rejected these as outmoded and sought new forms of spirituality and religious expression.

THE IDEOLOGICAL VACUUM IN LATE NINETEENTH-CENTURY RUSSIA

In the last quarter of the nineteenth century Russians were suffering from a sort of ideological exhaustion. On the right, the ruling ideology of Orthodoxy, autocracy and nationality, which was revived in a hardened form (if that is not a contradiction in terms) after the assassination of the reforming Tsar Alexander II in 1881, met the intellectual and spiritual needs of no one. As we shall see, the institutional Orthodox Church was fully compromised by its bondage to the regime, and the reactionary Chief Procurator of the Holy Synod between 1880 and 1905, Pobedonostsev, chief educator of both Alexander III and Nicholas II, actively sought to prevent change not only to the Synodal system but also to every other area of Russia's cultural life, notably in the area of freedom of speech. Where possible, he aimed to reverse the effects of what he deemed to be the 'criminal' reforms of Alexander II's reign. He even viewed the intelligentsia's awakened interest in religion with alarm, and it was he who put an end to the communication between church and intelligentsia generated by Merezhkovsky's Religious–Philosophical Meetings of 1901–3.

On the left, it seemed that the radical intelligentsia had arrived at an impasse. The dominant ideology of Populism, with its focus on the creation of a uniquely Russian agrarian socialism based on the peasant commune and its emphasis on the moral duty of the economically and culturally privileged class to liberate the people from tsarist oppression, had suffered three kinds of defeat. The impressive attempt of idealistic radicals to educate the peasantry in the sources of their oppression, the 'going to the people' movement of 1874 (repeated in 1875), had mixed results, with peasants responding angrily to any denunciations of God or the tsar, cases of village elders reporting their educators to the authorities and, worse, mass arrests and trials by the government.[4] The subsequent development of terrorism as a means of attempting to influence or remove the powers that be backfired when Alexander's assassination provoked widespread revulsion among the public and instigated twenty-five years of extreme political reaction under his successors, Alexander III and Nicholas II. Lastly, and fatally, economic developments finally rendered the Populist ideology redundant, rapid industrialisation (under Witte in the 1890s) depopulating the countryside and creating an urban proletariat, and the commune was fatally compromised by the pressures of agrarian capitalism and the appearance of the peasant landowner, the kulak. The stage was set, on the one hand, for Marxism to provide a new scientific basis for socialism and, on the other, for a rejection of all forms of socialism based on philosophical positivism and ethical utilitarianism, in short, of the intelligentsia ideology as it had become established in Russia since the 1850s.

Ideological exhaustion was felt and expressed most keenly in the arts. In particular, the realist aesthetic had reached the limits of its possibilities, and the age of the Russian realist novel was over. After 1877 and *Anna Karenina*

(1875–7), Tolstoy subordinated literature to his religious quest, and the didact largely usurped the place of the artist. Turgenev died in 1883, having written his last and unsuccessful novel *Virgin Soil* – about the Populists – in 1877. Dostoevsky died in 1881 without witnessing the regicide that his last novel, *The Brothers Karamazov* (1879–80), had anticipated. Of the canonical Russian prose writers, only Chekhov was on the ascendant in the 1880s, perfecting the genre of the short story. His artistic path is a symbol of his times. Realism had developed in tandem with the industrial age under the prevailing cultural imperative that the artist should 'serve' society by faithfully reflecting social conditions and ideological tensions under capitalism. Paradoxically, the cultural confidence of the age, supported by a still secure faith in the authority of human reason, had permitted talented writers to create novels which were great personal statements on the era: subjectivity was disguised as objectivity. The collapse of that confidence, which in Russia was reflected in the disillusionment with Populist ideology, compelled a reversal: Chekhov perfected an objective narrative point of view that disguised a new cultural subjectivism, a loss of authority to address the big questions and a forced return to the details revealed by forensic examination of the 'slice of life' ('this is what I see: draw your own conclusions'). This loss of authority, as much as reaction against the intelligentsia's ideal of service, accounts for the ascendancy in the 1890s of that most subjective of genres, the lyric poem.

RELIGIOUS TRENDS: THE RUSSIAN ORTHODOX CHURCH

If the Enlightenment project was burning itself out by the end of the nineteenth century, so far as the Russian Orthodox Church was concerned it appeared nevertheless to have succeeded in one of its main objectives: the fatal undermining of religious faith. The narrative of religious decline in Russia begins with the Great Schism in the Russian Orthodox Church that took place in 1666–7 as a result of the reforms of Patriarch Nikon and gave birth to the phenomena of Old Belief and Russian religious sectarianism. The future Peter the Great grew up watching the fall-out and concluding that this was what happened when the church operated independently of the state. On assuming power, he ended the Byzantine symphony of the Muscovite period by chopping off one of the eagle's heads: he transformed the church into an organ of the state, abolishing the patriarchate and placing a secular appointee, the Chief Procurator, at the head of the council of bishops – the Holy Synod, whose establishment is anticipated by the Ecclesiastical Regulation of 1721. The church hierarchy was assimilated to the Table of Ranks and the notion of state service; the clergy became a conduit for the 'spiritual', that is, the ideological, governance of the laity, who, as Vera Shevzov has argued, came to be regarded principally as the object of instruction.[5] The concepts of the state and the faith community were merged: believers became identical with subjects and religious belief the instrument of political compliance. Over time the church lost all vestiges of its independence and came to be held in contempt by all sections of society: the peasants, who had to contribute to the upkeep of the very priests who informed on them; the parish clergy, who were lorded over by appointed bishops drawn from the monastic orders, which many joined only nominally in order to advance their careers; their sons, whose experience of seminary education (the only kind their impoverished fathers could afford for them) drove them to atheism and political radicalism; the western-orientated, enlightened ruling elite for whom Orthodoxy became equated with peasant obscurantism; and, at the top of the hierarchy, the Chief Procurators themselves, who mostly despised the bishops on the Synod and who came to preside over a bureaucratic system of diocesan clerks that bypassed the bishops altogether. This is the Russian Orthodox Church that was the object of Solovev's sustained attack in the name of a papal theocracy in the 1880s and the focus of the rejection of traditional Christianity at the turn of the century by the 'artists', the people of the so-called 'new religious consciousness'.

Still, rumours of the death of religion generally prove to be much exaggerated. Even the official Russian Orthodox Church was preparing for major reform in the years to 1917. In the late nineteenth and early twentieth centuries pressure was building within the church for radical change. Some of the impetus for this came from the laity, not least the peasant laity, which, though devout, was not immune from the atmosphere of social unrest that pervaded Russia and aspired to a greater role in the running of the parish, including the election of its priest. The church authorities were aware that there were many defections to the Old Believers (*staroobriadtsy* – literally 'Old Ritualists') and the sects, which were far more democratic in their organisation. The decrees on religious tolerance of April 1905 and October 1906, which granted rights of self-government and property ownership to the dissenters, put these in a more privileged position than the established church and prompted Metropolitan Antony of St Petersburg to petition the tsar for permission to convoke an all-Russian church council of clergy and laity that would work out a system of autonomy for the church. The tsar's initial assent to this request was reversed by Pobedonostsev, and after the end of the latter's tenure the tsar continued to delay his permission. Still, a pre-conciliar commission met between March and December 1906 to hammer out the main issues. A majority favoured the restoration of the patriarch-ate. There was also a pre-conciliar conference in 1912. Finally, after the tsar's abdication, the council met in 1917, agreeing a range of major reforms in a very full programme of genuine debate before its premature end in September 1918, when the Bolsheviks confiscated the building it was meeting in.[6] There is no doubt that the church's will to reform facilitated the return to it of many members of the intelligentsia, some to the priesthood (Bulgakov, Florensky, Sventitsky, Ukhtomsky), and that, vice versa, the sustained discussion of religious issues in the journals of the day helped to revitalise the church.

RELIGIOUS DISSENT

Returning to a deeper historical perspective, it is clear that alongside that of the decline of the church, there are two equally long Russian religious narratives. One tells a story of untrammelled and rebellious life, another of disciplined and sober spiritual resurrection. The same Schism that led to the crippling of the official church also produced a vital tradition of religious dissent; indeed, it has often been said that Nikon's reforms alienated precisely the most spiritually committed, vibrant sector of the church, thus depriving it of a powerful resource for combating the ensuing onslaught of secularisation that so undermined it.[7] All this religious energy, fanned into fanaticism by successive waves of persecution, was directed into heterodox channels: initially the priestly and the priestless Old Believers (the *popovtsy* and *bespopovtsy*), then, out of the latter, the extraordinarily colourful religious sects (the Castrates, the Flagellants, the Milk-Drinkers, the Runners, the Spirit-Wrestlers, the Wanderers, and so forth). Since it was not in the interests of either church or state to admit the full extent of the Schism, numbers of dissenters were habitually underestimated, but in the middle of the nineteenth century the findings of special commissions forced Nicholas I's regime to revise the official figure upwards from 910,000 to 10 million, or a full quarter of the east-Slavic population of the empire.[8] In the late nineteenth and early twentieth centuries ethnographers devoted a great deal of research to the sectarians, and a series of important publications brought them to the attention of the Russian educated class.[9] The tradition of religious dissent in this way became one of the main streams that flowed into the religious revival of the Silver Age, where it fed precisely the tendency of religious rebellion against the church and state characteristic of the 'artists'.[10] Aleksandr Etkind has documented some of the specific contacts of members of Merezhkovsky's circle with the sectarian communities, for example, a visit by Merezhkovsky and Gippius to Lake Svetloiar in 1902 that convinced them of their spiritual affinity with the sectarians, whom they deemed to represent the true spirit of the Russian people, and of Rozanov to a community of Flagellants near Petersburg in 1904.[11] Points of affinity here include the following: the sectarians' radical apocalypticism and related chiliasm (which were born of their rejection of the established church as apostate, of Holy Russia as profaned and of the tsar as Antichrist); their historical association with anarchic political rebellion, or *bunt*; their communal spirit, democratic congregational structures and emphasis on collective salvation; the mystical rites (*radeniia*) of the Flagellants (the pursuit of ecstatic states through dance and chant), in which was sought the in-dwelling of the Holy Spirit; and, finally, their radical approach to sexuality and sexual relations, ranging from complete renunciation (castration – practised by the sect of Castrates) to experiments in free love. All of these are manifested very powerfully in the people of the 'new religious consciousness'.

The point is that the 'artists' did not merely elaborate a theory of a transcended Christianity, but sought to enact it in their own inner circle before disseminating it to society as a whole. Thus we find in Gippius's diaries an account of a ceremony involving Merezhkovsky, Gippius herself and Filosofov invented to inaugurate the Merezhkovskys' new 'Church of Flesh and Blood'. It took place on the Thursday of Holy Week 1901 and comprised a self-conscious refashioning of the Last Supper, with the taking of bread and wine. More importantly, it established the principle of Trinitarian *sobornost'* (community) as the foundation of the new church (whose emphasis was to be on collective salvation) with rites (kisses and the exchange of crosses) designed to symbolise the union without merging of the three founder-members.[12] Though this would all be blasphemous enough from an Orthodox perspective, the really radical element was the role played in the ceremony's symbolism by eros and gender, for the Trinity was conceived by Merezhkovsky's circle as a never-to-be-consummated erotic union, with the feminine principle being accorded the first place. The new church was to be founded on eros, not agape, in accordance with the pagan trinities (for example, of Osiris, Isis and Horus) which Merezhkovsky, likely following Schelling, believed had been deliberately usurped and distorted by the early Christian theologians. The Christian era, founded on a misplaced asceticism, was to be succeeded by the era of the Holy Spirit (the Christianity of the 'Third Testament'), founded on the concept of holy flesh, which would synthesise paganism and Christianity. It was desire that would deify the body and, once realised in society at large, establish the reign of God on earth. Gaidenko maintains that the secret purpose of the Religious–Philosophical Meetings was to expand the new church beyond its nuclear core but believes the Merezhkovskys were unclear as to how the erotic principle was to be realised socially, though she nevertheless alludes to the orgiastic turn allegedly taken by some of the rites of the Flagellants as a possible model.[13]

Meanwhile, across the city, at the home of the poet Minsky, Ivanov was instigating a Last Supper of his own. Etkind relates from the memoir literature how in May 1905 a group of Symbolists, including Ivanov, Rozanov and Berdiaev, sat on the floor in the dark, then began to turn in circles. A young Jewish musician who had volunteered for the role was next 'sacrificed' in a symbolic crucifixion, then cut by Ivanov at the wrist and his blood mixed in a cup with wine. The party all drank from the cup and exchanged kisses.[14] Etkind surmises that this rite was meant to inaugurate the apocalypse.[15] Certainly, the 'crucifixion' was supposed to express the symbolic equivalent of the sacrifices of Dionysus and Christ. Ivanov saw Dionysus (who, according to his cult – on which Ivanov was an expert – is half-human, half-divine, who is annually dismembered only to rise from the dead and whose flesh and blood are ritually consumed by his followers) as a forerunner to Christ. His call for the individual to be liberated from the constraints of personal boundaries into a mystical union with the cultic community through the communal pursuit of ecstatic states and his emphasis on the erotic, orgiastic dimension of such a pursuit clearly resonate with the practices of the Flagellants. As Michael Wachtel has pointed out, he also experienced his erotic life with his beloved second wife, Zinoveva-Annibal, as mystical, disclosing God.[16]

Rozanov sits rather awkwardly in the company of these Symbolist God-seekers. He was closely identified with Merezhkovsky's circle and played a leading role in the discussions at the Religious–Philosophical Meetings, but he refused to have anything to do with the Merezhkovskys' erotic utopia. Rozanov did not suffer from the problems of sexual identity that, in Olga Matich's persuasive interpretation, motivated his colleagues' sublimation of the sex drive. He was as vehemently opposed to the official church as they were, though this stemmed in his case to a quite significant extent from its refusal to let him divorce his first wife (Dostoevsky's former lover, Apollinaria Suslova) and establish his new family on a legitimate basis. Like the Merezhkovskys, he believed Christianity to be anti-sexual and life-denying, accusing Christ and His imitators, the monastic caste (from whom the church leadership was recruited), of sexual deviancy, and like them, he was inspired by pagan cults in his fight to restore eros to the centre of religion. But Rozanov's was a cult of biological heterosexual love, of the genitalia, semen, breasts and the pregnant belly, and despite his extraordinary lack of inhibition in elaborating on these, he conceived of sex in an essentially bourgeois manner, as holy in the sanctity of marriage and of the home. Rozanov was also profoundly ambivalent about Christ, revealing in his mature and best works – *Solitaria* (1911) and *Fallen Leaves* (1913–15) – great receptivity to the consolatory gifts of Christianity in the presence of suffering and death. The same works show Rozanov's love of the workaday rhythm of the liturgical life of the humble parish church, which he associates with the principle of the religio-ethnic community, of family. Ultimately, Rozanov is not, as the Merezhkovskys were, a revolutionary, but a religious conservative, notwithstanding his continuing power to shock.

THE HESYCHASTIC REVIVAL

The second alternative Russian religious narrative is one of spiritual revival within Orthodoxy, born of a rediscovery of the hesychastic tradition of mysticism or the quest for personal deification through the ascetic discipline of silent prayer. The theology and practice of hesychasm had first entered Russia in the fourteenth century with St Sergius of Radonezh, founder of the Trinity-St Sergius Lavra for which Rublev painted his famous icon, and contemporary of Palamas, the Byzantine theologian of hesychasm whose work led to the official endorsement of the tradition by the Orthodox Church. It had flourished in the fifteenth century among the Transvolgan Elders, whose spokesman was the hesychast Nil Sorsky, but had later fallen into abeyance. It was revived in the eighteenth century in the teeth of the Enlightenment and the aggressive secularisation of the Russian state through the efforts of Paisy Velichkovsky. Paisy began his theological training at the Kiev Academy but, frustrated by the Latin bias of that institution, left for Mount Athos, where he was exposed to the medieval ethos of Byzantine theology and to hesychastic practice. Paisy's influence was both theoretical and practical. He and the monks of his religious communities were prodigious translators of Greek patristic ascetical literature into Slavonic: in 1793 a Slavonic translation of the *Philokalia* (the *Dobrotoliubie*) was published at St Petersburg. This was a compilation of the ascetical writings of the eastern Christian mystics which had first been published, in their original Greek, in Venice in 1792. In the nineteenth century Paisy's spiritual descendants continued to make the Greek Fathers widely available to the Russian reading public. Notable in this regard is the Elder Makary's collaboration with the Slavophile Ivan Kireevsky in the 1840s and 1850s. The existence of such publications facilitated the rapprochement between the church and the intelligentsia in the early twentieth century and also fuelled the movement for reform within the church itself. The practical influence of Paisy lay in the great nineteenth-century revival of contemplative monasticism right across Russia as his disciples established themselves in the Russian monasteries. The Optina Pustyn hermitage (with its Elders Lev, Makary and Amvrosy) was only the best known of these, but its contribution is uniquely important in so far as throughout the nineteenth century it served as a point of contact with secular culture in the form of a string of visitors from Russia's cultural elite.[17] Through Kireevsky's collaboration with the hermitage the foundation of the mainstream of Russian religious thought was laid: the harmonious relationship of faith and reason on the model of the Greek Fathers. Through Dostoevsky's Zosima, an albeit very idiosyncratic image of the hesychast promoted the monastic vocation to a wide public. In addition to the Elders of Optina Pustyn, one should also mention the hesychast St Seraphim of Sarov (1759–1833), of whose existence and significance Russia was reminded on the occasion of his canonisation in 1903 and who was widely revered in the first decades of the twentieth century.[18]

The full significance of the hesychastic revival for the religious intellectual culture of the Silver Age has yet to be investigated. One of its dimensions is the impetus it gave, through the translation and dissemination of Greek patristics, to the reclamation of theology for Russian Orthodoxy as a vital pursuit conducted in the context both of the church and of the personal spiritual quest of the practitioner. It should be emphasised that since the seventeenth century Russian seminaries and theological academies, extra-ordinary though this may seem to the uninitiated, had been dominated by a Latinised curriculum (Aristotle and Aquinas) based on the Jesuit school system that came from the Kiev Academy, supplemented in the eighteenth century by a Protestant bias under the influence of Feofan Prokopovich. Only in the nineteenth century was Russian adopted as the language of instruction. There was little training in Greek, and even after nineteenth-century reforms the dominant theological trends were historicism and moralism rather than the creative development of patristic thought.[19] The full fruits of this theological revival appear only in the younger generation of expatriate theologians, to which, for example, Florovsky, V. Lossky and Meyendorff belong; but the link to this generation comprises the religious philosophers of the Silver Age, some of whom were lay Orthodox, others priests. Florensky's *The Pillar and Ground of the Truth* (1914) is a landmark work in this respect.[20] It departs from the assertion that dogmatic truth can be apprehended only in religious experience and, as its title indicates, is founded on the concept of ecclesiality (*tserkovnost'*), understood as the church community as the synthesis of truth and spiritual life. The book is saturated with references to the Greek Fathers and consistently foregrounds the Orthodox saint as the living embodiment of the fullness of truth, which is ultimately inseparable from spiritual beauty. At the same time, Florensky is neither afraid of secular culture nor dismissive of it, and he brings his formidable mathematical, philosophical and philological learning to bear on every aspect of his theology.

The hesychastic revival was also at the very least an important cultural context for a theological controversy in the decade leading up to the Revolution over 'name-worshipping' (*imiaslavie*).[21] This was a dispute over the assertion by Russian hesychasts on Mount Athos that the invocation of the name of God amounted to the invocation of God Himself, who was mystically present in His name. In hesychastic practice, monks seek an encounter with God through constant silent repetition of the name of Jesus (in the Jesus Prayer: 'Jesus, Son of God, have mercy on me, a sinner'). The name-worshippers founded their case on the distinction drawn by Palamas between God unknowable in His essence, yet knowable in His energies, claiming that it was the energy of God that was encountered in His name. Predictably, the official Russian church condemned the name-worshippers but, tellingly, they were supported by Evgeny Trubetskoy, Florensky and Bulgakov, who went on to write a work called *The Philosophy of the Name* (published posthumously in 1953). One might also mention in this connection that the Neoplatonist philosopher Losev, who also wrote a book called *Philosophy of the Name* (1927), though not involved in this controversy, has been shown to have made use of Palamite theology in his work.[22]

In the sphere of secular thought the hesychastic revival, through Kireevsky and (with some reservations) Solovev, contributed to the flowering of Russian religious philosophy, which, as I have indicated, confidently sought to demonstrate the inter-dependence of revealed and rational truth in the Platonist tradition of Greek patristics. In his revisionist work on Solovev, Evgeny Trubetskoy tries to rescue his friend from the un-Orthodox philosophical positions that the latter's gnostic and German mystico-philosophical orientation gets him into (see below) and to bring out the theologically more orthodox dimensions of his work. His brother Sergey, a specialist in pagan Greek philosophy, published two scholarly analyses of this subject, the second of which – *The Doctrine of the Logos:*

A History (1900) – focused on the influence of Platonism on Christian theology of the Hellenic period. In this work Trubetskoy defends the legitimacy and productiveness of bringing Greek metaphysics to bear on Christian revelation from the criticism of such nineteenth-century Protestant theologians as Ritschl and Harnack. Among the next generation of philosophers, both Frank and Nikolay Lossky adopt a Platonic ontological realism and develop an intuitivist epistemology that, while it owes a debt to Bergson, goes back to Solovev's 'intuition' and the Slavophiles' 'faith' as an organ of perception of absolute being. However, Frank's philosophy is tainted, from an orthodox Christian point of view, by the mystical pantheism that he shares with Solovev and that flows from conceiving the Absolute, in the manner of Schelling, as a total-unity. Lossky retains a theistic position by not identifying the subject with the Absolute and by distinguishing between intellectual intuition of universals and mystical intuition of the transcendent creator God. On the other hand, he defends the theologically disputed doctrine of the transmigration of souls. In general it is probably fair to say that Russian religious philosophy of the Silver Age struggles with the same set of difficulties faced by early Christian thought (the assimilation of Platonism, the struggle with gnosticism) and achieves varying degrees of success. But, unlike the work of the Greek Fathers, it is ultimately to be judged as philosophy, not as theology.

ESOTERIC SPIRITUALITY

In addition to the currents of spirituality deriving from Orthodoxy and religious dissent, the late nineteenth century was also characterised by huge popular interest in and engagement with the occult. In Russia this incorporated practices deriving from native pagan cultures – shamanism, divination of various kinds, astrology – but also practices and beliefs originating in the West, such as spiritualism, theosophy and anthroposophy. The latter in particular were taken very seriously by the educated elite: for example, Solovev was involved in spiritualist circles in his youth and exercised his mediumistic gift of automatic writing most of his life; Bely was a devotee of anthroposophy. Bernice Glatzer Rosenthal has drawn an analogy with Thomas Kuhn's theory of scientific paradigms to elucidate the phenomenon, likening it to the plethora of posited new paradigms that come into being when the old paradigm becomes inadequate to account for all the anomalies that begin to arise. The occult flourishes at times of cultural uncertainty until such time as a new belief system establishes itself.[23] Occult movements like theosophy, she says, spoke to the need for the resolution of the tension between science and religion and the need for *knowledge* of spiritual realities in the increasing absence of faith. Theosophy was a pseudo-religious movement founded in 1875 in New York City by Elena Blavatsky and propagated through her Theosophical Society. Maria Carlson considers it to be the 'most intellectually important' of the occult trends of the time.[24] Blavatsky's doctrine (set out in *Isis Unveiled* (1877) and *The Secret Doctrine* (1888)) aspired to be a 'synthesis of Science, Religion, and Philosophy'. In practice it was a syncretic amalgam of occult doctrines and eastern philosophies, but it served as an important channel into Russian culture for gnosticism in its manifold ancient and modern incarnations: Kabbalism, Hermeticism, Rosicrucianism and so forth. Though Solovev held *Isis Unveiled* in contempt, there are manifold parallels between theosophy and the aspirations and sources of his own work. Indeed, as Glatzer Rosenthal has pointed out, the entire Symbolist movement (which he in part inspired) is based on the occult idea of correspondences between the visible and invisible worlds.[25]

RUSSIAN INTELLECTUAL INFLUENCES

Dostoevsky was enormously influential on the Silver Age. Rozanov (1891), Merezhkovsky (1902), Shestov (1903) and Berdiaev (1923) all wrote monographs on him. Each fashioned him in his own image, but all saw him as uniquely relevant to the concerns of their own age, particularly to the religious concerns, in relation to which he was deemed by all to be a prophet. Solovev, who was personally acquainted with Dostoevsky and who famously accompanied him on his trip to Optina Pustyn in 1878, started the trend with the three speeches he wrote between 1881 and 1883 to commemorate Dostoevsky's death. In these Dostoevsky is cast in the role of artist-prophet, but, as Pamela Davidson has argued, not in terms of Dostoevsky's own nationalist Orthodox world-view but rather in terms of the ecumenical and theocratic ideals that Solovev was promoting at the time and of which he himself wished to be seen as the prophet.[26] Rozanov's *Dostoevsky and the Legend of the Grand Inquisitor* is testimony to his almost total identification with his hero at this early point in his career. Characterised by extensive quotation and paraphrase, it highlights Dostoevsky's defence of the personality against the depersonalising forces of his century and his emphasis on the psychological importance to humans of religion. Rozanov admires Dostoevsky's prescience and identifies the crisis of his own day as the widespread thirst for faith accompanied by the loss of the capacity for it. Rozanov's choice of the 'Legend' for commentary was itself rather prescient, as its theme of Antichrist, or 'mangodhood', was to come to be of seminal importance to Silver Age culture. Merezhkovsky, Shestov and Berdiaev all read Dostoevsky through the lens of Nietzsche. Merezhkovsky's comparison of the 'Dionysian tragedy' of Dostoevsky and the 'Apollonian epic' of Tolstoy is typical: Silver Age commentators habitually dismissed what was perceived as Tolstoy's outmoded preference for 'complete and stable forms' in favour of Dostoevsky's more contemporary feeling for the liminal, chaotic and degenerate, thus directly opposing the Populist Mikhailovsky's view of these Dostoevskian features as morbid. Or rather, Merezhkovsky celebrated Dostoevsky's morbidity as a 'sickness unto life' that was more authentic, and thus had greater spiritual potential, than Tolstoy's sham moral regeneration. Shestov's approach is directly to compare the philosophical trajectories of Dostoevsky and Nietzsche and evaluate the Russian according to how faithful he remains to his exilic insight into the illusoriness of all consolatory ideological constructs. Thus he celebrates Dostoevsky's sceptics and tortured doubters as the 'authentic' Dostoevsky, as courageous representations of the author's disillusionment with the Romantic idealism of his youth (the Underground Man is Shestov's favourite), and criticises as inauthentic and regressive the discourse of Dostoevsky's religious characters. Finally, Berdiaev shares Shestov's analysis of Dostoevsky's crisis of values but evaluates the artist's religious quest positively, as the struggle for godmanhood against the Nietzschean solution of the *Übermensch* or Overman. In accordance with his own views, he emphasises the centrality of freedom to Dostoevsky's world conception, while criticising the nationalistic and messianic dimension of his religious belief.

In the case of Leontev it is difficult to speak of any direct influence on the religious revival of the Silver Age, but equally it is impossible to leave him out of any contextual account of the phenomenon. The writer with whom he is most closely associated, and with whom he corresponded, is Rozanov: both have been likened to Nietzsche, a figure of major importance for the period, yet neither admits to the connection. Leontev's philosophy prefigures the paradoxical quality of the 'artists'' programme, its doomed striving to reconcile opposites, indeed the same fundamental opposites of aestheticism and Christianity. In contrast to them, however, Leontev was a profound pessimist, convinced of the inevitability not of the joyful transfiguration and immortalisation of culture and humanity but of death for both and divine judgement for mortals. The Christian pole of his world outlook was characterised by an asceticism motivated by fear and trembling, the embrace of suffering as due punishment, and was thus far removed not only from the 'artists', who were blind to the concept of sin, but also from the 'academics', for whom the ascetic path was one of love and service. Moreover, Leontev was neither a reformer, like the 'academics', nor a revolutionary, like the 'artists', but an unrepentant reactionary who valued the autocratic state as the guardian of cultural diversity and social division, to which he attributed great aesthetic value, Leontev's 'holy of holies'. It is this political conservatism (and its attendant virulent anti-westernism) that attracted the maverick Rozanov, alongside the quality of paradoxicality in Leontev, of which Rozanov was so proud in himself.

Fedorov's 'philosophy of the common task' has enjoyed a more fruitful reception in Russian culture.[27] Both Dostoevsky and Solovev were genuinely impressed by Fedorov's idiosyncratic genius. Solovev profoundly sympathised with Fedorov's most fundamental concern: that humanity should devote all its efforts to the pursuit of immortality not only for the present generation but also for the ancestors, without whose resurrection the task could not be said to have been completed. It has been argued that Fedorov's ideas influenced the generational theme in *The Brothers Karamazov*.[28] Fedorov's great project has common features with the theurgic orientation of the Silver Age 'artists'. He, as they, conceived of human destiny as resting with humans themselves: salvation was to be primarily through human agency and not through grace. Like the 'artists', Fedorov perceived nature as something to be overcome in the flight from mortality. He conceives the work of resurrection as an artistic one, which transforms the artist even as he or she brings dead matter to life, thus echoing the life-creation (*zhiznetvorchestvo*) agenda of the Symbolists.[29] He also shares the God-seekers' emphasis on the community, the social nature of the new religious order: his entire system is predicated on the very Russian notion of kinship (*rodstvo*). Finally, he conceives of this new order not as 'a new heaven and a new earth', but as the spiritualisation of the existing cosmos. Nonetheless, there were significant differences between Fedorov and the God-seekers. The latter, following Solovev, held the key to immortalisation to be unconsummated erotic love. As Matich has put it, 'accumulated erotic energy would be expended collectively', immortalising the body.[30] Fedorov disdained the sex act because it diverted energy away from the task, but attributed to filial, not erotic, love the power to reunite and to transform. Furthermore, Fedorov's task was conceived as long, painful, self-sacrificing labour, more akin to the ideal of the progressivist 'academics', while the revolutionary 'artists' looked to the moment of sudden and effortless, if cataclysmic, transformation for their salvation from the natural order. One further feature of Fedorov's task was alien to the Silver Age, but central to the utopian aspirations of the first Soviet generation, namely his belief in the role of science and technology in the future immortalisation of humanity.

Solovev's influence can be felt in almost every participant in the religious renaissance, which is scarcely surprising since his work contains, it seems, every single one of the phenomenon's ingredients. One way of looking at this is to separate him into philosopher, religious activist and artist. As a trained philosopher, he set an example (building on the academically unpolished, embryonic theories of the Slavophiles Ivan Kireevsky and Khomiakov) of respectable and philosophically rigorous religious thought, which greatly appealed to the academic Christians even where these rejected his philosophical premises and methodology. He also handed down to them conceptual tools for further creative development, chief among which were the concepts of total-unity (*vseedinstvo*), godmanhood (*bogochelovechestvo*) and Sophia. Solovev's social conscience, his commitment to effecting real social transformation through personal and collective action, and his respect for socialists who, he felt, though not believing in God were nevertheless carrying out his work more effectively than the church, harmonised with the Marxist background and/or political commitment of, for example, the *Landmarks* contributors Berdiaev, Bulgakov, Frank and Struve, as did his passionate polemic against the Russian Orthodox Church of the Synodal era. It is known, for example, that Bulgakov delayed entering the priesthood until after the church reforms. Merezhkovsky's circle shared Solovev's aversion to the institutional church and also (unlike Bulgakov and Florensky, who were inspired by the hesychast revival) to the monastic order. But it was as artist and mystic that Solovev entered the consciousness of the God-seekers among the Symbolists. They embraced his erotic cult of the divine feminine and were compelled by the gnostic dimension of his thought, especially in the form it took in his last, 'theurgic' decade. The key text for them was *The Meaning of Love* (1892–4), which set out a doctrine of immortalisation through chaste heterosexual love (the achievement of androgyny through the union-without-merging of male and female) that was to be extended to society and the cosmos in an erotic utopia. Solovev's last work, *A Short Tale of the Antichrist* (1900), articulated an apocalyptic vision that was the reverse face of his lifelong utopianism. This was a theme of the age. Social and cultural apocalypse was anticipated by all, but whereas the academic Christians dreaded it and sought to forestall it, the Symbolists eagerly awaited it and the positive religious-cultural transformation they believed it would bring about.

Another sense in which Solovev contained all the elements of the religious renaissance is that in many cases he served as a channel for sources which were simultaneously reaching the Silver Age generation from elsewhere. For example, his mystical utopianism was echoed in the beliefs and practices of the Russian sects and may have been in part inspired by them.[31] His doctrine of godmanhood, the divinisation of humanity through the in-dwelling of the Logos, set out in the *Lectures on Godmanhood* (1877–81), is derived from the Orthodox concept of deification that also theologically supported hesychasm, though it is known that Solovev disdained the latter as egotistical escapism and had discovered deification through firsthand knowledge of Greek patristics. His cosmological myth of the fallen Sophia was created out of his reading in the British Museum in 1875 of ancient gnostic and other esoteric literature, including the Jewish Kabbala, but also at second hand from the German Protestant mystics Böhme and Swedenborg and from his intimate knowledge of (and reliance on) Schelling. As I have indicated, gnostic systems and ideas were circulating independently of Solovev. So, too ,was German mysticism: Böhme became a seminal authority for Berdiaev when he discovered him in 1912.

WESTERN INTELLECTUAL INFLUENCES: GERMAN
SPECULATIVE IDEALISM

Gaidenko has traced Solovev's reception of Schelling, Schelling's reception (and the German idealists' reception generally) of seventeenth-century German mysticism and of Meister Eckhart and the mystics' reception of the gnostic systems, thus identifying perhaps the most important western stream of influence on the artistic-intellectual culture of the Silver Age.[32] The salient motifs here are the concept of the essential contiguity of the divine and material spheres and the related notion that humanity belongs simultaneously to both: materially, man belongs to nature but in his spiritual being he is divine. Or, equally: nature is itself divine, being the fallen manifestation of God's otherness, the tragic world soul, the gnostic Sophia who yearns to be reunited with her divine consort, the Logos. Thus, the cosmos is the suffering God in the process of becoming, a process in which humanity plays the defining role of the bringing to consciousness, the spiritualisation, of the world soul. According to Gaidenko, Schelling identifies his notion of God's radical otherness to Himself (the necessity for which, in his system as in Solovev's, arises out of the premise that God is an all-unity in which all opposites are reconciled) with Böhme's *Ungrund*, the 'dark nature' at the foundation of the Divine. This is unconscious and irrational will, out of which, for Schelling, comes the fall into material being.[33] Gaidenko also draws attention to the way in which Schelling's allocation of the Persons of the Trinity to the three aeons of the divinity's evolution – the pre-temporal, temporal and post-temporal – derives ultimately (via Angelus Silesius) from the twelfth-century heretic Joachim of Fiore, who preached the imminent arrival of the era of the Holy Spirit, in which God and man would be united on earth.[34] Solovev, too, looks to a third era of the restored total-unity, a fully realised Divine Humanity (*bogochelovechestvo*), imagined first as a theocracy but ultimately as the erotic utopia that was so influential for the religious Symbolists. The western European millenarian tradition, begun by Joachim and flourishing in the early modern period, arrives in Russia in the early twentieth century simultaneously and with equal force in both its modern guises: as the Marxist belief in the perfect society under communism and as the Romantic religious-philosophical myth of the divinised cosmos. This is why Merezhkovsky could claim that his spiritual revolution was more radical than that of the Bolsheviks.

The Sophia myth proved extraordinarily fecund in Silver Age culture among 'artists' and 'academics' alike. Through Florensky and Bulgakov it even found its way into the church. Despite the manifestly heterodox sources for Sophia, Solovev succeeded in establishing her as an essential component of the religious world-view of the generation that followed him. In *Lectures on Godmanhood* Sophia is incorporated into the Trinity as the passive principle of the second Person, the 'material' upon which the Logos eternally acts. She is the human principle in the pre-incarnate Christ, the ideal archetype of humanity, but also the ideal cosmos. The material cosmos comes into being as a result of her fall; history is the struggle of the fallen Sophia – apparently now identified with the material world – to be restored to the life of the Divinity, and the Incarnation marks the decisive moment when humanity becomes responsible for that task. Later, in his 'theocratic' period, Solovev tries to re-source his Sophia in the wisdom literature of the Old Testament and to distinguish more clearly between the eternally pure divine feminine and the fallen world soul. It was the untainted version that he saw in his visions and who became his poetic muse, while his earthly loves were revered as her incarnations. The poetic cult of Sophia was inherited by Blok, though for him the 'Beautiful Lady' was to metamorphose into the sinister 'Stranger'; his chaste marriage to Liubov Mendeleeva was framed by himself, Bely and Sergey Solovev as a mystical erotic union in the manner of *The Meaning of Love* that was to inaugurate the apocalyptic transfiguration of the world. I have already indicated how Solovev's late theurgic conception of Sophia feeds into the Merezhkovskys' erotic utopia. Meanwhile, both Bulgakov and Florensky took up the Sophia theme in their thinking seemingly independently of each other, though Florensky is often credited with having influenced Bulgakov in the direction of his theology.[35] In *Pillar and Ground of the Truth* Florensky is concerned to locate Sophia fully in the Orthodox liturgical and iconographic tradition and avoids recourse to the gnostic myth in his theological account of her. Nevertheless, this account is ambiguous: Sophia is the thought-content of the Logos and thus a fourth hypostatic element of the Trinity, yet she is not consubstantial with God, but created. In the various roles ascribed to her by Florensky she is always a mediator between heaven and earth, manifesting differently in each aspect. Bulgakov pursued the Sophianic idea throughout his life, producing his major theological works on her well after the Revolution, in exile. His failure (or unwillingness) clearly to delineate Sophia's status as either created or divine led the church to censure him both for pantheism and for introducing a fourth Person into the Trinity. Though a devout Orthodox Christian, he nevertheless remains bound to the Schellingian tradition bequeathed to him by Solovev.

NIETZSCHE

Nietzsche had a powerful liberating effect on Russia's literary elite, since he gave them permission to slough off the burden of artistic responsibility for the people and pursue personal artistic goals. He was used in the attack on the utilitarianism, positivism and rationalism of radical intelligentsia ideology, now perceived as stultifying. Shestov mimicked him in a sustained campaign against *all* consolatory constructs of the mind, including philosophical idealism. Nietzsche was a licence to indulge anti-bourgeois sentiments. His cult of beauty set the tone for the dominance of aesthetic over ethical criteria of excellence in the art of the Symbolist period. But more than anything else Nietzsche was understood religiously in Russia, almost because of, rather than despite, his polemic against Christianity. This was a thinker who took religion seriously. The manner of his proclamation of the death of God was worthy of an Old Testament prophet; it reflected in reverse the dramatic and extremist spirit of the Russian Schismatics who proclaimed the arrival of Antichrist. Nietzsche *did* proclaim the arrival of the Antichrist! His apocalyptic message resonated with the dissident Russian religious consciousness of Merezhkovsky's God-seekers, who, like Nietzsche (and informed by him), rejected conventional Christian ethics and attacked the ossified church. Even though these did so in the name of a new Christianity of the Holy Spirit, their vision of the new religion was imbued with Nietzschean values of creativity, destruction and the overcoming of conventional sexual mores. Nevertheless, Merezhkovsky's circle rejected Nietzsche's aristocratic individualism (though precisely this appealed to Berdiaev) and sought instead a new form of religious community united by eros. The Symbolists were very much attuned to the cultic and collectivist aspects of Nietzsche, as expressed in a text of seminal importance for them, the early *Birth of Tragedy from the Spirit of Music* (1872). As I have indicated above, the loss of self in Dionysian ecstasy resonated with the much-admired communal ecstasy pursued through the rites of the Flagellants. What was sought was not personal union with God, exemplified by the monk-ascetic and modelled, Merezhkovsky correctly perceived, on the divine-humanity of Christ, but collective ecstasy in the Spirit, union with God through religious revolution. It was also largely through *The Birth of Tragedy* that the people of the new religious consciousness embraced and interpreted pagan Hellenic culture. The Christian–pagan opposition, central to the thought of Ivanov, Merezhkovsky and Rozanov, contained the polarities of the times: ethics–aesthetics; agape–eros; spirit–flesh; heaven–earth; Christ–Antichrist. Each sought his own resolution of, and suffered his own ambivalence towards, these conflicting phenomena.

Nietzsche was important also for the academic Christians, but as a challenge to Christianity that had to be overcome, rather than an ally in the cause of religious revolution. He was not dismissed but actively engaged with by these thinkers as a worthy and serious opponent. Frank was one of the editors of his collected works (1909–12), and his ideas were treated at length in the essay collection *Problems of Idealism*, to which Berdiaev, Bulgakov and Frank all contributed. I would single out the sober religious humanism which this volume and its successor, *Landmarks*, elaborated, as the reasoned response to both the irresponsible (from the *Landmarks* camp's point of view) irrationalism of Russian Dionysianism, which lacked even the pagan corrective of Apollo, and the cult of the Overman that was discerned by some in the heroic pose of the atheist *intelligent*-revolutionary. Whereas the religious mysticism of the aesthetes was inspired by the sectarian communities, these thinkers drew from the wisdom of the Orthodox tradition. Of course, the Overman had an established Russian predecessor in the man-god, whom Dostoevsky had opposed to Christ, the God-man. Dostoevsky had anticipated Nietzsche in his exploration, through fictional characters such as Raskolnikov (*Crime and Punishment*, 1866) and Kirillov (*The Devils*, 1871–2), of the consequences of setting oneself above Christian ethics. If God does not exist, all is permitted for the one who dares. Dostoevsky had also set the image of a monk (Zosima) against the arguments of the rebel Ivan Karamazov and his Antichrist-like hero, the Grand Inquisitor, whose Jesuitical pseudo-paradise he believed anticipated socialist despotism. In his essay for *Landmarks* Bulgakov also draws on the ascetic ideal to argue for the *social* importance of the pursuit of personal moral perfection. In contrast to Solovev and Merezhkovsky's circle, he sees the ascetic ideal as compatible with work in and for the community, emphasising the values of patient personal labour and humility before God as the antidote to the moral nihilism and utopianism of the socialist intelligentsia that would lead Russia to ruin. Florensky, though a priest like Bulgakov, unlike him was close to Symbolist circles and shared their aestheticism: he looked to the Orthodox saint as an aesthetic counter-ideal to the decadence-prone extra-ecclesial pursuit of beauty by the Symbolists. He conceived the hesychast as an icon of spiritual beauty, purged of all traces of the demonic. This was his answer to the moral dangers of Nietzschean aestheticism.

FROM MARXISM TO IDEALISM

It might seem on first consideration that Marxism, as the last incarnation of the intelligentsia's revolutionary socialism, and one which was made fully to inherit the latter's entrenched atheistic bias, ought to remain outside the narrative of Silver Age religious revival. This is not in fact the case as far as many prominent 'academics' are concerned, since for these the embrace of Marxism proved to be the first stage in their development of a religious world-view. Several were active in the revolutionary movement in their youth, prompted by a strong social conscience that they never lost. Already as a student Struve was publishing articles in socialist journals. In 1896 he attended the International Socialist Congress in London, and he wrote the Manifesto of the (Marxist) Russian Social-Democratic Labour Party on its formation in 1898. In the same year Berdiaev was expelled from Kiev University for his involvement in student demonstrations, and he went on to spend three years in exile in Vologda because of his illegal activities as a Marxist. Frank was involved in revolutionary circles in Moscow until 1896 and was expelled from Moscow for writing a revolutionary pamphlet as late as 1899. The attraction of Marxism to these intellectuals in the 1890s was what was seen as the scientific rigour of its political economics, to which the subjective idealism of Russian Populism was unfavourably compared: both Struve and Berdiaev began their academic careers with a Marxist critique of Populism, and Bulgakov started with two works on economics from a broadly Marxist perspective. By the same token, Marxism over time lost its appeal precisely in so far as it failed to be consistently philosophically credible in their view. Struve, Bulgakov and Frank all rejected as intellectually fantastic the utopian, millenarian dimension of Marxism, the expectation of a dialectical leap from determinism to freedom after the Revolution, and insisted on an evolutionary approach that set them against the 'orthodox' Marxism of Plekhanov and Lenin. Further, if a positivist approach to economic questions was acceptable to them, the application of scientific methodology to social and ideological questions was not. The reception of Marxist thought by the revolutionary intelligentsia also threw the moral relativism inherent in a thoroughgoing materialism into high relief: the *Landmarks* symposium consistently criticised the radicals' subordination of ethical considerations to political goals and of the individual to social class. It was the primary concern philosophically to defend the unconditional value and freedom of the individual human being as a moral but also a creative agent that led these and other scholars eventually to embrace the neo-Kantian idealism that dominated academic philosophy in Germany and in Russia at the beginning of the twentieth century. The shift from Marxism to idealism is registered in *Problems of Idealism*, but some of the contributions to this volume show that even at this stage philosophical idealism was expanding into religious faith, with God being seen as the ultimate foundation and guarantor of the personality.

The former Marxists would develop their new-found Christian faith philosophically and theologically in very different directions, with a striking difference in their respective positions being evident already by the time of the October Revolution. At that point Struve was politically a right-wing liberal and philosophically still guided by neo-Kantian idealism, accepting the irrationality of the unknown noumenal world, upon the existence of which human freedom, the precondition for the morally responsible life, is predicated. As Gaidenko has pointed out, this essentially places him in the Protestant religious tradition out of which Kantianism arose.[36] Frank went on to repudiate Kantian dualism and to write *The Object of Knowledge* (1915), in which he begins to elaborate a metaphysics of total-unity that places him back in the tradition of German speculative idealism of the Schellingian kind, and *Man's Soul* (1917), a defence of the metaphysical dimension of the soul against the empirical psychological definition of it.[37] Berdiaev, under the influence of Ivanov and Chulkov's mystical anarchism and more decisively, from 1912, of Böhme, would develop an anarchic personalism that accorded freedom the highest value, posited that humans always already dwell in Christ and partake of His Sonship and attributed the same creative powers to humanity as those enjoyed by God (*The Meaning of the Creative Act*, 1916). He nevertheless continued to consider himself an Orthodox Christian.

Bulgakov married his liberal individualism to a politically engaged Christian socialism, seeking to reunite the aspirations of socialism with what he was convinced were their religious roots. He failed to find sufficient support for his attempts to enshrine this position in concrete organisations – the Christian Brotherhood of Struggle and the Christian Political Union – and became despondent about the diminishing prospects for success of Russian democracy. The Revolution found him preparing for the priesthood and turning in his thinking away from socio-cultural criticism and towards the theology that would dominate his output in exile: the transitional work *The Unfading Light* (1917) bears witness to this shift.

CONCLUSION

The religious renaissance was not allowed to continue long into the Soviet era. The pattern for its participants was generally exile or death, both not infrequently at the instigation of the state. Among the 'artists', the Merezhkovskys and Shestov left voluntarily as early as 1919 and Ivanov in 1924 (after four years as Professor of Classics at Baku University), while Rozanov died of hunger and despair in 1919. Many of the 'academics' were expelled from the Soviet Union on the 'philosophers' ships' of 1922: the passengers included Berdiaev, Bulgakov, Frank and Lossky. Florensky was spared for a time thanks to the contribution he could make as a scientist but was imprisoned in 1933 and shot in 1937. Remarkably, Losev survived – just – to make a life for himself as an academic in the Soviet Union: he died in 1988. It was left to the émigré community to take the renaissance forward into a new phase, and all of the figures I have discussed here did indeed continue to think, write and publish. A few achieved an international profile as philosophers (Berdiaev, Shestov) or theologians (Bulgakov). Penetration of their work into the Soviet Union was patchy. Now, in the post-Soviet era, all are being republished and discussed in the Russian academic community, but it remains to be seen whether their work may yet have the impact on the Russian people as a whole that they longed in vain for it to have during their lifetimes.

NOTES

1. Nicolas Zernov, *The Russian Religious Renaissance of the Twentieth Century* (London: Darton, Longman and Todd, 1963).
2. P. P. Gaidenko, *Vladimir Solov'ev i filosofiia Serebrianogo veka* (Moscow: Progress-Traditsiia, 2001).

3. Christopher Read, *Religion, Revolution and the Russian Intelligentsia 1900–1912: The Vekhi Debate and Its Intellectual Background* (London and Basingstoke: Macmillan, 1979), p. 13.
4. Lionel Kochan and Richard Abraham, *The Making of Modern Russia*, 2nd edn (Harmondsworth: Penguin Books, 1983), pp. 215–16.
5. Vera Shevzov, *Russian Orthodoxy on the Eve of Revolution* (New York: Oxford University Press, 2004), p. 18.
6. On the church reforms, see Shevzov, *Russian Orthodoxy*, pp. 12–53, and Zernov, *The Russian Religious Renaissance*, pp. 63–85.
7. See, for example, Dmitry Pospielovsky, *The Orthodox Church in the History of Russia* (Crestwood, N.Y.: St Vladimir's Seminary Press, 1998), pp. 75–6.
8. Pospielovsky, *The Orthodox Church*, p. 150.
9. Details of these can be found in George Ivask, 'Russian modernist poets and the mystic sectarians' in G. Gibian and H. W. Tjalsma (eds.), *Russian Modernism: Culture and the Avant-Garde 1900–1930* (Ithaca and London: Cornell University Press, 1976), pp. 85–106, especially p. 106.
10. The ground-breaking work on this subject is A. Etkind, *Khlyst: Sekty, literatura i revoliutsiia* (Moscow: Novoe literaturnoe obozrenie, 1998).
11. Etkind, *Khlyst*, pp. 191 and 184 respectively.
12. The event is recounted in Gaidenko, *Vladimir Solov'ev*, pp. 327–9.
13. Gaidenko, *Vladimir Solov'ev*, pp. 334–6.
14. Etkind, *Khlyst*, pp. 8–9. An account in English is available in Olga Matich, *Erotic Utopia: The Decadent Imagination in Russia's Fin de Siècle* (Madison: University of Wisconsin Press, 2005), pp. 260–2.
15. Etkind, *Khlyst*, p. 10.
16. Michael Wachtel, 'Editor's introduction' in *Viacheslav Ivanov: Selected Essays*, trans. and notes Robert Bird, ed. Michael Wachtel (Evanston: Northwestern University Press, 2003), p. viii.
17. For a full account of Velichkovsky's work and the hesychastic revival, see S. Chetverikov, *Starets Paisii Velichkovskii: His Life, Teachings, and Influence on Orthodox Monasticism*, trans. Vasily Lickwar and Alexander J. Lisenko (Belmont, Mass.: Nordland, 1980).
18. A discussion circle called the Orthodox Brotherhood of St Seraphim of Sarov, founded by S. A. Alekseev (Askol'dov), existed between 1921 and 1928. See Zernov, *The Russian Religious Renaissance*, p. 208.
19. On the history of religious education in Russia, see Georges Florovsky, *Ways of Russian Theology: Parts I and II*, trans. Robert L. Nichols (Belmont, Mass.: Nordland, 1979).
20. Zernov claims 'it marked the beginning of a new era in Russian theology': see Zernov, *The Russian Religious Renaissance*, p. 101.
21. On the name-worshipping controversy, see Rowan Williams (ed.), *Sergii Bulgakov: Towards a Russian Political Theology* (Edinburgh: T&T Clark, 1999), pp. 8–13, and Catherine Evtuhov, *The Cross and the Sickle: Sergei Bulgakov and the Fate of Russian Religious Philosophy* (Ithaca and London: Cornell University Press, 1997), pp. 210–18.

22. See, for example, Konstantin V. Zenkin, 'On the religious foundations of A. F. Losev's philosophy of music', *Studies in East European Thought*, 56 (2004), 161–72.

23. Bernice Glatzer Rosenthal (ed.), *The Occult in Russian and Soviet Culture* (Ithaca and London: Cornell University Press, 1997), p. 6.

24. Maria Carlson, 'Fashionable occultism: spiritualism, theosophy, freemasonry, and hermeticism in fin-de-siècle Russia' in Glatzer Rosenthal (ed.), *The Occult in Russian and Soviet Culture*, pp. 135–52; see p. 139. She has also written a monograph on the subject: Maria Carlson, *'No Religion Higher Than Truth': A History of the Theosophical Movement in Russia 1875–1922* (Princeton University Press, 1993).

25. Glatzer Rosenthal (ed.), *The Occult in Russian and Soviet Culture*, p. 12.

26. Pamela Davidson, 'Vladimir Solov'ev and the ideal of prophecy', *Slavonic and East European Review*, 78 (2000), 643–70. The relevant section is found on pp. 650–9.

27. Critical opinion is divided as to how influential Fedorov was for Russian culture. See Irene Masing-Delic, *Abolishing Death: A Salvation Myth of Russian Twentieth-Century Literature* (Stanford University Press, 1992), pp. 102–3. The chapter on Fedorov in this work serves as an accessible introduction to a complex philosophy: pp. 76–104.

28. See W. J. Leatherbarrow, *Fyodor Dostoyevsky: The Brothers Karamazov* (Cambridge University Press, 1992), pp. 27–30.

29. On this phenomenon, see Irina Paperno and Joan Delaney Grossman (eds.), *Creating Life: The Aesthetic Utopia of Russian Modernism* (Stanford University Press, 1994).

30. Matich, *Erotic Utopia*, p. 7.

31. See Etkind, *Khlyst*, pp. 167–79.

32. Gaidenko, 'Gnosticheskie motivy v ucheniiakh Shellinga i Vl. Solov'eva' in Sergei Bocharov and Aleksandr Parnis (eds.), *Vittorio. Mezhdunarodnyi nauchnyi sbornik, posviashchennyi 75-letiiu Vittorio Strady* (Moscow: Tri kvadrata, 2005), pp. 68–92.

33. Ibid., p. 79.

34. Ibid., pp. 85–6.

35. It is Williams who argues for Bulgakov's relative independence in this matter: see Williams, *Sergii Bulgakov*, pp. 120–6.

36. Gaidenko, *Vladimir Solov'ev*, p. 451.

37. Philip Boobbyer, *S. L. Frank: The Life and Work of a Russian Philosopher, 1877–1950* (Athens, Ohio: Ohio University Press, 1995), p. 93.

PART III

Themes and constructs

CHAPTER 9

The West

Vera Tolz

Since Peter the Great's reforms 'the West' (*zapad*) had become arguably the most important ingredient of modern Russian identity. Through debating Russia's relationship to this constructed category, the Russian elites pictured Russia as a nation and as an empire, identified paths for their country's modernising political, economic and social reforms, analysed the place of the individual in society and dwelt on the role of religion in the modern world.[1] In the period discussed in this chapter, the dichotomy between the West and the East (Orient) (*vostok*), or Europe and Asia, constituted an essential component of how all the European elites perceived their nations.[2] These categories are, of course, not fixed, objective entities. They are cultural and political constructs 'talked and written into existence'.[3] The geographical boundaries of these categories have changed as a result of historical events and often have depended on the arguments those evoking them aimed to advance.[4] While 'the West' and 'Europe' were sometimes identified as one and the same, on other occasions, as we will see in this chapter, 'the West' and true 'Europe' could be separated and contrasted. 'Europe' and 'the West' have never been purely geographical categories; rather, they are, above all, cultural and developmental (defined through common cultural, social and political traits and patterns of development), as well as temporal (as reflected, for instance, in the arguments that true European values were manifested in the past or would be realised in the future). These categories could be evoked in 'totalising' and 'essentialising' ways, particularly when they were used to designate the 'Other'. Yet, their heterogeneity could also be acknowledged, since one of their components could be viewed positively and another negatively.

Addressing the key issues facing Russia through the discourse on the West and Europe, the Russian elites were full participants in the European debates of their time; they responded to the ideas articulated by their counterparts elsewhere in Europe and, in turn, influenced Pan-European perceptions of Russia and Europe in many important ways. It is significant for the understanding of the construction of Russian images of the West and Europe that, at the time when 'the West' and 'Europe' were becoming the central components of Russian identity, in western Europe an image of the eastern periphery of Christian Europe (eastern Europe) was consistently presented as not quite European. Within the framework of this dichotomy between East and West within Europe itself, which Larry Wolff argued was fully formed during the Enlightenment period of the eighteenth century, only France, the Low Countries, northern Italy and Britain – that is to say, western Europe – were regarded as the true Europe.[5] Germany was also usually included in this category, but at times (during the First World War, for instance), the image of two Germanys, with one (militaristic) part excluded from Europe, was advanced.[6] In this vision, eastern Europe was represented as the intermediate zone between Europe and Asia, between barbarism and civilisation, and as a region marked by 'backwardness'. Eastern European intellectuals, with Russians at the forefront, struggled against this perception in the attempt to broaden the boundaries of Europe, rejecting the exclusionist claims of western Europeans. It should be remembered that they operated within the parameters of a Eurocentric vision, based on a belief in the superiority of 'European civilisation' as manifested in its cultural achievements and scientific and technological progress. The development of other societies was measured against the European yardstick. Belinsky summed up this perception thus: '[e]verything human is European, and everything European is human'.[7] It was only in 1869 that the Pan-Slavist Danilevsky became one of the first European thinkers to question such a view.

In the period discussed in this chapter, Russian thinkers often applied the techniques of othering through emphasising the difference between Russia and 'the West' (western Europe) and attacking various features of 'the West'. This rejection and criticism of the West was accompanied, however, by claims that Russia belonged, at least since the time of Peter the Great, to a wider European political and cultural realm. For most Russian thinkers, neither western Europe itself nor its specific civilisation was homogeneous. As the religious philosopher Bulgakov put it, western European civilisation, both historically and contemporarily, was a 'many-branched tree'.[8] Thus, one could choose from the western European heritage the parts which reflected 'true' European values, rejecting the 'false' ones. And with a particular messianic zeal, Russian intellectuals defined the salvation of Europe's own true ideals as Russia's historic mission.[9] Indeed, while postulating major differences between 'the culture [*prosveshchenie*] of Europe' and that of Russia, the early Slavophile Ivan Kireevsky made it clear that he meant 'the culture of the West' or western Europe, noting at the same time that it was 'impossible to imagine the development of intellectual life in Russia without its relationship with Europe and the intellectual development of Europe without its relationship with Russia'.[10] While castigating western Europe for forgetting Christ, Dostoevsky spoke at the same time about Russia's destiny as 'incontestably all-European' and argued that the Russians had two fatherlands – 'our Rus and Europe'.[11] The proponent of Official Nationality, Shevyrev, coined in 1841 the term 'rotten West' (*gniloi zapad*), whose common translation into English as 'rotten Europe' is misleading.[12] In turn, in 1880 the liberal historian Kavelin criticised those Westernisers of the 1840s who had tended to reduce Europe to its western core.[13] In sum, the full equation of Europe with the West and the consequent exclusion of Russia from Europe, as was the case with Chaadaev and to some extent Danilevsky, were exceptions rather than the norm in Russian thought of the imperial period.

In different periods of imperial Russian history different issues acquired particular importance in shaping the debate about the West and Europe and Russia's relationship to both. Since the middle of the eighteenth century Lomonosov, Fonvizin and Novikov had already started thinking, to use contemporary terminology, about how a society could modernise without succumbing to a slavish imitation of foreign models. From the 1820s onwards, in the aftermath of the French Revolution and Napoleonic Wars and under the impact of the German Romantic tradition, the issues of nationalism (how to define Russia as a nation culturally and politically) began to dominate the debate about Europe. Beginning in the late 1840s, and particularly in the aftermath of the 1848 revolutions, contemporary western Europe, industrialising and bourgeois, captured the imagination of Russian thinkers and turned their particular attention to the western European models of economic development. If Russians often felt defensive when comparing Russia as a nation with its western European counterparts, they were much more confident about Russia's achievements as an empire. After the humiliation of the Crimean War, Russian thinkers were particularly keen to emphasise that, in carrying out Europe's 'civilising mission in Asia', Russia held many advantages over the West. In the last decades of tsarist rule, in addition to debating all the above-mentioned subjects, a trend towards collapsing the boundaries between East and West was noticeable, based on the profound questioning of Eurocentric visions of the world that was to be fully expressed by the Eurasianist movement of the 1920s.

Having outlined this rough chronology of the Russian debates, this chapter will now look at specific spatial, cultural, political and economic images and definitions of the West and Europe articulated by Russian intellectuals.

SPATIAL CONSTRUCTIONS OF EUROPE

A discussion of the geographical boundaries between Europe and Asia, started by the Greeks and continued in medieval western Europe, was of little political and cultural significance for Russia before the early eighteenth century. Until then, the dominant European perception of the Tanais or Don as marking the boundary between Europe and Asia, placing a large portion of the historical core of Muscovy in Asia, was not a matter of particular concern, as is reflected in sixteenth- and seventeenth-century Russian cosmographical works. The situation changed with Peter's Europeanising reforms, which brought with them the perception that Europe was culturally and politically pre-eminent. It was the champion of Peter's policies, the historian Tatishchev, who in the 1730s, after affirming Europe's superiority over other parts of the world, suggested a new boundary between Europe and Asia along the Ural Mountains. This new geographical vision placed a large part of Russia within Europe and stressed the similarity between European empires, where the European metropolis and colonies were separated by a natural boundary (water), and Russia, where this boundary was a mountain range.[14] At the very same time, a Swedish officer, Johann von Strahlenberg, ensured that the boundary through the Urals was accepted in Europe at large.

Tatishchev's designation of Siberia as an Asiatic colony clearly separated from the Russian European metropolis began to be questioned by the Decembrists and was then rejected later in the nineteenth century.[15] It was, however, the Pan-Slavists Danilevsky and Lamansky who directly challenged this geographical outline of Europe. Following Alexander von Humboldt and other German and French scholars, they began to deny the existence of a natural boundary between Europe and Asia, which hitherto had been important for sustaining Europe's self-glorifying claim of being a separate continent. For them, Europe became geographically nothing but an extension of Asia, a point which provided a foundation for their attack on Europe's claims of cultural superiority. Their theories, of course, were particularly significant for Russia and, more broadly, the world of Slavdom, proclaimed by the Russian Pan-Slavists to be a self-contained, culturally unified geographical region.[16]

Danilevsky was a leading figure in the European arena in the revision of dominant Eurocentric perceptions of the world.[17] He was, however, also part of a broader trend to which orientalist scholars in Germany, Austria and Russia contributed particularly significantly.[18] One example of the emerging new vision was the incorporation of what used to be, from a European perspective, one of the main parts of 'the Orient', the Near East, into 'the West' in the writings of orientalist scholars. With obvious implications for the definition of Russia's place in the world, Bartold, the foremost Russian specialist on Islam, outlined in 1912 the following cultural geography of the West: 'The near East, including Egypt, which is usually meant in western Europe when [people] speak about the "East" (*vostok*) constitutes, in reality, despite frequent military clashes, one cultural-historical whole with Europe and together they constitute "the West" in relation to more eastern cultural states such as India and China.'[19]

Certainly for Bartold, Russia was culturally part of Europe and his newly defined 'West'. At the same time, as will be discussed in more detail below, late imperial Russian orientalists did a lot to undermine the East–West dichotomy both geographically and culturally, and thus constituted a link between Danilevsky and the 1920s Eurasianists.

CULTURAL CONSTRUCTIONS

However important the issue of the geography of Europe and the West was, the cultural definition of Europe was far more central to how Russia and the West were conceived. The identification of western Christians as Europeans goes back to at least the fourteenth century. In western Europe, during the time of the Enlightenment, the equation of the western Christian tradition with Europe and a negative view of the eastern Christianity of Byzantium were the dominant perceptions.[20] In the western Europeans' own overlying definition, Europe was equated with the lands of western Christianity; it was the heir to the western Roman Empire, distinguished from other parts of the world by such developments as the Renaissance and Reformation and by distinctive political institutions and legal systems. It was widely argued that these distinct developments created people who had a particular passion for freedom and rationality (a deeper affinity for reason in contrast to the unquestioning acceptance of authority and tradition).[21] Those western Christians (in eastern and central Europe) who were seen by their western European counterparts as not sufficiently manifesting this passion for political freedom were often represented as not quite European.[22]

Russian thinkers reacted to this self-perception of 'the West' as the only Europe with both acceptance and rejection. In his first 'Philosophical Letter', Chaadaev most famously reproduced this narrow definition of

Europe and then postulated Russia's otherness on the basis of its accept-
ance of Christianity from Byzantium. Chaadaev's Europe was that of
Latin Christendom, whose ideals of 'duty, justice, law and order' were
the result of particular historical developments 'which have formed
European society'.[23] The [western] European civilisation of which, for
Chaadaev, the British institutions were 'the most representative' was to
him 'the final destiny of the human species', which neither 'the [eastern]
Christianity of Abyssinians' nor the modernisation pursued by the
Japanese 'could bring about'.[24] This positive image of western
Christianity, in which western European cultural and political development was rooted, was advanced by other Russian Westernisers. For the
celebrated Moscow University Professor of History Granovsky, 'western
Christianity' was 'the enlightened form of Christianity', whereas for
Kavelin, despite his refusal to perceive the world of western Christianity
as the only Europe, western Christianity nevertheless represented 'the
active, reformatory side of Christianity' which had produced great cultural
and political achievements and not simply 'the pope and atheism' as late
Slavophiles such as Dostoevsky would have it.[25]

The Slavophiles, of course, also identified the West with the world of
Latin Christianity but viewed it largely negatively, or at least as inferior to
Russia with its eastern Christian roots.[26] Influenced by German
Romanticism and such critics of the state of Christianity in the West as
Franz von Baader, the Russian Slavophiles condemned the 'abstract rationality' (*otvlechennyi razum* and *rassudochnost*) of 'the West' and its excessive
focus on formal logic and science as being one-sided and failing to appreciate intuitive, non-discursive forms of thinking, which were particularly
well developed in pre-Petrine Rus.[27] For Kireevsky, the roots of this western
trait were to be found in the heritage of the pagan Roman Empire, which
represented the 'domination of material interests'. In contrast, Russia was
an heir of the Greek (Byzantine) enlightenment with its emphasis on things
spiritual.[28] Thus, the image of 'the West' as materialistic and non-western
societies as more spiritual was originally articulated in religious terms and
then incorporated in the analysis of contemporary socio-political realities.
Russian Christianity might be of the East, but western Christianity was
shaped by Roman paganism. This perception explains why the early
Slavophiles viewed St Petersburg, with its architectural appropriation of
Roman imperial symbolism, as a pagan city.[29] Even worse, in some contemporary western societies, particularly in France, Christ was forgotten
altogether. And Russian thinkers from Dostoevsky to Vladimir Solovev, as
well as the authors of the famous *Landmarks* collection on the historical role

of the Russian intelligentsia, suggested that it should be Russia's goal to resurrect Europe's Christian tradition.[30]

Even for the Slavophiles not everything in the culture of the West deserved to be criticised. Though the West's focus on scientific and technological progress could be perceived as excessive, the Slavophiles agreed that western Europe's advances in this area deserved a certain admiration.[31] Similarly, in terms of their knowledge of and pride in their own histories and traditions, the peoples of the West were far ahead of Russia, they argued. Somehow, western Europeans were able to preserve their national uniqueness (*samobytnost*) and be Europeans at the same time, whereas Russians tended to renounce their national past in order to become Europeans, Kireevsky noted with regret. While complaining that the Russian elites were always 'dressed in brand new clothes' (i.e. constantly rejecting the heritage of the past), Khomiakov praised Britain's respect for tradition.[32] So did Konstantin Aksakov, for whom: 'England is the best fruit of western civilisation ... all improvements take place peacefully ... It is a reason why England represents such a great example. Look at it, and we will see that its religious and moral foundations are strong ... England, while advancing so quickly, honours its past, preserves its traditions.'[33] At the same time, not only the Slavophiles but also some committed Westernisers, such as Belinsky, disliked the petty-bourgeois culture of contemporary Europe. Herzen, who combined the ideas of both intellectual currents, was a particularly vocal critic of bourgeois society.[34]

This cultural construction of Europe often had specific temporal dimensions. Since Fonvizin's *Letters from France* and subsequently in the writings of the most influential nineteenth-century thinkers, such as Chaadaev and Herzen, Europe had been depicted as old and decaying and thus could be unfavourably contrasted with Russia and the United States of America, whose youthfulness presented an advantage.[35] Just as, for most Europeans, the glory of 'the East' was in the past while the present was pitiful, the same was the case with Europe for many Russian thinkers. While contemporary western societies could be strongly criticised for their corruption of morals, excessive materialism, focus on narrowly understood personal interests, the hypocrisy of their political system and banality of their bourgeois culture, even the West's harshest critics, such as Danilevsky and the philosopher Leontev, greatly admired certain periods of western European history. According to Leontev, for whom the emerging egalitarian mass culture of western Europe was 'aesthetically repulsive',[36] the true Europe was that of the medieval western European knighthood and of the period between the Renaissance and the eighteenth century with its aristocratic cultural elite, which, in contrast to the Slavophiles, he much preferred to pre-Petrine Rus.[37] Danilevsky, in common with many conservative western European thinkers, looked with nostalgia to the seventeenth century, which for him represented the peak of creativity of the 'Germano-Romance cultural-historical type' which he equated with Europe.[38]

POLITICAL IMAGES

While the cultural affinity between post-Petrine Russia and Europe was self-evident to most Russian thinkers in the imperial period, the differences between Russia and 'the West' in the political realm, particularly after the French Revolution, were also universally acknowledged. In the nineteenth century, western Europe was increasingly perceived as the place of con-stitutionalism, development of formal democracy and parliamentary insti-tutions. As early as the 1780s, the historian Boltin was claiming the superiority of monarchy over a parliamentary system, noting that 'the diseases of monarchy are short-lived and light; the diseases of republicanism are harsh and fatal'.[39] Reinforced by Karamzin, the criticism of constitu-tionalism, parliamentarianism and democracy and the emphasis on their unsuitability for Russia were an important feature of the Slavophiles' writ-ings in the 1840s and the 1850s. Criticising any modern state power as corrupting, the Slavophiles posited the superiority of the Russian people over their western European counterparts because of the former's alleged lack of concern about political matters and interest in 'moral' rather than 'political' freedom. Democracy in the western sense was simply 'a game of counting votes' based on the incorrect assumption that 'truth was always on the side of the majority'.[40] Constitutionalism, Samarin argued, was simply a codification of current injustices.[41]

The Slavophiles were critical of the western European judicial systems, derived from Roman law, which had a logical 'external form' but lacked 'inner justice' (*vnutrenniaia spravedlivost*),[42] and denied that individuals in the West, whether historically or in the present, were freer than in Russia. Echoing Fonvizin's claim in the 1780s that formal political freedoms in reality had left poor French peasants less free than Russians,[43] Kireevsky denied that historically the individual (*lichnost*) was more respected in the West than in Russia. For him, in the West, the individual was simply a juridical category, a mere 'reflection of the right of [private] property' which constrained his life. In contrast, 'in Russian public life, the individual is the first element', he insisted.[44] In particular, the peasant commune in medieval Rus cherished the individual without suppressing him in any way.[45]

For the Slavophiles, Europe's political history, based on the violence of medieval knights, a conflict between church and state and an excessive concern about formal political freedoms, produced societies which were the amalgamation of atomised individuals not connected with each other by any moral bonds.[46] This negative view of formal political freedoms and the perception of western European parliamentary institutions as a façade masking social and economic inequalities and exploitation reached its apogee in the ideology of Populism in the late 1860s and 1870s. For this generation of Russian socialists, Britain ceased to provide any positive examples, as it often had done for the early Slavophiles. Instead, it was a place where western political institutions and capitalism were linked up particularly closely to represent the interests of only a small section of society.[47]

The alternative approach of the Westernisers, who saw western European constitutionalism as a model for Russia, can also be traced to eighteenth-century authors such as Radishchev, whose writings offered one of the first positive images of the United States in Russian thought, and Novikov, with his interest in Britain's constitutional monarchy. In the aftermath of the Napoleonic Wars, the Decembrists attempted to implement their political ideals based on western models, for which they were later accused by the Slavophiles of bringing 'the fruits of un-Russian elements' (*plod nerusskikh nachal*) to their country.[48] One of the Decembrist leaders, Muravev, mod-elled his ideal Russia on the federal system of the United States, while the Southern Society's leader, Pestel, advocated large-scale capitalist ownership on the basis of Adam Smith's political economic theory.[49] The Westernisers of the 1840s held a positive image of western bourgeois democracy. Granovsky particularly praised the West's 'dispassionate legal system' devel-oped on the foundation of the Roman law.[50] For him, as well as for other liberals such as Kavelin, Annenkov and Botkin, only the western European political framework granted people a wide range of civil and political rights and thus respected the individual. Therefore, according to Kavelin, one should trace the beginning of 'the principle of personality in Russian history' back to Peter's westernising reforms.[51]

While the Slavophiles searched for their political models in pre-Petrine Rus, from the second half of the 1840s onwards some of the Russian thinkers who looked for their models in the West began to find the values of the true Europe in the ideas of French socialists. One of the most original Russian thinkers, Herzen, argued that contemporary western Europe rep-resented 'an ironic abuse' of the French ideals of 'Liberty, Equality, Fraternity' and that Russia's legal system under Nicholas I was, in terms of its impact on people's lives, no different from the Napoleonic code.[52] Herzen was repelled by the contemporary 'petty-bourgeois state of Europe' and questioned the ability of contemporary western Europe to serve as an example to anyone.[53] This line of argument subsequently dominated Russian socialist thought from the classical Populists of the late 1860s and the 1870s through to Lenin, for whom '[t]he Europe of our day is advanced not *thanks to*, but *in spite of* the bourgeoisie ... In "advanced" Europe, the only advanced (*peredovoi*) class is the proletariat.'[54]

ECONOMIC IMAGES

The (in)appropriateness of western European economic models (that is, the capitalist form of industrialisation) was debated by Russian thinkers with arguably even greater passion than the political differences between Russia and western Europe. The criticism of the negative impact of modern industrial development and rapid urbanisation on people's lives in the Russian intellectual tradition can be dated back to Fonvizin's depiction of the horrors of the modern city (in his case Paris), where people 'who have not completely turned into beasts' could hardly survive.[55] Even the leading Westerniser Belinsky, while praising bourgeois democracy, 'disliked the bourgeoisie itself'.[56]

After the 1848 revolutions in Europe, Herzen's representation of the Russian peasant commune as the embodiment of western Europe's own ideals of egalitarianism and democracy shaped the subsequent debates among the Populists and impacted on Russian Marxists. Chernyshevsky, in his influential essay 'A Critique of Philosophical Prejudices against Communal Landholding' (1858), argued that 'the Germans, and the French, and the ancestors of the British, and the ancestors of the Italians, in a word all European peoples, had communal landholding in early periods of their history'. Under the influence of Hegel's philosophy of history, Chernyshevsky then argued that 'the highest stage of development is similar in form to the beginning from which it proceeds', hence socialism based on communes was the future of Europe in its entirety.[57] A negative image of western capitalism became central to the ideology of the classical Populists, whose ideas Andrzej Walicki aptly described as a 'response to the image of capitalist development in Western socialist thought ... by the democratic intelligentsia in a backward peasant country at an early stage of capitalist development'.[58] Like Herzen, the Populists idealised the peasant commune and, following Chernyshevsky, believed in the eventual return of western Europe to communal principles. Thus, Bakunin insisted that the attitude towards the land and principles of self-government in the Russian peasant commune '[i]n essence ... fully correspond[s] to the ideas which have of late been taking shape in the consciousness of the proletariat of Latin countries'.[59]

On the opposite side of the debate on western capitalism stood such liberal thinkers as Annenkov, who argued that '[t]he entire future of France lies in the hands of the bourgeoisie', and Botkin, who, being himself a son of a merchant, rejected Herzen's condemnation of the bourgeois order.[60] The Populist tendency to vilify western capitalism was also challenged by 'the father of Russian Marxism', Plekhanov, who, in his own words, was ready to stand 'under the banner of an intelligently conceived Westernism'.[61] A positive image of western capitalism was particularly well developed in the works of Struve, a leader of the Legal Marxists, in the 1890s.[62] It was no surprise that around 1900 the Legal Marxists, who were deeply committed to capitalism, would join forces with the liberals and in 1905 form Russia's main liberal party (the Constitutional Democratic Party), which would present the West of capitalism and constitutional monarchy as the main positive model for Russia.

IMAGES OF IMPERIAL EUROPE

While imagining Russia as a nation, Russian thinkers often had to struggle with its perception (externally and internally) as backward compared to 'the West'. In contrast, when Russia was depicted as empire and defined through its imperial mission in the East, Russian thinkers often betrayed great confidence vis-à-vis their western European counterparts. Indeed, in relation to Asia, Russian European identity seemed secure. In the first half of the eighteenth century Tatishchev was already claiming a profound similarity between Russia and other European empires, and at the beginning of the nineteenth Karamzin argued that Russia, like Europe, brought less developed people 'into the universal system of geography and history'.[63] Many nineteenth-century thinkers went on to believe that, in fact, Russians possessed certain qualities that allowed them to be at the forefront of carrying out Europe's 'civilising mission' in Asia.

Across Europe, in national(ist) and imperial discourses of the time both nations and empires were marked by distinct features, and the identifications of national and imperial specificities mirrored each other.[64] In the Slavophile tradition, both western European histories and their imperial conquests were presented as violent, in contrast to Russia's peaceful past. The Russian military officer and eminent orientalist scholar Veniukov depicted the creation of the Russian Empire as an 'organic' and 'natural' growth, while arguing that 'English colonisation ... was accompanied by the bloody destruction of whole races and the enslavement of many millions of people.' In Russia, 'Siberian savages were not hunted down by a Russian armed with a gun and accompanied by a dog, as the English did in New Zealand.'[65] Russian rule in Central Asia was perceived by many Russian thinkers as more humane than the exploitative and 'rapacious' British imperialism in India.[66] A leading orientalist and army general, Snesarev, claimed that one of his books gave Indians a voice of which they had been deprived by British imperialism.[67]

It was argued that Russians were superior imperialists because in their culture a Pan-European feature of universality, which entailed an ability to understand other (non-European) cultures, was particularly well developed. All Europeans possessed this quality but, as Dostoevsky passionately insisted in his famous Pushkin speech in 1880, western Europeans did not excel in this regard as much as the Russians.[68] Many Russian scholars believed that one of the reasons was that western European perceptions of the East were more racist than those of the Russians. In contrast to the Russians, who were happy to mix with Asians, the British in India 'do their utmost to avoid mingling with the natives', argued such orientalists as Snesarev, Veniukov and Semenov (Tian-Shansky).[69]

As with the debates about the Europe of nations, the depiction of the Europe of empires was not monolithic. The very same authors who compared western European and Russian imperialism unfavourably on other occasions presented western Europe's policy in 'the East' as superior to Russia's, particularly because they were convinced that the former was always based on a thorough scientific knowledge of 'the East'. According to this view, western governments fully appreciated the fact that 'knowledge is power', something the tsarist government consistently refused to understand.[70] While in the 1870s a leading Russian orientalist scholar with liberal political views could assert that among the peoples of Central Asia and India comparisons between Russia and Britain 'always turn out to be unfavourable to Britain',[71] by the beginning of the twentieth century, in the context of the growing domestic criticism of Russia's imperial policies, a veteran imperial administrator in Central Asia argued that '[t]hose [Central Asians] who had visited western Europe spoke ... about the grandeur and good order of European cities, about the prosperity and high cultural levels of the countries they had seen; about how much Russia, while being larger, but relatively poor and little cultured, was in fact lagging behind'.[72] In turn, whereas the British had managed fully to transform their colonies in North America and Australia into Europe, both politically and culturally, Russians, because of their cultural backwardness, had not achieved the same level of success even in Siberia, argued Iadrintsev, a leader of the Siberian regionalist movement (*oblastnichestvo*).[73]

While claiming to be less racist towards non-European peoples than their western European counterparts, Russian thinkers in fact were active participants in racially coloured[74] discourses which contrasted Europe with its colonial domains in Asia and Africa as they constructed their own image of an 'Aryan Europe', of which Russia was not on the periphery but at the core. The concept of 'Aryan', as opposed to Turanian and Dravidian, originated in linguistics as a way of describing different groups of related languages in Eurasia. The use of the term in ethnology; a common perception, particularly in continental European scholarship, of a direct link between language and ethnicity; the development of physical anthropology; Social Darwinism; a negative view of non-white colonial subjects in the wake of colonial conflicts since the mid-nineteenth century – all these factors resulted in the emergence of racial interpretations of the above-mentioned concepts.[75] Even those who criticised the practice of equating linguistic and racial groups and of finding explanations for cultural differences in biology used 'the language of their time, talking about the Aryan race'.[76]

The Aryan theory of European origin, locating the original 'Aryan homeland' in India, was supplanted by the 1850s by the view that 'the cradle of the Aryan civilisation' could be found rather in eastern or northern regions, such as Siberia, Central Asia, the Caucasus or Germany. Russian scholars took part in the search, rejecting the claims of some western European scholars about the non-Aryan origin of the Slavs. Thus, a leading Russian orientalist scholar, Grigorev, argued in 1876 that 'the current western and eastern Turkestan was in antiquity ... populated by a people physiologically different from the Turkic people, by a people who for various reasons one should recognise as Aryan'. He went on to argue that these Aryans were 'the ancestors of the Slavs, Germans and Lithuanians'. Thus, the Russian conquest of Central Asia was simply a reclaiming by Europe of its indigenous lands.[77] For Grigorev and the majority of other Russian thinkers interested in this issue, 'the cradle of the Aryan civilisation', that is, 'the cradle of Europe', was the Scythia of Herodotus (i.e. the Crimea). Catherine the Great herself depicted Herodotus' Scythians as the ancestors of the Russians and, on that basis, justified the Russian imperial conquest of the Crimea as a reclaiming of 'indigenous Russian lands'. She also presented this annexation as Russia's claim on the legacy of ancient Greece, an essential element of the modern European identity and, therefore, as a demonstration of Russia's belonging to Europe.[78] In contrast to the prevailing view of the Scythians in western European writings of the time as rude and barbarous people,[79] Catherine's image of them was positive. The criticism of the 'Aryan myth' by such scholars as Bartold notwithstanding,[80] in the late nineteenth and early twentieth centuries the image of an Aryan Europe with its cradle in the Scythian Crimea continued to be advanced in Russian thought with the aim of claiming Russia's central, rather than peripheral, position in Europe.[81]

REINTERPRETING THE BOUNDARIES BETWEEN EAST AND WEST

Meanwhile, from the 1880s and, particularly, during the First World War, scholars in Germany, Austria and other parts of what Russians perceived as 'the West' began to question common Eurocentric perceptions of the world and Europe's exclusive Greco-Roman and Judeo-Christian roots. European scholars began to claim oriental origins for European medieval art, while German Assyriologists 'discovered pre-biblical accounts of "God", "the Flood", and the "Sabbath"', generating 'new mythological speculations'.[82] Russian scholars were at the forefront of these revisions, offering new definitions of 'the West' which, as had been the case with the above-quoted image offered by Bartold of a West that included the Near East, were aimed at redefining the East–West boundary. In turn, the maverick linguist and famous archaeologist Marr offered in 1908 his own revision of Eurocentric perceptions, placing the origins of European civilisation in the ancient traditions of the aboriginal population of the Caucasus, 'the Orient' of Russian Romantic literature, which he termed 'Japhetic'.[83] Marr's culturally heterogeneous 'Japhetids' achieved the highest levels of civilisation at the time when 'Indo-Europeans were lingering somewhere in the far north of Europe. Greeks and Romans, who in the past had been perceived as the founders of ancient European culture, had not yet appeared.'[84] The fact that Marr found the cradle of his Japhetic civilisation in the Caucasus, whose ethnographic, cultural and linguistic variety in his opinion made the region a 'microcosm of Russia',[85] again allowed him to claim Russia's central, rather than peripheral, position in Europe vis-à-vis the traditionally defined West.

CONCLUSIONS

Confronted with the notion that Europe and 'the West' represented the pinnacle of modern civilisation, Russia was among the first societies whose elites had to deal with the question of how 'the non-West' could become part of the modern world other than by simply emulating western patterns of development. As Isaiah Berlin argued in his essay on the Russian Populist movement, Russian intellectuals who spoke about the atomisation of societies under the impact of industrialisation and urbanisation, who criticised the mass culture of bourgeois Europe and attacked Eurocentric perceptions of the world, provided 'acute insights into moral, social, and aesthetic problems' whose 'central importance' was fully realised by their counterparts in the West only in the second half of the twentieth century.[86]

In their reaction to 'the West', Russian thinkers articulated, to utilise Benedict Anderson's term, a specific 'modular model' of nationalism.[87] This was a form of 'reactive nationalism' developed in reaction to and in comparison with western societies. While admitting the technological superiority of western Europe and, more reluctantly, the effectiveness of its statecraft, Russian thinkers claimed the superiority of their own society in the spiritual domain, producing images of Russian national culture and history in opposition to what they perceived to be western patterns which they often bitterly criticised. In his influential critique of Anderson's argument that Europe 'supplied for all subsequent nationalisms a set of modular forms from which nationalist elites in Asia and Africa had chosen the ones they liked', Partha Chatterjee claimed the originality of non-European forms of nationalism on the grounds of their separation of the material domain (scientific and technological progress and effectiveness of political institutions) and the spiritual domain (culture and historical heritage). While admitting the West's superiority in the first sphere, national leaders of the colonial and post-colonial world constructed cultural identities of their nations not by imitating the West but by emphasising the difference to western models, Chatterjee pointed out.[88] In fact, in order to refute Anderson's argument, Chatterjee followed the common trend of reducing Europe to western Europe and overlooked the origins of the model he described in the eastern periphery of Europe, particularly Russia, in the eighteenth and the nineteenth centuries, when this region was the first to modernise in competition with the more economically and politically advanced 'West'.

NOTES

1. Liah Greenfeld, *Nationalism: Five Roads to Modernity* (Cambridge, Mass.: Harvard University Press, 1992), pp. 254–5, and Vera Tolz, *Russia: Inventing the Nation* (London: Arnold, 2001), pp. 69–71.
2. Following the publication of Edward Said, *Orientalism* (London: Penguin, 1995), the techniques of constructing European identities by claiming superiority over the 'eastern Other' and also incorporating this 'Other' as part of one's

own identity have been particularly well studied. The same techniques of othering, in fact, have been used when one European society was compared to its neighbours within Europe or when boundaries between East and West have been drawn within the body of the nation itself. See, for instance, John MacKenzie, *Orientalism: History, Theory and the Arts* (Manchester University Press, 1995), and Aleksandar Kiossev, 'The dark intimacy: maps, identities, acts of identification' in D. Bjelic and O. Savic (eds.), *Balkan as Metaphor* (Cambridge, Mass.: MIT Press, 2002), pp. 165–90.

3. Iver Neumann, *Russia and the Idea of Europe* (London: Routledge, 1996), p. 2.

4. For a survey of the history of the construction of these categories, see Martin Lewis and Karen Wigen, *The Myth of Continents. A Critique of Metageography* (Berkeley: University of California Press, 1997), particularly chapters 2 and 3.

5. Larry Wolff, *Inventing Eastern Europe. The Map of Civilization on the Mind of the Enlightenment* (Stanford University Press, 1994). On the changing perception of Russia in western Europe since the nineteenth century, see Martin Malia, *Russia under Western Eyes* (Cambridge, Mass.: The Belknap Press of Harvard University Press, 1999).

6. Suzanne Marchand, *Down from Olympus. Archaeology and Philhellenism in Germany, 1750–1970* (Princeton University Press, 1996), p. 232.

7. Quoted in Nicholas Riasanovsky, *The Image of Peter the Great in Russian History and Thought* (New York: Oxford University Press, 1985), p. 217.

8. Sergei Bulgakov, 'Geroizm i podvizhnichestvo' in *Vekhi. Sbornik statei o russkoi intelligentsii* (Frankfurt: Posev, 1967), p. 32.

9. B. H. Summer, 'Russia and Europe', *Oxford Slavonic Papers* 2 (1951), 1–16.

10. I. V. Kireevskii, 'O kharaktere prosveshcheniia Evropy i ego otnoshenii k prosveshcheniiu Rossii' in N. L. Brodskii (ed.), *Rannie slavianofily* (Moscow: Tipografiia Tovarishchestva I. D. Sytina, 1910), p. 8.

11. F. M. Dostoevsky, *The Diary of a Writer* (New York: George Braziller, 1954), p. 979.

12. See, for instance, Neumann, *Russia and the Idea of Europe*, p. 31.

13. K. D. Kavelin, 'A letter to F. M. Dostoevsky' in Marc Raeff (ed.), *Russian Intellectual History. An Anthology* (New York: Harcourt, Brace and World, 1966), pp. 306–7. In fact, even the early Westernisers were interested in 'other Europes' such as Spain and Italy. See Derek Offord, *Journeys to a Graveyard: Perceptions of Europe in Classical Russian Travel Writing* (Dordrecht: Springer, 2005), p. 12.

14. Mark Bassin, 'Russia between Europe and Asia: the ideological construction of geographical space', *Slavic Review*, 50 (1991), 1–7.

15. Mark Bassin, 'Inventing Siberia: visions of the Russian East in the early nineteenth century', *The American Historical Review*, 96 (1991), 763–94.

16. Bassin, 'Russia between Europe and Asia', 9–13.

17. On Danilevsky's possible impact on Oswald Spengler, see Pitirim Sorokin, *Modern Historical and Social Philosophies* (New York: Dover, 1963), pp. 50, 69, 73–82.

18. On the German orientalists' critique of Eurocentrism, see Suzanne Marchand, 'German orientalism and the decline of the West', *Proceedings of the American Philosophical Society*, 145 (2001), 465–73.

19. 'Ot redaktsii', *Mir Islama*, 1:1 (1912), 4. A similar view was expressed earlier in V. V. Vasil'ev, *Religii Vostoka* (St Petersburg: Tipografiia Imperatorskoi akademii nauk, 1873), p. 8.

20. A negative view of eastern Christianity and Byzantium was presented, for instance, in Edward Gibbon's highly popular *The Decline and Fall of the Roman Empire* (1776).

21. Lewis and Wigen, *The Myth of Continents*, pp. 73–85.

22. Wolff, *Inventing Eastern Europe,* and Maria Todorova, *Imagining the Balkans* (New York: Oxford University Press, 1997).

23. P. Ia. Chaadaev, 'Letters on the Philosophy of History. The First Letter', in Raeff (ed.), *Russian Intellectual History*, p. 165.

24. Ibid., p. 169.

25. Kavelin, 'A letter to F. M. Dostoevsky', p. 314.

26. For a comprehensive analysis of the views of the Slavophiles, see Nicholas Riasanovsky, *Russia and the West in the Teaching of the Slavophiles: A Study of Romantic Ideology* (Gloucester, Mass.: Peter Smith, 1965).

27. Kireevskii, 'O kharaktere prosveshcheniia Evropy', pp. 4–5.

28. Ibid., p. 11.

29. Brodskii (ed.), *Rannie slavianofily*, p. xii.

30. Dostoevskii, *Polnoe sobranie sochinenii*, 30 vols. (Leningrad: Nauka, 1972–90), vol. XXIX, part i, pp. 146–7; V. S. Solov'ev, 'Natsional'nyi vopros v Rossii' in his *Sobranie sochinenii* (St Petersburg: Obshchestvennaia pol'za, 1905), pp. 1–368; Bulgakov, 'Geroizm i podvizhnichestvo', p. 61.

31. Brodskii (ed.), *Rannie slavianofily*, pp. 115–16.

32. Ibid., pp. 64–5.

33. Ibid., pp. 120–1.

34. Particularly strong criticism of bourgeois society is to be found in Herzen's 'Letters from the Avenue Marigny'. For a comprehensive analysis of Herzen's views, see Martin Malia, *Alexander Herzen and the Birth of Russian Socialism* (New York: Glosset and Dunlap, 1965).

35. Chaadaev expressed this view in his 'Apologia of a Madman'. For an interesting discussion of the development of this view in Chaadaev's writings, see E. B. Rashkovskii and V. G. Khoros, '"Zapad-Rossiia-Vostok" v filosofskom nasledii P. Ia. Chaadaeva' in *Vostok-Zapad* (Moscow: Nauka, 1988), pp. 115–16. See also A. I. Gertsen, 'Staryi mir i Rossiia' in his *Sobranie sochinenii* (Moscow: Izdatel'stvo Akademii nauk SSSR, 1954–65), vol. XII, p. 169.

36. Andrzej Walicki, *A History of Russian Thought from the Enlightenment to Marxism*, trans. Hilda Andrews-Rusiecka (Oxford: Clarendon Press, 1980), p. 301, notes that Leontev anticipated the ideas of the existentialist writers of the twentieth century.

37. K. N. Leont'ev, *Sobranie sochinenii*, 9 vols. (Moscow: Tipografiia V. M. Sablina, 1912), vol. VI, pp. 431–2.

38. N. Ia. Danilevskii, *Rossiia i Evropa* (St Petersburg: Tipografiia brat. Panteleevykh, 1895).

39. Quoted in M. I. Koialovich, *Istoriia russkogo samosoznaniia* (Minsk: Luchi Sofii, 1997), p. 170.
40. K. S. Aksakov, 'Zapiska o vnutrennem sostoianii Rossii' (1855), and A. S. Khomiakov, 'Poslanie k Serbam' (1860) in Brodskii (ed.), *Rannie slavianofily*, pp. 70, 64.
41. Brodskii (ed.), *Rannie slavianofily*, p. lvi.
42. Kireevskii, 'O kharaktere prosveshcheniia Evropy', p. 14.
43. Offord, *Journeys to a Graveyard*, p. 60.
44. Kireevskii, 'O kharaktere prosveshcheniia Evropy', p. 37.
45. A. S. Khomiakov, 'Po povodu Gumbol'ta' (1849) in Brodskii (ed.), *Rannie slavianofily*, p. 51.
46. Brodskii (ed.), *Rannie slavianofily*, pp. 43, 45–7, 60–1.
47. James Billington, *The Icon and the Axe* (London: Weidenfeld and Nicolson, 1966), p. 378.
48. Aksakov, 'Zapiska o vnutrennem sostoianii Rossii', p. 86.
49. Walicki, *A History of Russian Thought*, pp. 60–3.
50. W. J. Leatherbarrow and D. C. Offord (eds.), *A Documentary History of Russian Thought: From the Enlightenment to Marxism* (Ann Arbor: Ardis, 1987), p. 165.
51. Walicki, *A History of Russian Thought*, pp. 144–50.
52. A. Herzen, 'The Russian People and Socialism' in Leatherbarrow and Offord (eds.), *A Documentary History of Russian Thought*, p. 148.
53. Ibid., p. 157.
54. V. I. Lenin, 'Otstalaia Evropa i peredovaia Aziia' in his *Polnoe sobranie sochinenii*, 55 vols. (Moscow: Politizdat, 1958–65), vol. XXIII, p. 166.
55. Quoted in Offord, *Journeys to a Graveyard*, p. 60.
56. Walicki, *A History of Russian Thought*, p. 144.
57. N. G. Chernyshevsky, 'A Critique of Philosophical Prejudices against Communal Landholding' in Leatherbarrow and Offord (eds.), *A Documentary History of Russian Thought*, pp. 205, 208.
58. Walicki, *A History of Russian Thought*, p. 225.
59. Quoted in Leatherbarrow and Offord (eds.), *A Documentary History of Russian Thought*, p. 279.
60. Walicki, *A History of Russian Thought*, pp. 145–6, and *The Controversy over Capitalism: Studies in the Social Philosophy of the Russian Populists* (Oxford: Clarendon Press, 1969).
61. Quoted in Neumann, *Russia and the Idea of Europe*, p. 93.
62. P. B. Struve, *Kriticheskie zametki k voprosu ob ekonomicheskom razvitii Rossii* (St Petersburg: Tipografiia I. N. Skorokhodova, 1894).
63. Raeff, *Russian Intellectual History*, p. 118.
64. On the close link between nation- and empire-building in Europe, see Frederick Cooper, *Colonialism in Question* (Berkeley: University of California Press, 2005), p. 172.
65. M. I. Veniukov, *Rossiia i Vostok* (St Petersburg: Tipografiia V. Bezobrazova, 1877), p. 114.

66. A. E. Snesarev, *Indiia kak glavnyi faktor v sredne-aziatskom voprose* (St Petersburg: Tipografiia A. S. Suvorina, 1906), p. 123.
67. Ibid.
68. Dostoevskii, 'Pushkin (ocherk)' in his *Polnoe sobranie sochinenii*, vol. XXVI, p. 146.
69. The quotation is from Veniukov in Milan Hauner, *What is Asia to Us? Russia's Asian Heartland Yesterday and Today* (London: Routledge, 1992), p. 43. See also Snesarev, *Indiia kak glavnyi faktor*, pp. 37, 128, 131, 135, 142.
70. Snesarev, *Indiia kak glavnyi faktor*, p. 7, and V. V. Grigor'ev, 'V oproverzhenie nekotorykh mnenii, vyskazannykh v poslednee vremia o prepodavanii vostochnykh iazykov v Rossii i ob izuchenii u nas Vostoka voobshche' in *Den'*, no. 18 (30 April 1865), 433.
71. I. P. Minaev, 'Rossiia i anglo-indiiskie interesy' in *Vostochnoe obozrenie*, no. 6 (6 May 1882), 1–3.
72. V. P. Nalivkin, *Tuzemtsy prezhde i teper'* (Tashkent: Tipografiia tovarishchestva pechatnogo dela, 1913), p. 120.
73. N. M. Iadrintsev, *Sibir' kak koloniia* (St Petersburg: Tipografiia M. M. Stasiulevicha, 1882), pp. 440, 443.
74. From the second half of the nineteenth century, scientific racism (a belief that race, as a category based at least partly on biological characteristics, can be used as an explanatory tool for differences in human abilities and development) was such an important part of Europe's intellectual tradition that it could not avoid impacting on Russian thought. On the importance of the concept of race to European science, see Nancy Stepan, *The Idea of Race in Science: Great Britain 1800–1960* (London: Macmillan, 1982).
75. Tony Ballantyne, *Orientalism and Race. Aryanism in the British Empire* (Houndmills: Palgrave, 2002), pp. 44–54.
76. Leon Poliakov, *The Aryan Myth: A History of Racist and Nationalist Ideas in Europe* (London: Chatto and Windus/Heinemann for Sussex University Press, 1974), p. 257.
77. *Trudy tret'ego mezhdunarodnogo s'ezda orientalistov v St Peterburge, 1876* (St Petersburg: Tipografiia brat. Panteleevykh, 1879–80), vol. I, pp. lv–lvi.
78. Andrei Zorin, 'Krym v istorii russkogo samosoznaniia', *Novoe literaturnoe obozrenie*, 31:2 (1998), 133.
79. Wolff, *Inventing Eastern Europe*, p. 10.
80. V. V. Bartol'd, 'Zadachi russkogo vostokovedeniia v Turkestane' in his *Sochineniia* (Moscow: Nauka, 1977), vol. IV, p. 529.
81. See Marlene Laruelle, *Mythe aryen et rêve impérial dans la Russie tsariste* (Paris: CNRS-Editions, 2005).
82. Marchand, 'German orientalism and the decline of the West', 468.
83. To describe this new linguistic and cultural family, Marr, in fact, used the term hitherto applied to Europe. St Jerome, for instance, claimed Europe to be the domain of Noah's son Japhet. From the eighteenth century, some scholars classified as Japhetic the languages which in the nineteenth century began to be commonly defined as Indo-European.

84. N. Ia. Marr, 'Kavkazovedenie i abkhazskii iazyk', *Zhurnal Ministerstva narodnogo prosveshcheniia*, 5 (1916), 1–27, and 'Chem zhivet iafeticheskoe iazykoznanie' in his *Izbrannye raboty*, 5 vols. (Leningrad: Izdatel'stvo GAIMK, 1933–5), vol. I, p. 171.
85. Quoted in Ia. V. Vasil'kov, 'Tragediia akademika Marr', *Khristianskii Vostok*, 2 (2001), 399–401.
86. Isaiah Berlin, *Russian Thinkers*, ed. Henry Hardy and Aileen Kelly (London: Hogarth Press, 1978), pp. 210–37. For an excellent analysis of Berlin's views, see Aileen Kelly, *Toward Another Shore: Russian Thinkers between Necessity and Chance* (New Haven: Yale University Press, 1998), p. 23.
87. Benedict Anderson, *Imagined Communities. Reflections on the Origin and Spread of Nationalism* (London: Verso, 1991).
88. Partha Chatterjee, *The Nation and Its Fragments* (Princeton University Press, 1993), pp. 5–6.

CHAPTER 10

The East

David Schimmelpenninck van der Oye

The Russian soul undeniably has an 'Asian stratification'.

Nikolay Berdiaev

'What is Asia to us?' Dostoevsky once famously asked.[1] The author wondered about the East's significance in a newspaper column he wrote after General Skobelev had stormed the Central Asian fortress of Geok Tepe in 1881. His answer was straightforward: '[It] provides the main outlet for our future destiny.' To this cheerleader for General Skobelev's glorious exploits in the sands of Turkestan, the East was something to be conquered for the greater glory of tsar and fatherland.

In this sense, Dostoevsky neatly fits into the late Edward Said's orientalist template, which argues that European perceptions of Asia are inextricably linked to colonialist conquest and control over a malevolent, inferior 'other'.[2] But if at first glance the novelist's thoughts appear to be in line with those of such European contemporaries as Cecil Rhodes and Jules Ferry, a deeper reading of his article betrays a more ambivalent view of Asia. Dostoevsky went on to explain, 'the Russian is not only a European but also an Asian'. Alluding to a common western perception of his nation as eastern, he added: 'We must free ourselves from this servile fear that Europeans will call us Asiatic barbarians and say that we are more Asian than European.'[3] There was clearly no shame in having a semi-oriental identity.

As Dostoevsky's musings suggest, there is no straightforward answer to the question of Asia's meaning in the Russian mind. More familiar with the continent than are its European neighbours to the west, Russians have invariably seen the East in a multiplicity of hues. Whether foe or friend, danger or destiny, other or self, or, as Vladimir Solovev put it, 'of Xerxes or of Christ',[4] the continent defies easy characterisation. As in the West, for the Russian imagination the Orient has often been the source of both dreams and nightmares, but greater intimacy with its people fashioned a unique symbiosis of fantasy and reality.

The most intriguing element of Russian thinking about Asia is the sense among many of a shared heritage. A number of distinguished noble lineages took pride in their Tatar bloodlines, and the population more generally has had far fewer qualms about intermarriage with alien races than many other Europeans. If few looked back nostalgically to two and a half centuries of submission to the Golden Horde, the 'Tatar Yoke' also left a legacy whose effects still remain the source of lively controversy. Meanwhile, ever since the Cossack Ermak and his heirs conquered Siberia some 400 years ago, the bulk of Russia's landmass has lain on the Asian continent. While his outlook was distinctly occidental, even Lenin understood that 'Russia is geographically, economically and historically related both to Europe and Asia'.[5]

Russian views of Asia therefore often reflect meditations on the nation's own identity, much like those about Europe. If the nineteenth-century debate between the Slavophiles and the Westernisers has received considerably more attention, the East has played a very similar role in Russia's ongoing quest to understand its true place in the world. Ultimately, these discussions about affinities with the Occident and the Orient are part of the same dialogue. And Asia's allure often increased as the West's diminished.

According to Nicholas Riasanovsky, ideas about Asia before the Soviet era evolved through three stages.[6] Until well into the seventeenth century, Russians tended to identify the Orient with the various nomadic peoples on their eastern frontier. Beginning at the turn of the eighteenth century, the efforts of Peter the Great and his heirs to transform Muscovy into a modern western power imbued Russians with a sense of superiority over the continent as they confidently considered themselves to be fully European. In the Romanov dynasty's troubled latter decades, however, some began to sense kinship with the East, a tendency that reached its apogee in the 1920s among the Eurasianists, a circle of émigrés who argued that Russia combined elements of both Europe and Asia. Although Riasanovsky's schema is somewhat simplistic, it is a good way to approach the question Dostoevsky posed about what Asia is to Russia.

BEFORE ASIA

For about the first 800 years of their recorded history, Russians largely thought about the East in terms of the steppe's Turkic and Mongol nomads. According to the chronicles the monastic scribes kept, encounters with these Inner Asian horsemen were invariably hostile, and the Slavic inhabitants of the forest suffered an unending succession of raids and wars. But this grim literature is deceptive, since the relationship between the forest and the steppe was not inherently antagonistic. While there were clashes, trade and intermarriage also characterised the European Slav's interaction with the Inner Asian nomad. Symbiosis rather than struggle was the order of the day. Even the two and a half centuries of the Mongol Golden Horde's rule were more benign than the histories compiled by churchmen in their wake would lead us to believe.[7]

The written evidence about attitudes to the East in the Muscovite era, however sketchy, likewise suggests antagonism, particularly to Islam. Much of this literature was also produced under the aegis of the Orthodox Church, which increasingly provided ideological support for the tsars' campaigns against Muslim foes.[8] Meanwhile, what little Russians knew about Asia tended to come from Byzantium until increased contact with the West in the reign of Peter the Great exposed them to a more secular outlook.[9]

If the church did not portray the Muslim East in a favourable light, neither did it monopolise Russian attitudes. Moscow's princes had long not only been intimately acquainted with the Golden Horde, but often acted as its leading Russian collaborator. As a result, if Byzantium shaped their view of God, the Mongols helped influence their understanding of secular politics.[10] Indeed, it was in part by assimilating the ways of the steppe that Moscow successfully conquered the khanates of Kazan and Astrakhan, two of the Golden Horde's successor states on the Volga, in the 1550s.[11]

Muscovy also absorbed elements of the Golden Horde more directly by welcoming its khans and lesser notables into the aristocracy.[12] Following the traditions of the steppe, Moscow had no qualms about integrating conquered nations and according the elites a similar status in their own society as long as they agreed to serve the ruler. And in choosing marriage partners among the upper class, caste generally trumped race. As a result, a variety of ethnic elements have long flowed in the veins of Russia's blue bloods.

Russian familiarity with the Golden Horde did not inevitably breed contempt. While the church increasingly championed hostility toward the Tatars, secular views tended to be more benign. Writing in the context of European relations with another Islamic foe, one scholar remarked, 'in the West something of a contradiction existed between the practical policies of governments *vis-à-vis* the Ottomans and the general tenor of published *turcica*: the former often reflected none of the hostility of the latter'.[13] The same was true of Muscovy and the Mongols.

More important, Russians were relatively late in developing a sense of national identity. In consequence, their sense of race tended to be much weaker than among western Europeans. Before the modern age, the *muzhik*'s primary allegiance was to his eastern Christian faith. But this loyalty was to the triple-barred Orthodox version, not the simpler Latin one. The Catholic *nemets* (western foreigner) was just as alien as the Muslim *basurman* (infidel). According to a well-known saying, 'Much woe has been wrought on us by the Crimean Khan and the Roman Pope.'[14]

Until the seventeenth century at the earliest, the steppe nomad dominated Russian perceptions of the Orient. But there were glimpses of other Easts, including the Levant, Turkey, Persia, India and eventually China. Some of them came from the chronographs (*khronografy*), or compilations of various histories of the world that were based on similar Byzantine digests.[15] Meanwhile, the reports of the tsar's envoys (*stateinye spiski*) to various oriental courts provided more objective firsthand accounts of Asian neighbours. However, these did not tend to have a wide readership at the time.[16]

THROUGH WESTERN EYES

Russia only truly became conscious of Asia as a separate continent when it began to regard itself as European during Peter the Great's reign. In turning to the West, Peter taught his subjects to think more systematically about the East. Motivated by geopolitical and commercial ambitions, not to mention his voracious curiosity, the tsar launched expeditions to Central Asia, Siberia and points beyond. Indeed, it was one of the tsar's more learned men, the polymath Tatishchev, who definitively set the continental boundary along the Ural Mountains.[17] And Peter launched orientology (*vostokovedenie*) as an academic discipline in his realm, albeit partly on the suggestion of the German philosopher Leibniz.[18]

Confident in their European identity, eighteenth-century Russians did not necessarily look to Asia with haughty disdain, for their age happened to coincide with the Enlightenment's philo-orientalism. French *philosophes* like Voltaire saw China as the apotheosis of rationalism, praising the Middle Kingdom's millennial culture for its emphasis on learning and toleration.[19] The anti-clerical spirit of the day also encouraged western thinkers to seek positive elements in Islam.[20] Culturally, *chinoiserie* and *turquerie* were all the rage in the decorative arts as European aristocrats built pagodas and commissioned portraits of themselves in Ottoman dress. Meanwhile, the publication of Galland's translation of the *Thousand-and-One Nights*, beginning in 1707, transformed western perceptions of the Near East from the Antichrist's realm to an exotic, fairy-tale wonderland.[21]

Eager to mimic Parisian fashions, well-heeled Russians under Catherine the Great in the latter half of the eighteenth century enthusiastically adopted France's Sinomania along with its powdered wigs and gallant manners.[22] The sovereign herself was one of the most assiduous followers of the vogue for *kitaishchina* (Sinophilia), building an entire village in the Chinese style at her summer residence of Tsarskoe Selo near St Petersburg, as well as adopting East Asian motifs in her literary creations and ordering translations of Qing law codes. Catherine also respected Near Eastern culture, although she was less sanguine about the Ottoman Empire's despotism. Emphatically rejecting the anti-Islamic policies of her predecessor, Empress Elizabeth, she even went so far as to encourage Muslim missionary activity among Kirghiz nomads on the steppe.[23] Subscribing to the Enlightenment ethos of confessional freedom, the *Nakaz* (*Instruction*) Catherine issued early in her reign stressed the need for 'prudent' religious toleration.[24]

Catherine emphatically considered Russia to be European. Paradoxically, the empress's *kitaishchina*, like her penchant for Classicism, was entirely bound up in her desire to impose western culture on her realm. As Dmitri Shvidkovsky has pointed out, 'China might be physically contiguous with Russia, but that boundary was far from St Petersburg, and for a Russian court pursuing Enlightenment modernisation it lay "in the wrong direction".'[25] The tsarina certainly did not allow her fondness for oriental culture and thought to sway her strategic ambitions with regard to her Ottoman and Qing neighbours.[26]

Russia's nascent intelligentsia shared their empress's orientalist tastes. Their members devoured translations of Chinese texts, while poets like Derzhavin played with eastern motifs in their verse. More ominously, some also began to imitate the western practice of writing about the Middle Kingdom Aesopically, as a veiled critique of domestic politics. For the time being, they invoked the East in a positive light, contrasting an idealised China with the shortcomings of their own order. Thus the playwright Fonvizin published a Confucian text about the ruler's obligations to his subjects, while the publisher Novikov more audaciously invoked a 'testament' of the Yongzheng Emperor subtly to disparage Catherine.[27]

DOUBTS ABOUT EUROPE

Educated Russians never identified themselves more closely with Europe than during Catherine the Great's reign.[28] But towards the end of her rule, even Catherine's enthusiasm for western ways began to sour as she learnt of the Bourbon monarchy's sanguinary end. The revolutionary turmoil that gripped France, followed by Napoleon's invasion in 1812, also led many others to question their ties to Europe. As Karamzin put it, 'Once upon a time we used to call all other Europeans *infidels*; now we call them brothers. For whom was it easier to conquer Russia – for *infidels* or for *brothers*? That is, whom was she likely to resist better?'[29]

The growing influence of German Romanticism in the early decades of the nineteenth century further encouraged speculation about Russia's place in the world. The discussion was spectacularly launched in 1836 by the publication of Chaadaev's first 'Philosophical Letter', which proclaimed that Russia was an orphan among the family of nations, without history or identity. Chaadaev's gloomy assessment initiated the stormy debate between the Westernisers and the Slavophiles of the mid-nineteenth century. The Westernisers believed that Russia should develop along western European lines towards an order based on rationalism, the rule of law and the primacy of the individual, while their opponents advocated rejecting Peter the Great's occidental turn and returning to what they saw as their nation's distinctly spiritual and paternalist course.[30] If the Slavophiles opposed western modernity, they did not suggest that Russia was Asian. What they championed was Orthodox, Slavic Europe rather than its Romano-German variant.[31]

There was one intriguing partial exception. Much as the German Romantic philosopher Friedrich von Schlegel had divided the world between Indo-European Aryans and non-Aryans, the Slavophile Khomiakov detected a fundamental dichotomy in mankind. One group, the Kushites, were descended from Noah's disgraced son Ham and had originated in northern Africa. According to Khomiakov, the Kushites embodied submission and nihilism and were in constant struggle with the Iranians, the race that represented freedom and spirituality. As a force of creative vitality, the Iranians had initially established both Greece and Rome. However, Khomiakov argued, successive waves of Kushites had subjected western Europe to their more repressive and heathen order. Only the Slavs had escaped the slavish dominion of the Kushites over the continent.[32] In Khomiakov's conception of history lay the roots of the notion, increasingly popular towards the turn of the twentieth century, that Russians retained the youthful vigour of their Scythian oriental ancestors.

Chaadaev, as he subsequently elaborated in his 'Apologia of a Madman', stood firmly in the camp of the Westernisers. 'We live in Europe's East', he wrote, 'but this fact does not make us eastern.' His aversion to the Orient was clear: 'In the East, docile minds that submitted to tradition spent themselves slavishly obeying some sacred principle and in the end … fell into a deep slumber, entirely ignorant of their destiny.'[33] Chaadaev's negative characterisation of Asia as mired in stagnant somnolence reflected a profound transformation from the Enlightenment's Sinophilia in European views of China at the turn of the nineteenth century. Beginning with Herder's contemptuous dismissal of the empire as 'an embalmed mummy, wrapped in silk, and painted with hieroglyphics', Romantic thinkers saw the Middle Kingdom as despotic, immobile, its people nothing but ants utterly devoid of free will or imagination.[34]

Kitaishchina now acquired a very pejorative sense in the Russian vocabulary. If in Catherine's day the noun evoked a playfully exotic China, during the nineteenth century it became associated with antediluvian tyranny, shameless corruption and utter immobility. Dal's dictionary of the Russian language included such definitions as 'rude, uneducated person' for the noun 'Asian' and 'savage, crude' for 'Asiatic'.[35] By the same token, *aziatchina* (Asianism) came to signify all of the continent's defects. In Chekhov's *The Cherry Orchard*, for example, the haughty student Trofimov dismissed Russia as 'nothing but filth, vulgarity, *aziatchina*'.[36]

Westernisers often invoked Asia as a warning or even a metaphor for tsarist reaction in their polemics. Belinsky had nothing but contempt for the Orient. He provided a detailed exposition of his views in a lengthy review of some books about Peter the Great and his father, Tsar Alexis, whose underlying theme was to praise the former's effort to turn Russia towards the West. Echoing Hegel's view that China and India lay outside of history, the critic remarked that 'Asia was the cradle of the human race and up to now has remained its cradle; its offspring grew up, but they are all still in the cradle, they acquired strength, but they still have to walk in leading strings.'[37]

According to Belinsky, only the Asian's ability to think and talk separated him from animals, but his intellect was primitive at best. 'Is something good or is it bad, reasonable or unreasonable – such questions don't enter into his head; they are far too weighty, too indigestible for his brain.' Even were he to be endowed with more sophisticated intelligence, the oriental's fatalism renders him inert. 'Why is everything the way it is, and not otherwise, and should it be thus rather than another way – he has never asked himself such things. Things have been like this for a long time, and they are so with everyone. It is Allah's will!'[38]

Like many of his generation, Belinsky did not trouble himself much to distinguish between the East's different nations. Even when he did, none was flattered by the comparison. Thus 'the Turk is indifferent when his ruler's displeasure causes him to be impaled or hanged'. Meanwhile, China's government, 'devoid of movement, represents itself as some petrified ancestor'. Belinsky never doubted the West's superiority: 'Asia is the land of so-called natural immediacy, Europe is the land of consciousness; Asia – the land of contemplation, Europe – of will and intellect.'[39]

Early nineteenth-century poets like Pushkin and Lermontov did not necessarily share such disdain for the Orient. Influenced by Byron's Romantic verse, they often portrayed a more colourful and attractive East. While its inhabitants might be violent savages ruled by cruel despots, their archaic culture had the virtue of being as yet uncontaminated by modernity's artifice and mediocrity. At the same time, Pushkin and his contemporaries had a deep respect for Asian civilisation. He was hardly disparaging the Islamic world when he penned his 'Imitations of the Koran'. Nevertheless, he also used Asia metaphorically to comment about affairs closer to home. In 'The Giaours [infidels] now praise Istanbul', a poem of 1830 that can be read as a lampoon of his countrymen who opposed western modernity, Pushkin sarcastically praised the Janissaries who had rebelled some twenty years earlier against the westernising reforms of the Ottoman Sultan Mahmud II.[40]

If the Slavophiles did not look to Asia as a model to be emulated, there were some Russians who did. According to Olga Maiorova, one of the first was a diplomat posted to Constantinople, Vladimir Titov.[41] Like a number of his colleagues at the Foreign Ministry, Titov was also active in St Petersburg's literary life. A member of Odoevsky's Society of Wisdom-Lovers, he wrote the prince a remarkable letter upon his arrival in the Turkish capital in 1836.[42] 'Looking back at Italy and Germany, I became much more of a Turk and an Asian', Titov announced. As he explained, the East had three advantages over the West: its strong religious convictions, its paternal government and its more sensual pleasures (*kaif*). These were all impossible for Europeans to achieve because of their feudal traditions and the Catholic Church. Fortunately, 'in Russia we did not have these two syndromes, nor their ... consequences; nevertheless, we suffered from another ailment – imitating Europeans'. Titov did not want to put the blame for this entirely on Peter the Great's shoulders. 'However', he proclaimed, 'it is time for us to return to our own ways and those of the East.'

While more ambivalent about Asia, the radical émigré Herzen came to share some of Titov's sympathies. Initially, he largely shared Belinsky's negative view of the East as the epitome of stagnation and tyranny, seeing the Orient as a metaphor for the harsh autocracy of Nicholas I. However, following his emigration to the West and subsequent disillusionment at the failure of the revolutions of 1848 to sweep away the old order, Herzen broke with the Westernisers and began to look eastward, to Russia's peasant commune, as his ideal society.[43] In the context of his evolving political ideas, Asia came to acquire for Herzen both a positive and a negative meaning. If, before his exile, Russian politics had been synonymous with oriental despotism, he now detected similarities between western Europe and East Asia. Chaadaev and Belinsky had always evoked immobile China as Europe's antithesis. But in the wake of the events of 1848, Herzen saw the latter's bourgeois philistinism and passivity as the occidental incarnation of *kitaishchina*.[44] Inverting Westerniser thinking, he invoked a favourite metaphor for the crippling conformity of Confucianism to deride Peter the Great's reforms: 'the Chinese shoes of German make, which Russia has been forced to wear for a hundred and fifty years, have caused many painful corns'. The damage was not permanent, Herzen added, 'since whenever [Russia] has had a chance of stretching out its limbs it has exuded a fresh young energy'.[45]

The 'fresh young energy' came from another Orient. Sharing Khomiakov's division of the world into a repressive and a free component, Herzen also saw the East as the source of rejuvenating vigour; not the stagnant Asia of the Chinese but its nomadic interior, the Turanian Asia of the Scythians and the Mongols. This was the *élan vital* that kept Russia young. In fact, the Tatar Yoke had been a blessing, since it had saved his nation from such invidious western institutions as feudalism and the Catholic Church.[46] Rather than being offended by the traditional European soubriquets of his countrymen as barbarians and Tatars, Herzen revelled in them. In a letter to the French anarchist Proudhon, he described himself as 'a barbarian … [both] by birth and by conviction'. 'Being a veritable Scythian,' he added, 'I delight in seeing the old world meet its doom.'[47]

ORIENTAL ROOTS

Many Russians saw their army's defeat in the Crimea in 1855 as a summons to renewed modernisation according to the western model. Considering their nation to be European, they believed that it had to be more like its occidental neighbours. The prevailing sentiment that such a course was vital to national survival enabled the new tsar, Alexander II, to introduce sweeping reforms that helped reshape the civic order along more occidental lines. But for others, St Petersburg's steady decline among Europe's great powers during the nineteenth century's second half made Asia all the more appealing. Lieutenant-General Blaramberg spoke for many when he proclaimed, 'Russia's future does not lie in Europe: it must look to the East.'[48] Some turned to the Orient as an arena for martial glory. Checked in the Near East by the Crimean War and again at the Congress of Berlin two decades later, they saw expansion into Central Asia and the Far East as a tonic for their empire's wounded pride. A smaller but nonetheless influential group began to argue that Russia's destiny lay in the East because it was essentially more Asian than European itself.

Notions of a manifest destiny in the Orient were hardly new to Russians. In his poem of 1848, 'Russian Geography', the poet and diplomat Tiutchev proclaimed its borders as stretching

> From the Nile to the Neva,
> From the Elbe to China,
> From the Volga to the Euphrates,
> From the Ganges to the Danube ...[49]

One of the more prominent advocates for a tsarist mission on the continent in the wake of the Crimean debacle was Pogodin. In addition to occupying the chair in Russian history at Moscow University, Pogodin also published a journal, *The Muscovite*, which he used as a platform for his conservative nationalism. Shortly after the war, he published a summons to imperial expansion further east. 'Leaving Europe alone, in expectation of more favourable circumstances', he wrote, 'we must turn our entire attention to Asia, which we have almost entirely left out of our considerations although it is precisely Asia that is predestined for us.' Like Tiutchev, he saw few limits for Russia's ambitions on the continent: 'to us belongs ... half of Asia, China, Japan, Tibet, Bokhara, Khiva, Kokand [and] Persia'.[50]

Pogodin did not consider his country's imperial ambitions to be in a different league from those of the other European powers. Convinced of the superiority of 'the tribe of Japheth', the white race descended from Noah's son according to biblical tradition, he believed its rightful destiny was to rule over 'the tribes of Shem and Ham'. Thus he sympathised with the British during the Indian Mutiny of 1857.[51]

St Petersburg's diplomatic humiliation at the Congress of Berlin in 1878, after another Turkish war, only reinforced enthusiasm for Asian conquest. Much like the other colonial powers during the age of high imperialism, many Russians were convinced of a special mission that justified their territorial expansion. Writing from Xinjiang in 1877, the explorer Przhevalsky reported, 'the local population constantly cursed their own government and expressed their desire to become Russian subjects. Rumours of how we brought order to Kokand and Ili spread far. The savage Asiatic clearly understands that Russian power is the guarantee for prosperity.'[52]

The most august proponent of such views was Nicholas II. In 1903, his Minister of War, General Kuropatkin, confided to his diary: 'Our sovereign has grandiose plans in his head: to absorb Manchuria into Russia, to begin the annexation of Korea. He also dreams of taking Tibet under his orb. He wants to rule Persia, to seize both the Bosporus and the Dardanelles.'[53] These sentiments would become less popular after Japan launched its attack on the tsar's naval base of Port Arthur in the Pacific Ocean a year later.

The nineteenth century saw a growing interest among Russians in their Asian past. Catherine the Great, in her 'Notes about Russian History', had already written about the Scythians, among the first people known to have lived on Russian territory.[54] Her description was so positive that one scholar recently suggested the empress might have been the first to claim the nomadic nation's ancestry for her adoptive homeland.[55] From the start, one of the driving forces of the academic discipline of orientology had been studying the Eastern elements of Russian history. At first, the scholars who pursued such interests were German – like Catherine herself. However, by the nineteenth century's second half, native Russian orientologists increasingly also became intrigued by the question. They included such prominent men as Vasily Grigorev, Veselovsky and Baron Rozen.[56] Meanwhile, the spectacular finds at Scythian burial mounds along the empire's southern periphery of intricate gold artefacts that blended entirely alien oriental styles with Classical Greek motifs further encouraged many to think about their Inner Asian ancestry, whether real or imagined.[57]

To be sure, pre-revolutionary historians tended not to dwell on Russia's links with the East. There were some exceptions. In the early 1800s the conservative Karamzin wrote that 'Moscow owes its greatness to the Khans.'[58] What he meant was that the Muscovite princes had adopted their autocratic regimentation of society – the strong centralised rule that had enabled Russia to achieve its pre-eminence – from the political tradition of the Mongols. Nevertheless, most nineteenth-century historians were distinctly uncomfortable with the idea that any good had come from the 'Tatar Yoke', as they disparagingly called the era of Mongol rule over much of Russia from around 1240 through the fifteenth century. Ideas about the influence of these Inner Asian conquerors were very much on the margins of the historiographical mainstream in Moscow and St Petersburg.

One influential figure who did see significant ties to the East in his nation's heritage was Vladimir Stasov. Historian, archaeologist, librarian, art critic and the tireless champion of the national school of Russian music, Stasov scandalised many of his compatriots when he suggested in a series of articles in 1868 that the *byliny* (medieval epics) were nothing more than imitations of tales that had originated in India and Persia, and 'emasculated' ones at that. 'Our bogatyrs [knights] merely convey various myths, legends and fairy tales of the ancient East', he concluded.[59] Stasov, as he dutifully acknowledged, derived the basic thesis about the oriental foundations of European epics from such scholars as the German Sanskritist Theodor Benfey. However, what distinguished the *byliny* was that they were much closer to the originals than the *Iliad, Nibelungenlied* or even Finland's *Kalevala*.

In other works, most notably his book *Russian Folk Ornament* of 1872, Stasov likewise stressed the similarities between Russian and Asian culture.[60] Despite the storm of controversy it initially aroused, 'On the Origins of Russian *Byliny*' earned the author the Imperial Academy of Sciences' prestigious Demidov prize and eventually gained many adherents, as did his related ideas.[61] The prominent French architectural historian Viollet-le-Duc based his book about Russian art on the notion, as he put it, that 'Russia has been one of the laboratories where the arts, having come from throughout all of Asia, have been joined to create an intermediary form between the oriental and occidental worlds.'[62]

Stasov was a man of relatively progressive views. Despite his fervent patriotism, his approach to Russia's cultural past tended to be scholarly. But there were others who looked to the East with more partisan motives. Just as Russian liberals saw western Europe's constitutional democracies as their political ideal, some conservatives advocated greater kinship with Asian autocracy. One of the most distinctive proponents of the latter policy was the mystical reactionary Leontev. As with Titov some three decades earlier, diplomatic service in the Ottoman Empire awoke in Leontev a passion for the Orient. The attraction was primarily aesthetic at first. As he explained in a letter to a friend: 'Only the life of Constantinople ... only this multifaceted existence could satisfy my *intolerably* refined tastes.'[63]

A spiritual crisis in the early 1870s led to a profound change of heart. Resigning from the Foreign Ministry, Leontev went on a lengthy retreat in the Orthodox monastic republic of Mount Athos. Eventually returning to Russia, he lived mostly on his estate until the final years of his life, when he was tonsured as a monk in the venerable Optina Pustyn Monastery. Leontev's credo was straightforward: 'More oriental mysticism and less European enlightened reason.'[64] In an age when many Russians subscribed to Pan-Slavism, a doctrine that advocated uniting all of eastern Europe's Slavs under the tsar's sceptre, he advocated a different course. For one thing, his nation had little in common with many of its Slavic cousins, who had already been deeply contaminated by Europe's poisonous liberalism:

The very character of the Russian people has very strong and important traits, which are more similar to those of Turks, Tatars and other Asian nations, or perhaps no one at all, than the southern and western Slavs. We are more indolent, fatalistic, much more submissive to our ruler, more dissolute, good-natured, insanely brave, unstable, and so much more inclined to religious mysticism than the Serbs, Bulgarians, Czechs and Croats.[65]

Rather than joining with its purported Slavic brethren, Russia's true destiny lay in restoring the Byzantine ideal of an empire that combined East and West, although its firmly autocratic political order would be distinctly more oriental. After all, as Leontev cautioned, 'no Polish rising, no Pugachev revolt can bring more harm to Russia than a most orderly and legal democratic constitution'.[66] With its capital in Tsargrad (Constantinople) rather than St Petersburg, the greater Russia he envisioned 'would be more cultured, that is, more true to itself; it would be less rational and less utilitarian, that is, less revolutionary'.[67] This new realm might well incorporate the other Slavs, but it would also join with it many Asian peoples, including Turks, Indians and Tibetans, thereby preserving its fundamentally eastern character.

THE ASIAN TEMPTATION

The turn of the twentieth century was for many Russians a time of even greater unease about the relationship with the West.[68] Outwardly, especially in the great cities, it seemed that the empire was becoming increasingly more European. Railways, factories, telegraphs and mass-circulation newspapers all heralded the coming of a new age. This occidentalisation was troubling, not just in the way it challenged the old order, but also because it seemed to emphasise Russia's inherent inferiority with respect to such modern industrial rivals as Great Britain and Germany. Yet if Russia looked to the West from a position of relative weakness, it could still face the East with confidence and strength.

As the nineteenth century drew to a close, Russia's new tsar, Nicholas II, became increasingly preoccupied with his empire's frontier on the Pacific. In the early 1890s, his father, Alexander III, had already decreed that a railway be built across Siberia to link St Petersburg with his distant Far Eastern territories. By the decade's end, Nicholas's diplomats had negotiated a secret treaty of alliance with China, in addition to a leasehold and extensive economic privileges in Manchuria. As the twentieth century dawned, it appeared to many Russians that the empire's destiny lay in Asia. Echoing Leontev, some influential political writers, the *vostochniki* (Asianists), even began to argue that Russia was fundamentally eastern rather than western in character.

One of the more prominent advocates of Asianism was Prince Esper Ukhtomsky, a newspaper publisher and poet. Close to Nicholas II – the prince had accompanied him on his oriental grand tour when he was still the tsarevich – Ukhtomsky exercised considerable influence on the emperor during the early years of his reign. On the pages of his daily *St Petersburg News* Ukhtomsky tirelessly advocated the Asianist cause.[69]

Even more than Leontev, the prince was convinced about Russia's kinship with Asia. 'The West', he wrote, 'is but dimly reflected in our intellectual life. The depths below the surface have their being in an atmosphere of deeply oriental views and beliefs.'[70] Like Asians, Russians relied more on faith than on reason. As Ukhtomsky explained: 'We feel our spiritual and political isolation from the Romano-Germanic countries overburdened by a too-exacting civilization. For us ... [as] for Asia, the basis of life is religious belief.'[71] At the same time, both Russians and Asians were repelled by materialism. But above all, the two were bound by a yearning for the ruler's firm, paternal hand: 'The East believes no less than we do ... [in] the most precious of our national traditions – autocracy. Without it, Asia would be incapable of sincere liking for Russia and of painless identification with her.'[72]

As an element of tsarist foreign policy, Asianism did not survive defeat during the war with Japan in 1905. But similar ideas about Russia's oriental nature flourished among the poets of the Silver Age, culminating with the Scythians, a literary movement in the Revolution's immediate aftermath.[73] To these versifiers, the Scythians came to represent the untamed vitality of their nation's soul, and verses lauding their putative ancestors proliferated. Among the first was Balmont, who praised the nomads' free spirit and martial prowess in 'The Scythians' (1899):

> We blessed hordes of freely roaming Scythians,
> Prize freedom above all else.
> Flying from Olvia's castle with its griffin statues,
> Hidden from the foe, we overtake him everywhere ...[74]

According to Ettore Lo Gatto, Silver Age authors had adopted an eastern identity to flout the West: 'In Russian ideological poetry, the terms Mongol, Scythian and Hun are terms with Slavophile connotations, and they were similarly brandished to proclaim Russia's distinct, so to speak Eurasian, character to the western world, Europe the damned, Europe the enemy.'[75] No one expressed this better than Blok in his defiant 'The Scythians'. Blok wrote the poem in early 1918 as a warning to the West not to interfere in the Bolsheviks' negotiations for a separate peace with the Central Powers at Brest-Litovsk:

You have your millions. We are hordes, and hordes, and hordes.
Just try it! Take us on!
Yes, we are Scythians! Yes, we're Asians too!
With slanting eyes bespeaking greed![76]

Asianism lost its appeal among policy-makers in St Petersburg after the catastrophic war with Japan, and the Scythians succumbed to tighter Bolshevik controls on literature in the early 1920s. In emigration, however, the Eurasianists revived many of these beliefs, but with one important difference. Rather than stressing its oriental nature, the Eurasianists argued that their nation was a world unto itself. For the Eurasianists, Russia was neither Asian nor European, but combined elements of both. Nevertheless, many of Eurasia's cultural facets, such as its rejection of materialism, its autocratic political nature and its spirituality, much more explicitly rejected the West.[77]

Based in Prague, the Eurasianist movement emerged in 1921 with the publication of a collection of essays, *Exodus to the East*.[78] Among the collaborators were a linguist, Prince Nikolay Trubetskoy, a geographer, Savitsky, a music critic, Suvchinsky, and the theologian Florovsky. A year later, they were joined by a promising young historian, George Vernadsky, who had just taken up work in the Czech capital.

Vernadsky boasted a distinguished academic provenance. His father, Vladimir, had been a leading Russian professor of mineralogy, and Vernadsky *fils* had attended the two leading departments, at Moscow and St Petersburg Universities, and also studied in Berlin and Freiburg. After five years in Prague, Vernadsky left Europe for America in 1927 to take up a newly established position in Russian history at Yale University.

Vernadsky wrote his most polemical Eurasianist works, *Characteristics of Russian History* and *A Preliminary History of Eurasia*, early in his career.[79] His focus was the vast prairie that stretches from Mongolia to Ukraine, the great Eurasian steppe. As he explained in these books, because of its flat topography the steppe was the meeting place for European and Asian peoples. The nomads who periodically swept westward from the depths of Inner Asia, such as the Scythians, the Huns and the Mongols, had intermarried with the more sedentary eastern Slavs. 'Each of these invasions', he explained in a subsequent work, 'brought new cultural patterns, and each, when it retreated years or centuries later, left its imprint indelibly on the land that was to become Russia.'[80]

Muscovite and tsarist conquest completed what Vernadsky called the 'millennial historical symbiosis' of the Slavs and the steppe nomads. According to the Eurasianists, together the Russians, Finns, Turks, Mongols and all the other nations that were spawned from the Inner Asian steppes had blended into a 'superethnos', a people they called 'Turanian'. Eurasia's peoples, the Turanian superethnos, had many characteristics in common, including related blood types and languages, but the most significant was a shared consciousness of the need for strong, autocratic government. All of Eurasia's most successful rulers, from the Scythians to the Romanov tsars, had governed with a firm hand. According to Vernadsky, 'The organisation of the Eurasian state, because of its enormous size, is very much along military lines.'[81] Furthermore, along with an instinctive yearning for firm rule, Eurasia's peoples were also united by a deep spirituality.[82]

In his later New Haven years, Vernadsky moderated some of his Eurasianist ideas. Although he continued to stress the importance of the steppe in Russian history, as his biographer Charles Halperin points out, his 'immigration to the United States ... purged [his] Eurasianism of its authoritarian, chauvinist, collectivist, and elitist aspects'.[83] However, for many Russians today it is not the mild-mannered Ivy League incarnation of George Vernadsky that intrigues them, but the young Eurasianist firebrand of Prague in the 1920s.

Even at their peak, the Eurasianists never attracted more than a small following among other émigrés. More prominent Russian intellectuals abroad, such as the distinguished historian Miliukov, strongly disagreed with the movement's anti-western bias.[84] However, the ideology has enjoyed a renaissance in the years following the collapse of communist rule. Its resurgence in the 1990s is closely linked to a profound disenchantment with the West among many Russians. The Canadian author Michael Ignatieff has pointed out that the dispute over whether Russia is European has once again emerged with a vengeance:

Since Pushkin, Russian intellectuals have argued bitterly about whether Russia is or is not part of European civilization. Slavophiles versus Westernisers, Dostoevsky versus Tolstoy – the argument goes to the very heart of Russian self-definition. For one side, the Europe of markets, parliamentary democracy, and individual rights represented Russia's only hope of escaping Asiatic backwardness and the madhouse of Slavic nationalism; for the other, Europe's capitalism represented the soulless, gimcrack, heartless individualism that the Russian soul should flee, as from the devil himself.[85]

Yet, despite Ignatieff's implication, it is not Slavophilism that has enjoyed a rebirth so much as the ideas of the Eurasianists. Several collections of Eurasianist essays have been issued in large printings. Meanwhile, the works of Lev Gumilev, a Brezhnev-era dissident with strong Eurasianist leanings, are everywhere, and translations of George Vernadsky's 'Yale History' are also now available in Russian bookshops.[86]

Eurasianism has found a strong following among both friends and opponents of the current regime, including communists and others who would restore Russia to its former Soviet glory. As John Dunlop, an American scholar who has long studied Russian nationalism, noted: 'The resurrection of a formerly obscure émigré ideology in the 1990s should, upon reflection, cause little surprise. With the effective demise of Marxism-Leninism as a "glue" for holding the Soviet Union together, "empire savers" were forced to cast about for substitutes.'[87]

One well-known cultural figure influenced by Eurasianism is the patriotic film director and sometime presidential candidate, Mikhalkov. In an interview in December 1991, Mikhalkov thundered against 'the [Russian] government's illusory notion that our state is based on the European political model'. He went on to proclaim: 'We are not Europe's backyard; we are Asia's front door.'[88] Mikhalkov's film *Close to Eden*, shot in 1992, is a clear expression of Eurasianism. *Close to Eden* describes the friendship of a wandering Russian truck driver and a Mongolian nomad who meet on the Inner Asian steppe. The encroaching capitalist materialism of the modern world (here in the guise of an Americanised Chinese city) is portrayed as impure and alien.

On the Russian right, the best-known neo-Eurasianists are Prokhanov and Dugin, editors of the tabloid *Tomorrow* and the journal *Elements: The Eurasian Review* respectively. More curious is the warm response Eurasianism has found among post-Soviet communists. Ziuganov, the chair of the Communist Party of the Russian Federation, speaks and writes gushingly about the movement: 'From its beginning, Eurasianism was the creative response of the Russian national consciousness to the Russian Revolution.'[89] Yet in the confusing politics of the post-Soviet era, this rehabilitation of an émigré intellectual current from the 1920s by communists in Moscow seven decades later makes perfect sense. The Russian political scientist Andrey Novikov has observed: 'Today people are studying the [Eurasianist geopolitical philosophy] of Lev Gumilev ... just as diligently as formerly they read Karl Marx's *Das Kapital*. Marxist historical determinism has been transformed into another kind of determinism, the national-geopolitical variant.'[90]

In 1997, Ziuganov published his strongest statement on Eurasianist ideas in *The Geography of Victory*. Written in the style of a textbook on geopolitics, the tract strongly attacks American primacy in global affairs. Like Leontev and Prince Ukhtomsky, Ziuganov urges his countrymen to reject the Occident and embrace Russia's oriental nature. 'To an important extent, Russia belongs to the East', he proclaims. He also finds much to admire in Confucian values. Echoing a hoary claim of tsarist propaganda, he argues that his compatriots have traditionally had much more pacific dealings with their neighbours in Asia than with Europeans. In a rare reference to his own party's former leaders, he adds: 'In Soviet times the traditional "turn to the East" … received a renewed impulse. It was precisely among the peoples of the Orient that Soviet Russia found allies in its struggle against western oppression and blackmail.' Today, Ziuganov believes, Russians must cement their ties with Asia because 'Russia and China are inexorably joined in a single historical destiny.'[91]

CONCLUSION

Certainly since their conversion to Christianity over ten centuries ago, most Russians would have denied being oriental. In their frequent warfare with Inner Asian nomads, medieval Russians saw themselves as defenders of the cross against the wicked pagans (*pogany*) of the steppe. From the eighteenth century, when Peter the Great and his heirs strove to impose western ways on their empire, educated Russians would have tended to agree with the Soviet leader Gorbachev's assertion that 'we are European'.[92]

The geography of Russia, as a land that straddles both of Eurasia's two continents, has nevertheless instilled some ambiguity about its continental identity among its inhabitants. In its earliest incarnation, as the Kievan principalities that flourished during the eleventh and twelfth centuries, Russia had cultural and commercial links with both European and Asian lands. Conquest and occupation by the Mongols in the thirteenth century effectively severed Russia's links with the West. Even after Muscovy freed itself from the Golden Horde 200 years later, it remained largely isolated from the rest of Europe.

When Peter the Great and his successors began attempting to return Russia to the European fold in the eighteenth century, they encountered strong resistance from many of their subjects. At first, this opposition came primarily from the clergy and other conservative social elements, who saw the West's Latin culture as anathema to their Orthodox faith. By the nineteenth century, however, some members of the educated elite, influenced by German Romanticism, also began to argue that Russia's place was not in the West. Earning the epithet of Slavophiles, they saw their society as fundamentally distinct from the sterile materialism and rationalism of the Latin world. At the same time, the Slavophiles did not consider their nation to be Asian.

Yet there were Russians who imagined a kinship with the Orient, such as Herzen and Stasov. Some began to detect a deeper affinity with Asia, like the *fin-de-siècle* poet Blok. Others, such as the nineteenth-century conservatives Leontev and Esper Ukhtomsky, identified with Asia in their distaste for European materialism and liberalism. One offshoot of this line of thinking was the early twentieth-century idea that Russia forms a separate 'Eurasian' continent, combining both Asian and European elements.

The advocates of Russia's oriental character had always been in a minority. But their ideas survived and now, after the fall of the Soviet Union, they can be found among prominent political movements in the Russian Federation. Profoundly uneasy about a 'new world order' dominated by the West's premier power, it is easy for nationalist Russians to believe that their country shares something with Asia as they reject the intrusive, materialist West, with its International Monetary Fund hotshots, its fast food, its pornography and its unruly parliaments. The 'Asian values' of autocracy, order and paternalism seem so much more appealing to those nostalgic for a mighty Russia. Rightist opposition parties – old-line communists, new-line fascists and extremist nationalists – often claim a racial affinity to the East. Even senior Kremlin officials occasionally invoke an Asiatic identity. One of Yeltsin's foreign ministers, Igor Ivanov, reminded his countrymen that 'Russia has been, is, and will be an Asiatic power.'[93] And under Putin and Medvedev, the Kremlin is still occasionally given to such posturing while ostentatiously trying to build anti-western coalitions with Asian powers.

NOTES

1. F. M. Dostoevskii, *Polnoe sobranie sochinenii*, 30 vols. (Leningrad: Nauka, 1972–90), vol. XXVII, pp. 32–6.
2. Edward A. Said, *Orientalism* (New York: Vintage, 1979).
3. Dostoevskii, *Polnoe sobranie sochinenii*, vol. XXVII, p. 33.
4. Vladimir Sergeevich Solovev, *Chteniia o Bogochelovechestve; Stat'i; Stikhotvoreniia i poema; Iz trekh razgovorov* (St Petersburg: Khudozhestvennaia literatura, 1994), p. 385.
5. Quoted in S. M. Mikhailova, *Kazanskii universitet v dukhovnoi kul'ture narodov Vostoka Rossii (XIX vek)* (Kazan: Izdatel'stvo Kazanskogo universiteta, 1991), p. 196.
6. Nicholas Riasanovsky, 'Asia through Russian eyes' in Wayne S. Vucinich (ed.), *Russia and Asia: Essays on the Influence of Russia on the Asian Peoples* (Stanford: Hoover Institution Press, 1972), pp. 3–29.
7. Charles Halperin, *Russia and the Golden Horde* (Bloomington: Indiana University Press, 1985); Donald Ostrowski, *Muscovy and the Mongols* (Cambridge University

Press, 1998); Richard Voorheis, 'The Perception of Asiatic Nomads in Medieval
Russia: Folklore, History and Historiography', unpublished PhD thesis (Indiana
University, 1982).

8. For an overview, see Halperin, *The Tatar Yoke* (Bloomington: Slavica, 1986).

9. Paul Bushkovitch, 'Orthodoxy and Islam in Russia', forthcoming in *Forschungen
zur osteuropäischen Geschichte*.

10. A classic discussion of the joint Byzantine and Tatar impact on Muscovite
thinking about statecraft is Michael Cherniavsky, '*Khan* or *Basileus*: an aspect
of Russian mediaeval political theory', *Journal of the History of Ideas*, 20 (1959),
459–76.

11. Edward Keenan, 'Muscovy and Kazan' 1445–1552: A Study in Steppe Politics',
unpublished PhD thesis (Harvard University, 1965), p. 400.

12. Paul Bushkovitch, 'Princes Cherkasskii or Circassian Murzas: the Kabardians
in the Russian boyar elite 1560–1700', *Cahiers du Monde russe*, 45 (2004), 28;
R. G. Landa, *Islam v istorii Rossii* (Moscow: Vostochnaia literatura, 1995),
pp. 56–8; Craig Kennedy, 'The Jurchids of Muscovy: A Study of Personal
Ties between Émigré Tatar Dynasts and the Muscovite Grand Princes in the
Fifteenth and Sixteenth Centuries', unpublished PhD thesis (Harvard
University, 1994), pp. 47–9.

13. Daniel Clarke Waugh, *The Great Turkes Defiance: On the History of the
Apocryphal Correspondence of the Ottoman Sultan in its Muscovite and Russian
Variants* (Columbus: Slavica, 1978), p. 188.

14. V. Dal', *Poslovitsy russkogo naroda* (Moscow: Gosudarstvennoe izdatel'stvo
khudozhestvennoi literatury, 1957), p. 348.

15. *Russkii khronograf. Polnoe sobranie russkikh letopisei* (Moscow: Iazyki slavianskoi
kul'tury, 2005), vol. XXII; I Iu. Krachkovskii, *Ocherki po istorii russkoi arabistiki*
(Moscow: Izdatel'stvo Akademii nauk SSSR, 1950), pp. 20–1; A. A. Zimin, *Russkie
letopisi i khronografy kontsa XV-XVI vv.* (Moscow: Moskovskii Gosudarstvennyi
Istoriko-Arkhivnyi Institut, 1960), pp. 8–9.

16. B. M. Dantsig, 'Iz istorii russkikh puteshestvii i izucheniia Blizhnego Vostoka v
dopetrovskoi Rusi' in *Ocherki po istorii russkogo vostokovedeniia* (Moscow:
Izdatel'stvo Akademii nauk SSSR, 1953), vol. I, pp. 209–13.

17. Mark Bassin, 'Russia between Europe and Asia: the ideological construction of
geographical space', *Slavic Review*, 50 (1991), 6–7. See also W. H. Parker,
'Europe: how far?', *The Geographical Journal*, 126 (1960), 278–97.

18. V. V. Bartold, *Sochineniia*, 9 vols. (Moscow: Nauka, 1943–77), vol. IX, pp. 24–41.

19. Jonathan Spence, *The Chan's Great Continent: China in Western Minds* (New
York: W. W. Norton, 1998), pp. 81–100.

20. Maxime Rodinson, *Europe and the Mystique of Islam*, trans. Roger Veinus
(Seattle: University of Washington Press, 1987), pp. 45–9.

21. Ibid., p. 44.

22. Barbara Widenor Maggs, *Russia and 'le rêve chinois': China in Eighteenth-Century
Russian Literature* (Oxford: The Voltaire Foundation, 1984); O. L. Fishman,
Kitai v Evrope: Mif i real'nost' (St Peterburg: RAN, 2003), pp. 368–94.

23. Bartold, *Sochineniia*, vol. IX, p. 411.

24. Isabel de Madariaga, *Russia in the Age of Catherine the Great* (New Haven: Yale University Press, 1981), p. 503.

25. Dmitri Shvidkovsky, *The Empress and the Architect: British Architecture and Gardens at the Court of Catherine the Great* (New Haven: Yale University Press, 1996), p. 176.

26. Maggs, *Russia and 'le rêve chinois'*, p. 146.

27. G. Makogonenko, *Nikolai Novikov i russkoe prosveshchenie XVIII veka* (Moscow and Leningrad: Gosudarstvennoe izdatel'stvo khudozhestvennoi literatury, 1952), pp. 167–70.

28. Madariaga, *Russia in the Age of Catherine the Great*, p. 588.

29. Nikolai Karamzin, *Karamzin's Memoir on Ancient and Modern Russia*, ed. Richard Pipes (New York: Atheneum, 1974), pp. 123–4.

30. Andrzej Walicki, *The Slavophile Controversy*, trans. Hilda Andrews-Rusiecka (University of Notre Dame Press, 1989), pp. 445–55.

31. Riasanovsky, 'Asia', pp. 9–10.

32. Riasanovsky, *Russia and the West in the Teaching of the Slavophiles* (Cambridge, Mass.: Harvard University Press, 1952), pp. 66–83, 215–18.

33. Chaadaev, *Polnoe sobranie sochinenii i izbrannye pis'ma*, 2 vols. (Moscow: Nauka, 1991), vol. I, p. 531.

34. Spence, *The Chan's Great Continent*, pp. 99–100; Ernst Rose, 'China as a symbol of reaction in Germany', *Comparative Literature*, 3 (1951), 57–65.

35. Kalpana Sahni, *Crucifying the Orient: Russian Orientalism and the Colonization of Caucasus and Central Asia* (Bangkok: White Orchid Press, 1997), p. 72.

36. See Dany Savelli, 'L'asiatisme dans la littérature et la pensée russe de la fin du XIXème siècle au début du XXème siècle', unpublished PhD thesis (Université de Lille III, 1994), p. 9.

37. V. G. Belinskii, *Polnoe sobranie sochinenii*, 13 vols. (Moscow: Izdatel'stvo Akademii nauk SSSR, 1953–9), vol. V, p. 98.

38. Ibid., p. 99.

39. Ibid., pp. 92–9.

40. V. A. Koshelov, 'Istoriosofskaia oppozitsiia "Zapad-Vostok" v tvorcheskom soznanii Pushkina' in E. P. Chelysheva (ed.), *Pushkin i mir Vostoka* (Moscow: Nauka, 1999), pp. 157–70.

41. Olga Maiorova, 'Intelligentsia views of Asia in the nineteenth century', paper presented at the Annual Meeting of the American Association for the Advancement of Slavic Studies, Philadelphia, 2008.

42. V. I. Sakharov (ed.), 'Rossiia – zveno Vostoka s Zapadom', *Mezhdunarodnaia Zhizn'*, 1998, no. 4.

43. Emmanuel Sarkisyanz, 'Russian attitudes toward Asia', *Russian Review*, 13 (1954), 246–7.

44. Susanna Soojung Lim, 'Chinese Europe: Alexander Herzen and the Russian image of China', *Intertexts*, 10 (2006), 56–9.

45. Ibid., 58.

46. Sarkisyanz, 'Russian attitudes', 246–7.

47. A. I. Gertsen, *Sobranie sochinenii*, 30 vols. (Moscow: Izdatel'stvo Akademii nauk SSSR, 1954–65), vol. XXIII, p. 175. Herzen's geography is not always

consistent. On another occasion, he likened Russians to a more occidental destructive force: 'Our relations with the Europeans ... bear some resemblance to those of the Germans and the Romans' (ibid., vol. XVI, p. 169).

48. See P. M. Shastitko *et al.* (eds.), *Russko-indiiskie otnosheniia v XIX v.: Sbornik arkhivnykh dokumentov i materialov* (Moscow: Vostochnaia literatura, 1997), p. 8.

49. See Roger Conant, *The Political Poetry and Ideology of F. I. Tiutchev* (Ann Arbor: Ardis, 1983), p. 34.

50. See Riasanovsky, 'Russia and Asia: two Russian views', *California Slavic Studies*, 1 (1960), 179–80.

51. Ibid., 178–9.

52. N. M. Przhevalskii, 'On the Current Situation in Eastern Turkestan', Memorandum, 6 June 1877, Archive of the Russian Geographical Society, *fond* 13, *opis'* 1, *delo* 26, p. 2.

53. A. N. Kuropatkin, 'Dnevnik A. N. Kuropatkina', *Krasnyi Arkhiv*, 2 (1922), 31.

54. Catherine II, *Sochineniia Imperatritsy Ekaterina II*, 12 vols. (St Petersburg: Tipografiia Imperatorskoi Akademii nauk, 1901–7), vol. VIII, pp. 17–20.

55. Andrei Zorin, *Kormia dvuglavogo orla* (Moscow: Novoe literaturnoe obozrenie, 2001), p. 110, n. 1.

56. A. I. Kononov, *Istoriia izucheniia tiurkskikh iazykov v Rossii* (Leningrad: Nauka, 1972), p. 39, n. 82.

57. I. Tolstoi and N. Kondakov, *Russkie drevnosti v pamiatnikakh iskusstva* (St Petersburg: A. Benke, 1889), vol. II; Véronique Schiltz, *La redécouverte de l'or des Scythes* (Paris: Gallimard, 1991), pp. 56–99.

58. N. M. Karamzin, *Istoriia gosudarstva rossiiskogo*, 12 vols. (St Petersburg: V tipografii Eduarda Pratsa, 1842–4), vol. V, p. 223.

59. V. V. Stasov, 'Proiskhozhdenie russkikh bylin', *Vestnik Evropy*, 3:2 (1868), 597.

60. Stasov, *Sobranie sochinenii*, 3 vols. (St Petersburg: Tipografiia M. M. Stasiulevicha, 1894), vol. I, pp. 197–212. See also Stasov, *Slavianskii i vostochnyi ornament po rukopisiam drevnego i novogo vremeni* (St Petersburg: Kartograficheskoe zavedenie A. A. Il'ina, 1887).

61. Vladimir Karenin, *Vladimir Stasov: Ocherk ego zhizni i deiatel'nosti* (Leningrad: Mysl', 1927), pp. 315–18. One notable exception was in Alfred Rambaud, *Russie épique: Étude sur les chansons héroïques de la Russie* (Paris: Maisonneuve, 1876), pp. 163–93.

62. E. Viollet-le-Duc, *L'art russe: Ses origines, ses ciments constitutifs, son apogée, son avenir* (Paris: A. Morel, 1877), p. 58.

63. Nicolas Berdiaev, *Constantin Leontiev*, trans. Hélène Iswolsky (Paris: Berg International, 1993), p. 49.

64. See Savelli, 'L'asiatisme', p. 46.

65. Leont'ev, *Vostok, Rossiia i Slavianstvo* (Moscow: Eksmo, 2007), pp. 606–7.

66. Ibid., p. 147.

67. Ibid., p. 636.

68. This section is adapted from my article 'Russia's Asian temptation', *International Journal*, 55 (2000), 603–23, with kind permission of the editor.

69. For more details about Prince Ukhtomsky, see the relevant chapter in my *Toward the Rising Sun: Russian Ideologies of Empire and the Path to War with Japan* (DeKalb: Northern Illinois University Press, 2001), pp. 42–60.

70. Prince Hesper Ookhtomsky [Ukhtomsky], *Travels in the East of Nicholas II when Cesarewitch*, 2 vols. (Westminster: Constable, 1896–1900), vol. II, p. 287.

71. Ibid., p. 32.

72. Ibid., p. 446.

73. The most detailed study in English is Stefani Hope Hoffman, 'Scythianism: A Cultural Vision in Revolutionary Russia', unpublished PhD dissertation (Columbia University, 1957). See also N. V. Kuzina, 'Ideologiia skifstva v russkoi obshchestvennoi mysli i literatury' in *Gosudarstvenno-patrioticheskaia ideologiia i problemy ee formirovaniia* (Smolensk: Izdatel'stvo Voennoi akademii, 1997), pp. 95–7.

74. K. D. Balmont, *Stikhotvoreniia* (Leningrad: Sovetskii pisatel', 1969), p. 150.

75. Ettore Lo Gatto, '*Panmongolismo* di V. Solovëv, *I venienti unni* di V. Brjusov e *Gli Sciti* di A. Blok' in Morris Halle *et al.* (eds.), *For Roman Jakobson* (The Hague: Mouton & Co., 1956), p. 300.

76. Aleksandr Blok, *Stikhotvoreniia i poemy* (Moscow: Khudozhestvennaia literature, 1968), p. 231.

77. Until recently, the most thorough study of the Eurasian movement was Otto Böss, *Die Lehre der Eurasier: Ein Beitrag zur russischen Ideengeschichte des 20. Jahrhunderts* (Wiesbaden: Otto Harrassowitz, 1961). However, in recent years there has been a renewed interest in the movement, especially in Russia. Two useful monographs are Margarita Georgievna Vandalovskaia, *Istoricheskaia nauka rossiiskoi emigratsii: 'Evraziiskii soblazn'* (Moscow: Pamiatniki istoricheskoi mysli, 1997), and O. D. Volkogonova, *Obraz Rossii v filosofii Russkogo zarubezh'ia* (Moscow: ROSSPEN, 1998). For a good account that takes the story up to the present, see Marlène Laruelle, *Russian Eurasianism: An Ideology of Empire* (Baltimore: The Johns Hopkins University Press, 2008).

78. P. N. Savitskii *et al.* (eds.), *Exodus to the East: Foreboding and Events: An Affirmation of the Eurasians*, trans. Ilya Vinkovetsky (Idyllwild: Charles Schlacks, 1996).

79. G. V. Vernadsky, *Nachertanie russkoi istorii. Chast' pervaia* (Prague: Evraziiskoe Knigoizdatel'stvo, 1927), and *Opyt istorii Evrazii s poloviny VI veka do nastoiashchego vremeni* (Berlin: Izdaniia evraziitsev, 1934).

80. Vernadsky, *A History of Russia* (New Haven: Yale University Press, 1961), p. 10.

81. Vernadsky, *Nachertanie russkoi istorii*, pp. 12–13, 18.

82. Ryszard Paradowski, 'The Eurasian idea and Leo Gumilëv's scientific ideology', *Canadian Slavonic Papers*, 41 (1999), 3.

83. Halperin, 'Russia and the steppe: George Vernadsky and Eurasianism', *Forschungen zur Osteuropäische Geschichte*, 36 (1985), 185.

84. See his spirited critique of Eurasianism in Paul Miliukov, 'Eurasianism and Europeanism in Russian history', *Festschrift Th. G. Masaryk zum 80. Geburtstag* (Bonn: Friedrich Cohen, 1930), vol. I, pp. 225–36.

85. Michael Ignatieff, 'Can Russia return to Europe?', *Harper's*, 284 (April 1992), p. 15.

86. Among such anthologies are L. N. Novikova and I. N. Sizemskaia (eds.), *Rossiia mezhdu Evropoi i Aziei: Evraziiskii soblazn* (Moscow: Nauka, 1993); I. A. Isaev (ed.), *Puti Evrazii: Russkaia intelligentsiia i sud'by Rossii* (Moscow: Russkaia Kniga, 1992); and N. N. Tolstoi (ed.), *Russkii uzel evraziistva: Vostok v russkoi mysli* (Moscow: Belovode, 1997).

87. John B. Dunlop, *The Rise of Russia and the Fall of the Soviet Empire* (Princeton University Press, 1993), p. 292.

88. Interview with Nikita Mikhalkov, *Rossiiskaia gazeta*, 14 December 1991.

89. Gennady Zyuganov, *My Russia: The Political Autobiography of Gennady Zyuganov* (Armonk: M. E. Sharpe, 1997), pp. 71–2.

90. Andrey Vladimirovich Novikov, 'Brak v kommunalke: Zametki o sovremennom evraziistve', *Zvezda*, 1998, no. 2, p. 230.

91. Ziuganov, *Geografiia pobedy: Osnovy rossiiskoi geopolitiki* (Moscow: n. p., 1997), pp. 182–3.

92. See Liah Greenfeld, *Nationalism: Five Roads to Modernity* (Cambridge, Mass.: Harvard University Press, 1993), p. 191.

93. Igor Ivanov, 'Dipkurer', *Nezavisimaia gazeta*, January 2000, p. 1.

CHAPTER II

The people

Derek Offord

Donald Fanger, in an essay on the representation of the peasantry in classical Russian literature, contends that the peasant

can only be approached from outside, by writers who, because they have *chosen* him as a subject, must find some significance in his existence. That significance is the writer's own invention or discovery; it answers *his* needs and is a part of *his* moral life. Thus the story of the peasant in Russian literature is the story of the changing moods and attitudes of the most influential segment of educated society, and it tells us much more about that society than about the peasant himself.[1]

In this chapter I shall apply a similar thesis more broadly to the corpus of classical Russian thought, which may be said to include imaginative literature. That is to say, I shall argue that the Russian common people, or *narod*, as conceived by the nineteenth-century intelligentsia, constituted not so much a clearly definable social entity as a construct fashioned in the minds of the intelligentsia. The function of this construct was to assist the intelligentsia in the urgent tasks of defining the identity and mission of Russia as a nation and of clarifying its own role within the nation. The emergence of the construct was one manifestation of the intelligentsia's attempt to solve the riddle of Russia's relationship with the West. In the writings of many thinkers the construct reflected an anxiety in the intelligentsia about the danger of social fragmentation in the wake of Russia's westernisation and the attendant industrialisation and urbanisation. At the same time, it could also betray a somewhat conflicting desire to overcome national backwardness and assume leadership on the European stage.

THE TERM *NAROD*

Like so many concepts that are embedded in the understanding that a people, social group, nation or state has of itself, the concept *narod* is elusive. This elusiveness is no doubt due partly to the fact that many such concepts have more emotional appeal than intellectual rigour. The difficulty is compounded, in this case, by the ambiguity which the term *narod* shares with its English, French and German equivalents ('the people', 'le peuple' and 'das Volk' respectively). That is to say, besides having the possible plural sense of 'people' or 'group of people' (as in the expression *mnogo narodu*, 'a lot of people'), the term may denote either the body of persons that comprises a community, tribe, race or nation, or, more narrowly, the common people, the mass of the community as distinguished from the nobility and the ruling or official classes.[2] The dictionary compiled by the nineteenth-century lexicographer Dal records these various meanings in a somewhat rambling entry:

people [*liud*] born in a certain space; people [*liudi*] in general; a people [*iazyk*], tribe; inhabitants of a country who speak the same language; the residents of a state [or] country which is under the same rule; the mass [*chern'*], the commonalty [*prostoliud'e*], the lower estates who pay the poll-tax [*podatnye*]; a multitude of people, a crowd.[3]

Essentially similar definitions are repeated in the *Dictionary of the Modern Russian Literary Language* published by the Soviet Academy of Sciences and in successive editions of Ozhegov's dictionary, albeit with the proviso in the latter that the meaning of commonalty (or oppressed mass, in Marxist-Leninist terminology) is applicable only in states with an exploitative ruling class.[4]

It is of some interest here, though, that in a volume of the *Dictionary of the Russian Academy* that came out in 1814, before the Golden Age of Russian literature and thought had properly begun, there is no allusion to the narrower meaning of common people that the term *narod* by itself came to acquire later in the nineteenth century and that it retains in the modern language. This early nineteenth-century lexicon gives only the meanings 'large number of people' and 'people, tribe, inhabitants of a state [or] some country being under the same laws and speaking the same natural language'. At the beginning of the nineteenth century, it would therefore seem, the substantive *narod* needed to be qualified with the adjective *prostyi* [*sic*] if it was to yield the meaning 'mass' or 'common people' [*prostoliudiny*].[5] There is evidence, then, to suggest that the range of meaning of the term was extended in the course of the nineteenth century, and this lexical evolution may throw light on the Russian search for and conception of national identity.

The practice adopted by Russian writers and thinkers of using the term *narod* sometimes to embrace the Russian people as a whole and sometimes to refer to the lower classes of that collectivity can, of course, cause difficulty. Moreover, the expression 'the people', when it is used in its first, comprehensive, sense and is combined with the adjective 'Russian' in the phrase *russkii narod*, may on close examination seem vague or misleading as an ethnic descriptor. For the ethnic origins, or partial ethnic origins, of those whom the term is likely to embrace may be extremely diverse (for instance, Lithuanian, Polish, Ukrainian or other Slav, Scandinavian, Tatar or other Turkic, and so forth). Equally problematic is the social scope of the term in its narrower meaning of labouring lower classes. No doubt all nineteenth-century Russian writers would have agreed that the term embraced the peasantry, and that the peasantry was the largest component of the *narod*. But did it embrace factory workers of various sorts, skilled, semi-skilled and unskilled, who were not at that time clearly differentiated in the minds of the intelligentsia from the peasantry, from which many seasonal workers (*prishlye rabochie*) in the towns in any case emanated? More broadly, did it include all or any part of the *meshchanstvo*, the lesser townspeople, such as petty traders, artisans, casual labourers and domestic servants? As so often when the student of Russian thought approaches material relating to the attempt at national self-definition, it seems easier to ascertain what a concept did not mean than what it did mean, and thus to reach a definition of it by an indirect route. That is to say, we can be fairly sure that 'the people', in the narrower sense of the term *narod*, were not nobility, *razno-chintsy*, *kupechestvo*, clergy, intelligentsia or any other professional or commercial elite or semi-elite. But then again, as Elise Kimerling Wirtschafter has convincingly argued, the social categories in late tsarist Russia were indeterminate, the boundaries between social groups were porous and the relationships between those groups were surprisingly fluid.[6] As a term objectively describing a real social stratum, therefore, *narod* remains an insubstantial thing, a baseless fabric liable to melt into thin air.

SLAVOPHILES

Towards the end of the eighteenth century, Russian writers, affected by the idylls of Gessner, 'the Swiss Theocritus', and by Rousseau's view that morals were corrupted in civilised societies, were already beginning to depict peasants in a sentimental light. Peasants figured not only as the victims of an unworthy nobility, as they did most famously in Radishchev's *Journey from St Petersburg to Moscow* (1790), but also – again in Radishchev and in Karamzin's 'Poor Liza' (1792) – as uncorrupted beings, healthy, virtuous beauties or hard-working ploughmen who were morally superior to their masters.[7]

However, the growth of interest in the *narod* in the classical period of Russian culture is a product not so much of Sentimentalism as of notions emanating from Germany about national distinctiveness. Particularly important in this respect was Herder's conception of a people as a natural community unspoilt by 'civilisation', in the pejorative sense of the word, and integrated primarily by possession of a common language.[8] Such notions had wide currency in early nineteenth-century Europe, especially among peoples such as the Czechs, Finns, Greeks, Magyars, Poles and Serbs, who were striving to assert their cultural or political independence from the more powerful peoples who dominated the states in which they found themselves.[9] In Russia the interest in national distinctiveness and the aspiration to cultural autonomy are already manifested in the Alexandrine period by the invention of the term *narodnost'*, 'nationality' or 'nationhood'. This translation of the French word *nationalité* was imported into Russian via Polish by the poet Viazemsky in 1819.[10] The concept of *narodnost'* was the subject of intense debate in literary circles in the 1820s and 1830s. Even Nicholas's Minister of Education, Uvarov, invoked it as one of the three pillars of the doctrine of Official Nationality, promoted from 1833. What the participants in the debate about *narodnost'* were seeking, though, was primarily a definition of the supposed essence that distinguished Russians in general from other peoples, rather than a definition of the Russian common people in particular.

It was the Slavophiles who took the lead in identifying the common people as the bearers of what was most distinctive and exemplary in the Russian national character. In one of the *loci classici* of their nationalism, Ivan Kireevsky's comparison of Russian and European civilisation (1852), for example, it is the 'simple people' (*prostoi narod*) whom Kireevsky depicts as having preserved the distinctive ancient customs, manners, Orthodox ways of thinking and communal mentality that he cherishes.[11] If one looked closely at the 'inner life' of the peasant hut, Kireevsky ventured to say, then one would see that no member of the family ever has his own personal interest in mind. On the contrary, each member

has completely cut off at the root any thought of personal gain. The integrity of the family is the only common aim and mainspring. Any surplus in the household goes to the head of the family alone, and he does not have to give any account of it; all private earnings are handed over to him in full and in good faith. Not that the mode of life of the family as a whole improves much, as a rule, as a result of the additional surpluses that come to the head of it [Kireevsky does not wonder whether he has stumbled here on evidence of self-interest and acquisitiveness that runs counter to his argument]; but the individual members do not look into how these surpluses are used and do not even try to find out how large they are: they carry on their eternal labour, taking just as much trouble [as before], with the same selflessness, as a duty of conscience, and upholding family harmony.[12]

Kireevsky's romantic conception of the *narod* was more fully developed by Konstantin Aksakov. In his memorandum of 1855 to Alexander II, Aksakov characterised the common people as serenely peaceable, apolitical and indifferent to western political aspirations such as revolution and constitutional government.[13] His copious philological writings on the Russian language were underpinned by the belief that the spirit of the common people found expression in it.[14] And in various historical writings he conceived of the village commune, through which the peasants managed their affairs and periodically redistributed the land at their disposal according to the changing needs of the households in their community, as a glorious 'moral choir'. For in the commune the individual personality renounced its 'exclusivity' for the sake of the general harmony.[15] This communal spirit, which Aksakov was sure the Russian people had possessed since time immemorial,[16] was a manifestation of true brotherly love and Christian religiosity. It enabled the people to live in a state as near as one could find in this world to moral perfection.[17]

Aksakov continued to reflect on the character of the 'common people' in an editorial that he wrote in 1857 for the ninth number of a short-lived Slavophile paper, *The Rumour*. He is concerned here, *pace* the Westernisers, as we shall see, to characterise the *narod* as a conscious entity, not an unconscious mass that can be turned in this direction or that. The people are an elemental force, to be sure, and a 'guardian of tradition and a custodian of antiquity'. However, they are not a servile 'blind worshipper of custom'. Rather, they are a 'rational element which has moral will'. What is of equal interest from our present point of view is that in the course of this eulogy Aksakov ceases to use the expression 'the simple people' (*prostoi narod*) and begins instead to use the word *narod* on its own in this sense. This shift in usage implicitly reveals Aksakov's fundamental point. The common people are not merely the 'basis of the country's whole social edifice' and 'the source of its material well-being' but also the sole bearers of true, primordial Russianness. Aksakov himself comments on the consequent redundancy of the epithet *prostoi*: the 'simple people', he writes, playing with the word *prostoi*, 'are *simply the people*, or the people properly speaking'.[18]

The nation as the Slavophiles prefer to conceive of it is therefore not primarily a territorial unit or a bureaucratic state or a union of social classes. A nation of that sort, denoted by the term *natsiia* in Aksakov's parlance, is a political concept which holds no attraction for them. What the Slavophiles yearn for instead is an organic community, an apolitical, moral utopia inhabited by the conservative, communal, peaceable Russian common people and permeated with the Orthodox Christian values that the people have preserved. A nation of this sort is a cultural concept denoted by the term *narod* in the narrower sense that Aksakov gives it.

Finally, in the cultural nation imagined by the Slavophiles, the upper classes, to which the Slavophiles themselves belonged, might find that they had no place, or at least they might struggle to be included in it. For this reason Samarin, in an article of 1847, exhorted members of society (*obshchestvo*) to 'get to know' the *narod*, in the hope of recovering from them truths which the urbanised elite, with their books and material comforts, had forgotten. The wealthy members of the educated class are represented here as have-nots who might benefit from an exchange of knowledge and experience with their poorer brethren, while the common people, despite their relative material poverty, turn out to be the haves.[19] Thus the interest of the Slavophiles in the common people, in the final analysis, could be construed as springing not so much from a philanthropic concern for the poor oppressed mass as from a more self-interested concern with their own integration into the nation as they conceived of it.

'WESTERNISERS'

Although it is conventional to contrast the Slavophiles with the Westernisers of the same generation, in truth both Slavophilism and Westernism were species of the nationalism generated in Russia in the first half of the nine-teenth century by the preoccupation with the notion of national distinctive-ness. All the same, the Westernisers, for the most part, refused to view the common people through a Romantic prism, as the Slavophiles had done. Rather, they looked upon them from a humanitarian standpoint, in the light of such foreign writings as the French physiological sketch and the utopian socialist tract, both of which became popular in Russia in the 1840s. The more liberal group among the Westernisers, in particular, tended to regard the *narod* as an unenlightened, indeterminate mass whose level of civilisa-tion would have to be gradually raised by means of governmental reform and through the efforts of the westernised elite. One prominent member of the more radical group of Westernisers, Herzen, on the other hand, took a view of the common people which, while in some respects different from that of the Slavophiles, was hardly less idealised than theirs.

The liberal Westernisers' relatively sober assessment of the character of the Russian people found expression in the late 1840s and 1850s in the view that ancient Russian society was organised on a principle quite different from the communal principle admired by the Slavophiles. In fact, Kavelin argued in an influential essay of 1847, it was a clan or kinship principle that underlay ancient Russian society. Then, from the period of the Tatar Yoke, Kavelin believed, this form of society began to be broken down as the Muscovite princes asserted the interests of the state over those of the family. At the same time, the notion of personal worth gained ground as a criterion for social status and political influence. Finally, Peter the Great created the conditions in which the autonomous individual personality could flourish. Thus social organisation in medieval Russia, according to Kavelin, was shaped not by the personality of a people more capable than others of brotherly love but by blood relationships and, at a later stage, by individual rulers who overcame the loyalties of the clan.[20]

In any case, the liberal Westernisers' acceptance of the need for a strong, centralised, authoritarian state and their reverence for supposedly benevolent autocrats such as Peter, whom they regarded as the main agents of progress in Russia, militated against an idealised view of the *narod*. Indeed, Kavelin, while seeing the Great Russian peasant as a fresh, gifted force, described him as still like 'Kaluga dough' (that is to say, something that could be kneaded) or as 'a sort of ethnographic protoplasm', living matter that was in the process of taking shape.[21] Similarly, the historian Granovsky believed that the popular masses, if left to their own devices, stagnated under the weight of 'historical and natural determinants'. Far from possessing some 'general, infallible reason' that found expression in their traditions, as the Slavophiles supposed, they were a force of nature, given to irrational impulses. Historical progress, for Granovsky, was measured by the degree to which this mass was broken down as members of it became enlightened and individualised.[22] Chicherin was shortly to take a similarly sceptical view of the peasant commune. He challenged the Slavophiles' representation of the commune as a Christian utopia originating in pre-Varangian times and defined it instead as an institution that, in its present form, had come into being only quite recently and whose function was to aid the collection of taxes.[23]

The leading radical Westerniser, Belinsky, also distanced himself from the Slavophile view of the *narod* as endowed with peculiar religiosity. In his furious response of 1847 to Gogol's homiletic *Selected Passages from Correspondence with Friends*, for instance, he asserted that the Russian people had 'no trace of religiosity'. On the contrary, they were 'by nature profoundly atheistic'. The Russian spoke the name of God while scratching his behind, Belinsky scoffed.[24] Elsewhere Belinsky contested the Slavophiles' view of the relationship between society and the common people, arguing that a people in the broad sense of the word can only develop when outstanding individuals, the 'flower and fruit' of the native soil, rise above the mass and promote its subconscious needs. Echoing Granovsky's words about the elemental nature of the impulsive crowd, he also denied that the common people on their own could constitute a nation (*natsiia*); rather, a nation was made up of all 'estates'. At the same time, Belinsky did seek some middle ground. He accepted that the lowest and most numerous part of the nation, the part of it that is not 'society' (*obshchestvo*), was the 'custodian of the essence' of a people, an instinctively conservative force that protected a people from anything that ran counter to its spirit. Indeed, he went further: the Russian people, he claimed, were 'one of the most capable and gifted peoples in the world', thanks in particular to their exceptional receptivity to the ideas of other peoples and their 'passion for emulation'.[25] Even in their indifference to matters of faith they seemed exemplary: their lack of mystical exaltation, their common sense and clear and positive mind, he asserted in his letter to Gogol, promised a great historical destiny.[26]

Belinsky's sentiments betoken the development of that veneration of the *narod* that would become characteristic of Russian radical thought in the age of Alexander II. Nowhere are the origins of such veneration more apparent in the late 1840s and early 1850s, though, than in the conception of the common people that emerges from a series of essays in which Herzen outlined his theory of 'Russian Socialism'. Herzen's conception is sharpened, just as Kireevsky's had been, by a contrasting characterisation of certain western peoples, or more particularly, in Herzen's case, by the characterisation that he offered in his *Letters from France and Italy* (1847–54) of the French bourgeoisie and their supposedly moribund civilisation. Whereas the western bourgeois, according to Herzen, was egoistic and mercenary, the Russian peasant was communitarian and relatively uninterested in material possessions. Thus the Frenchman, Herzen observed as he travelled through Provence, brazenly asserts an exclusive property right by marking the boundary of his land with high stone walls topped with broken glass (a sight that offended Herzen's Slavonic soul).[27] The Russian peasant, on the other hand, has a collectivist spirit that is expressed in his attachment to the commune, which – Herzen noted approvingly, as had the Slavophiles – does not recognise private property rights and administers its affairs in an apparently democratic way.[28] Herzen's peasant also has a pleasing aversion to written contractual arrangements of the sort that characterise bourgeois society and is correspondingly loath to enter into legal disputation.[29] He is strong, agile and intelligent, too, and, to complete the flattering portrait, he has 'an open, handsome countenance', 'a lively mind' and a 'beauty' that Herzen considers virile.[30] Herzen's peasants differ from the Slavophiles' peasants, it is true, inasmuch as their commune is a basis for a socialist utopia rather than an example of Christian brotherhood. And yet in other respects – their love of informality, their physical and mental dexterity, their apparent good sense and above all their communality – they are strikingly similar to the rural paragons imagined by the Slavophiles.

In the years following the Crimean War (1853–6), when debate was freer for a while and took a more overtly social and political turn, interest in the *narod* reached new heights. This interest was encouraged by the determination of the new emperor, Alexander II, to abolish serfdom. At the same time, the intelligentsia became much preoccupied with the gulf that separated it from the common people, who seemed no less alien than the western peoples whose countries and cultures the intelligentsia had been exploring in the age of Nicholas. By and large, the intense humanitarian concern for the *narod* was bolstered by positive conceptions of the people's character and potentiality. These conceptions typically informed the mentality of the revolutionaries active in the latter half of the age of Alexander, who may in general be classified as Populists, but at some level they also affected much broader swathes of the intelligentsia.

The heightened interest in the *narod* after the Crimean War was reflected in a prodigious volume of artistic activity that continued throughout the 1860s and 1870s, as well as in Russian thought. A school of young writers – including Levitov, Reshetnikov, Sleptsov and Nikolay Uspensky,[31] together with the established poet Nekrasov – described conditions in the countryside or in the factories that were now springing up in the Russian heartland. It is indicative of the growing importance of the life of the common people as a subject of fiction in the late 1850s that Dobroliubov devoted considerable attention to it in his literary criticism. In a number of essays he treated the peasant masses as serious-minded, practical, endowed with a moral purity that was lacking in the idle aristocracy and fit for the role of free citizen after the anticipated abolition of serfdom.[32] The interest of the intelligentsia in the common people was sustained in the 1870s by other imaginative writers, most notably Gleb Uspensky (a cousin of Nikolay), who portrayed the *narod* as 'patient and mighty in misfortunes', 'youthful in soul, man-like in their strength and child-like in their meekness', provided always that the mysterious '*power of the land*' held sway over them.[33] Nor was this interest confined to imaginative literature. Painters, especially members of the group known as the *peredvizhniki* (sometimes translated as The Wanderers), began to portray representatives of the masses with respect and compassion for their plight. Meanwhile, certain composers, under the influence of the critic Stasov, introduced folk motifs into their work, and Musorgsky, in his operas *Boris Godunov* and *Khovanshchina*, treated the *narod* as a powerful historical force.

Not all the great novelists, it is true, shared the general enthusiasm for the Russian peasant. Most notably Turgenev, whose socio-political views were close to those of the liberal Westernisers, took a sceptical view of the peasant's character, despite his humane and individualised literary representation of peasants in his *Sportsman's Sketches* (1847–52). Responding to Herzen's cycle of essays *Ends and Beginnings* (1862), in which Herzen had reiterated his long-held view about the decay of the bourgeois West and the bright futurity of Russia, Turgenev bluntly characterised the Russian peasant as instinctively bourgeois. The people whom Herzen worships, Turgenev complains, 'are conservative *par excellence*, and even bear the embryo of a bourgeoisie in a sheepskin coat and a warm, dirty peasant hut, with their bellies always stuffed to the point where they have heartburn and with revulsion for any civic responsibility and individual initiative'.[34] Turgenev accordingly conceived of the role of the intelligentsia in terms similar to those used by Granovsky: it would provide leadership, albeit of a modest kind, transmitting civilisation to the people so that they themselves could decide what to accept and what to reject.[35]

However, the two novelists who dominated the literary landscape in the 1860s and 1870s, Dostoevsky and Tolstoy, both of whom may be treated as thinkers in their own right, viewed the Russian common people in ways that were more typical in the post-Crimean age. Dostoevsky, as a nationalist who was convinced that the spiritual and social well-being of a people depended on their being conscious of their distinctive collective personality, regarded the *narod* as still unspoilt by the foreign ideas, values and fashions that were threatening to obliterate the identity of the educated elite.[36] In fact, it was the aim of Native-Soil Conservatism, or *pochvennichestvo*, the latter-day variant of Slavophilism, which Dostoevsky helped to propagate, to effect a reconciliation between the 50 million 'simple' Russians and the 100,000 members of the elite who, the *pochvenniki* believed, had been separated from the people by westernisation as a result of the Petrine reforms. The intelligentsia would take European culture to the *narod*, to be sure, Dostoevsky argued in his travelogue *Winter Notes on Summer Impressions* (1863); but it would also be fortified by contact with them, as Pushkin had been by his upbringing at the hands of his peasant nursemaid, Arina Rodionovna. The exemplary personality that Dostoevsky thought the people had preserved through centuries of suffering bore now familiar features: a capacity for self-abnegation, a sense of community, a striving for social harmony and an instinctive brotherhood (*bratstvo*) that is of a Christian kind, unlike the superficial *fraternité* to which the foreign socialist aspired.[37]

Dostoevsky continued to eulogise the common people and to underline the need for reconciliation of *obshchestvo* and *narod* in the following decade. Thus in *The Devils* (1871–2) Stepan Verkhovensky, a free-thinking 'man of the forties' modelled to some extent on Granovsky, eventually seeks meaning for his own life among the common people, once he has become dimly aware of the error into which his frivolous westernism has led him.[38] In his last novel, *The Brothers Karamazov*, Dostoevsky takes pains to emphasise the close connection between the simple Russian people and the novel's provincial monastic community, which upholds the values he cherishes.[39] He also used his *Diary of a Writer* to restate more explicitly his view about the need for and prospects of reconciliation. Arguing in the story 'Vlas' (1873) that Russia's destiny would not be decided by the elite of St Petersburg, he anticipated that the peasants would awaken from their present turpitude and save the intelligentsia, as well as themselves: 'light and salvation will shine forth from below', he predicted, in a way not expected by Russia's liberals.[40] It is said that when in his later years he was pressed by sceptical listeners in salon society, where he was now received as a sage, about his grounds for believing in the superiority of Russia over other nations, Dostoevsky would in a similar vein invoke the 'kitchen peasant' (*kufel'nyi muzhik*) who, he supposed, could enlighten the corrupted upper classes.[41]

Tolstoy, whose Gerasim in 'The Death of Ivan Ilich' (1886) was thought of as the eventual literary embodiment of Dostoevsky's 'kitchen peasant',[42] also presented an idealised view of the peasants. The most notable example is his portrait, in *War and Peace* (1865–9), of Platon Karataev, who makes such a profound impression on Pierre Bezukhov while they are both prisoners of the French invaders in 1812. Karataev is physically and spiritually robust. Both his practical skills (he can bake, cook, sew and mend boots) and his speech, which is peppered with proverbs and sayings that embody popular good sense, associate him with the peasant milieu and set him apart from the class from which Pierre comes. So, too, do his fondness for prayer and his piety: in fact, being a peasant is indistinguishable, for Karataev, from being a Christian. His ideal kindliness and simplicity and his lack of self-interest or ulterior motive are constantly manifested in his habit of sharing whatever he has, in his mode of expressing his thoughts (which is spontaneous and without forethought) and in his love of and ability to accommodate himself to everyone and everything with which life brings him into contact. The lack of self-absorption which enables Karataev to take an untroubled view of life as something that is merely to be lived makes him an exemplary figure for the troubled Pierre, in whose mind he would always remain 'a most intense and precious memory and personification of everything Russian, good and round'. In short, Karataev conforms to the image of the peasant that had become so pervasive in the Russian intelligentsia by the 1860s. He is an authentic being equally at ease in his community and the cosmos: his individual life has no meaning except 'as a particle of a whole which he constantly sensed'.[43]

Alongside all these artistic representations of the common people there sprang up a large corpus of related scholarly and ethnographic material, of which I shall mention only a few major examples. Shchapov wrote extensively about the peasant commune, the seventeenth-century assemblies of the land (*zemskie sobory*) and especially the Schism (*raskol*) in the Russian church in the second half of the seventeenth century, which he construed as a form of popular resistance to the oppressive tsarist state and the institution of serfdom.[44] Beliaev, in his *Peasants in Rus* (1859), examined the peasants' use of the land and their relationship with landowners and the state, arguing that in Muscovite times they had enjoyed relative freedom in Russian society, and contending, like the Slavophiles, to whom Beliaev was close, that the commune was an ancient institution central to the national way of life.[45] Petr Kireevsky's collection of Russian folk songs was first published posthumously in this period.[46] Dal published a collection, in 1862, of over 30,000 proverbs and sayings of the Russian people, whose language he had by then been studying for some three decades.[47] Afanasev, Buslaev and Miller, inspired by the Romantic approach to folklore as a collective expression of a people's consciousness, studied Russian fairy tales, popular legends, myth and the oral epos.[48] Historians and legal scholars (for instance, Efimenko, Semevsky, Sergeevich and Sokolovsky) interested themselves in such matters as the origins and history of serfdom, the tension between the people and the state, the history of the peasant commune and the ways in which Russian law impinged on the life of the common people.[49]

POPULISTS

The reservoir of material about the *narod* that was contained in the fiction, scholarship and journalism of the age of Alexander II provided an inexhaustible source of inspiration for Russian Populism, that is to say, for what came to be known as *narodnichestvo*. Populists shared with conservative thinkers such as Dostoevsky a desire for rapprochement between the two poles of the nation and a conviction that the common people had exceptional positive qualities. However, they interpreted these qualities as a pledge of a future socialist utopia rather than an Orthodox Christian one. According to this interpretation, the people's instinctive egalitarianism, expressed in the peasant commune and the workers' artel, could serve as a basis for a distinctive native form of socialism, to which Russia might proceed without passing first through the capitalist phase of development currently afflicting the West.

These classical Populist assumptions, which drew on Herzen's 'Russian Socialism', were put forward in a now neglected but at the time influential work, *The Condition of the Working Class in Russia* (1869), by an eccentric man of Scottish ancestry, Bervi, who wrote under the pseudonym Flerovsky. Using the term 'working class' in a very loose sense to mean all labouring people, Bervi defended the *narod* against those who branded them as idle, ignorant, promiscuous or prone to drunkenness. In fact, Bervi believes, the Russian common people are too patient and industrious for their own good. They are the least bellicose people in Europe. They possess sound judgement, 'natural wit, [a] vigorous, enterprising nature and an instinctive striving for civilisation'. They grasp new concepts much more quickly and surely than members of the nobility. They bear within themselves the great principle of cooperation, which will enable them to remain aloof from the divisive competitiveness characteristic of western capitalist societies. Like so many of his contemporaries, Bervi holds up the peasant commune as both an economically effective unit which makes judicious use of land and other shared resources and an expression of the indigenous socialistic instinct.[50]

It was Bakunin, though, who did most to convert the positive image of the *narod* that had been constructed by thinkers of various complexions over several decades into an inspirational revolutionary strategy. He reiterated the conception of the *narod* as the repository of a communal ideal that led them to see the land as the property of all who worked it and to aspire to self-government within their community. Admittedly, various factors – veneration of the tsar, the patriarchal nature of the Russian family and the Christian faith – tended to obscure the people's communality. And yet there were other phenomena in Russian life from which Bakunin took heart. One such phenomenon was brigandage, which he interpreted as a sign of the people's innate rebelliousness against the state. Most importantly, the *narod* seemed to Bakunin to be an elemental force, which had repeatedly erupted with great destructive power. He drew particular comfort from the uprisings led by Stenka Razin in 1670–1 and Emelian Pugachev in 1773–4. These *bunty*, Bakunin claimed, demonstrated that the ideal that the people strove to realise was 'really alive in their consciousness'. It was the task of revolutionaries now to try to incite further rebellion of this sort on a national scale by means of agitation among the peasant mass.[51]

Bakunin's chief rival for influence as a revolutionary strategist in the 1870s, Lavrov, could not be said to have contributed to the same degree to the cult of the people in the 1870s. For the role of the intelligentsia, in Lavrov's eyes, was not to follow the people but to provide them with leadership, by inculcating in them the socialist consciousness that the elite, thanks to its wealth and leisure, had been able to acquire. Elements of the mass, thus raised to the level of the intelligentsia, would be in a position, when the opportunity somehow arose, to put socialist ideals into practice. And yet Lavrov, too, provided a key component in the conception of the relationship between intelligentsia and *narod* that imbued Russian thought in the latter half of the reign of Alexander II. For he described the task of raising the consciousness of the *narod* as a moral debt incurred by the privileged minority as a result of its prolonged exploitation of the peasants' labour. By discharging this debt, or duty (the Russian word *dolg* has an ambiguity that is convenient in this context), Lavrov argued in a famous passage in the fourth of his *Historical Letters* (1868–9), the 'critically thinking minority' would expiate an evil.[52] Thus the *narod*, for the Populist Lavrov no less than for the Christian Slavophiles, are more than an object of curiosity and enquiry: they are a construct that serves a psychological need of the guilt-laden intelligentsia by offering a path to redemption.

Dissenters from the admiring view of the *narod* were few in the age of Alexander II. The most striking among them is the so-called 'Jacobin' or 'Blanquist' revolutionary, Tkachev. It is significant in this connection that although Tkachev repeated the Populist shibboleth that Russia would take its own path to socialism, bypassing a capitalist phase of development, he was one of the first Russian thinkers to endorse Marx's belief that culture was shaped by environment, particularly by the economic conditions obtaining in a given society.[53] This determinism led him to argue that the Russian common people were 'coarse, savage, [and] brutal' and that they would remain so until they ceased to be poor.[54] Tkachev did accept that the *narod*, as an oppressed mass, were in a sense ever ready for revolution. He also accepted that they nurtured a communal ideal, an embryonic communism, as it were. At the same time, he believed that they would be incapable of initiating a revolution, owing to their awe of the powers that be, their stoical passivity, silent obedience and innate conservatism. The intelligentsia therefore had no grounds for 'genuflecting before the people'. They would have to do without such 'idols' and should accordingly erase from their lexicon meaningless phrases leased from the Slavophiles about the *'people's genius'*.[55] This negative conception of the *narod* shaped Tkachev's revolutionary strategy, just as a positive conception had shaped Bakunin's. Revolutionaries should abandon their practice of going to the countryside with the aim of persuading the peasants to carry out what was described at this time as an 'economic' or 'social' revolution, a revolution from below. They should concentrate their energy instead on the creation from within their own social milieu of a highly disciplined force capable of carrying out a political revolution, a *coup d'état*, as a prelude to the imposition of a new order by decree, a revolution from above.[56]

Tkachev's essentially disparaging conception of the *narod* had negligible impact in the short term. It was the much more widespread positive conception of the *narod* advanced by so many imaginative writers, critics, painters, composers, ethnographers, lexicographers, folklorists, historians, legal scholars and social and political thinkers of the 1860s and 1870s that affected the idealistic students who took part in the 'going to the people' of 1874 and in further attempts to settle in the countryside in the second half of the decade. Only after the failure of the Populists to stir the masses either by propaganda and agitation or by the campaign of political terrorism that began in 1879 and culminated in the assassination of Alexander II on 1 March 1881 did a significant portion of the intelligentsia begin to lose faith in the peasantry. It was then that the previously dominant positive view of the *narod* began to be challenged by Marxists (though at first only by the émigrés led by Plekhanov in Switzerland), who considered the peasantry an instinctively conservative class. The notion of ethnic and cultural distinctiveness on which admiration of the peasantry rested had no place in the Marxists' 'scientific' outlook, which, it was claimed, was universally applicable. For Populists and their sympathisers, meanwhile, the collapse of their 'idol' (to use Tkachev's term) threatened more than the premises on which the revolutionary strategy of 'going to the people' had been based. For such was the psychological importance of the positive image of the *narod* in their lives, as Richard Wortman has argued, that the loss of faith in the peasant left many bereft and profoundly affected the view that they held of themselves.[57] The exceptional despondency of the intelligentsia during the 1880s might therefore be felt to be as much a product of the disintegration of a cherished construct as of the failure of The People's Will to overthrow the autocracy, the success of the police in suppressing the revolutionary movement and the reactionary policies of Alexander III.

CONCLUSION

What I have been concerned with in this chapter is not the plausibility, let alone the historical accuracy, of the views expressed by members of the nineteenth-century intelligentsia about the Russian common people but the nature of the intelligentsia's perceptions of them. Broadly speaking, two representations of the *narod* have emerged. One representation is highly positive. The common people are respected, or even venerated, for qualities such as innate goodness, sound judgement, devotion to an ancient, autochthonous way of life, communality and aversion to private property and material things. These qualities render them fit to inhabit a utopia, which may be either Christian or socialistic. Those who characterised the people in this way tended to believe that the intelligentsia should emulate them, or at least that it had much to learn from them. The other representation of the *narod* is more negative and less widespread. The common people are an indeterminate, backward mass and will only progress when the intelligentsia has brought to them from the outside the enlightenment that it has discovered in the West. On the whole, these two representations of the common people follow the lines laid down in the 1840s and 1850s by the Slavophiles and Westernisers respectively. However, it would distort the truth to press the dichotomy too far, for there were many variants to each type of characterisation of the *narod*. Nor should we try to identify either characterisation too closely with a position on the political spectrum. After all, the conservative Official Nationalist Pogodin, who in certain respects was close to the Slavophiles, did not revere the common people (perhaps because he himself was of peasant stock). On the other hand, the radical Westerniser Herzen (the illegitimate son of a very wealthy Russian nobleman and a bourgeois German woman) did idealise them, at least in his writings as an émigré.

The nationalism that found expression in the more positive conception of the *narod* that I have described, at least until the emergence of the Populist revolutionaries, was not, for the most part, nationalism of the political variety. Rather, it was cultural nationalism, as Susanna Rabow-Edling, drawing on the work of scholars such as John Hutchinson and Anthony Smith, has recently argued with reference to Slavophilism.[58] The proponents of this latter form of nationalism, in the main, are thinkers, artists and scholars rather than statesmen, legislators and agitators. They aspire to regenerate what they suppose to be – in the words of Smith, as he offers a definition of a 'nonwestern' conception of the nation – a 'community of common descent' in which birth, family ties and native culture are of paramount importance.[59] They seek – in Rabow-Edling's words now – 'to recover the "creative force" of the nation', substituting 'for the legal and rational concept of citizenship the much vaguer concept of "the people", which can only be understood intuitively'.[60] They regard the people, conceived in the narrower sense in which the term has been used in this chapter, as a 'final rhetorical court of appeal' and cherish vernacular culture, hence the prominent role among them, as Smith points out, of lexicographers, philologists and folklorists.[61] This exclusive, cultural or 'ethnic' conception of a nation was widespread among the nineteenth-century Russian intelligentsia. The Slavophiles, the Native-Soil Conservatives and the writers of various sorts who created the atmosphere in which Populism could flourish all subscribed to it.

Fewer Russian thinkers can plausibly be described as proponents of a more inclusive conception of the nation that takes a largely sceptical view of the capacities of the common people and invokes instead the 'people' in the broader sense of the term, offering a vision that accommodates all social classes. Some of the Westernisers, it is true, promoted a more 'western' model of the nation, in Smith's classification. According to this model, the rule of law is prized more highly than popular or demotic culture and the territorial nation is bound together by shared civic values and equal legal rights within a political community rather than by ethnic ties.[62] Chicherin and Turgenev were notable representatives of this way of thinking, together with Granovsky, who in an admiring essay on Alexander the Great expressed respect for civilising principles that might unite ethnic groups.[63] However, we cannot associate Herzen or Bakunin with such a vision: although they are often classified as two of the more radical Westernisers of the 1840s, in the final analysis they helped to inspire the Populist movement which in the 1870s clearly articulated the notion of Russian exclusiveness.

It may be useful, finally, to summarise the various contrastive ways in which the representations of the *narod* that I have outlined, or at least the more positive type of representation, helped the intelligentsia to construct a sense of identity for their young nation and to formulate a role for their own social group within it.

First, the imagined Russian common people (*narod* in the narrower sense of the term) could serve as a model of what a people as a whole (*narod* in its broader sense) might be like if they did not want to resemble the western peoples whom Russians were observing in the age of Nicholas. As conceived by the Slavophiles, Herzen, Dostoevsky and most of the Populists, the *narod* were far removed from the western bourgeois, especially in his French or English incarnations. Westerners, it was alleged, were individualistic, self-assertive, more concerned with rights than obligations, confrontational, formalistic and – in the opinion of Russian conservative thinkers – godless. Russians, as represented by common people, on the other hand, were indifferent to private property and material wealth and found fulfilment in the voluntary surrender of the ego to their community.

Second, the common people also stood at an opposite pole to the Russian state, against which the intelligentsia was beginning to pit itself in the age of Nicholas. That is to say, they could be conceived not merely as victims of the state but also as an indigenous antithesis to a ruling class that was alien in several respects. After all, since the eighteenth century the royal family had had German blood; many noblemen whose families originated from Baltic lands were prominent in the higher echelons of the imperial bureaucracy; and the court and the upper nobility, deeply affected by the French culture that had been in the ascendant in Europe since the age of Louis XIV, had adopted a foreign way of life. Konstantin Aksakov and Bakunin, from different standpoints on the political spectrum, both made much of this contrast between alien state and native people. Dostoevsky pointed it up, too, in *The Devils*, by drawing a derisive portrait of the eventually demented town-governor von Lembke, an official of Baltic German origin.[64] The common people, then, could be conceived as a bulwark against powerful home-grown aliens as well as aliens from beyond Russia's borders.

Third, the intelligentsia's perception of the *narod*, besides offering an alternative vision of the human condition to that which many Russian writers and thinkers associated with the western European peoples, afforded a tantalising glimpse of a type of personality and a way of life that were felt to have been lost by the jaded urban elite. For the peasants in their rural community, unlike the *intelligent*, were imagined as morally secure and spiritually whole and leading a life that was authentic and immediate. And yet there was a ray of hope for the intelligentsia, and the people provided it for writers and thinkers on both its Christian conservative and radical atheistic wings. The *intelligent*, too, might attain a state of well-being by performing some act of altruism or self-sacrifice, some exploit or *podvig*, for the people's benefit. (It was in these terms that many of the participants in the 'going to the people' conceived of their expedition.) Thus the common people became the object of a spiritual or moral aspiration. They were transmuted into an elevated collective being to whom service of the sort that the nobility had once performed for the autocratic state was now due. Perceived in this way, they endowed the lives of intellectuals with fresh purpose and meaning.

NOTES

1. Donald Fanger, 'The peasant in literature' in *The Peasant in Nineteenth-Century Russia*, ed. Wayne S. Vucinich (Stanford University Press, 1968), pp. 232–3.

2. These definitions are framed in the terms used in the entry on 'people' in the *Oxford English Dictionary*, 2nd edn (Oxford: Clarendon Press, 1989), vol. XI, pp. 504, 505. Compare the definition of the French word 'peuple' in *Le Nouveau Petit Robert* (Paris: Dictionnaires le Robert, 2002), p. 1923.

3. Vladimir Dal', *Tolkovyi slovar' zhivogo velikorusskogo iazyka*, 4 vols. (Moscow: Gosudarstvennoe izdatel'stvo inostrannykh i natsional'nykh slovarei, 1955; reprint of Izdanie knigoprodavtsa-tipografa M. O. Vol'fa, Moscow and St Petersburg, 1881), vol. II, p. 461.

4. *Slovar' sovremennogo russkogo literaturnogo iazyka*, 17 vols. (Moscow and Leningrad: Izdatel'stvo Akademii nauk SSSR, 1950–65), vol. VII, pp. 446–7; *Slovar' russkogo iazyka*, ed. S. I. Ozhegov, 11th edn (Moscow: Russkii iazyk, 1977), p. 355; see also, for example, 13th edn (1981), p. 342.

5. *Slovar' Akademii Rossiiskoi po azbuchnomu poriadku raspolozhennyi*, 6 vols. (St Petersburg: Pri Imperatorskoi Akademii Nauk, 1806–22), vol. III, pp. 1175–6.

6. See Elise Kimerling Wirtschafter, *Social Identity in Imperial Russia* (DeKalb: Northern Illinois University Press, 1997), especially p. ix and, on the 'labouring people', pp. 100–62.

7. *Puteshestvie iz Peterburga v Moskvu* in A. N. Radishchev, *Izbrannye sochineniia* (Moscow and Leningrad: Gosudarstvennoe izdatel'stvo Khudozhestvennoi literatury, 1949), especially pp. 150–9; 'Bednaia Liza' in N. M. Karamzin, *Izbrannye sochineniia*, 2 vols. (Moscow and Leningrad: Izdatel'stvo 'Khudozhestvennaia literatura', 1964), vol. I, pp. 605–21.

8. See F. M. Barnard, *Herder's Social and Political Thought: From Enlightenment to Nationalism* (Oxford: Clarendon Press, 1965), especially pp. 55–62, 73–4.

9. On the forms that this interest in cultural identity took, see Peter Burke, *Popular Culture in Early Modern Europe* (London: Temple Smith, 1978), chapter 1.

10. On the provenance of the term, see Lauren G. Leighton, *Russian Romanticism: Two Essays* (The Hague and Paris: Mouton, 1975), p. 49.

11. 'O kharaktere prosveshcheniia Evropy i o ego otnoshenii k prosveshcheniiu Rossii' in I. V. Kireevskii, *Polnoe sobranie sochinenii*, ed. M. Gershenzon, 2 vols. (Moscow: Tipografiia Imperatorskogo Moskovskogo Universiteta, 1911), vol. I, pp. 174, 203.

12. Ibid., p. 212.

13. 'Zapiska K. S. Aksakova "o vnutrennem sostoianii Rossii", predstavlennaia Gosudariu Aleksandru Imperatoru Aleksandru II v 1855 g.' in *Rannie slavianofily: A. S. Khomiakov, I. V. Kireevskii, K. S. i I. S. Aksakovy*, compiled by N. L. Brodskii (Moscow: Tipografiia T-va I. D. Sytina, 1910), pp. 69–96.

14. See vols. II and III of K. S. Aksakov, *Polnoe sobranie sochinenii* (Moscow: V tipografii V. Bakhmeteva (vol. I); V Universitetskoi tipografii (vols II–III), 1861–80).

15. Aksakov, 'Kratkii istoricheskii ocherk zemskikh soborov', *Polnoe sobranie sochinenii*, vol. I, p. 292.

16. See, for example, Akaskov, 'O drevnem byte', ibid., vol. I, pp. 59–124, especially pp. 79–83, 92–3, 112, 114, 122–4.

17. See *Rannie slavianofily*, p. 108.

18. Ibid., pp. 112–15; Aksakov's italics.

19. 'O mneniiakh "Sovremennika" istoricheskikh i literaturnykh' in Iu.F. Samarin, *Sochineniia*, 12 vols. (Moscow: Tipografiia A. I. Mamontova, 1877–1911), vol. I, pp. 28–108; see pp. 91–2.

20. 'Vzgliad na iuridicheskii byt drevnei Rossii' in K. D. Kavelin, *Sobranie sochinenii*, 4 vols. (St Petersburg: Tipografiia M. M. Stasiulevicha, 1897–1900), vol. I, cols. 5–66. The main Slavophile contribution to this debate was Samarin's essay cited in note 19 above, which was a rebuttal of Kavelin's.

21. Quoted by D. A. Korsakov in 'Konstantin Dmitrievich Kavelin. Materialy dlia biografii, iz semeinoi perepiski i vospominanii', *Vestnik Evropy*, 1886, no. 10, 745–6.

22. T. N. Granovskii, *Sochineniia*, 4th edn (Moscow: Tovarishchestvo tipografii A. I. Mamontova, 1900), p. 445.

23. See G. M. Hamburg, *Boris Chicherin and Early Russian Liberalism: 1828–1866* (Stanford University Press, 1992), pp. 87–8, 160.

24. See V. G. Belinskii, *Polnoe sobranie sochinenii*, 13 vols. (Moscow: Izdatel'stvo Akademii nauk SSSR, 1953–9), vol. X, pp. 212–20, here p. 215.

25. Ibid., pp. 367–70.

26. Ibid., p. 215.

27. *Pis'ma iz Frantsii i Italii* in A. I. Herzen, *Sobranie sochinenii*, 30 vols. (Moscow: Izdatel'stvo Akademii nauk SSSR, 1954–65), vol. V, p. 74.

28. 'La Russie', ibid., vol. VI, pp. 161–8.

29. Ibid., p. 173; 'Le peuple russe et le socialisme', ibid., vol. VII, pp. 286–7.

30. 'La Russie', ibid., vol. VI, pp. 162–3, 172; *Du développement des idées révolutionnaires en Russie*, ibid., vol. VII, p. 10.

31. On these writers, see Derek Offord, 'Literature and ideas in Russia after the Crimean War: the "Plebeian" writers' in *Ideology in Russian Literature*, ed. Richard Freeborn and Jane Grayson (Basingstoke: Macmillan and University of London, 1990), pp. 47–78.

32. 'O stepeni uchastiia narodnosti v razvitii russkoi literatury' in N. A. Dobroliubov, *Sobranie sochinenii*, 9 vols. (Moscow and Leningrad: Gosudarstvennoe izdatel'stvo khudozhestvennoi literatury, 1961–4), vol. II, pp. 218–72; 'Narodnoe delo', ibid., vol. V, pp. 246–85, especially pp. 284–5; 'Cherty dlia kharakteristiki russkogo prostonarod'ia', ibid., vol. VI, pp. 221–88, especially 224ff., 240ff., 266ff.; 'Povesti i rasskazy S. T. Slavutinskogo', ibid., vol. VI, pp. 49–64, especially 52ff.

33. *Vlast' zemli* in G. Uspenskii, *Polnoe sobranie sochinenii*, 6th edn, 6 vols. (St Petersburg: Izdanie T-va A. F. Marks, 1908), vol. V, p. 108. Uspenskii's italics.

34. See I. S. Turgenev, *Polnoe sobranie sochinenii i pisem*, 28 vols. (Moscow and Leningrad: Izdatel'stvo Akademii nauk SSSR, 1961–8), *Pis'ma*, vol. V, pp. 51–2.

35. Ibid., p. 51.

36. On the danger of such obliteration, see, for example, his articles 'Ob"iavlenie o podpiske na zhurnal "Vremia" na 1862 god' in F. M. Dostoevskii, *Polnoe*

sobranie sochinenii, 30 vols. (Leningrad: Nauka, 1972–90), vol. XIX, p. 149; 'Dva lageria teoretikov', ibid., vol. XX, pp. 6–7.

37. *Zimnie zametki o letnikh vpechatleniiakh*, ibid., vol. V, especially pp. 51–2, 79–80.
38. See *Besy*, part 3, chapter 7, ibid., vol. X, pp. 479–507.
39. For example, in Book 6, on 'The Russian Monk', ibid., vol. XIV, pp. 257, 266–7, 285.
40. Published in *Dnevnik pisatelia* for 1873; ibid., vol. XXI, pp. 31–41, especially pp. 34–6, 41.
41. 'O kufel'nom muzhike i proch' in N. S. Leskov, *Sobranie sochinenii*, 11 vols. (Moscow: Gosudarstvennoe izdatel'stvo khudozhestvennoi literatury, 1956–8), vol. XI, pp. 134–56; see especially pp. 146–53.
42. 'Smert' Ivana Il'icha' in L. N. Tolstoi, *Polnoe sobranie sochinenii*, 90 vols. and one supplementary vol. (Moscow and Leningrad: Gosudarstvennoe izdatel'stvo, 1928–64), vol. XXVI, pp. 61–113, especially pp. 95–9; see also Leskov, *Sobranie sochinenii*, vol. XI, pp. 154–5.
43. *Voina i mir* in Tolstoi, *Polnoe sobranie sochinenii*, vol. XII, pp. 44–51, here pp. 48 and 51 respectively.
44. See A. P. Shchapov, *Sochineniia*, 3 vols. (St Petersburg: Izdanie M. V. Pirozhkova, 1906–8), vol. I.
45. See I. Beliaev, *Krest'iane na Rusi: Issledovanie o postepennom izmenenii znacheniia krest'ian v russkom obshchestve* (Moscow: Universitetskaia tipografiia, 1860), republished with an introduction by E. N. Vakulina (Gosudarstvennaia publichnaia istoricheskaia biblioteka Rossii, 2002).
46. *Pesni sobrannye P. V. Kireevskim*, 3 parts, ed. P. A. Bessonov (Moscow: Obshchestvo liubitelei rossiiskoi slovesnosti, 1860–74).
47. Dal', *Poslovitsy russkogo naroda. Sbornik poslovits, pogovorok, rechenii, prislovii, chistogovorok, pribautok, zagadok, poverii i proch* (Moscow: v Universitetskoi tipografii, 1862), republished with an introduction by V. Chicherov (Moscow: Gosudarstvennoe izdatel'stvo khudozhestvennoi literatury, 1957).
48. For an English edition of Afanasev's work, which was first published in eight volumes in 1855–64, see *Russian Fairy Tales. Collected by Alexander Afanas'ev*, trans. Norbert Guterman, with commentary by Roman Jakobson (London: Sheldon Press, 1975); F. Buslaev, *Istoricheskie ocherki russkoi narodnoi slovesnosti i iskusstva*, 2 vols. (St Petersburg: Izdanie D. E. Kozhanchikova, v tipografii Tovarishchestva 'Obshchestvennaia pol'za', 1861; reprinted The Hague and Paris: Mouton, 1969); O. F. Miller, *Il'ia Muromets i bogatyrstvo kievskoe* (St Petersburg: Tipografiia N. N. Mikhailova, 1869).
49. On all these scholars, see Michael B. Petrovich, 'The peasant in nineteenth-century historiography' in Vucinich (ed.), *The Peasant in Nineteenth-Century Russia*, pp. 200–3, 211–15.
50. N. Flerovskii [V. V. Bervi], *Polozhenie rabochego klassa v Rossii* (St Petersburg: Izdanie N. P. Poliakova, 1869).
51. Bakunin, 'Appendix A' to *Statism and Anarchy* in W. J. Leatherbarrow and D. C. Offord (eds.), *A Documentary History of Russian Thought: From the Enlightenment to Marxism* (Ann Arbor: Ardis, 1987), pp. 278–85.

52. Ibid., pp. 261–8.
53. 'Retsenziia na knigi Iu. Zhukovskogo' in P. N. Tkachev, *Izbrannye sochineniia*, 5 vols. published (Moscow: Izdatel'stvo vsesoiuznogo obshchestva politkator-zhan i ssyl'no-poselentsev, 1932–), vol. I, pp. 69–70.
54. 'Razbitye illiuzii', ibid., vol. I, p. 369.
55. 'Nashi illiuzii', ibid., vol. III, pp. 242–3; 'Narod i revoliutsiia', ibid., vol. III, p. 267. Tkachev's italics.
56. See, for example, the programme of Tkachev's journal *Nabat* and his article 'Organizatsiia sotsial'no-revoliutsionnoi partii', ibid., vol. III, pp. 227ff. and 285–94 respectively.
57. Richard Wortman, *The Crisis of Russian Populism* (Cambridge University Press, 1967), p. x.
58. Susanna Rabow-Edling, *Slavophile Thought and the Politics of Cultural Nationalism* (Albany: State University of New York Press, 2006); J. Hutchinson, *The Dynamics of Cultural Nationalism: The Gaelic Revival and the Creation of the Irish Nation State* (London: Allen and Unwin, 1987); Anthony D. Smith, *National Identity* (London: Penguin, 1991).
59. Smith, *National Identity*, pp. 11–12.
60. Rabow-Edling, *Slavophile Thought*, pp. 64–5.
61. Smith, *National Identity*, p. 12.
62. Ibid., pp. 9–11.
63. Granovskii, *Sochineniia*, pp. 257–8.
64. See especially *Besy*, part 2, chapter 4, section 3, in Dostoevskii, *Polnoe sobranie sochinenii*, vol. X, pp. 241ff.

CHAPTER 12

The intelligentsia and capitalism

Wayne Dowler

The Russian intelligentsia wrestled with two related questions about the development of capitalism in Russia. First, given their knowledge of the economic and social disruptions and the exploitation of factory discipline caused by capitalism in western Europe, was it desirable or moral to promote capitalism in the empire? Second, could Russia survive in the modern world without a strong industrial base, higher levels of popular culture and the liberal social attitudes that capitalism appeared to foster? Aesthetic and ethical considerations jostled with pragmatic concerns as the intelligentsia struggled to cope, first with the idea of capitalism and by the 1880s with the thing in itself. The natural constituency of capitalism and liberalism, the urban middle class, was small in Russia and produced few articulate spokespersons for capitalism until the last years of the empire. The leading intelligentsia theorists frequently came from gentry or clerical backgrounds and did not hold middle-class values.

Principal features of capitalism in the nineteenth century were open competition of producers in a free market, free movement of labour and wage labour, protection of private property through rational laws that secured the inviolability of contracts, use of advanced technology in production, including factory organisation, and public access to the purchase of shares in business enterprises. The model capitalist nation was Britain, where the industrial revolution had farthest advanced and free trade found its strongest advocates. Those nations that followed Britain down the capitalist-industrial path found it difficult to overcome the advantage that Britain's head start provided. By the 1840s protectionist doctrines, designed to shield local producers from the competition of British manufactures, were widespread on the continent and growing in the United States.

When the generation of the Russian intelligentsia that became known as the 'men of the 40s' began to emerge, most features of modern capitalism were absent in Russia. Although the majority of workers in manufactories were wage labourers, they usually came from the enserfed peasantry. In poorer agricultural regions of central and northwest Russia, peasants supplemented their incomes by taking work, with the permission of landlords or the commune, in various occupations, including wage labour in industry. Some landlords employed serf labour in manufacturing enterprises on their estates. The state also used serf labour in state-owned manufacturing and mining enterprises. The merchant estate was organised in three guilds according to ability to pay an annual licence fee and declare capital at a set level. Nobles could register in the merchant estate, but the state protected merchants by restricting peasant trade in cities. Free movement of labour, choice of occupation and open competition were, therefore, limited in pre-emancipation Russia. Law was weakly developed in a country dominated by bureaucratic arbitrariness and corruption, and an enforceable commercial law barely existed by the 1840s. Only a handful of joint stock corporations functioned, and their shares were owned by families or small cartels and not publicly traded. The industrial revolution had only lightly touched Russian manufacture by the middle of the century. A supply of cheap labour and low demand for industrial products limited pressure for mechanisation of production.[1]

THE EARLY INTELLIGENTSIA

Since industrial capitalism scarcely existed in Russia before mid-century the nascent intelligentsia of the 1840s knew it not through direct experience but from reports from the West and visits abroad. As outsiders to the experience of capitalism, the early intelligentsia took less interest in it as an economic system than as a social formation. The disruptions to traditional social arrangements and occupations caused by early accumulative capitalism, the hardships of the wage system, the excesses of wealth enjoyed by the new bourgeoisie and the culture that wealth fostered made a painful impression on the Russian intelligentsia. The denunciation by western socialists of the competition and exploitation of capitalism, which political economists ardently defended as natural, reinforced their impression.

Herzen set the tone. In *Letters from the Avenue Marigny*, published in Russia in 1847, he excoriated the French bourgeoisie: though useful in destroying feudal ties and asserting the primacy of the individual, the bourgeoisie did not have 'a great past and it has no future'.[2] Lacking a true 'social religion', the bourgeoisie created a morality based solely on the power of money and the love of order.[3] Herzen denied that political economy, by which he meant the theoretical foundations of capitalism, was a sufficient basis for living. 'Science', he complained, 'put a bludgeon into the hands [of capitalists], with which to beat the poor consumer.'[4] The tools for economic and social harmony proposed by Adam Smith – individualism, competition, legal rights and minimal government regulation – appeared to Herzen to justify a rapacious economic system that elsewhere he called 'cannibalism in its educated form'.[5] For him the bourgeois order, which, he argued, the western proletariat benefited from and accepted, nourished a vulgar mass culture of consumption without redeeming values. Back in Russia, the critic Belinsky agreed with Herzen, at least in 1847. The capitalists, he said, had shamed France with their lack of patriotism and disregard for the common good.[6] Herzen's assessment of the bourgeoisie changed little over time. Bourgeois complicity in the suppression of the French workers during the revolution of 1848 only hardened his opinion. The most oppressive and intolerable atmosphere in Europe prevailed, he wrote, 'where the modern system is most developed, where it is most wealthy and most *cultured* – that is, most industrial'.[7] In 1848, however, Belinsky demurred: civil society could only grow in Russia when the Russian gentry was 'transformed into a bourgeoisie'.[8]

Following the revolutions of 1848, Herzen's despair about the direction of western civilisation turned into hope that Russia could avoid capitalism and the mass society it engendered. He counted on the chance survival of the *mir*. Its collectivist principles and practices seemed to contain the seeds of the socialist order that western socialists imagined but could not realise. The Slavophiles, who opposed a western path of development for Russia, also thought in terms of differences between Russia and the West. Whereas Herzen saw the peasant commune as a fortunate survival in Russia that had been lost in western Europe, the Slavophiles, who believed that a civilisation's underlying religious principles defined it, regarded the *mir* as a product of Orthodox religious culture. Catholic Europe had imbibed the rationalistic and legalistic culture of Rome that in time gave birth to individualism and the doctrine of individual rights. The unity of the Catholic Church rested on the authority of the Pope. Western society cohered through the external force of law. Protestantism represented the extreme expression of western individualism and atomism. Western capitalism and bourgeois society, based on competitive individualism and the rights of man, were symptoms of western religious history. By contrast, Russia's faith rested on *sobornost'*, which found powerful expression in the commune. Russian society cohered not through law but through internal religious conviction that excluded the social atomism of western bourgeois society.[9] Although the early Slavophiles wrote little about capitalism, their views about the religious differences between Russia and the West formed one pillar of 'Slavophile capitalism' in the post-emancipation period.

ATTITUDES TO CAPITALISM IN THE
POST-CRIMEAN PERIOD

The intelligentsia of the 1840s understood capitalism from afar. They poorly grasped capitalist economic theory and larded their thinking with German idealistic philosophy about national differences and the missions of nations in advancing world civilisation. With the defeat of Russia in the Crimean War and the declaration by the new emperor, Alexander II, in 1855 that the state intended to abolish serfdom, the discussion among the intelligentsia about Russian economic development took a more practical turn. The emancipation decree in 1861 conferred land in communal tenure on former serfs and burdened them with a shared obligation to redeem the landlords' alienated property through forty-nine years of redemption payments. Peasants remained legally and financially bound to the commune. But emancipation in other categories of serfdom and a willingness on the part of communes to permit members to depart for non-agricultural work generated a small pool of relatively free labour for industrial employment. A judicial reform in 1864 created a system of independent courts that established an enclave of rights-based justice within the administrative arbitrariness of the regime. The state initiated a programme of railway building in the second half of the 1850s. Foreign companies dominated in early railway construction, but the boom created opportunities for Russian entrepreneurs and investors. The growth of stock corporations reflected the new climate. Between 1853 and 1859, for example, 106 joint stock companies came into being.[10] The State Bank, which held a monopoly on banking and credit, began in the post-emancipation period to make more capital available. In the late 1860s private banks formed, further improving the investment atmosphere. In 1857 the government lowered tariffs on foreign imports, stimulating discussion of the merits of free trade or protectionism. Though far from fulfilling all of the conditions for capitalist growth, the climate of post-emancipation Russia presented new opportunities for entrepreneurship and opened the possibility that Russia was on the threshold of western capitalistic development.

Belinsky's ambivalence about the virtues of capitalism and the bourgeois society it supported was widely reflected in the debate about capitalism among the intelligentsia in the emancipation years. Herzen's antipathy towards the economic effects of capitalism on working people and the disintegrating social consequences of individual competitiveness made a deep impression on the intelligentsia. Typical was the introduction to a translation in 1861 of Elizabeth Gaskell's novel *Mary Barton* in *Time*, the journal edited by Fedor Dostoevsky and his brother Mikhail. The novel, the introduction asserted, exposed the way of life and the suffering of the English working class. Among all the peoples of Europe, only Russians were spared these misfortunes, thanks to the peasant commune that 'preserves us forever from that awful and everywhere gaping abyss that is called pauperism or proletarianism'.[11] However, the role of capitalism in overcoming absolutist regimes in western Europe, the freedom, order and legality of bourgeois society and the cultural and educational advances that capitalism fostered were attractive to some educated Russians oppressed by an autocratic-bureaucratic order that stifled freedom and initiative. Moreover, defeat in the Crimean War by the more advanced industrial nations of the West impressed on thinking Russians the importance of industry to national survival. Also writing in *Time*, the economist Shill linked the extent of a country's industrialisation directly with the well-being of its population and saw industry as an index of a nation's civilisation.[12] Later in *Time*, Razin predicted that Russia was not destined to be a 'purely agricultural state'.[13] The question for members of the intelligentsia across the ideological spectrum in these years was how to reap the benefits of capitalist economic development while at the same time avoiding or mitigating its harsher aspects.

German economists did much to shape Russian views about capitalism in this period. As capitalist industry developed in several German states, German theorists were forced to grapple with the problem of the late industrial start. Were the laws of capitalist development universal, requiring all nations to follow the British model, or were they modulated by local conditions and national history? In particular, was Adam Smith's advocacy of free trade a necessary condition of capitalist development? Wilhelm Roscher, Bruno Hildebrand and Karl Knies were instrumental in establishing a historical method for the study of economic development. They argued that effective economic policies depended on rooting them in place and time. Particularly influential in Russia was the work of Hildebrand. He argued that Smith had mistakenly tried to construct an economic theory applicable in all times and places. Instead, humans are the product of their history and culture. Economic organisation cannot be separated from its historical roots or expressed in purely abstract formulae. Hildebrand also doubted Smith's claim that personal egoism and individual economic competition were sufficient guarantees of the common good.[14] Such views confirmed the established preference of the Russian intelligentsia for doctrines about national differences rooted in geography and historical experience. They also reinforced Herzen's view that political economy could not provide a sufficient basis for right living. Writing in *Time* in

November 1862, Razin argued that political economy was not a science. It alone could not provide a goal or ideal for Russian development. The ideals of the English, French or Germans were not suited to a Russia shaped by its own climate, geography and history.[15]

Roscher also stressed the importance of balanced economic national development. Echoing him, Razin, writing in *Time* in 1863, maintained that great powers achieved their eminence through the simultaneous development of their physical resources, population, stores of wealth and elevation of popular culture. An agricultural country could not attain balanced growth and was destined for subordination to powers whose development was 'normal'. Moreover, industrial society promoted knowledge; without industry a country was for ever condemned to poverty and ignorance.[16] Others agreed. A certain V. V., writing in the Slavophile journal *Day* early in 1863, tied the expansion of the railway network directly to the growth of the material well-being and moral development of the masses.[17] On one point, though, most *intelligenty* parted with Hildebrand. He maintained that the lot of the working masses under capitalism was steadily improving. Citing Engels's *Condition of the Working Class in England* (1844), Poretsky, on the other hand, expressed a widely shared view among the intelligentsia that the impoverishment of a growing segment of the working class was a likely, if not inevitable, outcome of capitalist development.[18] Convinced that the material and moral development of the populace and the defence of the nation from colonial status required the development of industry, the intelligentsia nevertheless feared that industrial capitalism would visit on Russia the dislocation and poverty they witnessed in western European nations. That dilemma caused them to search in the particulars of Russian history for a principle to soften the negative effects of capitalism. Most found it in Russia's communal traditions. The academic and noble landowner Kavelin, an early liberal, provides a good example of the dilemma. In supporting emancipation in 1855, Kavelin defended property rights, which 'no state can destroy without compromising civil order and the community at its roots'. He condemned regulations that stifled industry and trade in Russia and deplored the ignorance of the masses and state officials. The abolition of serfdom, he argued, would facilitate the free movement of labour and normalise the market by ending unpaid serf labour that distorted both wages and prices.[19] Writing in 1859, Kavelin rejoiced that industry was burgeoning in Russia and linked industrialism to intellectual and moral growth among the populace. But he also believed that only a portion of the population could succeed in a capitalist environment. The rest would fall into pauperisation as western experience had proven. Kavelin saw in a modified version of the peasant commune a haven from capitalist competition. The existence of such an institution, he argued, 'neutralised the harsh and destructive consequences of the arduous industrial struggle' and preserved the social organism in a 'normal condition'.[20]

Similarly, the radical publicist Chernyshevsky recognised in capitalism an advance over pre-capitalist forms. He believed that capitalism was a transitional stage in a dialectical process leading from primitive communalism to a socialist society. Russia must take advantage of the capitalist experience of the West, especially its scientific and technological advances, in order to soften the effects of capitalism and shorten the period of transition to socialism. Like Kavelin, Chernyshevsky saw no contradiction between the preservation of the commune and the development of capitalism. His optimism about the positive role of capitalism arose from his understanding of the nature of capital. If capital consisted only of money and material things, capitalists were justified in appropriating nearly all productive wealth to themselves and leaving the workers a pittance. But Chernyshevsky defined capital as both material and moral. The greatest national capital was the intellectual and moral development of the people. 'In this moral capital', he wrote, 'is contained the source of all material capital.' Without it the capitalist can produce nothing.[21] For Chernyshevsky, the impoverishment of the working class was not necessary, indeed was harmful to economic development. He rejected the 'laws of nature', which supposedly informed laissez-faire economics. Laissez-faire approaches had cleared the way for a rational economics, but had outlived their time. The task of political economy was to determine the needs of the present and address them rationally. The question for Chernyshevsky was not whether something was natural but whether it met the test of utility by helping the society it served. To be a science, he contended, political economy had to take into account the interests of all and not solely those of any given private business.

While denying the universality of laissez-faire economics, Chernyshevsky accepted many of Smith's premises. The market does set the value of a product, and the division of labour is the key to high productivity. Personal interest does drive production. From these premises, Chernyshevsky argued that personal interest was in turn driven by the desire to own property. 'If that is the case', he wrote, 'then labour ought to be the sole owner of productive value.'[22] Production was best served when the producer fully owned the product of his labour. Productive labour creates goods necessary for human welfare; unproductive labour produces luxuries. If for Chernyshevsky production was guided by self-interest, then distribution rested on the maxim that the value of production is measured by its contribution to maximising social well-being and enjoyment. Equal distribution of the value of all production creates the greatest happiness for the greatest number. In capitalist theory and practice, therefore, Chernyshevsky discerned tools for a rational transition to a just and prosperous socialist order. In his view, governments were obligated to support rational and just actions. He therefore urged the Russian government to use State Bank loans to help workers set up production artels and workshops.[23]

With the deaths by 1860 of the leading early Slavophile theorists, the publicist Ivan Aksakov assumed the burden of advancing Slavophile ideas in the post-emancipation period. Convinced that capitalist development in Russia was necessary not only to compete with the West but to raise the intellectual and moral level of the Russian people, Aksakov formed an alliance with a small group of merchants and commercially minded noble entrepreneurs in Moscow. They resented the role that foreigners played in Russian commerce and industry and campaigned for protective tariffs to support their own industrial endeavours. They formed joint stock companies to compete with foreigners, especially in railway construction, and mobilised domestic capital through the establishment of the first private banks in Moscow. Chief among them was Chizhev, once an impoverished noble and amateur art historian, now a successful entrepreneur. Chizhev collaborated with Aksakov in the creation of 'Slavophile capitalism'.[24] Slavophile capitalists believed that in order to compete successfully with the western European states Russia had to produce its own manufactured goods. Domestic industry would not only guarantee Russia's economic independence, but also lift workers' wages and provide the masses with greater opportunities for education. Invoking Orthodox *sobornost'*, which the Slavophiles believed precluded the economic individualism and exploitation that underlay social relations in the West and gave capitalism its exploitative nature, Chizhev and Aksakov urged Russian merchants to treat their workers with benevolence.[25]

In practice, though, the Moscow merchants showed little inclination to treat the workers with the respect that the theory demanded. Chizhev attributed the failure to economic backwardness and the arbitrariness with which 'westernised' bureaucrats treated the merchants.[26] Moreover, Aksakov's hope that the merchants would look beyond their own narrow interests to the good of the nation as a whole was frequently disappointed. As late as 1884, he wanted to make his paper *Rus* an organ of the merchants that would advance the 'truly legitimate and rational interests of Russian trade and industry' rather than the 'narrow and egotistical' interests that a merchant-run paper would support.[27]

Even as Russian merchants began to transform themselves into modern capitalists, their reputation among the intelligentsia as dishonest, ignorant, narrow and petty tyrants was consolidated. Ostrovsky's play *The Thunderstorm* (1859) portrayed a regime of domestic tyranny in the merchant society of a Volga town so severe that one of its victims, the heroine Katerina Kabanova, committed suicide to escape it. Here was the realm of the *samodur*, the petty tyrant, who abuses power for no better reason than that he can. The radical literary critic Dobroliubov named it the 'kingdom of darkness', the product of the extreme 'abnormality of social relations' as a result of which its inhabitants lose all common sense in moral questions.[28] Although Dobroliubov meant the kind of social relations produced in a serf society, the 'dark kingdom' became synonymous with the world of the merchants.

Ostrovsky also associated *samodurstvo* with the pre-emancipation past and not a particular class. The *samodur* in his play *The Forest* (first performed 1871), for instance, comes from the impoverished landed gentry. With *Easy Money* (first performed 1870), Ostrovsky set out to characterise the capitalist of the post-emancipation era as opposed to the traditional merchant of his earlier plays. The hero is Vasilkov, a provincial businessman who arrives in Moscow and is smitten by the mercenary Lidia, the spoilt daughter of a bankrupt noble landowner. Vasilkov is not yet wealthy but maintains that 'at this moment in time any man with a few brains can [get rich]'.[29] Far from being sly and dishonest, Vasilkov declares that honesty is the best policy. 'In a practical age like ours, it's not only better to be honest, it's more profitable.' Fraud and deception, he says, do best in a Romantic age when passions run high and sharp practices work. The pragmatic capitalist is harder to fool.[30] Though in love to distraction, Vasilkov proudly keeps his head; in his pursuit of Lidia he refuses to 'go over budget'.[31] On her side, Lidia despises Vasilkov's 'economic laws' and concerns herself with the 'laws of fashion and good taste'.[32] But she also understands market value. 'All I have to do', she declares, 'is find out how much my caresses are worth in gold, and I'd better do that right now – I just can't live without money.'[33] Practicality triumphs. Despite Lidia's disdain for him, Vasilkov marries her because his business requires a society wife who can offset his own provincialism. She accepts 'that rough-hewn idol of toil and industry, whose name is budget' and becomes his wife/housekeeper because she must. The best husband, she concludes, is no longer the man who can squander money with style, but 'the man who can earn it, with no style whatsoever, and who calls himself a businessman'.[34] By no means flattering with its commodification of personal relationships, Ostrovsky's portrait of the new capitalist in *Easy Money* was drawn from life and helps to explain the popularity of his later plays with merchant audiences.

But the stigma of the 'kingdom of darkness' permanently marked the merchants in the eyes of the intelligentsia.

POPULISTS AND ANARCHISTS

A character in *Easy Money* says about Vasilkov: 'he scares me stiff; he's like some force of nature bearing down on you'.[35] By 1870 others felt the same way about the capitalism he represented. The influx of foreign capital since the mid-1850s, the growth of state and private credit, the rapid mechanisation of key industries that began in the late 1860s, the proliferation of Russian-owned stock corporations and especially the growing railway network that enabled large-scale shipments abroad of grain stimulated the growth of market forces in the country. Some observers detected momentous changes in the villages and began to fear that the commune could not withstand the capitalist onslaught. To them, Chernyshevsky's optimism that the rational outcome of capitalist progress was socialism seemed unfounded. Among the first to sound the alarm about the assault on the commune was Bervi-Flerovsky. In 1869 he published *The Condition of the Working Class in Russia*. In the working class Bervi included both peasants and urban workers, whose situation he found to be worse than that of the western proletariat. Working-class poverty, in his view, resulted from an excessive burden of state taxes, the greed of capitalist speculators and merchant middlemen who exploited artisans and peasants and the decline of equality in the commune as kulaks proliferated. Bervi argued that only the traditional, egalitarian commune could give peasants independence and promote the rational exploitation of the land. He also proposed the non-capitalist industrial development of the country through a modernised version of the traditional workers' artel. His larger message was that the western path of economic and social development was wrong for Russia. The fatal flaw in western civilisation was its individual competitiveness, its failure to nurture in people 'concepts and feelings that allow them to help each other'.[36] The answer was nation-wide solidarity and cooperation rather than capitalist class warfare.

The Populism that Bervi helped to inspire was motivated by the concern, first raised by Herzen, about the objectivity of the laws of laissez-faire economics and the inevitability of capitalist progress or of progress in general. Lavrov tried to address this concern in his *Historical Letters* (1868–9). He argued that historically the cultural and economic development of the minority was built on the labours of the majority. While enjoying the fruits of civilisation, the minority had too often neglected or even refused to disseminate the benefits of civilisation to the masses. Such neglect was not inevitable. Instead, it was an evil that had to be redeemed in the present through an effort by the minority to 'improve the condition of others'.[37] Desirable social outcomes were the result of human will informed by a rational and utilitarian assessment of the needs of all and of the best means to meet them. In the peasant commune, Lavrov saw a humane alternative to capitalist development.

Another major contributor to the 'subjective sociology' of Populism was Mikhailovsky. Whereas Lavrov rejected the inevitability of capitalism and cast doubt on its desirability as an economic and social system, Mikhailovsky attacked its premises. Goaded by the claims of Herbert Spencer and the Social Darwinists, he set out to redefine progress. Spencer had championed the division of labour or functional specialisation as the key to progress. The greater the heterogeneity of society and the more integrated the individual parts into the economic and social whole, the higher the level of development. Mikhailovsky countered that organic society, by integrating the individual into the whole, destroyed the many-sided personality. Against the integrated personality, Mikhailovsky champ-ioned the integral (*tsel'naia*) personality. In his view, societies passed through three types of development. The first type, called 'objectively simple cooperation', was the homogeneous society whose individual mem-bers were highly heterogeneous in function and personality. The division of labour created the second or 'eccentric' type of development. During it the feudal order perished; but with feudalism were destroyed small units of economic self-sufficiency. The Russian peasant commune had, however, survived. It provided the foundation for the third developmental type, 'subjectively simple cooperation'. Whereas capitalism sought to eliminate economic self-sufficiency and the small producers who owned the product of their labour, the commune resisted the division of labour on which capitalism feasted. The Russian peasant, though poor, met all of his own needs and led a rounded existence. Although the capitalist factory system represented a higher 'level' of economic development, the commune was a superior 'type' of human organisation. On the basis of his tripartite scheme, Mikhailovsky defined progress as 'the gradual realisation of the integral individual, of the fullest and most diversified division of labour possible among human organisms and the least possible division of labour among persons'. Whatever reduced the heterogeneity of society and increased the heterogeneity of its individual members was just; all that hindered that process was immoral and unjust.[38] By this definition, capitalism was the antithesis of human progress and the enemy of individualism. Lavrov, on the other hand, defended the division of labour as necessary if society were not to remain stagnant.

Fears about creeping capitalism prompted Tkachev to sound the alarm in 1875. In the programme of his journal *The Tocsin*, he contended that economic progress was undermining the commune, the very institution on which Russia's future depended. Capitalism was bringing into existence forms of bourgeois life: kulaks, merchant middlemen, individualism and egoism. Still weak, the enemies of the commune, he predicted, would become stronger; capitalist economic development would revitalise a moribund state. Tkachev anticipated a transition from autocracy to liberal constitutionalism that would entrench the state as the defender of property, big business and the interests of the bourgeoisie in general. He urged that the time to strike was when the enemies of the commune were weak and divided. He pleaded for a pre-emptive coup before the bourgeois world was realised in Russia.[39]

Revulsion at the capitalist bourgeois order was widespread among the intelligentsia. Herzen's aesthetic objections to mass society found many echoes in later decades. Even Leontev, a conservative thinker and novelist, was alarmed by bourgeois liberal developments in the Slav world. He ridiculed the grey dress and timid morals of the western bourgeoisie and bemoaned the rise of the 'middle, rational European'. He blamed the doctrine of rights for undermining social difference and promoting a bland cosmopolitanism. The most pressing need of his time, Leontev believed, was cultural independence. He wrote: 'Culture is nothing else but originality; and originality now almost everywhere is perishing at the hands of political freedom.'[40] Instead of rights and equality, Leontev advocated a hierarchy of social groups and classes and even opposed mobility from region to region.[41] His goal, like Mikhailovsky's, was the greatest diversity among individuals and ethnic groups and the strengthening of the unique personality, which capitalism erased.

In the 1870s Russian anarchists mounted their own critique of capitalism. Like Marx, Bakunin recognised the class basis of capitalist exploitation. He distinguished between productive and exploitative labour. Workers performed productive labour; capitalists, living on profits, rents and interest, did not. Inheritance was a key to class formation. It enabled the heirs of the capitalist to live without working. As long as property and capital existed, on the one hand, and labour existed, on the other, the worker would remain slave to the capitalist master. Like Marx, Bakunin believed that to survive, capitalist industry and banking must expand at the expense of smaller enterprises. Wealth concentrates in fewer hands and the working class inevitably gets poorer. Competition for work and an ever more numerous proletariat, as small producers fall into the working class, make a mockery of the notion of 'free' labour. The worker must sell his labour at the lowest price.[42] Like Tkachev, Bakunin recognised the role of the state in defending the interest of capitalists. Capitalist production, he argued, demanded the creation of a centralised state apparatus in order to subject millions of workers to exploitation. Just as capitalist enterprises must expand, so too do modern states seek to become universal. All states, Bakunin believed, are ruled by the intelligent minority who claim to know what the interests of the people are. Only the simultaneous destruction of capitalism and the state could liberate workers and put the products of their labour back into their own hands.[43]

Writing in the 1890s, Russia's other famous anarchist, Kropotkin, offered a different version of the success of capitalism. Capitalist wealth results from worker poverty. Lack of means among the poor and an abundance of labour compel workers to labour for capitalists. Who would work in a factory, he asked, if the needs of rural men and women were met?[44] Like Mikhailovsky, Kropotkin blamed the division of labour for the plight of workers. First came the broad division between producer and consumer; further subdivisions followed: manual and intellectual worker or agricultural and industrial worker. The capitalist division of labour deprived workers of their broad skills and reduced them to the tedium of making a tiny part of a thing. The initial results were dazzling and promoted the view that the goal of life is profit. People and nations resist specialisation, however. Diversity is the feature of nations and regions and of those who live in them.[45] Instead of a society based on division of labour, Kropotkin, like Mikhailovsky, advocated a society of integral labour, 'a society where each individual is a producer of both manual and intellectual work; where each able-bodied human being is a worker, and where each worker works both in the field and the industrial workshop'.[46] Kropotkin also rejected free trade and comparative advantage. Instead, each nation should produce and consume its own agricultural and manufactured products. With the restoration of broad self-sufficiency, people could satisfy their own basic needs and destroy the basis of capitalist exploitation. In his Christian anarchism, Tolstoy espoused similar views.[47]

Since the end of the Crimean War the intelligentsia had been aware of the need for native industry to secure national defence in a hostile world. In the West capitalism was the vehicle for industrialisation. Was capitalism also necessary in Russia or could a backward nation adopt other means to support industrialism? Chernyshevsky had argued that backward nations had no need to recapitulate all of the steps already taken by more advanced nations but could draw on the latter's experiences to shorten their own term of industrial development. He and others had also suggested that communal forms of industrialisation were possible. Lavrov, more explicitly than others, had decoupled industrialisation from capitalism. Until the 1880s, however, the discussion among Populists had focused on avoiding capitalism while developing communalist forms of manufacture. For instance, in 1882 Vorontsov contended that capitalism was impossible in Russia, arguing that its further development would impoverish peasant cottage and artisan producers and so stifle the domestic market. But the empire's late start also excluded Russian capitalists from foreign markets. Yet Russia still needed industry, and, following Chernyshevsky, Vorontsov held that backwardness enabled Russia to take advantage of the technological advances of the West and avoid the exploitation associated with early capitalism. He proposed the non-capitalist development of Russian industry through state initiative. The state should nationalise large-scale industries and assist small producers to form workers' artels. Cottage producers should unite in cooperatives and government ensure them a supply of raw materials and markets. In Vorontsov's view, production by independent small producers was a temporary means to avoid the pain of capitalist exploitation. The goal, however, was socialist production, which could be gradually realised as industrialisation advanced.[48] Vorontsov's 'Legal Populism' found support in the work of Danielson in the early 1890s. He believed that the further development of capitalism could only harm the interests of state and society and supported state-controlled industrialisation.[49]

MARXISTS

The Legal Populists were responding to two closely related developments in Russia. The first was the accelerating pace of capitalism in the empire from around 1880. By 1885 Russia entered a period of capitalist growth that mirrored the experience of other capitalist countries in their early years in nearly every detail and lasted until the outbreak of the First World War in 1914. Indeed, Russia out-performed, during its peak years of early capitalist growth, most of the more advanced nations in theirs.[50] The second development was the rise of Marxism in Russia. The intelligentsia had long been familiar with Marx's critique of capitalism, which it used to justify their campaign to avoid capitalist development in Russia. By the late 1870s, however, some Populists noticed that workers in Russian factories were more open to radical propagandising than peasants had been during the 'to the people' movement in the mid-1870s. The splintering of Land and Liberty into two factions in 1879, the assassination of Alexander II in 1881 and the harsh repression that followed facilitated a second look at Marx's work as a programme for revolution rather than as a critique of capitalism. Lavrov had already remarked on the potential of Russian workers for radicalisation. In 1879 some of his followers formed The Black Partition. Preferring exile to arrest in the wake of the emperor's assassination, some of the members of The Black Partition went abroad and formed links with Marxism. Among them were Plekhanov, Akselrod and Vera Zasulich, the first Russian Marxists.

In 1884 Russia's fledgling Marxists defined their differences with Populism, arguing that the latter was mistaken in its belief that Russia could avoid capitalism. The Populists' beloved commune had degenerated from a community of equals into class division. No coup could halt the progress of economic individualism once it had begun. Social revolution rested not on will but on the objective forces of social evolution. The emancipation of the serfs had set off in Russia a process similar to developments in western Europe. Not the peasants, who were essentially petty bourgeois, but the proletariat were the only revolutionary class. Their revolution had to be prepared in the school of capitalism.[51] Subsequently, Plekhanov argued that since the Russian bourgeoisie was weakly developed it would need the assistance of the proletariat to overthrow absolutism and establish liberal democracy and a full regime of capitalism. Only after a period of bourgeois capitalist rule would proletarian revolution become possible.[52] While both Marxists and Populists envisaged a socialist future for Russia, they disagreed about the way it would be realised. The Marxists accepted capitalism, whatever its costs in human displacement and suffering, as objectively necessary. The Populists deplored the immorality of such a stance and continued to seek the means to skip capitalism and pass directly into socialism.

Their disagreement turned less on the role of the workers, whom both Marxists and Populists courted, but on the fate of the peasantry and of small-scale rural production. The debate reached its climax following the famine and epidemic that swept through the empire in 1891–2. Populists argued that the famine resulted from ruinous tax and tariff policies that favoured capitalist factory production and undermined the position of cottage producers who relied on cottage manufacture for supplemental income. Marxists such as Struve saw in the famine proof that class differentiation in the village was well under way. A rural bourgeoisie was purchasing land and farming it with hired hands. A proletarian class of dispossessed peasants was in formation. What Struve saw in the country-side confirmed for him the accuracy of Marxist analysis about the inevitability of capitalism.[53]

The famine also played a critical role in Lenin's conversion from Populism to Marxism. The distress in the villages convinced him that a process of class differentiation was taking place there. A bourgeois upper stratum of kulaks had begun to dispossess the poorer peasants and create a landless proletariat. Although he had accepted Marxian class analysis, Lenin had not by 1893 arrived at Plekhanov's position that Russia must pass through a lengthy phase of liberal capitalism. Instead, like Vorontsov and Danielson, Lenin advocated the nationalisation of production. Unlike them, he rejected the autocratic state as the instrument of socialisation and called instead for a conspiratorial seizure of state power.[54]

With his work *The Development of Capitalism in Russia* (1898), Lenin moved towards a more orthodox Marxist position regarding the role of capitalism in preparing revolution. He disputed the Populists' claim that capitalism was an artificial imposition on Russia and so unsustainable. Capitalism was necessary and viable. As small producers went out of business they necessarily became consumers of factory goods, thus expanding the home market.[55] Lenin divided the home market into personal consumption and productive consumption, by which he meant consumption of goods to build the means of production. That sector, he said, had to grow faster than personal consumption and therefore formed an important part of the home market that would sustain capitalist growth. Lenin did not doubt that improvements in productive technology would also enable Russian capitalists to find foreign markets in an increasingly integrated world economy.[56] He denied that the divide between factory and handicraft industry identified by the Populists was real. The two formed a continuum, although the trend was in the direction of large-scale machine industry. Using statistical analysis, he also sought to demonstrate that the agrarian system in the country was already capitalist.[57]

Lenin welcomed capitalist development. Capitalism, he wrote, had a great mission to perform in Russia as elsewhere. Although it had a dark side, capitalism was a progressive phenomenon in a lengthy process of social transformation. Capitalism was progressive because it both increased the productive forces of labour and socialised labour.[58] Only the growth of large-scale machine industry could maximise the productive forces of labour. Industrial transformation occurred unevenly amid periods of boom and bust; individual industries failed but the whole advanced. Capitalism socialised labour by destroying small-scale economic units and gathering local markets into national and world markets. It concentrated production in agriculture, destroyed the forms of personal dependence that characterised feudal economies and facilitated the movement of labour. The proportion of the population working in agriculture shrank under capitalism and large industrial centres multiplied. Capitalism smashed local forms of association, divided society into groups occupying different places in production and gave impetus to organisation within those groups.[59] Most importantly, capitalism altered the mentality of the population. Labour migration drew the masses 'into the whirlpool of modern social life'.[60] Commerce and industry raised the standard of living and the level of culture of workers, who grew to disdain the peasant mentality. The working class attained new family forms and higher 'spiritual and material requirements'. The hard conditions capitalism imposed on women and juveniles in production served to inspire social legislation that regulated working conditions, shortened the working day and guaranteed workplace safety. Capitalism destroyed the patriarchal isolation of women and juveniles, stimulated their development, fostered their independence and liberated them from patriarchal immobility.[61] So great were the gains conferred by capitalism that in comparison the scruples of the Populists looked reactionary and morally retrograde.

Economic gains by European workers and the success of the German Social Democratic Party at the polls in the 1890s sparked a re-examination among European Marxists of Marx's theory of revolution. Revisionists argued that legislation could protect workers from inevitable impoverishment and that socialism could be realised through democratic evolutionary political processes rather than through Marxian social revolution. Such views soon penetrated the ranks of Russian Marxists. Writing in 1902, Tugan-Baranovsky reflected on Marx's 'iron law of wages'. The condition of the English working class had since the middle of the nineteenth century steadily improved. Labour legislation, trade unions, the cooperative movement, the vast increase in labour productivity that technology fostered, all worked together to promote the welfare of the working class. In England trade unions had forced capitalism into concessions. In Germany the government played a similar role. Even the German Social Democrats had struck the iron law of wages from their programme.[62] Government measures to regulate relations between labour and capital had demonstrated the bankruptcy of Adam Smith's preference for minimal government interference in economic life. Friedrich List had long before demonstrated that the national interest took precedence over private economic interests. Experience had also demonstrated that free international trade was not to the advantage of backward nations. Instead, it reduced them to suppliers of raw materials to advanced nations and trapped them in agricultural economies.

For all the progress of workers under capitalism, however, Tugan-Baranovsky believed the jury was still out on the 'iron law of wages'. Marx, he said, had been right on much: class tensions still underlay economic relations despite superior management of them. Although, contrary to Marxism, small and middle-sized farming had prevailed over large-scale agriculture, the concentration of industrial capital that Marx had predicted was at the turn of the century a fact, and large-scale production was growing faster than small-scale industry. Since everywhere industry was becoming more important economically than agriculture, Tugan-Baranovsky concluded, Marx was by no means entirely wrong.[63]

Despite efforts by Struve and other 'Legal Marxists' to win him to the side of revisionism, Lenin stoutly resisted. In the preface to a new edition of *The Development of Capitalism in Russia* in 1907 he reasserted the law of impoverishment. Capitalist societies inevitably generate 'an insignificant minority of small producers [who] wax rich, "get on in the world", turn bourgeois, while the overwhelming majority are either utterly ruined and become wage-workers or paupers, or eternally eke out an almost proletarian existence'.[64]

Trotsky also remained a revolutionary Marxist, but of dubious orthodoxy. In his view, English and Russian capitalism had little in common. Far from repeating a broadly similar course of development from one country to another, capitalism was a worldwide phenomenon that seized on countries lying in its path and created in each an amalgam out of local conditions plus the universal requirements of capitalism. 'The new Russia', he argued, 'acquired its absolutely specific character because it received its capitalist baptism in the latter half of the nineteenth century from European capital, which by then had reached its most concentrated and abstract form, that of finance capital.'[65] Trotsky held that European capital had created Russian industry in only a few decades. The result was a fatally enfeebled Russian bourgeoisie. The petty bourgeoisie, born of a lengthy process of capitalist development, which had joined with a nascent working class to overthrow French absolutism, was largely absent in Russia.[66] European capital abroad could not recapitulate its own long history. Instead, it began at the point at which it arrived.[67] It focused industry around the machine. In the proletariat it created in Russia it instilled the revolutionary energy that in other places had belonged to the bourgeoisie. The time for national revolutions, Trotsky concluded, had passed. In an age of imperialism it was no longer the bourgeoisie against old regimes but the international proletariat versus the idea of the bourgeois nation.[68] Trotsky's argument for the specificity of capitalism in particular countries and the imperial nature of capitalism in the twentieth century paved the way for Lenin's case at the beginning of the First World War that as the weakest capitalist link in the imperial chain, Russia, despite its low level of capitalist development, was a legitimate subject for proletarian revolution and a catalyst for revolution elsewhere.[69]

EARLY TWENTIETH-CENTURY LIBERALS

Few Russian liberals in the early twentieth century were prepared to accept capitalism unequivocally, despite Russia's economic progress and the amelioration of capitalist exploitation in the West. Like Kavelin in the 1850s, many Russian liberals remained ambivalent about making a clean break with traditional collectivism. Typical was Miliukov, who from 1905 led the Constitutional Democratic Party (Kadets). Lecturing abroad in the early weeks of the 1905 revolution, Miliukov asserted the basic compatibility of Russian liberalism with socialism. Russian liberals, he maintained, were strongly democratic and many Russian socialists preferred class reconciliation to working-class revolution.[70] He agreed with Populists who argued that capitalist factory industry had deprived the peasant small producer of income. An unfair tax burden further condemned the peasant to poverty.[71] Tariff protection for Russian industry reduced competition and kept prices high without increasing the purchasing power of the population. Lack of domestic demand created production surpluses. Unable to compete with foreigners for markets abroad, Russian industry was in perpetual crisis.[72] Economic growth depended on raising agricultural productivity through the technical education of peasants in order to create a market for industry. Although Miliukov wished to remove arbitrariness in communal decision-making, he continued to defend communal forms of land use, as did the Kadet party after the 1905 revolution. Kavelin had viewed property as inviolable; Miliukov went so far in 1905 as to endorse the confiscation of gentry land for distribution to the peasants.[73] As late as 1913, an editorial in the liberal newspaper *The Russian Gazette* pointed to individualistic tendencies among the peasantry that resulted from capitalist development in the country 'with all its routine and profoundly negative aspects'.[74]

The strongest liberal critic of the intelligentsia in general and of its attitude to capitalism in particular was Struve, once a Legal Marxist, but before the 1905 revolution a convert to liberalism. In March 1909 Struve and other former Social Democrats published *Landmarks*, a critique of the values of the Russian intelligentsia. The thrust of the collection was that the intelligentsia had sought solutions to Russia's problems in social engineering rather than in the development of the intellectual and moral resources of individuals. Effective political and social change depended on the prior spiritual education of citizens. Individual contributors attacked the intelligentsia's indifference to philosophy, which they subordinated to politics, their ignorance of the social effect of religion, their disregard for creative personality, their fawning to the masses, their lack of legal awareness and their suspicion of the state.[75] Late in 1908 Struve had prefaced the assault of *Landmarks* on the intelligentsia in a lecture, in which he assailed its attitude to economic development. Economic progress, he argued, rested on the system of production of a country. Efficient production was rooted in personal advantage, which entailed the co-ordination of the advantages of all persons in the system of production. In Russia the intelligentsia raised the idea of the equality of non-responsible individuals above the idea of personal advantage. In particular they looked on capitalism from the point of view of distribution or consumption and not production. In so doing they failed to grasp the significance of industrial capitalism, in which they saw inequality in distribution and the exploitation of labour instead of a superior productive system.[76] Not only was capitalism more productive of material goods, but it also created 'the very foundations of culture'. Neither class struggle nor oppressive government could provide the basis for society. Reversing Herzen's belief that capitalism was an insufficient basis on which to build a civilised society, Struve argued that only the high level of capitalist productivity that flows out of the pursuit of individual advantage can provide the foundations of civilisation.[77]

Though sweeping and unfair to some *intelligenty*, Struve's broad indictment of intelligentsia attitudes to Russia's economic development was perceptive. An anti-capitalist discourse preceded the arrival of capitalism in Russia. Its persistence prevented most members of the intelligentsia from gaining more than a rudimentary grasp of the underlying assumptions and principles of capitalism. Disdain for bourgeois culture, politics and social arrangements supported anti-capitalism. Apologists for the autocratic-bureaucratic regime shared the radical intelligentsia's disregard for constitutionalism, individual rights and the rule of law and saw capitalism as a source of state revenue more than as a desirable economic system. Together bureaucrats and intelligentsia radicals stifled the few voices that over the years spoke in defence of liberal economics and politics. Widely shared intelligentsia notions about Russian exceptionalism, rooted in the country's communalist traditions, struck at the heart of capitalism. It could thrive only in a competitive but rule-based environment that was receptive to individual enterprise and reward. Long absent, just such an environment was coming into being after the revolution of 1905, as Marxists, ex-Marxists and lifelong liberals recognised. It needed decades to be realised; instead, fate provided only a few years. The outbreak of the First World War in 1914 cut short the already stunted prospects for Russian capitalism and liberal democracy in their infancy.

NOTES

1. On industrialisation, see W. L. Blackwell, *The Beginnings of Russian Industrialization, 1800–1860* (Princeton University Press, 1961).
2. A. Herzen, *Letters from France and Italy, 1847–1851*, trans. J. Zimmerman (Pittsburgh University Press, 1995), p. 29.
3. Ibid., p. 30.
4. Ibid., p. 56.
5. Ibid., p. 164.
6. Derek Offord, *Portraits of Early Russian Liberals. A Study of the Thought of T. N. Granovsky, V. P. Botkin, P. V. Annenkov, A. V. Druzhinin and K. D. Kavelin* (Cambridge University Press, 1985), p. 96.
7. A. Herzen, *The Memoirs of Alexander Herzen. My Past and Thoughts*, ed. D. Macdonald (Berkeley and Los Angeles: California University Press, 1973), p. 397.
8. Cited in A. Walicki, *The Controversy over Capitalism. Studies in the Philosophy of the Russian Populists* (Oxford University Press, 1969), p. 163.
9. On the early Slavophiles, see N. V. Riasanovsky, *Russia and the West in the Teaching of the Slavophiles* (Cambridge, Mass.: Harvard University Press, 1952).
10. Blackwell, *Beginnings of Russian Industrialization*, p. 94.
11. Anon., 'Mary Barton', *Vremia* (April 1861), 523.
12. I. Shill', 'Kuda devalis' nashi den'gi?', *Vremia* (February 1861), 112.
13. Anon. [A. E. Razin], 'Nashi domashnie dela', *Vremia* (October 1862), 41.
14. Anon. [A. U. Poretskii], Review of Bruno Hildebrand's 'Politicheskaia ekonomiia nastoiashchego i budushchego', *Vremia* (March 1861), 74–92.
15. Anon. [Razin], 'Nashi domashnie dela', *Vremia* (November 1862), 91.
16. Anon. [Razin], 'Nashi domashnie dela', *Vremia* (February 1863), 95.
17. V…V., 'Otchego u nas malo zheleznykh dorog?', *Den'* (23 February 1863), 6–7.
18. Anon. [Poretskii], Review of Bruno Hildebrand's 'Politicheskaia ekonomiia', 85.
19. K. D. Kavelin, 'Zapiska ob osvobozhdenii krest'ian v Rossii' in *Sobranie sochinenii K. D. Kavelina*, 4 vols. (St Petersburg: M. M. Stasiulevich, 1898), vol. II, cols. 5, 25–9, 41.
20. Kavelin, 'Vzgliad na russkuiu sel'skuiu obshchinu' in *Sobranie sochinenii*, vol. II, col. 183.
21. N. G. Chernyshevskii, 'O nekotorykh usloviiakh, sposobstvuiushchikh umnozheniiu narodnogo kapitala' in *Izbrannye ekonomicheskie proizvedeniia*, 3 vols. (Moscow: Gosudarstvennoe izdatel'stvo, 1948), vol. I, pp. 377–8.

22. Chernyshevskii, 'Kapital i trud' in *Izbrannye ekonomicheskie proizvedeniia*, vol. I, p. 344.
23. Ibid., p. 371.
24. See Thomas C. Owen, *Dilemmas of Russian Capitalism. Fedor Chizhov and Corporate Enterprise in the Railroad Age* (Cambridge, Mass.: Harvard University Press, 2005), pp. 8 and 81–2, and *Capitalism and Politics in Russia. A Social History of the Moscow Merchants, 1855–1905* (Cambridge University Press, 1981), chapter 2.
25. Owen, *Dilemmas*, p. 80.
26. Ibid., p. 81.
27. I. S. Aksakov, *Ivan Sergeevich Aksakov v ego pis'makh*, 3 vols. (Moscow: Russkaia kniga, 2003–4), vol. III, p. 441.
28. N. A. Dobroliubov, 'Temnoe tsarstvo' in *Izbrannoe* (Moscow: Detskaia literatura, 1970), p. 68.
29. Quoted from A. Ostrovsky, *Crazy Money [Easy Money]* in *Four Plays*, trans. S. Mulrine (London: Oberon, 1997), p. 170.
30. Ibid., p. 177.
31. Ibid., p. 184.
32. Ibid., p. 194.
33. Ibid., p. 220.
34. Ibid., p. 262.
35. Ibid., p. 181.
36. N. Flerovskii [V. V. Bervi], *Polozhenie rabochego klassa v Rossii* (St Petersburg: Izdanie N. P. Poliakova, 1869), p. 453.
37. P. L. Mirtov [P. L. Lavrov], *Istoricheskie pis'ma* (Moscow: Tipografiia A. Kotomina, 1870), pp. 63–4.
38. N. K. Mikhailovskii, 'Chto takoe progress?' in *Sochineniia*, 6 vols. (St Petersburg: Russkoe bogatstvo, 1896–7), vol. I, col. 150.
39. P. N. Tkachev, 'Nabat (Programma zhurnala)' in *Sochineniia*, 2 vols. (Moscow: Akademiia nauk SSSR, Izdatel'stvo sotsial'no-ekonomicheskoi literatury, 1976), vol. II, pp. 89–102.
40. K. N. Leont'ev, *Sobranie sochinenii*, 9 vols. (Moscow: V. M. Sablin, 1912), vol. VI, p. 40.
41. Ibid., p. 53.
42. M. A. Bakunin, *The Political Philosophy of Bakunin: Scientific Anarchism*, ed. G. P. Maksimoff (London: Free Press, 1964), pp. 180–6.
43. Ibid., pp. 210–11.
44. P. A. Kropotkin, *The Essential Kropotkin*, ed. Emile Capouya and Keitha Tompkins (New York: Liveright, 1975), pp. 228–9.
45. Ibid., pp. 244–5.
46. Ibid., p. 245.
47. See L. N. Tolstoy, 'The Meaning of the Russian Revolution' in Marc Raeff (ed.), *Russian Intellectual History. An Anthology* (New York: Harcourt and Brace, 1966), pp. 323–57.
48. Walicki, *The Controversy over Capitalism*, pp. 114–20.

49. Ibid., pp. 121–5.
50. P. R. Gregory, *Before Command. An Economic History of Russia from Emancipation to the First Five-Year Plan* (Princeton University Press, 1994), pp. 9, 36.
51. G. V. Plekhanov, *Nashi raznoglasiia* in *Izbrannye filosofskie proizvedeniia*, 5 vols. (Moscow: Akademiia nauk SSSR, 1956), vol. I, pp. 322–5.
52. Walicki, *The Controversy over Capitalism*, pp. 155–6.
53. R. Pipes, *Struve: Liberal on the Left, 1870–1905* (Cambridge, Mass.: Harvard University Press, 1970), pp. 60–1, 116.
54. Ibid., pp. 129–30.
55. V. I. Lenin, *The Development of Capitalism in Russia* in *Collected Works*, 47 vols. (Moscow: Progress, 1960–80), vol. III, pp. 39–44.
56. Ibid., pp. 54–5.
57. Ibid., p. 540.
58. Ibid., p. 505.
59. Ibid., pp. 595–8.
60. Ibid., p. 545.
61. Ibid., pp. 545–6.
62. M. I. Tugan-Baranovskii, *Ocherki iz noveishei istorii politicheskoi ekonomii i sotsializma* in *Ekonomicheskie ocherki* (Moscow: Rosspen, 1998), pp. 167–8.
63. Ibid., pp. 272–3.
64. Lenin, *The Development of Capitalism*, p. 32.
65. Leon Trotsky, *1905* (New York: Vintage Books, 1971), p. 50.
66. Ibid., p. 293.
67. Ibid., p. 51.
68. Ibid., p. 322.
69. Lenin, 'On the Slogan for a United States of Europe' in *The Lenin Anthology*, ed. Robert C. Tucker (New York: W. W. Norton, 1975), p. 203.
70. P. Miliukov, *Russia and Its Crisis* (New York: Collier Books, 1962), p. 248.
71. Ibid., pp. 322–3.
72. Ibid., pp. 338–40.
73. Ibid., p. 383.
74. *Russkie vedomosti*, no. 252 (1 November 1913), 1.
75. See Marshall S. Shatz and Judith Zimmerman (eds. and trans.), *Signposts: A Collection of Articles on the Russian Intelligentsia* (Irvine: Charles Schlacks, 1986). 'Signposts' here is a translation of *Vekhi*, which is perhaps more accurately rendered as 'Landmarks' in the text.
76. P. B. Struve, 'Na raznye temy' in *Collected Works*, 15 vols., ed. Richard Pipes (Ann Arbor: University Microfilms, 1970), vol. VIII, pp. 203–5.
77. Ibid., p. 206.

CHAPTER 13

Natural science

Charles Ellis

'Not one Russian has appeared, whose name deserves to be recorded in the history of the Arts and the Sciences.'[1] So writes the explorer and astronomer the abbé Jean-Baptiste Chappe d'Auteroche in the course of his lengthy and arduous journey from Paris via St Petersburg to Tobolsk in Siberia, which he had undertaken at the invitation of the St Petersburg Academy of Sciences in order to observe the 1761 transit of Venus. With no shortage of time on his hands during his overland journey, Chappe had ample opportunity to compile a travelogue[2] that describes the vast Russian hinterland beyond St Petersburg in which the local population subsists in conditions of unimaginable poverty and privation through the nine-month Siberian winter, a wretched condition exacerbated by the near-slavery to which despotism and serfdom have reduced it. This leads Chappe to one of the explanations he offers in his travelogue for the underperformance of Russian science up to the mid-eighteenth century: 'Despotism debases the mind, damps the genius and stifles every kind of sentiment.'[3] Chappe regards the constitution of the eighteenth-century Russian state as being inimical to the spirit of independent thought in general, and of progressive scientific enquiry in particular.

If an index of a country's scientific achievement may reasonably be drawn from the recognition accorded its scientists by scientific institutions and writers elsewhere in the wider world scientific community, then Chappe's initial contention can be granted, for at the time of his writing the international recognition of Russia's contribution to world science was indeed very low.[4] The explanation for this that Chappe offers is possibly interesting and worthy of further examination, but there is clearly a more present and obvious explanation that he does not consider, which is the commonplace that Russia, owing to its peculiar historical experience, is a latecomer to the modern, western world of scientific Enlightenment. This surely is an observation so uncontroversial that it needs here but the briefest of rehearsals.

What Chappe could have mentioned but did not, by way at least of a partial explanation for Russia's failure to date to produce scientists of world-ranking stature, was that until comparatively recently there had existed little if anything in Russia that could have been dignified with the name of a native scientific culture or indeed of a scientific culture at all. A number of factors had combined to exclude Russia from all but the barest exposure to the cultural and intellectual experience of western Europe, to the extent that Russia had taken little if any part in any of those cultural processes that are now in retrospect designated the Renaissance, the Reformation and the Enlightenment. In addition to having been bypassed by these aspects of the western cultural and intellectual experience now recognised to have been essential steps along the western path towards a modern scientific culture, Russia, unlike the West, had no church with any tradition of rational enquiry to offer. Orthodox Christianity had neither brought with it, nor met with upon its arrival in the Russian lands in the late tenth century, any tradition of scientific enquiry. Orthodoxy rejected science, and rationalism in general, as secondary and debased forms of intellectual activity[5] in a way that western Christianity, the sole inheritor of Classical wisdom in the West, did not. Chappe himself, as a scientific researcher as well as a Catholic abbé, provides an obvious and immediate example of this distinction between the attitudes towards science of western and eastern churches.

Before the pivotal reign of Peter I, Russia had had but little by way of a canonical view of science, next to nothing by way of a secular science and no obvious cultural resources whereby any indigenous scientific culture was going to take root in Russia of its own accord. For Russia to break in upon the world of modern science, a scientific culture was going to have to be *imposed* from above, and by imperial *diktat*. This is what Peter was to provide.

The driving motivation behind the career of Peter the Great was that his Russia should, after its history of detachment from the modern, western world, become part of that world and take its proper place in it on terms commensurate with the weight of Russia's territory, population and potential wealth. For this to be achieved, the application of science to military technology and practice was essential, as Peter well recognised. In particular, the practice of modern warfare had become such that military technology needed to become industrialised, informed by mathematics and science, as he had discovered at first hand in the course of his Grand Embassy of 1697–8 to the Netherlands and to England.[6] 'The inextricable link between war and reform', Lindsey Hughes observes, 'lies at the heart of most interpretations of Peter's reign.'[7]

The immediate exigencies of war were to require the establishment of military and naval colleges in Russia,[8] but Peter's ambition for the development of science and scientific education in Russia extended beyond the narrowly martial. Russia was also to be equipped to take its proper part in the western scientific Enlightenment more widely considered. This ambition was first embodied in his project for the establishment of an Academy of Sciences in St Petersburg to emulate institutions such as the Royal Society in London or the Académie des Sciences in Paris, and this project was realised early in 1726 during the brief reign of Peter's widow and successor Catherine I. With no resource to draw upon of appropriately qualified Russian candidates for academic posts, the Academy was at the outset staffed by foreigners, mainly Germans, but Peter's declared intention had been that this should only be a temporary measure, as is depicted by Lomonosov in his anniversary ode of 1747 to the Empress Elizabeth Petrovna. Russia, Lomonosov writes, must find from among its own population such people as it has hitherto summoned from elsewhere so that the Russian lands can engender their own 'Platos and sharp-witted Newtons'.[9]

Chappe's condemnation of despotism in Russia as something that paralyses the spirit and practice of scientific enquiry might strike one as ill-judged, ungracious even, in view for instance of Peter's explicit and determined measures to promote science, or of the generous sponsorship bestowed upon Chappe's own expedition by Peter's admittedly less energetic and less scientifically committed daughter, the Empress Elizabeth.[10] Chappe's criticism is possibly, then, more usefully to be regarded not as being specifically directed towards the figure of the despot himself or herself, but rather towards the wider political and economic circumstances that attended autocratic rule in Russia. Peter's modernising reforms provoked resentment and opposition from deeply conservative elements in all estates of eighteenth-century Russian society, the liberty and privileges of all of which had been circumscribed in the interests of Peter's increasingly regimented, militarised and centralised state. Where he had sought to lead, traditional Russia proved reluctant or unequipped to follow.

EIGHTEENTH-CENTURY ATTITUDES TOWARDS SCIENCE IN RUSSIA

The nobility, particularly the provincial nobility, showed little if any enthusiasm for learning of any kind, as is entertainingly portrayed by Kantemir in his first satire (1729) and over fifty years later by Fonvizin in his play *The Minor* (1782). The peasantry was, as might be expected, all but excluded from any more than the most rudimentary education. In addition to this, there scarcely existed in Russia any native entrepreneurial middle class to engage in the modern scientific and technological enquiry and experimentation that underlay the industrial revolution in England and in parts of western Europe. In other words, there was little if any private sector interest in the development of Russian science.

The remaining estate in Russia gave voice to outright and explicit opposition to modern science. Although it was noted above that the Russian Orthodox Church had had no tradition of scientific thought to defend, it might equally have been noted that there had until now been no corpus of secular scientific thought in Russia that it had ever needed to oppose. Now there was, for Copernicus, Galileo, Huygens and Newton were in Russia on the march, and their findings were, in large part thanks to Peter, becoming recognised and publicised. It is even suggested that Peter himself contributed to the introduction of the first translation into Russian of Christiaan Huygens's *Kosmotheoros*,[11] a work that promoted a Copernican, heliocentric view of the universe, arguing in particular that any or all of the planets now reliably understood to be orbiting the sun instead of the earth could well be capable of supporting intelligent life, and indeed, as Huygens contended, most likely did support intelligent life. This was the issue raised by secular scientific enquiry that particularly outraged the Russian church, and it gave rise to an impassioned controversy during much of the eighteenth century. It was, however, a battle that the church was for the most part losing, largely at the hands of Lomonosov.

Lomonosov, an accomplished writer of poetry as well as a practising experimental scientist, wrote a number of works celebrating from a deistic point of view the magnificence of creation as it is apprehended by the modern Enlightenment scientist, and in so doing advancing the Copernican system and its wider scientific implications. First among these works were his morning and evening meditations upon the majesty of God (1743).[12] In these meditations Lomonosov speculates about the immensity and splendour of creation in the morning as he contemplates the sunrise and in the evening as he observes the Northern Lights and ponders their possible causes. In the 'Evening Meditation' Lomonosov raises specifically the issue of life on other planets: 'There is a multiplicity of worlds out there. Innumerable suns burn out there, and these worlds are inhabited by mortal beings. In confirmation of the greater glory of God, the laws of science are universal.' Lomonosov celebrates the majesty of God not through any scriptural revelation, but instead by means of direct reference to the awesome magnitude, rational orderliness and splendour of His creation.

Further, he asserts that it is for mankind a duty of piety to investigate God's creation by means of scientific enquiry,[13] and this is how he concludes the 'Morning Meditation': 'Creator, extend to me the rays of your wisdom, for I am still beset by ignorance. Teach me always to do what is seemly to you, and teach me how, when I look upon your creation, to give praise to you, my immortal Sovereign.'

Lomonosov's meditations are works that promote an Enlightenment deistic standpoint, but that do not directly confront traditional clerical authority on matters of science. However, other works of the eighteenth century do challenge reactionary and obscurantist clerical attitudes towards science and learning. For instance, the conservative cleric Crito from Kantemir's first satire has this to say about those who pursue science and learning: 'They discuss and want to know the grounds and cause of everything, and they do not put enough faith in sacred authority. They have abandoned proper morality and no longer drink *kvas*.'[14] Not only does science here threaten the authority wielded by the church (and its wealth),[15] it threatens traditional morality and it is moreover *un-Russian* (i.e. in that they no longer drink *kvas*). Kantemir's testimony concerning the ignorance, obscurantism and venality of the clergy is repeated, and in terms considerably less temperate, in Lomonosov's notorious and scurrilous 'Hymn to the Beard' (1757).[16]

The most comprehensive of Lomonosov's popularisations of science is his 'Epistle on the Value of Glass' (1752), in which his polemic against clerical obscurantism over matters of science is more measured and less gratuitously offensive than is the 'Hymn to the Beard', but it is nonetheless effective. In this poem of 440 lines Lomonosov repeats the testimony of the meditations and goes on to celebrate the manifold benefits that applied science confers upon mankind. The 'Epistle' catalogues the various uses of glass from the trivial to the more substantial, from beads and mirrors and glazed pottery through window glass and spectacles and on to navigational and scientific instruments such as barometers, telescopes and microscopes. More importantly, the 'Epistle' at its philosophical core[17] presents the literal clarity of glass as a metaphor for the spirit of clarity that inspires Enlightenment science and reaffirms the validity of the Copernican heliocentric system as it has been discovered by mankind by means of the glass used to make scientific instruments. Opposing geocentric clerical views are dismissed not only because they are misguided, but further because they are blasphemous. The blasphemy of such views lies in the fact that their presentation of creation diminishes the status of God to that of a capricious miracle-worker in a rather small and restricted geocentric cosmos. True piety, on the other hand, lies in the scientist's striving to apprehend the rationality, grandeur and boundless immensity of God's creation, and hence the greater magnificence of God himself, as these are celebrated in the meditations and revealed through the use of glass in particular and the pursuit of scientific enquiry in general. The contest over the issue concerning the Copernican system can be regarded as irrevocably lost by the clerical reactionaries when in 1786 the teaching of the Copernican system was established as part of the school syllabus in Russia.[18] This was progress in Russian *scientific* thought, but was this progress that was going to be matched by any corresponding progress in the political or social spheres?

All the eighteenth-century writers so far considered – Kantemir, Lomonosov, Fonvizin – were, in one way or another, establishment figures, on the state payroll and with a stake in the *status quo*. Though in places critical of some of its current shortcomings, none of them called into question the principle of autocracy as such and they all proposed that the advancement of science and learning would lead to the improved functioning, to the benefit of all of its inhabitants, of the Russian state as currently constituted. To these writers, the Enlightenment science they promoted was quite of a piece with the current political system they upheld. This had not so much been the case in western countries: for example, the French *philosophes* did identify scientific rationalism as an integral part of a wider rationalist outlook, an outlook that ultimately was to inform the revolutionary government in France. An equally striking example is that of Benjamin Franklin in America. An accomplished practising scientist, Franklin, as one of the foremost contributors to the Declaration of Independence and to the American Constitution, clearly extended his rationalist vision well beyond the confines of natural science.[19]

Scientific thought in Russia remained neutral towards, or often indeed complaisant with, the ideology of autocracy, and its exercise brought to the Russian Empire, actually or potentially, considerable advances to its power, wealth and international prestige. Such was the perception of the status of the sciences for the greater part of the reign of Catherine II. Catherine was a fervent enthusiast for science, and as a patroness and correspondent of the great French *philosophes* had taken an active interest in all aspects of Enlightenment thought. Indeed, in 1759 she engaged Aepinus, the distinguished German physicist and astronomer from the St Petersburg Academy, as her personal scientific tutor[20] at a time when scientific education of any sort was by no means expected of someone destined to become a tsar's consort.

In spite of Chappe's slight concerning the quality of Russian scientists, and in general of the manners, morals and aptitudes of the Russian people, against which Catherine herself wrote a detailed and impassioned rebuttal,[21] Catherine enthusiastically backed expeditions throughout the Russian territories by scientists from abroad to observe the recurrence of the transit of Venus in 1769.[22] Such expeditions had formed a significant part of Russian scientific endeavour from Peter's reign onwards, and their organisation and conduct had from the outset been designated one of the primary functions of the St Petersburg Academy of Sciences. They represent perhaps the greatest and most conspicuous achievements of the early years of the Academy.[23] The obvious and immediate motivation behind the expeditions was naturally one of mapping the rapidly expanding territories of the empire, and of measuring and describing its human and natural resources, but a further consideration would no doubt have been one of advertising to the world how Russia was, or was becoming, a participant in scientific research to be taken seriously in international terms. Catherine, notoriously a consummate self-propagandist, sponsored the 1769 expeditions to no fewer than eleven locations in her empire with her characteristically ostentatious largesse.[24] Such showcase (but not necessarily any less valuable for that) enterprises apart, the uptake by native Russians of careers in science continued to proceed only rather slowly: attitudes towards science, and the limited accessibility to scientific education in Russia, remained little advanced from what has been described above. Among native Russians there persisted a shortage of people qualified to teach the natural sciences, and also of those willing or financially able to subscribe to any such courses. This shortfall still had to be made good by foreign teachers, many of whose students were themselves the sons of expatriates, but nonetheless there were areas of scientific enquiry in which Russia, through its own scientists, was beginning to lay the foundations of a world-class scientific culture.

The expeditions to observe the transits of Venus in 1761 and 1769 had nourished an enthusiasm for research in astronomy, which was to culminate in the establishment some time later, in 1839, of the observatory at Pulkovo near St Petersburg, possibly the most advanced of its time. Also, the magisterial presence at the Academy of the Swiss mathematician Leonhard Euler (1707–83), who served at the Academy from 1726 to 1741 and again from 1766 to 1783, established an uninterrupted tradition in mathematics in Russia among whose leading lights in the century to follow were to be the world-renowned Lobachevsky, Ostrogradsky and Chebyshev.[25]

In that they had remained detached from social and political debate, science and scientists had constituted no threat to Catherine's regime, and indeed Russian scientific endeavour had served to enhance the international reputation both of Catherine herself and of her empire. However, political events elsewhere, drawing their inspiration one way or another from wider aspects of Enlightenment thought, were to call into question the entire Enlightenment project as it was perceived in Russia.

FROM THE ENLIGHTENMENT TO DARWINISM

Following the revolution and regicide in France, Catherine in the last few years of her reign became disenchanted with the Enlightenment philosophy that she had earlier so enthusiastically espoused. After her death, the Enlightenment was further seen to be discredited on account of the Terror in France, the Napoleonic violation of sacred Russian soil and the Decembrist uprising of 1825. These outrages to Russian autocratic sensibilities, all conducted in the name of Enlightenment, were to lead in Russia to a reining-in of Enlightenment values, the unrestrained pursuit of science included, that persisted well into the notoriously repressive reign of Nicholas I. Intellectuals, who under other circumstances might have taken an interest in natural science, were now turning their attention away from Enlightenment concerns, at a time when the government of Nicholas I with its coercive apparatus of Official Nationality was repudiating Enlightenment thought yet more explicitly.[26] Science was still acknowledged as indispensable to the state, but now more as something of a necessary evil, and scientific education was increasingly becoming subjected to rigid state control, with university departments being denied any autonomy over scientific curricula. Additionally, from 1828 biology, physiology, chemistry and geology were no longer taught in the gymnasiums, resulting in a marked decline in the number and quality of university students in these sciences.[27] However, mathematics did still flourish both as an 'intellectual sanctuary from political oppression'[28] and on account of the continuing legacy of Euler. The St Petersburg Academy fared somewhat better than did other educational institutions, though its activities were still subjected to strict state direction determined by state demands to investigate current practical needs, with the result that the emphasis of its researches lay overwhelmingly on applied rather than pure or speculative science. The Academy still had the good fortune to maintain a number of highly distinguished scientists from abroad and, as in Catherine's time, was promoted as a showcase to the world of Russian scientific achievement and endeavour, again with great expeditions of discovery by land and sea such as those of Humboldt and von Baer[29] featuring prominently.

Still, as events were to reveal, Russian scientific progress in the first half of the nineteenth century was to fall yet further behind that of the West. The humiliation of Russian arms in the catastrophe of the Crimean War provided graphic testimony to just how moribund, except at all but the highest level, had become the sciences in Russia under the shackles of Official Nationality and the persistent interference of government in academic affairs. After the death of Nicholas I in 1855 and the succession of his son, Alexander II, the 1860s saw a significant if short-lived liberalisation in the arts and sciences in Russia that sought eagerly and rapidly to make good the stagnation of the previous fifty years or so. This liberalisation was centred on the momentous political reform of 1861, the emancipation of the serfs. In particular, the idea of continuing political progress was in the air, and, unlike in the previous century, scientific progress in Russia was now coming to be regarded as a necessary and inseparable concomitant of a more general political and social progress.

Foremost in looking towards the methods of rational, positive science as a panacea for the shortcomings of Russian society were the nihilists in their scientistic contention that 'the methods used in studying natural sciences should be employed also in investigating all aspects of human behaviour and condition, e.g. in philosophy and social sciences'.[30] Chernyshevsky's 'Anthropological Principle in Philosophy' (1860) can be regarded as the manifesto of scientism in mid-nineteenth-century Russia, and it remained even in Soviet times an oft-quoted and highly respected text. Chernyshevsky presents his scientism in terms such as these:

That part of philosophy which deals with the problems of man, just like the other part which deals with the problems of external nature, is based on the natural sciences. The principle underlying the philosophical view of human life and all its phenomena is the idea, worked out by the natural sciences, of the unity of the human organism; the observations of physiologists, zoologists and medical men have driven away all thought of dualism in man. Philosophy sees him as medicine, physiology and chemistry see him.[31]

And it was just at this historical moment, when sociological and natural-scientific processes were being identified by the likes of Chernyshevsky as governed by one and the same principle, that there appeared a scientific work that proposed a model of progress that was inbuilt into the natural world itself. Darwin's *On the Origin of Species* (1859) put forward a comprehensive and coherent account (and one that has to this day triumphantly stood the test of time and of all manner of religious or otherwise ignorant or vexatious opposition) of how complex life forms have developed over time from their less complex ancestors, a process that was readily accepted as constituting a force for *progress* inherent in the natural world, and a force for progress with a clear analogue to be imputed into the world of human affairs. Moreover, and congenially for the nihilists and their allies, Darwin's account is entirely materialist and studiously non-miraculous, which indeed it has to be, for otherwise it would not be natural science.[32]

The case study described above of the reception in Russia of the Copernican system, later culminating in the Newtonian system, shows a view of a universe that is subject to immutable laws and governed by a supremely benign and rational autocrat. The eighteenth-century writers here considered found in the rational workings of Newton's universe a ready analogue in the polity of the enlightened Catherine's Russia. However, the case study discussed below of the reception of Darwinism in Russia does call into question the idea of tsarist autocracy as being the last word in Russian political debate. It explores how Russian writers looked to progress in the natural world, such as Darwin was apparently promising, for the promise of progress in Russian society beyond that of the tsarist autocracy they so detested.

DARWINISM AND PROGRESS

Darwin's theory was [very sympathetically] received in Russia. While in western Europe it met firmly established old traditions which it had first to overcome, in Russia its appearance coincided firmly with the awakening of our society after the Crimean War and here it immediately received the status of full citizenship and ever since has enjoyed wide popularity.[33]

Here the celebrated comparative embryologist Kovalevsky, whose work had been acknowledged and admired by Darwin himself, confirms succinctly much of the foregoing discussion of the relationship between scientific thought and of more general philosophical, social and political concerns in Russia. In addition, Kovalevsky identifies the historical moment, 'the awakening of our society after the Crimean War', with the appearance of Darwin's seminal publication. This was indeed to introduce into Russia a remarkable development in the pursuit of the life sciences, for the nihilist scientistic view of the nature of human psychology inspired the researches into animal behaviour of Sechenov, followed by Pavlov,[34] who were to achieve recognition as world leaders in the investigation of the physiological basis of animal and, importantly by extension, human psychology and behaviour. In this line of research it was clearly necessary for these scientists to have at hand a model of the development of complex forms of life with complex psychological constitutions that owe nothing to factors other than those purely physiological. Darwin's is just such a model. Although Darwinism was illuminating and uncontentious for many of the life scientists in Russia, it turned out to be less so for radical political commentators of the 1860s onwards, many if not most of whom were quite limited in their scientific background or expertise. The trouble for them was the particular mechanism responsible for Darwin's 'descent with modification', which is that of natural selection. For all that natural selection offers a model of progress in the natural world, it does not bring with it quite the right kind of progress that commentators such as Chernyshevsky were demanding. Most vehement (and arguably least scientifically competent) among those objecting to the model of natural selection was Chernyshevsky himself, to whom the apparent sociological and political implications of Darwinian theory were simply too unpalatable, and too much at odds with Chernyshevsky's own vision for the future course of development of Russian society.

Official interference in scientific debate was often a matter of the authorities' unwillingness to regard scientific thought in isolation from its actual or perceived philosophical, social and political implications; and Chernyshevsky maintained in effect that very same view, though with his own radical socialist agenda in mind: 'Political theories, and all philosophical doctrines in general, have always been created under the powerful influence of the social situation to which they belonged, and every philosopher has always been a representative of one of the political parties which in his time contended for predominance in the society to which the philosopher belonged.'[35] In this spirit Chernyshevsky dismisses the Darwinian model of the struggle for existence as no more than the apologia of a complacent and comfortable English bourgeois for competitive capitalism, a model of social development that Chernyshevsky and many of his fellow radical writers expressly wished to exclude from their programmes for the social and economic development of post-1861 Russia.[36] A particular focus for the revulsion of Chernyshevsky and others towards Darwinism, as Daniel Todes comprehensively examines,[37] is the reference Darwin makes in *Origin of Species* to the gloomy political economist Thomas Malthus: 'A struggle for existence inevitably follows from the high rate at which all organic beings tend to increase ... It is the doctrine of Malthus applied with manifold force to the whole animal and vegetable kingdoms.'[38]

This principle of the struggle for existence is to Chernyshevsky not only morally repugnant, but scientifically unjustifiable in the face of his universal anthropological principle. The argument from the anthropological principle appears to run something along these lines (although Chernyshevsky is not always the most coherent of writers): the laws governing progress in nature are identical to those governing progress in society; all conduct in society is governed by rational self-interest; the sum of the rational self-interests of all members of a society is greatest where conflict between them is least; societies naturally progress, or necessarily gravitate towards an optimum; Malthus's model of society is a model of conflict; so Malthus's model must be wrong; so the Darwinian doctrine of the struggle for existence must be wrong. Simple as that. Instead of making his appeal to a discredited political economist, says Chernyshevsky, Darwin would have done better to have looked to the as yet unrefuted work of a biologist, Lamarck. Indeed, in keeping with his dismissal of Darwinism as an apologia for bourgeois capitalism, Chernyshevsky ascribes the rejection of Lamarckian transformism in France to the greater acceptability, both on political and religious grounds, of the Cuvierian anti-transformist doctrine of essentialism in natural types.[39]

Aside from its not having any disagreeable Malthusian connotations, the Lamarckian model of 'soft inheritance'[40] is appealing to Chernyshevsky in that it proposes that changes in the form of an organism are driven by the environment in which it lives, whereas in Darwinism they are random with respect to the environment. The Lamarckian view is clearly consistent with the finding of the 'Anthropological Principle' that human actions are *adaptive physiological responses to social circumstances*. Better still, such changes are invariably beneficial, whereas in Darwinism they are normally the opposite and it is owing to natural selection that these are eliminated and that only the occasional variations advantageous with respect to the environment are preserved. Transferring Lamarck's model to human society – and remember that the essence of the anthropological principle is that the same laws apply to man as apply to nature – Chernyshevsky can contend that socialism is possible; that given the right social environment, man will *of physiological necessity* evolve socialist inclinations. Chernyshevsky, then, could not but reject the Darwinian struggle for existence on account of its misguided or pernicious endorsement of Malthus, but writers of the same generation, who broadly sympathised with Chernyshevsky's moral and political persuasions, made more of an attempt to accommodate their views within the Darwinian model.

The so-called subjective sociologists, foremost among them Lavrov and Mikhailovsky, remain respectably faithful, along with Chernyshevsky and with Darwin himself, to the notion that life and behaviour, grounded as they are in physiology, which is itself grounded in chemistry and more fundamentally even than that in physics and mathematics, are non-miraculous processes amenable to scientific investigation and indeed at the time already yielding to the researches of natural scientists such as Sechenov and Pavlov. They were, however, prepared to introduce other terms into the discussion.

CRITICAL THOUGHT AND MUTUAL AID

'Any hypothesis of the creation of living beings by the supernatural powers of a deity is just as unthinkable from the scientific point of view as is the proposition of the existence of this deity in the first place.'[41] So writes Lavrov in his *Essay on the History of Modern Thought*, and in this unequivocal and incontrovertible declaration there is clearly no immediate point of departure from what Chernyshevsky has contended. What the subjective sociologists do introduce into the debate, and what Chernyshevsky by his own confession cannot, is the element of *critical thought* (Lavrov's term, but a concept that Mikhailovsky will readily accept), which is the defining feature of their 'subjective sociology' and is what distances them from the 'objective materialism' of Chernyshevsky. This capacity for critical thought remains for them, though, a purely biological product, for that is all it can be, in that in the nature of its *origin* it does not and cannot differ from any other of the myriad characteristics that the (human) individual possesses. However, in the nature of its *performance*, the capacity for critical thought does differ *qualitatively* from the more brute physical characteristics of the human organism, and in this sense it has become a separate category for *sociological*, rather than biological, enquiry.

Critical thought is a property *emergent* from the evolutionary development of increasingly complex forms of society, whereby once human society has attained a certain level of complexity, there has needed to arise in the human brain a level of complexity corresponding to that of the society its possessor inhabits. Thus far this is impeccably Chernyshevskian. However, this level of complexity brings with it, accidentally, or emergently, a capacity to *assess from without*, rather than simply to *behave within*, society, and here is the point where the subjective sociologists part company with Chernyshevsky. That is, critical thought is the capacity, possibly for the time being unique to humanity, to make judgements and to have preferences, whereby people can strive *actively to define* rather than merely *passively to receive* the form that society takes, or, to use Lavrov's expression, 'to act in history'. In the brief illustrations that follow from each writer's work, it is clear that although the terminology they use may differ, and that although they are arguing towards different but not incompatible conclusions, the use to which they put this notion of 'critical thought' in their discussions of the sociological implications of Darwinian theory is essentially the same.

'And accepting the law of struggle from Darwinism as a fact, we must impose on ourselves a moral law of a struggle against struggle, against selection, against useful adaptations, against divergence of character.'[42] This is a central contention of Mikhailovsky's 'Observations on Darwinism' (1870), which is a critique of 'Social Darwinism', with Herbert Spencer as its chief apostle,[43] who had enlisted Darwinian theory in support of the capitalist notions of competition and of the division of labour. Mikhailovsky is telling us here that for all that Darwinism is true, the 'subjective method', emergent from the evolutionary process, allows humanity to *do something about it*, to kick against the pricks, to 'struggle against the struggle for existence' and to act on its own behalf to bypass that which the Social Darwinists proclaim to be the natural and inevitable order of society. Critical thought enables mankind to strive instead towards the goal of the subjective definition of progress in human society with which Mikhailovsky concludes his essay *What is Progress?* (1869):

To the question that we asked, 'What is progress?', we answer: 'Progress is the step-by-step approach towards the wholeness of the individual, towards the fullest and most comprehensive division of labour between the organs [of the individual body] and the least possible division of labour between people. Anything that holds this process back is immoral, unjust, harmful and irrational. Only that which diminishes the heterogeneity of society and at the same time increases the heterogeneity of its individual members is moral, just, rational or useful.'[44]

In biological terms, the increased complexity of the human organism is to be welcomed, but in sociological terms the implied concomitant process of capitalism and the division of labour is to be resisted, since this atrophies the full potential of the human individual, and this is Mikhailovsky's concern about the sociological implications of Darwinism. The subjective method, the struggle against the struggle for existence, must therefore be enlisted in order to avert the vicissitudes of capitalism in general, and the division of labour in particular, that Social Darwinists such as Herbert Spencer promote and misguidedly applaud as being inevitable.

Mikhailovsky's ally Lavrov uses a very similar line of argument but less with a view to opposing particular malign aspects of capitalism and its effects upon the growth and fulfilment of the individual in society than towards promoting the possibility of a more benign socialism. In his *Essay on the History of Modern Thought* he contends that 'It is quite proper to recognise that biological processes are the starting-point for social processes, since communal life is one of the manifestations in which life is found and one of the weapons in the struggle for existence between organisms.'[45] Communal life has arisen from the struggle for existence. That much is uncontroversial, but Lavrov has to go further in order to secure his desired conclusion that the struggle for existence will favour a socialist form of communal life. When he found that biological evolution by itself was insufficient as a guarantor of progress towards ever more communal forms of living, he identified the development of the capacity for conscious thought in mankind as signalling a point of departure from this purely biological process. This is a point at which biology begins to give way to sociology, and where begins an analogous process of natural selection that may take place between different forms of society according to the degree of critical thought that takes place within them. This is, Lavrov proposes, a process that may lead to the ultimate triumph of socialism, for instance, in that a socialist society wastes fewer of its energies in the prosecution of internal conflict. Lavrov is here faintly echoing Chernyshevsky and more distinctly foreshadowing Kropotkin

Using the same apparatus of critical thought, of the struggle against the struggle for existence or of biology giving way to subjective sociology, both writers have reconciled their sociological science with Darwin's biology, adding to it a moral dimension that accords with their aspirations for the future development of Russian society and to which there is no obvious reason to suppose that Darwin himself would have objected. They have come to terms with what had been at first sight the inconvenient and unpalatable consequences of the theory of the struggle for existence that had so troubled Chernyshevsky. The subjective sociologists' accommodation with Darwinism is modest, reasonable and humane, and is surely echoed in this more modern testimony: 'We, that is our brains, are separate and independent enough from our genes to rebel against them … There is no reason why we should not rebel in a large way, too.'[46] In a way that Chernyshevsky could never have allowed, we can, at least to an extent, become the masters rather than the servants of our physiological constitution.

The anarchist Prince Kropotkin was perhaps less in need of such testimony than had been Mikhailovsky and Lavrov. With more conviction than Lavrov could muster, Kropotkin in his *Mutual Aid* (1896)[47] presents Darwinian natural selection as a law of nature that when transposed on to human society will necessarily favour a communal mode of living and penalise more competitive forms of society. Kropotkin, unlike Chernyshevsky, Mikhailovsky or Lavrov, had been a practising natural scientist, taking part in expeditions to study the wildlife and other natural resources of Siberia. His experience of nature had differed significantly from Darwin's, and this led him to draw significantly different conclusions about the nature of the struggle for existence. Darwin had observed the struggle for existence in temperate and tropical regions, in environments that seemed for ever to be filled to capacity with living organisms. Within such environments it seemed natural to suppose that the Malthusian population principle was at all times operating with unrelenting force and that this would in large part be realised in the form of direct competition. Were an additional individual or species to be able to find a place in such a natural economy, it seemed inevitable that this would have to be at the price of the death of an existing individual or the extinction of an existing species. Kropotkin, on the other hand, had made his field observations in the barren and sparsely populated landscapes of Siberia, where the idea of competition born of overcrowding seemed to be quite inappropriate, since species populations there evidently never attained numbers that got near to the capacity of the landscape to accommodate them.[48] Instead of witnessing competition within animal populations, Kropotkin was continually impressed by the mutual support he observed in their common struggle against predators and against the vicissitudes of the abiotic environment.[49]

Kropotkin's analogous account of the course of human history describes how periods in which mutual aid has predominated, where social arrangements have proceeded according to mankind's biologically inherited cooperative disposition, have been the most peaceful, productive and progressive; but these have been punctuated by periods in which an authoritarian state has predominated, the Russia of Kropotkin's day of course being a conspicuous example of this. During those periods when the state arrogates to itself the rules by which its members cooperate, in the form of a legislative apparatus upheld by actual or threatened violence, individuals are left to exercise on their own behalf only the residual competitive aspect of their evolutionary inheritance, and to Kropotkin the anarchist any such social arrangement is unnatural and malign.[50] Biology has told Kropotkin that for cooperation to take place in human society needs no legislation, and that it is periods of mutual aid in society that are the more consonant with man's evolutionary inheritance. In his eyes, it is the periods when the state predominates that are the pathological condition. Kropotkin admits that he cannot with scientific certitude extend the mutual aid principle to the whole of mankind, but he still looks upon this ideal as being something more substantial than a pious hope, as he tells us in the concluding passage of *Mutual Aid*: 'In the practice of mutual aid, which we can trace to the earliest beginnings of evolution, we thus find the positive and undoubted origin of our ethical conceptions; and we can affirm that in the ethical progress of man, mutual support – not mutual struggle – has had the leading part. In its wide extension, even at the present time, we also see the best guarantee of a still loftier evolution of our race.'[51] Kropotkin hereby asserts that aspirations for the development of Russian society to proceed along more communitarian lines have in no way been confounded by evolutionary theory, and that Darwinism understood properly, seen in the light of Kropotkin's own Siberian field evidence, by no means inevitably implies that competitive capitalism is the natural order of modern society.

This greater concern of Kropotkin and of other Russian writers for the political and sociological, rather than the religious (or straightforwardly scientific) assumptions and implications of Darwinism, significantly differentiates the debate in Russia from that in the West. It also goes some way towards illustrating a more general distinctiveness in the attitudes of Russians towards the place of science in their culture.

THE DISTINCTIVENESS OF THE RUSSIAN SCIENTIFIC DEBATE

The most impassioned and 'non-rational' criticisms came not from official representatives of the church but from devout laymen [such as] Danilevsky and Strakhov whose opposition to Darwinism was interwoven, not only with their religious views, but, perhaps more importantly and directly, with their Russian nationalism and anti-Westernism.[52]

Here George Kline observes that, unlike in the West (and particularly, even unto this day, in the United States), there was no articulated tradition of biblical creationism for the evolutionists in Russia to overcome. The writers discussed above clearly identified that there was no religious case to be considered, first in that none had been made by the Orthodox Church, and then in that, as self-declared atheists all, they had no apologies to make in that direction anyway. The lines of battle in the Russian debate were to be drawn elsewhere, and at a place where a distinctive Russianness in science confronts, and needs to be evaluated apart from, for instance British, French, American or German science, which did not (at least until the 1930s in Germany) advertise themselves as being anything other than universally applicable.

One of the foreign scientists to adorn the Academy in the dark days of the reign of Nicholas was Karl Ernst von Baer, whose acolyte Danilevsky accompanied him on his expeditions of scientific research and was influenced by von Baer's teleological account of embryonic development.[53] Von Baer's teleology had furnished Danilevsky with a ready metaphor for his historical treatise *Russia and Europe* (1869).[54] In this work Danilevsky describes the historical experience of Russia and Europe not as two manifestations of a single process of development common to all human societies, which is what might be a more natural application of the Darwinian principle of common descent, but as two distinct processes of development – Cuvierian *embranche-ments*, if you will.[55] In common with the Slavophiles of earlier years, Danilevsky cherished a belief in the innate superiority of specifically Slavic virtues not present in western cultures, and to this he added the notion of historical development as a teleological process analogous to that of von Baer's notion of embryonic development. Putting the two together, Danilevsky could now advance the highly appealing prospect of a sort of Russian 'Manifest Destiny', of an ultimate triumph in history of Slavic cultural values over decadent or degenerate western values and practices. Darwinian theory Danilevsky dismissed as the morally flawed product of a vicious, competitive, culturally inferior strand of historical development, here indeed having Chernyshevsky as an unlikely and perhaps not altogether welcome bedfellow. They had both demonstrated how the scientific debate in Russia could not be divorced from wider concerns about the distinctive nature of Russia and of Russianness.

Chappe in the 1760s identified in the Russian people no enthusiasm for the pursuit of science. To the extent that this was to be attributed to the dead hand of autocracy and serfdom dampening the Russian genius, perhaps the burgeoning of internationally accredited Russian scientific achievement from the 1860s onwards following the abolition of serfdom might up to a point vindicate his case. Additionally, in the intellectual ferment of the 1860s other previously dormant currents of Russian thought were reasserting themselves with no less vigour, including a renewed examination, reminiscent of the Slavophilism of the 1830s and 1840s, of a notion of Russianness, of a Russian national destiny grounded in specifi-cally Russian insight and experience for ever to be set apart from national consciousnesses elsewhere. At the same time that science was reasserting itself in Russia, such currents of thought were calling into question the place of science in the Russian intellectual landscape, and the very Russianness of science. Writers such as Dostoevsky and the yet more explicitly religious commentators Berdiaev and Solovev, while not gainsay-ing the value of scientific progress, contended that the specific Russian cultural genius lay elsewhere than in science, in a realm of spiritual insight such as western cultures had never known and could now never hope to attain. Science remained to them an alien and inferior means of apprehending the truth about the world, just as it had been for the early Orthodox missionaries to the Russian lands.

As Dostoevsky records in his *Winter Notes on Summer Impressions* (1863), he found the products of scientific and technological progress on show at the Great Exhibition in London awesome in both senses of the word – provoking at the same time both wonder and dread. The wonder needs no explanation, but what Dostoevsky dreads is how in the face of science rampant, any notion of a spiritual dimension to the human personality is becoming marginalised. The very question of how we should live, which ought to be the central focus of human moral enquiry, is in danger of becoming reduced to a natural scientific investigation undifferentiated in kind from any other natural scientific investigation. This is a concern he further addresses in *Notes from Underground* (1864).[56] However, the truths and potency of science cannot be wished away; and perhaps a more promising approach to Dostoevsky's anxiety than that of the Underground Man can be found in the writings of the Russian chemist Mendeleev, who identified in 1869 the Periodic Table of the Elements. Mendeleev's contribution to the advance of the science of chemistry was as ground-breaking as had been Darwin's to the science of biology ten years earlier.[57] A liberal rather than a radical, Mendeleev pays due tribute to the value in Russian culture of distinct but complementary areas of enquiry such as religion and the arts, but insists that their findings are valid only in so far as they remain consistent with the truths of natural science.[58] Scientific principles, as Dostoevsky regrets and Mendeleev justifiably and confidently asserts, had by now become the primary standard for validation of philosophical discourse.

SCIENCE UNBOUND

The historian of Russian science Alexander Vucinich is little short of exultant in celebrating how science in Russia has come of age: 'The essential change during the 1860s was that science ceased to be a secondary force in Russian intellectual culture and became as important as the anti-rationalist tradition in understanding the full spectrum of Russian thought.'[59] Those Russian writers who resisted this coming of age of science in Russia were fighting a rearguard action. The most illustrious among them, Dostoevsky, could not inveigh against science from any position of strength. The wishfully thinking indignation of his Underground Man is readily to be regarded as petulant, feeble and ultimately pathetic. Unlike in the eighteenth century, where the scientific debate had been isolated from the political debate, in the latter half of the nineteenth century its horizons expand and it proceeds to become the leading factor in the re-examination of long-held religious, political and sociological assumptions. Unleashed, science was nevermore to be confined by medieval superstition or by sentimental nationalism. From the 1860s onwards science in Russia had achieved a momentum that was not to be arrested, and Russia, and later the USSR, was to proceed to establish for itself a scientific tradition and potential quite comparable with those of developed western nations, our intrepid abbé's own homeland not excluded.

NOTES

1. H. Woolf, *The Transits of Venus: A Study of Eighteenth-Century Science* (Princeton University Press, 1959), citing *A Journey into Siberia* (see note 2 below).
2. J-B. Chappe d'Auteroche, *A Journey into Siberia* (London, 1770; reprinted New York: Arno Press, 1970).
3. Ibid., p. 332.
4. Lomonosov's acceptance into the Bologna Academy in 1764 was, if not the very first, certainly among the first international recognitions of scientific achievement by Russians.
5. See A. Vucinich, *Science in Russian Culture: A History to 1860* (Stanford University Press, 1963), pp. 4–5.
6. See Lindsey Hughes, *Russia in the Age of Peter the Great* (London: Yale University Press, 1998), pp. 22–7.
7. Ibid., p. 63.
8. Ibid., chapter 3.
9. M. V. Lomonosov, *Polnoe sobranie sochinenii*, ed. S. I. Vavilov, 10 vols. (Moscow and Leningrad: Izdatel'stvo Akademii nauk SSSR, 1950–9), vol. VIII, pp. 196–207, stanza 22. See also Ludmilla Schulze, 'The russification of the St Petersburg Academy', *British Journal of the History of Science*, 18 (1985), 305–35, especially 309.
10. Chappe does, though, acknowledge Elizabeth's generosity in funding and facilitating his expedition: see *A Journey into Siberia*, p. 26.
11. See Valentin Boss, *Newton and Russia, the Early Influence, 1698–1796* (Cambridge, Mass., Harvard University Press, 1972), pp. 50–7.
12. Lomonosov, *Polnoe sobranie sochinenii*, vol. VIII, pp. 117–23.
13. See Joachim Klein, *Puti kul'turnogo importa* (Moscow: Iazyki slavianskoi kul'tury, 2005), part 2, chapter 6.
14. 'Na khuliashchikh ucheniia: k umu svoemu' (1729) in Antiokh Kantemir, *Sobranie sochinenii* (Leningrad: Sovetskii izdatel', 1956), pp. 57–67, lines 33–5.
15. Ibid., lines 142–5.
16. Lomonosov, *Polnoe sobranie sochinenii*, vol. VIII, pp. 618–26, and see the editor's endnotes.
17. Ibid., pp. 508–22, for example, lines 268–332.

18. See Klein, *Puti kul'turnogo importa*, p. 492.
19. J. C. Ellis, 'The Scientific Revolutions of Copernicus and Darwin and Their Repercussions on Russian Political and Sociological Writing', unpublished PhD thesis (University of Bristol, 1999), pp. 29–33.
20. R. W. Home, 'Science as a career in eighteenth-century Russia: the case of F. U. T. Aepinus', *Slavic and East European Review*, 51 (1973), 75–94.
21. See Woolf, *Transits of Venus*, p. 124 and n. 78.
22. Whether or not to any extent influenced by Chappe's disparaging account of Russian science, the French Academy of Sciences declined to take part in any of these expeditions. For the record, Chappe in 1769 made highly successful observations from Mexico, but he and most of his expedition perished there from typhus.
23. See Loren R. Graham, *Science in Russia and the Soviet Union* (Cambridge University Press, 1993), pp. 2, 25; see also Vucinich, *Science in Russian Culture: A History to 1860*, chapters 2–3.
24. See Woolf, *Transits of Venus*, pp. 179–82.
25. See Vucinich, *Science in Russian Culture: A History to 1860*, pp. 240, 264, 309–10, and entries for these mathematicians in the *Dictionary of Scientific Biography* (New York: Charles Scribner and Sons, 1972).
26. See W. J. Leatherbarrow and D. C. Offord (eds.), *A Documentary History of Russian Thought: From the Enlightenment to Marxism* (Ann Arbor: Ardis, 1987), p. 61.
27. Vucinich, *Science in Russian Culture 1861–1917* (Stanford University Press, 1970), p. 35.
28. See Graham, *Science in Russia and the Soviet Union*, p. 41.
29. *Dictionary of Scientific Biography*.
30. From the entry for 'scientism' in *Chambers Dictionary* (Edinburgh: Harrap, 1993).
31. 'Antropologicheskii printsip v filosofii' in N. G. Chernyshevskii, *Polnoe sobranie sochinenii*, 15 vols. (Moscow: Gosudarstvennoe izdatel'stvo 'Khudozhestvennaia literatura', 1939–50), vol. VII, pp. 222–95, here p. 240.
32. See J. A. Rogers, 'Darwinism, scientism and nihilism', *Russian Review*, 19 (1960), 10–23.
33. A. O. Kovalevskii, as quoted in Daniel P. Todes, *Darwin without Malthus* (Oxford University Press, 1989), p. 23.
34. See the *Dictionary of Scientific Biography* entries on Sechenov and Pavlov.
35. Chernyshevskii, *Polnoe sobranie sochinenii*, vol. VII, p. 223.
36. Chernyshevskii, 'Proiskhozhdenie teorii blagorodnosti bor'by za zhizn'' (1888) in *Polnoe sobranie sochinenii*, vol. X, pp. 737–72.
37. Todes, *Darwin without Malthus*.
38. Charles Darwin, *On the Origin of Species by Means of Natural Selection*, ed. J. W. Burrow (London: Penguin, 1985), pp. 116–17.
39. Chernyshevskii, *Polnoe sobranie sochinenii*, vol. X, p. 744, and see Ellis, 'The Scientific Revolutions', pp. 51–2. See Ernst Mayr, *The Growth of Biological Thought* (Cambridge, Mass., and London: Harvard University Press, 1982),

pp. 364–5 for a discussion of Cuvier's notions of essentialism and embranchments in animal species.

40. See Mayr, *The Growth of Biological Thought*, pp. 358–62, 700–1.
41. P. L. Lavrov, *Opyt istorii mysli novogo vremeni*, 2 vols. (Geneva: Vol'naia russkaia tipografiia, 1888–91), vol. I, p. 179.
42. 'Zametki o darvinizme' in N. K. Mikhailovskii, *Sochineniia*, 6 vols. (St Petersburg: Russkoe bogatstvo, 1896–7), pp. 270–300, especially p. 300.
43. Mayr quite justifiably insists that the more appropriate term here should be 'Social Spencerism': see Mayr, *The Growth of Biological Thought*, p. 386 and p. 536, n. 4. Mayr's contempt for Spencer's contribution to the debate on Darwinism is uninhibited.
44. Mikhailovskii, *Chto takoe progress?* in *Sochineniia*, vol. I, pp. 1–150, here p. 150.
45. Lavrov, *Opyt istorii mysli*, vol. I, p. 281.
46. Richard Dawkins, *The Selfish Gene* (Oxford University Press, 1989), p. 332.
47. P. A. Kropotkin, *Mutual Aid* (London: Allen Lane, 1972).
48. This is a point particularly stressed by S. J. Gould, 'Kropotkin was no crackpot' in *Bully for Brontosaurus: Further Reflections in Natural History* (London: Penguin, 1992). But see Ellis, 'The Scientific Revolutions', p. 158.
49. See Kropotkin, *Mutual Aid*, pp. 60–1.
50. See M. A. Miller, *Kropotkin* (University of Chicago Press, 1976), pp. 184ff.
51. Kropotkin, *Mutual Aid*, p. 251.
52. G. L. Kline, 'Darwinism and the Russian Orthodox Church' (1955) in Ernest J. Simmons (ed.), *Continuity and Change in Russian Thought* (New York: Russell, 1967), p. 327.
53. Mikhailovsky is convincing in his denial of teleology in natural processes (though not specifically in rejoinder to von Baer or Cuvier). See Ellis, 'The Scientific Revolutions', pp. 126–8.
54. N. Ia. Danilevskii (ed.), *Rossiia i Evropa* [1869] (New York and London: Johnson Reprint Corporation, 1966).
55. Todes, *Darwin without Malthus*, p. 41, appropriately draws this parallel in his discussion of Danilevsky's work.
56. See Diane Oenning Thompson, 'Dostoevskii and science' in W. J. Leatherbarrow (ed.), *The Cambridge Companion to Dostoevskii* (Cambridge University Press, 2002), chapter 10.
57. See the prologue to Paul Strathern, *Mendeleyev's Dream* (London: Penguin, 2001).
58. Vucinich, 'Mendeleev's views on science and society', *Isis*, 18 (1967), 342–51, especially 345.
59. Vucinich, *Science in Russian Culture 1861–1917*, chapter 15.

PART IV

The afterlife of classical thought

CHAPTER 14

Continuities in the Soviet period

Galin Tihanov

Intellectual history presents a bundle of continuities and discontinuities enacted, sometimes simultaneously, within cultures that evolve over time. In this essay I focus on the continuities that permeate – often hidden behind dramatic political changes – the scene of philosophy and social thought in the Soviet period, from the October Revolution in 1917 to the demise of the USSR in 1991. Limitations of space mean that difficult decisions have had to be made as to what ought to be included and what could be left out. Since the dominant intellectual paradigm of the period was Marxism, it was beyond doubt that any serious engagement with the question of continuity must not simply address Marxism but should actually put it right at the centre of attention. Ignoring Marxism and preferring instead to explore solely various non-Marxist discourses would have resulted in a failure to grasp the crucial place of Marxism in the often subterranean dynamics of stability and change which sustained and shot through the public discourses of philosophy and the social sciences in the Soviet period. With reference to Marxism, the continuity inscribed in this dialectic of permanence and transformation had two important aspects: the self-awareness and positioning of Soviet Marxism vis-à-vis western non-Marxist philosophy, and through this, but also independently of it, vis-à-vis pre-1917 Russian thought.

The second part of the essay examines various discourses of exceptionalism, concentrating on the revival of Slavophilism, *pochvennichestvo* (a current of thought that crystallised in the 1860s and displayed some affinities with Slavophilism but was more unambiguously conservative and at times also anti-Semitic) and Eurasianism. The emphasis here is deliberately on developments in the Soviet Union. I have elected not to include a separate overview of émigré currents of thought, because this would have reproduced the wrong notion of Russian émigré intellectuals as being the only heirs to the pre-1917 tradition, thus also reinforcing the long-maintained – and rather misleading – picture of a constant and unbridgeable chasm between Soviet and émigré intellectual life. The diaspora and the mainland were involved in a historically changing dynamic of impact, with Soviet culture and thought being more influential among the diaspora before the Second World War, followed, especially since the 1960s, by an extended period in which émigré thought (both of pre- and post-Second World War provenance) was increasingly consequential for the Soviet debates. The detailed identification of the impact of Soviet intellectual developments on the various émigré currents of thought, as well as the thorough examination of the relevance of the latter for Soviet intellectual life, are all tasks for the future (a comprehensive study, to take just one important example, of the reception of Soviet Marxism in the Russian diaspora before 1945 is yet to be written). Here I can only begin to set the overall agenda, sketching very briefly the (dis)continuities revealed in the revival of Eurasianism in the Soviet Union. (Other instructive cases, well researched by now, concern the overlaps and exchanges between émigré thinkers and intellectuals living in the Soviet Union involved in the appropriation – in Harbin, Prague, Paris, Moscow, Kaluga, Petrograd and Minsk (to name only a few of the locations) – of Fedorov's ideas, as well as the impact of Berdiaev's émigré works, particularly his *New Middle Ages*, in the 1960s when, together with Djilas's *The New Class*, they became an inspiration for the opposition group VSKhSON (the All-Russian Social-Christian Union for the Liberation of the People), established in Leningrad in 1964.)[1]

Finally, for the purposes of this chapter I have decided to focus on the continuities with pre-1917 Russian thought. This qualification is not trivial. The seven decades of Soviet history were long enough for continuities to begin to develop between focal points of thought elaborated after the October Revolution. But this process was hampered by various factors and, on the whole, began to come to prominence only at the very end of the Soviet period, around 1990, reaching fruition in the years afterwards. Thus throughout the formative stages of the Tartu–Moscow School of semiotics and cultural theory neither Shpet (who in the 1920s published important work foreshadowing various tenets of structuralism and semiotics), nor Losev (one of the first philosophers in the Soviet Union to ponder concepts such as 'sign' and 'structure') were actively appropriated by Lotman and his colleagues. Losev even complained in 1968 that he was not being cited in their works.[2] Only Florensky seemed to have been received and appropriated more intensely by the Tartu–Moscow School. Contrast this largely broken line of continuity in the 1960s with the impact of Bakhtin towards the end of the 1980s. Not only did he leave a visible trace in a string of more specialised historical and literary studies in the 1970s and 1980s by pre-eminent intellectuals such as Likhachev, Averintsev and

Gurevich, but by 1991, the year of the collapse of the Soviet Union, his theory of dialogism had become the cornerstone of Bibler's doctrine of 'dialogue of cultures', which assisted Bibler and his associates in developing new school curricula and a new philosophy of education.[3] Thus, while in the epilogue I add one more significant example of Soviet philosophy of history and culture engaging with earlier Soviet thought, the exposition remains largely concerned with continuities that form a bridge to pre-revolutionary intellectual developments.

CONTINUITIES WITHIN SOVIET MARXISM

The political rupture of 1917 and the ensuing consolidation of Marxism as a ruling ideology have long served to obscure several important points of continuity with the past. To begin with, until 1930, when Losev's *The Dialectics of Myth* was published in Moscow (containing a qualification of dialectical materialism as an 'outright absurdity'),[4] philosophising in a non-Marxist key and publicising the results of such activity continued to be a legitimate business. Second, the backbone of philosophical education continued to include, well into the 1940s, both pre-revolutionary textbooks and the works of a significant number of non-Marxist philosophers (many of them – but not all – drawn into the orbit of materialism and dialectics like their predecessors). At the end of the 1920s even at the leading Institute of Red Professors the old pre-1917 textbooks on the history of philosophy were still being widely used;[5] when logic was restored to the curriculum in 1946, the use of a pre-revolutionary textbook by Chelpanov was permitted.[6] According to figures supplied by Mitin, one of Stalin's most powerful official philosophers, in the period 1897–1916 Aristotle's works were published in a total of 1,000 copies, Hegel's in 4,500 copies and Spinoza's in 7,700 copies. In 1917–38 these figures rose, respectively, to 78,300, 200,500 and 55,200.[7] As late as 1936 the required reading for the postgraduate oral examinations in philosophy at the Institute of History, Philosophy and Literature included – along with Marx, Lenin and Stalin – Kant, Hegel, Aristotle, Bacon, Hobbes, Locke, Descartes, Spinoza, Leibniz and Hume.[8] The only demonstrable weakness of the philosophy curriculum, apart from the rigidly controlled ideological interpretation, was the neglect of twentieth-century western philosophy. Even after the list of canonical western names was extended further, following suggestions for a curriculum reform in 1938, it still stopped with Nietzsche (whose year of death – 1900 – appropriately indicated the disregard for twentieth-century non-Marxist philosophy).[9]

But most importantly, well into the 1920s Soviet Marxism still bore the birthmarks of a tradition of thought originating at the crossroads of Russian 'Legal Marxism', 'Christian socialism' and various attempts to reconcile Marxism with neo-Kantianism and the philosophy of Mach. Three of the most illustrious representatives of Russian religious thought in the twentieth century – Berdiaev, Sergey Bulgakov and Frank – had actually started their intellectual careers as sympathisers of Marxism and the socialist idea. Others, notably Lunacharsky and Gorky, had engaged with Marxism as part of a social platform that presented a powerful mixture of religious idealism and radical Nietzschean activism (the resulting doctrine, vestiges of which continued to be influential into the mid-1920s, is usually referred to as *bogostroitel'stvo* (God-building)). Others still, especially Plekhanov and Bogdanov, had anchored Marxism in a paradigm of thought that was either more broadly sociological (Plekhanov) or rooted in a more sympathetic appropriation of contemporary western philosophy (Bogdanov). While Bogdanov was never really admitted to the canon of official Soviet Marxism (he was criticised in the 1920s for wishing to dissolve Marxism into his own 'general science of organisation', the so-called *tektology*)[10], Plekhanov, whose work fell almost entirely in the pre-1917 period, enjoyed a more uneven reputation. It reflected the waves of relaxation and ossification in official doctrine and the successive mobilisations of Marxism for the purposes of establishing Stalin's authority and advancing the agenda of nation-building. For most of the 1920s Plekhanov remained an authority for all those seeking to inscribe Marxism in a materialist tradition of thought that could lay claim to a serious pedigree going back to Spinoza. (Deborin even drew a distinction between Lenin and Plekhanov, describing the latter – approvingly – as 'the theoretician', while Lenin was praised for being 'the man of action, the politician, the leader'.)[11] In the early 1930s, however, Plekhanov fell from grace for exactly the same reason: he was chastised for considering dialectical materialism a mere strand of materialism, not essentially different from other varieties of materialism in western thought. At the same time, he became unacceptable also because of his admonition (towards the end of his life) that Soviet Russia had not had a sufficiently long capitalist evolution, and that therefore socialism had not been allowed to emerge as the result of a natural process of radicalising the contradictions of capitalism. Yet in the early 1940s, amid a new wave of nationalist propaganda during the war, Plekhanov resurfaced once again as part of the canon of Russian Marxist thought. Pavel Iudin praised him in 1943 as 'the greatest and most distinguished Marxist, after Marx and Engels, of the pre-Lenin epoch', a 'great patriot' and a thinker who had enriched 'Russian national culture'.[12]

Plekhanov's consistent and, in the 1920s, still influential attempt to derive Marxism, including its understanding of society and social change, from the tradition of western materialism is a helpful reminder of the larger continuities characteristic of the Soviet period. The evolution of Soviet Marxism was marked by an incessant need to deal with its presumed and actual forefathers; the work of establishing the intellectual genealogy of Marxism continued after 1917 and was the one aspect of Marxist thought in the Soviet Union that did not lose momentum even in the decades of Stalinism. Two figures of western philosophy became the main points of reference in this debate, Hegel and Spinoza, although the search for legitimate predecessors was often extended to encompass Feuerbach, as well as the major representatives of nineteenth-century German idealism.[13] Both Spinoza and Hegel have been generic concerns for Marxism (as the work on Spinoza by western Marxists, notably Althusser and Balibar, and on Hegel by Lucio Coletti and Antonio Negri among others, testifies), but the Soviet debates were particularly intense. By the early 1930s Russian literature on Spinoza exceeded in quantity that of any country in the West.[14] The publication of Lunacharsky's *From Spinoza to Marx* (1925), which restated some of Lunacharsky's positions from the time of his *bogostroitel'stvo*, was part and parcel of the growing polemic about Spinoza that took place in the second half of the 1920s. Coming from very different methodological perspectives, and reaching very different conclusions, Liubov Akselrod (the major philosopher of the mechanists, also known by the pseudonym 'Orthodox') and Deborin (the leader of the opposite camp, which was to become known by his name) both sought to determine the relationship between Spinoza's philosophy and Marxist materialism. Much later, Ilenkov re-engaged with Spinoza in his innovative studies of Marx. He even planned to write a book on Spinoza, but the project did not materialise.[15]

The persistent preoccupation with Hegel was of particular importance for Soviet Marxism, because it would put it in an initially direct (then increasingly mediated) contact with a very long tradition of Russian non-Marxist philosophical appropriations of the German philosopher, stretching from the Slavophiles to Ivan Ilin, who just a year after the October Revolution had published a two-volume study of Hegel and the 'concreteness of God and man'. Lenin, whose own *Philosophical Notebooks* (published posthumously in 1929) contained ample evidence of his ambition to master Hegel's methodology, is said to have liked the book so much that he decided to release Ilin from prison (which did not save him from deportation in 1922).[16]

Interest in Hegel was further motivated by the necessity to gauge the originality of the Marxist dialectical method. Deborin made the first sustained effort to do that in his book *Marx and Hegel* (1923), which was later criticised on the grounds that it overemphasised Hegel's role. Realising Hegel's significance for the principles and even the vocabulary of Soviet Marxism (the important concept of *partiinost'* was little more than a replica of Hegel's *Parteilichkeit*),[17] a Party resolution envisaged the speedy publication of a fifteen-volume edition of his works by 1932 (not completed, in fact, until well after the Second World War).[18] Hegel also figured prominently in the famous third volume of the collective *History of Philosophy* (1943), which gained the nickname 'the grey horse' (describing both the colour of its binding and its intellectual power). The chapter on Hegel occupied more than ninety pages (equalling the combined space allocated to the five thinkers discussed under the heading 'utopian socialism'), stressing his central position in the pre-history of Marxism and arguing for Hegelian dialectics as the 'pinnacle of all bourgeois thought' and the achievement of a 'genius thinker'.[19] As was the case with Plekhanov's rising stock, the nationalist ideological campaign of the war years clearly affected the fate of 'the grey horse'. Although seven volumes were conceived (and the volume on Russian philosophy, number six in the series, was already in preparation), and although the authors had been awarded the Stalin Prize in 1942 for the two preceding volumes, the Party in 1944 decreed that the third volume had been a serious mistake, allegedly failing to expose the limitations of Hegel's idealist dialectics and to criticise his glorification of the Germans as a 'chosen people'. Thus the whole multi-volume project came to an end.[20] Lukács, a prominent exile in Stalin's Moscow, at the end of 1942 defended a professorial dissertation on the young Hegel as an important forebear of Marxism. After the Party resolution of 1944, attempts to publish Lukács's dissertation as a book in Russian invariably failed (it was only in 1956 that a portion of *Young Hegel* appeared in *Problems of Philosophy*; the book in its entirety was not published in Russian until 1987). In 1947 Zhdanov declared at an official gathering of Soviet philosophers that the Hegel issue had been settled.[21]

Yet the need to keep alive the internal dialogue of Marxism with the traditions of western thought – and through this also, if not always directly, with pre-1917 Russian philosophy – was acutely felt once again during the revival of Marxist philosophy after Stalin's death. Beginning in the mid-1930s and through to the early 1950s, the serious study of Marxism in the Soviet Union had suffered neglect. In 1935 the 'Marx, Engels, Lenin' Institute suspended publication of the German-language edition of the collected works of Marx and Engels, with only twelve of the planned forty volumes published. Work on the Russian-language edition continued until 1947.[22] The decade from 1947 (the year that saw the public condemnation, led by Zhdanov, of G. F. Aleksandrov's *History of Western Philosophy*) until the mid-1950s, when the 'thaw' years began, could confidently be regarded as the direst time for philosophy in the Soviet Union. When in the early 1950s a group of young philosophers at Moscow State University (MGU), including Ilenkov and the future dissident writer and sociologist Aleksandr Zinoviev, began to study the logic of Marx's *Capital*, both Hegel and Spinoza were revived once again. Ilenkov and his colleagues were soon stigmatised as 'gnoseologists', for they believed that philosophy should above all be a method of cognition rather than an all-encompassing outlook. Ilenkov was not allowed to teach at MGU, and the publication of his dissertation was delayed until 1960.[23] Two years later Ilenkov published his celebrated article 'The Ideal', which tried to carve out a set of specifically ideal (as opposed to simply mental) phenomena and to argue the case for their objective existence anchored in human activity. (He expanded this thesis in the mid-1970s, without adding significantly to the original forcefulness of the argument.)[24] It was precisely in the early 1960s that Ilenkov did his best work, persistently marked by a deep interest in Hegel. The starting-point of his study of Marx's *Capital* was Hegel's question: 'Who thinks abstractly?' Ilenkov argued that our first encounter with an object is always an encounter with the abstract (not with the concrete, as the empiricist materialists believed), the result of an abstraction that categorises the object without being able to penetrate into the multitude of forms, processes and contradictions that the concrete life of the object involves. Thus he described Marx's thought as an ascent from the abstract to the concrete, and as an oscillation between the historical and the logical.

While an innovator in the interpretation of Marx, Ilenkov had distinctly conservative ideas in the realm of aesthetics. He was a lifelong admirer of Wagner but rejected pop art and Andy Warhol (his mistrust of pop art was shared by his older friend Lifshits). Having seen an exhibition of contemporary art in Vienna in 1964, Ilenkov came back subdued, his belief in the ability of art to serve as the vehicle of humanism severely dented.[25] Rather than a dissident, Ilenkov was perhaps the best mind of the 'people of the sixties' (*shestidesiatniki*), the generation that came on the crest of the short-lived 'thaw' and suffered throughout the years of Brezhnev's stagnation without giving up its hope that the system could be reformed from within. Having prepared in the mid-1970s a typewritten translation of Orwell's *1984*, Ilenkov still believed that this was a book tracing the latent tendency towards totalitarianism in capitalist societies, not a communist dystopia.[26]

Not much younger than Ilenkov, but with his formative years spent in a very dissimilar way, Mamardashvili largely shared Ilenkov's non-dissident orientation, yet he did not intend his work in philosophy as a tool for the renewal of Marxism. If anything, Mamardashvili's philosophising (much of it done in the form of lectures rather than in print) signalled the end of Soviet Marxism's claim to an intellectual monopoly. The gulf between his and Ilenkov's disposition probably stemmed from the fact that Mamardashvili was still too young to be called up during the Second World War; further-more, his Georgian upbringing and his early love for French culture were reasons enough for him to be perceived as more cosmopolitan and less prepared to get immediately involved in the civic agenda of Soviet philo-sophy. Touched by privilege and luck, Mamardashvili served in the 1960s on the editorial staff of the Prague-based journal *Problems of Peace and Socialism.* He could travel to France and Italy, made the acquaintance of Althusser (with whom he later corresponded and met on occasion), and became an admirer of jazz and Proust. Philosophically, too, Mamardashvili thought he had moved away from Ilenkov by turning his back on the dominant influence of Hegel. In fact, he referred to Ilenkov's philosophy as 'too Hegelian'.[27] This, however, could not conceal the fact that Mamardashvili's first book, *Forms and Content of Thinking* (1968), drew inspiration precisely from Hegel in order to articu-late an understanding of consciousness as a supra-individual phenomenon that has its binding forms (objective Spirit), existing as it were in 'estrange-ment' from the consciousness of the individual. Ironically, it was this anti-psychologism, which Mamardashvili learnt from Hegel and Marx rather than from Husserl, that later guided him to question their idea of 'iron necessity' and to ask how we can avoid nihilism if we admit that our actions are causally determined. In the words of an astute Russian commentator, Mamardashvili's question became how to reconcile a scientific (Marxist) approach to history and consciousness 'with the phenomenon of freedom, the uniqueness of our personality, our dignity'.[28] In his bid to solve the conundrum, Mamardashvili outlined a typology of rationality, which forms the focal point of what is probably his best book.[29] The 'classic ideal of rationality' separates the thinking subject from the reality he aspires to know. This is meant to be a guarantee of the objectivity of knowledge, but it actually amounts to a crippling dualism: the thinking human being is pushed as if beyond and outside the world he strives to understand; all his subjective experiences are also expelled in the process. The 'non-classic ideal of ration-ality' restores to the individual his lawful place in the world. As the thinking person gets reinstated as an integral part of reality, consciousness and cogni-tion cease to be a reflection (and even refraction) of that reality; they are now seen ontologically, as events that take place and unfold in the world. Consciousness becomes an effort, a creative act that no longer tries to banish our subjective experiences; instead, it underwrites the existence of freedom. In his lectures on Proust (1984–5) Mamardashvili took this argument further, demonstrating that in the creative event of consciousness the past, present and future are no longer clearly demarcated. Were it not for our effort, the future might not come to be; it is not simply available to us in the mode of ontological certainty. On the other hand, in the act of a creative effort (consciousness) the past may come alive once again. This is where Mamardashvili begins to leave behind Soviet Marxism as a cultural and social project. On the surface, his assertion of human effort and activity is only a reformulation of Marx's famous theses on Feuerbach. In truth, Mamardashvili's praise of effort is also an admission of uncertainty, an embrace of open-endedness, coloured by an optimistic vision of self-fashioning but equally tinged by an anxious realisation that the pursuit of happiness cannot be a collective project.

What is even more significant for our argument is the fact that with Ilenkov and Mamardashvili Soviet Marxism had once again reached the point – for the first time since the 1930s – of self-reflexive engagement with the non-Marxist philosophical tradition in Russia. (In 1943 the mediocre but powerful Party philosopher Iovchuk had organised the first Soviet chair in the History of Russian Philosophy,[30] but this amounted to little more than fuelling Russian nationalism while guarding the purity of Marxist-Leninist dogma.) In the latter half of the 1950s Ilenkov was the centre of a circle of young intellectuals – many of them later to confirm their credentials as conservative and even nationalist thinkers – which included, among others, Davydov, Kozhinov, Gachev, Bocharov and Palievsky.[31] Ilenkov's essay of that time, 'Cosmology of Spirit' (first published posthumously in 1988), has been interpreted as exhibiting a number of parallels with Fedorov's anti-positivist and anti-individualist philosophy of nature, although the question of whether Ilenkov had actually read Fedorov remains open.[32] It is well documented, however, that he was familiar with the work of the Bakhtin Circle, displaying enthusiasm for Medvedev's *The Formal Method in Literary Scholarship* (1928) but remaining indifferent towards Bakhtin's *Problems of Dostoevsky's Poetics* (1963).[33]

More importantly, while Ilenkov did not sympathise with the Slavophiles and, provoked by Kozhinov, voiced disapproval of both Ivan Kireevsky's works and his countenance,[34] his view of Marxism as the offspring of a long western cultural tradition (he called Marx a 'son of the West' and described Lenin in exactly the same words)[35] no doubt implied a certain antagonism between Marxism and the currents of Russian thought whose legacy had come to be tested after the Revolution. Unlike Berdiaev, Ilenkov did not hold Communism to be the organic outgrowth of specific eastern (Russian) circumstances; but in calling Lenin a 'son of the West' he nonetheless evoked the old framework of opposition between Westernisers and Slavophiles that had served to organise the discussion of Russian intellectual life for several decades before 1917.

Mamardashvili shared Ilenkov's suspicion regarding a Russian *Sonderweg* in philosophy. He places Chaadaev at the beginning of modern Russian thought, but notes at the same time that Chaadaev failed to generate a tradition; his work faded without yielding further impulse. Philosophy as an autonomous enterprise, Mamardashvili believed, commenced with Solovev. Not unlike Shpet before him, Mamardashvili was convinced that philosophy cannot exist and flourish where the struggle for social justice takes the upper hand. This is why he contends that Russian philosophy either never existed, or only began to emerge at the end of the nineteenth century, denying Soviet philosophy autonomy and considering it part of what he terms, borrowing from Althusser, 'the ideological state apparatus'. Mamardashvili was equally sceptical of the time-honoured practice of substituting nineteenth-century Russian literature for philosophy; in particular, Dostoevsky was to him a helpless 'idiot' as soon as he moved on to the level of philosophical reflection. Tolstoy, on the other hand, was granted the status of a great religious thinker.[36]

The singling out of Solovev as the inceptor of autonomous Russian philosophy is not accidental. While careful to distinguish between Russian philosophy and Russian literature, Mamardashvili – despite his pronounced secularism and predilection for western philosophy – is more willing to see the complex mediations between philosophy and religious thought in the Russian context. The two, he believed, intersected and overlapped above all in the field of eschatology. The 'eschatological note' continued to be present into the 1920s, embodied by thinkers and writers shaped by the Silver Age.[37] In the same lecture, delivered in Leningrad on 2 December 1988, Mamardashvili paid tribute to a host of Russian religious thinkers, notably Berdiaev, Shestov and, above all, Rozanov, whose *Apocalypse of Our Time* received special praise.[38] Thus instead of drawing an impenetrable boundary between philosophy and religious thought in Russia, Mamardashvili essayed to see them as discursive formations that often occupied the same territory and were involved in a dialectic of exchange and competition.

DISCOURSES OF EXCEPTIONALISM

If Soviet Marxism was thus able to remain in dialogue with non-Marxist Russian thought, or at least to exhibit a degree of self-awareness and reflexivity vis-à-vis the traditions of pre-1917 Russian thought, other intellectual currents were much more prominent in their role as guardians of the tradition. In addition to a host of nineteenth-century intellectuals actively appropriated and often interpreted in a rather strained fashion by Soviet Marxism as early exponents of revolutionary thinking (Belinsky, Herzen, Chernyshevsky, Pisarev), a wider alternative corpus of Russian thought was gradually being reassembled in the Soviet Union. At first, this included solely nineteenth-century thinkers and writers: five previously unknown 'Philosophical Letters' by Chaadaev were published as early as 1935, along with Leontev's autobiography (all in vols. 22–4 of the prestigious series *Literaturnoe nasledstvo*). Later, during the 'thaw' years, Lossky's and Zenkovsky's histories of Russian philosophy appeared in the Soviet Union in small print runs (in 1954 and 1956, respectively); dissemination was restricted on both occasions to people in the Party hierarchy and to those entrusted with leading positions in Soviet ideological life.

The rediscovery of Russian religious thought began in earnest in the late 1960s and early 1970s, with a series of articles written for the five-volume Soviet *Philosophical Encyclopaedia* by Losev, Averintsev, Asmus, Khoruzhy and others. The article on Solovev in the final volume (1970) was, much to everybody's surprise, longer than even the entry on Engels.[39] This particular volume also contained articles on Khomiakov, Florensky, Shestov, Fedorov and other religious thinkers, all of them written informatively and in a respectful tone. A two-volume edition of Skovoroda's works appeared in 1973, followed by a volume of Kireevsky's writings in 1979. The first half of the 1980s saw editions of some of the essays of Konstantin and Ivan Aksakov, but probably the most tumultuous event of the 1980s, still before Gorbachev commenced his reforms in 1985, was the appearance in 1982 of a volume of selected essays by Fedorov, edited by the renowned Kant and Schelling scholar Arseny Gulyga and withdrawn from the bookshops soon after publication.[40] Together with Losev (who by the time of his death in 1988 had managed to write a short introduction and a more extensive book on Solovev),[41] Gulyga had started work in the 1970s on a three-volume edition of Solovev's principal works, which was to materialise as a two-volume selection in 1988. The same year saw a Politburo resolution decreeing that a series of republications of Russian non-Marxist philosophy be launched in 1989. Berdiaev, Shpet, Bakunin, Chaadaev, Florensky,

Frank, Rozanov, Losev, Kropotkin, Ern, Iurkevich, as well as the important collective volumes *Landmarks* and *Out of the Depths*, were all published in this series in 1989–91.

Crucially, however, this chronology of rediscovery must not conceal the fact that, as Vladimir Smirnov notes in his memoirs of Asmus, the pre-1917 editions of Russian philosophy had actually always been freely available in the public libraries; they never formed part of the special depositories and, what is more, in the years following the Second World War these pre-1917 editions could also be bought in second-hand bookshops.[42] When at the beginning of the 1970s clandestine religious circles began to be formed in Leningrad, the works of Berdiaev, Florensky and Sergey Bulgakov were all discussed in the meetings (attended sometimes by thirty to fifty people).[43] Similarly, when the organised meetings of the Anthroposophical Society resumed in Moscow in 1969, Russian and western pre-1917 works were once again read and examined.[44] Russian pre-1917 thought was thus revived and studied in waves of appropriation and accommodation that were no doubt politically conditioned and subject to considerable censorship but had nonetheless been in evidence long before the more propitious time of the 1980s.

Let me illustrate this argument with a brief look at the appropriation in the Soviet Union of two powerful pre-1917 discourses of exceptionalism, Slavophilism and *pochvennichestvo*. For some two decades after 1917, Slavophilism seemed entirely forgotten; its conservative charge meant that it was considered squarely incompatible with the tenets of Soviet ideology. In the early 1920s, while ideological control was still rather lax, Shpet famously claimed that it was the Slavophiles who had formulated 'the only original problems of Russian philosophy'.[45] Bakhtin, in his lectures on Russian literature given privately in the 1920s, recommended Slavophilism as 'a significant phenomenon in the history of Russian thought', calling Westernism 'just a soap bubble that produced nothing but phrases before bursting'.[46] At the State Academy of Artistic Sciences (GAKhN), where Shpet served as Vice-President from 1924 to 1929, Losev gave in March 1928 an apparently intriguing paper on the aesthetics and language theory of Konstantin Aksakov.[47] Yet it was only in the late 1930s, as Stalin's politics of russification and nation-building gathered pace and the discourse of *narodnost'* surfaced once again in public discussions, that Slavophilism was put on the agenda in earnest. The key issue was how to evaluate Slavophilism historically, how to discern – from a Marxist perspective – the progressive and the retrograde in the platform of the Slavophiles. This debate began in 1939 with an article by Nikolay

Druzhinin, on 'Herzen and the Slavophiles', in which he made the telling (but inaccurate) claim that no research had been published on the Slavophiles since 1917.[48] Two years later Sergey Dmitriev contributed to the same journal an article which, while branding Slavophilism 'a variety of reactionary-nationalist Romanticism', took the liberty of noting some progressive features and concluded that, objectively, the Slavophiles were in favour of a 'Prussian route' for Russian capitalism. This relativisation of the opposition between Slavophiles and Westernisers was a novel element, and it was unambiguously criticised in the ensuing discussion.[49]

The mainstream view of the Slavophiles as upholders of tradition and thinkers with unmistakably conservative leanings was not overturned during the 1940s, but it was defended with arguments that could potentially destabilise the official ideology. Lidiia Ginzburg, one of the most distinguished liberal intellectuals of the Soviet age, turned her attention in a book published in 1940 to Lermontov,[50] who knew Samarin and Khomiakov and whose poetry was favoured in Slavophile circles. In fact, Ginzburg produced arguments undermining the case for affinity between Lermontov and the Slavophiles. But while doing that, she arrived at a subversive version of the official Soviet literary canon. According to Ginzburg, in the 1840s there was a trend among the left-wing Westernisers to prefer Lermontov, in contrast to a distinctive Slavophile preference for Pushkin.[51] Thus in Ginzburg's account Pushkin's supremacy and reserved seat in the canon were subjected to scrutiny and put in question, becoming tainted by association with the conservative Slavophile camp.

Ginzburg's book is important in one more respect. It points to the fact that debates on Slavophilism in the Soviet Union would begin, as was also often the case before 1917, as debates on literature and aesthetics but would end up as debates on ideology and philosophy. This was not just because the Slavophiles were themselves literati (not very successful ones), but also because questions of identity, culture and language were so central to their endeavours and to those of the Soviet philosophers, historians and literary scholars who examined their work. Literature and aesthetics became the focal point of the second defining moment in Soviet debates on Slavophilism, and a springboard for attempts to re-evaluate the overall cultural and political significance of Slavophilism. This second discussion took place at the end of the 1960s, starting in 1968 in *Problems of Literature* and continuing in the same journal and in *New World* in 1969, the year that saw the publication in Leningrad of a representative volume of Khomiakov's poems and plays.[52] Among the participants were two literary scholars, Boris Egorov and Vadim Kozhinov, representing two very different orientations in the Soviet intellectual landscape. While Egorov was close to Lotman and the Tartu School (after Lotman's death Egorov wrote his biography), Kozhinov had already set off on a journey that would make him one of the principal revivers of *pochvennichestvo*. In the wake of the discussion, Egorov conceived an article that inscribed the culture and the outlook of the Slavophiles and the Westernisers in a wider semiotic system, thus projecting and emphasising a typological similarity rather than a set of non-negotiable differences between the two.[53] Kozhinov, too, sought to relax the opposition between Slavophilism and Westernism, but he went much further than Egorov. Kozhinov saw the underlying characteristic of Slavophilism as its insistence on Russia's uniqueness and originality rather than as the espousal of traditionalism and aristocratic values. He was adamant that this doctrine had no 'political colouration'; rather, it was shared by thinkers from across the ideological spectrum: Populists, monarchists, socialists, aristocrats and democrats alike. The same variety, Kozhinov believed, could also be observed within Westernism. This invites the conclusion that no 'ideological watershed' ran between Slavophilism and Westernism as such: they both strove to 'understand objectively the essence of Russia's historical path and culture'; each of the two grasped certain aspects of the truth, while missing others.[54] (This complementarity no doubt reminds the reader of Berdiaev's dictum: 'both sides loved Russia; the Slavophiles as a mother, the Westernisers as a child'.)[55] Drawing on Kireevsky, Kozhinov submits that the Slavophiles continued the Platonic rather than the Aristotelian line in philosophy; their suspicion vis-à-vis the undivided authority of rationalism and the seminality of abstract thought and their attention to a holistic notion of the human being enabled them to foreshadow certain features of twentieth-century Existentialism. On the other hand, their organic vision of the people, of a historically evolving collectivity, and of the need to enrich the life of the people with the practical benefits of philosophy separated them clearly – and safely – from the Existentialists. The Slavophiles were admittedly idealists, but that was no reason to disqualify and exclude them from the history of Russian thought, where idealism (as opposed to materialism) was the ground 'on which a plethora of deep philosophical discoveries were born, which were needed by mankind'.[56]

This forceful rehabilitation of the Slavophiles at the end of the 1960s marked at the same time the beginning of the revival of *pochvennichestvo* in the Soviet Union, a process that by the end of the 1980s was drawing into its orbit not just Kozhinov, one of the inveterate 'pochvenniks or neo-Slavophiles' (as Bakhtin called Kozhinov, while trying to shield him from accusations of anti-Semitism),[57] but even the renowned historian of western (in particular German) philosophy Arseny Gulyga. During the late 1970s and early 1980s Gulyga gradually refocused his attention on Russian nineteenth-century thinkers (Fedorov and Solovev), joined the proponents of Russian exceptionalism, contributing to the conservative periodical *Our Contemporary* an essay that read at the time like a catalogue of nationalist demands,[58] and eventually arrived – while maintaining that he was no religious 'fanatic' – at a preference for Russian Orthodoxy as a form of Christianity that 'endows man, more than western versions of Christianity, with freedom of will'.[59] In an article written in 1990, he asserted that the philosophical centre of the world had been shifting towards Russia since the 1870s, a process that lasted until the 1920s, thanks to the universality of Russian religious thought and its three distinctive features: love, faith-informed collectivity (*sobornost*) and cosmic addressivity.[60]

The reawakening of the conservative idea of Russian uniqueness some-times drew explicitly on emblematic nineteenth-century Russian thinkers and writers, chiefly Dostoevsky (although, as the work of the liberal Grigory Pomerants demonstrates, Dostoevsky was not the exclusive property of the exceptionalists).[61] Iury Davydov, another intellectual who had begun as an expert in, and connoisseur of, German thought and had written illuminating pieces on Spengler and Max Weber, remobilised Dostoevsky's well-known praise for the Russian spirit as naturally – and uniquely – disposed towards 'all-humanness' (note the tension between universalism and uniqueness in this claim). All nations, Davydov wrote in 1982, borrowing from Dostoevsky's arguments, are inherently orientated towards universality; they all exist in a dual mode, poised between the native soil and the moral absolute of 'all-humanness'. Each nation has its own destiny and its own path towards universality. From this Davydov inferred that different nations are likely to travel at a different pace and to find themselves at different stages on their journey to the moral absolute.[62] The West, once united with Russia by the sublime moral idea inviting self-sacrifice for the all-human good, had long since given up the goal of attaining the absolute, and all that is left behind are the dead monuments of its past greatness of spirit; this is how Davydov (following here Spengler) interprets Ivan Karamazov's desire to visit Europe, that 'dear cemetery'. Russia's destiny, on the other hand, is to complete the journey, to attain for the world the moral absolute that all nations are called upon to seek, but only a few (one, in Davydov's account) can really reach. Turning to Dostoevsky's *The Devils*, Davydov evokes Shatov's conviction of the uniqueness of the Russian people: 'If a great people does not believe that in it alone the truth resides (in it alone and exceptionally in it), if it does not believe that it alone is able and called to resurrect and save all through its truth, then it ceases immediately to be a great people and turns at once into ethnographic material rather than a great people.'[63] Davydov's messianism is thus nurtured by Dostoevsky's appeal to Russia as the sole surviving nation that is immediately involved in the pursuit of the moral absolute; no one else accompanies the Russian people on this arduous journey, and they alone are destined to a self-sacrificial struggle on behalf of all other peoples. Davydov's original (albeit not very convincing) twist to this otherwise trite story is the attempt to revise and smooth out the opposition between Dostoevsky and Tolstoy (the classic statement of which was worked out in the Silver Age, notably by Merezhkovsky, and had since become one of the *topoi* of aesthetic conservatism, not least in Germany, where it was adopted by Moeller van den Bruck and Spengler). Tolstoy is now positioned not as an antagonist but as the receiver of a set of shared values which his heroes materialise. The moral resurrection that was beyond the reach of Dostoevsky's 'demonic' characters is achieved by Tolstoy's protagonists, shot through by ideas of labour, soil and solidarity.[64] What is more, Davydov produces here a direct link between Tolstoy and the 'great moral philosophy' that allegedly informs the works of Astafev, Rasputin and other conservative writers of the 'village prose' movement. In praising them, he declares himself against the 'abstract-"globalist"', or 'universal-"cosmic"', understanding of the world, implying a move backwards to the time-honoured and 'truly moral' love for the real (Russian) world of one's neighbours, one's kin and one's colleagues (Davydov chooses the obsolete form *sosluzhivtsev*).[65]

This elevation of Russian literature of the nineteenth century to a reservoir of indispensable philosophical ideas, the desirability of which Davydov notes in his book[66] (and the undesirability of which Mamardashvili, as we have seen, highlights with reference to Dostoevsky), had been a feature of the restoration of discourses of exceptionalism since the late 1960s. At that time Georgy Gachev, drawing inspiration from Tiutchev (arguably the poet he quotes most frequently), Danilevsky, Spengler, Gumilev and Dostoevsky (whose 'cosmos' he discussed in an early essay),[67] began to explore the elusive entity that he termed 'cosmo-psycho-logos', an indivisible and primordial unity of psychology, language and specific world outlook characteristic of each nation and manifest in the various forms of national life. Starting in January 1967, Gachev wrote down his lectures, in the form of dialogue, on the everyday embodiments of national cultures (food, sound, bodily movements, home interiors and exteriors, etc.). Earlier, in 1966, he had laid the foundations of his long-term project with an article on 'Language as the Voice of a Nation's Essence'. Gachev's approach was disarmingly eclectic:

a mixture of (implicit) Slavophile admiration for the Russian language, a German Romantic confidence in language as capable of conveying directly the original features of a nation's psyche and a self-confessed revival of the ancient Greek doctrine of the four elements (earth, water, air and fire), which, in different combinations and with different specific weights, are present in the metaphoric arsenal of each language, giving this particular language its own uniqueness. Gachev's work leaves the impression of an uncontrollable play of associations. He is sometimes witty, sometimes excruciatingly dilettantish (and often both). Among his signature 'discoveries' is the metathesis 'mother-darkness' (*mat'-t'ma*), establishing a rich field of associations between femininity, birth and depth, night, opacity and secrecy (ultimately their identity), of which the Swiss anthropologist and cultural historian Bachofen would no doubt have approved. '"Matter" (a philosophical category) originally means a beginning, maternal and dark', Gachev concludes, exploiting the alliteration built on *mat'*.[68] Language is seen by Gachev as a 'portable cosmos'; one does not need to travel abroad to 'grasp another nation's mentality: one simply needs to listen to that nation's language'.[69] He is thus torn between an ultimately soil-rooted view of national cultures and a realisation of the potential of language to liberate these cultures from the confines of their monadic existence.

Because nations present different cosmo-psycho-logic entities, they also have different images of the world and of other nations. These images mirror the claim to uniqueness that all nations seem to enjoy in Gachev's cultural theory. Gachev is not a straightforward exceptionalist. At first sight, Russia's claim to uniqueness is as legitimate as that of any other nation. Where Gachev does part company with this tolerant view is in the adoption and propagation of a xenophobic and at times anti-Semitic philosophy of Russian history. He proffers a 'negative' version of exceptionalism: unlike any other great nation, Russia has always been in need of a strong foreign ruler: Tataro-Mongols, Germans (during Peter the Great's reign), 'the German-Jewish socialism' of Lenin's time, 'the Georgian Dzhugashvili' and then a string of Ukrainian leaders (*khokhly-malorossy*, in Gachev's language), beginning with Khrushchev.[70] The collapse of the Soviet Union was judged by Gachev to be both a loss (of empire) and a gain (of the autonomy of nationhood), a dialectical give-and-take between *Rossiia* and *Rus'*.

This oscillation between empire and nation also marked the writings of Lev Gumilev, especially during his later years. His work is important for our argument, as it reveals the complex modifications of émigré Eurasianism and the ensuing (dis)continuities informing Gumilev's understanding of Russian history. The son of Nikolay Gumilev and Anna Akhmatova (suffering over many years a traumatic estrangement from his mother), Gumilev was arrested four times and spent years in the Gulag, eventually enjoying relative stability and freedom of research after 1956 and even a spell of autumnal glory during the late 1980s and early 1990s (still fostered today by his numerous followers in Russia). Best known for his book *Ethnogenesis and the Biosphere of the Earth*, defended as a second doctoral dissertation in 1974 but only published officially in 1989,[71] Gumilev owed much to Danilevsky and, with considerable qualification, also to some of the inter-war representatives of Eurasianism (mostly to Savitsky, Vernadsky and, to a lesser extent, Nikolay Trubetskoy). Danilevsky's line can indeed be traced throughout the history of Eurasianism (originally an intellectual movement of Russian émigré intellectuals founded in Sofia, influential at various points among segments of the emigration in Prague, Paris, Belgrade, the Baltic and China (1921–38), then resurrected in post-Soviet Russia in a version that exhibited only limited similarity with the pre-Second World War Eurasian platform). Trubetskoy took for granted Danilevsky's fragmentation of history into relatively insulated cultural types.[72] He also shared Danilevsky's scepticism regarding the existence of 'universal civilisation' ('Universal civilisation does not and cannot exist', Danilevsky wrote),[73] developing this statement into a battle cry against what he termed the 'cultural imperialism' of the Germano-Romanic type. Savitsky, on the other hand, embraced Danilevsky's interest in the spatial aspects of history, introducing the concept of *mestorazvitie* ('place of development' but also 'place that develops') to address the specific environment that enables the evolution of a given cultural-historical type and itself changes with the latter's development.[74] Gumilev accepted Danilevsky's thesis of the essentially closed existence of the cultural-historical types, although he did recognise that at times a symbiosis between different ethnic communities is possible. But at the same time he distanced himself from the very notion of type: the entity that conformed to the self-sufficient mode of existence envisaged by Danilevsky was the ethnos, not the cultural-historical type. This substitution signalled Gumilev's determination to write from the standpoint of the exact sciences, which he considered superior to the humanities. The introduction of the ethnos as the basic unit of analysis went hand in hand with a staunch determinism that saw no room for free will, perfection or modification. Unlike Savitsky (with whom Gumilev corresponded from 1956, two decades after Savitsky had ceased working actively on his Eurasian doctrine, until the latter's death, although they met only once, in 1966 in Prague),[75] Gumilev was interested in the cosmic and biological factors shaping history (or, more appropriately, the 'course of events'), much less so in the geographical environment or the economic framework.

Gumilev inherited from Danilevsky (and Spengler) the belief that each particular ethnos (cultural type; civilisation) existed only for a limited time. The question for him was not whether an ethnos would fade away, but rather how it came to be in the first place. The explanation he offers, despite his claim to scientific rigour, cannot be tested or falsified, and it very much betrays a style of reasoning characteristic of an essayist claiming for himself the honourable title of 'ethnosopher' (Savitsky preferred to call himself not a geographer but a 'geosopher'). According to Gumilev, the ethnogenesis should be attributed to a cosmic push that transmits 'passionarity' (*passionarnost*), the creative energy that compels the human species to act against the instinct of self-preservation and thus propels them into new, previously unavailable and uncharted territories. The great conquests take place when an ethnos is at the peak of its passionarity; then the phases of 'inertia' (much like Spengler's 'decline') and 'obscurity' follow, until in the end an ethnos disappears altogether.[76] None of this, of course, was part of classic Eurasianism. Although he flirted with the title of 'the last Eurasian',[77] Gumilev insisted that his theory of passionarity, combining as it did cosmic impulses and genetic pools in order to explain the fate of different ethnic collectives, was completely novel compared with the much more traditional humanistic outlook of the Eurasians. In this respect, he was no Eurasian at all, for his overall episteme was indeed rather different.[78] And yet, like the Eurasians, he believed in Russia's suitability to develop as a complex 'super-ethnos' (empire of different peoples and races, in the language of the pre-war Eurasians); like Vernadsky, he also evaluated positively the Mongol invasion, interpreting the ensuing regime not as a yoke but as a symbiosis that proved beneficial for Russia (while discarding Kievan Rus as too European). Finally, he, too, was full of suspicion when it came to the role played by the West: while the Russian ethnos was compatible with the Turkic, the West was no partner for Russia. Continuing Trubetskoy's assault on 'Germano-Romanic' civilisation, Gumilev prophesied: 'The Turks and the Mongols can be genuine friends, but the English, the French and the Germans, I am convinced, can only be cunning exploiters ... Let me tell you a secret: if Russia is to be saved, then it will only be as a Eurasian power, and only through Eurasianism.'[79]

EPILOGUE

Philosophy and social thought in the Soviet Union were, in the fitting words of Evert van der Zweerde,[80] the product of a specific historical culture. When it comes to the social settings in which philosophy operated, the Soviet regime was justly criticised as oppressive.[81] A look at the historical *durée*, however, might suggest a rather dispiriting continuity. Examining the processes of philosophical education, Frances Nethercott has established substantive parallels between the Soviet Union and tsarist Russia. As in the Soviet Union, the teaching and the study of philosophy in nineteenth-century Russia was far from unconstrained. It was severely limited at the universities following the Decembrist uprising of 1825, banned after 1848, resurrected in 1863 and banned again in 1884, to mention only a few of the disturbingly many milestones along the road.[82] These successive 'hot and cold showers', as Nethercott puts it, led to the spontaneous formation of informal circles, of a philosophical 'underground', where the quality of instruction, or of production for that matter, was not necessarily high. The true legacy of the Soviet intellectual culture may thus be the cultivation of an emerging civil society, the grass-roots reform of the public sphere that at least two generations of dissidents have shouldered since the 1960s, preparing Russia for the non-patriarchal age of freedom without guidance or guarantees. As the post-Soviet years confirm, however, things have proved to be much more complicated. The discourses of exceptionalism continue to thrive, rivalled by the comparatively feeble voices of liberal or democratic pluralism. At the same time, the intellectual attractiveness of Marxism seems to have faded for all but a small minority.

Yet sifting through the debris of Soviet Marxism – or its illicit hybrids that were undermining Marxist orthodoxy from within – one might still stumble upon veritable examples of high intellectual endeavour that deserve to survive the tectonic shifts of history. I wish to conclude by mentioning briefly a fascinating and rare case of continuity, as early as the late 1960s, between Soviet Marxism and earlier Soviet thought, a case where what was meant as a *bona fide* piece of Marxist historical science ended up transcending the boundaries of disciplines and crushing the shell of orthodox Marxism. Boris Porshnev, arguably the most sophisticated Russian philosopher of history to emerge during the second half of the twentieth century, wrote in the late 1960s *On the Beginning of Human History*, a book published posthumously in an abridged version.[83] With this book, Porshnev, an early Soviet admirer of Foucault and at the time already enjoying international recognition as a historian of seventeenth-century France (more so abroad, where he had earned praise from Fernand Braudel, than in the Soviet Union, where many of his colleagues considered him a dogmatic, if not an outright, Stalinist, while others ridiculed him as an indefatigable enthusiast for the Yeti),[84] ventured into an area which he termed 'paleopsychology'. Designed as the middle part of a large three-part work to be titled *A Critique of Human History*,[85] the book was intended to address the question of anthropogenesis, thus establishing (in fact, shortening radically) the true duration of human history and using this new premise to address the law of acceleration that Porshnev believed to be at work, as well as its implications for Marxism and for communist society. Although often questionable in its anthropological hypotheses, Porshnev's book – indeed his entire unfinished project – displayed a major forte: in marrying history and paleopsychology, Porshnev was committed to historicising the very foundation of history – the human species that had so far been taken as an immutable substance. He found support in the work of Nikolai Marr (whose semantic paleontology informed the study of language, folklore and prehistoric artefacts in the 1930s, and whom Porshnev praised openly at a time when Marr's ideas had long been confined to oblivion by the establishment),[86] as well as in Pavlov's theory of the 'second signal system', Ukhtomsky's 'dominant' and Vygotsky's model of the development of consciousness in the child. Yet Porshnev was interested not only in historicising the human species, but also – equally important – in locating the inner propeller and mechanisms of history. In an article sketching what was envisaged as one of the central arguments of the trilogy, Porshnev, drawing on his earlier work on social psychology, contends that human history can be explained from the workings of suggestion (*suggestiia*), the nuclear psychic activity (but also for Porshnev the nuclear act of oppression) that made man distinguishable from the animal kingdom. Human history is interpreted by Porshnev as an epic struggle between consecutive series of socially produced suggestions (involving corresponding acts of counter-suggestion).[87] Not class struggle as such, but the push–pull sequence of suggestion and counter-suggestion is the constantly working engine of history. The alienation of man from man under capitalism is only a variety of a large-scale counter-suggestion, a manifestation of which Porshnev sees in the introduction of more advanced money-based (i.e. increasingly indirect) relationships. In this context, laughter, just as in Bakhtin, has a dual nature for Porshnev, too: it acts as a mechanism of suggestion (team- and nation-building, where Porshnev also notes the role played by feasts, collective celebrations, excessive eating and drinking), but also as a mechanism of counter-suggestion (parodying and excommunicating others, instilling suspicion or a sense of superiority against a rival community or vis-à-vis a 'sacred' message), revealing its joyfulness and oppressiveness in the same breath.[88] This incessant struggle which man has waged right from the start of history (in Porshnev, there is no 'golden age' of primitive freedom and equality) is supposed to end only with communism, when science and the truthfulness of Marxism would finally remove the need for man to sift the environment and the information one constantly receives through the 'filter of mistrust'.

If this sounds too optimistic or too naïve, it is no more so than any other prophecy about the end of history – which might serve as a reminder that the history of thought in the Soviet period, too, should remain open, as a source of inspiration and admonition.

NOTES

1. See Michael Hagemeister, *Nikolaj Fedorov: Studien zu Leben, Werk und Wirkung* (Munich: Otto Sagner, 1989), pp. 241–457; Hagemeister, 'Russian Cosmism in the 1920s and today' in Bernice Glatzer Rosenthal (ed.), *The Occult in Russian and Soviet Culture* (Ithaca and London: Cornell University Press, 1997), pp. 185–202; Anastasiia Gacheva, 'Religiozno-filosofskaia vetv' russkogo kosmizma' in A. Gacheva, O. Kaznina and S. Semenova, *Filosofskii kontekst russkoi literatury 1920–1930-kh godov* (Moscow: IMLI RAN, 2003), pp. 79–125; Svetlana Semenova, *Filosof budushchego veka: Nikolai Fedorov* (Moscow: Pashkov dom, 2004), pp. 463–553. For Berdiaev's impact on VSKhSON, see John B. Dunlop, *The New Russian Revolutionaries* (Belmont: Nordland Publishing Company, 1976), which contains an analysis and a translation of the organisation's programme (its Russian text was first published by Dunlop a year earlier in Paris), as well as the account of one of VSKhSON's leaders: Evgenii Vagin, 'Berdiaevskii soblazn ("Pravye" v oppozitsionnom dvizhenii 60–70-kh godov)', *Nash sovremennik*, 4 (1992), 172–8 (Vagin also mentions the importance of Frank, Solovev and Fedotov).
2. See Boris Egorov, *Zhizn' i tvorchestvo Iu. M. Lotmana* (Moscow: Novoe literaturnoe obozrenie, 1999), p. 140.
3. See V. S. Bibler, *Mikhail Mikhailovich Bakhtin, ili Poetika kul'tury* (Moscow: Progress, 1991); see also Caryl Emerson, *The First Hundred Years of Mikhail Bakhtin* (Princeton University Press, 1997), pp. 274–5.
4. A. Losev, *Dialektika mifa* (Moscow: Mysl', 2001), p. 63. See also James P. Scanlan, *Marxism in the USSR. A Critical Survey of Current Soviet Thought* (Ithaca and London: Cornell University Press, 1985), p. 12.
5. See more in L. A. Kozlova, 'Institut Krasnoi Professury (1921–1938). Istoricheskii ocherk', *Sotsiologicheskii zhurnal*, 1 (1994), 96–112.
6. See Gustav Wetter, *Dialectical Materialism. A Historical and Systematic Survey of Philosophy in the Soviet Union*, trans. Peter Heath (London: Routledge & Kegan Paul, 1960), p. 525.
7. M. B. Mitin, *Filosofskaia nauka v SSSR za 25 let. Doklad, prochitannyi na sessii Akademii nauk SSSR. 18 noiabria 1942 g.* (Moscow: Ogiz; Gospolitizdat, 1943), p. 22.
8. Iu. P. Sharapov, *Litsei v Sokol'nikakh. Ocherk istorii IFLI – Moskovskogo instituta istorii, filosofii i literatury imeni N. G. Chernyshevskogo (1931–1941 gg.)* (Moscow: AIRO-XX, 1995), p. 26.

9. For this list, see John Somerville, *Soviet Philosophy: A Study of Theory and Practice* (New York: Philosophical Library, 1946), p. 235.

10. For an English translation, see [A. A. Bogdanov], *Bogdanov's Tektology* [Book 1], ed. Peter Dudley (Hull: Centre for Systems Studies, 1996).

11. A. M. Deborin, *Lenin kak myslitel'*, 3rd expanded edn (Moscow: Gosudarstvennoe izdatel'stvo, 1929), p. 26.

12. P. Iudin, *Georgii Valentinovich Plekhanov (K 25-letiiu so dnia smerti)* (Moscow: OGIZ; Gospolitizdat, 1943), pp. 18, 20.

13. See in this regard Valentin Asmus's major work, *Ocherki istorii dialektiki v novoi filosofii* (Moscow and Leningrad: Gosudarstvennoe izdatel'stvo, 1930). In his review of the book, Berdiaev was so impressed with Asmus's knowledge and philosophical culture that he thought Asmus was an adherent of Marxism 'solely by accident' (quoted in V. V. Sokolov, 'V. F. Asmus i dramaticheskie momenty ego filosofskogo tvorchestva i filosofskoi zhizni', *Voprosy filosofii*, 2 (2009), 97–102, here 99).

14. See George L. Kline's 'Introduction' in Kline (ed.), *Spinoza in Soviet Philosophy* (London: Routledge & Kegan Paul, 1952), p. 1.

15. For Ilenkov's planned book on Spinoza, see S. N. Mareev, *E. V. Il'enkov* (Moscow and Rostov-on-Don: MarT, 2005), p. 7. On his enduring fascination with Spinoza, see A. G. Novokhat'ko, 'Pochemu imenno Spinoza' in V. I. Tolstykh (ed.), *Eval'd Vasil'evich Il'enkov* (Moscow: ROSSPEN, 2008), pp. 70–83. In 1977, Ilenkov published in the journal *Communist* (under a pseudonym) a co-authored article on Spinoza entitled 'Three centuries of immortality'.

16. See Ivan Il'in, *Filosofiia Gegelia kak uchenie o konkretnosti Boga i cheloveka*, 2 vols. (Moscow: G. A. Leman and S. I. Sakharov, 1918); Lenin's approval of the book is recorded by Tschiževsky in *Hegel bei den Slaven* (Reichenberg: Gebrüder Stiepel, 1934), p. 374, n. 15.

17. See Evert van der Zweerde, *Soviet Historiography of Philosophy: Istoriko-filosofskaia nauka* (Boston: Kluwer, 1997), p. 30.

18. RGASPI (Moscow), f. 374, op. 1, d. 5, l. 98.

19. G. F. Aleksandrov *et al.* (eds.), *Istoriia filosofii*, vol. III, *Filosofiia pervoi poloviny XIX veka* (Moscow: Ogiz; Gospolitizdat, 1943), p. 210.

20. On the designation 'grey horse' (*seraia loshad'*) and the campaign against the volume, see more in G. S. Batygin and I. F. Deviatko, 'Sovetskoe filosofskoe soobshchestvo v sorokovye gody: pochemu byl zapreshchen tretii tom "Istorii filosofii"', *Vestnik Rossiiskoi Akademii Nauk*, 63:7 (1993), 632–3.

21. For more on this and on the polemics around Hegel in the Soviet Union, see Galin Tihanov, 'Revising Hegel's phenomenology on the left: Lukács, Kojève, Hyppolite', *Comparative Criticism*, 25 (2004), 67–95.

22. See V. E. Evgrafov *et al.* (eds.), *Istoriia filosofii v SSSR*, vol. V, book 2 (Moscow: Nauka, 1988), pp. 38–9.

23. It was translated into English as *The Dialectics of the Abstract and the Concrete in Marx's Capital* (Moscow: Progress, 1982).

24. The most reliable version of the mid-1970s text that reflects the additions and rests on a surviving manuscript is Eval'd Il'enkov, 'Dialektika ideal'nogo', *Logos*, 1 (2009), 6–62.

25. See more on this in David Bakhurst, 'The living and the dead in Ilyenkov's philosophy' in Vesa Oittinen (ed.), *Evald Ilyenkov's Philosophy Revisited* (Helsinki: Kikimora Publications, 2000), pp. 23–37.

26. Ilenkov showed the translation to his close friend Mareev; see S. N. Mareev, 'Sotsializm: teoriia i praktika' in Tolstykh (ed.), *Eval'd Vasil'evich Il'enkov*, p. 269.

27. Merab Mamardashvili, *Kak ia ponimaiu filosofiiu* (Moscow: Progress, 1990), p. 35. See also Nikolai Veresov, 'Vygotsky, Ilyenkov and Mamardashvili: searching for the monistic theory of mind (methodological notes)' in Oittinen (ed.), *Evald Ilyenkov's Philosophy Revisited*, pp. 131–45. In a series of interviews recorded in French in November 1989, Mamardashvili confirmed his later departure from Hegel: 'German philosophy! Rise, hat off! No, for me the last interesting philosopher in Germany is Kant. Well, maybe also Schopenhauer, that's all' (M. K. Mamardashvili, 'Mysl' pod zapretom. Besedy s A. E. Epel'buen', *Voprosy filosofii*, 5 (1992), 100).

28. V. A. Smirnov, 'M. K. Mamardashvili: Filosofiia soznaniia' in V. A. Lektorskii (ed.), *Filosofiia ne konchaetsia ... Iz istorii otechestvennoi filosofii: XX vek*, 2nd edn (Moscow: ROSSPEN, 1999), vol. II, pp. 480–97, here p. 489. Smirnov's article, first published in 1991, remains probably the best concise introduction to Mamardashvili's philosophy, admirably sensitive to his evolution as a thinker.

29. Mamardashvili, *Klassicheskii i neklassicheskii idealy ratsional'nosti* (Tbilisi: Metsniereba, 1984).

30. See Z. A. Kamenskii, 'O "Filosofskoi entsiklopedii"' in Lektorskii (ed.), *Filosofiia ne konchaetsia*, vol. II, pp. 43–82, here p. 68.

31. See Mareev, *E. V. Il'enkov*, p. 13.

32. See ibid., pp. 25–8.

33. See V. Kozhinov, 'Gnoseologiia i tragediinost' bytiia' in Tolstykh (ed.), *Drama sovetskoi filosofii. Eval'd Vasil'evich Il'enkov (Kniga-dialog)* (Moscow: [Institut filosofii RAN], 1997), pp. 100–6, here pp. 105–6.

34. Ibid., p. 104.

35. See E. V. Il'enkov, 'From the Marxist-Leninist point of view' in Nicholas Lobkowicz (ed.), *Marx and the Western World* (University of Notre Dame Press, 1967), pp. 391–407, here pp. 392 and 394. Ilenkov was invited to this colloquium (held in April 1966 at the University of Notre Dame) but could not attend. According to the editor of the volume, he fell ill and was 'hospitalised' (*Marx and the Western World*, p. xii); in the introduction accompanying the first publication of the text in Russian (*Voprosy filosofii*, 1988, no. 10) it is unambiguously suggested that the authorities had actually not allowed him to travel.

36. See Mamardashvili, 'Mysl' pod zapretom', 113–14.

37. References here are to Mamardashvili's 1988 lecture 'Filosofiia i religiia' in Mamardashvili, *Moi opyt netipichen* (St Petersburg: Azbuka, 2000), pp. 258–79, here p. 277.

38. See Mamardashvili, 'Filosofiia i religiia', pp. 273–4.
39. This detail and the rest of the factual information on the publications of non-Marxist thinkers in the Soviet Union until 1991 are drawn from Stanislav Dzhimbinov, 'The return of Russian philosophy' in James P. Scanlan (ed.), *Russian Thought after Communism. The Recovery of a Philosophical Heritage* (Armonk and London: M. E. Sharpe, 1994), pp. 11–22 (originally published in Russian in 1992).
40. Nikolai Fedorov, *Sochineniia*, ed. A. Gulyga (Moscow: Mysl', 1982).
41. A. F. Losev, *Vladimir Solov'ev* (Moscow: Mysl', 1983) and *Vladimir Solov'ev i ego vremia* (Moscow: Progress, 1990).
42. See Smirnov's entry in 'V. F. Asmus – pedagog i myslitel' (materialy "kruglogo stola")' in Lektorskii (ed.), *Filosofiia ne konchaetsia*, vol. II, pp. 292–327, here p. 319.
43. See Evgenij A. Pazuchin, 'Studium und Entwicklung der Tradition der russischen religiösen Philosophie vom Anfang des 20. Jahrhunderts im Milieu der religiösen Leningrader Intelligenz von den 70-er Jahren bis heute' in Eberhard Müller and Franz Josef Klehr (eds.), *Russische religiöse Philosophie. Das wiedergewonnene Erbe: Aneignung und Distanz* (Stuttgart: Akademie der Diözese Rottenburg-Stuttgart, 1992), pp. 33–50, here p. 38. The circle in question was founded by Tatiana Goricheva in 1975; the last meeting was held in 1980. In January 1976, the circle began to issue a journal (*37*: the number of the apartment where the meetings took place); the poet Viktor Krivulin became one of its editors. A number of private philosophical seminars and circles in the Soviet Union are mentioned in Zweerde, *Soviet Historiography of Philosophy*, p. 52.
44. See Renata von Maydell, 'Die anthroposophische Gesellschaft in Russland. Entstehung (1913), Auflösung (1923) und Neugründung' in Müller and Klehr (eds.), *Russische religiöse Philosophie*, pp. 171–83, here p. 176.
45. Gustav Shpet, *Ocherk razvitiia russkoi filosofii. Pervaia chast'* (Petrograd: Kolos, 1922), p. 37.
46. Mikhail Bakhtin, *Sobranie sochinenii*, 7 vols. (Moscow: Russkie slovari, 1996–), vol. II, p. 427.
47. Losev's paper survives only as an extended summary organised around bullet points: 'Filologiia i estetika Konstantina Aksakova' (1928) in Losev, *Imia: izbrannye raboty, perevody, besedy, issledovaniia, arkhivnye materialy*, ed. A. A. Takho-Godi (St Petersburg: Aleteia, 1997), pp. 94–100.
48. N. Druzhinin, 'Gertsen i slavianofily', *Istorik-marksist*, 1 (1939), 125–45, 197–200, here 125. By the mid-1930s, Mark Azadovskii had published the correspondence between Petr Kireevsky and Iazykov (Moscow: Izdatel'stvo Akademii nauk SSSR, 1935) and an article on the two, 'Kireevskii i Iazykov', republished in a slightly altered version in his *Literatura i fol'klor* (Leningrad: Khudozhestvennaia literatura, 1938).
49. See S. S. Dmitriev, 'Slavianofily i slavianofil'stvo', *Istorik-marksist*, 1 (1941), 85–97. On the discussion, with contributions by fifteen speakers, see I. Ganichev, 'Obsuzhdenie doklada S. S. Dmitrieva 'Slavianofily i slavianofil'stvo'. Informatsiia o diskussii', *Istorik-marksist*, 1 (1941), 97–100. See also Dmitriev's article 'Zapadniki i slavianofily', *Molodoi bol'shevik*, 11 (1941), 39–49.

50. L. Ginzburg, *Tvorcheskii put' Lermontova* (Leningrad: Gosudarstvennoe izdatel'stvo 'Khudozhestvennaia literatura', 1940). Chapter 7 is entitled 'Spor o Lermontove' and discusses Lermontov and the Slavophiles.

51. Ginzburg, *Tvorcheskii put' Lermontova*, pp. 219–20.

52. A. S. Khomiakov, *Stikhotvoreniia i dramy*, ed. B. F. Egorov (Leningrad: Sovetskii pisatel', 1969).

53. See Egorov, 'Slavianofil'stvo, zapadnichestvo i kul'turologiia' in *Trudy po znakovym sistemam*, vol. VI, pp. 265–75 (Uchenye zapiski Tartuskogo gosudarstvennogo universiteta, 308 (1973): *Sbornik nauchnykh statei v chest' Mikhaila Mikhailovicha Bakhtina (k 75-letiiu so dnia rozhdeniia)*, ed. Iu. Lotman). The article was first drafted in the form of theses published in 1970 (see Egorov, 'Slavianofil'stvo, zapadnichestvo i kul'turologiia' in Iu. Lotman (ed.), *Tezisy dokladov IV Letnei shkoly po vtorichnym modeliruiushchim sistemam, 17–24 avgusta 1970* (Tartu: Tartuskii gosudarstvennyi universitet), pp. 88–9).

54. All quotations are from Vadim Kozhinov, 'O glavnom v nasledii slavianofilov' in V. A. Fateev (ed.), *Slavianofil'stvo: Pro et Contra*, 2nd edn (St Petersburg: Izdatel'stvo Sankt-Peterburgskogo universiteta, 2009), pp. 877–99, here pp. 881–2 (first published in *Voprosy literatury*, 10 (1969), 113–31).

55. Nicholas Berdyaev, *The Russian Idea* (London: Geoffrey Bles, 1947), p. 39.

56. Kozhinov, 'O glavnom', pp. 895–6.

57. V. D. Duvakin, *Besedy s Bakhtinym* (Moscow: Soglasie, 2002), p. 247.

58. See A. Gulyga, 'Russkii vopros', *Nash sovremennik*, 1 (1990), 168–76. On the role of *Nash Sovremennik* in the Soviet ideological life of the time of *glasnost'* and *perestroika*, and on the complex co-optation of nationalism in the Party agenda, see Yitzhak M. Brudny, *Reinventing Russia: Russian Nationalism and the Soviet State, 1953–1991* (Cambridge, Mass.: Harvard University Press, 1998), pp. 199–203.

59. Arsenii Gulyga, *Russkaia ideia i ee tvortsy* (Moscow: Soratnik, 1995), p. 16; see also Gulyga's defence of *sobornost'* against the critique by liberal thinkers such as Grigorii Pomerants and Boris Groys (ibid., p. 19).

60. See Gulyga, 'Russkii religiozno-filosofskii renessans', *Nash sovremennik*, 7 (1990), 185–7.

61. See Grigorii Pomerants, *Dostoevskii: Otkrytost' bezdne* (Moscow: Sovetskii pisatel', 1990; first published New York, 1989); see also Pomerants's essay 'Mysliteli chitaiut Dostoevskogo', *Oktiabr'*, 3 (1993), 185–9. Pomerants had gained popularity as a dissident defender of liberal values and an opponent of the native-soil conservative ideas of Solzhenitsyn. On the status of Dostoevsky as a thinker and for an inscription of his work in the Russian philosophical context, see James Scanlan, *Dostoevsky the Thinker* (Ithaca: Cornell University Press, 2002).

62. Iurii Davydov, *Etika liubvi i metafizika svoevoliia (problemy nravstvennoi filosofii)* (Moscow: Molodaia gvardiia, 1982), p. 268.

63. This is my translation of the quotation from *Besy* adduced by Davydov (Davydov, *Etika liubvi*, p. 270).

64. Ibid., p. 273. Davydov talks explicitly about the need to revise the opposition between Dostoevsky and Tolstoy (mentioning Merezhkovsky) in the introduction to the book, p. 8.

65. Ibid., p. 274. On Davydov's neo-*pochvennichestvo*, see also Evert van der Zweerde, 'Die Rolle der Philosophiegeschichte im "neuen philosophischen Denken" in der UdSSR', *Studies in Soviet Thought*, 40 (1990), 66–70.

66. Davydov, *Etika liubvi*, pp. 6–7.

67. G. D. Gachev, 'Kosmos Dostoevskogo' in S. S. Konkin (ed.), *Problemy poetiki i istorii literatury* (Saransk: Mordovskii gosudarstvennyi universitet imeni N. P. Ogareva, 1973), pp. 110–24. The volume was a *Festschrift* on Bakhtin's seventy-fifth birthday; Gachev, together with Kozhinov and Sergey Bocharov, was responsible for the rediscovery of Bakhtin in the Soviet Union in the first half of the 1960s.

68. Gachev, 'Iazyk kak golos natsional'noi prirody' [September 1966] in Gachev, *Kosmo-psikho-logos* (Moscow: Akademicheskii proekt, 2007), pp. 184–208, here p. 205, n. 1.

69. Ibid., p. 185.

70. Gachev, 'Kosmosofiia Rossii' [1990] in Gachev, *Kosmo-psikho-logos*, pp. 459–64, here p. 462. Gachev's appreciation of Jewish culture and thought is often dotted with outbursts of condescension and contempt (see his essay 'Evreiskii obraz mira', ibid., pp. 484–503). By 1991 Gachev had prepared a 700-page typescript on the Jewish mentality (see Gachev, *Mental'nosti narodov mira* (Moscow: Eksmo Algoritm, 2008), p. 527). Little of it has been published to date; for more on Gachev's anti-Semitism, see Vadim Rossman, *Russian Intellectual Anti-Semitism in the Post-Communist Era* (Lincoln: University of Nebraska Press, 2002), pp. 178–81.

71. There is an abridged English translation under the title *Ethnogenesis and the Biosphere* (Moscow: Progress, 1990).

72. Danilevsky formulated the principle of discrete cultural-historical types (ten in total) in his 1869 work *Rossiia i Evropa*; see N. Danilevskii, *Rossiia i Evropa*, 6th edn (St Petersburg: Glagol, 1995), p. 73.

73. Danilevskii, *Rossiia i Evropa*, p. 104.

74. For more on this, see Tihanov, 'Cultural emancipation and the novelistic: Trubetzkoy, Savitsky, Bakhtin', *Bucknell Review*, 43:2 (2000), 47–67.

75. These facts can be found in Gumilev's biography: Sergei Lavrov, *Lev Gumilev: sud'ba i idei* (Moscow: Svarog i K, 2000).

76. Gumilev, *Etnogenez i biosfera zemli* (Leningrad: Gidrometeoizdat, 1990), pp. 288–9.

77. See Gumilev, 'Zametki poslednego evraziitsa', *Nashe nasledie*, 3 (1991), 19–34.

78. This point is made very well by Marlène Laruelle in her book *Russian Eurasianism: An Ideology of Empire* (Baltimore: The Johns Hopkins University Press, 2008), pp. 56–70.

79. Gumilev, *Ritmy Evrazii: epokhi i tsivilizatsii* (Moscow: Ekopros, 1993), p. 31 (I quote here Mischa Gabowitsch's translation from Laruelle, *Russian Eurasianism*, p. 73).

80. See Zweerde, *Soviet Historiography of Philosophy*, especially pp. 26–31; see also Nikolai Plotnikov, 'Sovetskaia filosofiia: institut i funktsiia' in Mikhail Ryklin

et al. (eds.), *Uskol'zaiushchii kontekst: russkaia filosofiia v postsovetskikh uslo-viiakh* (Moscow: Ad Marginem, 2002), pp. 287–302.

81. See Iegoshua Iakhot, *Podavlenie filosofii v SSSR (20–30 gody)* (New York: Chalidze Publications, 1981), where the reader will find more factual informa-tion about the canonisation of Marxism-Leninism, including a discussion of the important Party resolution of 1931 (about the journal *Under the Banner of Marxism*) and the infamous *Short Course* (1938).

82. See Nethercott's account in her essay, 'Philosophieren unter Stalin und unter Nikolaj I' in Klaus-Dieter Eichler and Ulrich Johannes Schneider (eds.), *Russische Philosophie im 20. Jahrhundert* (Leipziger Universitätsverlag, 1996), pp. 23–34, here p. 30.

83. Boris Porshnev, *O nachale chelovecheskoi istorii: problemy paleopsikhologii* (Moscow: Mysl', 1974); this abridged edition was followed by a fuller but textologically not entirely reliable edition (St Petersburg: FERI-V, 2006). References here are to the most recent, unabridged and texto-logically more rigorous edition prepared by Oleg Vite (St Petersburg: Aleteia, 2007).

84. See Z. A. Chekantseva, 'Retseptsiia tvorchestva B. F. Porshneva vo Frantsii i v Sovetskom Soiuze' in *Frantsuzskii ezhegodnik 2007* (Moscow: LKI, 2008), pp. 12–26, here pp. 15–17. From the narrower perspective of the guild, Aron Gurevich recognised Porshnev's enormous talent and compel-ling interdisciplinary breadth but thought his ideas spurious and untested by scrupulous research (A. Gurevich, *Istoriia istorika* (Moscow: ROSSPEN, 2004), pp. 25–8). Gurevich, who had attended Porshnev's seminars on his-torical psychology, refused to admit that Porshnev's 1966 book *Sotsial'naia psikhologiia i istoriia* was, by Soviet standards, a pioneering work which preceded by several years his own work on historical psychology (see I. S. Filippov, 'B. F. Porshnev i politicheskaia ekonomiia feodalizma' in *Frantsuzskii ezhegodnik 2007* (Moscow: LKI, 2008), pp. 87–129, here p. 127). It was in *Sotsial'naia psikhologiia i istoriia* that Porshnev praised Foucault for the first time, calling his *Folie et déraison* 'an outstanding work' (see Porshnev, *Sotsial'naia psikhologiia i istoriia* (Moscow: Nauka, 1966), p. 8, n. 7); Porshnev also refers to Foucault's book in *O nachale chelovecheskoi istorii* (Porshnev, *O nachale*, p. 395).

85. See Porshnev, *O nachale*, p. 11. In an unpublished piece, Porshnev dates the idea of the trilogy back to 1924 (see Oleg Vite, '"Ia – schastlivyi chelovek". Kniga "O nachale chelovecheskoi istorii" i ee mesto v tvorcheskoi biografii B. F. Porshneva' in Porshnev, *O nachale*, pp. 576–706, here p. 577).

86. See Porshnev, *O nachale*, pp. 41–2, 442. (Porshnev's praise of Marr is even stronger in an earlier article outlining the methodological foundations of the book: B. F. Porshnev, 'O nachale chelovecheskoi istorii' in *Filosofskie prob-lemy istoricheskoi nauki*, ed. A. V. Gulyga and Iu. A. Levada (Moscow: Nauka, 1969), pp. 80–112, here p. 97.) After Marr's dethronement in 1950, Porshnev's opponents sought to uncover in his work vestiges of Marr's by

then deplorable 'new teaching'. In the mid-1960s, Porshnev wrote an article on Marr's centenary which remained unpublished (see Vite, "'Ia – schastlivyi chelovek'", p. 585).

87. See Porshnev, 'Kontrsuggestiia i istoriia' in Porshnev and L. I. Antsyferova (eds.), *Istoriia i psikhologiia* (Moscow: Nauka, 1971), pp. 7–35.

88. Ibid., p. 25.

CHAPTER 15

Dialectical materialism and Soviet science in the 1920s and 1930s

Daniel Todes and Nikolai Krementsov

With the Bolshevik coup in October 1917 and victory in the Civil War four years later, the philosophy underlying Marxism, dialectical materialism, became a cultural resource – not just a philosophy, but also a ruling ideology and language of accommodation to the regime's policies and priorities. State officials, political figures, ideologues, philosophers and scientists all drew upon this cultural resource to pursue their ends – to seek truth, to display loyalty to the regime, to struggle for resources, power or survival. Dialectical materialism itself became a terrain of contention and was constantly redefined as it was incorporated into Soviet culture in the 1920s and 1930s.

A non-reductionist materialism that emphasises unceasing historical development and the interplay and mutual transformation of opposites, dialectical materialism provided numerous interpretative moments to those employing it as a philosophy and ample flexibility to those deploying it as a language of struggle, justification and accommodation. Being and consciousness, base and superstructure, material continuity and dialectical discontinuity, necessity and freedom, analysis and synthesis, theory and practice, philosophy and science – all these relationships could be interpreted and deployed in various ways. It is difficult, therefore, to imagine any scientific discovery or line of investigation that would be acceptable in terms of the dominant philosophy in western science – positivism – that could *not* be interpreted or justified using the lexicon of dialectical materialism. Dialectical materialism proved notoriously amenable to varied usages, including penetrating (but often sharply differing) analyses and the justification of the morally unjustifiable.

Dialectical materialists manifested varying styles – defining and employing central concepts and terms differently as a result of their differing biographical trajectories, characters, interests and contexts. Engels was famously more 'positivistic' than Marx, Lenin was criticised by many 'orthodox Marxists' as insufficiently materialist (as voluntarist), and he himself famously characterised leading Bolshevik theoretician Bukharin as not 'fully Marxist' since 'he has never made a study of dialectics, and I think never fully appreciated it'.

Stalin's notoriously wooden style is often attributed to his seminary training and psychological characteristics. Those who learnt their dialectical materialism from Marx and Engels imbibed a very different doctrine than did the much greater number of Russians who by the late 1920s learnt theirs from Stalin's *Foundations of Leninism.*

During the 1920s the regime promulgated dialectical materialism in Soviet society; during the Great Break (1929–32) it imposed a particular version of it, and in the aftermath of the Great Break it imposed yet another version. During that first decade various versions of dialectical materialism flourished, but the dominant, semi-official style (which suited the evolutionary approach to socialist construction enshrined in Lenin's New Economic Policy, or NEP) favoured the materialist moment – emphasising, for example, the continuity of humans and the animal kingdom, the primacy of being over consciousness and of base over superstructure. The official dialectical materialism of Stalin's Great Break was imposed by Communist Party *diktat* and, in keeping with the spirit of the Great Break ('there are no fortresses the Bolsheviks cannot storm'), emphasised the dialectical moment (the qualitative differences between humans and other animals, the sometimes decisive role of conscious human activity). The Great Break ended with an affirmation of the central role of 'practice' as the final arbiter of theory. That, in principle, could have a variety of meanings, but in effect meant that the time for debating broad issues had passed and that of simply deciphering and following directives from Stalin and his minions had begun. Official dialectical materialism became a matter of citing approved authorities and quotations. Yet whatever version of dialectical materialism prevailed in specific periods, its commonly accepted features provided the parameters for Soviet public discourse.[1]

How, then, did the Communist Party's efforts to encourage the use of dialectical materialism in the 1920s and to impose it in the 1930s influence Soviet scientific thought? The most common reaction was that Soviet scientists adapted rhetorically to official pressure by adding Marxist terms to their scientific works, appeals for state support and explanations of their research. Yet that research remained substantially unchanged and continued to develop long-standing orientations and traditions. A few figures such as the physiologist Pavlov and the biogeochemist Vernadsky, protected by their privileged status, publicly denounced both Marxism and its imposition, and made no attempt to cast their work in terms of the official ideology. Finally, some scientists, most frequently among the *vydvizhentsy*, the new proletarian intellectuals nurtured and promoted by Soviet policies in the 1920s and 1930s, sought genuinely to approach scientific issues from a dialectical materialist perspective. In this essay we will use our own research and that of other historians to sketch the rhetorical and philosophical uses of dialectical materialism and then to explore one case study of each.

SCIENCE AND THE BOLSHEVIKS

The Bolshevik coup of October 1917 replaced a Provisional Government that enjoyed the enthusiastic support of Russian scientists with a regime towards which they were almost unanimously hostile. Yet scientists were 'bourgeois specialists' especially important to the Bolsheviks' vision and plans for modernisation, so in the years of War Communism and NEP the Bolsheviks sought to preserve, expand and co-opt this community while preparing a successor generation through recruitment from the working classes. Under NEP, the Soviet state funded science generously, purchasing needed scientific equipment abroad, securing foreign publications, sponsoring conferences and periodicals and creating by 1929 some 1,200 scientific institutions.[2]

As the economy recovered under NEP, scientists who did not actively oppose the regime were able to pursue their work under unprecedentedly propitious conditions. The prestige of science soared, the number of popular science journals exploded and items about science appeared frequently in *Pravda* and *Izvestiia*. The Bolsheviks and Russia's scientific community, then, found in the NEP years a common language that expressed broadly common beliefs about the key role of science in the enlightenment of the population, the resolution of practical tasks and social progress in general.[3]

A new element, of course, was the dialectical materialism promulgated by the Bolshevik state. As Lenin put it in 1922: 'No natural science, no materialism can withstand the struggle against the pressure of bourgeois ideas and the bourgeois worldview without a sound philosophical basis. In order to be able to withstand the struggle and to accomplish it successfully, a scientist must be an up-to-date materialist, a deliberate follower of the materialism presented by Marx, that is, he must be a dialectical materialist.'[4]

The authorities actively propagandised dialectical materialism with the help of the Communist Academy and various societies (the Society of Mathematicians-Materialists, the Society of Biologists-Materialists, the Society of Marxist-Agrarians and so on), and the adoption of Marxist phraseology became one way for scientists to curry favour with the authorities: for example, when seeking funding for a project or institution. The militant, dogmatic culture within the Communist Academy and the nation's educational institutions – where a new generation of scientists was being prepared – contrasted sharply with the broad latitude within public discourse.[5]

The flexibility of dialectical materialism was fully displayed in discussions of scientific issues in the 1920s, including those concerning the most ideologically charged scientific subjects: quantum mechanics and relativity theory, psychology and the complex of issues surrounding genetics, inheritance of acquired characteristics and evolutionary theory. Established pre-revolutionary specialists Bekhterev (b. 1857) and Kornilov (b. 1879) were almost certainly adapting rhetorically to their Bolshevik patrons when, in 1925, they framed their long-standing, and very different, approaches to psychology within a Marxist lexicon. The much different approach espoused by Vygotsky (b. 1896) and his student Luria (b. 1902) clearly resulted, on the other hand, from a genuine grappling with Marxist philosophy. Vygotsky found in dialectical materialism a fruitful approach to problematic antinomies in aesthetics, psychology and child development. In psychology, for example, he creatively followed Marx's lead in his attempt to transcend disputes between psychologists and philosophers who advocated a reductionist approach to mind and those who insisted on the study of consciousness itself. Russia's vigorous eugenics movement, as Mark Adams has demonstrated, included both established pre-revolutionary specialists such as Filipchenko and Koltsov, and younger Bolshevik scientists such as Volotskoy (b. 1893) and Serebrovsky (b. 1892). Committed dialectical materialists expressed the same diversity of views on such subjects as the inheritance of acquired characteristics, the chromosomal theory and approaches to eugenics as did older specialists – and differed among themselves regarding the compatibility of eugenics with Marxism. As David Joravsky has noted, in the 1920s Soviet Marxists proved 'eclectically broadminded' on other issues as well. In the pages of the Communist Academy's journal *Under the Banner of Marxism*, arguments about set theory in mathematics, quantum physics and relativity, genetics, psychology and Freudian theory were all couched in Marxist language – but were no less varied than those expressed in the West.[6]

The lack of unanimity concerning the new physics is particularly revealing since Lenin himself had pronounced polemically and at length on that subject in his *Materialism and Empirio-Criticism* (1908). Lenin had not contested physicists' findings themselves – these, he thought, constituted exciting new scientific advances in understanding the nature of matter – but polemicised against the relativist ontological and epistemological conclusions drawn by some scientists and philosophers, most notably his fellow Bolshevik Bogdanov, who had argued famously that 'matter is disappearing'. For Lenin, such views constituted a new form of idealism, the ideology of the class enemy. While recognising a connection between science and philosophy, Lenin distinguished between science itself and the philosophical conclusions drawn from it.[7]

In the 1920s, Marxist philosophers expressed a wide variety of views about quantum mechanics and relativity. Arkady Timiriazev, a physicist and mechanistic Party philosopher, rejected relativity on both scientific and philosophical grounds, and intensified his criticism of quantum mechanics at mid-decade when Nils Bohr's principle of complementarity and Werner Heisenberg's uncertainty principle combined in the so-called Copenhagen interpretation. On the other hand, Semkovsky, a Marxist philosopher at the Ukrainian Academy of Sciences, argued that modern physics confirmed some basic Marxist concepts. As Joravsky puts it, he 'felt that great revolutions in natural science coincided with periods of great social revolutions, and he recalled Engels' insistence that materialism must take on a new form with every advance in the scientific understanding of matter. Dialectical materialism must accordingly absorb the new insights provided by the theory of relativity.' Einstein's *Relativity: The Special and General Theory* was translated into Russian in 1921 and reprinted four times over the next two years, fuelling a great variety of views. As with quantum theory, concludes Alexander Vucinich, Marxist philosophers proved 'the most active – and inconsistent – interpreters of Einstein's theory'.[8]

Some Soviet physicists, such as Fock and Fridman, contributed to relativity theory and quantum mechanics in the 1920s, and those who engaged the philosophical issues raised by the new physics shared the 'philosophical turmoil' and diverse responses of their colleagues in the West. Leading physicists such as Ioffe and Sergey Vavilov occasionally made rhetorical gestures in the direction of dialectical materialism, 'obviously trying to placate authorities and protect physics and physicists', but physicists of the so-called Leningrad school 'produced many direct and indirect signals indicating [their] firm belief that there was no way to establish sound cooperative relations between modern physics and dialectical materialism'. Most physicists had little contact with Marxist philosophy, took relativity and quantum mechanics for granted or worked in specialities unaffected by them, living 'in amorphous isolation from ideological issues and activities'.[9]

Throughout the 1920s, Bolshevik leaders assured scientists that they need not adopt dialectical materialism as long as they toiled loyally on their research. Some established scientists tacked to the political winds, but most seem to have taken the authorities at their word and proceeded in their research much as they had earlier. They and their institutions were, as

Joravsky has put it, 'almost as little Bolshevik or Marxist at the end of the twenties as they had been at the beginning', and the much-vaunted new generation of 'red specialists' had made very little progress.[10]

That changed with Stalin's *velikii perelom*, the Great Break of 1929–32, during which the Party tightened its control over every aspect of Soviet society – suppressing the market, establishing a state monopoly of resources and production and launching campaigns for rapid industrialisation, forcible collectivisation of agriculture and 'cultural revolution'. The Great Break in Soviet science involved a stunning increase in the number of scientists and scientific institutions and the establishment of a centralised system of bureaucratic control. The cultural revolution featured a 'sharpening of the class struggle' and broad campaigns against 'bourgeois specialists' in all fields and a concomitant promotion of the *vydvizhentsy* who had been recruited and cultivated over the previous decade.

In April 1929 Pokrovsky, director of the Communist Academy, declared an end to peaceful coexistence with non-Marxist naturalists and 'fetishism before bourgeois scientists'. Soon thereafter began the campaign against 'mechanistic materialism and menshevising idealism' – a campaign that was personally endorsed by Stalin in philosophy and expanded into mathematics, chemistry, geology, biology, psychology, history and other fields. Stressing the 'class nature of science', this campaign identified the class enemy with vaguely and flexibly defined philosophical and methodological trends in scholarly fields. Insufficiently dialectical 'mechanistic materialism' was associated with the 'right deviation' of Bukharinism, while insufficiently materialist 'menshevising idealism' was associated with the 'left deviation' of Trotskyism. Conducted by such organisations as the All-Union Association of Scientific and Technological Specialists for Assisting Socialist Construction, these campaigns facilitated the politicisation of scientific discourse, purges of scientific institutions and the imposition of dialectical materialist language upon scientists. An important landmark in the establishment of the Stalinist science system was the Bolshevisation of the Academy of Sciences in 1928–30, during which an aggressive public campaign culminated in the expansion of the Academy and coerced 'election' of Communist academicians, the institution's first unified plan of work and the adoption of a statute committing its members to dialectical materialism.[11]

Pressured and terrorised, 'bourgeois specialists' were also, as the State Planning Commission put it in 1930, 'dissolved in a sea of new forces'. Higher education expanded at a staggering pace between 1928 and 1932, and the *vydvizhentsy* now flooded scientific institutions. The academic year 1928–9 was 'the year of the thousand' youthful Communist militants who entered universities with little regard for academic prerequisites; they were joined by 2,000 more in 1929–30 and by still more in subsequent years. The avenue for many of the *vydvizhentsy* into scientific employment was *aspirantura*, the new expanded graduate training programmes that were created, for example, at the newly Bolshevised Academy of Sciences. Many of the most promising young militants supplemented that training with programmes at Moscow's and Leningrad's Communist Academy, where they learnt to apply dialectical materialism to their particular speciality.[12]

The cynical assessment of one militant that 'the threat [to a professor] of losing his academic ration can, in the time span of a single course, transform even the most inveterate counter-revolutionary into a Marxist' was of course true only in the most limited sense. As Pavlov put it in a letter to Molotov objecting to the 'cruel insult' of requiring Russian scientists to use the official philosophy in their scientific research: 'Of course, [scientists] don't do this in their investigations, but introduce into the presentations of their works slavish words and phrases about dialectical materialism.' A scientist could be compelled to adopt Marxist phraseology, but not to pursue a Marxist approach to his or her subject; and the Party officials and philosophers who thundered about 'mechanism', 'dialectics' and the *partiinost'* (Party-mindedness) of science were not sufficiently familiar with the substance of scientific research to do so themselves.[13]

The most widespread result of the imposition of dialectical materialism during the Great Break, then, was a set of political – fundamentally, rhetorical – responses. Philosophers sought to establish their role as transmitters and enforcers of official ideology in the scientific community, and scientists adapted in various ways to this new political demand upon them. All philosophers expressed the basic views enunciated in Lenin's *Materialism and Empirio-Criticism*: that modern physics represented a dialectical leap in the development of scientific knowledge, that the physical micro-universe of quantum mechanics was a true reflection of objective reality, that historically bounded definitions of 'matter' were constantly changing, but that matter itself, as an epistemological category with ontological reality independent of consciousness, continued to exist and that the idealist Copenhagen interpretation of quantum mechanics reflected the interests of the reactionary bourgeoisie in an era of capitalist crisis. Yet within these parameters philosophers differed in their emphasis and assessment of key issues, frustrating attempts to impose any uniform position.[14]

Leading physicists made good use of the flexibility of dialectical materialism and their own mastery of esoteric knowledge to minimise intrusions into their discipline while demonstrating loyalty to the regime. For example, Tamm, writing for *Under the Banner of Marxism* in 1933, complained that the philosophers were much too 'scientifically illiterate' to fruitfully apply dialectical materialism to modern physics. Vavilov and Ioffe, both eminent physicists considered politically loyal, each delivered papers to a conference of 1934 convened by philosophers on the twenty-fifth anniversary of the publication of Lenin's polemic to enforce ideological uniformity in physics. Yet Ioffe's contribution to that meeting was a defence of Heisenberg's principle of indeterminacy and Bohr's complementarity principle – each, he claimed, constituted a 'brilliant confirmation and enrichment of dialectical materialism'. Deploying Lenin, Ioffe criticised those who allied modern science with bourgeois ideology, but also warned Marxist philosophers against damaging science by crusading against phantom idealist threats. At that same conference, Vavilov analysed the nature of light (his speciality) as an illustration of both Bohr's complementarity principle and the dialectical materialist principle of the 'unity of contradictions'. On another occasion, Vavilov lauded Einstein's conception of space-time as both a turning-point for physics and a victory for dialectical materialism. 'In Einstein's theory', he noted, 'space-time is an inseparable attribute of matter, and cannot exist without matter.' The attempt of Party philosophers to purge physics of 'idealistic rubbish' through a campaign and conference in 1937 foundered upon the same shoals.[15]

Yet, as Loren Graham has observed, dialectical materialism was no less plausible than other philosophies of nature that have demonstrably influenced scientific enquiry. Just as mechanistic materialism had inspired many scientifically orientated Russian youths in the 1860s, so were many *vydvizhentsy* 'attracted to the relationship of Marxism and science in the early, idealistic period of Soviet history before Stalinist ideological controls squeezed out much of the intellectual content in dialectical materialism'. Graham has analysed their 'authentic' use of that philosophy in a broad range of sciences. His most fully elaborated case study is that of the physicist Fock, whose Marxism played a fundamental role in his defence of relativity theory and the Copenhagen interpretation and in his development of an idiosyncratic mathematical method ('harmonic co-ordinates') to separate them from the idealist and relativist philosophical positions within which they were often framed in the West.[16]

'MARXIST-DARWINISM' AS A CULTURAL RESOURCE

Despite the popularity of both Darwinism and Marxism in Russia, the decades before the Bolshevik seizure of power witnessed few efforts to establish connections between the two doctrines. That changed dramatically after the Revolution, as a result of the largely independent, but converging efforts by both Russian biologists and Russian Marxists.

During the Civil War, Narkompros had already moved to reform existing curricula to include teaching of Marxism in every educational institution and sponsored the publication of countless booklets, pamphlets and leaflets popularising Marxism, including separate editions and excerpts from and compilations of works by Marx, Engels and Lenin. State and Party agencies established a number of specialised institutions of 'Communist learning' – the Communist Academy, Communist universities and 'institutes of red professors' to prepare the cadres for disseminating Marxism.[17] The Bolsheviks spared no effort to combat illiteracy and to 'bring science to the masses'.[18] They supported the publication of brochures, books and popular magazines which disseminated basic knowledge in various fields of science, from astronomy and geography to chemistry and hygiene. Biology became a particular focus of the new state's educational efforts: popular treatises on the chemistry and physiology of the human body, the 'mechanics' of mental processes, the origins of life and human origins constituted an important part of the Bolsheviks' militant anti-religious campaign.[19]

It was within these huge educational/propagandistic campaigns that the first systematic attempts to forge links between Darwinism and Marxism took place. In 1923, in a series entitled Problems of Marxism, the Bolshevik historian Ravich-Cherkassky published a compilation entitled *Darwinism and Marxism*. In the preface, he explained the necessity of studying Darwinism for any 'conscientious Marxist': 'It is hardly possible to consider the learning of Marxism to be not only completed, but even generally serious and sufficiently deep, if one did not learn – at least on an elementary level – the historical and philosophical relation of Marxism to Darwinism.'[20] During subsequent years, a number of publications with similar titles appeared in Russia.[21] Many of them emphasised the parallels between Darwinism and Marxism famously inaugurated by Engels, who in his eulogy at Marx's grave had equated Darwin and Marx as scientific geniuses, each of whom had accomplished a revolution by bringing 'historical method' to his field. Trotsky reiterated in 1923 that 'in relation to social phenomena Marxism occupies the same position as Darwinism does in relation to the plant and animal world'.[22] Some propagandists moved beyond simple parallels to incorporate Darwinism into Marxism. They began to hail Marxism as a comprehensive 'materialistic world-view' (dialectical materialism) that explained not only economic and political developments, but any and every kind of development, including biological evolution. Following the lead of Marx and Engels, who had portrayed Darwin's works as the 'materialistic explanation' of biological evolution, they began to present Darwinism as an important component of Marxism itself. As a result, Darwinism was included in courses on the history of philosophy and on Marxism at educational institutions.

The Communist Academy became the main instrument for the introduction of Marxism to the Russian scientific community. In 1922, in the first issue of its mouthpiece, *Under the Banner of Marxism*, the editorial board called upon Marxists to 'unfold the banner of militant materialism' and to launch a broad attack on 'idealism' in scientific research.[23] The journal's third issue carried an article, 'On the Significance of Militant Materialism', by Lenin himself, who charged scientists with the task of 'the struggle against the pressure of bourgeois ideas and the bourgeois worldview' and insisted that every 'scientist must be an up-to-date materialist, a deliberate follower of the materialism presented by Marx, that is, he must be a dialectical materialist'.[24] Lenin's article became the manifesto of Communist scholars, and some took upon themselves the task of rooting out 'idealistic' conceptions of biological evolution. By June 1925 a resolution of the Central Committee of the Communist Party had recorded that 'the infusion of dialectical materialism into entirely new fields (biology, psychology, natural sciences in general) has begun'.[25]

This early campaign for the 'infusion of dialectical materialism' into biology was carried out primarily by professional Marxists, with one notable exception – 'Darwin's Russian bulldog', Kliment Timiriazev, father of the physicist mentioned above. In mid-1919, in the journal *Proletarian Culture*, Timiriazev published an article, 'Ch. Darwin and K. Marx', which would become a model for many of the subsequent treatments of the issue.[26] Timiriazev was the first to note that Darwin's *Origin of Species* and Marx's *Contribution to the Critique of Political Economy* had appeared in the same year, 1859, and to maintain that 'it was more than a simple chronological coincidence'. According to Timiriazev, both Darwin and Marx based their theories not on 'theology and metaphysics', but on science: on 'scientifically explored' and 'material' phenomena. Darwin studied the 'economy of plants and animals' and Marx the 'economy of human societies'. Both explained 'evolution' – Darwin, biological and Marx, social – as the result of 'material', 'economic' conditions and factors: 'Both of them marched under the banner of natural sciences.'

Unlike Timiriazev, most Russian biologists greeted the Bolshevik Revolution with distrust, suspicion and open hostility. Very soon, however, they developed a functioning symbiosis with the new government.[27] They joined the Bolsheviks' campaign for the popularisation of science, producing popular accounts of various biological subjects, with the issues of biological evolution and heredity occupying a prominent place. Biologists quickly capitalised on the Bolsheviks' active science policy to increase greatly their institutional base.

As part of this remarkable institutional growth, a new discipline of genetics emerged in Soviet Russia. Three enterprising scientists, Filipchenko, Koltsov and Nikolay Vavilov, mobilised the resources of Narkomzdrav (People's Commissariat of Public Health), Narkompros (People's Commissariat of Enlightenment) and Narkomzem (People's Commissariat of Agriculture) to organise research laboratories, convene conferences, create periodicals, publish textbooks and train a new professional generation. To legitimise their discipline-building efforts, geneticists conducted a large publicity campaign, popularising both the actual achievements of genetics in uncovering mechanisms of heredity – including Mendel's 'hybridisation laws' and T. H. Morgan's 'chromosomal theory' – and lauding their discipline's potential for 'gaining control over the nature' of plants, animals and humans. An important feature of this legitimisation campaign was geneticists' 'contribution to Darwinism'.[28]

The first two decades of the twentieth century witnessed wide-ranging international debates over the validity of Darwin's views on evolution and the proliferation of 'alternative' concepts, which historians have described as the 'eclipse of Darwinism'.[29] Critics proposed several 'alternative' concepts to correct the perceived deficiencies of Darwin's natural selection: orthogenesis – evolution on the basis of regularities; neo-Lamarckism – evolution on the basis of the inheritance of acquired characteristics; mutationism – evolution on the basis of mutations; and isolationism – evolution on the basis of isolation.

Russia's biological community enthusiastically engaged in these debates, with geneticists taking a very active part, particularly in their advocacy of mutationism and their concerted critique of Lamarckism.[30] In mid-1924 Koltsov published a long article advancing his arguments against Lamarckian inheritance in general and its Russian proponents in particular.[31] Soon Filipchenko joined the battle by publishing a booklet entitled 'Are Acquired Characteristics Inheritable?', which included a Russian translation of an article by the leading US geneticist T. H. Morgan and an article by Filipchenko himself.[32] Both articles answered the question posed in the title of the booklet in the negative.

Although geneticists adamantly rejected the inheritance of acquired characteristics, several Russian biologists defended Lamarckism. They launched a counter-attack on genetics, which they saw merely as a modern version of preformationism, presenting their own views as a kind of epigenesis.[33] They regularly reviewed and abstracted works by western proponents of Lamarckism, including the notorious experiments of the Austrian biologist Kammerer.[34] In 1925 Kammerer's voluminous treatise on 'General Biology' appeared in Russian translation with a sympathetic (though anonymous) foreword.[35] In 1927 the entomologist Smirnov published a lengthy survey of 'the problem of the inheritance of acquired characteristics'.[36] The same year, two different publishers almost simultaneously released Russian translations of Kammerer's book *The Enigma of Heredity*.[37] Geneticists responded to the growing popularity of Lamarckism by producing highly critical accounts of their opponents' research and publications. A student of Koltsov, Serebrovsky, offered a detailed critique of major publications by Russian Lamarckists, while a student of Filipchenko, Dobzhansky, provided an analysis of the concept of the inheritance of acquired characteristics.[38]

Although the debates over 'alternative' evolutionary concepts had originated within the biological community, professional Marxists soon joined the fray.[39] In his 1923 edition of Plekhanov's collected works, the Marxist historian Dmitry Riazanov criticised Plekhanov's supportive remarks on mutationism.[40] Another Marxist, Sarabianov, disagreed with Riazanov and defended not only mutationism, but also orthogenesis and Lamarckism.[41] Other Marxists soon joined the polemics, publishing arguments *pro* and *contra* mutationism in *Under the Banner of Marxism*.[42] Some criticised Darwinism for its attachment to gradualism and neglect of the 'revolutions' embodied in sudden mutations, while others attacked mutationism for its neglect of the environmental influences on evolutionary processes embodied in the inheritance of acquired characteristics.

The Sverdlov Communist University, the Timiriazev Biological Institute (renamed in 1924 the Timiriazev Scientific-Research Institute for the Study and Propaganda of the Scientific Foundations of Dialectical Materialism) and the Communist Academy constituted the stronghold of Lamarckism. Two Marxist societies organised in 1924 under the auspices of the Moscow University medical school, the 'Circle of Materialist-Physicians' and 'Leninism in Medicine', also lent support.[43] In late November 1925 Professor Boris Zavadovsky of the Sverdlov Communist University delivered a long report to the Communist Academy on 'Darwinism and Marxism', advocating a 'synthesis' of Lamarckism and genetics.[44] The Academy leadership even planned a special laboratory to prove the existence of the inheritance of acquired characteristics and invited Kammerer to head it. Kammerer accepted the invitation, but on the eve of his departure to Russia, faced with accusations of scientific fraud, he committed suicide, and so the projected laboratory never materialised.

Several geneticists, notably Serebrovsky, joined the Communist Academy to lead the criticism of Lamarckism from the inside. In January 1926 Serebrovsky delivered there a long talk on 'Morgan's and Mendel's Theory of Heredity and Marxists', arguing that modern genetics represented a 'truly materialist', and hence 'Marxist', view of heredity and variability, while Lamarckism was 'anti-Marxist'.[45] In subsequent years geneticists and their critics regularly debated the interrelations among genetics, Lamarckism, Darwinism and Marxism within the Academy, with proceedings appearing on the pages of the Academy's publications.[46]

The polemics over Lamarckism raged from 1924 to 1930. Geneticists and their Marxist supporters clearly won the debate. Serebrovsky's untiring crusade against Lamarckism within the Communist Academy 'converted' to genetics a number of young Marxists, including the founder of the 'Circle of Materialist-Physicians', Levit, and the rising science administrator Agol, who had previously subscribed to Lamarckism. Each of the 'converts' published extensive critiques of their former comrades 'from the viewpoint of dialectical materialism'.[47] As a result, the supporters of Lamarckism became marginalised and lost their institutional strongholds, most importantly the Timiriazev Institute (Agol became its director in early 1930) and the Communist Academy, which came to be dominated by geneticists and their Marxist allies.

The results of the 1920s debates over Lamarckism proved far more profound than any simple victory for the geneticists. In the course of these debates a group of Marxists specialising in 'dialectics of nature' attempted 'to develop the dialectical-materialist methodology' for biology.[48] This group introduced a new 'Marxist' lexicon and a new polemical style into discussions of evolutionary issues. Like similar polemics in other fields of knowledge, the debates quickly moved from issues concerning the validity of certain scientific concepts, such as Lamarckism and genetics, to issues regarding which of the competing concepts (and, respectively, its advocates) was more 'Marxist' – and hence more 'Darwinist' (or vice versa) – than the other. As Agol stated in his 1930 monograph *Dialectical Method and Evolutionary Theory*: 'Darwinism is an intrinsic materialistic dialectics of biology ... Darwinism as a method of studying animal and plant kingdoms is one of the areas of the application of the dialectical method.'[49] The actual content of competing biological concepts became subordinate to their perceived philosophical/ideological foundations.

In many polemical writings, references to 'sacral texts' by Marx, Engels and Lenin replaced the invocation of scientific observations and experiments. Professional Marxists with no biological training saw fit to enter the debates and pass judgements on questions of biological evolution using only Engels's *Dialectics of Nature* as a reference. In 1926 the director of the Marx-Engels Institute, Deborin, published a series of articles in *Under the Banner of Marxism* on 'Engels and dialectics in biology'.[50] Along with Marx, Engels and Lenin, a number of Marxist polemicists began to hail Timiriazev as a 'founding father of Darwinism', using his statements to support their own, often diverging, views on evolution, variability and heredity.[51] Thus, debates began to revolve not around scientific facts, hypotheses and conceptions *per se*, but rather around which concepts better corresponded to the pronouncements of the 'founding fathers' of both Marxism and Darwinism.

Just as the two parallel systems of scientific institutions – 'academic' and 'communist' – coexisted in the 1920s, so, too, did traditional scientific and 'Marxist' treatments of evolutionary issues coexist in different settings: the former appeared mostly in professional periodicals, the latter in Party publications and the popular press. During the 1920s the majority of Soviet biologists stayed clear of Marxist debates. At the three congresses of Russian zoologists, anatomists and histologists (1922, 1925 and 1927), the links between 'Marxism' and 'Darwinism' were completely absent from discussions, although questions about evolution, heredity and variability occupied almost half of their proceedings. Similarly, in a jubilee account of the development of Darwinism during the first decade of the Soviet regime, Russia's leading evolutionary morphologist Severtsev did not even mention Marxism.[52] Furthermore, the first Soviet edition of Darwin's collected works issued in 1928–9 under the editorship of Russia's foremost ornithologist, Menzbir, contained not a single reference to Marxism.[53]

One can see a clear generational divide in the involvement of Soviet biologists in the discussions over 'Marxism and Darwinism': while older scientists largely abstained from using Marxist vocabulary and adopting 'communist' polemical culture, many of their younger colleagues eagerly entered the debates. It is indicative that not a single figure among the first generation of geneticists, including Koltsov and Filipchenko, utilised the Marxist lexicon or took part in the debates over 'Darwinism and Marxism'. In contrast, many of their students, including Serebrovsky, Boris and Mikhail Zavadovsky, Agol and Levit, became actively engaged in 'Marxist' polemics. For some biologists, such as Serebrovsky and Levit, dialectical materialism perhaps indeed became a genuine source of inspiration and influenced their research programmes and scientific writings. But at the same time, for them as for many others, Marxism provided a convenient rhetorical cover for advancing their personal research interests, institutionalising their own approaches or simply promoting their own careers within the Soviet science system. The younger generation of Soviet biologists struggled to establish and maintain their own institutions and careers when available institutional niches within the academic science system had already been occupied by their older colleagues. References to the philosophical/ideological value of their work may have helped younger biologists to bolster their appeals for state support by displaying their loyalty to their employer – the Bolshevik state.

Yet the 1920s debates over 'Darwinism and Marxism' produced more than convenient rhetoric. The debates effectively 'grafted' Darwinism on to Marxism in Russia. The resulting hybrid – 'Marxist-Darwinism' – emerged as a powerful cultural resource employed by every interested party for its own advantage.[54] 'Marxist-Darwinism' appeared very influential in intellectual and institutional battles of the time owing to the considerable flexibility of its constituent components, both Marxism and Darwinism. The label 'Darwinism' covered a variety of theoretical constructions on the issues of biological evolution, with adherents of every competing doctrine – be it mutationism, isolationism, orthogenesis or Lamarckism – claiming that their own views represented 'true Darwinism' while those advocated by their opponents exemplified 'anti-Darwinism'. Similarly, the label 'Marxism' covered a number of often contradictory statements, declarations and assertions produced by various individuals and groups, each of which claimed to advance dialectical materialism as originated by Marx, Engels and Lenin. The fierce polemics over the content of Marxism that raged within the community of Soviet Marxists during the 1920s added great volatility to the actual contents of 'Marxist-Darwinism'.

The debates over Lamarckism, coupled with the active propaganda of both Darwinism and Marxism, transformed specialised, often esoteric knowledge about the laws and principles of evolution, heredity and variability into a *public* cultural resource – 'Marxist-Darwinism' – readily available not only to professional biologists and professional Marxists, but also to any graduate of the Soviet educational system and, most importantly, to state and Party officials at all levels. The inclusion of Darwinism as a part of Marxism in curricula of educational institutions helped disseminate a simplified, stripped-down knowledge of evolution, heredity and variability. Similarly, the inclusion of 'Marxist evaluations of Darwinism' in biology curricula helped spread the particular Marxist lexicon that had emerged within the 1920s debates over Lamarckism. Although the 1920s discussions of evolutionary questions in terms of Marxism represented only a fraction of research and publications on evolution, heredity and variability in the country, they set definitive parameters for ensuing debates over these issues, including the range of participants and the type of arguments used to defend/attack particular intellectual positions and institutional actions.

The public nature of 'Marxist-Darwinism' made its meanings highly dependent on specific institutional, intellectual and ideological contexts, within which the competing groups exploited this cultural resource. In their competition for resources interested parties deployed 'Marxist-Darwinism' as a convenient language shared by the biological community and its Party/ state patrons, defining and redefining its vocabulary according to the current political, ideological and economic priorities of the regime. Competition over which of the many interest groups would set the terms, forms and norms of the meaning of 'Marxist-Darwinism' characterised much of the subsequent development of Soviet biology. It was the ability of Lysenko and his supporters to exercise their control over 'Marxist-Darwinism' that secured their victory in competition with geneticists over agricultural institutions during the 1930s.

PAVLOV'S COMMUNISTS: DIALECTICAL MATERIALISM AS METHODOLOGY AND PHILOSOPHY

Pavlov (1849–1936) was Russia's sole Nobel prize-winner and the country's most internationally acclaimed scientist in the 1920s and 1930s. Having seriously considered emigration after the Bolshevik seizure of power, he had remained in Russia for a variety of reasons – his patriotism, the impossibility of recreating his large laboratory enterprise abroad and Lenin's pledge (which he and his successors fully redeemed) of essentially unlimited support. The Bolsheviks sought to reap propaganda value from having this Nobel laureate flourish in revolutionary Russia and also valued his scientific work as a contribution to the materialist world-view. Protected by his special status, Pavlov cultivated contacts with the state that enabled him to expand his scientific enterprise to an unprecedented degree while at the same time constantly criticising the regime. A very rare voice of public criticism throughout the 1920s, he lambasted the Bolsheviks in private and semi-private forums in the 1930s, undeterred by his knowledge that these were monitored by the secret police. To the end of his days, Pavlov criticised the regime's repression, dogmatism, persecution of religion and incompetence; but in his last years, particularly after the Nazi seizure of power in

1933, he changed his tone and also praised it for important achievements, most notably its lavish support for science.[55]

Were it not for his special status, Pavlov would have provided an ideal target for the Great Break's campaign against mechanical materialism. Constantly equating organisms with complex machines, and dogs with humans, he insisted on the fundamental continuity between physical, chemical, biological and psychological processes. He dismissed as 'animism and dualism' the dialectical materialist view of emergent qualities at different levels of organisation, and, when asked his opinion of that philosophy in 1935 by the visiting luminary H. G. Wells, he responded with 'comic gestures of disgust'. Pavlov was sharply criticised as a mechanist at the Conference on Behaviour convened in 1930, but his defenders were also quite vocal. In any case, the larger policy considerations behind his special status prevailed over such relatively minor doctrinal issues.[56]

The Communists who entered Pavlov's laboratories from the early 1920s, and in growing numbers with the Great Break, were, then, unable simply to impose dialectical materialist ideas or rhetoric upon their chief as did their comrades in other venues. A number of them instead engaged him intellectually by bringing their notion of dialectical materialism into close, creative contact with the real substance of Pavlovian investigations – and they succeeded to some degree in substantially influencing his investigations and views.

During the 1930s nine Communists worked regularly in Pavlov's laboratories. They represented the new generation of Soviet scientists that Lenin had envisioned a decade earlier: working-class Party militants who had taken advantage of educational opportunities in the 1920s to acquire the necessary skills to replace their bourgeois predecessors. Dedicated and competent young scientists, they earned Pavlov's trust in the laboratory. Some earned the chief's high compliment of being 'a thinking person' and contributed novel perspectives to laboratory research. Having mastered the difficult lexicon and procedures of conditional reflexes research, they were prepared, in the spirit of the Great Break, to push Pavlov beyond the confines of what they saw as his bourgeois mechanist views.

One such figure was Maiorov (1900–64), who worked with Pavlov from 1925 until the chief's death in 1936. The son of a cobbler, Maiorov had joined the wave of Red Army veterans who flooded Petrograd's Military-Medical Academy after the Civil War. As a medical student, he worked in Pavlov's laboratory there, earning the chief's offer of a precious paid position as his assistant and then organising the physiological laboratory at Pavlov's new science village outside Leningrad, the Institute of Experimental Genetics of Higher Nervous Activity in Koltushi.

'An active Party comrade well-prepared in Marxism', Maiorov was dispatched by his Party cell in August 1929 to the Leningrad branch of the Communist Academy. From 1929 to 1932 he combined his laboratory and political work with graduate studies of the history of philosophy, theories of knowledge, genetics, variability and evolution – all with an eye towards Pavlovian experimental practice and doctrine. He completed his training by writing two reports: *Physiology and Psychology* and *A Critique of the Methodological Foundations of the Pavlov School.* These were circulated and discussed among Maiorov's comrades in Pavlov's laboratories.[57]

Composed under the supervision of Communist Party instructors charged with preparing new proletarian cadres to replace bourgeois specialists and revolutionise science in a Marxist spirit, Maiorov's *Critique* offered a detailed analysis of Pavlovian research and a programme of action for Pavlov's Communists in the era of the Great Break. For Maiorov, Pavlov's great service was developing a new branch of physiology that dealt a 'fatal blow' to spiritualist views and revealed experimentally the material foundations of psychic activity. Pavlov avoided philosophical discussions and professed a positivist separation of philosophy and science. Yet the design and interpretation of experiments were limited by his reductionism and his conviction that the organism was but a complex machine.

Pavlov could, however, be moved by the 'spontaneous dialectics of facts', especially if experimental results were forcefully called to his attention and interpreted in correct dialectical fashion. So, for example, his long-standing mechanistic notion of 'the struggle and balance' between excitation and inhibition was yielding increasingly to the concept of 'mutual induction'. This principle had been urged upon him in the 1920s by Fursikov, a non-Party dialectical materialist who later became director of the Institute of Higher Nervous Activity at the Communist Academy. According to the 'law of mutual induction', the opposed processes of excitation and inhibition interacted with and conditioned one another. So, for example, the effect of a conditional exciter was often enhanced if it immediately followed a conditional inhibitor, and vice versa. Fursikov had endured two years of the chief's hostility and ostracism before finally convincing him that experimental data were better explained by the principle of 'mutual induction' than by that of 'struggle and balance'. Fursikov's law, which he had urged upon Pavlov without any dialectical materialist phraseology, thereafter became central to Pavlovian explanations.[58]

Maiorov identified three fundamental issues in the struggle between mechanistic and dialectical approaches to Pavlovian research. First, the relationship between physiological and social phenomena: Pavlov and a number of his co-workers were guilty of 'physiological imperialism', that is, of reducing social phenomena to physiological processes. Pavlov's concepts of the 'reflex of goal', 'reflex of freedom' and 'reflex of slavery' were notorious examples, surpassed only by the unpublished but well-known public addresses in which he had deployed his studies of conditional reflexes 'to explain social phenomena and to reach several reactionary political conclusions'. A number of his co-workers had followed Pavlov's lead, such as Savich, author of the 'accursed book' *Foundations of Human Behaviour* (1924, 1927), in which he argued that 'social relations are a consequence of reflexive reactions', analysed morality as a purely biological function and attributed revolutions to the sexual instinct and compared them to amoeboid reactions.[59]

A second key issue was the relationship between physiological and psychological phenomena, and the related question of the similarities and differences between higher functions in dogs and humans. Here Maiorov found Pavlov's views insufficiently dialectical (of course), but free of two errors manifested by many of his co-workers. In his essay on 'Physiology and Psychology', Maiorov had developed the traditional dialectical materialist view that the objective and subjective (i.e. physiological and psychological) processes represented a 'dialectical unity' – each was real and each represented an aspect of the same unitary process. Pavlov, he noted, was in basic agreement with this and, unlike some of his co-workers, did not deny or discount the subjective realm, understanding that (as Pavlov himself had put it) 'the subjective world exists and that it is the task of science not to ignore this subjective world but to learn how to explain it'. Pavlov also recognised the highly developed cortex in man as the main feature separating humans from other animals. So, although he believed that the same basic laws applied to both, he was more careful than many of his co-workers in extending to humans the results of experiments on dogs. Yet Pavlov understood the unity of physiology and psychology mechanistically, thought naïvely that his conditional reflexes methodology would fully elucidate the relations of mind and body and sought to avoid a metaphysical commitment to materialism, characterising himself instead as a 'monist'.[60]

The third fundamental problem concerned 'analysis and synthesis', both in higher nervous activity and in scientific enquiry itself. For the dialectical materialist, Maiorov observed, the brain and correct scientific investigation each moved both from the simple to the complex (analysis) and from the complex to the simple (synthesis). The understanding of any complex whole required knowledge of its parts as well as of the whole (which, having its own dynamics, was not the simple sum of its parts). As a mechanist, Pavlov had pursued an almost entirely analytical path of research – breaking down the higher nervous activity of animals into its component parts (unconditional and conditional reflexes and the laws governing them) and attempting mechanistically to construct from these an understanding of the whole (higher nervous activity). So, Pavlov's conception of higher nervous activity rested almost entirely upon experiments on the dynamics of individual conditional reflexes.

Recently, however, Pavlov himself had recognised the limitations of this approach and the need to investigate more fully the synthetic qualities of the cerebral cortex. This was clear, for example, in the emerging importance of the concept of 'systematicity'. If, for example, a series of conditional reflexes was established (say, the buzzer as a conditional exciter, electrical shock as a conditional inhibitor and the metronome as a conditional inhibitor) any variation in the order of those exciters changed the response to *each*. The cortex, in other words, responded not just to a single exciter but to the system of exciters as a whole. This holistic moment resulted from the interaction of the individual reflexes and constituted 'one of the essential qualities of cortical activity'. Pavlovian research had thus already revealed 'much that is new and of fundamental importance' about the synthetic dimension of cortical activity, but progress was limited by the chief's one-sidedly analytical cast of mind.

For Maiorov, attention to this synthetic dimension was the great contribution of modern Gestalt theory and, especially, of Wolfgang Köhler, who insisted that the intelligence displayed by chimpanzees could not be explained by simple reflexive mechanisms. Köhler's one-sided Gestaltism and preoccupation with 'synthesis' mirrored Pavlov's one-sided associationism and preoccupation with 'analysis'. A 'dialectically understood' physiology of higher nervous activity would synthesise the two on a materialist foundation, a task that required both a more expansive investigative methodology and a broader interpretative framework than Pavlov's. Experiments on the conditional reflexes of dogs could advance the study of higher nervous activity only so far; other methods and other model organisms were necessary.

What, then, was to be done? Maiorov suggested three principal lines of investigation through which Communists could educate Pavlov and his co-workers while expanding Pavlovian investigations beyond the bounds of its originator's ideological convictions and methodological imagination: first, to develop systematic investigations of higher nervous activity 'below and above the classical dog; that is, to develop in all possible ways the comparative physiology of higher nervous activity of animals on the basis of materialist dialectics'. Second, Communists should concentrate their efforts on the Biological Station at Koltushi, where the research agenda was conducive to pitting the 'Marxist-Leninist worldview against the mechanistic conception of Pavlov'. Koltushi's focus on the genetics of the higher nervous activity of animals brought to the fore issues related to genetics and the influence of the environment that 'will lead the Pavlovian school far beyond the boundaries of physiology to the sphere of broad biological questions'. Communist leadership was also especially necessary there to resist the 'great danger of the mechanical transfer to man of conclusions acquired in experiments and observations on dogs'. Finally, Communists should initiate investigations of higher nervous activity in humans, which would 'inevitably involve a rejection of outmoded Pavlovian methodology'. This process, indeed, had already begun in a division of Pavlov's enterprise directed by his Communist co-worker Dolin: 'the Division of Pathophysiology of the Higher Nervous Activity of Man *organised by us*, the work of which is built upon dialectical materialist methodology'. In sum, by highlighting the 'synthetic' dimension of cortical activity, the differences between this synthetic dimension in various organisms and the role of the broader environment Communist Pavlovians could expand Pavlovism beyond the chief's mechanistic limitations.

In their scientific research, Pavlov's Communists pursued *precisely* this agenda. Maiorov himself capitalised on the chief's long-standing interest in the roles of nature and nurture in determining 'nervous type' (personality) by collaborating with a non-Communist co-worker in experiments on dogs at Koltushi that demonstrated to the chief's satisfaction that the environment in which a pup was raised (whether 'free' to roam the fields or 'imprisoned' in a kennel) fundamentally influenced its nervous type.[61]

His comrade Denisov brought the chimpanzees Roza and Rafael to Koltushi in summer 1933 and collaborated with Pavlov on experiments that gradually forced the chief to appreciate the qualitative differences between dogs and primates (and to amend his doctrine accordingly). Pavlov had resisted repeated entreaties to study the conditional reflexes of anthropoids at the primate colony in Sukhumi, Abkhazia, so Denisov instead brought the mountain to Mohammed. Of the seven or eight co-workers who researched conditional reflexes in anthropoids during Pavlov's lifetime, at least *five* were Communists – who also clustered disproportionately around research on 'systematicity' and humans – and two more were attached to the Communist Academy.[62]

The research interests of another Communist co-worker, Dolin, read like a check-list of Maiorov's priorities. Having studied primates at Fursikov's Institute of Higher Nervous Activity at the Communist Academy, he served as senior assistant at Pavlov's Nervous Clinic, directing a laboratory there devoted to the investigation of higher nervous activity in humans. Here Dolin attempted also to develop a new methodology for investigating conditional reflexes in humans (since salivary fistulas were impractical). With Pavlov's support, he became head of the Division of Physiology of Higher Nervous Activity at Leningrad's Institute for the Study of the Brain, where he continued the work on comparative physiology that he had begun at the Sukhumi Primatological Centre and the Communist Academy. As assistant to Pavlov's long-time collaborator and lover, Maria Petrova, in her Department of Physiology and Pathology of Higher Nervous Activity at Leningrad's Institute for the Improvement of Physicians, Dolin and his co-workers elaborated the principle of cortical systematicity through studies of nervous pathology and its treatment in humans. His experiments on humans, together with Denisov's and Pavlov's collaborative experiments on chimpanzees, proved instrumental in the chief's abandonment of his long-standing identification of 'conditional reflexes' and 'associations' – a development that signalled important changes in Pavlov's thinking about the relationship of physiology and psychology in the final months of his life.[63]

The complex dynamics of the Communists' intellectual influence on Pavlov's research and views cannot be discussed in this brief essay, but it was clearly substantial. In the years 1929–36 Pavlov's research featured an increasing concentration on systematicity, the self-conscious combination of analytical and synthetic approaches (which the chief came to justify in the very same terms as in Maiorov's *Critique* – as a synthesis of the elements of truth in both associationism and Gestalt) and an increasingly pointed comparison of results achieved upon dogs, chimpanzees and humans. During his final months the preliminary results of these lines of investigation combined to raise in Pavlov's mind some of the fundamental questions that his Communists had hoped to bring to the fore – complicating his views about the nature of the conditional reflex and the relationship between physiology and psychology, and preparing the ground for a considerable broadening of his doctrine to tackle and explain what he came to see as important differences between dogs, chimpanzees and humans.[64]

Pavlov, however, died in February 1936. His Communists and his doctrine were gripped soon after by features of Stalinist culture far more fundamental than dialectical materialist doctrine.

CONCLUSION

Our discussions of 'Marxist-Darwinism' and 'Dialectical Materialist Pavlovism' have each emphasised one aspect of the complex use of dialectical materialism as a cultural resource.

Marxist-Darwinism was indeed a flexible cultural resource by which biologists sought the favour of state patrons and protection from competitors and demagogues, and through which Party officials informed the scientific community of the latest twists in the Party line – yet for some scientists it also provided a new way of thinking about evolutionary processes, finding new approaches to their research subjects and resolving exciting intellectual issues. In the 1920s Serebrovsky's search for a non-reductionist solution to the problem of integrating a population as a basic unit in evolutionary processes and a gene mutation as a basic evolutionary event led him to develop the concept of 'gene fund' (*genofond*) as a cumulative expression of all the genes and their variants in a population. As Mark Adams has convincingly demonstrated, this concept proved highly instrumental in the 'new synthesis' of genetics and Darwinism in the 1930s and 1940s.[65] Similarly, a decade later, the search for a non-reductionist explanation of relationships among embryonic development, genetic transmission and evolution led the prominent Soviet biologist Schmalhausen to his concept of 'norm of reaction', as a range of phenotypic expression for any given genotype in different environments. According to Garland Allen, this concept helped Schmalhausen to formulate his ideas of 'dialectical interaction' between the 'dynamic' and 'stabilising' forms of natural selection, which appeared very influential in the subsequent investigations of the issues.[66]

Pavlov's Communists indeed used dialectical materialism authentically to challenge their chief's mechanistic and reductionist views, and to devise specific lines of investigation that would broaden those views by engaging them on a scientific terrain – but they also deployed it to demonstrate their loyalty to the Party line, to defend themselves against the charges of 'mechanism' levelled against the chief and to prepare for the day when Pavlov himself passed from the scene. Maiorov conceded to Marxist critics of Pavlov during the Great Break that there was indeed a 'crisis' in Pavlovian studies, but hoped that Communist attempts to broaden Pavlovism would demonstrate that this was not the fatal crisis of a bourgeois doctrine but rather a 'crisis of development'. In other words, that the scientific orientation to which Pavlov's Communists had hitched their fates merited support even after the chief's death. The fate of these Communists' scientific contributions to Pavlov's doctrine remains to be studied, but months after Pavlov's death the Great Terror transformed the terrain upon which they operated. Denisov and his comrade Nikitin were both denounced as Trotskyists – Denisov was shot and Nikitin cheated the NKVD by committing suicide. The genuine intellectual issues raised and pursued in the 1930s would play little role in public discourse amid the political struggle that culminated in the 'Pavlovian session' of 1950, which enshrined both Pavlov and his doctrine as icons in the image of official late Stalinist dialectical materialism.[67]

NOTES

1. For dialectical materialism as philosophy of science, see David Joravsky, *Soviet Marxism and Natural Science, 1917–1932* (New York: Columbia University Press, 1961), and Loren Graham, *Science, Philosophy, and Human Behavior in the Soviet Union* (New York: Columbia University Press, 1987); for dialectical materialism as a broader cultural resource, see Nikolai Krementsov, *Stalinist Science* (Princeton University Press, 1997); Krementsov, 'Big revolution, little revolution: science and politics in Bolshevik Russia', *Social Research*, 73:4 (2006), 1173–204; and Alexei Kozhevnikov, *Stalin's Great Science: The Times and Adventures of Soviet Physicists* (London: Imperial College Press, 2004).

2. Krementsov, *Stalinist Science*, pp. 16–30; Vera Tolz, *Russian Academicians and the Revolution: Combining Professionalism and Politics* (New York: St Martin's Press, 1997).

3. Richard Stites, *Revolutionary Dreams: Utopian Vision and Experimental Life in the Russian Revolution* (New York and Oxford: Oxford University Press, 1989); James Andrews, *Science for the Masses: The Bolshevik State, Public Science, and the Popular Imagination in Soviet Russia, 1917–1934* (College Station: Texas A&M University Press, 2003).

4. V. I. Lenin, 'O znachenii voinstvuiushchego materializma', *Pod znamenem marksizma* (hereafter *PZM*), 3 (1922), 29.

5. Michael David-Fox, *Revolution of the Mind: Higher Learning among the Bolsheviks, 1918–1929* (Ithaca: Cornell University Press, 1997); Krementsov, *Stalinist Science*, pp. 23–9.

6. Joravsky, *Soviet Marxism*, especially pp. 65–6, 221–2, 299–300, 310; Mark B. Adams, 'Eugenics in Russia, 1900–1940' in Adams (ed.), *The Wellborn Science: Eugenics in Germany, France, Brazil, and Russia* (New York: Oxford University Press, 1990), pp. 153–201; and Krementsov, 'Big revolution, little revolution', 1173–204, see especially 1193. On Vygotsky, see Graham, *Science, Philosophy, and Human Behavior in the Soviet Union*, pp. 168–76, and Joravsky, *Russian Psychology: A Critical History* (Oxford: Basil Blackwell, 1989), pp. 238–70.

7. V. I. Lenin, *Materialism and Empirio-Criticism: Critical Comments on a Reactionary Philosophy* (New York: International Publishers, 1927). Lenin did not comment on relativity theory. For an influential historical analysis of the ideological context of the new physics in the West, see Paul Forman, 'Weimar culture, causality, and quantum theory: adaptation by German physicists and mathematicians to a hostile environment', *Historical Studies in the Physical Sciences*, 3 (1971), 1–115.

8. Joravsky, *Soviet Marxism*, p. 284; Alexander Vucinich, *Einstein and Soviet Ideology* (Stanford University Press, 2001), p. 34.

9. Joravsky, *Soviet Marxism*, pp. 275–6; Vucinich, *Einstein*, p. 55.

10. Joravsky, *Soviet Marxism*, pp. 221–2.

11. Sheila Fitzpatrick, *Education and Social Mobility in the Soviet Union, 1921–1932* (Cambridge University Press, 1979); Fitzpatrick (ed.), *Cultural Revolution in Russia, 1928–1931* (Bloomington: Indiana University Press, 1978); Krementsov, *Stalinist Science*, pp. 31–54; Loren Graham, *The Soviet Academy of Sciences and the Communist Party, 1927–1932* (Princeton University Press, 1967); F. F. Perchenok, 'Akademiia Nauk na Velikom Perelome' in G. V. Belkova *et al.* (eds.), *Zven'ia: Istoricheskii al'manakh*, vol. I (Moscow: Progress, 1991), pp. 163–235.

12. Joravsky, *Soviet Marxism*, p. 238; Krementsov, *Stalinist Science*, p. 40.

13. The cynical comment is from a discussion of the manipulation of food rations to encourage political loyalty, in *Arkhiv Rossiiskoi Akademii Nauk*, St Petersburg, *fond* 2, *opis'* 1–1917, *delo* 43, *list* 54 (hereafter: ARAN 2.1–1917.43:54). Draft letter from Pavlov to Molotov, probably written in December 1935, ARAN 259.1a.39:14.

14. Vucinich, 'Soviet physicists and philosophers in the 1930s: dynamics of a conflict', *Isis*, 71:257 (1980), 236–350 (see especially 237, 239).

15. Joravsky, *Soviet Marxism*, pp. 275–95; Vucinich, 'Soviet physicists', 242, 244; Vucinich, *Einstein*, pp. 71, 77, 84; David Holloway, 'Physics, the state, and civil society in the Soviet Union', *Historical Studies in the Physical and Biological Sciences*, 31:1 (1999), 173–93.

16. Graham, *Science, Philosophy, and Human Behavior in the Soviet Union*, p. xi. See also Graham's *Science in Russia and the Soviet Union: A Short History* (Cambridge University Press, 1993), pp. 99–120; and, especially, his article 'Do mathematical equations display social attributes?', *The Mathematical Intelligencer*, 22 (1999), 31–6.

17. David-Fox, *Revolution of the Mind*.

18. Andrews, *Science for the Masses*.

19. G. Ia. Graf, *Ot biblii k Darvinu* (Leningrad: Gosudarstvennoe izdatel'stvo, 1925).

20. M. Ravich-Cherkasskii, 'Predislovie k pervomu izdaniiu' in Ravich-Cherkasskii (ed.), *Darvinizm i Marksizm* (Kharkov: Gosudarstvennoe izdatel'stvo Ukrainy, 1925), p. 6.

21. B. M. Zavadovskii, *Darvinizm i marksizm* (Moscow: Gosudarstvennoe izdatel'stvo, 1926).

22. L. Trotskii, 'K pervomu vserossiiskomu s''ezdu nauchnykh rabotnikov', *Izvestiia*, 24 November 1923, p. 1.

23. 'Ot Redaktsii', *PZM*, nos. 1–2 (1922), 3–4, here 4.

24. Lenin, 'O znachenii voinstvuiushchego materializma', p. 29.

25. 'O politike partii v oblasti khudozhestvennoi literatury', *Zvezda*, no. 4 (1925), 256–9 (see 257).

26. K. A. Timiriazev, 'Darvin and Marks', *Proletarskaia kul'tura*, nos. 9–10 (1919), 20–5.

27. Krementsov, *Stalinist Science*.

28. Mark B. Adams, 'Through the looking glass: the evolution of Soviet Darwinism' in Leonard Warren and Hilary Koprowski (eds.), *New Perspectives on Evolution* (New York: Wiley-Liss, 1991), pp. 37–63.

29. Peter J. Bowler, *The Eclipse of Darwinism* (Baltimore: The Johns Hopkins University Press, 1983).
30. A. E. Gaissinovitch, 'The origins of Soviet genetics and the struggle with Lamarckism, 1922–1929', *Journal of the History of Biology*, 13 (1980), 1–51.
31. N. K. Kol'tsov, 'Noveishie popytki dokazat' nasledstvennost' blagopriobreten-nykh priznakov', *Russkii evgenicheskii zhurnal*, 3:2–3 (1924), 159–67.
32. T. H. Morgan and Iu. A. Filipchenko, *Nasledstvenny li priobretennye priznaki* (Leningrad: Seiatel', 1925). For Morgan's original article, 'Are acquired characteristics inherited?', see *Yale Review*, 13:4 (1924), 712–29.
33. *Preformizm ili epigenezis?* (Volodga: Severnyi pechatnik, 1926).
34. E. S. Smirnov, Iu. M. Vermel' and B. S. Kuzin, *Ocherki po teorii evoliutsii* (Moscow: Krasnaia nov', 1924). On Kammerer's work, see Sander Gliboff, 'The case of Paul Kammerer: evolution and experimentation in the early 20th century', *Journal of the History of Biology*, 39 (2006): 525–63.
35. P. Kammerer, *Obshchaia biologiia* (Moscow and Leningrad: Gosudarstvennoe izdatel'stvo, 1925).
36. E. S. Smirnov, *Problema nasledovaniia priobretennykh priznakov: Kriticheskii obzor literatury* (Moscow: Izdatel'stvo Komakademii, 1927).
37. P. Kammerer, *Zagadka nasledstvennosti* (Leningrad: Priboi, 1927; Moscow: Gosudarstvennoe izdatel'stvo, 1927).
38. A. Serebrovskii, 'E. S. Smirnov, Iu. M. Vermel', B. S. Kuzin, Ocherki po teorii evoliutsii', *Pechat' i revoliutsiia*, no. 4 (1925), 257–8; F. G. Dobrzhanskii, *Chto i kak nasleduetsia u zhivykh sushchestv?* (Leningrad: Gosudarstvennoe izdatel'stvo, 1926).
39. For an early analysis of this debate, see Joravsky, 'Soviet Marxism and biology before Lysenko', *Journal of the History of Ideas*, 20:1 (1959), 85–104.
40. See his commentaries in G. V. Plekhanov, *Osnovnye voprosy marksizma* (Moscow: Gosudarstvennoe izdatel'stvo, 1923), pp. 120–2.
41. V. Sarab'ianov, 'Nazrevshii vopros', *Sputnik kommunista*, no. 20 (1923), 215–34.
42. Compare, for instance, D. Gul'be, 'Darvinizm i teoriia mutatsii', *PZM*, nos. 8–9 (1924), 157–66, with F. Duchinskii, 'Darvinizm i mutatsionnaia teoriia', *PZM*, no. 3 (1925), 128–39.
43. See, for instance, the article by the founder of the society 'Leninism in Medicine' Petr Obukh, 'Nauka i organizatsiia meditsiny', *Pravda*, 3 February 1923, 2.
44. Zavadovskii, 'Darvinizm i lamarkizm i problema nasledovaniia priobreten-nykh priznakov', *PZM*, nos. 10–11 (1925), 79–114.
45. Serebrovskii, 'Teoriia nasledstvennosti Morgana i Mendelia i marksisty', *PZM*, no. 3 (1926), 98–117.
46. For example, I. I. Agol, 'Dialektika i metafizika v biologii', *PZM*, no. 3 (1926), 118–50; M. M. Mestergazi, 'Epigenezis i genetika', *Vestnik Kommunisticheskoi Akademii*, no. 19 (1927), 187–252; F. Duchinskii, 'Darvinizm, lamarkizm i neodarvinizm', *PZM*, nos. 7–8 (1926), 95–122.
47. For example, Agol, *Vitalizm, mekhanisticheskii materializm i marksizm* (Moscow: Moskovskii rabochii, 1928), and *Dialekticheskii metod i evoliutsionnaia*

teoriia (Moscow: Izd. Komakademii, 1930); S. Levit, 'Evoliutsionnye teorii v biologii i marksizm', *Meditsina i dialekticheskii materializm*, no. 1 (1926), 15–32, and 'Dialekticheskii materializm v meditsine', *Vestnik sovremennoi meditsiny*, no. 23 (1927), 1481–90.

48. 'Ot redaktsii' in *Dialektika v prirode* (Vologda: Severnyi pechatnik, 1926), vol. II, p. viii.

49. Agol, *Dialekticheskii metod*, p. 150.

50. See A. Deborin, 'Engel's i dialektika v biologii', *PZM* (1926), nos. 1–2, 54–89; 3, 5–28; 9–10, 5–25.

51. See N. S. Poniatskii, *Velikii uchenyi-revoliutsioner, Kliment Arkad'evich Timiriazev* (Moscow and Leningrad: Gosudarstvennoe izdatel'stvo, 1923); Duchinskii, 'K. A. Timiriazev kak darvinist', *PZM*, no. 7 (1925), 86–97; for a historical analysis of Timiriazev's views on genetics and their uses by various interested parties, see A. E. Gaissinovitch, 'Contradictory appraisal by K. A. Timiriazev of Mendelian principles and its subsequent perception', *History and Philosophy of the Life Sciences*, 7 (1985), 257–86.

52. A. N. Severtsev, 'Istoricheskoe napravlenie v zoologii' in *Nauka i Tekhnika v SSSR, 1917–27* (Moscow: Rabotnik prosveshcheniia, 1928), pp. 143–93.

53. See M. A. Menzbir (ed.), *Polnoe sobranie sochinenii Charlza Darvina*, 4 vols., each in 2 parts (Moscow and Leningrad: Gosudarstvennoe izdatel'stvo, 1928–9).

54. See Mark B. Adams, 'Darwinism as science and ideology' in John G. Burke (ed.), *Science and Culture in the Western Tradition: Sources and Interpretations* (Scottsdale: Gorsuch Scarisbrick, 1987), pp. 199–208.

55. Daniel P. Todes, 'Pavlov and the Bolsheviks', *History and Philosophy of the Life Sciences*, 17:3 (1995), 379–418.

56. Pavlov's dismissal of dialectical materialism as 'animism and dualism' is recorded in F. P. Maiorov, *Kritika metodologicheskikh osnov Pavlovskoi Shkoly* [1931–2], in ARAN 225.4a.24:12. See Wells's letter of 1 October 1935 to C. E. M. Joad in David Smith (ed.), *The Correspondence of H. G. Wells*, vol. IV (London: Pickering and Chatto, 1998), p. 36. For two Communist co-workers' defence of Pavlov at the Congress on Behaviour, see Maiorov, 'Uchenie akademika I. P. Pavlova ob uslovnykh refleksakh', *Vrachebnaia gazeta*, 1930, no. 1, 61–8, and L. N. Fedorov, 'Metod uslovnykh refleksov v izuchenii vysshei nervnoi deiatel'nosti', *Chelovek i priroda*, 1930, no. 4, 21–6.

57. Maiorov, *Kritika metodologicheskikh osnov Pavlovskoi Shkoly* and *Fiziologiia i psikhologiia* [1931 or 1932], in ARAN 225.4a.24.

58. Maiorov, *Kritika*, pp. 32–3; D. S. Fursikov, 'Iavlenie vzaimnoi induktsii v kore golovnogo mozga', *Arkhiv biologicheskikh nauk*, 23 (1923), 195–216; and his 'O sootnoshenii protsessov vozbuzhdeniia i tormozheniia', *Trudy fiziologicheskikh laboratorii im akademika I.P. Pavlova*, 1:1 (1924), 3–45; Rita Rait-Kovaleva, 'Vospominaniia ob akademike I. P. Pavlove' (unpublished manuscript written in 1970), p. 17, in archive of Dom-Muzei Akademika I. P. Pavlova (Riazan).

59. Maiorov, *Kritika*, pp. 18–23; V. V. Savich, *Osnovy povedeniia cheloveka* (Leningrad, 1924, 1927); for a brief discussion of one of Pavlov's public addresses, see Todes, 'Pavlov and the Bolsheviks', 384–6.

60. Maiorov, *Kritika*, pp. 23–6.
61. S. N. Vyrzhikovskii and F. P. Maiorov, 'Materialy k voprosu o vospitanii na sklad vysshei nervnoi deiatel'nosti u sobak', *Trudy fiziologicheskikh laboratorii im akademika I. P. Pavlova*, 5 (1933), 171–92.
62. Pavlov, 'Intellekt chelovekoobraznykh obez'ian' (unpublished manuscript, probably written in early 1935), in ARAN 259.1.52; P. K. Denisov, 'Analizatornaia i sinteticheskaia funktsiia bol'shikh polusharii shimpanze', *Zhurnal vysshei nervnoi deiatel'nosti*, 8:6 (1958), 345–54; and L. A. Orbeli (ed.), *Pavlovskie sredy*, vol. II (Moscow and Leningrad: Akademiia nauk SSSR, 1949), pp. 385, 517, 573–4.
63. Biographical information on Dolin is from his files at ARAN 259.7.221 and Tsentral'nyi gosudarstvennyi arkhiv istoriko-politicheskikh dokumentov St. Peterburga 1728.385023.
64. This is evident, for example, in 'Intellekt chelovekoobraznykh obez'ian', another unpublished manuscript, 'Psikhologiia kak nauka' (in ARAN 259.1.66), and his remarks recorded in *Pavlovskie sredy*, vol. III, pp. 261–3, 392–3, and 414–15. Relations between Pavlov and the Communists in his laboratories are explored in more detail in Todes's forthcoming biography of Pavlov.
65. Mark B. Adams, 'From "gene fund" to "gene pool": on the evolution of evolutionary language' in William Coleman and Camille Limoges (eds.), *Studies in the History of Biology*, vol. III (Baltimore: The Johns Hopkins University Press, 1979), pp. 241–85.
66. Garland E. Allen, 'Mechanistic and dialectical materialism in 20th century evolutionary theory: the work of Ivan I. Schmalhausen' in Warren and Koprowski (eds.), *New Perspectives on Evolution*, pp. 15–36.
67. On later scientific developments, see Graham's discussion of Petr Anokhin, a Communist co-worker of Pavlov's in the 1920s, in *Science, Philosophy, and Human Behavior*, pp. 200–11. On Pavlov as Stalinist icon, see Krementsov, *Stalinist Science*, pp. 260–75, and *Nauchnaia sessiia posviashchennaia problemam fiziologicheskogo ucheniia akademika I. P. Pavlova* (Moscow: Akademiia nauk SSSR, 1950).

CHAPTER 16

Afterword

James Scanlan

From the time of Peter the Great, Russian social thought has been persistently both introspective and forward-looking – that is, it has been dominated by attention to its own land and to that land's future. However disparate the world-views of the individual thinkers discussed in this volume, the progressives and the conservatives alike were preoccupied with hopes, fears, dreams, warnings, forecasts and other anticipations of what the future held in store for Russia. The progressives dreamt of achieving a prosperous and powerful nation through enlightenment and modernisation, on the model of the western European states of the day. The conservatives, too, looked forward to a rich and strong nation, but one that, by preserving and nurturing the distinctive features of Russian culture, would avoid what they saw as the errors and diseases of the western world.

After all the attention in this volume to what Russia would, should or might become, it may be worthwhile in conclusion to compare our thinkers' visions with what Russia *has* become in the three centuries since Peter the Great's modernising efforts began. How close did these thinkers come to anticipating the subsequent development of their country? What did they accurately foresee, and what did they miss? Which of their hopes and fears came true, and which did not? Entertaining questions of this sort may throw some light on the complex link between social thought and historical reality, not only in the case of Russia but in regard to other modernising nations as well.

This cannot be an effort to pronounce a definitive 'verdict of history' on the Russian thinkers' visions, for history, unlike courtroom trials, is open-ended. It is said that Mao Zedong, once asked whether the French Revolution brought humanity more good than harm, replied thoughtfully that it was too soon to tell. Yet in the present case a qualified verdict, at least, appears to be possible. Leaving aside the future still to come, let us ask how today's Russia compares with the imagined Russias sought or feared by the thinkers of the past three centuries of the nation's history. Which of those thinkers, if any, were right about the forces shaping their country's future and the results those forces would produce?

Virtually all of them – even Chaadaev, despite his gloomy 'Philosophical Letters' (as William Leatherbarrow explains in chapter 5) – correctly foresaw a strong and flourishing Russia ahead, though few had any inkling of the enormous human cost of that progress and none, with the possible exceptions of Dostoevsky and Danilevsky, anticipated the full global impact of Russia's power and resources. Peter the Great's dream of an educated, technically advanced, militarily powerful, wealthy and influential Russia came true, not nearly as smoothly as he may have hoped but to a degree surely unimaginable in his day.

As concerns military power and technological modernisation, even the somewhat diminished Russia of post-Cold-War times remains an undoubted global presence and force. One of the two nuclear superpowers, with a large stockpile of ballistic missiles, the country is rivalled only by the United States as a potential agent of destruction in the world. A pioneer in space exploration, Russia is a partner of the United States in the construction and operation of the International Space Station – a partner on which the American space-shuttle programme is heavily dependent. Moreover, as Charles Ellis has described in chapter 13, Russia does not lag behind the western world in the basic science behind the country's military and other technological achievements.

The material prosperity now increasingly seen in post-Soviet Russia, if not yet broadly distributed or fully secure, is also something Peter the Great would applaud. Granted, it has rested thus far in large part on what are loosely called (by a linguistic coincidence Peter might enjoy) 'petrodollars' – the income gleaned from the exportation to the West of petroleum and natural gas; the country has huge reserves of both. According to one recent estimate, roughly 60 per cent of the Russian government's annual budget is covered by the income from the export tax on oil and gas.[1] But the growing prosperity is also, of course, a function of the western-inspired privatisation and acceptance of capitalist market mechanisms that followed the fall of communism and the break-up of the Soviet Union.

Only now on the cusp of capitalist development in Russia is still another great natural resource – arable land, in which the world's largest country is immensely rich, most of it under-used from an agricultural point of view and a great deal of it not used at all. Legal institutions that facilitate the buying and selling of land are finally being introduced, and the old collective farms are being broken up and sold – not typically to individual farmers for private family farming (as some of our nineteenth-century theorists would have hoped), but to investors, domestic and foreign, who are reassembling the plots into large corporate factory farms to gain economies of scale and apply advanced equipment and the principles of modern agronomy. With no comparable mass of unused or under-used arable land available anywhere else in the world, one specialist predicts that within ten or fifteen years, if the capitalist reforms continue, Russia will be the leading force in world agriculture.[2]

Since these successes are the fruits of modernisation, which in Russia meant westernisation, we would seem obliged to give the palm to the Westernist progressives as the best prognosticators of Russia's future to the present date. No doubt it was their science and technology and their socio-economic reforms – most dramatically, the Great Reforms of the 1860s and the sudden restoration of capitalism at the end of the twentieth century – that set the stage for Russia's development in the twenty-first century. It is certainly true that much of the Westernist agenda has been achieved effectively and beneficially in Russia. And if we add to this picture of progress the fact that the Russian state today enjoys broad public support under a written constitution that has all the appearance of guaranteeing the human rights and freedoms that Westernist liberals in Russia have championed since the days of Radishchev, the triumph of Westernist visions might seem not only salubrious but complete.

But there is much more to the story. 'Westernist visions' is far too broad a rubric to merit blanket congratulations for historical foresight and benign influence on Russia. For one thing, it includes attractive but utopian schemes that were never so much as tried, such as the programmes of agrarian socialism advocated by the Populists and others under the influence of the French socialists. More darkly, it has produced schemes that were tried but proved damaging and consequently had to be abandoned. The most obvious and devastating example of the second category is, of course, the whole, long Marxist experiment, which was grounded in the last word in political economy as pronounced by one wing of western socio-political thought. Over the course of a century, from Lenin's youth to Gorbachev's overthrow, this attempt to follow in Russia a western-devised socio-economic blueprint for universal human fulfilment, despite some evident successes in industrialisation, literacy and general education that cannot be denied, produced unprecedented brutality and suffering on a massive scale and eventually collapsed through its own incapacity to change.

Most significant today, however, is still another category of Westernist visions that have failed thus far – namely, the visions that have triumphed in form only, not in substance. Despite the overthrow of tsarist and communist autocracies, despite fundamental changes in the Russian economy and despite the recent adoption of a constitution that explicitly endorses the classic liberal socio-political programme advanced by the Russian Westernisers, that programme is far from being realised in Russia. Popular sovereignty, constitutional limits on the power of the ruler, individual human rights and liberties, representative government, the separation of powers, the separation of church and state – these liberal ideals, urged repeatedly by the Westernist thinkers discussed in this volume, have been acknowledged in principle but not yet effectively institutionalised in Russian socio-political reality.

The first attempt to preach liberal principles but practise authoritarianism followed the elimination of Russia's autocratic monarchy in 1917. The Communist government promulgated a succession of 'constitutions', of which the best known is the so-called 'Stalin constitution' (1936–77), which gave ringing endorsements to a multitude of group and individual rights and liberties (including freedom of speech, expression, religion and assembly) and guaranteed 'the inviolability of the person' (Articles 118–33). Yet the document itself provided clues as to how little it meant in reality when it singled out 'working people' as those to whom printing presses and paper would be made available (Article 125) and specified that the right to form public organisations was to be exercised 'in conformity with the interests of the working people' (Article 126) – as defined, of course, by the Communist Party. And, under Stalin, to guarantee 'the inviolability of the person' can only be considered a cruel joke.

The end of Marxist rule and the collapse of the USSR gave Russia the best chance in its history of achieving the goals sought by the liberal Westernisers, and in 1993 the new Russian Federation, headed by a democratically inclined if impulsive Boris Yeltsin, announced a new constitution that raised great hopes. Although the document provides for a relatively strong executive, it explicitly circumscribes the government's powers with such declarations as 'The bearer of sovereignty and the only source of power in the Russian Federation shall be its multinational people' and 'Russia is a democratic, federal, law-bound state with a republican form of government.' 'The supreme, direct expression of the power of the people', the constitution affirms, 'shall be referenda and free elections' (Articles 1–3). It goes on to proclaim freedom of conscience, speech, religion (an established religion is prohibited) and association and in general makes it the obligation of the state to recognise, observe and protect individual rights, including the rights of judicial appeal and land ownership.

Despite all these pious declarations, however, not long after Vladimir Putin was elected president in 2000 we began to see formal and informal changes in the structure and operation of the Russian government, all in the direction of strengthening the Kremlin's power. After 2004, in Putin's second term in office, the pace of such alterations quickened. Among the more significant structural changes was the passage in 2004 of an amendment to the constitution that eliminated direct popular election of the governors of Russia's eighty-eight provinces and republics and replaced it with presidential appointment, thus giving the Kremlin direct control over the administration of the regions. Other major changes were effected not by amendment but by creative manipulation of the constitution's existing provisions. When, in 2008, Putin was approaching the term limit of his presidency, there was much debate about whether he would in fact relinquish his position of power or would, rather, seek to have the constitution changed to permit him to remain as president. In fact, he did neither. He gave up the presidency but he remained in power by exploiting a convenient loophole in the constitution. He endorsed for president his own loyal chief of staff, Dmitry Medvedev, who upon election promptly appointed him (with the consent of the Duma) to the position of 'prime minister' (officially, 'Chairman of the Government of the Russian Federation'), with constitutional duties sufficiently sweeping to give him enormous power when serving under a compliant president and legislature.

Recent observers have catalogued a growing list of features that comprise what the journalist David Remnick has called 'the authoritarian eco-system of Vladimir Putin'.[3] Over and above adjustments and creative uses of the constitution, these include less visible changes in the law and its administration, such as reducing the number of crimes that call for trial by jury and extending the definition of treason (one of the crimes no longer eligible for jury trial) to include any action that harms Russia's 'constitutional order', 'sovereignty' or 'territorial integrity' – all terms that are left undefined.[4] Economic levers, too, are freely used by the Putin administration to maintain control, in a system that increasingly resembles state capitalism. The great natural-resource firms such as Gazprom and Rosneft, as well as virtually all of the major national and regional television networks in Russia, are now owned by the government or its staunch supporters.

Economic control of television, along with other types of pressures on the mass media generally – extending, some charge, to the elimination of troublesome journalists (there have been twenty unsolved murders of journalists in Russia since 2000) – helps the government to discredit and stifle dissenting parties, allowing Putin's party – United Russia – and others closely allied with it to govern without significant opposition.[5] The liberal parties taken together, polls show, are backed by no more than 20 per cent of the population. One prominent liberal leader, Nikita Belykh, has been neatly co-opted by Putin: weary of the arrests and other forms of intimidation to which he and his now-disbanded party, the Union of Right Forces, had been subjected, Belykh in late 2008 accepted Putin's offer to appoint him governor of the Kirov region in return for a pledge that he would not work against United Russia.[6]

Putin's authoritarian eco-system prospers by absorbing elements of civil society into the body of the state, and no element has proved more amenable to co-option than the Russian Orthodox Church. A special church–state bond, as we have seen, has a lengthy history in Russia. Forged by Peter the Great, it was developed by his successors in a way that changed their autocracy into what David Saunders in chapter 2 calls 'a quasi-theocracy'. Nor did the wrenching shift from quasi-theocracy to Communism in 1917 break that bond, for Stalin found a way to exploit the connection even in an atheistic state. Now it is continued in still another form in a state that, officially, advantages no particular faith or absence of faith.

The post-Soviet (1993) constitution affirms that 'The Russian Federation is a secular state. No religion may be established as a state or obligatory one.' 'Religious associations', the text goes on, 'shall be equal before the law' (Article 14). 'Equality before the law', however, appears not to rule out an intimate partnership between the Russian Orthodox Church and the Russian state – sometimes described now as their acting 'in symphony' – that clearly works to the advantage of Orthodoxy over other denominations. On the national level, the principal voices in this 'symphony' have been Putin himself and the late Patriarch Aleksiy II, who headed the Orthodox Church from 1990 until his death on 5 December 2008. Putin openly affirms his own Orthodox faith and endorses legal restrictions on the missionary and other activities of the non-Orthodox denominations. Aleksiy, for his part, publicly supported Putin and praised him on national television for selecting Medvedev to succeed him as president. Medvedev declared the day of Aleksiy's funeral a day of national mourning. For a three-day period, television broadcasting was dominated by documentaries on the patriarch's life, talk shows discussing him, and live coverage of the elaborate funeral ceremony, which was attended by both Putin and Medvedev.[7]

Much of the day-to-day discouragement of other denominations takes place at the regional and local levels, beneath the radar of the national and international media, with the blessing and frequently the active support of the regional executives (appointed by the president) as well as of their legislatures. In the Belgorod region, for example, new laws severely limit Protestant proselytising and require that all children in state schools take what is essentially a Russian Orthodox religion course. In many regions, the national laws that require all churches to be registered and to have licences for their land, buildings and activities are administered with particular severity, amounting to the virtual limitation of their activities to prayer meetings in private apartments. Often, local authorities will defer to the Orthodox bishop of the region on disputed questions concerning religious matters, and the bishop is typically not eager to see land allotted or construction permits given to the congregations of other faiths.[8]

In general, there is no question but that Orthodoxy is flourishing in Russia in the nurturing environment of the church–state symbiosis. Church attendance remains low, but more and more citizens of the recently atheistic state identify themselves as not only believers but Russian Orthodox believers: the number of those confessing Orthodoxy is up, according to one survey, from 53 per cent in 2003 to 71 per cent in 2008.[9] Growth of the Russian Orthodox print media – magazines and newspapers published by or about the church and its activities – has been exponential in recent years: roughly 500 such publications now appear regularly. Nor is the Internet untouched by the information explosion: there are an estimated 3,500 websites associated with the Orthodox Church, including blogs by individual priests. Commentators have also noted the extent to which Orthodoxy has been embraced by influential figures well beyond the political elite – film stars and other celebrities – and is promoted in glossy magazines. As one critic observes: 'Glamorous people must believe, go to church, have icons and go on pilgrimages to places like Optina Pustyn and Valaam and tell everyone about it.'[10]

Beyond religious feelings and fashion, however, there is still another major dimension of the current vogue for Orthodoxy in Russia, and that is nationalism. Russian nationalism, in the sense of a special devotion to the interests of Russia as a nation and to Russians as people (at the expense of others, if necessary), appears to be gaining force in the country, encouraged by the leadership, from Putin downwards, and broadly welcomed by the citizenry, or at least by the great majority who are of Russian descent. Such devotion contributes to the power of Orthodoxy when the latter is viewed, as increasingly it is, as bound up with Russian national identity. As a Russian Baptist minister put it recently, describing prevailing attitudes: 'This is how they think: If you are a Russian person, it means you have to be Russian Orthodox.'[11]

For some seventy years the rulers of the USSR made an effort to transfer the nationalistic sentiments of Russians from Russia to the Soviet Union, but their attempts to create a 'Soviet people' to replace the Russian people were so half-hearted that they had little effect, and the sense of national humiliation produced by the loss of their empire in the late twentieth century was virtually guaranteed to promote attitudes favourable to the restoration and flourishing of a proudly Russian nation. The Putin administration's defence of all things Russian, from Russian Orthodoxy to the Russian-majority populations of South Ossetia and the Crimea, is an integral part of that broad pattern.

Another part of the pattern is the contribution of Russian nationalism to the strengthening of authoritarian tendencies. In its most disingenuous form, this may be seen in the unquestioning acceptance of the country's autocratic past as a standard of judgement concerning social policy. A revealing moment came in a recent press interview when Putin was asked how he would respond to charges of stifling the Russian media: 'Very simply', he replied. 'We have never had freedom of speech in Russia, so I don't really understand what could be stifled ... there must exist certain boundaries.'[12] The fact that restrictions on the press have been normal in Russian history is considered justification in itself for continuing them, as if they reflect something endemic to the land and its people. This is particularly evident in the case of authoritarian practices associated with things of which today's Russians can be proud, above all the defeat of Nazi Germany in the 'Great Patriotic War', as the Second World War is called in Russia. For his role in that heroic Russian triumph, Stalin, despite his crimes and mistakes, is still revered as a great leader by millions of Russian citizens.

Jonathan Brent's book *Inside the Stalin Archives* (Atlas, 2008) describes the extent to which, despite the reopening of many Soviet archives, nationalistic impulses continue to have a dampening effect on historical scholarship. Scholars, both Russian and foreign, still often face insuperable obstacles in seeking access to archives that might throw light on uncomplimentary aspects of tsarist and Soviet rule, and those researchers who succeed are subject to further pressures. Some report, as Joseph Tartakovsky writes, being 'bullied over insufficient reverence toward the Red Army'. One scholar concludes from his experience that 'the order has been given to rehabilitate Russian and Soviet statehood in all epochs'.[13]

If this pattern of interlocking authoritarianism, Orthodoxy and nationalism in the socio-political culture of Putin's Russia looks familiar to readers of this volume, they have only to return to Leatherbarrow's description in chapter 5 of the doctrine of 'Official Nationality' in order to be reminded of the paradigmatic statement of this value-system in nineteenth-century Russia under Nicholas I. In many ways, Uvarov's slogan – 'Orthodoxy, autocracy, nationality' – applies just as well to Putin's Russia as it did to the Russia of Nicholas. One cardinal difference, however, is that then, the elements of the tripartite formula were explicitly endorsed, without apology, as state policy. Now, the aim appears to be to promote these same features of Russian reality while at the same time claiming allegiance to their opposites – secularism, democracy and internationalism.

Of course, the authoritarian dimension of the Putin regime today is no match for the undisguised autocracy of Nicholas – or of Stalin after him. Neither Nicholas nor Stalin would have tolerated the Internet, as Putin thus far has done, and Nicholas and Stalin had more efficient ways of neutralising political opponents than bribing them with regional gover-norships. Yet the parallels are unmistakable, and one advantage of reflect-ing on them is that it suggests the enduring significance of traditional patterns of culture – in this case, the elements of 'Official Nationality' (by whatever name) – as organic features of a culture, not simply options that might or might not be promoted, depending on one's interests.

Scholars and statesmen of a Westernist bent have tended to view Uvarov's three principles as describing accidental, deliberately changeable features of Russian culture that conservatives, in their own interests, wished to make permanent. But what if, in view of the apparent recurrence of Uvarov's pattern over the centuries and into the present, we focus on its elements as deeply rooted, enduring facts about Russia, resilient features of Russian culture and mentality that antedated and long outlived Nicholas I and cannot be treated as simple social options like items on a menu? Uvarov himself, of course, regarded the three principles not as optional choices for Russia but as features that defined Russia. He called them, as quoted by Leatherbarrow above, 'principles which form the distinctive character of Russia, and which belong only to Russia' – that is, a unique set of features that describes the essence of the Russian nation.

The nineteenth-century liberal Westernisers largely agreed with Uvarov's characterisation of the Russia of their day as Orthodox, autocratic and nationalistic, but their failure to appreciate the endurance of these features is illustrated by such things as Belinsky's belief that the Russian common people were really not *fundamentally* religious. The Westernisers for centuries have underestimated the power of cultural inertia – the burden of history – in undermining their reforms. In the case of secularisation, for example, even the most severe and massive campaign to wipe out religion in the USSR did not destroy the attraction of Orthodoxy, and the Communist rulers were eventually forced to enlist its support; the present generation of rulers continues that tradition without being forced. The Westernisers were wrong about the staying power of all three of Uvarov's quintessential, organic features of the Russian nation, most dramatically in believing that autocracy could be surgically excised from Russia, at any time, by revolution or reform.

The substantial and apparently growing evidence of the survival of Uvarov's three marks of Russianness in twenty-first century Russia under Putin clearly necessitates a reassessment of the degree to which today's Russia has been transformed or foreseen by Westernisers. Scientific, technological, educational and economic modernisation are undoubted fruits of westernisation that bear out the Westernisers' hopes and predictions. In the socio-political sphere, however, Russia remains a mere approximation or semblance of the liberal, secular, constitutional state that many of the thinkers discussed in this volume imagined for Russia. Each side has had some successes – the liberals in the realms of intellectual enlightenment, the Great Reforms of Alexander II and the capitalist revolution of the 1990s; the conservatives in the preservation of major cultural and institutional elements of 'Official Nationality'.

The ideas of the liberals have not died in Russia. Public expression of them continues, especially on the Internet and in the print media, where pressures, official and unofficial, are not as severe as in broadcasting. Opposition political parties still exist, however hobbled by the overwhelmingly dominant party, United Russia. Yet these other parties have little influence. Trying to explain the weak appeal of Solidarity – a liberal movement organised by chess champion Garry Kasparov and Boris Nemtsov – one Russian scholar offers a simple explanation: 'The problem that Solidarity faces is that, while many of its criticisms are true, its leaders are not perceived by the vast majority of the population as representing the average person's interests.'[14]

Does this mean that westernisation in Russia has permanently stalled at the point of technical, educational and economic modernisation, without achieving the socio-political reforms championed by the liberals? To echo Mao, it is too soon to tell. Cultural patterns do change. But Russia has been modernising for three centuries now without eliminating authoritarian rule. Modernisation took place haltingly under tsarist rule, rapidly but disastrously under Communist rule and now is continuing with some promise on a capitalist basis – but still without the law-governed state and the effective constitutional protection of civil liberties that characterise capitalist societies in the West. Is there any reason to expect a paradigm shift that will bring Russia into line with the western experience?

One such reason offered by some western scholars today is applicable not only to Russia but to all authoritarian societies in the process of modernisation. These scholars argue that it is not possible to sustain technical, educational and economic progress without eventually 'completing' westernisation – that is, without abandoning an essentially authoritarian political structure. The educated, informed and relatively prosperous citizenry that an advanced market economy requires and nurtures, the argument goes, will eventually refuse to tolerate the corruption, inefficiency and restrictions on initiative that authoritarianism generates, and hence will demand political reforms. As applied to Russia, the conclusion is that the modernisation already achieved in the country has made westernisation of the political variety very likely. The economist Anders Åslund, for one, endorses this argument, contending that what he calls (according to a published summary of a 2008 address) the 'fragile authoritarian government' of Putin is no match for the 'strong and growing market economy' of Russia.[15] If Åslund is right, we can reasonably expect that something close to full westernisation will be achieved in Russia, sooner rather than later.

These remarks were made, however, earlier in 2008, before it became evident later that year that a deep global recession was under way. Since that time we have seen a precipitous drop in the world prices of oil and gas, Russia's principal money-makers, and we have seen turmoil in the Russian currency and share markets – turmoil created in part by the Kremlin's continuing push to renationalise the great petroleum and natural gas firms to bring them under Kremlin control.[16] If the same state-capitalist approach that is being taken to the oil and gas companies should be taken to the recently freed agricultural lands as well, those lands may not live up to their full economic promise. Add to this the many signs of creeping autocracy in the socio-political and cultural spheres that we have seen above, and we may suspect that the contest between free-market capitalism and authoritarianism might better be characterised as the reverse of Åslund's formula. Perhaps what is 'fragile' in Russia is the market economy, not Putin's authoritarian government, and what is 'strong and growing' is that government, not the market economy. If so, what we may expect is not the extension of westernisation to the political sphere but its retrenchment in the economic sphere. Even if we grant the principle that economic and political liberalisation go hand in hand, in the light of history it seems at least as likely that, in Russia, an authoritarian government will hobble economic potential as it is that a vibrant capitalist economy will produce political liberalisation.

Thus the issues concerning modernisation that have animated the debates between Westernisers and conservatives discussed in this book have by no means been resolved. The social realities that have provoked the intellectual confrontations of three centuries are still present in Russia today, albeit in different forms. At the moment, evidence points to the persistence of some variety of authoritarian rule, to the detriment of both liberal political values and further economic progress. The spirit of Count Uvarov's trilogy remains a force to be reckoned with in twenty-first-century Russia.

NOTES

1. Andrew H. Kramer, 'Gazprom set to halt gas shipments to Ukraine', *New York Times*, 1 January 2009 (online edition).
2. Kramer, 'Russia's collective farms: hot capitalist property', *New York Times*, 31 August 2008 (online edition).
3. David Remnick, 'Echo in the dark. A radio station strives to keep the airwaves free', *The New Yorker*, 22 September 2008, p. 37.
4. 'Editorials: Soviet echoes', *Columbus Dispatch*, 23 December 2008, p. A8.
5. Remnick, 'Echo in the dark', p. 43.
6. Clifford J. Levy, 'Russia's liberals lose their voice', *New York Times*, 24 December 2008 (online edition).
7. Sophia Kishkovsky, 'Patriarch Aleksy II, Russian Orthodox leader, dies at 79', *New York Times*, 6 December 2008 (online edition); Kishkovsky, 'With Orthodoxy's revival in Russia, religious media also rise', *New York Times*, 25 December 2008 (online edition).
8. Clifford J. Levy, 'At expense of all others, Putin picks a church', *New York Times*, 24 April 2008 (online edition).
9. Ibid.
10. Kishkovsky, 'With Orthodoxy's revival'.
11. Levy, 'At expense of all others'.
12. Remnick, 'Echo in the dark', p. 40.
13. Joseph Tartakovsky, 'Documents and disorder: inside the Stalin archives', *The Wall Street Journal*, 2 December 2008, p. A17; Clifford J. Levy, 'Nationalism of Putin's era veils sins of Stalin's', *New York Times*, 27 November 2008 (online edition).
14. Levy, 'Russia's liberals lose their voice'.
15. F. Joseph Dresen, 'Russia's capitalist revolution: why market reform succeeded and democracy failed', *Kennan Institute Meeting Report*, vol. XXV, 18 November 2008, p. 1.
16. Kramer, 'Gazprom, once mighty, is reeling', *New York Times*, 30 December 2008 (online edition); Associated Press, 'Ruble continues to slide, to record lows', *New York Times*, 30 December 2008 (online edition).

Biographical details of thinkers and writers

Dates of works by the thinkers and writers described in the following entries are dates of first publication unless otherwise stated.

The references at the end of the entries are to items cited in the bibliography. Most of these items are to be found in the sections of the bibliography containing secondary sources, especially the sections on studies of thinkers or on the history of the revolutionary movement or the literary context, but a few are to be found among the translations of primary sources cited there. In the case of scholars who have authored more than one work cited in the bibliography we give the date of the relevant publication in brackets in the biographical entry.

We do not cite in the biographical entries the following major reference works on Russian literature: Cornwell (1998), Mirsky, Moser (1992), Terras (1985, 1991). However, material on all of the imaginative writers to whom a biographical entry is devoted will be found in most of these works, and in Terras (1985), which uses a broad definition of 'literature', material on most of the thinkers will be found as well.

Aksakov, Ivan Sergeevich (1823–86). Brother of Konstantin Aksakov (*q.v.*). Journalist, editor and publisher; Slavophile and, in the 1870s and 1880s, Pan-Slavist. Ivan Aksakov edited the first volume of the *Moscow Miscellany* (1852) and was *de facto* editor of the journal *Russian Colloquy* in 1858–9 and subsequently publisher and editor of various Moscow newspapers, including *The Day* (1861–5) and *Rus* (1880–6). He was also one of the leading figures of the so-called Moscow Slavonic Benevolent Committee (1858–78), of which he took over the presidency from Pogodin (*q.v.*) in 1875. Aksakov sought to apply the ideas of the early Slavophiles in the post-reform conditions, hoping for a rapprochement of the various social strata in a society that he conceived as organic. See Lukashevich (1965), Riasanovsky (1965), Walicki (1975).

Aksakov, Konstantin Sergeevich (1817–60). Brother of Ivan Aksakov (*q.v.*). Historian, philologist, poet, playwright and journalist, and, together with Khomiakov and Ivan Kireevsky (*qq.v.*), one of the most important early Slavophiles. In 1855 Aksakov submitted a 'Memorandum on the Internal State of Russia' to the new tsar Alexander II. In 1857 he edited the short-lived Slavophile journal *The Rumour*. His particular interest was the character of the Russian common people and their supposedly communal way of life in pre-Petrine times, when he imagined that the state and the people had coexisted in harmony. He also wrote extensively on the Russian language. See Christoff (1982), Rabow-Edling, Riasanovsky (1965), Walicki (1975).

Annenkov, Pavel Vasilevich (1813–87). Nobleman, dilettante and a leading figure among the mid-nineteenth-century liberal Westernisers. In the 1840s Annenkov wrote minor works of short prose fiction and rather colourless travel sketches of journeys to western Europe (*Letters from Abroad* (1841–3) and *Parisian Letters* (1847–8)). In 1855–7 he published a seven-volume edition of Pushkin's works, including an introductory biography, which was emblematic of the views of those older members of the intelligentsia who continued to commend art as an end in itself. His memoirs, *Literary Reminiscences* (1880), provide one of the most important accounts of mid-nineteenth-century Russian cultural and intellectual life, especially of the role and personality of Belinsky (*q.v.*). See Offord (1985).

Bakhtin, Mikhail Mikhailovich (1895–1975). Philosopher, philologist, theorist of literature, language and culture. Bakhtin has become established as one of the foremost critical theorists of the twentieth century, whose influence is discernible in practically all disciplines of the arts and humanities, yet he defined himself as a philosopher first and foremost, and for much of his time lived a politically precarious life in isolation as an unpublished educator in the provinces of the Soviet Union. A precocious intellect and fluent in German from childhood, Bakhtin familiarised himself with the German philosophical tradition as a youth, but trained as a classicist under Zelinsky at university in Petrograd. After the 1917 Revolution he became the intellectually charismatic leader of philosophical discussion groups based successively in Nevel, Vitebsk and Leningrad, the last of which, attended also by Medvedev and Voloshinov, became primarily Marxist and linguistic in orientation. Paradoxically, but not without reason, Bakhtin was arrested in 1929 as a religious intellectual and lived in official and unofficial exile thereafter, returning to Moscow only as a result of ill health in 1969. The rediscovery of his 1929 monograph *Problems of Dostoevsky's Art* in the late 1950s, its republication in 1963 and the publication of *Rabelais and His World* in 1965 marked the beginning of the belated but extraordinarily rapidly expanding recognition of Bakhtin's theoretical genius, first in Russia, then in the West. See Brandist, Clark and Holquist, Coates, Morson and Emerson.

Bakunin, Mikhail Aleksandrovich (1814–76). Anarchist thinker and revolutionary organiser and agitator. From a privileged noble family of Tver province, Bakunin abandoned a military career and threw himself into the study of German philosophy. In the 1840s he became prominent both in Russian intellectual life, being associated with the radical Westernisers, and in the European socialist movement. In 1849 he participated in revolutionary uprisings in Prague and Dresden, where he was arrested. In 1851 he was extradited to Russia and imprisoned in St Petersburg, where he wrote a 'confession' to Nicholas I. In 1857 the new tsar, Alexander II, commuted his sentence to exile in Siberia, from where he escaped in 1861, travelling via Japan and North America to London. There he began to collaborate with Herzen (*q.v.*), with whom, however, he soon came to disagree over revolutionary strategy. From 1864 he lived mainly in Italy and then, from 1867, in Switzerland. In 1869–70 he was associated with the Machiavellian conspirator Nechaev and may have lent a hand in the writing of the notorious 'Catechism of a Revolutionary', which upheld the axiom that for the revolutionary the end justifies the means. In the years 1868–72 he clashed with Marx over the direction of the First Workingmen's International. Bakunin invoked the peasant revolts of Russian history as manifestations of a rebellious spirit among the Russian people, which he urged revolutionaries to rekindle. He was the author of numerous articles and pamphlets, many of them fragmentary. His most important work was perhaps the tract *Statism and Anarchy* (1873). His writings and revolutionary career, notwithstanding its conspicuous failure, were inspirational to the Populist revolutionaries of the 1870s. See Berlin (2008), Carr (1961), Copleston, Kelly (1982), Lampert (1957), Leier, Shatz's introduction in Bakunin (1990), Venturi.

Belinsky, Vissarion Grigorevich (1811–48). Son of a naval doctor, brought up in Penza province. The leading literary critic of the reign of Nicholas I, Belinsky profoundly affected the development of Russian imaginative literature and thought in its golden age. In 1838–40, while under the influence of Hegel, he briefly took a conservative position, advocating 'reconciliation with reality', and demanded that artists eschew a partisan view of reality, thus furnishing a basis for a view of art as an end in itself. However, he subsequently came to oppose the autocratic regime, aligning himself with the radical wing of the Westernisers and espousing utopian socialism. In the last five or six years of his life he accordingly demanded that art play a civic role. His major essays include 'Literary Reveries' (1834, written under the influence of Schelling), 'On the Russian Novella and the Novellas of Mr Gogol' (1835), 'Menzel, a Critic of Goethe' (1840), two essays on Lermontov (1840–41, written as Belinsky was freeing himself from Hegelianism), 'Nikitenko's Speech on Criticism' (1842), a cycle of eleven essays on the work and literary-historical significance of Pushkin (1843–6) and annual surveys on the state of Russian literature (1840–7). His famous 'Letter to Gogol' (1847), in which he attacked Gogol for allegedly betraying the vocation of the writer in Russia, was considered his testament (he died of lung disease at the age of thirty-six). He was acknowledged by contemporaries to have played the leading role in shaping the character of the Russian intelligentsia as a morally intense group committed to promotion of social justice and fulfilment of a national mission, variously conceived. See Berlin (2008), Bowman, Copleston, Freeborn (2003), Lampert (1957), Offord (in Rydel 1999), Proctor, Randall (1987), Terras (1974).

Berdiaev, Nikolay Aleksandrovich (1874–1948). Religious Existentialist philosopher. Berdiaev was an aristocrat of mixed Russian and French descent who rejected the court career intended for him for an independent academic life. In his youth he became a Marxist and joined the Social Democratic Party. His studies in law at Kiev University were brought to an end in 1898 by a two-year stint in exile in Vologda for illegal political activity. From about 1900 his Marxism evolved into philosophical idealism and eventually Orthodox Christianity, though he prided himself on remaining intellectually independent of the church. For a time he moved between Symbolist and academic circles. He worked as a freelance philosopher and journalist until the October Revolution: his intellectual evolution can be traced in several collections of articles (e.g. *Sub Specie Aeternitatis* (1907) and *The New Religious Consciousness and Society* (1907)) and in his early philosophical works (e.g. *The Meaning of Creativity* (1916)). After 1917 Berdiaev briefly headed a Free Religious–Philosophical Academy in Moscow before being expelled from the Soviet Union in 1922. In exile he became a prolific religious Existentialist philosopher and Russian intellectual historian, attracting an extensive non-Russian readership. See Berdyaev, Pyman, Zernov.

Botkin, Vasily Petrovich (1811–69). Son of a tea-merchant, Botkin was a central figure in mid-nineteenth-century Russian cultural life. Although he was particularly close to Belinsky (*q.v.*; their correspondence is a valuable source for Russian literary and intellectual history), Botkin was one of the more moderate, liberal voices in the Westernist camp. He was the author of an important example of travel writing (*Letters on Spain*, 1847–51) and of essays on music and painting as well as literature. He also translated Thomas Carlyle's *On Heroes, Hero-Worship and the Heroic in History* (his translation was published in 1855–6), which seemed emblematic of an elitist and poetic view of the world in the utilitarian industrial age. When views on literature polarised in Russia in the late 1850s, Botkin became a leading representative of the art for art's sake tendency (the 'Pushkin school' of Russian literature). See Moser (1989), Offord (1985, 2005).

Bulgakov, Sergey Nikolaevich (1871–1944). Political economist, philosopher, theologian. Bulgakov was born into a priestly family in Orel province but, following an established intelligentsia tradition, left the seminary upon conversion to atheism and studied economics and law at Moscow University as a Marxist. Subsequently, he pursued an academic career as a political economist, first at Kiev Polytechnic, later at Moscow University's Institute of Commerce, from which he resigned in protest at government interference in 1911. However, Bulgakov early became critical of the materialistic basis of Marxist ideology, and for a time sought a synthesis of Marxist economic theory and idealist epistemology: this was expressed politically as Christian socialism (Bulgakov was an elected representative of the Second Duma in 1907). Bulgakov's intellectual output prior to 1917 largely took the form of scholarly journal articles, some of which appeared in the collections *From Marxism to Idealism* (1903) and *Two Cities* (1911), but after his ordination as a priest of the Russian Orthodox Church in 1918 and subsequent expulsion from the Soviet Union in 1923 (after which he served as Dean and Professor of Dogmatic Theology at the Institute of Orthodox Theology in Paris), he wrote extensive and doctrinally controversial theological works in which Sophia occupies a central place. See Evtuhov, Valliere, Williams, Zernov.

Chaadaev, Petr Iakovlevich (1793 or 1794–1856). Son of a nobleman and grandson of Prince Shcherbatov (*q.v.*), Chaadaev was an important thinker who helped to precipitate the debate of the 1840s between the so-called Westernisers and Slavophiles. He took part in the Battle of Borodino (1812) and other late battles in the Napoleonic Wars. In the years 1823–6 he travelled in western Europe. He was attracted to Catholicism and to the philosophy of Schelling. He was the author of eight witty, jaundiced 'Philosophical Letters', written in French. The first of these letters (written in 1829 but not published until 1836, and the only one of the cycle to be published in Chaadaev's lifetime) represents a landmark in Russian thought. It poses the question of Russia's relationship to the West and takes an unremittingly bleak view of Russia as a nation outside the mainstream of civilised humanity. The authorities declared Chaadaev insane on account of these views and placed him under house arrest. His 'Apologia of a Madman', written in 1837, in which he protests that he does have faith in Russia's future, is perceived as a partial recantation. See Copleston, Freeborn and Grayson, McNally (1971), Walicki (1979).

Chekhov, Anton Pavlovich (1860–1904). Major short-story writer and dramatist. Chekhov was the grandson of a serf and the son of a brutal Taganrog shopkeeper who became bankrupt while Chekhov was still at school. He began to write in order to support his family and himself while studying medicine in Moscow (1879–84), being paid by the line for satirical sketches for humour magazines such as *The Dragonfly* and *Fragments*. As he gradually came to take himself seriously as a writer, the thematic range, complexity and length of his stories increased: he began publishing in newspapers, notably Suvorin's *New Time*, and in 1886 dropped his use of pseudonyms. His prose evolved from satire to nuanced psychological observation; his narrators became increasingly objective as his characters began to reveal themselves in all their ordinary moral ambiguousness, inconclusiveness and, frequently, unhappiness: Chekhov famously resisted solutions, answers and closure. While continuing to mature as a writer of short prose, from 1887 (with *Ivanov*) he established himself also as a dramatist, and by the time of his premature death from tuberculosis had produced four great plays – *The Seagull* (1896), *Uncle Vanya* (1899), *Three Sisters* (1901) and *The Cherry Orchard* (1904). In these Chekhov elaborated an innovative (and initially mistrusted) approach to theatre, eliminating the melodramatic and heroic and focusing on the minutiae of personal relationships, the predominant failure of people to communicate with each other. See Rayfield (1997, 1998).

Chernyshevsky, Nikolay Gavrilovich (1828–89). The son of a priest from the provincial city of Saratov on the Volga, Chernyshevsky was the leading Russian radical thinker of his generation. He studied at St Petersburg University from 1846 to 1850 and after a brief spell teaching in a school in Saratov returned to St Petersburg in 1853. He then began to contribute to *The Contemporary*, of which he shortly became the guiding force. He demanded that artists treat contemporary reality and that art serve social and political ends. He propounded Benthamite utilitarianism (to which, however, he gave a socialist orientation) and a crude philosophical materialism, denying the existence of a spiritual dimension to human beings. He wrote extensively on the practice of communal landholding, which he favoured, helping to lay foundations for the later Populist movement. Through articles on French politics he obliquely attacked the advocates of liberalism in Russia in the years leading up to the emancipation of the serfs in 1861. In 1862 he was arrested on suspicion of complicity in the organisation of revolutionary activity. While in prison he wrote his influential novel *What is to be Done?* (1863), in which he propagated his rational egoism in fictional form. The novel also provided inspirational portraits of the 'new people' who would help to usher in a utopian, cooperative society, and depicted a wilful proto-revolutionary figure, Rakhmetov, who would later make a profound impression on Lenin. In 1863 Chernyshevsky was exiled to Siberia, where he remained until 1883, when he was allowed to move to Astrakhan. His major works, apart from *What is to be Done?*, include his dissertation 'The Aesthetic Relations of Art to Reality' (1855), a cycle of 'Essays on the Gogol Period of Russian Literature' (1855–6) and his articles 'A Critique of Philosophical Prejudices against Communal Landholding' (1858) and 'The Anthropological Principle in Philosophy' (1860). See Copleston, Lampert (1965), Paperno (1988), Pereira, Proctor, Randall (1967), Walicki (1979), Woehrlin.

Chicherin, Boris Nikolaevich (1828–1904). Nobleman from a high-ranking family of Tambov province, historian, legal philosopher and one of the most important nineteenth-century Russian liberal thinkers. Chicherin's major works include *Russia's Regional Institutions in the Seventeenth Century* (1857), *Essays on the History of Russian Law* (1859), *Essays on England and France* (1859), *The History of Political Doctrines* (5 vols., 1869–1902), *Science and Religion* (1879), *On Popular Representation* (1899) and *Philosophy of Law* (1901). Chicherin took the étatist view commonplace in Westernist historiography, according to which the state had played the decisive role in Russian history. He was influenced by the German notion of a *Rechtsstaat*, or constitutional state. His contemporaries, even those liberals to whom he was intellectually close, felt there was something cold and alien about him. On the whole, it became conventional in twentieth-century scholarship to disparage him as a blind believer in Hegelian teleology and to view him as a conservative thinker, although in his time he offended the authorities as well as the radical and liberal intelligentsia. See Hamburg, Kelly (1998), Lampert (1965), Schapiro (1967), Walicki (1979).

Danilevsky, Nikolay Iakovlevich (1822–85). Conservative thinker, Pan-Slavist and natural scientist (ichthyologist). In his major work *Russia and Europe* (1869) Danilevsky dealt with the subject of the relationship between Russia and western European civilisation in the light of his theory of distinctive culturo-historical types. (His theory foreshadows twentieth-century writings by Oswald Spengler, Arnold Toynbee and Samuel Huntington.) Presenting the western character as aggressive and the Russian character as peaceable, and rejecting the notion that a successful universal civilisation was feasible,

Danilevsky anticipated an inevitable struggle between Russia and Europe and looked forward to the establishment of a Slav federation in which Russia would enjoy hegemony. See Macmaster, Thaden, Walicki (1979).

Dobroliubov, Nikolay Aleksandrovich (1836–61). The son of a priest, Dobroliubov was the most influential literary critic of the early years of the reign of Alexander II. From 1856 until his death, from lung disease, at the age of twenty-five, Dobroliubov wrote for *The Contemporary* and from 1857 was in charge of its critical section. He worked closely with Chernyshevsky (*q.v.*), with whom he had a great intellectual affinity. His many essays include famous reviews of Goncharov's *Oblomov* ('What is Oblomovism?', 1859), Ostrovsky's plays ('The Kingdom of Darkness', 1859), Turgenev's *On the Eve* ('When Then Will the Real Day Come?', 1860) and Ostrovsky's *Thunderstorm* ('A Ray of Light in the Kingdom of Darkness', 1860). Dobroliubov interpreted works of literature as a reflection of social conditions and processes, irrespective of their authors' intentions, and he used criticism to bring these conditions and processes to light, interesting himself particularly in what could be considered typical of contemporary society rather than idiosyncratic or coincidental. He set no store by art whose significance he considered purely aesthetic, such as the lyric poetry of Fet. See Lampert (1965), Moser (1989), Proctor, Walicki (1979), Wellek in Simmons.

Dostoevsky, Fedor Mikhailovich (1821–81). One of the great classical novelists and also, in the last twenty years of his life, a prolific journalist and conservative nationalist thinker. Dostoevsky won glowing praise from Belinsky (*q.v.*) for his first work of prose fiction, the epistolary novel *Poor Folk* (1846). In 1849 he was arrested for participation in the Petrashevsky circles, which discussed utopian socialism, and, with others, he was sentenced to death for allegedly plotting against the government. The sentence was commuted at the last moment, as the execution was about to take place, to imprisonment in Siberia, where Dostoevsky spent the years 1850–4, and then exile as a soldier in Semipalatinsk (in modern Kazakhstan, 1854–9). Following his return to St Petersburg, Dostoevsky founded and became *de facto* editor of the journals *Time* (1861–3) and *The Epoch* (1864–5). He now became one of leading exponents of Native-Soil Conservatism (*pochvennichestvo*). His post-Siberian prose writings include: a semi-fictional account of his years in prison (*Notes from the House of the Dead* (1861)); an account of his first journey to the West in 1862 (*Winter Notes on Summer Impressions* (1863)); the short novels *Notes from Underground* (1864) and *The Gambler* (1866); the long novels *Crime and Punishment* (1866), *The Idiot* (1868), *The Devils* (1871–2; also translated as *The Possessed*), *A Raw Youth* (1875; also translated as *An Accidental Family*) and *The Brothers Karamazov* (1879–80); and some shorter prose fiction, including 'Bobok' (1873), 'A Gentle Creature' (1876) and 'The Dream of a Ridiculous Man' (1877). In the 1870s, still intensely interested in topical social, political and moral questions, he devoted much energy to a further journalistic enterprise, the *Diary of a Writer* (1876–81; also translated as *A Writer's Diary*). In his fiction Dostoevsky catches individuals at moments of spiritual crisis in their lives, exploring with profound psychological insight such matters as loss of faith and the importance of belief, ideological delusion, crime, madness, suicide, human motivation and freedom and responsibility for moral choice. At the same time, his treatment of these questions of universal importance is firmly rooted in sharply focused consideration of the problems confronting Russia in his age. Dostoevsky's political beliefs, after his youthful flirtation with socialist teachings, are conservative and intensely nationalistic, although he perhaps always remained, in his own phrase, a 'child of [his] age of unfaith'. See Carter, Copleston, Dowler (1982), Frank, Malcolm Jones, Jones and Miller, Jones and Terry, Leatherbarrow (1981, 1992, 2002), Masaryk (vol. III), Mochulsky, Peace (1971), Scanlan (2002), Ward, Wasiolek (1964).

Florensky, Pavel Aleksandrovich (1882–1937). Physicist, theologian, philosopher, philologist. Born in Azerbaidjan and educated in Tiflis (Tbilisi), Florensky graduated in 1904 from Moscow University's Department of Physics and Mathematics. A convert to Orthodoxy from 1899, he went on to study at Moscow Theological Seminary in Sergiev Posad and was ordained in 1908. His reputation as a polymath and as a uniquely gifted new kind of Orthodox theologian was established by the publication in 1914 of his epistolary work, *The Pillar and Ground of the Truth*, a development of his doctoral dissertation. In the period up to 1921 Florensky served as priest to the Church of St Mary Magdalene in Sergiev Posad, simultaneously lecturing in philosophy at the Seminary and in mathematics and cosmography at the Women's Gymnasium. After the October Revolution, he was employed as a scientist by the Soviet regime, working for the Soviet Electrification Plan and for GlavELEKTRO on the development of insulation materials. Though he famously came to work in his priest's cassock and cross, he escaped final arrest until 1933. He was moved between three prison camps, the last of which was Solovki Monastery on the White Sea, and was executed by firing squad at Levashovo near Leningrad in December 1937. See Kornblatt and Gustafson, Pyman.

Fonvizin, Denis Ivanovich (1745–92). Russia's leading dramatist in the age of Catherine the Great. In his satirical comedies *The Brigadier* (completed 1769) and *The Minor* (1782) Fonvizin satirises philistine provincial nobles who do not understand the obligations to their nation that nobility entails and seek to evade service. His many other writings include two cycles of letters on travels to the West and a daring treatise on the fundamental laws of state (in which he envisaged laws that might avert the despotism towards which he and his patron, Nikita Panin, thought Catherine was inclining in the later years of her reign). He also translated French works on the subjects of Confucianism and Stoicism, by which he was much attracted. See Moser (1979), Offord (2005).

Frank, Semen Liudvigovich (1877–1950). Frank was Jewish by birth but converted to Orthodoxy and was baptised in 1912. As a youth he was active as a Marxist, and his arrest in 1899 for engagement in anti-government propaganda forced him to abandon his study of law at Moscow University. He finished his education in Germany, where he studied economics and philosophy, and

Kazan. As with Bulgakov (*q.v.*), neo-Kantian idealism facilitated Frank's transition from Marxism to Christianity. From 1901 he devoted himself to philosophy: he collaborated with Struve (*q.v.*) in a variety of publishing projects, including the editing of the journals *The Pole Star*, *Freedom and Culture* and *Russian Thought* (1905–6); he contributed to all three of the symposia *Problems of Idealism* (1902), *Landmarks* (1909; also translated as *Signposts*) and *Out of the Depths* (1918); and taught philosophy at the Universities of St Petersburg, Saratov and Moscow (1912–22). In 1922 he was expelled from the Soviet Union. Frank's mature philosophy, articulated in *The Object of Knowledge* (1915), *The Ineffable* (1939) and *Light in the Darkness* (1949), is a metaphysics of total-unity that owes its greatest debt to Neoplatonism and to Solovev (*q.v.*). See Boobbyer, Zenkovsky, Zernov.

Gogol, Nikolay Vasilevich (1809–52). Son of minor land-owning Ukrainian gentry, one of the major imaginative writers of the age of Nicholas I. Gogol's writings include the collections of short stories *Evenings on a Farm near Dikanka* (1831–2), *Mirgorod* (1835) and *Arabesques* (1835), the short stories 'The Nose' (1836) and 'The Overcoat' (1842), and the play *The Government Inspector* (1836). His masterpiece is his novel *Dead Souls* (1842), conceived as the first part of a Dantesque trilogy that would point the way to Russia's moral regeneration. The central character of the novel, Chichikov, travels through provincial Russia attempting to buy up the entitlement to serfs ('souls') who have died since the last census, with a view to relocating and fraudulently mortgaging them. Gogol's depiction of his trivial characters (themselves 'dead souls' of another sort) and their stagnant environment was taken as a bitter indictment of Russian reality. Unable to make progress with the second part of the novel, Gogol attempted to articulate his moral message, including his view of the Russian nobleman's responsibilities, in his *Selected Passages from Correspondence with Friends* (1847). However, his defence of the Orthodox Church and the institution of serf-ownership caused outrage, prompting Belinsky (*q.v.*), who had previously championed him, to write his famous testamentary letter to him. In continuing spiritual torment, Gogol starved himself to death during Lent. See William Brown (1986, vol. IV), Erlich, Fanger, Maguire, Nabokov, Peace (1981).

Goncharov, Ivan Aleksandrovich (1812–91). Major classical novelist, travel writer, critic and memoirist; also a civil servant from 1835–67 and official censor. Goncharov wrote three novels: *A Common Story* (1847), *Oblomov* (1858–9) and *The Precipice* (1869). In *Oblomov*, which was famously reviewed by Dobroliubov (*q.v.*), he portrayed in his eponymous hero the literary type of the 'superfluous man' at his most indolent and ineffectual. The character came to be perceived as a metaphor for the inertia that prevented the nobility from taking decisive action. Goncharov also wrote a notable account of a voyage that he made to the Far East as a member of a Russian diplomatic mission (*The Voyage of the Frigate Pallada*; first published in 1855 as *Russians in Japan at the End of 1853 and the Beginning of 1854*, revised edition under new title in 1858). See Ehre, Freeborn (1973).

Granovsky, Timofey Nikolaevich (1813–55). Historian who occupied the chair of World History at Moscow University from 1839 to 1850 and the leading liberal Westerniser of the age of Nicholas I. His public lectures on medieval European history in 1843–4 were a major cultural event, for they had resonance for an audience living in a society in which serfdom persisted. Granovsky believed that western civilisation had gradually progressed through the spread of enlightened ideas into law and government. He wrote in praise of the medieval institution of knight-errantry as a source of refined values. At the same time, he admired the powerful visionary ruler with a unifying mission, such as Alexander the Great or Charlemagne. Himself a quixotic figure (but also prone to gambling), he served as a model for Stepan Verkhovensky, the embodiment of the free-thinking 'man of the 40s' whom Dostoevsky portrayed, for the most part, in cruelly negative terms in his novel *The Devils*. See Offord (1985), Roosevelt (1986), Schapiro (1967), Walicki (1979).

Grigorev, Apollon Aleksandrovich (1822–64). Major literary critic of the early years of the reign of Alexander II and, together with Dostoevsky (*q.v.*), one of the leading exponents of Native-Soil Conservatism (*pochvennichestvo*). In 1851–5 Grigorev played a major role on the editorial board of the conservative nationalist journal *The Muscovite*, which was edited by the historian Pogodin (*q.v.*). In 1858–9, after travelling in Italy, France and Germany, he edited *The Russian Word* and then contributed, in 1861–3 and 1864 respectively, to Dostoevsky's journals *Time* and *The Epoch*. Grigorev developed a type of criticism that apprehended art as the 'organic' product of a particular people and their age and culture. He wrote influentially about contemporary writers such as Nekrasov, Ostrovsky, Tolstoy and Turgenev (*qq.v.*) and also about the literary-historical significance of earlier writers such as Pushkin and Gogol (*qq.v.*). Some of his views (e.g. on the assertive character of western peoples and the meek nature of the Russian people) strongly affected Dostoevsky. See Dowler (1995), Moser (1989).

Herzen (Russian Gertsen; father's surname Iakovlev), Aleksandr Ivanovich (1812–70). Social and political thinker, essayist, writer of prose fiction, journalist and autobiographer. Having suffered periods of internal exile as a result of his political views in the 1830s and early 1840s, Herzen emerged in the mid-1840s as one of the radical Westernisers, but his later idealisation of the Russian peasant also lends him some affinity with the Slavophiles. In 1847 he travelled with his family to the West, where he immediately began vehemently to attack the bourgeois economic and social order and, in 1848, witnessed the revolutionary events in Italy and France. His radical political sympathies made it impossible for him to return to Russia after 1848. In 1852, following the defeat of revolutionary forces in France and personal losses (the death of his mother, one of his sons and his wife, Natalie), Herzen settled in England, where he founded a free Russian press. From 1857, together with Ogarev, he edited *The Bell*, a periodical publication which served as a mouthpiece for uncensored news and debate in the years when major reform was being discussed in Russia. In 1865 he returned to continental Europe and settled in Switzerland. By the 1860s Herzen's thought seemed outmoded and elitist to the radical younger generation of the Russian intelligentsia, and his standing and influence declined. His major works include: *Dilettantism in Science* (1842–3); *Letters on the Study of Nature* (1845–6); the novel *Who is to Blame?* (1845–6); *Letters on France and Italy* (first Russian edition 1854; this is his account of the western bourgeois order before, during and immediately after the revolutions of 1848); a cycle of essays on 'Russian Socialism' (1849–54, which laid the foundations for Populism); *From the Other Shore* (original German edition 1850, first Russian edition 1855, in which Herzen argued, on the whole, against historical inevitability and a teleological view of history); *Ends and Beginnings* (1862–3); *Letters to an Old Comrade* (published posthumously in 1870), in which he distanced himself from Bakunin's revolutionism; and his autobiography, *My Past and Thoughts* (only partially published in his lifetime). See Acton, Berlin (2008), Copleston, Aileen Kelly (1998, 1999), Malia (1961), Venturi, Walicki (1979).

Karamzin, Nikolay Mikhailovich (1766–1826). Major writer, journalist, thinker and historian of the late Catherinian and Alexandrine ages. In the 1790s Karamzin wrote popular short prose fiction in the sentimentalist (Pre-Romantic) manner, especially 'Poor Liza' (1792) and 'Natalia, the Boyar's Daughter' (1792) and a Gothic tale, 'The Island of Bornholm' (1794). He also produced a seminal work of travel literature, *Letters of a Russian Traveller* (1797–1801), loosely based on his journeying in the German states, France, Switzerland and England in 1789–90. He compiled various anthologies and almanacs and in 1802–3 edited *The Messenger of Europe*. From 1803, when he was appointed court historian, he devoted himself to the study of Russian history. The fruit of this labour was his monumental, though unfinished, *History of the Russian State* (vols. I–VIII were published in 1816–18, vols. IX–XI in 1821–4 and vol. XII posthumously, in 1829). Karamzin argued in this work that firm autocratic government was necessary in Russia. He also wrote a *Memoir on Ancient and Modern Russia*, an essay in political thought of a conservative complexion which he presented to Alexander in 1811. See Black, Cross (1971), Kochetkova, Martin, Offord (2005).

Kavelin, Konstantin Dmitrievich (1818–85). Son of a Russian nobleman and a Scottish mother, Kavelin was a historian, jurist, academic lawyer and philosopher, and one of the leading liberal Westernisers of the 1840s. His 'Brief Survey of the Juridical Way of Life of Ancient Russia' (1847) articulated the Westernist view of personality. In the new climate after the death of Nicholas I, Kavelin wrote a 'Memorandum on the Emancipation of the Peasants in Russia' (1855). He was a leading representative of the moderate intelligentsia who wished for reform from above but were loath to press the government to introduce sweeping change for fear of causing instability. His caution was reflected in his tendency always to seek compromise between opposing points of view and doctrines (e.g. idealism and materialism). His most important works in the post-reform period were *Problems of Psychology* (1872) and *Problems of Ethics* (1884). See Offord (1985), Walicki (1979), Zenkovsky.

Khomiakov, Aleksey Stepanovich (1804–60). Together with Konstantin Aksakov and Ivan Kireevsky (*qq.v.*), one of the leading early Slavophiles and the main theologian among them. Khomiakov served in the army in his youth and fought in the Russo-Turkish War of 1828–9. He believed that only Orthodoxy maintained the freedom and unity of the early Christian Church, whose spirit was manifested in the principle of conciliarism (*sobornost*). In Catholicism, on the other hand, freedom had been sacrificed for the sake of unity, Khomiakov believed, while in Protestantism unity had been sacrificed for the sake of freedom. In both cases rationalism had triumphed. Khomiakov produced several tragedies and much poetry (of a philosophical, patriotic and even civic nature), as well as theological and philosophical essays. He also wrote some unfinished *Notes on Universal History* (three volumes were published post-humously, in 1871–3), in which he distinguished between peoples whose civilisations were supposedly based on the principle (which he termed 'Iranian') of inner freedom and peoples whose civilisations were based on the 'Kushite' principle of coercion. He died of cholera contracted while treating peasants during an epidemic. See Christoff (1961), Copleston, Rabow-Edling, Riasanovsky (1965), Walicki (1975).

Kireevsky, Ivan Vasilevich (1806–56). One of the leading early Slavophiles and the most accomplished philosophical writer among them. In the 1820s Kireevsky was one of the founder-members of the circle of Wisdom-Lovers (*liubomu-dry*), who admired the philosophy of Schelling. In the reign of Nicholas I, having begun to view European civilisation through the prism of Orthodox religiosity, Kireevsky wrote some of the most important expositions of Slavophile ideas, such as 'A Reply to Khomiakov' (1839), 'On the Nature of European Culture and Its Relation to the Culture of Russia' (1852) and 'On the Need for and Possibility of New Principles for Philosophy' (1856). A fragment of an unfinished utopian story, 'The Island', written in the late 1830s, also survives. See Christoff (1972), Copleston, Gleason (1972), Rabow-Edling, Riasanovsky (1965), Walicki (1975).

Kropotkin, Prince Petr Alekseevich (1842–1921). Geographer, zoologist, historian, revolutionary of international standing and a leading anarchist thinker. From 1862–7 Kropotkin served as an army officer and took part in geographical expeditions in the Far East. In the late 1860s and early 1870s he served in the Royal Geographical Society in St Petersburg. Following a visit to Switzerland in 1872, where he was impressed by the voluntary associations of the Swiss watchmakers of the Jura Mountains, he participated in circles conducting revolutionary propaganda among the workers in St Petersburg. In 1874 he was arrested but in 1876 escaped abroad. He remained in exile until 1917, mainly in Switzerland, France and, from 1886, England, where he befriended George Bernard Shaw and William Morris and made many contributions to *The Times* and *Encyclopaedia Britannica*. His major expositions of anarchist doctrine include *Conquest of Bread* (1892), *Fields, Factories and Workshops* (1899) and *Mutual Aid: A Factor of Evolution* (1902), in which he argued, *pace* Darwin, that cooperation rather than competition is the chief factor in species' evolution. See Avrich, Cahm, Miller, Woodcock, Woodcock and Avakumović.

Lavrov, Petr Lavrovich (pen-name Mirtov; 1823–1900). Professor of Mathematics, philosopher, sociologist and political thinker who exercised a strong influence on Populist revolutionaries in the 1870s. Together with Mikhailovsky (*q.v.*), Lavrov represented a 'subjective' school of sociology that contrasted the objective method of the natural sciences with the method of the social sciences, in which thinkers could not help promoting their ideals and indeed had a duty to promote them. In his *Historical Letters* (1868–9) he argued that the 'critically thinking minority' had a moral debt to the masses on whose toil over many generations the minority's privilege rested. Having escaped from internal exile in Vologda in 1870 he went abroad and, in 1873–7, edited a journal, *Forward!* (first in Switzerland, then in London), thus helping to stimulate and guide the movement 'to the people' in the 1870s. His other major writings include 'Knowledge and Revolution' (1873–4), *From the History of Social Doctrines* (1873–4) and *The State Element in the Society of the Future* (1875–6). See Copleston, Pomper (1972), Scanlan's introduction in Lavrov (1967), Venturi.

Leontev, Konstantin Nikolaevich (1831–91). Writer of prose fiction, and social and political thinker of extreme conservative complexion. Leontev served as a military surgeon in the Crimean War and from 1863 to 1873 as a Russian consular official at various places in the Ottoman Empire. In essays that were eventually collected in the volume *The East, Russia and Slavdom* (1885–6), he deplored the effects of industrialisation and democratic levelling on European culture. He regarded European civilisation as in a state of terminal decline and considered this decline inevitable because of the laws by which civilisations grew, blossomed and decayed. Resisting the further incursion of this civilisation into post-reform Russia, he advocated authoritarian monarchic government and rigid social stratification and explored the possibility that Russia could find an alternative based on a Byzantine tradition with which it was losing touch. From 1887 he lived near the Optina Pustyn hermitage, where he secretly took monastic vows. See Copleston, Freeborn and Grayson, Thaden.

Lomonosov, Mikhail Vasilevich (1711–65). The outstanding figure in Russia's mid-eighteenth-century Enlightenment. Son of an entrepreneur from the port of Kholmogory near the White Sea, Lomonosov became a polymath: a scientist of international reputation who wrote on physics, astronomy, chemistry, metallurgy, geology and geography, but also a student of Russian history, prosody and language. In an ode of 1739 celebrating a Russian military victory, he applied new rules of versification that he himself outlined in an epistle written at the same time. His writings also include: two meditations on the majesty of the universe (written in 1743); a further ode, of 1747, celebrating the anniversary of the accession of the Empress Elizabeth to the throne (in gratitude for her increased financial support for the Academy of Sciences); an 'Epistle on the Value of Glass' (1753); a eulogy to Peter the Great (1755); a scurrilous 'Hymn to the Beard' (written in 1756–7), in which he attacks the resistance of the church to Enlightenment values; and an essay 'Preface on the Value of Church Books in the Russian Language' (1757), which codified the embryonic Russian literary language. He played a major role in the founding of Moscow University in 1755. See William Brown (1980), Menshutkin, Rogger, Vucinich (1963).

Merezhkovsky, Dmitry Sergeevich (1865–1941). Poet, novelist, dramatist, literary critic and religious philosopher. Husband of Symbolist poet Gippius. Merezhkovsky was one of the most influential figures of the Silver Age. He came to prominence not so much as an artist but as a propagandist for the new literary movement of Symbolism, the metaphysical idealism of which he extolled in the manifesto-like essay 'On the Reasons for the Decline and on the New Trends in Contemporary Russian Literature' (1893). In 1899 he and his wife embraced a highly idiosyncratic version of Christianity, which preached the reconciliation of the pagan principle of the flesh with the Christian principle of the spirit in a new synthesis which would characterise the fast-approaching era of the Third Testament. The Religious–Philosophical Meetings of 1901–3, instigated by the Merezhkovskys to proselytise for their new church, were landmark events that brought together members of the Orthodox Church hierarchy with the intelligentsia in debate for the first time. After the 1905 revolution, Merezhkovsky became politicised, writing in sectarian spirit of the unholy alliance between church and tsar that would be swept away in the revolution which he viewed as the apocalypse that would inaugurate an era of spiritual anarchy. Ardently opposed to Bolshevism, the Merezhkovskys left Russia in 1919. See Matich, Pyman, Rosenthal (1975).

Mikhailovsky, Nikolay Konstantinovich (1842–1904). Journalist, literary critic, sociologist and political thinker whose writings helped to drive the revolutionary movement of the 1870s and 1880s. Like Lavrov (*q.v.*), Mikhailovsky represented a 'subjective' school of sociology, resisting the rational egoism of Chernyshevsky and Pisarev (*qq.v.*) and arguing, for example in his essay 'What is Progress?' (1869), that the work of the social scientist should be informed by ideals. He also promoted the major tenets of Populism, insisting that Russia needed to avoid a capitalist phase of development and that socialism could be built on the institution of the peasant commune. From 1869 Mikhailovsky was a contributor to the journal *Notes of the Fatherland* and from 1877 until its closure by the authorities in 1884 he was one of its editors. In the early 1880s he was close to the leaders of the revolutionary organisation The People's Will and he was the author of 'political' letters published in two numbers of the organisation's journal, in which he urged the government to grant political freedoms. From the early 1890s until his death he contributed to the journal *Russian Wealth*. See Billington (1958), Proctor.

Nekrasov, Nikolay Alekseevich (1821–78). One of the major nineteenth-century poets; also an important journalist and editor, whose political sympathies were radical. Nekrasov was one of only two poets who continued to write successful verse in the age of Alexander II, when the intelligentsia was demanding that writers address topical issues in a realistic manner. Unlike the other poet active in that period, Fet (who wrote personal lyric poetry devoid of topical content), Nekrasov addressed civic issues, especially the character and plight of the peasant masses, in such works as his narrative poems 'The Pedlars' (1861), 'Red-Nosed Frost' (1864) and the unfinished 'Who Can be Happy and Free in Russia?' (1866–76). In 1847, together with Ivan Panaev, he took over *The Contemporary*, which after the Crimean War became the leading organ for the expression of radical opinion. In 1868, following the closure of *The Contemporary* by the authorities in 1866, Nekrasov took over *Notes of the Fatherland*, which he managed until his death. See Birkenmayer.

Novikov, Nikolay Ivanovich (1744–1818). Son of a middle-ranking nobleman; journalist, publisher, educator, freemason, philanthropist and one of the main contributors to the Russian reception of the Enlightenment in the age of Catherine the Great. Inspired by the eighteenth-century English practice, Novikov published satirical journals. In *The Drone* (1769–70) he raised the issue of the injustice of serfdom and drew attention to official corruption, and in *The Painter* (1772–3) he debated with Catherine herself (who had set up her own paper, *All Sorts*) whether satire should be denunciatory or simply playful. In 1777 he published the weekly *St Petersburg Learned Gazette*, devoted to literary and scientific topics, and then, from 1777 to 1780, the didactic *Morning Light*, the proceeds of which were devoted to the establishment of primary schools in St Petersburg. In 1779 he moved to Moscow to rent Moscow University Press and greatly intensified book production there, as well as expanding the book trade and overseeing several new periodical publications. He fell into disfavour after the outbreak of the French Revolution in 1789 and when Catherine ceased to tolerate freemasonry, into which Novikov had been initiated in 1775. In 1792 he was arrested and sentenced to fifteen years' imprisonment. In 1796 he was released by Catherine's son Paul on his accession, but he retired to his estate and did not resume his broad cultural activity. He had, however, played a major role in promoting reading and in bringing public opinion into being in Russia. See Gareth Jones (1984), Marker.

Odoevsky, Vladimir Fedorovich (1804–69). Writer of short prose fiction, music critic and minor composer, amateur scientist, educationist, philanthropist and salon host. Prince Odoevsky was an eccentric dilettante but also a well-connected cultural figure who played an important role in the transmission of German Romanticism to Russia in the age of Nicholas I. In the 1820s he co-edited the almanac *Mnemosyne*, acquired extensive knowledge of German Romantic philosophy and began to write short prose fiction, much of which would be innovatory in form. In the 1830s and 1840s he published satirical tales (e.g. 'The Brigadier', 1833), society tales (e.g. 'Princess Mimi', 1834), 'artistic biographies' (e.g. 'Sebastian Bach', 1835), Gothic stories (e.g. 'The Kosmorama', 1840) and wrote proto-science fiction (e.g. *The Year 4338* (first published in 1926)). He produced two collections of tales, *Variegated Tales*

(1833), which combines satirical and fantastic elements, and *Russian Nights* (1844). In the latter collection, sometimes described as a 'philosophical novel' or 'philosophical frame-tale', various short stories (most of them previously published) are held together by discussion of aesthetic and social matters and by consideration of the possibility that Russia might refresh the dystopian utilitarian civilisation of the West. See Cornwell (1986).

Ostrovsky, Aleksandr Nikolaevich (1823–86). Major dramatist whose many plays include *It's a Family Affair: We'll Settle it Ourselves* (1849), *The Poor Bride* (1852), *Keep to Your Own Sledge!* (1853), *Poverty's No Vice* (1854), *A Profitable Position* (1857), *The Thunderstorm* (1859; famously reviewed by Dobroliubov (*q.v.*) and the basis for Janáček's opera *Káťa Kabanová*), *Easy Money* (first performed 1870), *The Forest* (first performed 1871) and *Without a Dowry* (1878). In the main, these plays deal in a remorselessly realistic way with the life and mores of the materialistic Muscovite merchantry, among whom Ostrovsky was brought up. In the early 1850s Ostrovsky helped to edit *The Muscovite*, an organ of Official Nationality managed by Pogodin (*q.v.*), and later, in the early 1860s, he was close to the Native-Soil Conservatives, Dostoevsky and Grigorev (*qq.v.*). Besides greatly enlarging the Russian dramatic repertoire he was active in theatre management, being closely associated with the Malyi Theatre in Moscow. In 1874 he founded an Association of Russian Playwrights and Operatic Composers, of which he was president until his death, and in the last year of his life he was appointed director of the Moscow imperial theatres. See Dowler (1982, 1995), Hoover.

Petrashevsky (more accurately Butashevich-Petrashevsky), Mikhail Vasilevich (1821–66). Son of an eminent surgeon and a god-child of Alexander I, Petrashevsky was an eccentric nobleman who from 1845 propagated the teachings of French utopian socialists, especially Charles Fourier, at weekly social gatherings at his house in St Petersburg. Petrashevsky's 'Fridays' were frequented by men of letters, government officials, artists, teachers and students. (Danilevsky and Dostoevsky (*qq.v.*) were among the guests.) Petrashevsky contributed to the compilation of *A Pocket Dictionary of Foreign Words That Have Entered the Russian Language* (1845–6), through which radical ideas could be explained in apparently innocent entries in a compendium. In 1849 he was arrested, the authorities having placed an informer in his circle. He was among twenty-one people sentenced to death; the sentence was commuted to indefinite exile in Siberia, where he died. See Evans, Frank (1976), Seddon, Venturi, Yarmolinsky.

Pisarev, Dmitry Ivanovich (1841–68). Literary critic, radical thinker and leading representative of the 'nihilism' that affected the radical intelligentsia in the 1860s. Pisarev's work appeared in *The Russian Word* from 1861 until the authorities closed the journal in 1866. For most of that time (1862–6), Pisarev was in the Peter and Paul Fortress, where he was imprisoned for writing a pamphlet in which he welcomed the prospect of the overthrow of tsarist government. He shared the enthusiasm of Chernyshevsky (*q.v.*) for the method of the natural sciences. He also subscribed to Chernyshevsky's utilitarian view of art, his materialism and his rational egoism, which he, too, expounded in articles such as 'Scholasticism of the Nineteenth Century' (1861), 'The Destruction of Aesthetics' (1865) and 'The Thinking Proletariat' (1865), a review of Chernyshevsky's novel *What is to be Done?* However, Pisarev lent Chernyshevsky's ideas a more impatient and destructive tone. He also championed the individual rather than the collective. In his articles 'Bazarov' (1862) and 'Realists' (1864) he favourably reviewed the novel *Fathers and Children* (1862) by Turgenev (*q.v.*), which he saw as depicting the sceptical, practical younger generation as he himself wished it to be. He was drowned bathing in the Baltic at the age of twenty-six. See Lampert (1965), Moser (1989), Proctor, Venturi, Wellek in Simmons.

Plekhanov, Georgy Valentinovich (1856–1918). Revolutionary who played the main role in introducing Marxism to the Russian intelligentsia in the late nineteenth century. In the 1870s Plekhanov participated in the Bakuninist Land and Liberty organisation (1876–9), and in 1876 he was one of the chief organisers of a demonstration outside the Kazan Cathedral on Nevsky Prospekt in St Petersburg. He then became one of the leaders of the organisation The Black Partition (founded in 1879) but was forced to flee from Russia after arrests weakened that organisation. In 1880 he settled in Switzerland, where he became the leader of the small so-called 'Emancipation of Labour' Group, founded in 1883, which set about promoting Marxism to a Russian readership. In *Socialism and Political Struggle* (1883) and *Our Differences* (1885) he attempted to demonstrate the applicability of Marxism to Russia as well as to the more industrialised countries of western Europe. Plekhanov split with Lenin following the division of the Russian Social-Democratic Labour Party into Bolshevik and Menshevik factions after its second congress in 1903, and he failed in subsequent attempts to reunite the party. See Baron, Copleston, Harding, Offord (1986), Walicki (1969, 1979).

Pobedonostsev, Konstantin Petrovich (1827–1907). Son of an Orthodox priest; government official and extreme conservative political thinker. From 1859 to 1865 Pobedonostsev occupied a chair of Civil Law in Moscow University and in 1865 moved to St Petersburg to serve as tutor to the sons of Alexander II. (Later he would also serve as tutor to Alexander's grandson, the future Nicholas II.) In 1880 he was appointed Chief Procurator of the Holy Synod, i.e. lay head of the Russian Orthodox Church. After the assassination of Alexander II by terrorists of The People's Will on 1 March 1881 he played an important role, during the reign of his former pupil, now Alexander III (1881–94), in shaping the government's reactionary policies. He sought to bolster autocracy and defend Orthodoxy from all rival beliefs, pressing for the Russianisation of ethnic and religious minorities in the empire. He resisted social mobility and opposed aspirations to constitutional and democratic government. His advocacy of authoritarian rule was based on a deeply pessimistic view of human nature. His religious, social and political ideas are most fully expressed in his *Moscow Collection* (1896). See Byrnes, Thaden.

Pogodin, Mikhail Petrovich (1800–76). The son of a serf emancipated by his master in 1806, Pogodin is chiefly remembered as a historian, journalist and conservative nationalist thinker. He was a member of the Wisdom-Lovers (*liubomudry*), who studied the philosophy of Schelling in the years 1823–5. In the period 1827–30 he edited *The Moscow Messenger* and, from 1841 to 1856, *The Muscovite*, in which the doctrine of Official Nationality was propagated. From 1835 to 1844 he also occupied a chair of Russian History at Moscow University. He was a prolific, if unaccomplished, writer, producing short prose fiction, historical dramas, an account of his extensive travels in western Europe and many articles on political topics, as well as a large corpus of scholarship on early Russian history, which he viewed as characterised by a harmony between rulers and ruled that was lacking among the western peoples. See Offord (2005), Riasanovsky (1959).

Prokopovich, Feofan (1681–1736). Churchman and prolific writer who played a major role in establishing the supremacy of secular over ecclesiastical power and in founding a western literary and intellectual tradition in Russia. Prokopovich was born in Kiev and studied in Rome as well as his native city, becoming exceptionally widely read, for a Russian of that time, in classical, theological and philosophical literature. As an ardent supporter of the reforms of Peter the Great, he was called to St Petersburg in 1715. In 1718 Peter appointed him Bishop of Pskov and in 1720 Archbishop of Novgorod. His Ecclesiastical Regulation prepared the ground for the establishment in 1721 of the Holy Synod, of which Prokopovich himself was effectively the first head. In his play *Vladimir* (performed in 1705) he used the historical account of the conversion of Russia to Christianity by the Kievan Grand Prince in the tenth century as a means of ridiculing the opponents of change in Peter's time. His treatise *The Justice of the Monarch's Will* (1722) dealt with the law of succession. He was also the author of various orations that celebrated Peter's achievements or asserted the need for enlightened absolutism in Russia and of a funeral oration to Peter in which he eulogised the late monarch in biblical terms. Prokopovich influenced the satirist Kantemir and the historian Tatishchev, with whom he tried to defend Peter's reforms during the constitutional crises after Peter's death. See William Brown (1980), Cracraft (1971).

Pushkin, Aleksandr Sergeevich (1799–1837). Almost invariably acknowledged as Russia's greatest poet and a seminal influence on classical Russian literature. Pushkin's poetic *oeuvre* spans numerous genres. He wrote a large number of lyric poems and a dozen narrative poems, of which the most renowned are the light-hearted fairy story 'Ruslan and Liudmila' (1820), the Romantic 'southern' poems 'The Prisoner of the Caucasus' (1822), 'The Fountain of Bakhchisaray' (1824) and 'The Gypsies' (1827), the historical poem 'Poltava' (1829), which concerns Peter's decisive battle of 1709 with the Swedes in the Great Northern War, and 'The Bronze Horseman' (written in 1833; first published in 1841), in which he explores the plight of the little man in the face of great forces of nature and historical destiny. His masterpiece is perhaps the 'novel in verse' *Eugene Onegin* (1823–31), whose eponymous hero came to be seen as one of the prototypes of the 'superfluous man'. He also wrote a historical drama, *Boris Godunov* (1831; written in 1824–5), which was set at the beginning of the Time of Troubles in the early seventeenth century, and a number of 'little tragedies', most notably *Mozart and Salieri* (written in 1830). Towards the end of his life Pushkin turned from poetry to prose, in which he aspired to conciseness. His main works of prose fiction are a group of five light stories under the title *The Tales of Belkin* (1831), the tale 'The Queen of Spades' (1834) and the historical novel *The Captain's Daughter* (1836), set at the time of the Pugachev Revolt (1773–4). He also left a travel sketch, *A Journey to Arzrum* (1836), literary critical essays, some historical writing, especially a *History of Pugachev* (1835), and much elegant correspondence. Pushkin's writings profoundly affected the development of the nineteenth-century Russian literary language. Exiled to the southern borderlands in his twenties and often at odds with the court, where he was given a minor position in his last years, Pushkin was killed at the age of thirty-seven in a duel with the adopted son of the Dutch ambassador. See Briggs, William Brown (1986, vol. III), Todd (1986), Vickery.

Radishchev, Aleksandr Nikolaevich (1749–1802). Nobleman sent by Catherine the Great to study law in Leipzig (1767–71), where he was affected by western Enlightenment notions which led him on his return to question the legitimacy of the political and social order in his native land. Influenced by the theories of natural law and social contract, Radishchev wrote a fictional travelogue in the Sentimentalist manner, *A Journey from St Petersburg to Moscow*, printed on his private press in 1790. In this tract he railed against numerous abuses of autocratic government and Russian officialdom (especially arbitrariness, lawlessness and corruption) and put forward economic and moral arguments against the institution of serfdom. For publishing his *Journey* (which appeared shortly after the outbreak of the French Revolution), Radishchev was tried and sentenced to death, then exiled to Siberia. After Catherine's death he was allowed, in 1797, to return to European Russia. However, crushed by his experiences, he committed suicide a few years later by drinking sulphuric acid. Radishchev subsequently served as a model of what came to be known as the 'repentant nobleman' (*kaiushchiisia dvorianin*) plagued by a sense of guilt towards his social inferiors. See William Brown (1980), Clardy, Lang, McConnell.

Rozanov, Vasily Vasilevich (1856–1919). Writer, literary critic, journalist. Rozanov was born in Kostroma province into an impoverished family. He was rescued from life as a provincial school-teacher by the influential critic Strakhov, who was impressed by the potential of his first work (the obscure *On Understanding*) and secured him a post in the Civil Service in the capital. Rozanov eventually earned his living as a journalist, selling his work unscrupulously to both reactionary and liberal journals. He became a central figure in the Symbolist circle of Merezhkovsky (*q.v.*) and his wife and was one of the most prolific and provocative contributors to the Religious–Philosophical Meetings of 1901–3.

Rozanov's themes were sex and religion. He opposed what he saw as the ascetic foundation of Christianity and the Russian Orthodox Church (which he accused – in *Apocalypse of Our Time* (1917–18) – of enfeebling Russian culture and making possible the Revolution), in the name of a mysticism of sex, family and nation inspired by pagan fertility cults and Old Testament Judaism. His most remarkable and, from a formal point of view, original works are *Solitaria* (1911) and *Fallen Leaves* (1913–15). See Matich, Pyman.

Samarin, Iury Fedorovich (1819–76). Son of a wealthy noble family, one of the leading early Slavophiles. Samarin studied philosophy at Moscow University before entering government service. He was the author of an essay published in 1847 that was seen as the Slavophiles' riposte to the étatist conception of Russian history outlined by the Westerniser Kavelin (*q.v.*). In 1853–4 he wrote a proposal for the emancipation of the serfs, a project to which he gave much thought after his retirement from government service in 1853. He also wrote on numerous other subjects, ranging from Russian relations with other ethnic groups in the Baltic region of the Russian Empire to Prussian finance. A man noted for his integrity, Samarin remained active in public life, taking part in his later years, for example, in the organisation of popular education and discussion of reform of the poll tax. See Christoff (1991), Riasanovsky (1965), Walicki (1975).

Shcherbatov, Prince Mikhail Mikhailovich (1733–90). Descendant of an ancient noble family, statesman, defender of the privileges of the upper nobility, historian and conservative political thinker. Shcherbatov wrote *A History of Russia from the Earliest Times* (seven volumes published between 1770 and 1791, covering the subject up to the early seventeenth century), using numerous primary sources that he himself had brought to light. He also wrote an unfinished utopian tract, *A Journey to the Land of Ophir* (written in 1783–4), in which he imagined a strictly policed state governed by a monarch with the aid of the hereditary upper nobility. In his jaundiced treatise *On the Corruption of Morals in Russia* (probably written in 1786–7 and first published posthumously, in expurgated form, in 1858) Shcherbatov deplored the decadence that he believed had taken root in Russia since the seventeenth century and which he attributed in particular to the introduction of foreign goods and customs. See Lentin in Shcherbatov, Madariaga (1981, 1998), Walicki (1979).

Solovev, Vladimir Sergeevich (1853–1900). Both as religious philosopher and poet, Solovev was one of the most significant intellectual influences on Russian Symbolism and the Silver Age. He achieved considerable recognition in his lifetime despite the fact, or perhaps because of it, that his religious belief, philosophical methodology and political convictions ran counter to the prevailing culture. Solovev devoted his life to the Christianisation of culture in pursuit of the ideal of a divinised humanity, or mangodhood (articulated most clearly in a celebrated series of public lectures published as *Lectures on Divine Humanity* (1878)). The son of the prominent historian Sergey Mikhailovich, he initially pursued this ideal as an academic philosopher, building on the work of the Slavophiles Ivan Kireevsky and Khomiakov (*qq.v.*) and also on Hegel and Schelling, in his elaboration of a historico-cultural-religious theory of total-unity in *Philosophical Principles of Integral Knowledge* (1877) and *Critique of Abstract Principles* (1880). In 1881 an appeal to Alexander III to show clemency to the assassins of his predecessor forced Solovev's departure from academia, after which he directed his attention towards the reunification of Eastern and Western Christianity. This phase of his career took him away from Slavophilism: he conducted a polemic against religious nationalism in the thick journals and cultivated a relationship with the Catholic Church through the Croatian Bishop Strossmeyer, which led him to be accused of apostasy from Orthodoxy. In the last decade of his life Solovev abandoned his ecumenical project and returned to philosophy (*The Justification of the Good* (1897)) and esoteric mysticism, his poetry and prose (*A Short Tale of the Antichrist* (1900)) taking on increasingly apocalyptic tones. See Copleston, Kornblatt and Gustafson, Sutton, Valliere, Zenkovsky.

Struve, Petr Berngardovich (1870–1944). Influential political journalist, economist. Struve came from an outstanding academic family. He studied law at the University of St Petersburg, but following the publication of *The Economics of Prices* (1913–16) obtained a doctorate in economics and became a professor at the Moscow Polytechnic Institute and a member of the Academy of Sciences. He became a Marxist at university. His first monograph, published when he was just twenty-four, was a Marxist critique of Populist economics; he wrote the first Manifesto of the Russian Social-Democratic Party, and he collaborated on the translation of Marx's *Capital* into Russian. Abandoning Marxism in 1900 for philosophical idealism and political liberalism, Struve moved gradually towards the political right. From Germany between 1901 and 1905 he published the journal *Liberation*, which led to the formation of the Constitutional Democratic (Kadet) Party. He returned to Russia in 1905, became the editor of *Russian Thought*, and, like Bulgakov (*q.v.*), was elected to the Second State Duma. After the Revolution he joined the White movement and after its defeat fled to western Europe. See Pipes (1970, 1980), Zernov.

Tiutchev, Fedor Ivanovich (1803–73). Major poet and representative of conservative nationalism who was close to Gogol and the Slavophiles. Tiutchev served as a diplomat from 1822 to 1841 (much of this period he spent in Munich and Turin). He also served for long periods as a censor. The surviving corpus of his verse (he destroyed some of his poems in 1833) consists mostly of short lyric poems, of which 'Silentium' and 'A Dream at Sea' are among the best-known poems in the Russian language. Affected by the philosophy of Schelling, Tiutchev reflects on love, nature and the transcendent. In the late 1840s and early 1850s he also wrote political verse, in which he expressed Slavophile or Pan-Slav views and contrasted the revolutionary West with conservative Russia and published a number of articles of similar complexion in French. See William Brown (1986, vol. IV), Conant, Gregg.

Tkachev, Petr Nikitich (1844–85, or 1886 NS). One of the leading radical political thinkers and revolutionary strategists in the age of Alexander II and also a prolific literary critic of the utilitarian school. In 1868–9 Tkachev was associated with the political conspirator Nechaev and in 1869 he was arrested. In 1873, after his release from prison, he fled to Switzerland. Like other revolutionaries of his time, Tkachev believed that it would be increasingly difficult to introduce socialism as capitalism took hold in post-reform Russia and that a revolution therefore had to be carried out urgently. He differed, though, from most of his radical contemporaries in refusing to pin any hopes on the Russian peasantry, arguing instead that revolution could be effected only if the revolutionary minority created a highly centralised and disciplined clandestine organisation and carried out a *coup d'état*. He expounded this view, known as 'Jacobinism' or 'Blanquism', in numerous articles in his journal *The Tocsin*, which was published first in Geneva and then London over the period 1875–81. In 1882 Tkachev was admitted to a home for the mentally ill in Paris and there he died. See Hardy (1977), Venturi, Weeks.

Tolstoy, Lev Nikolaevich (1828–1910). One of the great classical writers of prose fiction, dramatist, essayist and, during the last thirty years of his life, an exponent of a pacifist variety of anarchism. After service in the army (1852–6), including participation in the Crimean War (1853–6), and foreign travel (1857, 1860–61), Tolstoy settled at his estate at Iasnaia Poliana, near Tula. His shorter prose writings include a trilogy of autobiographical reflections, *Childhood, Boyhood, Youth* (published separately in 1852, 1854, 1857), 'Sebastopol Stories' (1855–6, based on his experience in the Crimea), 'Family Happiness' (1859) and 'The Cossacks' (1863). The first of his novels is *War and Peace* (1865–9), in which he deals with the life of the Alexandrine nobility against the backcloth of the Napoleonic Wars and Napoleon's invasion of Russia in 1812 and addresses the question of historical causation, musing on the role of 'great men', providence, chance and necessity. In his second novel, *Anna Karenina* (1875–7), the adultery and ostracism of his eponymous heroine occasion a contrast of the shallow, hypocritical values of high society with the supposedly authentic life to be lived on the rural estate, close to the peasants and the land they cultivated. After the publication of *Anna Karenina* Tolstoy spurned the life he had led as an aristocrat and began to offer a more explicit, unsubtle critique of his society. He wrote a self-analytical *Confession* (1879–81) and moralising tracts such as 'What Men Live By' (1885) and urged that evil be resisted by non-violent means. Abjuring art produced for aesthetic pleasure, he also made a plea, in *What Is Art?* (1896), for didacticism. His most substantial work in this later period was his novel *Resurrection* (1899), in which he attacked his society's institutions, notably its judicial and penal systems and the Orthodox Church (from which he was excommunicated in 1901). He also now wrote some of his finest works of shorter prose fiction, including 'The Death of Ivan Ilich' (1886), 'The Kreutzer Sonata' (1890) and 'Khadzhi Murat' (published posthumously in 1912), in which he again attempts to make readers recoil from the horrors and senselessness of war. Tolstoy's advocacy of a simple and peaceful life attracted many followers in the guilt-ridden intelligentsia. Disciples also set up communities inspired by his teachings in foreign countries. In 1910, at the age of eighty-two, shortly before his death, he abandoned Iasnaia Poliana in a final act of self-rejection. See Avrich, Berlin (2008), Christian, Copleston, Freeborn (1982), Gifford, Jones and Miller, Kalb and Ogden, Layton, Masaryk (vol. III), Morson (1987), Orwin, Wasiolek (1978), Woodcock.

Turgenev, Ivan Sergeevich (1818–83). One of the major prose writers of the classical age and a moderate Westerniser who was close to Annenkov (*q.v.*) and, in the late 1840s, to Belinsky (*q.v.*). His main works are *A Sportsman's Sketches* (1847–52; also translated as *Sketches from a Hunter's Album*), the novellas 'Asia' (i.e. the name of the heroine; 1858) and 'First Love' (1860), the play *A Month in the Country* (1855) and the novels *Rudin* (1856), *A Nest of Gentry* (1859), *On the Eve* (1860), *Fathers and Children* (1862, which he dedicated to Belinsky), *Smoke* (1867) and *Virgin Soil* (1877). Turgenev's novels were felt vividly to portray the dilemmas and changing character of the mid-nineteenth-century Russian educated class. Nevertheless, Turgenev always aspired to create art of timeless beauty and resisted the utilitarianism pressed upon writers by radical critics such as Chernyshevsky and Dobroliubov (*qq.v.*) in the reign of Alexander II, when most of his major work was written. He spent the greater part of the last thirty years of his life in western Europe. See Freeborn (1963), Schapiro (1978).

Selected bibliography

With the exception of editions of major primary sources (i.e. works by the Russian thinkers and writers whom the volume examines), the works cited in this bibliography are all in English. There is, of course, a vast secondary literature in Russian on the subjects dealt with in this volume and considerable corpora of scholarship in other languages, in particular French and German, as well.

We have for the most part confined ourselves to citation of books, although a few articles and chapters in books are also cited, especially when they concern subjects on which not much else has been written.

PRIMARY SOURCES

RUSSIAN EDITIONS OF THINKERS' WORKS

[Aksakov, I. S.] *Ivan Sergeevich Aksakov v ego pis'makh*, 3 vols. (Moscow: Russkaia kniga, 2003–4).

[Aksakov, I. S., *et al.*] *Rannie slavianofily. A. S. Khomiakov, I. V. Kireevskii, K. S. i I. S. Aksakovy*, compiled by N. L. Brodskii (Moscow: Tipografiia T-va I. D. Sytina, 1910).

Aksakov, [K. S.], *Polnoe sobranie sochinenii* (Moscow: V tipografii V. Bakhmeteva (vol. I); V Universitetskoi tipografii (vols. II–III), 1861–80).

[Annenkov, P. V.] *P. V. Annenkov i ego druz'ia: Literaturnye vospominaniia i perepiska 1835–1885 godov* (St Petersburg: Izdanie A. S. Suvorina, 1892).

Literaturnye vospominaniia (Moscow: Gosudarstvennoe izdatel'stvo khudozhestvennoi literatury, 1960).

Parizhskie pis'ma, ed. I. N. Konobeevskaia (Moscow: Izdatel'stvo 'Nauka', 1983).

Bakhtin, M. M., *Sobranie sochinenii v semi tomakh*, 5 vols. published to date (Moscow: Russkie slovari, 1996–).

Belinskii, V. G., *Polnoe sobranie sochinenii*, 13 vols. (Moscow: Izdatel'stvo Akademii nauk SSSR, 1953–9).

Chaadaev, P. Ia., *Sochineniia i pis'ma P. Ia. Chaadaeva*, 2 vols., ed. M. Gershenzon (Moscow: Tovarishchestvo tipografii A. I. Mamontova, 1913–14).

Chernyshevskii, N. G., *Polnoe sobranie sochinenii*, 16 vols. (Moscow: Gosudarstvennoe izdatel'stvo khudozhestvennoi literatury, 1939–53).

Sobranie sochinenii, 5 vols. (Moscow: Izdatel'stvo 'Pravda', 1974).

Danilevskii, N., *Rossiia i Evropa*, 6th edn (St Petersburg: Glagol, 1995).

Dobroliubov, N. A., *Sobranie sochinenii*, 9 vols. (Moscow and Leningrad: Gosudarstvennoe izdatel'stvo khudozhestvennoi literatury, 1961–4).

Dostoevskii, F. M., *Polnoe sobranie sochinenii*, 30 vols. (Leningrad: Nauka, 1972–90).

Fedorov, N. F., *Sochineniia*, ed. A. Gulyga (Moscow: Mysl', 1982).

Flerovskii, N. [V. V. Bervi], *Polozhenie rabochego klassa v Rossii* (St Petersburg: Izdanie N. P. Poliakova, 1869).

Fonvizin, D. I., *Sobranie sochinenii*, ed. G. P. Makogonenko, 2 vols. (Moscow and Leningrad: Gosudarstvennoe izdatel'stvo khudozhestvennoi literatury, 1959).

Gachev, G., *Kosmo-psikho-logos* (Moscow: Akademicheskii proekt, 2007).

Gertsen: *see* Herzen

Gogol', N. V., *Polnoe sobranie sochinenii*, 14 vols. (Moscow: Izdatel'stvo Akademii nauk SSSR, 1940–52).

Goncharov, I. A., *Sobranie sochinenii*, 8 vols. (Moscow: Gosudarstvennoe izdatel'stvo khudozhestvennoi literatury, 1952–5).

Granovskii, T. N., *Sochineniia*, 4th edn (Moscow: Tovarishchestvo tipografii A. I. Mamontova, 1900).

Gumilev, L., *Etnogenez i biosfera zemli* (Leningrad: Gidrometeoizdat, 1990).

Ritmy Evrazii: epokhi i tsivilizatsii (Moscow: Ekopros, 1993).

Herzen, A. I., *Sobranie sochinenii*, 30 vols. (Moscow: Izdatel'stvo Akademii nauk SSSR, 1954–65).

Kantemir, Antiokh, *Sobranie sochinenii* (Leningrad: Sovetskii izdatel', 1956).

Karamzin, N. M., *Istoriia Gosudarstva rossiiskogo*, 12 vols. (St Petersburg: Voennaia tipografiia Glavnogo shtaba, 1816–29).

Pis'ma russkogo puteshestvennika, ed. Iu. M. Lotman, N. A. Marchenko and B. A. Uspenskii (Leningrad: Nauka, 1984).

Sochineniia, 2 vols. (Leningrad: Khudozhestvennaia literatura, 1984).

Kavelin, K. D., *Sobranie sochinenii*, 4 vols. (St Petersburg: Tipografiia M. M. Stasiulevicha, 1897–1900).

Khomiakov, A. S., *Polnoe sobranie sochinenii*, 4th edn, 8 vols. (Moscow: Tipografiia I. N. Kushnereva, 1900–4).

Izbrannye sochineniia, ed. N. S. Arsen'ev (New York: Izdatel'stvo imeni Chekhova, 1955).

Stikhotvoreniia i dramy, ed. B. F. Egorov (Leningrad: Sovetskii pisatel', 1969).

Kireevskii, I. V., *Polnoe sobranie sochinenii*, 2 vols., ed. M. Gershenzon (Moscow: Tipografiia Imperatorskogo Moskovskogo Universiteta, 1911).

Lavrov, P. L., *Izbrannye sochineniia na sotsial'no-politicheskie temy*, 4 vols. published (Moscow: Izdatel'stvo vsesoiuznogo obshchestva politkatorzhan i ssyl'no-poselentsev, 1934–5).

Leont'ev, K. N., *Sobranie sochinenii*, 9 vols. (Moscow: V. M. Sablin, 1912).

Lermontov, M. Iu., *Izbrannye proizvedeniia*, 2 vols. (Moscow: Gosudarstvennoe izdatel'stvo khudozhestvennoi literatury, 1963).

Lomonosov, M. V., *Polnoe sobranie sochinenii*, 10 vols. (Moscow and Leningrad: Izdatel'stvo Akademii nauk SSSR, 1950–9).

Losev, A. F., *Imia: izbrannye raboty, perevody, besedy, issledovaniia, arkhivnye materialy*, ed. A. A. Takho-Godi (St Petersburg: Aleteia, 1997).

Mamardashvili, Merab, *Klassicheskii i neklassicheskii idealy ratsional'nosti* (Tbilisi: Metsniereba, 1984).

Kak ia ponimaiu filosofiiu (Moscow: Progress, 1990).

Mikhailovskii, N. K., *Sochineniia N. K. Mikhailovskogo*, 6 vols. (St Petersburg: Russkoe bogatstvo, 1896–7).

Nekrasov, N. A., *Sobranie sochinenii*, 8 vols. (Moscow: Izdatel'stvo 'Khudozhestvennaia literatura', 1965–7).

Pisarev, D. I., *Sochineniia*, 4 vols. (Moscow: Gosudarstvennoe izdatel'stvo khudozhestvennoi literatury, 1955–6).

Plekhanov, G. V., *Sochineniia*, 3rd edn, 24 vols. (Moscow and Leningrad: Gosudarstvennoe izdatel'stvo, 1923–7).

Izbrannye filosofskie proizvedeniia, 5 vols. (Moscow: Akademiia nauk SSSR, 1956).

[Pogodin, M. P.] Barsukov, Nikolai, *Zhizn' i trudy M. P. Pogodina*, 22 vols. (St Petersburg: Tipografiia M. M. Stasiulevicha, 1888–1910).

Pushkin, A. S., *Polnoe sobranie sochinenii*, 16 vols. (Moscow and Leningrad: Izdatel'stvo Akademii nauk SSSR, 1937–49).

Radishchev, A. N., *Polnoe sobranie sochinenii*, 2 vols. (Moscow and Leningrad: Izdatel'stvo Akademii nauk SSSR, 1938–41).

Samarin, Iu. F., *Sochineniia*, 12 vols. (Moscow: Tipografiia A. I. Mamontova, 1877–1911).

Shchapov, A. P., *Sochineniia*, 3 vols. (St Petersburg: Izdanie M. V. Pirozhkova, 1906–8).

Solov'ev, V. S., *Chteniia o Bogochelovechestve; Stat'i; Stikhotvoreniia i poema; Iz trekh razgovorov* (St Petersburg: Khudozhestvennaia literatura, 1994).

Tkachev, P. N., *Izbrannye sochineniia*, 5 vols. published (Moscow: Izdatel'stvo vsesoiuznogo obshchestva politkatorzhan i ssyl'no-poselentsev, 1932–).

Sochineniia, 2 vols. (Moscow: Akademiia nauk SSSR, Izdatel'stvo sotsial'no-ekonomicheskoi literatury, 1976).

Tolstoi, L. N., *Polnoe sobranie sochinenii*, 90 vols. (Moscow and Leningrad: Gosudarstvennoe izdatel'stvo, 1928–58).

Tugan-Baranovsky, M. I., *Ekonomicheskie ocherki* (Moscow: Rosspen, 1998).

Turgenev, I. S., *Polnoe sobranie sochinenii i pisem*, 28 vols. (Moscow and Leningrad: Izdatel'stvo Akademii nauk SSSR, 1961–8).

ENGLISH TRANSLATIONS OF WORKS BY RUSSIAN THINKERS

Anthologies

Edie, James M., Scanlan, James P., and Zeldin, Mary-Barbara (eds.), with the collaboration of George L. Kline, *Russian Philosophy*, 3 vols. (Chicago: Quadrangle Books, 1965).

Leatherbarrow, W. J., and Offord, D. C. (eds.), *A Documentary History of Russian Thought: From the Enlightenment to Marxism* (Ann Arbor: Ardis, 1987).

Leighton, Lauren Gray (ed. and trans.), *Russian Romantic Criticism: An Anthology* (New York, Westport and London: Greenwood Press, 1987).

Matlaw, Ralph E. (ed.), *Belinsky, Chernyshevsky, and Dobrolyubov: Selected Criticism* (Bloomington: Indiana University Press, 1976).

Poole, Randall A. (ed. and trans.), *Problems of Idealism: Essays in Russian Social Philosophy* (New Haven: Yale University Press, 2003).

Proffer, Carl, and Proffer, Ellendea (eds.), *The Silver Age of Russian Culture: An Anthology* (Ann Arbor: Ardis, 1975).

Raeff, Marc (ed.), *Russian Intellectual History: An Anthology* (New York, etc.: Harcourt, Brace and World, 1966).

Savitskii, P. N., *et al.* (eds.), *Exodus to the East: Foreboding and Events: An Affirmation of the Eurasians*, trans. Ilya Vinkovetsky (Idyllwild: Charles Schlacks, 1996).

Schmemann, Alexander (ed.), *Ultimate Questions: An Anthology of Modern Russian Religious Thought* (New York: St Vladimir's Seminary Press, 1977).

Segel, Harold B. (ed. and trans.), *The Literature of Eighteenth-Century Russia: An Anthology of Russian Literary Materials of the Age of Classicism and the Enlightenment from the Reign of Peter the Great (1689–1725) to the Reign of Alexander I (1801–1825)*, 2 vols. (New York: Dutton, 1967).

Shatz, Marshall S., and Zimmerman, Judith (eds. and trans.), *Signposts: A Collection of Articles on the Russian Intelligentsia* (Irvine: Charles Schlacks, 1986).

Shein, Louis J. (ed.), *Readings in Russian Philosophical Thought* (The Hague and Paris: Mouton, 1968).

Individual thinkers and writers

Annenkov, P. V., *The Extraordinary Decade: Literary Memoirs*, ed. Arthur P. Mendel, trans. Irwin R. Titunik (Ann Arbor: University of Michigan Press, 1968).

[Bakhtin, Mikhail] *The Dialogic Imagination: Four Essays by M.M. Bakhtin*, ed. Michael Holquist, trans. Caryl Emerson and Michael Holquist (Austin: University of Texas Press, 1981).

  Problems of Dostoevsky's Poetics, ed. and trans. Caryl Emerson (Minneapolis: University of Minnesota Press, 1984).

[Bakunin, M. A.] *The Political Philosophy of Bakunin: Scientific Anarchism*, ed. G. P. Maksimoff (London: Free Press, 1964).

  Selected Writings, trans. Steven Cox and Olive Stevens, ed. and introduced by Arthur Lehning (London: Jonathan Cape, 1973).

  The Confession of Michael Bakunin, trans. R. C. Howes (Ithaca: Cornell University Press, 1977).

  Statism and Anarchy, trans. Marshall Shatz (Cambridge University Press, 1990).

Belinsky, V. G., *Selected Philosophical Works* (Westport: Hyperion Press, 1981).

Berdyaev, N., *Dream and Reality: An Essay in Autobiography* (London: Geoffrey Bles, 1950).

[Bogdanov, A. A.] *Bogdanov's Tektology*, ed. Peter Dudley (Hull: Centre for Systems Studies, 1996).

[Chaadaev, P. Ia.] *The Major Works of Peter Chaadaev*, ed. and trans. Raymond T. McNally (University of Notre Dame Press, 1969).

Chernyshevsky, N. G., *Selected Philosophical Essays* (Westport: Hyperion Press, 1981).

What is to be Done?, trans. Michael R. Katz, annotated by William G. Wagner (Ithaca and London: Cornell University Press, 1989).

Dobroliubov, N. A., *Selected Philosophical Essays*, trans. J. Fineberg (Westport: Hyperion Press, 1983).

Dostoevsky, F. M., *Winter Notes on Summer Impressions*, trans. David Patterson (Evanston: Northwestern University Press, 1988).

A Writer's Diary, trans. and annotated by Kenneth Lantz, and with an introductory study by Gary Saul Morson, 2 vols. (Evanston: Northwestern University Press, 1993–4).

Dostoevsky's Occasional Writings, trans. and with an introduction by David Magarshack (Evanston: Northwestern University Press, 1997).

Florovsky, Georges, *Ways of Russian Theology: Parts I and II*, trans. Robert L. Nichols (Belmont, Mass.: Nordland, 1979).

Fonvizin, D. I., *The Political and Legal Writings of Denis Fonvizin*, trans. with notes and an introduction by Walter Gleason (Ann Arbor: Ardis, 1985).

Gogol, N. V., *Selected Passages from Correspondence with Friends*, trans. Jesse Zeldin (Nashville: Vanderbilt University Press, 1969).

[Grigor'ev] Grigoryev, Apollon, *My Literary and Moral Wanderings*, trans. Ralph E. Matlaw (New York: Dutton, 1962).

Gumilev, L., *Ethnogenesis and the Biosphere* (Moscow: Progress, 1990).

[Herzen, A. I.] Alexander Herzen, *'From the Other Shore' and 'The Russian People and Socialism'*, trans. Moura Budberg and Richard Wollheim (London: Weidenfeld and Nicolson, 1956).

My Past and Thoughts: The Memoirs of Alexander Herzen, 4 vols., trans. Constance Garnett, revd Humphrey Higgens (London: Chatto and Windus, 1968).

Ends and Beginnings, selected and ed. with an introduction by Aileen Kelly (Oxford University Press, 1985).

Letters from France and Italy, 1847–1851, trans. J. Zimmerman (Pittsburgh University Press, 1995).

Ilyenkov, E. V., *The Dialectics of the Abstract and the Concrete in Marx's Capital* (Moscow: Progress, 1982).

[Ivanov, V. I.] *Viacheslav Ivanov: Selected Essays*, ed. Michael Wachtel, trans. and with notes by Robert Bird (Evanston: Northwestern University Press, 2003).

[Karamzin, N. M.] *Karamzin's Memoir on Ancient and Modern Russia: A Translation and an Analysis*, ed. and trans. Richard Pipes (Cambridge, Mass.: Harvard University Press, 1959).

Nikolai Karamzin: 'Letters of a Russian Traveller', ed. and trans. Andrew Kahn (Oxford: Voltaire Foundation, 2003).

Kropotkin, P., *Memoirs of a Revolutionist*, with a preface by George Brandes (London: Smith, Elder, 1899).
Mutual Aid (London: Allen Lane, 1972).
The Essential Kropotkin, ed. Emile Capouya and Keitha Tompkins (New York: Liveright, 1975).
The Conquest of Bread and Other Writings, ed. Marshall Shatz (Cambridge University Press, 1995).
Lavrov, P. L., *Historical Letters*, trans. and with an introduction and notes by James P. Scanlan (Berkeley: University of California Press, 1967).
Lenin, V. I., *Materialism and Empirio-Criticism: Critical Comments on a Reactionary Philosophy* (New York: International Publishers, 1927).
Collected Works, 47 vols. (Moscow: Progress, 1960–80).
The Lenin Anthology, ed. Robert C. Tucker (New York: W.W. Norton, 1975).
Pisarev, D. I., *Selected Philosophical, Social and Political Essays* (Moscow: Foreign Languages, 1958).
Plekhanov, G. V., *Selected Philosophical Works*, 5 vols. (London and Moscow: Lawrence & Wishart and Foreign Languages Publishing House (vol. I); Moscow: Progress Publishers (vols. II–V), 1961–81).
[Radishchev, A. N.] Aleksandr Nikolaevich Radishchev, *A Journey from St Petersburg to Moscow*, trans. Leo Wiener, ed. Roderick Page Thaler (Cambridge, Mass.: Harvard University Press, 1958).
Shcherbatov, Prince M. M., *On the Corruption of Morals in Russia*, ed. and trans. A. Lentin (Cambridge University Press, 1969).
Stasov, Vladimir Vasilievich, *Selected Essays on Music*, trans. Florence Jonas (New York: Praeger, 1968).
Struve, P. B., *Collected Works*, 15 vols., ed. Richard Pipes (Ann Arbor: University Microfilms, 1970).
Tolstoy, *Recollections and Essays*, trans. Aylmer Maude (London: Oxford University Press, 1961).

SECONDARY LITERATURE

HISTORICAL CONTEXT

General histories, periods, rulers

Anisimov, Evgenii V., *The Reforms of Peter the Great: Progress through Coercion in Russia*, trans. and with an introduction by John T. Alexander (Armonk: M. E. Sharpe, 1993).
Cracraft, James, *The Revolution of Peter the Great* (Cambridge, Mass.: Harvard University Press, 2003).
Dixon, Simon, *The Modernisation of Russia 1676–1825* (Cambridge University Press, 1999).
Dunlop, John B., *The Rise of Russia and the Fall of the Soviet Empire* (Princeton University Press, 1993).

Florinsky, M. T., *Russia: A History and an Interpretation*, 2 vols. (New York: Macmillan, 1953).

Hosking, Geoffrey, *Russia: People and Empire, 1552–1917* (London: Fontana Press, 1997).
Russia and Russians: From Earliest Times to 2001 (London: Penguin Books, 2001).

Hughes, Lindsey, *Russia in the Age of Peter the Great* (New Haven and London: Yale University Press, 1998).

Kappeler, Andreas, *The Russian Empire: A Multi-Ethnic History* (Harlow: Longman, 2001).

Lieven, Dominic (ed.), *The Cambridge History of Russia*, vol. II (Cambridge University Press, 2006).

Lincoln, W. Bruce, *Nicholas I, Emperor and Autocrat of All the Russias* (London: Allen Lane, 1978).

McConnell, Allen, *Tsar Alexander I: Paternalistic Reformer* (New York: Thomas Y. Crowell, 1970).

Madariaga, Isabel de, *Russia in the Age of Catherine the Great* (London: Weidenfeld and Nicolson, 1981).

Malia, Martin, *Russia under Western Eyes: From the Bronze Horseman to the Lenin Mausoleum* (Cambridge, Mass.: The Belknap Press of Harvard University Press, 1999).

Mosse, W. E., *Alexander II and the Modernisation of Russia* (London: English Universities Press, 1958; 2nd edn, London and New York: IB Tauris, 1992).

Pipes, Richard, *Russia under the Old Regime* (London: Weidenfeld and Nicolson, 1974).

Saunders, David, *Russia in the Age of Reaction and Reform, 1801–1881* (London and New York: Longman, 1991).

Seton-Watson, H., *The Russian Empire, 1801–1917* (Oxford: Clarendon Press, 1967).

Vernadsky, G., *A History of Russia*, 5th revd edn (New Haven and London: Yale University Press, 1961).

Vucinich, Wayne S. (ed.), *Russia and Asia: Essays on the Influence of Russia on the Asian Peoples* (Stanford: Hoover Institution Press, 1972).

Zaionchkovsky, Peter A., *The Russian Autocracy under Alexander III*, ed. and trans. David R. Jones (Gulf Breeze: Academic International Press, 1976).
The Russian Autocracy in Crisis, 1878–1882, ed., trans. and with a new introduction by G. M. Hamburg (Gulf Breeze: Academic International Press, 1979).

Economic, institutional, political and social history

Balzer, H. D. (ed.), *Russia's Missing Middle Class: The Professions in Russian History* (Armonk: M. E. Sharpe, 1996).

Blackwell, W. L., *The Beginnings of Russian Industrialization, 1800–1860* (Princeton University Press, 1961).

Blum, Jerome, *Lord and Peasant in Russia from the Ninth to the Nineteenth Century* (Princeton University Press, 1961).

Daly, Jonathan W., *Autocracy under Siege: Security Police and Opposition in Russia, 1866–1905* (DeKalb: Northern Illinois University Press, 1998).

The Watchful State: Security Police and Opposition in Russia, 1906–1917 (DeKalb: Northern Illinois University Press, 2004).

Dukes, Paul, *Catherine the Great and the Russian Nobility* (Cambridge University Press, 1967).

Emmons, Terence, *The Russian Landed Gentry and the Peasant Emancipation of 1861* (Cambridge University Press, 1968).

The Formation of Political Parties and the First National Elections in Russia (Cambridge, Mass.: Harvard University Press, 1983).

Emmons, Terence, and Vucinich, Wayne S. (eds.), *The Zemstvo in Russia. An Experiment in Local Self-Government* (Cambridge University Press, 1982).

Engel, Barbara Alpern, *Women in Russia, 1700–2000* (Cambridge University Press, 2004).

Field, Daniel, *The End of Serfdom: Nobility and Bureaucracy in Russia, 1855–1861* (Cambridge, Mass., and London: Harvard University Press, 1976).

Rebels in the Name of the Tsar, 2nd edn (Boston, etc.: Unwin Hyman, 1989).

Gerschenkron, Alexander, *Europe in the Russian Mirror: Four Lectures in Economic History* (Cambridge University Press, 1970).

Gregory, P. R., *Before Command. An Economic History of Russia from Emancipation to the First Five-Year Plan* (Princeton University Press, 1994).

Hamburg, G. M., *Politics of the Russian Nobility 1881–1905* (New Brunswick: Rutgers University Press, 1984).

Hartley, Janet M., *A Social History of the Russian Empire, 1650–1825* (London and New York: Addison Wesley Longman, 1998).

Johnson, R. E., *Peasant and Proletarian: The Working Class of Moscow in the Late Nineteenth Century* (New Brunswick: Rutgers University Press, 1979).

Jones, Robert E., *The Emancipation of the Russian Nobility 1762–1785* (Princeton University Press, 1973).

LeDonne, John P., *Ruling Russia: Politics and Administration in the Age of Absolutism, 1762–1796* (Princeton University Press, 1984).

Absolutism and Ruling Class: The Formation of the Russian Political Order, 1700–1825 (Oxford University Press, 1991).

Lincoln, W. Bruce, *In the Vanguard of Reform: Russia's Enlightened Bureaucrats 1825–1861* (DeKalb: Northern Illinois University Press, 1982).

The Great Reforms: Autocracy, Bureaucracy, and the Politics of Change in Imperial Russia (DeKalb: Northern Illinois University Press, 1990).

Madariaga, Isabel de, *Politics and Culture in Eighteenth-Century Russia: Collected Essays* (London and New York: Longman, 1998).

Monas, Sidney, *The Third Section: Police and Society in Russia under Nicholas I* (Cambridge, Mass.: Harvard University Press, 1961).

Moon, David, *The Russian Peasantry 1600–1930: The World the Peasants Made* (London and New York: Longman, 1999).

Owen, Thomas C., *Capitalism and Politics in Russia. A Social History of the Moscow Merchants, 1855–1905* (Cambridge University Press, 1981).

Dilemmas of Russian Capitalism. Fedor Chizhov and Corporate Enterprise in the Railroad Age (Cambridge, Mass.: Harvard University Press, 2005).

Pushkareva, Natalia, *Women in Russian History: From the Tenth to the Twentieth Century*, ed. and trans. Eve Levin (Armonk: M. E. Sharpe, 1997).

Roosevelt, Priscilla R., *Life on the Russian Country Estate: A Social and Cultural History* (New Haven and London: Yale University Press, 1995).

Sahni, Kalpana, *Crucifying the Orient: Russian Orientalism and the Colonization of Caucasus and Central Asia* (Bangkok: White Orchid Press, 1997).

Schimmelpenninck van der Oye, D., *Toward the Rising Sun: Russian Ideologies of Empire and the Path to War with Japan* (DeKalb: Northern Illinois University Press, 2001).

Squire, P. S., *The Third Department: The Establishment and Practices of the Political Police in the Russia of Nicholas I* (Cambridge University Press, 1968).

Vucinich, Wayne S. (ed.), *The Peasant in Nineteenth-Century Russia* (Stanford University Press, 1968).

Wirtschafter, Elise Kimerling, *Structures of Society: Imperial Russia's 'People of Various Ranks'* (DeKalb: Northern Illinois University Press, 1994).

  Social Identity in Imperial Russia (DeKalb: Northern Illinois University Press, 1997).

Wortman, Richard, *The Development of a Russian Legal Consciousness* (University of Chicago Press, 1976).

Zelnik, R. E. (ed.), *Labor and Society in Tsarist Russia: The Factory Workers of St. Petersburg, 1855–1870* (Stanford University Press, 1971).

The intelligentsia, relations between state and intellectuals

Billington, James, 'The intelligentsia and the religion of humanity', *American Historical Review*, 65:4 (1960), 807–21.

Brower, Daniel R., 'The problem of the Russian intelligentsia', *Slavic Review*, 26:4 (1967), 638–47.

Chamberlain, Lesley, *Lenin's Private War: The Voyage of the Philosophy Steamer and the Exile of the Intelligentsia* (New York: St Martin's Press, 2007).

Confino, M., 'On intellectuals and intellectual traditions in eighteenth- and nineteenth-century Russia', *Daedalus*, 101 (1972), 117–49.

Engel, Barbara, *Mothers and Daughters: Women of the Intelligentsia in Nineteenth-Century Russia* (Cambridge University Press, 1983).

Fink, L., Leonard, S.T., and Reid, D. M. (eds.), *Intellectuals and Public Life: Between Radicalism and Reform* (Ithaca: Cornell University Press, 1996).

Finkel, Stuart, *On the Ideological Front: The Russian Intelligentsia and the Making of the Soviet Public Sphere* (New Haven: Yale University Press, 2007).

Kelly, Aileen, 'Self-censorship and the Russian intelligentsia, 1905–1914', *Slavic Review*, 46:2 (1987), 193–213.

Knight, Nathaniel, 'Was the intelligentsia part of the nation? Visions of society in post-emancipation Russia', *Kritika: Explorations in Russian and Eurasian History*, 7:4 (2006), 733–58.

McConnell, Allen, 'The origin of the Russian intelligentsia', *Slavic and East European Journal*, 8:1 (1964), 1–16.

Nahirny, Vladimir C., 'The Russian intelligentsia: from men of ideas to men of convictions', *Comparative Studies in Society and History*, 4:4 (1962), 403–35.

Pipes, Richard (ed.), *The Russian Intelligentsia* (New York: Columbia University Press, 1961).

Pollard, Alan P. 'The Russian intelligentsia: the mind of Russia', *California Slavic Studies*, 3 (1964), 1–6.

Pomper, Philip, *The Russian Revolutionary Intelligentsia* (New York: Thomas Y. Crowell Company, 1970; 2nd revd edn, Wheeling: Harlan Davidson, 1993).

Raeff, Marc, *Origins of the Russian Intelligentsia: The Eighteenth-Century Nobility* (New York: Harcourt, Brace and World, 1966).

Riasanovsky, Nicholas V., *A Parting of Ways: Government and the Educated Public in Russia, 1801–1855* (Oxford: Clarendon Press, 1976).

The revolutionary movement

Cahm, Caroline, *Kropotkin and the Rise of Revolutionary Anarchism: 1872–1886* (Cambridge University Press, 1989).

Evans, John L., *The Petraševskij Circle, 1845–1849* (The Hague and Paris: Mouton, 1974).

Geifman Anna, *Thou Shalt Kill: Revolutionary Terrorism in Russia, 1894–1917* (Princeton University Press, 1993).

Entangled in Terror: The Azeff Affair and the Russian Revolution (Wilmington: Scholarly Resources, 2000).

Getzler, I., *Martov: A Political Biography of a Russian Social Democrat* (London: Cambridge University Press, 1967).

Haimson, L. H., *The Russian Marxists and the Origins of Bolshevism* (Cambridge, Mass.: Harvard University Press, 1955).

Hardy, Deborah, *Land and Freedom: The Origins of Russian Terrorism, 1876–1879* (New York: Greenwood Press, 1987).

Keep, J. L. H., *The Rise of Social Democracy in Russia* (Oxford: Clarendon Press, 1963).

Mazour, A. G., *The First Russian Revolution, 1825. The Decembrist Movement. Its Origins, Development and Significance* (Stanford University Press, 1962).

Morrissey, Susan K., *Heralds of Revolution: Russian Students and the Mythologies of Radicalism* (Oxford University Press, 1998).

Naimark, Norman M., *Terrorists and Social Democrats: The Russian Revolutionary Movement under Alexander III* (Cambridge, Mass.: Harvard University Press, 1983).

Offord, Derek, *The Russian Revolutionary Movement in the 1880s* (Cambridge University Press, 1986).

O'Meara, Patrick, *K.F. Ryleev: A Political Biography of the Decembrist Poet* (Princeton University Press, 1984).

The Decembrist Pavel Pestel: Russia's First Republican (Basingstoke: Palgrave Macmillan, 2004).

Pipes, Richard, *The Russian Revolution* (New York: Knopf, 1990).

Pomper, Philip, *Sergei Nechaev* (New Brunswick: Rutgers University Press, 1979).

Radkey, Oliver H., *The Agrarian Foes of Bolshevism: Promise and Default of the Russian Socialist Revolutionaries, February to October 1917* (New York and London: Columbia University Press, 1958).

Raeff, Marc, *The Decembrist Movement* (Englewood Cliffs, N.J.: Prentice-Hall, 1966).

Schwartz, S. *The Russian Revolution of 1905: The Workers' Movement and the Formation of Bolshevism and Menshevism*, trans. G. Vakar (Chicago University Press, 1967).

Seddon, J. H., *The Petrashevtsy: A Study of the Russian Revolutionaries of 1848* (Manchester University Press, 1985).

Stites, Richard, *The Women's Liberation Movement in Russia: Feminism, Nihilism, and Bolshevism, 1860–1930* (Princeton University Press, 1978).

Surh, Gerald D., *1905 in St. Petersburg: Labor, Society, and Revolution* (Stanford University Press, 1989).

Venturi, Franco, *Roots of Revolution: A History of the Populist and Socialist Movements in Nineteenth Century Russia*, trans. F. Haskell (London: Weidenfeld and Nicolson, 1960).

Wildman, A., *The Making of a Workers' Revolution: Russian Social Democracy, 1891–1903* (Chicago University Press, 1967).

Yarmolinsky, Avrahm, *Road to Revolution: A Century of Russian Radicalism* (New York: Collier Books, 1962).

CULTURAL CONTEXT

Education, fine arts, gender, identity, journalism, literacy, music, religion

Bird, Alan, *A History of Russian Painting* (Oxford: Phaidon Press, 1987).

Bowlt, J. E. (ed.), *Russian Art of the Avant-Garde: Theory and Criticism* (London: Thames and Hudson, 1988).

Brooks, Jeffrey, *When Russia Learned to Read. Literacy and Popular Literature, 1861–1917* (Princeton University Press, 1985).

Brower, Daniel R., *Training the Nihilists: Education and Radicalism in Tsarist Russia* (Ithaca and London: Cornell University Press, 1975).

Brumfield, W. C., *A History of Russian Architecture* (Cambridge University Press, 1994).

Cracraft, James, *The Church Reform of Peter the Great* (London: Macmillan, 1971). *The Petrine Revolution in Russian Architecture* (University of Chicago Press, 1990). *The Petrine Revolution in Russian Imagery* (University of Chicago Press, 1997).

Cracraft, James, and Rowland, Daniel, *Architectures of Russian Identity: 1500 to the Present* (Ithaca: Cornell University Press, 2003).

Edmondson, Linda (ed.), *Gender in Russian History and Culture* (Houndmills and New York: Palgrave, 2001).

Faggionato, Raffaella, *A Rosicrucian Utopia in Eighteenth-Century Russia: The Masonic Circle of N. I. Novikov* (Dordrecht: Springer, 2004).

Franklin, S., and Widdis, E. (eds.), *National Identity in Russian Culture: An Introduction* (Cambridge University Press, 2004).

Freeze, G. L., *The Parish Clergy in Nineteenth-Century Russia* (Princeton University Press, 1983).

Gray, Camilla, *The Russian Experiment in Art, 1863–1922* (London: Thames and Hudson, 1986).

Gray, Rosalind P., *Russian Genre Painting in the Nineteenth Century* (Oxford: Clarendon Press, 2000).

Jones, W. Gareth, *Nikolay Novikov, Enlightener of Russia* (Cambridge University Press, 1984).

Kassow, Samuel, *Students, Professors, and the State in Tsarist Russia* (Berkeley: University of California Press, 1989).

Kelly, C., *Refining Russia: Advice Literature, Polite Culture and Gender from Catherine to Yeltsin* (Oxford University Press, 2001).

Kelly, C., and Shepherd, D. (eds.), *Constructing Russian Culture in the Age of Revolution: 1881–1940* (Oxford University Press, 1998).

Kivelson, V. A., and Greene, R. H., *Orthodox Russia: Belief and Practice under the Tsars* (University Park: Pennsylvania State University Press, 2003).

McReynolds, Louise, *The News under Russia's Old Regime: The Development of a Mass-Circulation Press* (Princeton University Press, 1991).

Marker, Gary, *Publishing, Printing, and the Origins of Intellectual Life in Russia, 1700–1800* (Princeton University Press, 1985).

Marsh, Rosalind, *Women and Russian Culture: Projections and Self-Perceptions* (New York and Oxford: Berghahn, 1998).

Martinsen, Deborah A. (ed.), *Literary Journals in Imperial Russia* (Cambridge University Press, 1997).

Pospielovsky, Dmitry, *The Orthodox Church in the History of Russia* (Crestwood, N.Y.: St Vladimir's Seminary Press, 1998).

Riasanovsky, Nicholas V., *The Image of Peter the Great in Russian History and Thought* (Oxford University Press, 1985).

Russian Identities: A Historical Survey (Oxford University Press, 2005).

Rogger, Hans, *National Consciousness in Eighteenth-Century Russia* (Cambridge, Mass.: Harvard University Press, 1960).

Rzhevsky, N. (ed.), *The Cambridge Companion to Modern Russian Culture* (Cambridge University Press, 1998).

Sarabianov, D., *From Neo-Classicism to the Avant-Garde: Painting, Sculpture, Architecture* (London: Thames and Hudson, 1990).

Seaman, Gerald R., *History of Russian Music*, vol. I, *From Its Origins to Dargomyzhsky* (Oxford: Basil Blackwell, 1967).

Smith, Douglas, *Working the Rough Stone: Freemasonry and Society in Eighteenth-Century Russia* (DeKalb: Northern Illinois University Press, 1999).

Valkenier, Elizabeth Kridl, *Russian Realist Art: The State and Society: The Peredvizhniki and Their Tradition* (Ann Arbor: Ardis, 1977).

Ware, Timothy, *The Orthodox Church* (Harmondsworth: Penguin, 1963).

Wortman, Richard, *Scenarios of Power: Myth and Ceremony in Russian Monarchy*, 2 vols. (Princeton University Press, 1995–2000).

Zernov, Nicolas, *The Russian Religious Renaissance of the Twentieth Century* (London: Darton, Longman and Todd, 1963).

Science

Adams, Mark B. (ed.), *The Wellborn Science: Eugenics in Germany, France, Brazil, and Russia* (New York: Oxford University Press, 1990).
  'Through the looking glass: the evolution of Soviet Darwinism' in *New Perspectives on Evolution*, ed. Leonard Warren and Hilary Koprowski (New York: Wiley-Liss, 1991), pp. 37–63.
Andrews, James, *Science for the Masses: The Bolshevik State, Public Science, and the Popular Imagination in Soviet Russia, 1917–1934* (College Station: Texas A&M University Press, 2003).
David-Fox, Michael, *Revolution of the Mind: Higher Learning among the Bolsheviks, 1918–1929* (Ithaca: Cornell University Press, 1997).
Gaissinovitch, A. E., 'The origins of Soviet genetics and the struggle with Lamarckism, 1922–1929', *Journal of the History of Biology*, 13 (1980), 1–51.
  'Contradictory appraisal by K. A. Timiriazev of Mendelian principles and its subsequent perception', *History and Philosophy of the Life Sciences*, 7 (1985), 257–86.
Graham, Loren, *The Soviet Academy of Sciences and the Communist Party, 1927–1932* (Princeton University Press, 1967).
  Science, Philosophy, and Human Behavior in the Soviet Union (New York: Columbia University Press, 1987).
  Science in Russia and the Soviet Union: A Short History (Cambridge University Press, 1993).
Holloway, David, 'Physics, the state, and civil society in the Soviet Union', *Historical Studies in the Physical and Biological Sciences*, 31:1 (1999), 173–93.
Joravsky, David, 'Soviet Marxism and biology before Lysenko', *Journal of the History of Ideas*, 20:1 (1959), 85–104.
  Soviet Marxism and Natural Science, 1917–1932 (New York: Columbia University Press, 1961).
  Russian Psychology: A Critical History (Oxford: Basil Blackwell, 1989).
Kozhevnikov, Alexei, *Stalin's Great Science: The Times and Adventures of Soviet Physicists* (London: Imperial College Press, 2004).
Krementsov, Nikolai, *Stalinist Science* (Princeton University Press, 1997).
  'Big revolution, little revolution: science and politics in Bolshevik Russia', *Social Research*, 73:4 (2006), 1173–204.
Todes, Daniel P., *Darwin without Malthus: The Struggle for Existence in Russian Evolutionary Thought* (Oxford University Press, 1989).
  'Pavlov and the Bolsheviks', *History and Philosophy of the Life Sciences*, 17:3 (1995), 379–418.
Vucinich, A., *Science in Russian Culture: A History to 1860* (Stanford University Press, 1963).
  Science in Russian Culture 1861–1917 (Stanford University Press, 1970).
  Einstein and Soviet Ideology (Stanford University Press, 2001).

Reference works on and general histories of Russian literature

Brown, William Edward, *A History of 18th-Century Russian Literature* (Ann Arbor: Ardis, 1980).
  A History of Russian Literature of the Romantic Period, 4 vols. (Ann Arbor: Ardis, 1986).
Cornwell, Neil (ed.), *Reference Guide to Russian Literature* (London and Chicago: Fitzroy Dearborn, 1998).
  The Routledge Companion to Russian Literature (New York: Routledge, 2001).
Gillespie, Alyssa Dinega (ed.), *Russian Literature in the Age of Realism* (*Dictionary of Literary Biography*, vol. 277) (Detroit: Gale, 2003).
Jones, Malcolm V., and Miller, Robin Feuer (eds.), *The Cambridge Companion to the Classic Russian Novel* (Cambridge University Press, 1998).
Kalb, Judith E., and Ogden, J. Alexander (eds.), with the collaboration of I. G. Vishnevetsky, *Russian Writers of the Silver Age, 1890–1925* (*Dictionary of Literary Biography*, vol. 295) (Detroit: Gale, 2004).
Kalb, Judith E., and Ogden, J. Alexander (eds.), *Russian Novelists in the Age of Tolstoy and Dostoevsky* (*Dictionary of Literary Biography*, vol. 238) (Detroit: Gale, 2001).
Karlinsky, Simon, *Russian Drama from Its Beginnings to the Age of Pushkin* (Berkeley: University of California Press, 1985).
Kelly, Catriona, *A History of Russian Women's Writing, 1820–1992* (Oxford: Clarendon Press, 1994).
Leach, Robert, and Borovsky, Victor (eds.), *A History of Russian Theatre* (Cambridge University Press, 1999).
Mirsky, D. S., *A History of Russian Literature*, ed. Francis J. Whitfield (New York and London: Knopf and Routledge & Kegan Paul, 1949).
Moser, Charles A. (ed.), *The Cambridge History of Russian Literature*, revd edn (Cambridge University Press, 1992; first published 1989).
Rydel, Christine A. (ed.), *Russian Literature in the Age of Pushkin and Gogol: Prose* (*Dictionary of Literary Biography*, vol. 198) (Detroit: Gale, 1999).
Terras, Victor (ed.), *Handbook of Russian Literature* (New Haven and London: Yale University Press, 1985).
  A History of Russian Literature (New Haven and London: Yale University Press, 1991).

Literary movements, topics, themes, genres

Andrew, Joe, *Writers and Society during the Rise of Russian Realism* (London and Atlantic Highlands, N.J.: Macmillan and Humanities Press, 1980).
  Russian Writers and Society in the Second Half of the Nineteenth Century (London and Atlantic Highlands, N.J.: Macmillan and Humanities Press, 1982).
  Women in Russian Literature, 1780–1863 (London: Macmillan, and New York: St Martin's Press, 1988).
Chances, Ellen B., *Conformity's Children: An Approach to the Superfluous Man in Russian Literature* (Columbus: Slavica, 1978).

Freeborn, Richard, *The Rise of the Russian Novel from 'Eugene Onegin' to 'War and Peace'* (Cambridge University Press, 1973).
    The Russian Revolutionary Novel: Turgenev to Pasternak (Cambridge University Press, 1982).
Freeborn, Richard, and Grayson, Jane (eds.), *Ideology in Russian Literature* (Basingstoke: Macmillan and University of London, 1990).
Heldt, Barbara, *Terrible Perfection: Women and Russian Literature* (Bloomington and Indianapolis: Indiana University Press, 1987).
Holmgren, Beth (ed.), *The Russian Memoir: History and Literature* (Evanston: Northwestern University Press, 2003).
Layton, Susan, *Russian Literature and Empire: Conquest of the Caucasus from Pushkin to Tolstoy* (Cambridge University Press, 1994).
Levitt, Marcus C., *Russian Literary Politics and the Pushkin Celebration of 1880* (Ithaca: Cornell University Press, 1989).
Marsh, Rosalind (ed.), *Gender and Russian Literature: New Perspectives* (Cambridge University Press, 1996).
Masing-Delic, Irene, *Abolishing Death: A Salvation Myth of Russian Twentieth-Century Literature* (Stanford University Press, 1992).
Mathewson, Rufus W., *The Positive Hero in Russian Literature* (New York: Columbia University Press, 1958; revd edn, Stanford University Press, 1975).
Morson, Gary Saul (ed.), *Literature and History: Theoretical Problems and Russian Case Studies* (Stanford University Press, 1986).
    Narrative and Freedom: The Shadows of Time (New Haven and London: Yale University Press, 1995).
Moser, Charles A., *Antinihilism in the Russian Novel of the 1860's* (The Hague: Mouton, 1964).
Pyman, Avril, *A History of Russian Symbolism* (Cambridge University Press, 1994).
Todd, William Mills, III, *Fiction and Society in the Age of Pushkin: Ideology, Institutions, and Narrative* (Cambridge, Mass.: Harvard University Press, 1986).
Todd, William Mills, III (ed.), *Literature and Society in Imperial Russia, 1800–1914* (Stanford University Press, 1978).
Welsh, David J., *Russian Comedy 1765–1823* (The Hague: Mouton, 1966).
Wirtschafter, Elise Kimerling, *The Play of Ideas in Russian Enlightenment Theater* (DeKalb: Northern Illinois University Press, 2003).

Individual classical writers

Birkenmayer, Sigmund S., *Nikolai Nekrasov: His Life and Poetic Art* (The Hague and Paris: Mouton, 1968).
Briggs, A. D. P., *Alexander Pushkin: A Critical Study* (London: Croom Helm, 1983; reprinted Bristol Classical Press, 1991).
Christian, R. F., *Tolstoy: A Critical Introduction* (Cambridge University Press, 1969).
Conant, Roger, *The Political Poetry and Ideology of F.I. Tiutchev* (Ann Arbor: Ardis, 1983).

Cornwell, Neil, *The Life, Times and Milieu of V. F. Odoevsky, 1804–1869* (London: Athlone Press, 1986).

Cross, A. G., *N. M. Karamzin: A Study of His Literary Career, 1783–1803* (Carbondale: Southern Illinois University Press, and London: Feffer and Simons, 1971).

Ehre, Milton, *Oblomov and His Creator: The Life and Art of Ivan Goncharov* (Princeton University Press, 1973).

Erlich, Victor, *Gogol* (New Haven: Yale University Press, 1969).

Fanger, Donald, *The Creation of Nikolai Gogol* (Cambridge, Mass.: The Belknap Press of Harvard University Press, 1979).

Freeborn, Richard, *Turgenev: The Novelist's Novelist* (Oxford University Press, 1963).

Gifford, Henry, *Tolstoy* (Oxford University Press, 1981).

Gregg, Richard, *Fedor Tiutchev: The Evolution of a Poet* (New York and London: Columbia University Press, 1965).

Hammarberg, Gitta, *From the Idyll to the Novel: Karamzin's Sentimentalist Prose* (Cambridge University Press, 1991).

Hoover, Marjorie L., *Alexander Ostrovsky* (Boston: Twayne, 1981).

Jones, Malcolm V., *Dostoevsky after Bakhtin: Readings in Dostoevsky's Fantastic Realism* (Cambridge University Press, 1990).

Jones, M. V., and Terry, G. M. (eds.), *New Essays on Dostoevsky* (Cambridge University Press, 1983).

Leatherbarrow, William J., *Fedor Dostoevsky* (Boston: Twayne, 1981).

   Fyodor Dostoyevsky: The Brothers Karamazov (Cambridge University Press, 1992).

Leatherbarrow, William J. (ed.), *The Cambridge Companion to Dostoevskii* (Cambridge University Press, 2002).

Maguire, Robert A., *Exploring Gogol* (Stanford University Press, 1994).

Menshutkin, Boris N., *Russia's Lomonosov: Chemist, Courtier, Physicist, Poet* (Princeton University Press, 1952).

Mochulsky, Konstantin, *Dostoevsky: His Life and Work*, trans. Michael A. Minihan (Princeton University Press, 1967).

Morson, Gary Saul, *The Boundaries of Genre: Dostoevsky's 'Diary of a Writer' and the Traditions of Literary Utopia* (Austin: University of Texas Press, 1981).

   Hidden in Plain View: Narrative and Creative Potentials in 'War and Peace' (Stanford University Press, 1987).

   'Anna Karenina' in Our Time: Seeing More Wisely (New Haven: Yale University Press, 2007).

Moser, Charles A., *Denis Fonvizin* (Boston: Twayne, 1979).

Nabokov, Vladimir, *Nikolai Gogol* (Oxford University Press, 1989; first published 1944).

Orwin, Donna Tussing, *Tolstoy's Art and Thought, 1847–1880* (Princeton University Press, 1993).

Peace, Richard, *Dostoevsky: An Examination of the Major Novels* (Cambridge University Press, 1971).

   The Enigma of Gogol: An Examination of the Writings of N. V. Gogol and Their Place in the Russian Literary Tradition (Cambridge University Press, 1981).

Rayfield, D., *Anton Chekhov: A Life* (London: HarperCollins, 1997).
  Understanding Chekhov (London: Bristol Classical Press, 1998).
Schapiro, Leonard, *Turgenev: His Life and Times* (Oxford University Press, 1978).
Vickery, Walter N., *Alexander Pushkin* (Boston: Twayne, 1970; revd edn 1992).
Wasiolek, E., *Dostoevsky: The Major Fiction* (Cambridge, Mass.: MIT Press, 1964).
  Tolstoy's Major Fiction (University of Chicago Press, 1978).

RUSSIAN THOUGHT
General histories, collections of essays, wide-ranging studies

Anderson, Thornton, *Russian Political Thought: An Introduction* (Ithaca: Cornell University Press, 1967).
Berlin, Isaiah, *Russian Thinkers*, ed. Henry Hardy and Aileen Kelly, 2nd revd edn (London: Penguin, 2008; first published London: Hogarth Press, 1978).
Brudny, Yitzhak M., *Reinventing Russia: Russian Nationalism and the Soviet State, 1953–1991* (Cambridge, Mass.: Harvard University Press, 1998).
Copleston, Frederick, *Philosophy in Russia: From Herzen to Lenin and Berdyaev* (University of Notre Dame Press, 1986).
Gershenzon, Michael, *A History of Young Russia*, trans. James P. Scanlan (Irvine: Charles Schlacks, 1986).
Greenfeld, Liah, *Nationalism: Five Roads to Modernity* (Cambridge, Mass.: Harvard University Press, 1993).
Kelly, Aileen M., *Toward Another Shore: Russian Thinkers between Necessity and Chance* (New Haven and London: Yale University Press, 1998).
Kline, George L. (ed.), *Spinoza in Soviet Philosophy* (London: Routledge & Kegan Paul, 1952).
Lossky, N. O., *History of Russian Philosophy* (New York: International Universities Press, 1951).
McLean, Hugh, Malia, Martin E., and Fischer, George (eds.), *Russian Thought and Politics* (Cambridge, Mass.: Harvard University Press, 1957).
Masaryk, Thomas Garrigue, *The Spirit of Russia: Studies in Literature, History and Philosophy*, 2nd edn (London: Allen and Unwin, 1955 (vols. I–II); New York: Barnes and Noble, 1967 (vol. III)).
Moser, Charles A., *Esthetics as Nightmare: Russian Literary Theory, 1855–1870* (Princeton University Press, 1989).
Neumann, Iver B., *Russia and the Idea of Europe: A Study in Identity and International Relations* (London and New York: Routledge, 1996).
Offord, Derek, *Journeys to a Graveyard: Perceptions of Europe in Classical Russian Travel Writing* (Dordrecht: Springer, 2005).
Scanlan, James P., *Marxism in the USSR. A Critical Survey of Current Soviet Thought* (Ithaca and London: Cornell University Press, 1985).
Scanlan, James P. (ed.), *Russian Thought after Communism: The Recovery of a Philosophical Heritage* (Armonk: M. E. Sharpe, 1994).

Schapiro, Leonard, *Rationalism and Nationalism in Russian Nineteenth-Century Political Thought* (New Haven and London: Yale University Press, 1967).

Simmons, Ernest J. (ed.), *Continuity and Change in Russian Thought* (New York: Russell, 1967).

Somerville, John, *Soviet Philosophy: A Study of Theory and Practice* (New York: Philosophical Library, 1946).

Stacy, Robert H., *Russian Literary Criticism: A Short History* (Syracuse University Press, 1974).

Tolz, Vera, *Russia: Inventing the Nation* (London: Arnold, 2001).

Utechin, S. V., *Russian Political Thought: A Concise History* (London: Dent, 1964).

Walicki, Andrzej, *A History of Russian Thought from the Enlightenment to Marxism*, trans. Hilda Andrews-Rusiecka (Stanford University Press, 1979; Oxford: Clarendon Press, 1980).

Wetter, Gustav, *Dialectical Materialism. A Historical and Systematic Survey of Philosophy in the Soviet Union*, trans. Peter Heath (London: Routledge & Kegan Paul, 1960).

Zenkovsky, V. V., *A History of Russian Philosophy*, 2 vols., trans. George L. Kline (London: Routledge & Kegan Paul, 1953).

Zweerde, Evert van der, *Soviet Historiography of Philosophy: Istoriko-filosofskaia nauka* (Boston: Kluwer, 1997).

Individual thinkers and groups of thinkers

Acton, E., *Alexander Herzen and the Role of the Intellectual Revolutionary* (Cambridge University Press, 1979).

Ascher, A., *Pavel Axelrod and the Development of Menshevism* (Cambridge, Mass.: Harvard University Press, 1972).

Avrich, Paul, *The Russian Anarchists* (Princeton University Press, 1967).

Baron, Samuel H., *Plekhanov: The Father of Russian Marxism* (London: Routledge & Kegan Paul, 1963).

Besançon, Alain, *The Intellectual Origins of Leninism*, trans. Sarah Matthews (Oxford: Basil Blackwell, 1981).

Billington, James H., *Mikhailovsky and Russian Populism* (Oxford: Clarendon Press, 1958).

Black, J. L. (ed.), *Essays on Karamzin: Russian Man-of-Letters, Political Thinker, Historian, 1766–1826* (The Hague and Paris: Mouton, 1975).

Boobbyer, Philip, *S. L. Frank: The Life and Work of a Russian Philosopher, 1877–1950* (Athens, Ohio: Ohio University Press, 1995).

Bowman, Herbert E., *Vissarion Belinski, 1811–48: A Study in the Origins of Social Criticism in Russia* (Cambridge, Mass.: Harvard University Press, 1954; republished New York: Russell and Russell, 1969).

Brandist, Craig, *The Bakhtin Circle: Philosophy, Culture, and Politics* (London: Pluto Press, 2002)

Brown, Barry A., *et al.* (eds.), *Bakhtin and the Nation: Bucknell Review* (Bucknell University Press, 2000).

Brown, Edward J., *Stankevich and His Moscow Circle, 1830–1840* (Stanford University Press, 1966).

Byrnes, Robert F., *Pobedonostsev: His Life and Thought* (Bloomington: Indiana University Press, 1968).

Carlson, Maria, '*No Religion Higher Than Truth': A History of the Theosophical Movement in Russia, 1875–1922* (Princeton University Press, 1993).

Carr, E. H., *Michael Bakunin* (New York: Vintage Books, 1961).

   The Romantic Exiles: A Nineteenth-Century Portrait Gallery (Harmondsworth: Peregrine Books, 1968; first published London: Victor Gollancz, 1933).

Carter, Stephen K., *The Political and Social Thought of F. M. Dostoevsky* (New York and London: Garland, 1991).

Chmielewski, Edward, *Tribune of the Slavophiles: Konstantin Aksakov* (Gainesville: University of Florida, 1961).

Christoff, Peter K., *An Introduction to Nineteenth-Century Russian Slavophilism*, vol. I, *A. S. Xomjakov* ('s-Gravenhage: Mouton, 1961).

   An Introduction to Nineteenth-Century Russian Slavophilism, vol. II, *I. V. Kireevskij* (The Hague and Paris: Mouton, 1972).

   An Introduction to Nineteenth-Century Russian Slavophilism, vol. III, *K. S. Aksakov* (Princeton University Press, 1982).

   An Introduction to Nineteenth-Century Russian Slavophilism, vol. IV, *Iu. F. Samarin* (Boulder, San Francisco and Oxford: Westview Press, 1991).

Clardy, Jesse V., *The Philosophical Ideas of Alexander Radishchev* (London: Vision, 1964).

Clark, Katerina, and Holquist, Michael, *Mikhail Bakhtin* (Cambridge, Mass.: The Belknap Press of Harvard University Press, 1984).

Coates, Ruth, *Christianity in Bakhtin: God and the Exiled Author* (Cambridge University Press, 1998).

Dowler, Wayne, *Dostoevsky, Grigor'ev, and Native-Soil Conservatism* (University of Toronto Press, 1982).

   An Unnecessary Man: The Life of Apollon Grigor'ev (University of Toronto Press, 1995).

Emerson, Caryl, *The First Hundred Years of Mikhail Bakhtin* (Princeton University Press, 1997).

Etkind, Alexander, 'Whirling with the other: Russian Populism and religious sects', *Russian Review*, 62:4 (2003), 565–88.

Evtuhov, Catherine, *The Cross and the Sickle: Sergei Bulgakov and the Fate of Russian Religious Philosophy* (Ithaca and London: Cornell University Press, 1997).

Fadner, Frank, *Seventy Years of Pan-Slavism in Russia: Karazin to Danilevskii, 1800–1870* (Georgetown University Press, 1962).

Fischer, George, *Russian Liberalism: From Gentry to Intelligentsia* (Cambridge, Mass.: Harvard University Press, 1958).

Frank, Joseph, *Dostoevsky: The Seeds of Revolt, 1821–1849* (Princeton University Press, 1976).

   Dostoevsky: The Years of Ordeal, 1850–1859 (Princeton University Press, 1983).

   Dostoevsky: The Stir of Liberation, 1860–1865 (Princeton University Press, 1987).

   Dostoevsky: The Miraculous Years, 1865–1871 (Princeton University Press, 1995).

Dostoevsky: The Mantle of the Prophet, 1871–1881 (Princeton University Press, 2002).

Freeborn, Richard, *Furious Vissarion: Belinskii's Struggle for Literature, Love and Ideas* (London: School of Slavonic and East European Studies, 2003).

Gerstein, Linda, *Nikolai Strakhov* (Cambridge, Mass.: Harvard University Press, 1971).

Gleason, Abbott, *European and Muscovite: Ivan Kireevsky and the Origins of Slavophilism* (Cambridge, Mass.: Harvard University Press, 1972).

Young Russia: The Genesis of Russian Radicalism in the 1860s (New York: Viking Press, 1980).

Hamburg, G. M., *Boris Chicherin and Early Russian Liberalism: 1828–1866* (Stanford University Press, 1992).

Harding, Neil, *Lenin's Political Thought*, 2 vols. (London: Macmillan, 1977–81).

Hardy, Deborah, *Petr Tkachev: The Critic as Jacobin* (Seattle and London: University of Washington Press, 1977).

Hudspith, Sarah, *Dostoevsky and the Idea of Russianness: A New Perspective on Unity and Brotherhood* (London and New York: RoutledgeCurzon, 2004).

Joll, J., *The Anarchists* (London: Eyre and Spottiswoode, 1964).

Katz, Martin, *Michael N. Katkov: A Political Biography, 1818–1887* (The Hague and Paris: Mouton, 1966).

Kelly, Aileen, *Mikhail Bakunin: A Study in the Psychology and Politics of Utopianism* (Oxford: Clarendon Press, 1982; New Haven: Yale University Press, 1987).

Views from the Other Shore: Essays on Herzen, Chekhov, and Bakhtin (New Haven and London: Yale University Press, 1999).

Kochetkova, Natalya, *Nikolay Karamzin* (Boston: Twayne, 1975).

Kohn, Hans, *Pan-Slavism: Its History and Ideology*, 2nd revd edn (New York: Vintage Books, 1960).

Kornblatt, Judith Deutsch, and Gustafson, Richard F. (eds.), *Russian Religious Thought* (Madison: University of Wisconsin Press, 1996).

Lampert, E., *Studies in Rebellion* (London: Routledge & Kegan Paul, 1957).

Sons against Fathers: Studies in Russian Radicalism and Revolution (Oxford: Clarendon Press, 1965).

Lang, David Marshall, *The First Russian Radical: Alexander Radishchev, 1749–1802* (London: Allen and Unwin, 1959).

Laruelle, Marlène, *Russian Eurasianism: An Ideology of Empire* (Baltimore: The Johns Hopkins University Press, 2008).

Leier, Mark, *Bakunin: The Creative Passion* (New York: St Martin's Press, 2006).

Lih, Lars T., *Lenin Rediscovered. 'What is to be Done?' in Context* (Leiden: Brill, 2006).

Lukashevich, Stephen, *Ivan Aksakov, 1823–1886: A Study in Russian Thought and Politics* (Cambridge, Mass.: Harvard University Press, 1965).

N. F. Fedorov (1828–1903): A Study of Russian Eupsychian and Utopian Thought (Newark: University of Delaware Press, 1977).

McConnell, Allen, *A Russian 'philosophe': Alexander Radishchev, 1749–1802* (The Hague: Nijhoff, 1964).

MacMaster, Robert E., *Danilevsky: A Russian Totalitarian Philosopher* (Cambridge, Mass.: Harvard University Press, 1967).

McNally, R. T., *Chaadayev and His Friends: An Intellectual History of Peter Chaadayev and His Russian Contemporaries* (Tallahassee: Diplomatic Press, 1971).

Malia, Martin, *Alexander Herzen and the Birth of Russian Socialism, 1812–1855* (Cambridge, Mass.: Harvard University Press, 1961).

Martin, Alexander M., *Romantics, Reformers, Reactionaries: Russian Conservative Thought and Politics in the Reign of Alexander I* (DeKalb: Northern Illinois University Press, 1997).

Matich, Olga, *Erotic Utopia: The Decadent Imagination in Russia's Fin de Siècle* (Madison: University of Wisconsin Press, 2005).

Mendel, Arthur P., *Dilemmas of Progress in Tsarist Russia: Legal Marxism and Legal Populism* (Cambridge, Mass.: Harvard University Press, 1961).

Miller, M. A., *Kropotkin* (University of Chicago Press, 1976).

Morris, B., *Bakunin: The Philosophy of Freedom* (Montreal: Black Rose Books, 1993).

Morson, Gary Saul, and Emerson, Caryl, *Rethinking Bakhtin: Extensions and Challenges* (Evanston: Northwestern University Press, 1989).

  Mikhail Bakhtin: Creation of a Prosaics (Stanford University Press, 1990).

Offord, Derek, *Portraits of Early Russian Liberals: A Study of the Thought of T. N. Granovsky, V. P. Botkin, P. V. Annenkov, A. V. Druzhinin, and K. D. Kavelin* (Cambridge University Press, 1985).

Oittinen, Vesa (ed.), *Evald Ilyenkov's Philosophy Revisited* (Helsinki: Kikimora Publications, 2000).

Olkhovsky, Yuri, *Vladimir Stasov and Russian National Culture* (Ann Arbor: UMI Research Press, 1983).

Paperno, Irina, *Chernyshevsky and the Age of Realism: A Study in the Semiotics of Behavior* (Stanford University Press, 1988).

Pereira, N. G. O., *The Thought and Teachings of N. G. Černyševskij* (The Hague: Mouton, 1975).

Petrovich, M. B., *The Emergence of Russian Panslavism 1856–1870* (New York: Columbia University Press, 1956).

Pipes, Richard, *Struve: Liberal on the Left, 1870–1905* (Cambridge, Mass.: Harvard University Press, 1970).

  Struve: Liberal on the Right, 1905–1944 (Cambridge, Mass.: Harvard University Press, 1980).

Pomper, Philip, *Peter Lavrov and the Russian Revolutionary Movement* (University of Chicago Press, 1972).

Poole, Randall (ed.), *Neo-Idealist Philosophy in the Russian Liberation Movement: The Moscow Psychological Society and Its Symposium 'Problems of Idealism'* (Washington, DC: Kennan Institute for Advanced Russian Studies, 1996).

Pozefsky, Peter C., *The Nihilist Imagination: Dmitrii Pisarev and the Cultural Origins of Russian Radicalism (1860–1868)* (New York and Oxford: Peter Lang, 2003).

Proctor, Thelwall, *Dostoevskij and the Belinskij School of Literary Criticism* (The Hague: Mouton, 1969).

Rabow-Edling, Susanna, *Slavophile Thought and the Politics of Cultural Nationalism* (Albany: State University of New York Press, 2006).

Randall, Francis B., *N. G. Chernyshevskii* (New York: Twayne, 1967).

Vissarion Belinskii (Newtonville: Oriental Research Partners, 1987).

Read, Christopher, *Religion, Revolution and the Russian Intelligentsia 1900–1912: The Vekhi Debate and Its Intellectual Background* (London and Basingstoke: Macmillan, 1979).

Riasanovsky, Nicholas, *Nicholas I and Official Nationality in Russia, 1825–1855* (Berkeley and Los Angeles: University of California Press, 1959).

Russia and the West in the Teaching of the Slavophiles: A Study of Romantic Ideology (Gloucester, Mass.: Peter Smith, 1965).

Roosevelt, Priscilla R., *Apostle of Russian Liberalism: Timofei Granovsky* (Newtonville: Oriental Research Partners, 1986).

Rosenthal, Bernice Glatzer, *D. S. Merezhkovsky and the Silver Age: The Development of a Revolutionary Mentality* (The Hague: Martinus Nijhoff, 1975).

Rosenthal, Bernice Glatzer (ed.), *The Occult in Russian and Soviet Culture* (Ithaca and London: Cornell University Press, 1997).

Scanlan, James P., *Dostoevsky the Thinker* (Ithaca and London: Cornell University Press, 2002).

Stockdale, M. K., *Paul Miliukov and the Quest for a Liberal Russia, 1880–1918* (Ithaca: Cornell University Press, 1996).

Sutton, Jonathan, *The Religious Philosophy of Vladimir Solovëv – Towards a Reassessment* (London: Macmillan Press, 1988).

Terras, V., *Belinskij and Russian Literary Criticism: The Heritage of Organic Aesthetics* (Madison: University of Wisconsin Press, 1974).

Thaden, Edward C., *Conservative Nationalism in Nineteenth-Century Russia* (Seattle: University of Washington Press, 1964).

Valliere, Paul, *Modern Russian Theology: Bukharev, Soloviev, Bulgakov: Orthodox Theology in a New Key* (Grand Rapids: William B. Eerdmans Publishing Company, 2000).

Walicki, Andrzej, *The Controversy over Capitalism: Studies in the Social Philosophy of the Russian Populists* (Oxford: Clarendon Press, 1969).

The Slavophile Controversy: History of a Conservative Utopia in Nineteenth-Century Russian Thought, trans. Hilda Andrews-Rusiecka (Oxford: Clarendon Press, 1975).

The Legal Philosophies of Russian Liberalism (Oxford: Clarendon Press, 1987).

Ward, Bruce K., *Dostoyevsky's Critique of the West: The Quest for the Earthly Paradise* (Waterloo, Ontario: Wilfred Laurier University Press, 1986).

Weeks, Albert L., *The First Bolshevik: A Political Biography of Peter Tkachev* (New York University Press and University of London Press, 1968).

Whittaker, Cynthia H., *The Origins of Modern Russian Education: An Intellectual Biography of Count Sergei Uvarov, 1786–1855* (DeKalb: Northern Illinois University Press, 1984).

Williams, Rowan (ed.), *Sergii Bulgakov: Towards a Russian Political Theology* (Edinburgh: T&T Clark, 1999).

Woehrlin, W. F., *Chernyshevskii: The Man and the Journalist* (Cambridge, Mass.: Harvard University Press, 1971).

Woodcock, George, *Anarchism: A History of Libertarian Ideas and Movements*, new edn (Harmondsworth: Penguin, 1986).

Woodcock, George, and Avakumović, Ivan, *The Anarchist Prince: A Biographical Study of Peter Kropotkin* (London and New York: T. V. Boardman, 1950).

Wortman, Richard, *The Crisis of Russian Populism* (Cambridge University Press, 1967).

Index